1998 GLOBAL TELECOMS TAX PROFILES

1998 GLOBAL TELECOMS TAX PROFILES

SECOND EDITION

A RESOURCE FOR BUSINESS, TAX AND MARKET STRATEGIES

PRICEWATERHOUSECOOPERS

Global Telecoms Tax Network

Editor

Dennis J. McCarthy
Tax Partner
New York

Regional Editors

Nicasio del Castillo (Latin America)
Tax Partner
New York

Tim T.K. Leung (Asia/Pacific)
Tax Partner
Hong Kong

Barry J. Marshall
Tax Partner

John Wiley & Sons, Inc.

New York • Chichester • Weinheim • Brisbane • Singapore • Toronto

CONTENTS

PREFACE

In the realm of telecommunications, one value links many countries around the world: the recognition that competition brings with it prospects for economic growth and improved services at home, and for greater participation in the global economy. Although countries face many of the same issues, they are at widely varying points in their approaches to and timetables for liberalization. Some countries, though they have embraced liberalization in principle, remain strongly protective of their national telecoms monopolies. Others have fully competitive and active marketplaces for telecoms services. And in between are many stages and conditions.

Certainly other trends can be identified: 1997 witnessed a historic commitment to liberalization by the members of the World Trade Organization (WTO). All over the world, cross-border investments in telecoms infrastructure and service operations proliferated, with acquisitions continuing at a brisk pace and with joint ventures an increasingly important vehicle for entering markets. And there was near-dizzying uptake of cellular technologies, the Internet and value-added services.

Experienced telecoms investors and newcomers to the industry are finding that as the telecommunications business grows more exciting and attractive, the more important it becomes to engage in detailed tax and business planning. A patchwork of regulations, tax regimes, and business environments span the globe. Each country still has its own rules governing telecoms investment, and each has its own tax rules for various types of telecoms businesses. Income tax rates, VATs and withholding on remittances vary significantly from country to country. Where privatization of telecoms is just occurring, companies and investors may be dealing for the first time with complex accounting tax standards and tax rules.

The issue of when a telecoms operator becomes subject to tax (permanent establishment) grows in complexity. Although the OECD definition of permanent establishment applies in most countries, interpretations can be difficult, particularly in the kinds of cross-border activities now enabled by the evolving Internet, wireless and networking technologies.

PricewaterhouseCoopers (PwC) is helping investors gain the understanding they need to operate in these new, dynamic markets. In this, the second edition of the *Global Telecoms Tax*

Profiles, we provide an in-depth look at the market environments, investment opportunities, and tax structures pertaining to telecommunications in 43 countries. Building on the format we pioneered in our first edition (1997), we have added to each chapter tables and new sections that describe the players in a market and provide a feel for the business climate there.

Among the new players in telecoms markets are a variety of parties. In several countries, utilities (including gas and electric companies) and railways are investing substantially in telecommunications, using their considerable capital and in some cases employing their own networks and rights of way to provide telecommunications services. Cable-TV operators in several countries are entering the business as well. In some countries, large retailing concerns and banking institutions are investing in telecommunications ventures.

Going into 1998, it appeared that in most countries there will be significant new investment in wireless, including PCS and wireless-in-the-local-loop technologies. Worldwide subscriber growth in cellular amounted to a compound 10-year growth rate of about 60% by year-end 1996, and 40% growth was predicted for 1998, to bring the total to 196 million global users, for a 3.5% worldwide penetration rate. Asia was the hottest spot for cellular growth, with about 45% of the world's new subscribers in 1996. It remains to be seen how the Asian financial crisis will affect telecoms development in the short run. Over the long run, demand forecasts suggest that 40% of all new subscriptions in the world will come from Asia. In the U.S., meanwhile, the fast pace of new licensing is expected to subside now as a period of consolidation begins.

In terms of technology, the move worldwide is strongly toward digital technologies and deployment of fiber optic cables. Networks using fiber optics are being built to carry both regional and international traffic. Submarine fiber optic systems, which can be deployed more quickly than some types of installations, have been particularly successful and will eventually account for 75% of all fiber optic networks. Some industry analysts expect growth rates in fiber optic deployment of around 20% per year internationally through 2002. The traffic carried on these networks includes both voice and data; demand for additional fiber is surging as non-voice traffic grows. International voice services have grown at a rate of about 12% in recent years;

data and video services are growing at rates as high as 90% per year.

Rapid growth in the non-broadcast satellite services market is expected over the next few years as several countries open these markets to foreign investors and as a number of high-profile projects come on-line. Large increases in data and voice traffic via satellite can be expected over the next decade, with the total market reaching US$200 billion by 2010. Mobile voice and data services will likely be carried by satellite.

The Internet, meanwhile, is increasingly an international tool of business. The global network has grown in importance as a way of reaching customers and as a means of carrying out activities between companies and between subsidiaries of companies located in different countries. Tax authorities and companies alike are seeking to determine how these new inter-company and inter-group activities will be viewed for tax purposes. Electronic commerce is not yet widely established in most countries, but sufficient activity exists to have raised a welter of questions about customs duties and consumption taxes and how they will be applied to cross-border sales of goods and services. For the most part, countries are seeking to apply existing rules regarding place of supply and residence of users, but it is proving difficult for many to determine how to tax the sales of goods distributed electronically using the same rules written to cover traditional distribution. Several countries are reviewing their rules regarding these issues, and modifications and new rules can be expected in the near term. Investors and their tax planners need to be apprised of these and other developments.

The pace of change is not subsiding. On January 1, 1998, the members of the European Union (EU) opened their national telecoms markets to competition and instituted a common approach to value-added tax and import duties. Complicated and possibly contentious discussions lie ahead as EU members consider whether to adopt a single European currency (currently scheduled to be introduced in January 1999). The chief benefits of monetary union are expected to be savings in transaction costs, a boost in intra-European trade, and the removal of currency risk premiums. The European Monetary Union (EMU) will pose a serious systems challenge for telecoms operators, who are already faced with expensive systems changes to cope with year-2000 issues.

This year the signatories to the WTO Basic Telecoms Agreement began opening their telecoms markets to foreign operators under the same conditions and terms as those offered to domestic operators. Each of the 69 signatories has committed to a schedule for liberalization, with deadlines ranging from 1998 to 2002.

PricewaterhouseCoopers believes strongly that to succeed in this global environment, investors must view tax planning as an integral part of their business planning processes. Effective tax planning should start with a clear understanding of strategy and market restraints. It should take into account the structural and financing alternatives available to the planned venture as well as the tax and business objectives of all the parties involved. Whenever possible, tax planning should be completed before value is created. This permits investors to adopt structures appropriate to the market and to avoid costly changes later.

We believe the *1998 Global Telecoms Tax Profiles,* the only book of its kind, will be a valuable resource to business planners and tax planners. Each chapter is authored by PwC telecommunications and tax specialists in the local countries. For ease of use and comparability, the information for each country is presented in a consistent format resembling the business process for a foreign investment.

To our readers, we extend our hope that you may be well-informed and thus successful in your endeavors.

ACKNOWLEDGMENTS

To produce a book of this magnitude requires the continued commitment and cooperation of our global network of telecommunications tax, consulting and administrative professionals. I take great pride in the efforts of my PwC colleagues around the world. Their contributions reflect both the depth and breadth of our Firm's grasp of conditions in these many markets.

All of the authors mentioned within the chapters, along with their staffs, deserve special acknowledgement for devoting their time and expertise and for providing up-to-date information regarding the players and the tax issues in each of the markets they watch. Regional coordinating teams in London for Europe (David Attwood, Richard Clitherow, Sarah Deboo, Dennis Knowles, Barry Marshall, Hazel Platt and John Steveni); Hong Kong for Asia/Pacific (Vanessa Lee and Tim Leung); and New York for Latin America (Nico del Castillo and Paulo Espindula) provided many hours of coordination and review in their respective regions. Maria Brindlmayer, director of our Global Telecoms Group, offered her vision and expertise throughout the planning and execution of the book.

Of course, no book can be produced without quality editorial and research professionals and we were particularly fortunate to have the talent and commitment of our editing team of Christy Barbee, Sharon Kaufman and Mike McCullough, our copy-editing and proofreading team of Marc Farre and Brian Matthews, and our research expert, Mimi Calter, who provided supplemental research on a moment's notice.

Clearly, this publication would not exist without a gifted knitting together of the various processes that result in a seamless and comprehensive work. I am very grateful to Maggie Burke for the overall project management, quality control and completion of this project.

We are also deeply indebted to our Philadelphia office's Strategic Technology Group (yes, the entire department!) for their frequent and patient technical support throughout the project, and to Angelo Maiale for his guidance and assistance in distribution.

And to those who make us look good—marketing and public relations support were provided by Peter Birnbaum and Shelly Slack; with special thanks to Maureen McCafferty for chapter design.

My thanks to you all.

Dennis J. McCarthy
Tax Partner
PricewaterhouseCoopers
New York

1998 GLOBAL TELECOMS TAX PROFILES

Part One
Asia/Pacific

Australia
China (People's Republic of)
Hong Kong
India
Indonesia
Japan
Korea
Malaysia
New Zealand
Philippines
Singapore
Taiwan
Thailand
Vietnam

Australia

Telecommunications Tax Profile
by Gordon Thring
Tax Partner, Melbourne

Overview of the Telecommunications Market

Historical Background

Prior to 1989, the Australian telecommunications sector was a monopoly, with three separate government-owned companies responsible for domestic, international and satellite services. The Telecommunications Act of 1989 created a separate regulatory authority, opened competition in equipment supply and installation, and liberalized the provision of value-added services. The Telecommunications Act of 1991 introduced limited competition. The fixed-network monopoly of Australia's basic service and international providers ended when Optus Communications was granted a 25-year license, in November 1991. Competition came to mobile services when Optus and Vodafone Group Plc were granted wireless licenses in November 1991 and December 1992, respectively.

In 1993 Australia's former monopoly provider was restructured as Telstra Corporation Ltd. In 1996 the government further amended the Telecommunications Act and opened all sectors of the market to full competition. It also privatized one-third of Telstra.

Current Status

Australia's telecommunications market has experienced significant growth. In 1996–1997, Australian telecommunications industry services generated AUD 18 billion in revenue, and equipment manufacturers generated AUD 5.7 billion. Continued strong growth in service revenues and in the number of competitors is expected to result in total industry sales reaching AUD 30 billion by 2004, representing an annual growth rate of 6%. Strong competition exists in all sectors of the market. Non-carrier service providers now compete vigorously for business customers.

Optus has achieved greater success in the mobile markets than in the fixed market because of the enormous growth in the mobile telecommunications sector (obtaining new customers has been less difficult than converting existing Telstra customers). Optus has also been successful in selected lucrative international call routes.

The privatization of Telstra is underway. It will not be broken up and sold separately; rather, one-third ownership was to be sold through a public float of AUD 14 billion. Telstra is intended to remain under Australian control and to maintain its community and universal service obligations. It will also continue contributions to a universal service levy and maintain existing price caps. The government will be granted the right to obtain financial information and influence the company's strategic decisions.

Virtually all Australian homes and businesses are connected to approximately 200 digital switches. As of June 30, 1997, Telstra's fiber optic broadband network passed 2.1 million homes, in line with its target of 2.5 million by the end of 1997. Optus aimed to pass 3.5 million homes in the same time frame. Recently, though, there has been a significant slowing of the rollout because of a shortfall in the anticipated number of subscriptions to the networks.

At this stage, both analog and digital cellular technologies are in use. The analog system is scheduled to be phased out by the year 2000.

Current Liberalization Status

In the World Trade Organization (WTO) negotiations in February 1997, Australia committed to full liberalization and adherence to a common set of regulatory principles by 1998. Government policy provides no limits on the number of fixed and mobile carriers. Carriers have guaranteed access to network facilities, including customer equipment controlled by other carriers. Reasonable access to carrier networks and infrastructure is guaranteed for service providers. Competition and price regulation are now monitored by the Australian Competition and Consumer Commission (ACCC).

Type of Service	Degree of Liberalization	Key Legislation	Date of Actual or Expected Liberalization
Local			
Long Distance			
International	Fully liberalized	Telecommunications Act of 1996	1996
Cellular			
Paging			
Value-added			

Competitive Environment

The Australian telecommunications market is considered to be one of the most competitive in the world.

Type of Service	Entire Market		Top Two Players		
	Market Size (1995–96)	Number of Players	Names	Annual Revenue (1995–96)	Ownership
Local	AUD 4.4 billion	2	Telstra	AUD 4.4 billion	1/3 publicly traded, 2/3 government*
			Optus	AUD 25 million (for 1996–97)	Mayne Nickless Ltd. 25%, Cable & Wireless 49%, AMP Society 10.3%, AIDC Fund 6.1%, National Mutual Holdings 9.6%**
Long Distance	AUD 3.3 billion	50	Telstra	AUD 2.5 billion	See * above
			Optus	AUD 640 million	See ** above
International	AUD 1.5 billion	50	Telstra	AUD 1.3 billion	See * above
			Optus	AUD 160 million	See ** above
Cellular	AUD 2.8 billion	3	Telstra	AUD 1.7 billion	See * above
			Optus	AUD 765 million	See ** above
Paging	AUD 126 million	3	Hutchison Telecom	AUD 42 million	Hutchison Whampoa (HK) 56%, Robert Thomson Family 24%, Motorola 20%
			Link	AUD 46 million	PT Bakrie Communications, Link Corporation
Value-added	AUD 5 billion	600 plus	Telstra	AUD 4.7 billion	See * above
			Optus	AUD 233 million	See ** above

Sources: Paul Budde Communication Pty. Ltd., Telstra share offer prospectus reports, Telstra Annual Report 1996, Optus Statement of Accounts.

Licensing Requirements

Under rules that took effect in July 1997, the Australian Telecommunications Authority (AUSTEL) was disbanded, and restrictions on the number of fixed and mobile competitors were lifted. Australia's newly elected government has indicated that it supports the thrust of the previous government's telecommunications industry reforms, which was to refrain from limiting the number of fixed and mobile carrier licenses and to ensure that no financial or technical hurdles prevented potential market entrants from gaining carrier licenses after deregulation occurs.

Telecommunications carriers are now required to obtain licenses from the Australian Communications Authority (ACA), the amalgamation of AUSTEL and the Spectrum Management Agency. Service providers are not required to obtain licenses. Licenses are not required for equipment supply, information services, paging or facilities management services.

There will be no new mobile licenses or global system for mobile communications (GSM) licenses. More carrier licenses will be issued. Notification of intent is required for most services.

Potential for Foreign Ownerships/Relationships

All restrictions on foreign ownership were lifted in August 1997, except for investment in Optus, Vodafone and Telstra. No more than 35% in the publicly traded shares in Telstra may be owned by foreign investors, and no foreign individual can own more than 5%.

Optus and Vodafone are required (by earlier legislation) to be majority Australian-owned and controlled. The recent relaxation of the rules will mean that Cable & Wireless can take a majority share in Optus and that Vodafone will not have to sell down to a minority share by 2003 as was originally required.

Potential for Upcoming Liberalization/Investment Opportunities

The important targets for investment in the post-1997, deregulated Australian telecommunications market will be:

- The mobile market, which is expected to have 8 million subscribers by 2000. The market is expected to benefit from the coming introduction of personal communications networks.

- Value-added services, such as facilities management/outsourcing, virtual private network services, electronic data interchange (EDI) services and electronic funds transfer.

Forms of Doing Business

Permanent Establishment

Permanent establishment (PE) is defined in the tax legislation as being a place at or through which a person carries on any business. The legislation includes and excludes certain types of situations. In particular, a PE includes a place where:

- A person carries on business through an agent.

- A person has, is using, or is installing substantial equipment or substantial machinery.

- A person is engaged in a construction project.

A similar definition of PE, based on the OECD Model Convention, is found in most of Australia's tax treaties. Telecommunications services can cover a broad range of activities, which may or may not constitute PEs. Some examples follow:

- The provision of long-distance telephone services by a foreign company to local customers without any local presence generally does not constitute a PE.

- The licensing by a foreign company of technology and know-how to a local company without any permanent presence generally does not create a PE. Some or all of the payments received by the foreign telecommunications company are characterized as a royalty and subject to withholding tax.

- The presence of a foreign telecommunications company's employees for the operation of an Australian resident telecommunications company, including the provision of technical assistance, technological services and network management services by the foreign company to the local company, in exchange for service fees, is likely to create a PE. Some or all of the payments received by the foreign telecommunications company are characterized as a royalty and subject to withholding tax. When the persons providing the operator services and technical support become employees of the local entity, there will usually not be a PE.

- The leasing of telecommunications equipment (without other supporting activities in Australia) to a local company generally does not constitute a PE. When the lease payments include an interest component under a hire purchase agreement, this could create a PE, and the Australian tax authorities may seek to subject the interest component to withholding tax. Most of Australia's tax treaties specify that the equipment must be used in Australia continuously for more than 12 months to be deemed a PE. The Taxation Office has indicated that in certain perceived tax-avoidance situations, it may treat lease payments as royalties subject to withholding tax.

- The provision of call reorganization/turnaround services generally does not create a PE if the telephone cards are provided through an independent agent and the foreign telecommunications company has no substantial equipment in Australia.

- The provision of Internet access services may not create a PE, depending on the extent of a foreign company's operations in Australia. For instance, if a foreign entity merely sells or provides Internet access software to Australian customers without a presence in Australia, it generally is not characterized as a PE. Further, the proceeds from the sale of software are not normally characterized as a royalty, provided such a sale simply involves the right to use the software without any additional rights (e.g., the right to further develop the software).

- When a foreign entity owns an access server located in Australia, this may be sufficient to constitute a permanent establishment.

- Having a website located on a server in Australia that is owned and operated by another company is unlikely to be considered a PE. The mere availability to Australian consumers of a website on a server outside Australia does not constitute a PE, regardless of whether it is accessible to Australian residents or non-residents only.

- The laying of fiber optic cable and the construction of telecommunications switching equipment (a) for sale to a local company, or (b) to be operated by a foreign telecommunications company for a local company in exchange for a fee, generally constitutes a PE.

If the provision of any of the services described above does not create a PE, the only local tax to which a foreign entity is likely to be subject is withholding tax (see "Operating Considerations"). Withholding tax is levied on dividends, royalties and interest paid to a non-resident.

If the provision of any of the services described above does create a PE, a foreign telecommunications company is taxed as a branch.

Business Entities

Local Branch and Locally Incorporated Subsidiary of a Foreign Company. Foreign investors can conduct telecommunications business in Australia through either a branch or a locally incorporated subsidiary. However, common commercial practice favors a subsidiary. Employees, government authorities and lending institutions typically prefer to deal with a subsidiary corporation. In addition to general commercial considerations, a variety of Australian tax factors may influence the choice between a branch and a subsidiary. The key tax differences between a branch and a subsidiary can be summarized as follows:

- *Repatriation of profits.* No withholding tax applies to the repatriation of profits from a branch since Australia taxes branch profits at the corporate tax rate. Dividends by a corporate subsidiary may be subject to withholding tax, depending on the extent of franking.

- *Grouping.* Branches cannot transfer losses to offset profits of other resident companies within the same group. Wholly owned resident subsidiaries can transfer losses to other wholly owned resident companies.

Joint Venture. The term "joint venture" refers to a distinct type of business structure, although, informally, any joint business

may be referred to as a joint venture. The concept of joint venture refers to an arrangement in which the participants share the output of the project. An unincorporated joint venture pays no tax and does not file a tax return. The participants in a joint venture include their compensation on their individual tax returns. Against this income they would also claim deductions for their individual expenditures.

By entering into a joint venture with a local partner, a foreign telecommunications company may create a PE, depending on the extent to which the joint venture's business requires activity or presence of the joint venture in Australia.

When participants share income, partnership taxation rules apply. Although the partners, and not the partnership, pay tax, the partnership must file a return. Accordingly, partners must make the same election for most partnership items that require elections. Incorporated joint ventures and limited liability partnerships are taxed as corporations.

Local Funding Alternatives

Debt versus Equity

Generally, foreign investors prefer shareholder debt financing over equity financing because interest payments to non-residents are subject to a lower withholding tax. Furthermore, investors can deduct interest payments on debts that satisfy the thin capitalization rules (see "Thin Capitalization Rules"), whereas no deduction is allowed for dividends. In determining whether an instrument should be characterized as debt or equity, the legal form of the arrangement will generally prevail over its economic substance.

Acquisition Financing. The acquisition of an Australian telecommunications company by a foreign company may be financed through a newly formed Australian acquisition company to allow the acquired company to benefit from interest deductions on the acquisition debt. Specifically, the acquisition company could borrow the necessary funds for the acquisition and, pursuant to group relief provisions, the acquired business could obtain the benefit of the interest deductions relating to the acquisition debt. Foreign exchange gains and losses realized on the debt will generally be assessable and deductible.

Alternatively, once an acquisition has occurred, the acquisition company could merge with the acquired business on a tax-free basis (although a stamp duty may be required), which would also allow the acquired company to benefit from the interest deductions.

Foreign Shareholder Financing and Withholding Taxes on Interest. Australian law generally imposes a withholding tax of

10% of the gross amount of interest paid to non-residents. This is not reduced under current tax treaties. Unrealized exchange gains on debt denominated in foreign currencies are not recognized on an annual basis. Similarly, unrealized exchange losses on such debt are not deductible on an annual basis.

Local Australian Financing. When debt is incurred locally, an investor can deduct interest expense, and no withholding tax is due. Interest is deductible even if the debt is guaranteed by a non-resident shareholder of a local subsidiary, provided the guaranteed debt is not foreign debt.

Equity Financing and Withholding Taxes on Dividends. A dividend paid by an Australian resident company to a non-resident shareholder is generally subject to withholding tax to the extent that it has not been franked. Australia imposes dividend withholding tax at the rate of 30%. This rate is normally reduced to 15% by a tax treaty. No deduction is allowed for the payment of dividends.

Thin Capitalization Rules. The availability of a tax deduction may be restricted or denied for interest on debt associated with thinly capitalized foreign investments in Australia. The thin capitalization rules apply to Australian companies or other business enterprises in which non-residents, together with their associates, have at least a 15% interest in the control, capital or income of the enterprise. These rules may also apply to foreign investors with investments such as branch operations, rental investments or joint ventures in Australia.

Previously, the restriction on interest deduction applied to the extent that the ratio of relevant interest-bearing debt to relevant foreign equity exceeded 3 to 1. Legislation, which at the time of publication had not yet been passed by Parliament, would reduce this ratio to 2 to 1 after July 1, 1997.

If an Australian company borrows from an overseas third-party financial institution with the debt guaranteed by a foreign affiliate of the company, the pending legislation would treat the foreign debt as if it were foreign related-party debt, subjecting it to the thin capitalization rules.

Exchange Controls

Australia generally imposes no exchange controls on transfers of Australian or foreign currency. Thus, there are no currency restrictions on payments of interest, principal, dividends or returns of capital to non-residents. Unlimited quantities of foreign currency may be bought and sold provided that the dealings are conducted with an institution authorized by the Reserve Bank of Australia. No reserve requirements exist with respect to loans issued by non-residents.

Business Acquisitions and Dispositions

Capital Contributions into an Existing Local Entity

A capital contribution into a local entity is not subject to local tax. There are no limitations to the value of intangibles that a foreign entity can contribute to an existing local entity. A capital contribution should not affect existing shareholders, unless a change in majority ownership occurs.

If a foreign entity owns only a minority interest in a local entity, most tax attributes are normally available. Protection is available under some double-tax treaties.

If a telecommunications business transfers services or technology from an external source in exchange for an ownership interest in an Australian business, withholding tax may be payable when the ownership interest is received by the transferor in the form of a royalty. Withholding tax should not be payable when an ownership interest is provided in return for a transfer of inventory.

Purchase or Sale of Shares in a Local Entity

A foreign corporation can acquire the shares of an Australian company. A resident vendor, selling the shares in the local entity, will be subject to capital gains tax (CGT). A non-resident vendor will be subject to CGT on the sale of shares in most unlisted companies. A non-resident vendor will also be subject to CGT if, at any time during the previous five years, it owned not less than 10% of the share capital of an Australian resident company listed on any stock exchange.

The purchaser will not receive a step-up in the tax basis of the underlying assets of the acquired company for CGT purposes. The acquired company should retain the benefit of any foreign tax credits carried forward as well as accumulated dividend imputation credit and eligibility for tax concessions. The purchaser assumes all existing liabilities, including any that may be undisclosed.

Stamp duty on the transfer of shares generally applies at concessional rates of either 0.3% for listed shares or 0.6% for unlisted shares (other than for land-rich entities).

Purchase or Sale of Assets

A foreign corporation can also acquire an Australian company's assets. The purchase price is allocated to individual assets, with market value used to establish depreciation deductions. The purchaser can recover the cost of most intellectual property (e.g., patents, copyrights or registered designs) over the estimated life of the property, but not goodwill. By acquiring a company's assets, a purchaser can normally avoid assuming any undisclosed liabilities of the target business. Stamp duty payable on the transfer of assets can be substantial, costing as much as 5.5% of the value of the assets.

A local entity selling assets of a business will generally be subject to capital gains tax if the assets were acquired after September 19, 1985. In addition, recoupment provisions in relation to previously deducted amounts apply to items such as depreciation and intellectual property amortization. The profit on the sale of trading stock is normally taxable.

Generally, the only tax-free alternatives for disposition are group rollovers in cases in which the underlying ownership of the assets has not changed.

Acquiring a Partnership Interest. The acquisition of a partnership interest is treated as a partial acquisition of partnership assets for capital gains tax purposes. The purchaser will, therefore, be able to obtain a step-up in the basis of the interest in the partnership assets. Similarly, the selling partner will be treated as having disposed of an interest in each partnership asset. A new partner can normally avoid assuming any undisclosed liabilities of the partnership, and may share in the current-year losses or profits. Plant, equipment and inventories can receive a step-up in cost to market value.

Start-up Business Issues

Pre-operating Losses and Start-up/Construction Costs

Fees incurred in establishing a business, such as license fees and franchise fees, are deductible to the extent that they are incurred in producing assessable income. However, to the extent that these fees are capital in nature, they are not deductible. Fees that result in an enduring benefit will generally be characterized as being capital in nature. For instance, the cost of conducting a feasibility study is unlikely to be deductible.

In relation to the construction of a telecommunications network or facility, direct costs and direct overhead must be capitalized. The outright deductibility of finance costs, such as interest, incurred in funding start-up or construction costs is currently subject to the outcome of litigation. To be deductible or amortizable, the costs would need to be borne by a local entity (including a local branch) and not by a foreign parent. Withholding tax would be payable only on a charge by a foreign parent to a subsidiary to recover such costs if they represented a royalty.

Customs Duties and VAT

Most imported telecommunications equipment is subject to customs duty at a rate of 5% of customs value. The valuation of goods is based on the General Agreement on Tariffs and Trade (GATT) valuation code. In most cases, the customs value is determined according to the free-on-board (FOB) price of the goods from the place of export.

When there is no equivalent or substitutable Australian manufactured product that competes with an imported product, it may be possible to obtain a tariff concession order, thus reducing the duty on the imported product to 3%. A range of concessions is also available for various types of goods, including capital equipment. Customs duties may also be reduced on individual components of major plant items. State-of-the-art capital equipment that is not ordinarily made in Australia may also be imported free of duty.

Australia imposes a 22% sales tax on imported and domestically manufactured goods, including computer hardware and electronic/mechanical equipment, such as switches and motor vehicles. Although most commercial goods are taxed at 22%, certain goods are exempt, including most building materials and software.

Goods are ordinarily subject to tax when sold wholesale in Australia. If a wholesale sale does not occur, alternate taxing points exist; when the goods are imported directly by the user, for instance, tax is imposed at the time of importation. The value on which tax is payable is the wholesale selling price or, when an alternate taxing point applies, an equivalent amount.

There is no sales tax imposed on services such as regular telephony and Internet telephony. Australia does not impose a value-added tax.

Loss Carryovers

Losses incurred after July 1, 1990, may be carried forward indefinitely. (Australia previously imposed a seven-year limit.) Losses may not be carried back.

Prior-year losses or losses incurred in any part of the current year can be deducted if there is a continuity of ownership or the company continues to conduct the same business activity. Therefore, a local company may be unable to utilize its carried-forward tax losses if there has been a majority change in ownership or if it has changed its business activity (including, possibly, a change from wireline telephony to a mobile business).

Within a corporate group, losses can be transferred between two resident companies when either one company entirely owns the other or both are wholly owned by another company. The group company relationship must be satisfied throughout the year the loss was incurred, the year of transfer and any years in between.

Operating Considerations

Corporate Income Taxes

The federal income tax rate is 36% for both resident and non-resident companies. A resident company is taxed on income from all sources. A non-resident company is assessed only on income from sources in Australia.

Capital Gains Taxes

Capital gains tax applies to assets acquired on or after September 20, 1985. Capital gains and losses are recognized when assets are disposed or deemed to be disposed of (for example, by sale, gift or grant of interest). When corporations cease to be residents of Australia, they are deemed to dispose of certain assets at that time. The sale of shares in an Australian company creates a capital gains tax liability to the extent that the sale price exceeds the cost basis of the shares. This exposure may be avoided under some tax treaties.

Capital gains are calculated after allowing for inflation (i.e., the cost base of the asset is indexed to the consumer price index). Capital losses are calculated without indexation. Any net capital gain for the year (i.e., the aggregate of capital gains less allowable capital losses) is included in the company's taxable income and taxed at regular rates. Any net capital loss for the year is carried forward to offset future capital gains or may be transferred by one resident corporation to another resident corporation within the same wholly owned corporate group (subject to certain restrictions).

Tax Holidays and Exemptions

Industrial Research and Development Incentives. Resident companies are entitled to special tax concessions for research and development (R&D) activities undertaken to acquire new knowledge or to create new or improved materials, devices, products, processes or services. To obtain the tax concessions, a company must be registered with the Industry Research and Development Board. The incentives include:

- A 125% (previously 150%) immediate deduction for expenditures incurred directly for research and development activities

- A 125% deduction over three years of the capital cost of the plant used exclusively for research and development purposes

- A deduction over the term of the related R&D activity for expenditure incurred to acquire pre-existing "core technology" (however, the deduction in a particular year cannot exceed one-third of the amount of R&D expenditure incurred in that year on the related R&D activity)

There are two categories of eligible R&D activities:

- Core activities, which are defined broadly to include systematic, investigative and experimental activities involving innovation or high levels of technical risk, and which are carried on for the purpose of acquiring new knowledge or creating new or improved materials, products, devices, processes or services

- Supporting activities, including other activities carried on for a purpose directly related to the carrying on of core activities

Technology is considered to be core technology in relation to particular R&D activities if the purpose of the activities is to obtain new knowledge based on that technology or to create new or improved materials, products, devices, processes, techniques or services based on that technology, or if the R&D activities are an extension, continuation, development or completion of the activities that produced the technology.

For software development costs to be eligible for the R&D concession, there must be an intention that the software be licensed to two or more independent parties.

Regional Headquarters. Certain concessions are available to encourage multinational corporations to locate their regional headquarters (RHQ) in Australia. To become an RHQ, a company must apply to the Federal Treasurer and demonstrate that it intends to establish facilities in Australia for the main purpose of providing regional headquarters support (including management-related services, data services or software support services) to associated companies located outside Australia.

Depreciation/Cost-Recovery Conventions/Accelerated Deductions

Both the straight-line method (also known as the prime-cost method) and the diminishing-balance method are acceptable for tax purposes. There is limited accelerated depreciation available. The depreciation rules apply on a "unit of property" basis. Depreciation deductions are allowed where plant or articles have been used by the taxpayer during the year of income for the purpose of producing assessable income or, alternatively, have been installed ready for use for that purpose and held in reserve.

The annual depreciation rate, for units of depreciable property purchased after February 26, 1992, is determined by reference to the property's effective life in accordance with established rates, as reflected in the following table:

	Annual Depreciation Percentage	
Effective Life in Years	Prime Cost Method	Diminishing Balance Method
Fewer than 3	100%	100%
3 to fewer than 5	40%	60%
5 to fewer than 6 2/3	27%	40%
6 2/3 to fewer than 10	20%	30%
10 to fewer than 13	17%	25%
13 to fewer than 30	13%	20%
30 or more	7%	10%

The taxation law requires a taxpayer to self-assess the depreciation rate applicable for specific units of property based on the taxpayer's estimation of the reasonable length of time the property is capable of being used for income-producing purposes in the taxpayer's business. Given the impracticality of doing this for every unit of property, the Commissioner of Taxation publishes safe-haven rates. However, there are few such rates published for telecommunications equipment. The rates (shown in table at page bottom) have been gleaned from prior experience and should be seen as only approximate.

Australian Taxation Office practice is to permit a tax deduction outright for application software purchased. However, software integral with the computer system, including most software embedded in telecommunications equipment, is depreciated at the same rate as the equipment to which it relates. Investors can normally deduct marketing and advertising expenses, including payments made directly or indirectly through sales agents to contract customers. No special rules exist for these costs.

Transfer Pricing Rules

The transfer pricing provisions apply to transactions between separate legal entities when these four conditions are satisfied:

- There is an acquisition or supply of property or services under an international agreement.

- Two or more of the parties to the agreement were not dealing with each other at arm's length.

- The consideration, in the case of the supply of property or services, is less than, or in the case of the acquisition of property or services, exceeds the arm's-length consideration. The Commissioner of Taxation has issued guidelines establishing acceptable methodologies for determining what amounts to an arm's-length consideration.

- The Commissioner of Taxation has determined that the transfer pricing provisions apply.

The Revenue Department recently began actively enforcing the transfer pricing provisions and has instigated transfer pricing audits.

Transfers of Patents, Trademarks and Software

The taxation implications of a transfer of technology depend on the nature of the sale. When the entire right to a technology is transferred, the amount received may be characterized as a capital receipt and be assessed in accordance with the capital gains tax provisions. If a telecommunications company merely transfers the right to use the technology, the amount received is characterized as revenue and assessable as ordinary income.

Royalty payments and software licensing fees are deductible, except when they are of a capital nature. Royalties paid to non-residents will be subject to withholding tax of 30% of the gross amount of royalties. When the royalties are paid to a resident of a country with which Australia has a tax treaty, the maximum rate is usually reduced to 10%.

Service Fees

Service fees are generally deductible, provided they are incurred in earning assessable income or in carrying on a business for the purpose of gaining or earning assessable income.

Unit of Telecommunications Equipment	Estimated Effective Life	Prime Cost Depreciation Rate	Diminishing Value Depreciation Rate
Coaxial cable systems	10–15 years	17% or 13%	25% or 20%
Optical fiber cable systems	15–25 years	13%	20%
Switching equipment (e.g., gateway exchange)	5–7 years	27% or 20%	40% or 30%
Multiplexers	5–10 years	27%–17%	40%–25%
Sound and video equipment	10 years	17%	25%
Data transmission equipment	5–10 years	27%–17%	40%–25%
Satellite equipment (earth station, mobile and maritime)	8–20 years	20%–13%	30%–20%

If the fees are paid for the supply or use of pre-existing technical information or know-how, the fee may be more correctly considered to be a royalty (which, for tax purposes, is defined broadly) and consequently be subject to withholding tax.

Value-Added Tax, Sales Tax and/or Other Pertinent Taxes

Sales tax is federal tax imposed on tangible goods that are manufactured in, or imported for use in, Australia. The tax is a single-stage tax designed to fall primarily on sales by manufacturers or by wholesalers to retailers. Sales tax is payable on the normal taxable value, which is generally the equivalent of a fair wholesale price.

The general tax rate is 22%, unless the goods are specifically listed as being exempt or taxable at some other rate, being either 12%, 26%, 32% or 45%.

Australia does not impose VAT.

Local and Provincial Taxes

Stamp Duty. Each state and territory imposes duties on a wide range of certain documents and transactions, such as transfers of property, sales of securities and leasing and hiring arrangements. Rates for real estate can range up to 5.5%, rates for marketable securities are generally 0.6%, and rates for other business assets can reach 5.5%.

Land Tax. Each state and the Australian Capital Territory impose land tax. The tax rates vary by jurisdiction and are applied to the unimproved value of the land on either a flat rate or a progressive rate.

Payroll Tax. Each state and territory imposes payroll tax on the value of a business's payroll, subject to certain thresholds and exemptions.

For Additional Information, Contact:

Gordon Thring
Tax Partner
333 Collins Street
Melbourne 3000
Australia
Telephone: 61 (3) 9633 3621
Fax: 61 (3) 9633 3999
E-mail: Gordon_Thring@au.coopers.com

John Montgomery
Management Consulting Partner
Coopers & Lybrand Tower
580 George Street
Sydney 2000
Australia
Telephone: 61 (2) 9285 7859
Fax: 61 (2) 9285 5093
E-mail: John_Montgomery@au.coopers.com

China
(People's Republic of)

Telecommunications Tax Profile
by Marina Y. P. Wong
Partner, Hong Kong

Overview of the Telecommunications Market

Historical Background

The Ministry of Posts and Telecommunications (MPT), which is a functional department of the State Council, has traditionally acted as the principal regulatory and supervisory body for the telecommunications sector in China. In addition to its administrative departments, the MPT has several business enterprises, including the China National Posts and Telecommunications Industry Corp. (PTIC). Since its founding in 1980, PTIC has established many companies that design and manufacture telecommunications equipment and related products, such as cables, telephone exchange equipment, transmission equipment and terminal equipment.

Prior to February 1994, the Directorate General of Telecommunications (DGT) functioned as the head office of the MPT's telecommunications division. At that time, the State Council approved a reorganization of the MPT, which resulted in DGT's becoming an "entity of an enterprise nature," with accounting responsibilities independent of the MPT. On April 27, 1995, DGT registered as an "enterprise with legal responsibility" with the State Administration of Industry and Commerce under the name Directorate General of Telecommunications, P&T, China (China Telecom).

Due to the historical lack of a widespread telecommunications infrastructure throughout China, the Ministry of Railways (MR), the Ministry of Electronics Industry (MEI), the Ministry of Power Industry (MPI) and the People's Liberation Army have undertaken the task of constructing and operating their own telecommunications networks.

In July 1994, permission was granted to several consortia to enter and compete in the telecommunications equipment and service markets:

- Lian Tong, which is the United Telecommunications Corporation Ltd. (China Unicom), was established in July 1994 to provide competition in the fixed and wireless telecommunications arenas. At that time, it was given permission to offer basic services. Principal shareholders are the MR, MEI and MPI. There are a large number of other shareholders from various central and provincial level organizations.

- Ji Tong Communications Co. Ltd. (Ji Tong), which is owned by 26 state institutions and is the contractor of the Golden Projects, China's national information infrastructure projects, was granted permission to provide information networks. Shareholders include the MEI, as well as provincial and city governments.

Because these consortia are composed of government ministries, competition in China's telecommunications sector remains relatively controlled. In 1995, China Unicom began competing for digital cellular customers.

Current Status

Growth of the telecommunications industry has always been regarded as an important factor in stimulating continued economic development in China. In 1996, the national economic growth rate was being outpaced by that of the telecommunications sector. In that year, China's annual economic growth rate was 9.7%, while the post and telecommunications sector's revenues increased 35.4% over 1995 results to US$16.08 billion. Overall 1996 investment in the post and telecommunications industry is reported to have been US$12.48 billion, representing a 5.1% increase over 1995.

Infrastructure enhancements are being made to meet the growing demand for telecommunications services. By the end of 1996, 61.79 million people had telephones, representing an approximate 5.15% penetration of the current population, and a 39.4% increase in the number of people with telephones over 1995.

The major infrastructure enhancements being made in China's public switched telephone network are fiber optic, satellite, and microwave links. In 1995, six newly built fiber optic cable trunks across Beijing, Shenyang, and Harbin; Xian, Lanzhou, and Urumqi; Urumqi and Yiming; Beijing, Chengde, Fuxin, Baicheng and Qiqihar; Beijing, Wuhan and Guangzhou; and Jinan and Qingdao went into trial or formal operation. Fourteen satellite earth stations were constructed or upgraded the same year. In 1995, additional fiber optic cables were deployed to support the increased demand for digital transmission capabilities throughout China.

In 1996, infrastructure enhancement in China's public switched telephone network continued. China installed four major fiber optic lines. During the same period, thirty-one satellite earth stations were constructed or upgraded. By the end of 1996, the length of national fiber optic line stretched 130,000 km, while the length of digital microwave links amounted to 52,000 km.

China's switching capacity reached 109 million subscribers in 1996, with computer-programmed control provided 99.5% of the time. During the same year, the switching capacity of mobile telecommunications reached 7.16 million subscribers, with digital switches serving 2.74 million subscribers. Global system for mobile communications (GSM) is the prevailing technology employed at present in China.

Demand for wireless service continues to dramatically increase. By the end of 1996, the number of mobile phone subscribers reached 6.85 million, an annual growth rate of 88.8%. Digital cellular service is also developing rapidly, with its subscriber base accounting for 24% of the total cellular subscriber base. Paging services have been deployed throughout China and, by year-end 1996, were being used by 25.41 million subscribers, a 45.8% increase over 1995.

Current Liberalization Status

As previously stated, China Unicom was established in July 1994 to provide competition in the fixed and wireless telecommunications arenas. Given the fact that China Telecom (previously DGT) had been the only public telecommunications services provider for decades and that it remains an operational arm of the MPT, which regulates the industry, China Unicom faces an entrenched competitor that is also a regulator. Under these circumstances,

China Unicom's development has not approached initial projections and it poses little competition to China Telecom.

In October 1993, the State Council issued Document 55, which established provisional measures for the liberalization of value-added services. Radio mobile communications services require an MPT license, while EDI (electronic data interchange), e-mail, audiotex, videotex and other information services require only the approval of the MPT.

Type of Service	Degree of Liberalization	Key Legislation	Date of Actual or Expected Liberalization
Local	Partially liberalized	State Council Decision	1994
Long Distance	Partially liberalized	State Council Decision	1994
International	Partially liberalized	State Council Decision	1997
Cellular	Partially liberalized	State Council Decision	1994
Paging	Liberalized	State Council Document 55	1993
Value-added	Liberalized	State Council Document 55	1993

Competitive Environment

Although China Unicom has been authorized to operate public telephone networks, it is expected to take several more years before the company will be able to implement its own telecommunications infrastructure. As stated earlier, China Unicom poses no significant competition to China Telecom, particularly with respect to local, long-distance and international services. In addition, little public information on China Unicom's operational results is available. Therefore, no information on China Unicom, except for cellular service, is included in the table below.

	Entire Market		Top Two Players		
Type of Service	Market Size (1996)	Number of Players	Names	Annual Revenue (1996)	Ownership
Local	In excess of Rmb 47 billion	2	China Telecom China Unicom	Rmb 47 billion Not available	State-owned State-owned
Long Distance	In excess of Rmb 46.43 billion	2	China Telecom China Unicom	Rmb 46.43 billion Not available	State-owned State-owned
International	In excess of Rmb 22.72 billion	2	China Telecom China Unicom	Rmb 22.72 billion Not available	State-owned State-owned
Cellular	Not available	2	China Telecom China Unicom	Not available Not available	State-owned State-owned
Paging	Not available				
Value-added	Not available				

Source: MPT, *1996 Bulletin on Statistics on Telecommunications Development.*
Rmb = Renminbi (currency)

Licensing Requirements

Although the MPT is the regulatory agency officially responsible for telecommunications development within China, the State Council took the liberalization initiative to authorize Ji Tong and China Unicom to provide telecommunications competition to the state monopoly. Many provincial telecommunications administrations have independently entered into negotiations with joint venture partners. Ultimately, however, these administrations report to the DGT.

New entrants to the telecommunications equipment sector must apply for relevant licenses or permits, usually from a provincial post and telecommunications administration. In cases where the investment is significant or the product is deemed critical, authorization from the MPT is required.

Licenses to new entrants in telecommunications operations are given at the discretion of the State Telecom Industry Leading Group, a committee under the State Council; these do not seem realistic in the foreseeable future.

Potential for Foreign Ownerships/Relationships

Until recently, foreign participation in China's telecommunications market has been relatively limited because foreign investors are not allowed to own or operate telephone networks and/or paging systems directly. That situation is changing, although certain sectors remain closed to foreign involvement. For example, on June 30, 1993, the MPT imposed a complete ban on foreign investment in the operation of telecommunications services.

Conversely, over the last decade, the Chinese government has gradually allowed foreign funds to be utilized for modernizing the telecommunications sector, and has approved loans on favorable terms from foreign governments and international financial organizations and other types of direct investment by foreign investors.

In 1994, the MPT issued a notice that encouraged the use of foreign funds but again reiterated a ban on any involvement in network operations. Foreign investors may participate on a fixed-period-of-return basis or for a percentage of the operating profits according to the proportion of investment.

Foreign investors are also allowed to participate in the manufacture of certain types of equipment. Many joint ventures have been set up between foreign equipment vendors and local Chinese enterprises, usually the PTIC or MEI. Some foreign companies have also successfully set up joint ventures with either China Unicom or Ji Tong to provide network consulting services to the Chinese government in return for a share of the profits.

In June 1994, the MPT announced that foreign funds invested in the telecommunications sector since 1984 amounted to US$5.7 billion. At the end of 1995, the MPT announced that it would use additional foreign funds of US$2.1 billion and US$5 billion to implement its ninth five-year plan (1996–2000).

Potential for Upcoming Liberalization/Investment Opportunities

Over the next few years, China Unicom and Ji Tong will continue to be seen by many foreign investors as potential joint venture partners for entering China's telecommunications market. Future development of China's telecommunications infrastructure will emphasize deployment of modern technology for synchronous automation, digital mobile telecommunications, asynchronous transmission and broadband systems.

According to China's *Foreign Investment Industrial Guidance Catalogue,* which was issued in mid-1995, foreign investment is encouraged in certain types of projects such as the manufacture of certain communications equipment, and the provision of information and consulting services.

According to an internal document issued by the State Leading Group of Information, China Unicom is encouraged to compete with China Telecom on equal terms. China Unicom has been authorized to be involved in local, long distance and international business as well as wireless operations. The document also obligates the MPT to provide necessary interconnections to China Unicom to help it compete. In addition, the document allows for foreign funds to be received through an offshore joint venture, with foreign investors receiving returns based on a percentage of operating profits, according to the proportion of investment. However, merger and/or acquisition activities are not expected in the foreseeable future.

Forms of Doing Business

Permanent Establishment

According to the laws and regulations of the People's Republic of China (PRC), permanent establishment (PE) refers to management organizations; business organizations; representative offices and factories; places where natural resources are exploited; places where contracted projects of construction, installation, assembly and exploration are operated; places where labor services are provided; and business agents.

Under most tax treaties concluded between China and other countries, there are provisions concerning PEs. For example, a foreign company with no formal presence in China will be deemed to have a PE in China if the following situations, inter alia, occur:

• Where a foreign company has a building site, a construction, assembly or installation project, or supervisory activities in connection therewith, but only where such site, proj-

ect or activities continue for a period of more than six months.

• Where the furnishing of services, including consultancy services, by a foreign company takes place through employees or other personnel engaged by the company for such purposes, but only where such activities continue (for the same or a connected project) within China for a period or periods aggregating more than six months within any 12-month period.

Telecommunications services can cover a broad range of activities, which may or may not constitute PE, as discussed below:

Long-Distance Telephone Services and Call Reorganization/Turnaround Services. When these services are rendered outside of China by a foreign company to local Chinese customers without any presence or advertising in China, the telephone fee for services rendered outside of China is not subject to tax in China. However, if any of these services were rendered by a foreign company on a regular basis through its employees or dependent agents in China, the foreign company would be regarded as having a PE and would be subject to Foreign Enterprise Income Tax (FEIT) at 33% (subject to certain concessionary treatments) on profits derived from sales of telephone services conducted by such agents. In addition, business tax of 3% would be levied on the gross service fee income received.

Licensing of Technology and Know-How. A foreign company that provided a local Chinese company the right to use its technology and know-how and received a royalty or a license fee would not be regarded as having a PE. However, such royalty or license fee would be subject to withholding tax at a rate of 20%. This rate may be reduced to 10% under a tax treaty or if the fee is received from a company set up in one of the PRC's special tax regions.

Technical Assistance and Technological Services. If a foreign company provides technical assistance and technological services, including operator services and/or network management services, to a local company by sending its own employees to China in exchange for service fees, a PE is deemed to exist and such service fees will be subject to FEIT at a rate of 33% on a deemed profit basis. In addition, business tax will be imposed at 5% on the gross service income.

However, if the foreign company is established in a jurisdiction that has entered into a double-tax treaty with China, it will generally be deemed to have a PE only if such activities performed by its own employees in China continue for a period or periods aggregating more than six months within any 12-month period. If the six-month threshold is met, the foreign company will be subject to FEIT at a rate of 33% on a deemed profit basis on income for services in China and business tax of 5% on the gross service income. If the six-month threshold under the double-tax treaty is not met, the foreign company will not be deemed to have a PE in China and will not be subject to FEIT. However, the service income will still be subject to business tax.

Furthermore, if a portion of the fee payment includes consideration for the transfer of technology from the foreign company to the local company, that portion will be subject to withholding tax at a rate of 20%, which could be reduced under a double-tax treaty or if the local company paying the fee is resident in a special tax region in China.

Leasing of Telecommunications Equipment. A foreign company that leased telecommunications equipment to a local Chinese company and received rental income would not be considered to have a PE. Nevertheless, it would be subject to withholding tax at a rate of 20% on the gross amount of the rental income received from the Chinese company, which could be reduced to 10% by a tax treaty or if the rental income were received from a company set up in one of the special tax regions.

Internet Access Software and Services. The sale of Internet access software by a foreign company to a local Chinese person or entity without any intermediaries would not constitute a PE. If, however, the sale of the software had been arranged as the licensing of an intangible and the foreign company received a royalty payment, the provision of the right for a Chinese individual or company to use in China the intangible owned by the foreign company would be similar to the provision of licensing of technology or know-how (as discussed above) and the foreign company would not be regarded as having a PE. However, the gross amount of the royalty payment would be subject to withholding tax of 20%, which could be reduced by a tax treaty or if it had been received from a company or person resident in a special tax region.

There are currently no specific rules and regulations in China concerning the tax treatment of Internet access services. As such, the general rule regarding PEs may be applied when determining the taxability of the time charges incurred by a user of Internet access services.

For example, if the server or switch is located in China, a PE may be deemed to exist whether or not any other personnel are sent to China, and the time charges for the server access services would be subject to FEIT at 33% on deemed profit, and business tax at 3% on gross service income.

If a website is located on a server in China, a PE may be deemed to exist regardless of whether it is accessible by customers in China, or only accessible by customers outside of China. The time charges for the server access services would then be subject to FEIT at 33% on deemed profit, and business tax at 3% on gross service income.

If a website were located on a server outside China, it could be argued that no PE had been created even if the website were accessible by customers in China. Due to lack of case precedence in the area of Internet access services, the tax authorities should be consulted on a case-by-case basis until the relevant tax polices have become more developed.

Laying of Fiber Optic Cable and Construction of Telecommunications Equipment. Where a foreign company lays fiber optic cable and constructs telecommunications switching equipment in China either (a) for sale to a local Chinese company or (b) under a contracting project in exchange for a fee, the foreign company is considered to have a PE, because it has maintained a place or places where labor services for laying cable and constructing equipment are provided or where contracted projects of installation and construction are operated.

Under arrangement (a), a foreign company would be subject to FEIT of 33% on a gain derived from the sale, and to business tax of 5% on any gross proceeds attributable to the transfer of any immovable structures/properties. Under (b), a foreign company would be subject to FEIT of 33% on a deemed profit basis and to business tax of 3% on the gross fee income received. In addition, stamp tax of 0.03% and 0.05% would be levied on any sales and purchase contract, and construction contract, respectively, concluded in China.

Business Entities

The telecommunications industry in China is highly regulated. Foreign investors are not permitted to own or operate telecommunications services in China. They may, however, make capital investments in projects with Chinese companies that hold telecommunications licenses in return for revenue sharing. Network consulting projects that fall under the telecommunications business sector would only be approved in China if they were being undertaken as a joint venture with investments from Chinese and foreign companies. Foreign investment in plants for the manufacture of telecommunications equipment would be allowed if they were in the form of a joint venture.

Many foreign companies will establish representative offices in China as an initial step toward investing. Establishment of branch offices by foreign companies in China has been restricted mainly to foreign banks, insurance companies and law firms. Other common forms of foreign investment in China include equity joint ventures, cooperative joint ventures and wholly foreign-owned enterprises, which are collectively referred to as foreign investment enterprises (FIEs). Formation of FIEs is subject to various layers of government approval depending on the industry, location and capital investment amounts of the projects.

Representative Office. A representative office is a foreign company's formal presence in China. It is not a separate legal entity. A representative office is technically not allowed to conduct any profit-making business activities. It is only allowed to perform various promotional and liaison functions. A representative office may be taxable in China depending on the nature of the activities carried out both by itself and by its foreign head office.

Equity Joint Ventures. Foreign investors are permitted to form equity joint ventures (EJVs) with Chinese companies, enterprises or other economic organizations whereby the foreign and Chinese partners jointly manage the operations and take shares in a limited liability company registered in China. The duration of an equity joint venture is limited, depending on the industry and the terms of the joint venture agreement, although it may be extended upon approval by the Chinese authorities.

Profits and losses are shared according to the proportion of investment contributed by each partner. The contributions by the foreign partner, which are normally in the form of cash, machinery and equipment or technology transfer, cannot amount to less than 25% of the registered capital. In China, the term "registered capital" refers to the equity of the joint venture parties. It is distinguished from the concept of total investment, which means the total of registered capital and outstanding loans.

EJVs should file separate tax returns based on their own profits and losses. Consolidation of profits and losses of different companies is not allowed for tax purposes. A foreign company entering into an EJV with a local partner would not be deemed to have a PE.

Cooperative Joint Ventures. Cooperative joint ventures (CJVs) may take any form agreed upon between the Chinese and foreign partners. CJVs are commonly used for special projects such as joint construction and management of hotels and commercial complexes, offshore oil drilling and related services, and the manufacture of specialty goods. They may be structured as legal entities with limited liabilities or without a corporate form. The latter, however, is now being discouraged by the Chinese government. Cooperative joint ventures may or may not be appropriate for telecommunications investments, depending upon the circumstances.

For CJVs that do not constitute legal entities, each partner must assess and pay its income tax separately. Chinese parties assess and pay their income tax in accordance with laws and regulations for domestic enterprises. Foreign parties are deemed enterprises having PEs and pay FEIT. CJVs that did not constitute legal entities would not be regarded as FIEs, and therefore would not be able to enjoy the preferential tax treatments available for FIEs. (See "Operating Considerations.") CJVs that constitute legal entities may, upon approval of the local tax authorities, be subject to FEIT and enjoy preferential tax treatments available for FIEs.

CJVs which constitute legal entities should file separate tax returns based on their own profits and losses. As with EJVs, the consolidation of profits and losses of different companies is not allowed for tax purposes. The foreign company entering into a CJV with a local partner would not be deemed to have a PE.

Local Funding Alternatives

Debt versus Equity

The operation of an FIE may be financed through a capital contribution by its shareholders and/or by borrowing. If financing is done through a capital contribution by the shareholders, the shareholders will receive their return on investment by means of dividends out of after-tax profits of the FIE. Dividends paid to foreign investors of FIEs are not subject to withholding tax.

Under the corporate income tax law in China, an FIE may not deduct any interest expense incurred on equity capital raised by its shareholders. Also, if the foreign investors of an FIE fail to contribute the total registered capital of the FIE within the prescribed time period but provide interest-bearing loans to FIE instead, the FIE may not claim as a tax deduction the amount of interest expense equal to the interest payable on the difference between the total registered capital as required and the actual amounts contributed. However, interest on loans borrowed by the FIE for financing production or business operations would be deductible in determining its taxable income. If this debt is guaranteed by a shareholder, it is viewed as an external borrowing.

Chinese law permits an FIE to obtain financing either locally or from overseas, including its non-resident investors. Interest paid to non-resident investors is subject to withholding tax in China at a rate of 20%, which may be reduced by a tax treaty. Whether a debt is classified as internal or external borrowing does not affect the deductibility of the related interest expenses.

In some circumstances, shareholder debt financing—as opposed to equity financing—may result in a better tax position for FIEs and their foreign investors. While the foreign investors providing the debts to the FIEs are subject to withholding tax of 20% (or 10%) in China in respect to the interest income on the debts, the FIEs paying the interest will be able to claim a deduction for corporate income tax, which is 33% (or 15%). The existence, extent or timing of the possible tax benefits are, however, subject to other factors, such as whether the FIEs are entitled to tax holiday periods, the location of the FIEs in China, the tax treatments applicable to the interest income in the foreign investors' home country tax jurisdictions, and the view of the PRC local tax authorities on the interest payments from a transfer-pricing perspective.

Exchange gains and losses arising from debt financing are treated as ordinary income and expenses for determining the FIE's taxable income. The required debt-to-equity ratio for joint venture investment must be the higher of column (A) or (B):

Total Investment	Minimum Percentage of Registered Share Capital (A)	Minimum Required Share Capital (B)
US$3 million or less	70.0%	—
US$3–10 million	50.0%	US$2.1 million
US$10–30 million	40.0%	US$5.0 million
Over US$30 million	33.3%	US$12.0 million

Therefore, the amount of borrowing is generally restricted to the difference between total investment and registered capital. An FIE can also borrow foreign currency from domestic and foreign lenders. External debts (i.e., foreign currency borrowing) must be registered with the State Administration of Exchange Control (SAEC) in order for the FIE to obtain a debt registration certificate to open a special foreign exchange account in China for future remittance of repayment of the loan principal and interest.

Exchange Controls

New foreign exchange regulations were introduced on July 1, 1996. Foreign exchange control is exercised in China and administered by the SAEC and its branches. The major features of exchange controls in China are as follows:

- FIEs are allowed to settle and purchase foreign exchange at either designated foreign exchange banks or swap centers.

- Control over capital account items is stringent. Foreign exchange borrowing by FIEs is required to be registered with the SAEC or its branches and subsequent repayment approved by the SAEC.

- Control over current account items is more relaxed. SAEC approval is not required for most such foreign exchange payments.

- Repatriation of after-tax profits and dividends is a current account item.

Business Acquisitions and Dispositions

Organizations, enterprises or individuals outside of China, as well as foreign investment enterprises in China, are not permitted to invest in, operate or participate in the operation of telecommunications businesses in China. In the future, if this restriction is relaxed, the tax issues would be as discussed below.

Capital Contributions into an Existing Local Entity

A capital contribution by a foreign company into a local company would generally not be subject to taxes, including business tax and FEIT in China. A foreign company can contribute cash, buildings, premises, equipment or other related materials, industrial property, or intangible assets (such as know-how or the land use right of a site) as investment into a local company. If the local company is an FIE, the portion of intangible assets contributed as capital cannot exceed 20% of its registered capital. However, no withholding tax is payable.

For the existing shareholders of an FIE, an additional capital contribution by the existing or new shareholders into the FIE would not have any tax consequences, as the existing shareholders would not have, in effect, transferred their equity interest.

Purchase or Sale of Shares in a Local Entity

The purchase of shares in an FIE would not give rise to FEIT or turnover tax issues for the non-resident purchaser. On the other hand, any gains derived from the sale of equity interest in an FIE by its non-resident investors would be subject to withholding tax of 20% (or 10%) in China. Business tax of 5% may be levied, at the discretion of the local tax authorities, on any identifiable part of intangible and/or immovable assets attributable to the equity interest transferred. Furthermore, stamp tax of 0.05% is payable on the transfer consideration by both seller and purchaser.

Subject to the approval of the relevant authorities, the FIE may revalue its assets to the extent of the premium for goodwill included in the share transfer price. However, if the FIE charges depreciation and amortization based on the revalued amounts of the assets, adjustments should be made to restore the depreciation and amortization amounts before revaluation for determining the FIE's FEIT.

Purchase or Sale of Assets

The purchaser of the assets shall record the purchase prices of the respective assets as their costs for depreciation and amortization purposes. If there are no allocated values to the respective assets, the purchaser may record the costs based on the net book values reflected in the seller's accounts before the asset transfer. The difference between the total purchase price of the assets (or the entire business) and such net book values may be treated as goodwill and amortized according to the relevant tax regulations.

On the other hand, any gain on the sale of assets by an FIE is subject to FEIT of 33%. If there are intangible or immovable assets involved, especially land and buildings, other taxes may also be applicable (e.g., business tax, land value appreciation tax, stamp tax). Used tangible assets are not subject to value-added tax.

A stamp tax of 0.03% is payable on the transfer consideration by both seller and purchaser.

Transfer of Shares versus Assets

The main difference in tax treatment is that a gain from the transfer of shares in an FIE by foreign investors will be subject to withholding tax while a gain from the transfer of assets by an FIE will be subject to FEIT.

Furthermore, if an FIE disposes of all its assets (or its business), it may be regarded as having ceased operations and any tax holiday benefits previously enjoyed by the FIE will have to be repaid to the China tax authorities if the operating period of the FIE is less than the prescribed minimum requirement. However, if the shares of an FIE are transferred, the FIE's legal identity continues and the FIE can enjoy the remaining tax holiday, if any.

Other than the above differences, the choice between transfer of shares and transfer of assets may be a commercial decision. For example, a transfer of assets can be a selective process where only the desired assets and/or liabilities are transferred. With a transfer of shares, such flexibility does not exist and there may be a hidden liabilities risk.

Start-up Business Issues

Pre-operating Losses and Start-up/ Construction Costs

Start-up expenses refer to expenses related to setting up an enterprise from the date the project is approved to the date production or business operations begin. The costs of purchasing and constructing fixed assets are excluded from start-up expenses. Start-up expenses should be capitalized and amortized over a minimum period of five years. There is no maximum period.

Infrastructure costs, such as network development, construction and building, should be capitalized and are subject to depreciation starting from the month they are put into operation, using the straight-line method for a period of 5, 15 or 20 years. (See "Depreciation/Cost-Recovery Conventions/ Accelerated Deductions.")

Interest expense incurred on loans made for construction or purchase of assets should be capitalized during the construction period. Interest on loans made for other purposes during the construction period are considered to be pre-operating expenses. Interest incurred after the completion of construction and the commencement of operations shall be considered a financial expense and charged to the profit and loss account in the period when it is incurred.

Customs Duties and VAT

The importation of telecommunications equipment, as well as telecommunications materials and parts, into China is subject to import duty and VAT. Import duties are levied based on the landed cost (i.e., cost, insurance and freight, or CIF) value of imported goods and are payable by the importer. Duty rates vary depending on the categories of goods concerned. There are two tiers of import duty rates: most-favored nation (MFN) rates and general rates. MFN rates, which range from 12% to 25%, apply to imports from countries that are eligible for MFN treatment. As of April 1, 1996, the general duty rates for various telecommunications equipment range from 20% to 40%. However, FIEs that obtained their business licenses prior to this date may be exempted from duties and VAT.

Import VAT is levied based on the CIF price of imported goods plus customs duty payable. The general import VAT rate for all equipment, materials and parts is 17%. There is no distinction between regular telephony and Internet telephony for the purposes of VAT.

Loss Carryovers

Operating losses incurred by FIEs and foreign enterprises with PEs in China may be carried forward for a period not to exceed five years. Losses may not be carried back. If a change of business activity is allowed, the FIE's legal identity continues and the operating losses can be carried forward.

Operating Considerations

Corporate Income Taxes

Under FEIT law, FIEs and foreign enterprises with PEs in China are subject to FEIT at a rate of 30% on their net taxable profits.

Withholding Tax. Any foreign enterprise that does not have a PE in China but derives interest, rent, royalties or other income (i.e., gains from alienation, which is the balance of the transfer value after deduction of the original value of properties such as premises and buildings as well as gains from disposal of an equity interest in an FIE) from sources in China, is subject to withholding tax on such income at a rate of 20%. This rate may be reduced to 10% if the income is sourced in Special Economic Zones, Economic and Technological Development Zones or the Shanghai Pudong New Area.

The tax rate may also be reduced under certain circumstances. For example, fees arising from the transfer of technology for China's key construction projects in communications development or for fiber optic communications may be taxed at a preferential rate of 10%. Tax exemption may even be granted if the technology is regarded by the Chinese authorities as advanced technology and is provided on preferential terms. It should be noted that these withholding tax reductions and exemptions are not granted automatically. They require approval by the Chinese tax authorities.

Capital Gains Taxes

There is no separate capital gains tax in China. Capital gains are taxed as part of ordinary income.

Tax Holidays and Exemptions

FIEs are eligible for various tax holidays and other tax reductions and exemptions under FEIT law. Some of the major tax incentives include a lower income tax rate of 15% or 24% for FIEs located in Special Economic Zones or in Economic and Technological Development Zones. Foreign investors are currently exempted from withholding tax when they repatriate after-tax profits in the form of dividends from FIEs. Research and development costs are deductible when incurred and are capitalized only after they are patented. If previously incurred research and development costs have been expensed, no recapture of expensed costs will generally be required when patented.

Production-Oriented Enterprises. FIEs that are regarded as production-oriented enterprises are eligible for a two-year exemption of income tax starting with the first profit-making year (after all previous losses are recouped) and a 50% reduction in income tax during the subsequent three years for those corporations with an operating term of not less than ten years. Production-oriented enterprises include FIEs involved in the manufacture and production of telecommunications equipment and related products.

Technically Advanced and Export-Oriented Enterprises. FIEs, including telecommunications entities, that are classified as technically advanced enterprises may apply for a three-year extension of the 50% tax reduction. Those FIEs that export 70% or more of their output in a given year are eligible, on the expiration of the ordinary tax holiday, for a 50% reduction in that year. However, the minimum reduced tax rate is 10%.

Service Enterprises. FIEs of a service nature (including telecommunications service businesses) located in Special Economic Zones that have foreign investments exceeding US$5 million and a contract life of 10 years or longer are exempt from income tax in the first profit-making year. They are then permitted a 50% tax reduction in the following two years. Service enterprises located in other areas are not entitled to tax holidays, other than the ones discussed above.

Tax Rebates on Reinvestment. A foreign investor in an FIE that reinvests its share of profit in China for a period of not less than five years may obtain a tax rebate of 40% of the income tax paid on the amount of the reinvestment. If the reinvestment is made for establishing or expanding an export-oriented enterprise or a technically advanced enterprise in China, the tax rebate is 100%.

Depreciation/Cost-Recovery Conventions/Accelerated Deductions

Fixed assets shall generally be depreciated using the straight-line method based on the cost of the fixed asset minus the estimated residual value of 10% of the cost. Premises, buildings and structures are depreciated over 20 years; trains, ships, machinery and other production equipment are depreciated over 10 years; and electronic equipment, transportation equipment other than ships and trains, appliances, tools and furniture are depreciated over five years. Intangible assets, such as patents, technical know-how, trademarks and copyrights, are amortized over the term of the contract or over a period of not less than 10 years. The required depreciation period may be shorter under certain circumstances.

Telecommunications equipment, such as transmitters, is generally depreciated over 10 years. There are no special depreciation rules for purchased software embedded in telecommunications equipment. If the software forms part of the hardware equipment purchase, the software costs are usually included as part of the tangible asset costs. If the software is separable and identifiable from the hardware equipment, it may be treated as an intangible asset and amortized accordingly.

Research and development costs are classified as general and administration expenses and are deductible for FEIT purposes in the period incurred. Marketing and advertising costs, including payments made directly or indirectly to attract customers, are classified as selling expenses and are also deductible for FEIT purposes in the year incurred.

Transfer Pricing Rules

FEIT law stipulates that all fees and charges arising from business transactions between FIEs or foreign enterprises in China and their associated enterprises (which are entities with which they have direct or indirect connections) must be made in the same manner as between independent parties. When the parties fail to meet this stipulation, and a reduction of taxable income results, the tax authorities are empowered to make reasonable adjustments.

The question of whether transactions are at arm's length or not is generally regarded as a question of fact. However, the tax authorities have acknowledged that determining a reasonable transfer price tends to be a process of negotiation, rather than one based on industry pricing information. It appears that there is no standard procedure with respect to the handling of information collected. The local tax bureaus are expected to analyze the information and take appropriate actions based on their expertise and experience.

Notwithstanding the above, there are certain inter-company transactions, which must meet the arm's-length test, that are specifically provided for in the FEIT law. They are the:

• Price for purchase and sale transactions

• Interest rate for financing transactions

• Charge rate for services

• Price or charge for the alienation of property or property rights

In the past, the Chinese tax authorities have been able to identify only the most obvious offenders to the arm's-length standards. However, as part of the efforts of the Chinese tax authorities to tighten tax administration and to stem the loss of state tax revenues, there has recently been a noticeable increase in the number of transfer pricing investigation cases targeted at FIEs. The following characteristics are considered targets for transfer pricing investigations:

• Suffering continuous losses for two or more years

• Dealing with associated enterprises established in tax havens

• Showing fluctuating profits

• Having a lower profit margin as compared to enterprises engaged in similar industries in the same area

• Having a lower profit margin as compared to enterprises within the same group

Under current law and practice, no penalties or interest charges are imposed for tax assessed pursuant to transfer pricing adjustments except in cases where tax evasion is involved.

Transfers of Patents, Trademarks and Software

A license to operate in the telecommunications service industry may not be transferred or sold by the owner. The transfer or as-

signment of patented rights, non-patented technology, trademark rights and copyrights from a foreign investor to an FIE in China is subject to business tax of 5% and withholding tax of 20% on any gains from the transfer (i.e., proceeds net of original cost).

Based on Chinese domestic law and most tax treaties, any payments of royalties or license fees made by FIEs to foreign investors that do not have a PE in China for sharing information concerning industrial, commercial or scientific experience would be subject to withholding tax at a rate of 20%. This rate may be reduced under certain circumstances. Under most double-taxation treaties, the withholding tax rate would be reduced to 10%.

Payments of royalties or software licensing fees to foreign investors are deductible by FIEs for income tax purposes, provided the amounts incurred are determined to be reasonable by the local tax authorities. However, royalty payments from a branch to its foreign head office are not deductible for tax purposes. FIEs should deduct a withholding tax of 20% of the gross amount of each royalty payment or software licensing fee made to a foreign enterprise. Many Sino-foreign tax treaties provide for a lower withholding tax rate of 10% on different types of passive income (e.g., royalty or loan interest income) paid by FIEs in China to foreign enterprises.

Service Fees

Services fees paid by an FIE to foreign investors are generally tax-deductible, provided the amounts are reasonable. China does not generally impose withholding tax on service fees paid to non-residents. If services were rendered by foreign investors or by other employees inside China, this would constitute a PE and the service income received by the foreign investors would be subject to FEIT. Under current practice, FEIT is assessed on a deemed-profit basis. The deemed-profit rate ranges from 10% to 40%, depending on the nature of the services and local regulations. In addition, business tax of 5% will be levied on the gross amount of the service income.

Value-Added Tax, Sales Tax and/or Other Pertinent Taxes

Value-Added Tax. VAT is levied on the importation and sale of goods and the provision of processing, repairing and maintenance services. In essence, it is a tax on consumption, as it is the final consumer who bears the burden of the tax. Although the final consumer will ultimately pay the tax, VAT is collected at each stage of the production and distribution chain. In principle, there is no VAT on exports. In other words, the exporters should be able to claim from the PRC government a refund of VAT they have paid to the suppliers. However, subject to the reduction in the VAT export refund rate, the exporters are now required to bear part of the VAT paid or they may transfer the burden to overseas consumers by raising the export prices, if possible.

Enterprises engaging in the manufacture of telecommunications equipment will pay VAT on the cost of the goods supplied (e.g., parts and components) and will charge VAT on the selling price of goods (e.g., telephone sets). The VAT paid on inputs (purchases) can be offset against the VAT collected on outputs (sales).

Transfers of intangible properties (e.g., patent rights, technology, trademarks and copyrights) or immovable properties (e.g., premises and buildings) are not subject to VAT. The general VAT rate is 17%. For running water, heating, liquid petroleum gas and natural gas, the VAT rate is reduced to 13%.

Input VAT paid on the purchase of fixed assets (e.g., VAT paid on the importation of machinery and equipment) or on the purchase of goods or services used in non-taxable activities is non-creditable against the VAT payable (i.e., output VAT net of input VAT) to the government. VAT would not apply to payments for the provision of Internet access or Internet telephony services.

Stamp Tax. Stamp tax is levied on taxable documents (e.g., installation contracts and technology contracts) concluded or enforced in China. It is payable by all contracting parties based on the gross value of the contracts, at rates ranging from .03% to .1%.

Business Tax. Contrary to VAT, business tax is imposed on enterprises in the services, transport and other non-production industries, as well as on the transfer of properties and intangible assets. Business tax is levied on gross revenue at rates between 3% and 5%, except for entertainment businesses.

The business tax rate applicable to enterprises engaging in the provision of telecommunications services is 3%. For those enterprises providing consulting services relating to telecommunications, the business tax rate is 5%.

The transfer of intangible assets and the sale of tangible assets are subject to business tax at a rate of 5%. However, any tangible or intangible asset that is contributed as a capital investment in an FIE is exempt from business tax.

Local and Provincial Taxes

In addition to the FEIT, companies are subject to a local surtax of 3% on their net taxable profits.

For Additional Information, Contact:

Marina Y. P. Wong
Partner
Sunning Plaza
10 Hysan Avenue
Hong Kong
Telephone: 852 2839 4321
Fax: 852 2576 5356
E-mail: marina_wong@hk.coopers.com

Hong Kong

Telecommunications Tax Profile
by Tim Leung
Tax Partner, Hong Kong
Ian Sanders
Consulting Director, Hong Kong

Overview of the Telecommunications Market

Historical Background

For nearly 26 years, the Hong Kong telecommunications sector was dominated by monopoly service providers. Local fixed-line telephone services were provided exclusively by Hong Kong Telephone Company Ltd. (HKTC) and international circuits and services by Hongkong Telecom International Ltd. (HKTI). Since 1992, the Hong Kong government has taken a number of steps to liberalize the industry.

In 1993 the government transferred authority for regulation of the industry from the Postmaster General to an independent organization, the Office of the Telecommunications Authority (OFTA). OFTA determines its own priorities and courses of action and is not legally bound to pursue a given path of deregulation.

HKTC's fixed-line monopoly ended in 1995. In July 1995 the government introduced a new category of fixed telecommunications network services (FTNS) licenses, which were granted to HKTC and three new market entrants (Hutchison Communications Ltd., New T&T and New World Telephone Ltd.). At the same time, the government stated that it would not invite further applications for FTNS licenses for at least three years after they were first granted. That period lapses in 1998.

HKTI's international service monopoly is protected until September 30, 2006. (*Editor's note: In January 1998, HKTI agreed to end its monopoly on international services six years earlier than the required date. The effect will be the elimination of all telecoms monopolies in Hong Kong in the year 2000.*) International simple resale (ISR) of voice services and public video telephone services connected to the public switched telephony network (PSTN) are not allowed, but the following services are permitted:

- Simple resale (i.e., resale of circuits that connect to the PSTN at either end) of HKTI's international private leased circuits for fax and data services (allowed from January 1, 1998)

- Virtual private networks for internal communications of companies and organizations

- Videoconferencing services and customers' terminals for mobile-satellite services

- Call-back services

- Self-provided circuits (external circuits for transmission of the licensee's traffic only, as contrasted with "private circuits" used to transmit intra-company or intra-organizational traffic)

- OFTA has issued 18 public non-exclusive telecommunications service (PNETS) licenses to call-back service providers and 55 international value-added network (IVAN) services licenses.

Current Status

Although the market for fixed-line basic service (access and local calls) is now open to competition, the three new FTNS providers have been slow to build market share. They are attempting to build their subscriber bases by offering international call-back services. It was unclear as yet whether this strategy would be effective.

Despite its monopoly status, HKTI's share of the international outgoing call market has been reduced by the introduction of call-back services by other providers and by the authorization granted companies to self-provide external circuits for their internal corporate traffic. HKTI's dominance is expected to drop further following the issue in 1997 of 14 licenses for virtual private networks (VPNs).

The demand for mobile telecommunications is rising rapidly in Hong Kong. As of October 31, 1997, there were four cellular telephone service providers operating five networks—three GSM (global system for mobile communications), one AMPS (advanced mobile phone system) and one CDMA (call division multiple access)—and six PCS (personal communications service) providers (using digital cellular system-1800, or DCS-1800), plus 31 paging service operators. Demand for paging services has been decreasing gradually since October 1996. With the launch of competitive pricing for PCS services during the second and third quarters of 1997, the market share of paging services was expected to shrink further.

The telecommunications equipment supply market in Hong Kong is largely deregulated, although importers and sellers of radio equipment must be licensed. Equipment supplied for use in Hong Kong must be type-accepted or type-approved by the government.

Current Liberalization Status

In the World Trade Organization (WTO) negotiations of February 1997, Hong Kong committed to full liberalization and to adherence to a common set of regulatory principles by January 1, 1998. Hong Kong's specific WTO commitments are divided into two parts: local services and international services. In local services, Hong Kong already has a liberalized regime. It noted in its commitment the limit of four FTNS licenses until June 30, 1998, and its intention to review the issue of more licenses thereafter. In international services, Hong Kong committed to allow unlimited international simple resale of fax and data, virtual private networks and call-back services.

Type of Service	Degree of Liberalization	Key Legislation or Administrative Decree	Date of Actual or Expected Liberalization	Comments
Local	Liberalized	Telecommunications Ordinance 106	June 1995	The issue of further licenses will be reviewed in June 1998.
Long Distance and International	Monopoly, partially deregulated. (There are no long-distance services within Hong Kong.)	Telecommunications Authority statement on "The Regulatory Status of Call-Back Services," March 1995	2006*	Call-back services are permitted. Full liberalization is expected by 2006,* when HKTI's exclusive license expires.
Cellular	Liberalized	Telecommunications Ordinance 106	1985	
Paging	Liberalized	Telecommunications Ordinance 106	1970	
Value-added	Liberalized		1994	International simple resale of fax data and VPN services is permitted.

* Editor's note: HKTI had been granted a monopoly until 2006, but recently agreed to end its monopoly by 2000 in return for certain concessions.

Competitive Environment

Type of Service	Entire Market		Top Two Players		
	Market Size*	Number of Players	Names	Annual Revenue	Ownership
Local	Not available	4 FTNS providers	HKTC	HK$4.068 billion domestic revenue**	Hongkong Telecom (Cable & Wireless 53.7%, China International Trust & Inv. 10.08%, China Telecom 5.5%, publicly traded)
Long Distance and International	Not available	1 international service provider, 18 call-back providers and 14 VPN providers	HKTI	HK$16.593 billion in international service revenue**	Hongkong Telecom (Cable & Wireless 53.7%, China International Trust & Inv. 10.08%, China Telecom 5.5%, publicly traded)
Cellular	Not available	4 cellular phone providers operating 5 networks; 6 PCS service providers (licensed in 1996)	Hongkong Telecom CSL SmarTone Telecommunications Holdings Ltd.***	HK$2.088 billion*** HK$3.308 billion****	Hongkong Telecom Cellular 8 (36.71%), AT&T (24.75%), Town Khan (12.38%), publicly traded
Paging	Not available	31	Hutchison Star Paging	Not available Not available	Hutchison Telecom Star Telecom International Holding Ltd.
Value-added	Not available	120 Internet service providers, 54 international value-added network service operators. The 14 VPN licensees also provide value-added services.	Not available	Not available	

* Total telecommunications revenues in Hong Kong in 1996 were US$5.093 billion, according to the 1997 report of the International Telecommunications Union (ITU)
** Hongkong Telecom, annual report 1996
*** ITU, 1997
**** SmarTone, annual report 1997

Licensing Requirements

OFTA issues licenses for all operators of public telecommunications networks and services. Licensees may have to pay royalties, license fees or spectrum utilization fees, depending on the type of license granted.

On July 1, 1997, the Basic Law of the Hong Kong Special Administrative Region of the People's Republic of China (PRC) came into effect, providing that the laws in force in Hong Kong prior to this date would be adopted as laws of the region, except for those that contravene the Basic Law. Similarly, all documents, certificates and contracts in effect prior to this date continue to be recognized and protected by the region, provided they do not contravene the Basic Law.

Potential for Foreign Ownerships/Relationships

There are currently no foreign ownership restrictions on investments in telecommunications, and Hong Kong has made a commitment to the WTO to continue this policy.

Potential for Upcoming Liberalization/Investment Opportunities

The government remains committed to encouraging the widest range of telecommunications services in Hong Kong, so that it remains the leading telecommunications hub in Asia-Pacific. The limit on the number of FTNS licensees will expire June 30, 1998. In October 1997 a statement by a spokesperson for the

Secretary for Economic Services suggested that additional domestic telecommunications licenses would not be issued when the review of Hong Kong's fixed-line market was undertaken in June 1998. The spokesperson agreed with the three new operators' assertions that they needed more time to establish effective fixed networks across Hong Kong.

Because of the competitive nature of the cellular market and the increased number of operators (six new PCS licenses in 1996), consolidation of the operators is anticipated. OFTA announced in January 1997 that the licensing of cordless access service as public telecommunications services would be deferred. The situation was to be reviewed 12 months hence and OFTA was then to decide whether to invite new applications.

Forms of Doing Business

Permanent Establishment

A foreign company's liability for profits tax does not depend on whether the company has a permanent establishment (PE) in Hong Kong. Rather, liability depends on whether the company carries on a business in Hong Kong, and whether that business earns Hong Kong-sourced profits. However, the existence of a PE in Hong Kong may indicate that the foreign company is carrying on a business in Hong Kong.

PE is defined to mean a branch, management or other place of business, but does not mean an agency unless the agent has, and habitually exercises, a general authority to negotiate and conclude contracts on behalf of his principal or has a stock of merchandise from which he regularly fills orders. The PE factor is relevant in quantifying the assessable profits of a foreign company that are subject to profits tax by virtue of having a business in Hong Kong. In the absence of proper accounts for tax purposes, the assessable profits of a foreign company that has a PE may be estimated by applying a ratio to the company's worldwide profits (i.e., Hong Kong turnover to worldwide turnover).

In determining whether a foreign company carries on a business in Hong Kong, such factors as the existence of a profit-making motive and the frequency and scale of transactions are relevant. A business may be carried on in Hong Kong by a foreign company itself (e.g., by its employees) or through its agent in Hong Kong.

If a foreign company does not carry on a business in Hong Kong, it will not be subject to profits tax, even though profits may be derived from Hong Kong (see "Specific Scope of Profits Tax" under "Corporate Income Taxes"). Telecommunications services can cover a broad range of activities, which may or may not attract taxes. Some examples follow:

- When long-distance telephone services, operator services, call reorganization/turnaround services, technical assistance, or technological services including network management are rendered by a foreign telecommunications company that does not have any business presence in Hong Kong, the service fees are not taxable. No withholding tax is charged on the service fees. On the other hand, if any of these services are rendered by a foreign company on a regular basis through its employees or agents in Hong Kong, the foreign company is considered to be carrying on a business in Hong Kong and a portion of the fees attributable to the services rendered in Hong Kong is subject to profits tax.

- When technology and know-how are licensed, royalty payments for the use or the right to use certain intellectual property in Hong Kong are subject to withholding tax.

- When telecommunications equipment is leased, sums received by or accrued to a foreign company by way of hire, rental or similar charges for the use of or right to use movable telecommunications equipment in Hong Kong are subject to profits tax.

- A foreign Internet access provider is subject to profits tax if it regularly sells access software in Hong Kong or has servers located in Hong Kong.

- If a foreign service provider installs a server or switch in Hong Kong but does not have any personnel in Hong Kong, this amounts to a business in Hong Kong. Whether the profits are sourced and thus taxable in Hong Kong would depend on the nature of the income and the activities undertaken in Hong Kong by the foreign service provider to earn the income. Sourcing of profits depends on where the critical activities to earn the profits take place. The type of income is determined by the type of activity entailed. If the service provider merely leases the server or switch, then the location of the server or switch will dictate the source of the lease income. If the service provider uses the server or switch in providing other services, then the source of the income depends on what type of income is entailed and on other facts and circumstances. There are no clear rules yet for a call-back service provider as to whether the location of the switches will dictate the source of the income.

- A website located on a server in Hong Kong, whether or not accessible by customers in or outside Hong Kong, would amount to a business in Hong Kong. Whether the profits are sourced and thus taxable in Hong Kong depends on the nature of the income and the activities undertaken in Hong Kong by the foreign service provider to earn the income.

- In the absence of other activities in Hong Kong, a website located on a server *outside* Hong Kong but accessible by customers in Hong Kong does not amount to a business in Hong Kong.

- When a foreign telecommunications company carries out a project in Hong Kong involving the design, manufacturing, installation and testing of a fiber optic cable system for sale to a local telephone company, the foreign company is considered to be carrying on a business in Hong Kong.

Business Entities

Local Branch of a Foreign Company. This option is available to applicants for FTNS and other non-exclusive licensees. A foreign company operating a branch in Hong Kong is subject to profits tax on the Hong Kong-sourced profits from the whole company. If the branch acts as an agent for the head office and earns Hong Kong-sourced income, then the profits booked under the head office can also be exposed in Hong Kong on the same basis, and at the same tax rate, as a locally incorporated company. As a branch would constitute a PE, certain rules may be applicable for quantifying the assessable profits of the foreign company in the absence of proper accounts. The Hong Kong taxable profits or losses of the same entity from different lines of business will be grouped for assessment. However, group relief between companies is not allowed.

The legal liability to an investor operating through a Hong Kong branch would depend on whether the entity were set up as a separate legal person and/or as a limited liability entity or otherwise in its home country, and on the terms of each individual business agreement or guarantee that the investor undertook.

Locally Incorporated Subsidiary of a Foreign Company. A foreign investor can operate a telecommunications business by setting up a Hong Kong subsidiary. Companies carrying on a business in Hong Kong are subject to profits tax on the same basis, whether or not they are incorporated or resident in Hong Kong. The Hong Kong-taxable profits or losses of the subsidiary from different lines of business can be grouped for assessment. However, group relief between companies is not allowed.

The legal liability of the investors in a Hong Kong subsidiary depends on whether the subsidiary is set up as a limited liability entity or otherwise. A company in Hong Kong is a separate legal person.

Joint Venture. A joint venture is not considered to be a separate legal or taxpaying entity in Hong Kong; it merely connotes a contractual arrangement between the venturers to share the output of the venture. In this situation, each venturer would account for its share of the output of the joint venture in its own tax return.

Generally, however, the joint ventures existing in Hong Kong are formed as companies or partnerships, and are treated accordingly for profits-tax purposes. Both forms of joint venture file separate tax returns. Joint ventures between foreign and local investors in the telecommunications industry more commonly take the form of Hong Kong-incorporated companies. The use of joint venture companies is subject to any regulatory restrictions on foreign ownership applicable in each particular market.

Local Funding Alternatives

Debt versus Equity

A return on equity (e.g., a dividend) representing a distribution of profit or a withdrawal of capital is not deductible by the payor company for profits-tax purposes. The raising of equity in a company may also be subject to capital duty and premium duty, each at the rate of 0.3% of the increase in authorized share capital and share premium, respectively. There are legal restrictions on reducing the amount of share capital. Therefore, foreign investors may favor debt financing as it may give rise to interest deductions to the payor. Interest deductions are subject to certain restrictions.

There are no thin capitalization rules in Hong Kong. Taxpayers can deduct interest incurred in the production of assessable profits. Interest costs must also satisfy one of the following conditions to be deductible:

- The money has been borrowed by a financial institution (FI).

- The money has been borrowed by a public utility company.

- The money has been borrowed from a person other than an FI or an overseas FI, and the interest is subject to profits tax for the payee.

- The money has been borrowed from an FI or an overseas FI and the repayment of the borrowing is not secured or guaranteed directly or indirectly against an offshore deposit made with that or any other FI or overseas FI.

- The money has been borrowed wholly and exclusively to finance plant, machinery or inventory, and the lender is not associated with the borrower.

- The interest is payable by a corporation on listed debentures or similar instruments.

Interest expenses of a capital nature are not deductible. Neither dividends nor interest payments are subject to withholding tax. In general, debt financing from related parties, including a shareholder, attracts more restrictions on deductibility than debt financing from unrelated parties. Interest paid to a foreign shareholder is often not deductible because the corresponding interest income is non-taxable in Hong Kong in the hands of the foreign shareholder unless it satisfies any of the other conditions listed above.

Exchange gains or losses pertaining to the loan principal, whether borrowed from a related party or not, are regarded as capital in nature and non-taxable or non-deductible. The tax treatment of exchange gains or losses pertaining to interest payments accords with that of the underlying interest payments.

Exchange Controls

Hong Kong does not impose exchange controls on inbound or outbound transfers of Hong Kong or other currencies. The Basic Law safeguards the flow of capital into and out of the region.

Business Acquisitions and Dispositions

Capital Contributions into an Existing Local Entity

An investor may contribute cash, tangibles or intangibles as capital to a Hong Kong company. In general, a capital contribution does not trigger a profits-tax liability to the investor or the company. However, stamp duty may be payable if the assets contributed consist of Hong Kong-landed properties or Hong Kong-registered securities (see "Value-Added Tax, Sales Tax and/or Other Pertinent Taxes").

A capital contribution involving an increase in the authorized share capital or share premium account of the Hong Kong company is subject to capital duty or premium duty at a rate of 0.3% of such increase. Contribution of intellectual property is not subject to withholding tax if all rights attaching to the intellectual property are contributed.

A capital contribution does not usually affect the existing shareholders of the Hong Kong company from a profits-tax or duty perspective. If, however, the contribution involves an exchange of Hong Kong-landed properties or Hong Kong-registered securities, then stamp duty will be payable.

Purchase or Sale of Shares in a Local Entity

Profits arising from the sale of shares that were held as capital assets are not subject to profits tax. If the seller of the shares is a foreign investor having no business in Hong Kong, then it can have the additional cover for non-taxability of the sale profits. There is no difference for tax or duty purposes between a sale of substantial and a sale of minority shares.

Both the purchaser and the seller of Hong Kong-registered shares pay stamp duty at the rate of 0.15%. While the parties are free to use any value as the consideration value (e.g., related parties may use a nominal value), the stamp duty is imposed on the higher of the consideration for or the market value of the shares.

For profits-tax purposes, there is no change in the value of depreciable assets or inventory of the local company caused by a change in shareholding. Generally, the premium paid by an investor for intangibles such as goodwill cannot be recovered as a deductible expense by the local company. All the liabilities (including any undisclosed liabilities) of the local business remain with the local company in the case of a purchase or sale of shares.

Purchase or Sale of Assets

Profits from the sale of current assets or short-term investments are subject to Hong Kong profits tax, but profits from the sale of fixed assets or long-term investments are not. However, the sale proceeds (restricted to cost) of the fixed assets are reduced from the tax written-down values for depreciation allowances if the assets were previously ranked for depreciation allowances. Any excess of the sale proceeds (restricted to cost) over the tax written-down values is taxable.

The purchaser may reasonably allocate the purchase price to individual depreciable assets or inventory. To determine the basis for such allocation, the purchaser should first refer to any split indicated in the agreement. If there is none, then the purchaser can use any reasonable basis, including fair market value. Any amount not allocated to individual assets representing goodwill is not deductible. Tax losses sustained in the local business are not available to the purchaser of business assets.

Under the Transfer of Business (Protection of Creditors) Ordinance, the purchaser is liable for all the liabilities (including undisclosed liabilities) of the business. However, its exposure to any undisclosed liabilities may be limited by giving public notice in accordance with the ordinance or by securing indemnities from the seller.

A partnership is considered to be a separate taxpaying entity in Hong Kong. The purchase of an interest in a partnership does not generally give rise to significant profits taxes. Certain rules are, however, specifically applicable to the utilization of partnership losses. Capital contribution to a partnership is not subject to capital duty or stamp duty.

It is possible to structure a tax-free disposition of a sale of shares by interposing one or more tiers of offshore holding companies and selling the shares in the intermediate holding company, instead of directly selling the shares in the target.

Start-up Business Issues

Pre-operating Losses and Start-up/ Construction Costs

Expenses and payments, including license fees and franchise fees, are deductible to the extent that they are incurred in the production of assessable profits. Generally, expenses of a capital nature (i.e., that pertain to creating a fixed asset or an enduring benefit) are not deductible, and no amortization of such expenses is allowed.

Expenses incurred before a business commences are generally considered to be of a capital nature and therefore not allowable as deductions. In practice, the Commissioner of Inland Revenue may allow the deduction of such expenses on a case-by-case basis, provided that the expenses would be deductible if they had been incurred after the commencement of the business. Preliminary expenses for feasibility studies representing part of the costs of establishing a new source of profits are generally considered to be of a capital nature and therefore not deductible, whether they are incurred before or after the commencement of business.

Interest expenses incurred during the construction of a building or plant are of a capital nature. Interest expenses incurred in the construction of a building, before the building was used in the production of profits, are of a capital nature.

Capital expenditures for plant or machinery, industrial buildings or structures, or commercial buildings or structures are eligible for depreciation allowances. If such expenditures were incurred for a business that was about to begin, the expenditures would be deemed incurred at the commencement of the business and depreciated accordingly.

Subject to the above rules, start-up/construction costs incurred by a foreign company outside Hong Kong may be deducted by the local company by means of a recharge. The recharge would not be subject to withholding tax unless it involved the right to use intellectual property or movable property in Hong Kong.

Customs Duties and VAT

Customs duties are not payable on the import of telecommunications equipment into Hong Kong. There is no value-added tax in Hong Kong.

Loss Carryovers

A loss sustained by a corporation for any fiscal year is carried forward and set off against the assessable profits of the corporation for subsequent tax years. There is no time limit on the carryforward of losses. The carryback of losses is not allowed.

When there is a change in the shareholding in a corporation and the sole or dominant purpose of the change is to utilize losses sustained in that corporation, the Commissioner of Inland Revenue may disallow the set-off of losses against any profits that have been accrued to that corporation as a direct or indirect result of the change in shareholding. A change of business activity would not affect the carryforward of losses.

Operating Considerations

Corporate Income Taxes

The Inland Revenue Ordinance imposes profits tax, property tax and salaries tax. The Basic Law provides for an independent taxation system in Hong Kong, and the PRC does not levy taxes in the region.

General Scope of Profits Tax. A person carrying on a business in Hong Kong is subject to profits tax on its assessable profits arising in or derived from Hong Kong. A "person" is defined to include a corporation (whether resident or incorporated in Hong Kong or not), partnership or body of persons. The rate of profits tax for a corporation for the year of assessment 1997–1998 is 16.5%.

Specific Scope of Profits Tax. If a person does not carry on a business in Hong Kong, it is generally not subject to profits tax except if it sells goods in Hong Kong through an agent. Any person who sells any goods in Hong Kong on behalf of a non-resident person shall withhold from the sales proceeds and pay quarterly a sum equal to 1% of the gross proceeds from such sales or a lesser sum as agreed to by the Commissioner. In practice, the Commissioner would accept a sum of 0.5% of the gross proceeds as the final tax liability of a non-resident.

Withholding Tax. There is no withholding tax on the repatriation of profits or on payments that are in the nature of interest, dividends or management fees. Withholding tax is imposed only on sums (not otherwise chargeable to profits tax) received by or accrued to a person:

(a) For the use of or right to use in Hong Kong a patent, design, trademark, copyrighted material, secret process, formula or other similar property; or for imparting knowledge connected with the use of such property

(b) By way of hire, rental or similar charges for the use of or the right to use movable property in Hong Kong

When the sums for (a) are derived from a related party, the amount that would be deemed to be the assessable profits of the recipient would depend on whether the relevant property had at any time been owned by any person carrying on a business in Hong Kong. If so, then 100% of the sums would be deemed to be assessable profits and would be effectively taxed at the rate of 16.5% (for the year of assessment 1997–1998). In other cases, 10% of the sums would be deemed to be the assessable profits; that is, the sums would be effectively taxed at the rate of 1.65%.

The withholding tax rate for sums for (b) is not specifically prescribed in the ordinance. In practice, the Commissioner applies the normal profits tax rate to 10% of such sums; that is, the tax payable is effectively 1.65% of the sums for the year of assessment 1997–1998. The non-resident can alternatively offer to be taxed on the actual profit or loss from the leasing operation in (b).

Capital Gains Taxes

There is no capital gains tax in Hong Kong. Profits from the sale of capital assets and profits of a capital nature are also exempt from profits tax.

Tax Holidays and Exemptions

There are no special tax exemptions or incentives applicable specifically to the telecommunications industry, but the following may be relevant to a telecommunications business:

- Sums expended for the registration of a trademark, design or patent used in a business that produces assessable profits, including expenses of a capital nature, are deductible.

- Certain expenditures (excluding expenditures for land or buildings) incurred by a person for scientific research relating to its business that produces assessable profits, including expenses of a capital nature, are deductible. If any of the expenditures were incurred outside of Hong Kong and the business was carried on partly in and partly out of Hong Kong, the deduction would be limited to that part of the expenditure that was reasonable in the circumstances. "Scientific research" is defined to mean any activities in the fields of natural or applied science for the extension of knowledge. Software development could fall within this definition.

- Expenditures incurred for the purchase of patent rights or rights to any know-how for use in Hong Kong in the production of assessable profits, including expenses of a capital nature, are deductible.

- Dividend income from a corporation that is assessable for profits tax is specifically exempt from profits tax.

Depreciation/Cost-Recovery Conventions/Accelerated Deductions

Capital expenditures for plant or machinery, industrial buildings or structures, or commercial buildings or structures used in the production of taxable income are eligible for depreciation allowances in the form of deductions, as described below:

Plant or Machinery. Plant or machinery is defined to include electric cables, electronics manufacturing plant and machinery, electronic data processing equipment and plant or machinery used for the purposes of a public telephonic or telegraphic service. Capital expenditures incurred for the provision of plant or

machinery for the purposes of producing assessable profits are eligible for an initial allowance of 60% of the expenditure. An annual allowance of either 10%, 20% or 30% of the written-down value of the expenditure, depending on the type of plant or machinery, will also be granted if the taxpayer owns or has owned, and has or had put into use, the plant or machinery.

The treatment of the fixed assets may vary according to the type of telecommunications business. The ranking of the fixed assets for 10%, 20% or 30% annual allowance is listed in the Inland Revenue Rules. For example, electronic data processing equipment or electronics manufacturing equipment is eligible for a 30% annual allowance, and plant or machinery, including switches, routers, cells, satellite equipment used in a public telephone service, and electric cables are eligible for a 10% annual allowance. Switches, routers, cells, and satellite equipment used in other industries generally qualify for a 20% annual allowance. Annual depreciation allowances for assets in a network can be claimed when the assets have actually been put into use.

The taxation treatment of software has not been specified in the Inland Revenue Rules. It is generally accepted that system software would be capital expenditure forming part of an electronic data processing system and would be eligible for 30% annual allowance, whereas application software would be a revenue expense and deductible. Purchased software embedded in telecommunications equipment would be accorded the same treatment as that of the underlying equipment.

Industrial Building or Structure. Capital expenditures incurred in the construction of an industrial building or structure are eligible for an initial allowance of 20% of the expenditure. An annual allowance of 4% of the expenditure is generally available to any person who is, at the end of the taxation period, entitled to an interest in the industrial building or structure. An industrial building or structure is defined to include any building or structure (or part thereof) used for the purposes of:

- A business that consists of the manufacture of goods or materials

- A public telephone or telegraph service

- Scientific research in relation to any business

Commercial Building or Structure. Capital expenditures incurred in the construction of a commercial building or structure are eligible for an annual allowance of 2% of the expenditure. Generally, any person who is, at the end of the taxation period, entitled to an interest in the commercial building or structure is eligible for the allowance. A commercial building or structure is defined to mean any building or structure (other than industrial ones) used for the purposes of a business.

Marketing and Advertising Costs. These are generally deductible if they are incurred in the course of producing taxable profits. If they created an enduring asset or benefit, then they would be regarded as capital in nature and non-deductible. Payments made directly or indirectly through sales agents to attract customers are deductible.

Transfer Pricing Rules

The main transfer pricing provision in Hong Kong applies when a non-resident person carries on business with a closely connected resident person. If the resident person derives less than the ordinary profits that might be expected to arise in Hong Kong, the non-resident person is deemed to carry on business in Hong Kong. Thus, the non-resident person is subject to profits tax in accordance with the provisions of the Inland Revenue Ordinance. Because of its complexity, this provision has rarely been applied by the Commissioner.

Expenses and payments are deductible only to the extent that they are incurred in the production of assessable profits. The Commissioner has more often applied this rule to counteract transfer pricing arrangements by denying deductions for excessive expenditure.

There are also general anti-avoidance provisions that the Commissioner may use to counteract artificial or fictitious transactions and transactions that are entered into with the sole or dominant purpose of obtaining a tax benefit.

Transfers of Patents, Trademarks and Software

The profits tax treatment for payments for intellectual property, software or technology is uncertain. Generally, when all rights in intellectual property are transferred, the transaction is treated as a sale. Certain expenditures relating to trademarks or patents are deductible (see "Tax Holidays and Exemptions").

On the other hand, when the payments are made for a partial transfer of rights (e.g., when the owner has retained his ultimate rights over the intellectual property but granted part of his rights to a party who will exploit the property commercially), the payments will generally be treated as royalties or license fees. Patent, trademark and software licensing fees are deductible to the extent they are incurred in the production of chargeable profits and the expenses are not of a capital nature.

Depending on its nature, income earned by a Hong Kong business from the transfer of technology outside of Hong Kong may not be subject to profits tax if the income is derived from outside of Hong Kong or the income is of a capital nature.

Service Fees

There is no withholding tax on payments of service fees. However, service fee income derived from services rendered in Hong Kong, by a business carried on in Hong Kong, is subject to profits tax.

Value-Added Tax, Sales Tax and/or Other Pertinent Taxes

There is no VAT or sales tax in Hong Kong. Stamp duty is chargeable on the instruments for the following types of transactions:

- Conveyance on sale, agreements for sale and leases of immovable property in Hong Kong

- Sale, purchase or transfer of Hong Kong securities

- Issue of Hong Kong bearer instruments

- Duplicates or counterparts of any of the above

When the consideration or market value exceeds HK$4,413,830 (for the year of assessment 1997–1998), the rate of stamp duty applicable to a purchase of immovable property is 2.75% of the higher of the consideration for, or market value of, the property. Lower rates apply to immovable property of a lower value. The rate of duty for Hong Kong securities is currently 0.15% each for the purchaser and the seller on the higher of the consideration for, or market value of, the securities.

Local and Provincial Taxes

There are no local or municipal taxes in Hong Kong.

For Additional Information, Contact:

Tim Leung
Tax Partner
23/F Sunning Plaza
10 Hysan Avenue
Hong Kong
Telephone: 852 2839 4321
Fax: 852 2576 0942
E-mail: tim_leung@hk.coopers.com

Ian Sanders
Director, Telecoms and Media Consulting
Address: Same as above
Telephone: 852 2504 6606
Fax: 852 2890 3313
E-mail: ian_sanders@hk.coopers.com

India

Telecommunications Tax Profile
by Nityanath P. Ghanekar and P. R. V. Raghavan
Tax Directors, Bombay

Overview of the Telecommunications Market

Historical Background

The government began to liberalize certain sectors of the telecommunications industry in 1984, commencing with the equipment market. In 1985 the Department of Telecommunications (DOT) was created to manage the telecommunications sector. The DOT established two corporations, each of which was wholly owned by the central government. Videsh Sanchar Nigam Limited (VSNL) was formed for international services, and Mahanagar Telephone Nigam Limited (MTNL) for domestic basic services in Bombay and Delhi. Domestic basic services in all other parts of India were managed directly by the DOT. In 1986 VSNL and MTNL were spun off from the DOT, with the government retaining ownership.

In 1992 India began a general economic liberalization program, which included the privatization of several previously nationalized sectors. The DOT liberalized value-added services, including cellular telephony, radio paging, very small aperture terminals (VSATs), voice mail, e-mail and videoconferencing. In 1994 India issued its National Telecom Policy, which opened basic services (local telephone services) to competition. Two cellular operators were awarded licenses in 1994 to operate in each of the four Indian metropolitan areas.

Current Status

Telecoms "circles," the geographic allocation of basic telecommunications, cellular and paging services, are administered by the DOT. There are 24 circles for cellular and paging services and 20 circles for basic telecommunications services. In each circle, the DOT/MTNL and an additional private-sector operator are permitted to offer basic telecommunications services. For cellular services, two private operators are permitted to operate in each of the telecoms circles, and the DOT reserves the right to be the third operator. In paging, licenses were awarded for 27 cities initially, and thereafter for each of the telecoms circles (excluding the cities for which licenses had already been issued). Two to four operators have been granted licenses for each city/circle, depending on the socioeconomic profile of the region. The DOT has been building and modernizing India's basic services infrastructure to meet the increased demand created by the proliferation of computers in businesses and homes throughout India.

Call reorganization/turnaround services for the public are not yet open to private-sector participation.

The digital GSM cellular and paging service operators have begun offering services in most of the circles. Electronic data interchange (EDI), e-mail and VSAT licensees have also commenced operations. The basic services licensees were awaiting approvals from the DOT and regulatory authorities, and were likely to begin setting up infrastructure at the end of 1997 or beginning of 1998.

Foreign equipment companies participate in India's telecommunications market by making capital contributions and loans to local companies and by selling or licensing equipment, technology and know-how to local companies. Although India permits a foreign company to license telecommunications equipment to local companies, in practice, much of this type of licensing is authorized only for contracts with VSNL.

The Indian network consists of 21,000 telephone exchanges, 12 million lines and more than 16,000 kilometers of optical fiber. Cellular networks operate on the GSM standard, and the backbone of cellular operators is mainly microwave link or fiber optic cable. In basic services, operators are expected to use wireless-in-local-loop technology. Subsequently, copper usage is expected.

Current Liberalization Status

India committed to the World Trade Organization (WTO) in early 1997 that it would review DOT's monopoly over domestic long-distance services by 1999 and that of VSNL over international telecoms carrier services by 2004. Government sources have indicated that the domestic long-distance services market may open before 2004. The following table summarizes the progress of liberalization in India in the various telecommunications segments.

Type of Service	Degree of Liberalization	Key Legislation	Date of Actual or Expected Liberalization	Comments
Local	Deregulation underway	Indian Telegraph Act, 1885 Indian Wireless Act, 1933	1996	Licenses awarded for a few circles. Operations likely to commence in 1998.
Long Distance	Monopoly		1999 (as agreed with WTO)	
International	Monopoly		2000 (as agreed with WTO)	
Cellular	Fully liberalized		1994	
Paging	Fully liberalized		1994	
Value-added	Fully liberalized		1994	

Competitive Environment

The following table provides information regarding the top players in each sector of the telecommunications industry, their revenue and ownership.

Type of Service	Entire Market		Top Two Players		
	Market Size*	Number of Players	Names	Annual Gross Revenue*	Ownership
Local	Rs42 billion	1, with 2 expected per circle	MTNL	Rs42 billion	Government
Long Distance	Rs97 billion	1	DOT	Rs97 billion	Government
International	Rs60.87 billion	1	VSNL	Rs60.87 billion	Publicly traded (government is major shareholder)
Cellular	Not available	2 per circle	Reliance Telecom	Not available	Reliance Group of Industries
			BPL Telecom	Not available	Privately owned
Paging	Not available	2–4 per city/state	BPL Telecom	Not available	Privately owned
			Hutchison	Not available	Hutchison Telecom
Value-added	Not available	10 to 20	Wipro	Rs450 million expected	Publicly traded
			Hughes Escort	Not available	Hughes Network

Source: *Indian Business Intelligence* and other public reports.
* Year ending March 31, 1997.

Licensing Requirements

The Telecom Regulatory Authority of India (TRAI), an autonomous body, was recently set up to regulate the telecoms sector. The TRAI ensures technical compatibility and effective interconnection between different service providers, regulates revenue-sharing arrangements among service providers, and monitors compliance with license conditions. It is also charged with facilitating competition, promoting efficiency in the operation of telecoms services, and protecting consumer interests.

Operators of basic, wireless and of most of the value-added services (e.g., e-mail and VSAT networks) must obtain licenses from the DOT. For some of these services, there is a restriction on the number of licenses to be awarded (for instance, one private basic service licensee for each circle). There is no restriction on the number of VSAT services that may be licensed in a geographic area.

At the end of 1997, all licenses for paging and cellular services had been awarded, with the exception of two circles, the Jammu and Kashmir circle and the Andaman and Nicobar Islands circle. For basic services, letters of intent had been granted for eight circles. The licenses for the remaining 12 circles had yet to be finalized, and the DOT was considering inviting bids from private operators shortly.

Recently, some foreign companies with equity stakes in Indian telecommunications companies (attained by purchasing shares of such companies) have sold their equity stakes to other companies. International telecommunications companies have entered the Indian telecoms sector by acquiring equity stakes in the existing cellular service licenses as well as in value-added services licenses. For value-added services that do not involve use of the radio frequency spectrum, non-exclusive licenses are granted by the government's Telecommunications Commission.

Potential for Foreign Ownerships/Relationships

Foreign ownership is restricted for both telecommunications services and equipment. Approval for equity ownership in these sectors requires authorization from the Foreign Investment Promotion Board (FIPB) and the Reserve Bank of India (RBI). Foreign parties are permitted to have equity participation in these sectors only through an Indian joint venture company (JVC). Foreign equity in a JVC that manufactures equipment is restricted to a maximum of 51% of total share capital; for basic, cellular or paging services, foreign equity participation is restricted to 49% of total share capital.

If proposed legislation (the revised Companies Act) is passed, mechanisms to increase the voting control of a foreign shareholder above these levels may become available through the use of non-voting equity instruments allocated to the Indian equity holders.

Potential for Upcoming Liberalization/ Investment Opportunities

Significant demand for telecommunications services exists in India, with the number of telephones in service expected to triple between 1995 and 2000. Much of the investment required to meet this demand is likely to be generated by the private sector. On average, one person in 100 is connected to the network, compared with the average world density of 10 lines per 100 persons. The chart below illustrates the pattern of increasing demand for basic services.

In order to meet the DOT targets for numbers of direct exchange lines for the period 1995–2004, total funding of US$80 billion is needed, according to Credit Lyonnais Securities Asia. Although all licenses for telecoms circles have been awarded to Indian JVCs, non-resident joint venture participants could be added with FIPB and DOT approval.

Many of the value-added services that are commonly available internationally remain unavailable in India, and this is likely to be an important target for investment. Cellular services are still at a nascent stage, with a history of about two years in major metropolitan areas and about one year in other cities. As of March 31, 1997, the number of cellular subscribers was estimated at 369,050, an increase of 45.8% over the preceding quarter.

Forms of Doing Business

Permanent Establishment

The term "permanent establishment" (PE) does not appear in domestic tax law, but the concept is contained in the double-taxation treaties India maintains with more than 40 countries. A similar concept with a rather nebulous definition is referenced in the law as a "business connection." Courts have interpreted it broadly to include as taxable income, not only income derived

Year	Number of Exchanges	Telephone Lines (thousands)	Percentage Increase in Registered Demand	Waiting List (thousands)
1990–91	15,091	5,075	11.6	1,960
1991–92	16,091	5,810	15.1	2,290
1992–93	17,455	6,797	19.1	2,850
1993–94	18,956	8,026	9.1	2,500
1994–95	20,169	9,795	13.6	2,150
1995–96	21,152	11,978	19.3	2,280

Source: Centre for Monitoring Indian Economy

from business carried on in India, but also income derived from business carried on "with India." The following discussion is limited to the common concept of PE and related issues.

If a foreign company is treated as having a PE under its country's double-taxation treaty with India, the company is subject to tax on its net profits. If a foreign company's business activity in India does not result in a PE treatment, the payments that the company receives from such activity are likely to be subject to withholding taxes imposed on their gross amount.

The PE provision in Indian double-taxation treaties typically differs from the OECD Model Convention in that it requires a lesser nexus with a country before a PE is determined to exist. The provision contains the standard definition of "a fixed place of business through which the business of an enterprise is wholly or partly carried on." It also contains a non-exclusive list of fixed places of business that constitute PEs, some of which do not appear in the OECD Model's provisions. Among other items, the list includes a place of management, branch, workshop, warehouse providing storage facilities and a store or sales outlet. The definition also includes a building site; a construction, installation or assembly project; or related supervisory activities if continued for a period prescribed in a treaty (normally 180 days) within a 12-month period.

Participation in the telecommunications services and equipment sector involves a number of different activities and contractual relationships that may or may not result in a foreign company being treated as having a PE. Several examples are discussed below:

- PE does not usually arise for a foreign telecommunications company that derives income from the international revenue settlement process, either for originating international long-distance telephone calls that terminate in India or for terminating India-originated calls in its home country. A foreign company is generally not permitted to provide long-distance telephone services directly from India.

- The licensing of technology and know-how to a local company by a foreign company having no physical presence in India generally does not amount to a PE.

- The provision of technical assistance and technological services by a foreign company to a local company for service fees under an operator services agreement constitutes a PE because of the presence of the foreign company's employees in India. However, equity interest does not have an impact on PE status.

- A foreign company that owns and leases telecommunications equipment (without supporting activities in India) to VSNL or to another local company generally does not amount to a PE. If foreign company employees operate and maintain the equipment in India, however, the entire activity, including the leasing activity, could be attributed to a PE.

- Call reorganization/turnaround services provided by foreign companies to foreign nationals and companies with foreign currency accounts generally do not constitute PEs, provided that foreign company employees are not present in India and that no equipment is placed in India. Calling cards issued for this service would have to be marketed and sold through independent agents.

- The provision of Internet access services through the sale of software, if the sale were structured properly, would generally not create a PE in India. However, if a foreign company issued access software through a fixed place in India, the activity could be treated as a PE. The mere location of a server or a switch in India may not create a PE in India as the server/switch is not an asset that generates income to the foreign company. At the time of publication, VSNL had the only switch; private companies were not permitted to provide access. The TRAI has indicated that the restriction on other providers could be lifted in the near future.

- A foreign company having a website located on a server in India, whether or not it is accessible to customers in India, may be considered to have a PE. In practice, because of foreign-exchange restrictions, few Indian customers besides foreign expatriates can engage in transactions over websites. When exchange rules are liberalized, it is likely that a sale taking place via a website located on a server in India could result in PE exposure in India. If the website were not located in India, it is unclear how the rules would be applied.

- A turnkey telecoms installation project undertaken by a foreign company in India may constitute a PE, depending on the scope of activities that take place in India, the length of time during which a physical presence is required to perform such activities, and the manner of executing the contract.

- When the providing of services or licensing of equipment and technical know-how does not create a PE, a foreign telecommunications company could still be subject to withholding taxes levied on service fees or royalties at rates ranging from 10% to 20%, depending on the treaty country. If the company is from a non-treaty country, the rate is 20% (if a contract is made after May 31, 1997). Such withholding tax is levied on the gross amount of the payments. When such amounts are attributable to a PE in India, as is often the case with a transfer of technical know-how, the fees may be taxable at 48% on the gross income.

- If a sales contract is negotiated and concluded in India, the profits from the sale could be subject to tax since, generally, the sale will be through a fixed base in India; however, if the sale is negotiated and concluded and the title passes outside of India, the profit on the sale will not be taxable in India.

- The design, manufacture, installation and testing of fiber optic cable systems within the territorial waters of or on land in India for a period exceeding 90 days would cause a foreign company to have a PE. If the foreign company acted as a contractor carrying out these same activities, it, too, would have a PE. Similarly, the laying of fiber optic cable on local soil would result in a foreign company having a PE if the employees worked in India or the company had a fixed base for a period of time longer than that specified in a treaty. In the case of a foreign company stationing employees in India to operate a cable system of a local company for service fees, the foreign company would be treated as having a PE.

Through proper planning, a number of the above-mentioned projects, such as a turnkey fiber optic system sale and installation projects, could be structured so that a limited amount of income from the project were attributed to the Indian PE and taxed as such. For example, if a turnkey project were separated into a sale outside India and an installation inside India, the overall tax burden could be reduced, since the sale may not be viewed as being connected to the PE.

Business Entities

Local Branch of a Foreign Company. Foreign companies participating in India's telecommunications sector are generally not permitted to do so through a branch; however, foreign companies have been permitted to set up branches for fiber optic cable installation and operation. The branch of a foreign company is taxed at a rate of 48% on net taxable income. If fees paid to a foreign company are not connected with its PE in India, those fees are taxed at a rate of from 10% to 20% for tax-treaty countries, and 20% for non-treaty countries if the contract was entered into after May 31, 1997; and 30% if the contract was made prior to that date.

Locally Incorporated Subsidiary of a Foreign Company. In the telecommunications sectors, wholly owned subsidiaries of foreign companies are not permitted; however, limited equity participation by foreign companies is permitted (see "Joint Venture").

Joint Venture. Apart from license agreements, service agreements and sales contracts, the only vehicle through which foreign companies can participate in the Indian telecommunications sectors is a locally incorporated joint venture company (JVC). Equity participation by foreign companies is restricted to 49% in the telecommunications services sector and 51% in the telecommunications equipment sector. The JVC must be a limited liability company, whether private or public, incorporated in India.

Unlimited liability vehicles, such as partnerships, are not permitted in these sectors. Although a partnership entity can be formed in India, the unlimited liability feature precludes involvement by banks, financial institutions and the state-owned VSNL.

A local JVC, like all Indian domestic companies, is taxable at 35% of its taxable income. Under the minimum alternative tax rule, an Indian company's taxable income cannot be less than 30% of its book profit. A foreign joint venture participant that derives income through dividends declared by the JVC is not taxed in India, but the JVC is required to pay 10% of the amount of dividends declared. The JVC is required to file tax returns.

As either a public or private limited company, a JVC has limited liability and is regarded as an entity separate from its shareholders. As such, the treatment of a shareholder's other activities in India is generally not affected by its activity in a JVC.

Approvals from a number of government branches are necessary to form a JVC in the telecommunications sector. The government bodies are:

- *Foreign Investment Promotions Board.* The JVC and the foreign joint venture participant must obtain approval from the FIPB for a foreign equity investment.

- *Reserve Bank of India.* The JVC must obtain RBI approval to remit any payments outside of India to the foreign joint venture participant, regardless of the character of the payments (e.g., dividend distributions, royalties or fees for services).

- *Department of Telecommunications.* DOT approval is generally required for the provision of telecommunications services but not for telecommunications equipment manufacturing. Operation and maintenance of equipment leased to the JVC and/or VSNL may require DOT approval.

A foreign company's entering into equity collaboration with a local participant in a JVC generally does not result in a PE. To the extent that the foreign company transacts with or provides services for the JVC, however, it is possible that these activities would amount to a PE (see "Permanent Establishment").

Local Funding Alternatives

Debt versus Equity

Debt financing generally results in a tax deduction; however, the interest paid during the local company start-up must be capitalized. Equity financing, on the other hand, does not give rise to any tax deduction. Interest paid to non-residents is subject to a 20% withholding tax, unless a double-taxation treaty provides otherwise. For dividends paid, the payor must bear 10% of the amount distributed as tax on dividend. Further, because telecommunications services have now been categorized as "infrastructure facilities," it may be possible to obtain exemption from withholding tax from the Ministry of Finance against interest paid on foreign debt.

Under local tax laws, interest on funding that is approved by the government is exempt from local taxation upon fulfillment of certain conditions. Funding for infrastructure facilities may fall under such preferred funding, and interest payable on such funding could be exempt from Indian Income tax. If a funding that is not approved by the government is through an issue of Global Depository Receipt, the rate of withholding tax is only 10%.

No thin capitalization rules exist in India. Debt levels are governed by the regulations imposed by the commercial lending institutions. As with equity investments made by foreign companies, debt obligations to foreign companies also require prior approval from the government.

Foreign currency exchange losses or gains are typically the responsibility of the foreign lender. If a local company has acquired an asset from another country and if there is a change in the rate of exchange after the acquisition of the asset (i.e., if there is any increase or decrease in the liability relating to the acquisition of the asset as expressed in Indian currency), the difference can be added to or deducted from the actual cost of the asset.

Exchange Controls

Any raising of foreign currency loans must comply with the guidelines for external commercial borrowing (ECB) issued by the government, which cover bank loans, buyer's credit, supplier's credit, securitized instruments, credit from official export credit agencies and commercial borrowings from multilateral financial institutions.

The government imposes restrictions on the time to maturity and on amounts of ECBs. Approvals on ECBs for infrastructure projects, including telecommunications projects, have been given high priority, and certain restrictions are often eased.

Business Acquisitions and Dispositions

Capital Contributions into an Existing Local Entity

Subject to foreign ownership percentage restrictions and approval from the FIPB, foreign companies have generally been allowed to obtain equity interests in existing Indian companies for capital contributions of foreign currency and, in certain cases, contributions of equipment and/or technical services. Contributions of intangibles toward part of the allowed foreign ownership percentage are generally not permitted. A capital contribution into a local entity per se would not be subject to any local tax. Additional capitalization of the local entity does not produce tax consequences for existing shareholders.

Purchase or Sale of Shares in a Local Entity

The shareholder selling shares in a local entity is subject to tax on capital gains. The rate will depend on the shareholder's country of residence and applicable treaty provisions. The method for calculating capital gains depends on the method in which such shares were initially acquired. A purchase of shares, however, cannot result in a stepped-up basis in the underlying assets.

As a matter of tax planning, foreign companies often hold their equity interests in Indian companies through interposed Mauritius subsidiaries in order to take advantage of the India-Mauritius tax-treaty benefits. This treaty exempts Mauritius companies from the Indian capital gains tax. As a result, the foreign companies can have their Mauritius subsidiaries sell shares in the Indian company without being taxed in India.

Purchase or Sale of Assets

A foreign company cannot purchase assets of a local telecommunications company; it can purchase only the shares of such a company. If assets are transferred during the course of a restructuring, it is possible to transfer the assets without attracting any capital gains tax.

Because the manner of telecommunications sector investment is regulated and connected only with equity, allocation of purchase price to various assets does not arise for foreign companies seeking to do business in India. Because the partnership structure is generally not used in the telecommunications sector, the issue of acquiring a partnership interest generally does not arise.

Start-up Business Issues

Pre-operating Losses and Start-up/ Construction Costs

For accounting purposes, start-up costs incurred prior to incorporation of the local company are generally reported on the local company's books. These expenses include costs incurred for such activities as market surveys, engineering services and preparation of a feasibility report. Expenses such as license fees and franchise costs are accorded accounting treatment, depending on the terms of the company's agreement with the DOT and/or the tax authority.

For tax purposes, the pre-incorporation expenses are segmented into set-up expenses and capital expenses. The set-up expenses, as described above, are normally amortized over 10 years. Pre-incorporation capital expenses, including interest expenses (other than set-up expenses that are to be amortized over 10 years) are eligible for capitalization. Once these expenses are capitalized, they are eligible for depreciation.

For manufacturing concerns, after incorporation and before commencement of commercial operation, all costs incurred by a company can be capitalized and can form part of the cost of the assets, which are eligible for depreciation. However, for trading or service concerns, such costs cannot be capitalized, as they may not relate to any specific fixed assets.

If any of these expenses are incurred by a foreign company with the consent of a local company, only the local company can account for them. Accounting for and repatriation of money require the permission of the RBI. The withholding tax rate depends on the nature of the expenses and the payments made.

Generally, strict foreign exchange regulations make it difficult to claim deductions for costs incurred by a foreign company; thus, it is preferable for local costs to be incurred by a local, rather than a foreign, company.

India does not impose VAT on services; however, certain other VATs could be applicable within the telecommunications sector. A central excise duty is imposed on purchases of domestic capital goods and components, and a countervailing customs duty is imposed on purchases of capital goods and imported components. The countervailing customs duty matches the domestic excise tax imposed on domestic capital goods and components. These duties are eligible for rebates, called the modified value-added tax (MODVAT), against central excise duty liability on the finished goods. VATs such as central excise duty and sales tax are recoverable by the company from its customers.

Customs Duties and VAT

Currently, customs duties are 20% on parts and subassemblies of telecommunications equipment and 30% on finished equipment. The import duty on cellular phones, pagers and trunking handsets is 20%.

Telecommunications equipment imported as capital goods in connection with a project is eligible for a concessional rate of customs duty. The reduced rate of duty applicable to project-related imports is 20% ad valorem. Further, a countervailing duty is payable, equal to the amount of excise duty (excise duty is payable on goods manufactured in India) payable on similar goods manufactured in India. This is calculated on the landed cost of goods (CIF, or cost, insurance and freight) plus import duty. Recovery of additional customs duty under MODVAT is available.

No VAT is levied on imported goods if the goods are used by the purchaser.

Loss Carryovers

Unabsorbed losses, including depreciation, can be carried forward for a period of eight years and can be set off if there is no change in business activity. For private limited companies, ownership changes of more than 49% preclude the use of unabsorbed losses against company profits in the years after the ownership changes. Carryback of losses is not permitted.

Operating Considerations

Corporate Income Taxes

The federal taxes that apply to a telecommunications company are income tax and service tax. The corporate income tax rate is 35% for local companies (including JVCs). Foreign companies are taxed at the rate of 48% of their income attributable to Indian activities. The service tax rate is 5% of gross receivable telecommunications charges. Service tax is recovered by the telecommunications company from its customers.

Capital Gains Taxes

A foreign company that transfers all or part of its shares in a local company to anyone, regardless of residency, will be subject to capital gains tax. The applicable tax rate depends on the tax residence of the foreign company.

Write-off of License Fee Expense

In the tax year ending March 1996, for any up-front or periodic fees paid for a telecommunications operating license, an equal deduction will be allowed, starting from the year of payment (irrespective of the year the expense was incurred) and ending with the year in which the license ceases to be in force. The tax write-off of expenses may not occur before the start of commercial operation, but the language of the Income-Tax Act of 1961 suggests that this can be argued otherwise for write-off of a license fee.

Tax Holidays and Exemptions

Significant tax deductions may be available to a foreign company that sets up in an industrially backward district. If the company begins producing goods or services before March 31, 1999, up to 100% of the profits and gains for the first five years and 30% for the next five years may be deducted. The deduction also applies to any undertaking that starts providing telecommunications services before March 31, 2000.

Income in the form of dividends, interest or long-term capital gains of an infrastructure capital fund or an infrastructure capital company from investments made through shares or long-term financing in an enterprise providing telecommunications services on or after April 1, 1995, is exempt from tax.

Starting in the tax year 1997–1998, interest paid by a business providing telecommunications services on (a) money borrowed by the business from a financial institution in a foreign country and approved by the government or (b) money borrowed by the business in foreign currency from sources outside India under a loan agreement approved by the government, is exempt from tax in the hands of the recipient.

Minimum Alternative Tax

If a company's total income in any previous year commencing on or after April 1, 1996, is less than 30% of its book profit, the total income of the assessee is deemed to be 30% of its book profit. Book profit is defined as net profit shown in the profit and loss account after certain adjustments. When a license fee written off in the books is less than allowable, minimum alternative tax may be attracted, as book profit will be more than tax profit.

Accounting Treatment

Generally, capital expenditure on the acquisition of a license will be written off over the life of the license, starting in the year in which the expenditure was incurred and ending in the year in which the license expires.

However, a license fee paid after the commencement of business can be treated as a revenue expense and written off fully under Indian GAAP based on a contract signed with the Department of Telecommunications. Business would be said to have commenced in the year in which the assessee started to provide telecommunications services.

Depreciation/Cost-Recovery Conventions/Accelerated Deductions

All tangible assets are grouped under blocks. Depreciable assets must be grouped under one of the following blocks: land and building, plant and machinery, or furniture and fixture. Each block represents the rate at which these assets can be depreciated. Yearly depreciation is reduced from the opening balance, using the reducing balance method. Whenever an asset is acquired during the year, the cost thereof is added to the opening balance of the block, and whenever an asset is sold, the sale value of the asset is reduced from the balance value of the block.

The rate of depreciation for general plant and machinery is 25%. No special rates are available for telecommunications businesses. The software embedded in the telecommunications equipment cannot be separately identified. An asset is treated as placed in service when it is ready for commercial use.

A company engaged in the business of manufacturing telecommunications equipment will be allowed a weighted deduction of 125% of capital or revenue expenditures incurred on approved research and development activities. Costs incurred for construction of a research facility are not eligible for the above deduction. However, the same costs (except the cost of land) could be eligible for deduction at up to 100% under the tax law.

Marketing and advertising costs can be considered deferred revenue expenditures on the books; however, for tax purposes, these costs are considered revenue expenditures in the year in which they are incurred. Direct and indirect payments to sales agents are treated as revenue expenditures for tax purposes. However, accounting for the same could be as deferred revenue expenditure.

Transfer Pricing Rules

No specific transfer pricing policies exist in India; however, provisions exist in domestic tax laws to monitor transactions between resident and non-resident companies that are, in the opinion of the tax officer, arranged in such a manner as to reduce the profits normally made by the resident company in these types of transactions. These provisions are enforced quite rigorously by the tax authorities, particularly in the case of related entities.

Transfers of Patents, Trademarks and Software

There are no restrictions on the licensing of technology to a local company for royalty fees. However, the amount of royalty that can be paid is regulated. For royalty payments made outside India, government approval may be required.

In a sale of technology, the ownership of the technology passes to the buyer, and the buyer has the right to again sell or lease it to someone else; whereas in the licensing of technology, the licensee has the right only to use the technology and no right to sell or lease it to someone else.

Capital expenditures incurred for patents and copyrights are deducted over 14 years. Although payments of license fees to non-residents are not permitted for basic and cellular services, such fees may be paid for technology and know-how in the telecoms equipment manufacturing industry. The tax treatment for license fees relating to technology and know-how, which may include amounts paid for software, depends on whether the fees are considered a capital expenditure or a revenue-generating expenditure. An amount paid for the purchase of equipment or software can be treated as a royalty if the amount is contingent on the productivity or profits to be derived from the item.

Generally, license fees received by foreign companies are subject to tax at a rate of 20%, or at the rate specified in a treaty relating to the tax residence of the recipient. The entire tax is to be withheld.

Income generated from transfers of licenses, expertise and/or technology outside India will be taxable in India. However, subject to fulfillment of certain conditions, part of the income may be exempt from tax.

Service Fees

The withholding tax rates for service fees depends on the double-taxation avoidance agreement (DTAA) between India and the country from which the service is provided. These rates are generally in the range of 10% to 20% in the case of DTAA countries and 20% in the case of non-DTAA countries. The Indian company is permitted to take a deduction for service fee expense.

A local telephone company is liable for service tax payment at a rate of 5% of its gross fees from telecommunications services. Even engineering services rendered by a non-resident in India are liable for service tax.

Value-Added Tax, Sales Tax and/or Other Pertinent Taxes

States levy sales tax on the value of movable goods for which title is deemed to pass within the state from seller to buyer. Sales tax is not levied on services or immovable goods. Sales between states are subject to federal sales tax.

A works-contract tax is levied by states on the value of immovable goods for which title is deemed to pass from a contractor to a buyer within the state at the time of completion of a works contract. In other words, a works-contract tax is a charge on a composite contract for the supply and installation of a turnkey project. This tax is levied on the supply component of the total contract, and not on the service component. The rate of works-contract tax varies from state to state, ranging from 4% to 10%.

If a local telephone company leases various fixed assets from another entity, the lessor, which is exposed to a 4% lease tax, may recover such tax from the lessee telecommunications company. Similarly, when a local telecommunications company retains a contractor to install facilities, including equipment and other goods, the contractor, who is exposed to works-contract tax, will recover such tax from the local telecommunications company.

VAT will not apply to payments for the provision of Internet access. Internet access is considered telephony. (For more information regarding VAT, see "Pre-operating Losses and Start-up Construction Costs.")

Local and Provincial Taxes

Only the central government can tax income. States and provinces levy sales taxes. Municipal authorities can levy property tax on the assets owned by local telecommunications companies. They may also levy octroi (a tax on goods brought into a city for commercial purposes) on telecommunications equipment manufactured and sold locally.

For Additional Information, Contact:

Nityanath P. Ghanekar
Tax Director
Dubhash House
15, J.N. Heredia Marg
Ballard Estate
Bombay 400 038
India
Telephone: 91 (22) 261 8209
Fax: 91 (22) 261 3819
E-mail: nghanekar@hotmail.com

P. R.V. Raghavan
Tax Director
110/111 Shah & Nahar Indl. Premises Co op Soc. Ltd.
Dr. E. Moses Road
Worli
Bombay 400 018
India
Telephone: 91 (22) 496 0758
Fax: 91 (22) 495 1928
E-mail: coopers@giasbmo1.vsnl.in

Sharat Bansal
Management Consulting Director
Sandoz House
Annie Besant Road
Worli
Bombay 400 018
India
Telephone: 91 (22) 497 0202
Fax: 91 (22) 497 0404

Indonesia ◆

Telecommunications Tax Profile
by Sony B. Harsono
Senior Tax Partner, Jakarta

Overview of the Telecommunications Market

Historical Background

Before deregulation, Indonesia's telecommunications industry consisted of two state-owned companies: PT (Persero) Telekomunikasi Indonesia (Telkom), whose main focus was domestic telecommunications, and PT (Persero) Indonesian Satellite Corporation (Indosat), which owned and operated the satellite and international telecommunications links.

The Telecommunications Law of 1989 authorized private partnerships with Indosat and permitted private investors to become involved in network projects that were implemented and operated by Telkom. In 1991, Telkom began to undergo privatization. Since then, private-sector participation has been gradually extended, as follows:

- Minority stakes in both state-owned companies have been listed on the stock exchanges in Jakarta and New York.

- A competitor, PT Satelit Palapa Indonesia (Satelindo), has been licensed to operate in the international and satellite sectors and in cellular operations.

- Licenses have been issued to a limited number of private companies for cellular, paging and fixed cellular services.

- Five private consortia have been permitted to develop certain parts of the domestic wireline network under an unincorporated joint venture/joint cooperation agreement (a Kerja Sama Operasi, or KSO) with Telkom that is a build-operate-transfer (BOT) type arrangement.

- Licenses have been issued to various Internet, multimedia, direct-to-home and value-added network service providers.

One characteristic of this private-sector participation is that the major private telecommunications companies, such as Satelindo and the private companies operating the cellular systems, are not totally free agents. The government holds a minority stake in each of these companies, either through Telkom or Indosat. For example, between 20% and 35% of ownership in Indonesia's three private advanced mobile phone system (AMPS) joint ventures is held either by Telkom or its employee pension fund.

In August 1995, the government issued a decree (MTPT Decree 60/1995) that confirmed that Telkom would be allowed to retain a monopoly on local telecommunications services, including fixed wireless, for at least 15 years, and on long-distance services for at least 10 years.

Current Status

Two million of the six-and-a-half million domestic telephone lines scheduled for installation in Indonesia during the Repelita V1 Plan Period (1994–1999) will be provided by Telkom's private joint operating partners. These five KSOs are providing technical, managerial and operational expertise for the construction and initial operation of service in specific geographic regions under a BOT arrangement. Foreign telecommunications company participants in the KSOs include France Telecom, Singapore Telecom, Telstra Corporation Ltd. with Nippon Telegraph & Telephone Corporation (NTT), U S WEST and Cable & Wireless Plc. Telkom has retained exclusive responsibility for the Jakarta and Surabaya regions.

Direct competition exists in wireless services, and between Indosat and Satelindo in the international services sector. Because telecommunications tariffs are fixed by the government, competition is based upon quality of service, not price. Some tariff restrictions have been relaxed insofar as prices set by the government are maximums, particularly with respect to cellular services.

Competition is at an early stage, with private companies only recently coming into full operation on any scale. Indonesia's first global system for mobile communications (GSM) cellular operator, Satelindo, is only now beginning to face competition as the networks of the other GSM license holders, PT Telkomsel and PT Excelcomindo Pratama (Excelcom), are built throughout the country.

Dozens of regional or local paging licenses have been issued in an effort to bring coverage to all of Indonesia's 27 provinces. To date, of the ten companies granted licenses to operate national paging services, fewer than half have commenced operations. In 1995, the government authorized several large paging companies to participate with companies from other countries to offer paging services throughout Southeast Asia.

The government initiated a tendering process for personal communications network (PCN) licenses in the third quarter of 1997. Five licenses had been awarded: two national licenses for digital cellular system-1800 (DCS-1800) and three regional licenses for DCS-1800 and for Personal Handy-Phone System (PHS) services. Eleven additional regional licenses (DCS-1800 and PHS) were expected to be awarded in the first quarter of 1998: however, the tendering process has been indefinitely postponed by the government. In addition, a national license for code division multiple access-1900 (CDMA-1900) was awarded outside of the original PCN tendering process.

At the end of 1996, there were an estimated 4.5 million total lines in service. Domestic services have been growing at an average annual rate of approximately 30%. International services revenues have been growing at an approximately 20% rate annually. Line growth has been strong at 30% per year and is expected to continue at about 1.3 to 1.5 million lines added annually through 1999. International usage is expected to grow at a rate of 22% annually through 1999. Mobile subscriptions as of year-end 1996 were approximately 594,000. The number of mobile service customers is expected to reach 3 million.

Current Liberalization Status

In February 1997 at the World Trade Organization (WTO) conference on telecommunications, Indonesia committed to the regulatory principles outlined in the Reference Paper. Currently, foreign equity ownership of up to 35% is allowed in international long-distance, mobile, paging, payphone and value-added services providers.

The Telecommunications Law in 1989 formalized the rules for private participation in Indonesia's telecommunications sector. Market entry and competition are limited by government licensing controls and government control of customer tariffs.

Type of Service	Degree of Liberalization	Key Legislation	Date of Actual or Expected Liberalization	Comments
Local	Monopoly	Telecommunications Law 1989	Not before 2010*	
Long Distance	Monopoly	Telecommunications Law 1989	Not before 2006**	
International	Duopoly	Telecommunications Law 1989	Not before 2005	
Cellular	Restricted competition	MTPT Decree 94/1993	1991	5 GSM, 3 AMPS and 1 NMT operators
Paging	Restricted competition	Telecommunications Law 1989	1989	10 nationwide, 70 regional
Value-added	Restricted competition	Telecommunications Law 1989	1989	4, mainly using VSAT

* KSO providers have contracted to provide approximately 50% of Telkom's network for a period of 15 years from January 1996.

** Mobile providers have been authorized to transport their own domestic long distance calls.

Competitive Environment

The current market environment incorporates limited competition as set out below.

| Type of Service | Entire Market | | Top Two Players | | |
	Market Size (1996)	Number of Players	Names	Annual Gross Revenue (1996)	Ownership
Local and Long Distance	Rp (Rupiah) 6,082 billion* (estimated)	1	Telkom	Rp 5,076 billion** (approximately)	Publicly traded
International	Rp 1,227 billion*** (estimated)	2	Indosat	Rp 1,193 billion	Publicly traded
			Satelindo	Rp 34 billion***	Private
Cellular	Not available	7	Satelindo	Not publicly available	Private
			Telkomsel	Not publicly available	Private
Paging	Not available	80	PT Motorolain Corporation (Starko)	Not publicly available	Private
			PT Skytelindo Services (Skytel)	Not publicly available	Private

* Source: Telkom, Peregrine.
** Telkom has revenue-sharing agreements (KSOs) with private consortia in five regions of Indonesia.
*** Sources: Indosat, Merrill Lynch

Licensing Requirements

The Indonesian government retains extensive regulatory authority and supervisory control over the telecommunications sector through the Ministry of Tourism, Posts and Telecommunications (MTPT) and, to a lesser extent, through the Ministry of Finance (MOF). The telecommunications law and certain regulations and decrees establish the legal framework for the industry. However, most of the supervision and regulation of the industry is implemented through the general administrative powers of the MTPT. Within the MTPT, the Director General of Posts and Telecoms supervises the directors of telecoms, frequency management and standardization.

Licensing of services is currently regulated by classification as either basic or non-basic. Provision of basic services is restricted to so-called organizing bodies (Telkom or Indosat). Private companies can only provide basic services in direct or indirect cooperation with Telkom or Indosat. Non-basic services can be provided by private operators without participation (direct or indirect) by Telkom or Indosat. Basic and non-basic services are as follows:

Basic Services	Non-Basic Services
Local	Data transmission
Domestic long distance	Electronic mail
Mobile cellular	Store and forward facsimile
Fixed wireless	Abbreviated dialing
Leased line	Multi-call address
Packet switched data	Electronic data interchange
Telex	Paging
Telegraph	Videoconferencing

Potential for Foreign Ownerships/Relationships

The government recognizes that foreign investment is essential to obtaining the expertise, technology and finances necessary to expand telecommunications resources fast enough to keep pace with Indonesia's rapid economic development. Telecommunications is therefore a sector in which foreign investment is permitted, with the proviso that no foreigner can own more than 95% of a company operating in this sector.

In practice, foreign investment in the telecommunications sector has usually required a prospective investor to participate in a competitive bidding mechanism for a minority stake (typically in the range of 25% to 40%) in one of the Indonesian project companies.

Several foreign telecommunications companies that have participated in this process now hold minority stakes in the three GSM cellular companies serving Indonesia—DeTeMobil of Germany participates in Satelindo, PTT Telecom Netherlands holds a share of PT Telkomsel, and NYNEX participates in Excelcom.

Potential for Upcoming Liberalization/ Investment Opportunities

Although the Indonesian government has clearly shown its preference for retention of Telkom's domestic service monopoly over the next decade, it has also fostered liberalization and competition in other telecommunications sectors. In 1995, MTPT began pilot projects to test the feasibility of liberalizing customer premise equipment so that home and business users could select equipment other than that provided by Telkom and arrange for independent installation. MTPT is in the process of awarding licenses for PCN.

Forms of Doing Business

Permanent Establishment

The Indonesian tax authorities have not specifically stated their position regarding permanent establishments (PEs) for international telecommunications companies that derive income from Indonesian sources. To date, a foreign company that does not have a physical presence in Indonesia, but provides international transmission via satellite or other means, is not generally considered to have a PE.

Similar treatment may be expected for overseas Internet access providers (for providers of access to a website on an overseas server by an overseas party), and for call reorganization/turnaround providers. The licensing by a foreign company of technology and know-how will not normally, by itself, be considered to create a PE. However, associated activities—for example, the presence of foreign company personnel in Indonesia—may expose the overseas entity to tax liabilities. The leasing of telecommunications equipment on a simple rental or lease contract will be subject to similar considerations.

The presence of a server or switch (without personnel) belonging to an overseas business, or a website accessible by onshore or offshore customers, is likely to be considered a PE.

The provision by a foreign company of operator services, technical assistance or technology services, or network management services to a domestic company will, in most cases, create a PE. Similarly, the laying of fiber optic cable or the construction of telecommunications switching equipment, either for sale to a local company or for operation by a foreign telecommunications company for a fee, will create a PE. Exceptions may be made for projects of very short duration that may qualify for tax treaty relief.

A PE is subject to tax on profits at full domestic rates (up to a maximum of 30%) and to a 20% branch profits tax (which may be reduced to 0%–15% by a tax treaty). It is important to note that resident companies are required to impose a 20% withholding tax on services obtained from foreign parties—except in cases where the foreigner qualifies under a tax treaty for exemption or reduction in the rate of withholding tax, or has a local tax registration as a PE.

Business Entities

A telecommunications project generally must be in the form of a locally incorporated subsidiary or affiliate. Exceptions to the require-

ment of establishing a locally incorporated company are made in cases in which a foreign company is permitted to undertake:

- Government contracts as a PE

- Construction projects with a license from the Ministry of Public Works

In both cases, the work performed in Indonesia must be undertaken in association with a local partner.

Both Indonesian-incorporated companies and foreign-registered entities are subject to tax on profits at full domestic rates (up to a maximum rate of 30%). Distributions of profits are subject to withholding tax, as follows:

Branch of foreign company	20% of taxable profit less income tax on profits
Company dividend to a foreign shareholder	20% of dividend payable
Company dividend to an Indonesian company	0% of dividend payable
Company dividend to an Indonesian individual	15% of dividend payable

Dividends to non-residents may be reduced by tax treaty to 10%–15%. Tax losses of related subsidiaries cannot be grouped.

A foreign investor is not permitted by the Foreign Investment Law to become a partner in a business in the form of a partnership.

A joint operation is purely a contractual agreement to conduct a project—not a separate legal entity. Each party agrees to undertake certain aspects of a telecommunications project, with revenues or profits shared between the members on an agreed basis. Joint operations do not have limited liability. Each party is fully responsible for its own obligations and responsibilities as set out in the project agreement. The profits of the joint operation are taxable to its members (for a foreign company in the form of a PE) and the joint operation is not taxable on the profit from its activities. Joint operations may be subject to VAT and withholding tax obligations in relation to the project activities, but an income tax return of profits is not required.

Joint operations, or consortia, are the common structures used in the Indonesian telecommunications sector. A joint venture company, on the other hand, is one in which a local company has a foreign shareholder.

Local Funding Alternatives

Debt versus Equity

For company income tax purposes, interest on debt is deductible whereas dividend payments are not. Shareholder debt can provide an avenue to repatriate "trapped cash" where project cash flows exceed the levels of distributable profits. Dividends and interest payable to foreign residents are both subject to similar withholding taxes, at a general 20% rate, reduced to 10% or 15% when tax treaty relief applies.

Thin Capitalization Rules. The tax law imposes no thin capitalization limits. The Foreign Investment Law requires the planned debt equity level for a local incorporated company having a foreign investor to be submitted to the Investment Coordinating Board (Badan Koordinasi Penanaman Modal, or BKPM) for approval. For this purpose, a debt-to-equity ratio of 3 to 1 will normally be acceptable.

Shareholder Debt. Interest on shareholder debt is generally deductible, provided it represents an arm's-length rate. The tax authorities will treat excessive interest as a concealed dividend. The tax authorities do not generally challenge interest payable to a third-party bank, even though the loan is guaranteed by a shareholder.

Foreign exchange differences on conversion and translation of foreign currency loans (including loans from shareholders), both realized and unrealized, are treated as deductible expenses or taxable income. Special rules apply when an official currency revaluation occurs.

Exchange Controls

Indonesia has no restrictions on the remittance of funds overseas. Overseas borrowing levels are monitored by a team of senior government officials, whose approval is required for loans made to banks and other entities in which there is some form of government ownership or participation. Offshore borrowings of a company should be reported but are not subject to approval.

Business Acquisitions and Dispositions

Capital Contributions into an Existing Local Entity

There is no stamp duty or other tax on a contribution of capital. A contribution of assets in-kind, tangible or intangible, requires approval by the Investment Coordinating Board. The transfer of assets in exchange for shares will be subject to the normal tax requirements—that is, any import duties, VAT or withholding taxes applicable to the transfer of assets remain payable even though there is no cash consideration.

The issue of new shares has no direct tax impact on existing shareholders.

Purchase or Sale of Shares in a Local Entity

A gain on the sale of shares by a local individual or entity is subject to income tax. The gain is added to the person's other income for the year and taxed at the normal income tax rates. If, however, the sale is made through the stock market, tax is imposed at a fixed rate of 0.1% or 0.5% of the sale proceeds, depending on the circumstances when the seller acquired the shares. This tax is final, and no further tax is payable. The tax treatment is the same whether the transaction is for a majority or a minority stake.

A sale of shares by a non-resident is generally not subject to income tax in Indonesia, unless the non-resident has a PE in Indonesia:

- If the sale is made through the stock market, a final tax of 0.5% or 0.1% is imposed, depending on the circumstances when the seller acquired the shares.

- The law contains provisions, which have not been implemented to date, for imposing a withholding tax on the proceeds of transfers of property by non-residents. At present, no withholding tax is applicable.

Such taxes may be reduced if the seller is eligible for tax treaty relief. The tax basis in the assets remains unaltered in the event of a company acquisition.

Purchase or Sale of Assets

Like other government licenses, telecommunications licenses are granted to a specified entity and are not normally transferable. Consequently, an asset sale will only be possible if it is certain that the acquirer has its own license.

Any gain obtained by the vendor will be taxable as part of its annual profits. There are no roll-over or other reliefs to defer or reduce the tax impact.

Acquirers should allocate the purchase price to individual assets based on market values. Intangible assets, including goodwill, are depreciable over the useful life of the asset. The useful life of intangible assets for tax purposes will normally be the same as the useful life for book purposes. Indonesian accounting principles require goodwill to be depreciated over a three- to five-year period.

Asset acquisitions are often preferred by the acquirer in order to avoid any undisclosed liabilities and to increase the tax basis in the assets. For a vendor, an assets sale may not be attractive, as the proceeds are taxed twice—once as a profit of the company and again when the profit is ultimately distributed to individual shareholders. Over half the profit can thus be lost to taxes. Gains on the sale of partnership interests would also be taxable, but foreigners cannot acquire such interests.

Start-up Business Issues

Pre-operating Losses and Start-up/Construction Costs

Provided they are incurred for the purposes of the business, pre-operating costs and start-up costs are deductible for tax purposes:

- As a current expense, if the expense is of a routine nature and the future benefit lasts 12 months or less.

- By way of amortization, if the expenditure has a future benefit exceeding 12 months so that it is capitalized as a deferred cost or an intangible asset.

Construction costs are capitalized, together with interest during construction and such indirect construction costs as project management, site supervision and the like. On the other hand, selling, general, and administration costs relating to general management during the pre-operating phase are treated as current expense.

For assets under construction, depreciation commences in the financial period of completion of the assets. The period of amortization for tax purposes depends on the useful life of the expenditure, which normally will be consistent with the useful life adopted for book purposes.

Pre-operating costs can include costs incurred by a foreign company outside of Indonesia. To be deductible, the costs should be directly linked to the Indonesian project. The Indonesian company will need to settle any VAT and withholding taxes applicable to the expenditure when these are accounted for in its records, as if it had incurred the expenditure itself. VAT will be creditable for certain companies, but not for others, as discussed below. VAT incurred by overseas companies is not creditable.

For a number of reasons, it is generally better for the Indonesian entity to account for expenses directly, as far as this is possible.

Customs Duties and VAT

Imports of equipment, spares and other goods are subject to import duties at various rates: to VAT at 10%, and to income tax prepayment at 2.5%. Cellular telephones are excluded from the luxury sales tax on imports to which household electronic equipment is normally subject. There are no distinctions made for Internet telephony equipment.

Import duties and VAT are not payable for capital expenditures on equipment and related spare parts—items for which import reliefs have been approved by the Investment Coordinating Board.

VAT on imports may be creditable for some companies, but not others (see below). Income tax payable on imports can be offset against the company's year-end tax liability. In the pre-operating period, companies can apply for exemption from this tax.

Loss Carryovers

Losses can be carried forward against future profits, for up to five years following the year of loss. No tax grouping with affiliated companies or other loss relief is permitted. A change of ownership or business activity does not limit the use of previous-year losses.

Operating Considerations

Corporate Income Taxes

Company income tax at a rate of 30% applies to the total taxable income for the financial year. Lower rates apply on the first Rp 50 million of annual profits.

Foreign companies with a PE are subject to the same income tax rates. A branch withholding tax of 20% also applies, except if reduced by a tax treaty.

Interest and other income may be subject to special rules:

- Interest on bank deposits is subject to 15% tax at source, which is final.

- Rental of real estate is subject to 6% tax, which is final.

- Sales of listed shares are subject to either 0.1% or 0.5% tax at source, which is final.

Non-deductible expenses include expenditures on employee benefits in-kind, donations and provisions.

Capital Gains Taxes

Income tax is applied to capital gains, which are included in annual profits. Acquisition costs are deductible but cannot be adjusted for inflation. A transfer of land and buildings is subject to a 5% income tax, which is considered a pre-payment of the annual tax liability.

Tax Holidays and Exemptions

Tax incentives may be approved for companies operating in certain geographic areas. Generally, incentives are used to spur economic activity in the less-developed provinces of Indonesia. The incentives comprise:

• Depreciation at twice the normal rates

• Maximum period for a loss carryforward doubled to 10 years

• Withholding tax on dividends reduced to 10%

Companies that undertake government projects funded by aid are granted relief from income tax. Any income tax and branch withholding tax derived from aid-funded revenues are borne by the government and not paid by the company.

Tax holidays of up to 10 years will be initially granted to new investments in certain priority industries, which are selected by a team of ministers. Several companies in manufacturing and heavy industry have been granted tax holidays; to date, no tax holidays have been granted in the telecommunications sector.

Depreciation/Cost-Recovery Conventions/Accelerated Deductions

For tax purposes, assets are categorized into groups, based upon the nature of the assets and their expected useful lives, as shown in the table below. Note that land is not depreciable for tax purposes. These categories apply to all companies in the telecommunications sector, and almost all other sectors as well.

A company can elect to deduct tax depreciation on either a straight-line or declining-balance method for all assets except buildings. The method adopted must be applied consistently.

Purchased software will generally be categorized in Group 2. Research and development costs, including software development costs, are deductible as an expense unless they are considered to have a useful life of more than 12 months, in which case they should be treated as capital expenditure for tax purposes. The tax depreciation rate for such expenditures will depend into which of the non-building asset categories its useful life falls.

Tax depreciation normally commences when an asset purchase or construction is completed, irrespective of whether use commences at that time. Specific approval from the tax authorities is required to start tax depreciation from the date of use where it is different from the date of completion.

Marketing and advertising expenditures are generally deductible in the period incurred. Promotional gifts and certain types of other expenditures are not deductible.

Transfer Pricing Rules

Indonesia's self-assessment system relies on an extensive tax audit process. Related-party transactions are closely scrutinized in almost all audits. If auditors view inter-company charges as excessive, they will treat them as concealed dividends.

A related party is broadly defined in the tax law and includes:

• Companies with a 25% direct or indirect shareholding relationship

• Companies under common shareholdings of 25% or more

• Companies under common control as a result of technology or management factors

Official guidelines have been published to assist auditors in detecting transfer pricing manipulation. However, there is no procedure to obtain a pre-ruling on pricing arrangements, nor are there guidelines to assist companies in judging whether arrangements they have adopted represent an appropriate arm's-length basis.

Category	Years of Useful Life	Types of Assets	Straight-Line	Declining-Balance
Non-buildings				
Group 1	1 to 4	Furniture/loose tools	25%	50%
Group 2	5 to 8	Telecommunications and broadcasting equipment	12.5%	25%
Group 3	9 to 16	Equipment not included in other categories	6.25%	12.5%
Group 4	Over 16	Heavy equipment/pipelines	5%	10%
Buildings				
Permanent	20	Brick, cement or steel construction	5%	N/A
Temporary	10	Wooden construction	10%	N/A

Transfers of Patents, Trademarks and Software

These fees will be deductible, provided they are not considered excessive by tax auditors. Withholding tax applies at 15% on amounts payable to residents and 20% on amounts payable to non-residents, except when reduced by a tax treaty. VAT applies at 10%, and is self-imposed by the Indonesian entity. Charges for technology transfer should be at an arm's-length price. The tax authorities will treat an amount in excess of an arm's-length price as a concealed dividend.

Charges for use of technology are subject to withholding tax, whereas payments for purchases of technology are, in principle, not subject to withholding tax. However, the tax authorities are likely to take the position that all charges for technology are subject to withholding tax. Both purchase and usage charges are subject to VAT, applied by the Indonesian entity on a self-payment method.

Service Fees

Withholding tax at 20% applies to all fees payable to non-resident foreign parties for services performed both outside and inside the country. Tax treaties will often provide relief from this withholding tax. However, if a foreign company has a tax registration as a PE, the domestic withholding tax applies.

For service fees payable to residents, withholding tax applies at 4% or 6% for consulting and certain other services, and at 2% for construction services.

Value-Added Tax, Sales Tax and/or Other Pertinent Taxes

Value-added tax applies to telecommunications services at the standard rate of 10%. Telkom is subject to a special decree, under which its input VAT cannot be credited. This decree is understood to extend to activities conducted under a KSO or other joint arrangements with Telkom or Indosat.

Telecommunications companies that invoice customers directly—such as cellular, paging and Internet access companies—can follow the general VAT law and credit input VAT incurred on business expenditures. Cellular system operators also have an obligation to impose up to Rp 400,000 of VAT be-

fore activating a customer's handset in cases where the handsets were not purchased from an authorized importer/dealer or where a VAT invoice has not been shown.

Registration for VAT purposes is necessary to credit or obtain a refund of VAT. Parties unable to register, including overseas telecommunications companies, cannot recover VAT incurred. The VAT implications of international settlement processes have not been formally addressed in tax laws.

Land and Buildings Tax is an annual levy of 0.1% upon the market value of land and buildings.

Stamp duty is a small fixed amount (Rp 2,000 or Rp 1,000) that is applied to invoices, agreements, checks, receipts and other documents. No sliding-scale stamp duty exists.

Local and Provincial Taxes

Local and provincial taxes apply to miscellaneous transactions, such as motor vehicle registration, expatriate registration, and televisions. All are relatively minor costs relative to income tax, VAT and import duties.

For Additional Information, Contact:

Sony B. Harsono
Senior Tax Partner
and
Nicholas M. Bale
Tax Partner Advisor
Siddharta Siddharta & Harsono
32nd Floor Wisma GKBI
28, Jl. Jend. Sudirman
Jakarta 10210
Telephone: 62 (21) 574 2333/574 2888
Fax: 62 (21) 574 1777/574 2777

Robert Wilhelm
Principal Consultant—Telecoms & Media Practice
33rd Floor Wisma GKBI
28, Jl. Jend. Sudirman
Jakarta 10210
Telephone: 62 (21) 574 0060
Fax: 62 (21) 574 0150
E-mail: bob_wilhelm@asiamcs.coopers.com

Japan

Telecommunications Tax Profile
by Tsutomu Kikuchi
Tax Partner, Tokyo
and Al Zencak
Tax Manager, Tokyo

Overview of the Telecommunications Market

Historical Background

The liberalization and restructuring of Japan's telecommunications market began in 1985 with the Telecommunications Business Law (TBL), which enabled the privatization of Nippon Telegraph & Telephone Corporation (NTT), Japan's dominant telecommunications organization and the world's largest telecommunications company. The TBL ended NTT's domestic monopoly and Kokusai Denshin Denwa Co., Ltd.'s (KDD) monopoly on international service. Further, the TBL categorized telecommunications businesses as either Type I carriers (facilities-based) or Type II carriers (service providers leasing Type I circuits). Liberalization of the customer premise equipment business ushered in vigorous competition among many suppliers for consumer and business customers.

Current Status

Japan's telecommunications market is enjoying dynamic rates of expansion in a number of industry segments, including fixed-line telephone service; radio paging; high-speed digital transmission; integrated services digital network (ISDN); Internet access; the mobile, Personal Handy-Phone System (PHS) and telecommunications satellites. Today there are approximately 140 Type I carriers and more than 4,500 Type II carriers. This represents a 125% increase in the number of carriers from the prior year. The greatest number of Type I competitors are PHS, and cellular phone and radio paging network operators. There are also many providers of satellite, international, long-distance and regional services.

This expansion has resulted in a substantial increase in revenues generated in the communications industry. Revenue reported from both Type I and Type II telecommunications carriers

in 1994 and 1995 totaled ¥8,870,294 million and ¥10,629,941 million, respectively, of which ¥2,746,714 million and ¥4,146,856 million (respectively) were reported by carriers other than NTT and KDD. The anticipated revenues for 1996 were approximately ¥11,956,903 million, of which ¥5,437,903 million was anticipated to be earned by carriers other than NTT and KDD.

The Ministry of Posts and Telecommunications (MPT) announced on January 23, 1996, a deregulation plan entitled Promotion of Deregulations toward the Second Info-Communications Reform. The plan included a framework for restructuring NTT, in which a holding company would be established to hold 100% of the shares of NTT West, NTT East, and an NTT long-distance and international communications subsidiary. The above entities had not yet been established. The MPT will continue to revise tariffs for services other than mobile. The deregulation plans include a requirement that all mobile licensees issue prior notification of rates.

The MPT established a special committee to promote various forms of interconnection between telecommunications carriers and NTT's local network. In September 1996, the MPT authorized connection of leased circuits to the public telecommunications network at both ends, representing the complete deregulation of leased circuit usage. In December 1996, the Regulation for Enforcement of the Telecommunications Business Law was revised, establishing the mobile-telecommunications fees that are charged by Type I telecommunications carriers under an advance-notification system.

For Type I Telecommunications carriers that own fixed transmission facilities comprising more than 50% of the total number of subscriber lines at prefectural levels, the new rules introduce an interconnection tariff system, including interconnection charges and technical requirements. The rules also require preparation of accounting records concerning interconnection and disclosure of plans to revise or expand facility features or functions.

In addition, as a result of the agreement reached at the World Trade Organization (WTO) negotiations in February 1997, all limitations were eliminated for foreign investment in Type I telecommunications carriers, except for NTT and KDD, in which foreign investment was limited to less than 20%.

NTT continues to dominate the long-distance and local telephone markets. In addition, NTT began providing international telephone services in July 1997. Domestic service providers that compete with NTT include:

- Long-distance competitors Daini Denden Inc. (DDI), Japan Telecom (JT) and Teleway Japan. Nearly all domestic long-distance competitors reported substantially increased profits in 1996 as a result of their cellular subsidiaries' increased cellular phone sales and network expansion.

- Local/regional competitors Tokyo Telecommunications Network (TTNet), Osaka Media Port (OMP), Chubu Telecommunications Company (CTC) and nearly a dozen other providers of leased-line service. TTNet, a regional telephone carrier affiliated with Tokyo Electric Power Company, plans to lay fiber optic cable in the greater Tokyo area to link TTNet and NTT switching centers through leased lines and to build additional switching centers. Ultimately, TTNet envisions interconnecting with other regional new common carriers (NCCs) to build a network that can compete against NTT in local and long-distance service.

- Nearly 60 mobile service providers for PHS, which is a new type of digital, portable telephone developed in Japan.

- The introduction of the Internet telephone in late 1997 may add to competition and put pressure on rates, which are still the highest among member states of the Organization for Economic Cooperation and Development (OECD). As of January 1996, approximately 9.47 million host computers worldwide were connected to the Internet. Of these, 269,000 units were in Japan. As of December 1995, 278 Type II telecommunications carriers were providing Internet services, and only one Type I carrier, KDD, was providing such services. The international market is dominated by KDD, Japan's largest international communications carrier. In July 1997, KDD began to provide domestic local and long-distance services. Competitors include two domestic companies, International Digital Communications (IDC) and International Telecom Japan.

- The fiber-optic network covered approximately 12.9% of the population as of 1995, with installation mainly in prefectural seats. It is expected that by the year 2000, 20% of the population will be covered, with installation to 100% of the nationwide population expected by the year 2010.

Current Liberalization Status

A report by the OECD describes Japan as the most liberalized country in the telecommunications industry. Nonetheless, although there are generally no statutory restrictions, the MPT may enforce "invisible guidance" (i.e., placing restrictions on a verbal basis).

Type of Service	Degree of Liberalization	Key Legislation*	Date of Actual or Expected Liberalization
Local	Fully liberalized	TBL, NTT Corporate Law, WTO Agreement	1985, 1996, 1997
Long Distance	Fully liberalized	TBL, NTT Corporate Law, WTO Agreement	1997
International	Fully liberalized	TBL, NTT Corporate Law, WTO Agreement	1997
Cellular	Fully liberalized	TBL, NTT Corporate Law, WTO Agreement	1997
Paging	Fully liberalized	TBL, NTT Corporate Law, WTO Agreement	1997
Value-added	Fully liberalized	TBL, NTT Corporate Law, WTO Agreement	1997

* The TBL was effective in April 1985. As a result of an agreement reached at the WTO negotiations in February 1997, bills to revise the TBL were passed by the Diet. In addition, the NTT Corporate Law, which established NTT as a private enterprise, has been revised to allow NTT to operate internationally. Laws relating to the regulation of KDD were revised to allow both companies to operate domestically.

Competitive Environment

Type of Service	Entire Market		Top Two Players		
	Market Size	Number of Players	Names	Annual Revenue	Ownership
Local	¥7,481.5 billion (FY95 revenue for NTT, KDD and NCCs, including telephone, leased-circuit, cellular phone, and radio paging)	22	NTT	¥5,750.4 billion (3/97)	Publicly traded
			TTNet	¥61.163 billion (3/97)	Tokyo Electric, Mitsui & Co., Mitsubishi Corp., and Nissan Motor Co.
Long Distance	Not available	4	NTT	¥988.2 billion (3/97)	Publicly traded
			DDI	¥548 billion (3/97)	Kyocera Corp., Sony Corp., State Street Bank, others
International	¥344.8 billion (FY95 revenue for NTT, KDD and NCCs, including telephone and leased circuit)	5	KDD	¥248.300 billion (3/96)	Publicly traded
			IDC	¥52.326 billion (3/96)	NTT, Toyota Motor Corp., Itochu Corp., others
Cellular	¥1,418.7 billion (FY95 revenue for NTT, KDD and NCCs)	50	NTT DoCoMo	¥1,937.506 billion (total, including noncellular) (3/97)	NTT
			Cellular Group	¥532,754 (3/97)	DDI
Paging	¥288.9 billion (FY95 revenue for NTT, KDD and NCCs)	32	NTT DoCoMo	¥1,937.506 billion (total, including nonpaging) (3/97)	NTT
			Telemessage Group	¥111.810 billion (3/96)	JT, Mitsui & Co., Tokyo Electric, others

Sources: MPT *Annual Telecommunications Company Listing, 1996–1997*
MPT *Outline of Telecommunications Business in Japan. June 1997*

Licensing Requirements

Japan's telecommunications markets continue to be subject to stringent regulatory oversight by the MPT, which administers an extensive framework of fees and licensing procedures. Type I carriers must obtain a license from the MPT and establish tariffs. Type II companies are categorized as either general carriers or special carriers.

Special carriers are defined as Type II telecommunications businesses that (1) provide telecommunications services for an unspecified number of general subscribers and that have a scale exceeding the criteria prescribed by applicable cabinet ordinance (2000 circuits for 64 kbps conversion), or (2) that provide telecommunications facilities for communications with locations outside of Japan. Special carriers must register with the MPT and obtain approval for the types of services they plan to provide.

General carriers are Type II telecommunications businesses other than those defined as Special Type II telecommunications businesses. General carriers are required to notify the MPT only of the types of services that they will provide.

Potential for Foreign Ownerships/Relationships

Japan's telecommunications markets are open to foreign companies. There are no foreign ownership restrictions, except those applying to KDD and NTT, as noted in "Current Status."

Potential for Upcoming Liberalization/ Investment Opportunities

Important developments ahead in Japan's telecommunications market include further deregulation, more competition, and the likely expansion of mobile phone service. Also under consideration is the MPT proposal to break NTT into three separate companies, including two local telephone companies and one long-distance company.

The dynamic rates of expansion in the telecommunications sectors have created significant business opportunities. For example, DDI is working with Motorola's Iridium to develop the global personal satellite communications service. Opportunities also exist for Japanese and foreign manufacturers of telecommunications equipment, particularly advanced switching equipment and mobile phone equipment.

The government was considering the abolishment as early as fiscal year 1998 of the law that regulates KDD. This would remove the restrictions on foreign investment in KDD and enable KDD to merge with other companies without needing approvals from the MPT.

Forms of Doing Business

Permanent Establishment

Whether a foreign corporation is subject to Japanese corporation tax depends on whether it maintains a permanent establishment (PE) in Japan. Among the businesses that will be treated as PEs are:

- Those that own a branch, factory or other fixed place of business in Japan

- Those that carry out a construction, installation or assembly project for a period of more than one year in Japan or supervise this type of activity

- Those with an agent in Japan who is authorized to habitually conclude contracts, fill orders or negotiate on behalf of the foreign corporation

Japan-sourced income is taxable to a foreign corporation whether or not such business income is attributable to a fixed place of business, such as a branch. This rule may be modified by a tax treaty (e.g., a foreign corporation resident in a country with which Japan has a tax treaty and which is deemed to have a PE in Japan will be subject to tax on the income that is attributable to the PE in Japan). Following are examples of the concept of PE as related to telecommunications activities:

- The provision of long-distance telephone services by a foreign company having no local staff in Japan generally does not create a PE.

- The licensing of technology and know-how to a local company by a foreign company having no permanent presence in Japan generally does not result in a PE.

- The provision of technical assistance and operator services by a foreign company to a local company in exchange for service fees may result in a PE, whether or not the foreign company owns an equity interest in the local entity.

- The leasing of telecommunications equipment to a local company by a foreign company having no other activities in Japan does not result in a PE.

- The provision of call reorganization/turnaround services does not result in a PE if the telephone cards are provided through an independent agent and if the foreign telecommunications company has no fixed place of business in Japan.

- Whether a foreign company's provision of Internet access services in Japan results in a PE depends on the extent of the foreign company's operations in Japan. If the foreign entity merely sells access software to Japanese customers but has no other presence in Japan, it is not characterized as having a PE.

- Rules regarding the permanent establishment and tax status of websites and their locations and accessibility were still developing. The laying of fiber optic cable in Japan's territorial waters generally creates a PE, as does the construction of telecommunications switching equipment, either for sale to a local company or for operation by a foreign telecommunications company for a fee. Japanese tax law specifically includes in its definitions of a PE a place where a person is engaged in a construction project for a period of more than one year, subject to the provisions of relevant double-tax agreements.

If the provision of services does not create a PE for a foreign telecommunications company in Japan, the only tax to which the foreign entity is subject is withholding tax, which is levied on dividends, royalties and interest paid to a non-resident. If the provision of services does create a PE, then a foreign company is taxed as a branch, as described below.

Business Entities

Unregistered Liaison Representative Office. A foreign company that does not continuously engage in commercial transactions in Japan can carry on customer relations and general liaison activities through an unregistered liaison representative office. A representative office can be operated by an individual in Japan without any government reporting or corporate registration. Since the representative office is not permitted to engage in any commercial transactions, the foreign company will not be liable for any Japanese corporate taxes and is not required to file a corporate tax return.

Local Branch of a Foreign Company. Under certain circumstances, foreign companies may establish a branch office of a foreign corporation to provide telecommunications services in Japan. In most cases, the foreign corporation forms a new entity that will be the head office of the Japanese branch. The creation of the head office simplifies the determination of the income and expense allocation of the Japanese branch, including preparation of the branch's books and records in accordance with Japan's generally accepted accounting principles

(GAAP). The business and tax implications of operating in branch form, including tax rates and filing requirements, are similar to those of operating through a Japanese incorporated entity. There are several important tax differences, as follows:

- A Japanese branch is not subject to branch profits taxes on the repatriation of profits to a foreign head office; by contrast, a Japanese subsidiary is subject to withholding tax of 20% (which may be reduced by a tax treaty) on the distribution of dividends to a foreign corporation.

- A branch is taxable only on its Japanese-sourced income; a subsidiary is taxable on its worldwide income. Correspondingly, a branch can claim deductions only for Japan-sourced expenses, and a subsidiary may claim deductions for any expenses, regardless of source. In practice, it is more common to provide telecommunications services through a local subsidiary of a foreign corporation (as discussed below) than through a branch. Government authorities, lending institutions (e.g., banks) and employees generally prefer a local subsidiary, as it conveys a greater commitment to doing business in Japan.

Locally Incorporated Subsidiary of a Foreign Company. For Type II carriers, there is no limit on the amount of stock that a foreign company can own in a Japanese company. Therefore, a foreign Type II carrier may also establish a Japanese corporation. In almost all cases, the locally incorporated subsidiary is a kabushiki kaisha (KK), the main type of joint stock corporation.

In a KK, 50% of capital must be allocated to capital stock, but the remainder can be allocated to capital surplus. A registration tax is imposed on all initial and subsequent capital increases. This tax is equal to 0.7% of the increase in the capital stock account. Therefore, the registration tax can be reduced to the extent that a portion of the capital contribution (not to exceed 50%) is allocated to the capital surplus account.

Joint Venture. For Type I carriers, one-third of the capital of a Japanese company can be foreign capital. A joint venture normally takes the form of an equity interest in a Japanese KK corporation. Japan taxes a joint venture as it would a wholly owned Japanese corporation.

Telecommunications operators do not normally use other structures, nor do they usually use arrangements offering flow-through characteristics. Japanese law does allow for creation of two legal entities that are similar to partnerships: a gomei kaisha is similar to an unlimited partnership in that all partners are jointly and severally liable; a goshi kaisha is similar to a limited partnership in that some partners may have only a limited liability interest. Both entities are treated as separate taxable entities for corporate tax purposes. Profits and losses are not passed through to the investors. Both partnership forms also exhibit the least attractive characteristics of partnerships—unlimited liability with taxation at both the entity and investor levels. With both, a tax return must generally be filed within two months after the close of the corporation's accounting year.

Local Funding Alternatives

Debt versus Equity

From a Japanese corporation's tax perspective, interest payments are tax-deductible and dividend payments are not. Japan imposes a withholding tax on interest and dividends paid to foreign corporations at a rate of 20%, which may be reduced by a tax treaty.

Japan's thin capitalization rules provide for a 3-to-1 debt-to-equity ratio and apply to all companies and branches of foreign corporations having interest-bearing, foreign-related-party indebtedness. The portion of a Japanese company's interest expense that exceeds this ratio is generally not deductible. Further, withholding taxes will still be imposed on the portion of interest expense for which a deduction has been disallowed. These rules do not apply to third-party financing when they are guaranteed by a foreign-related party. Therefore, despite the thin capitalization rules, corporations can deduct interest expense even if the related debt is guaranteed by a non-resident shareholder of the Japanese corporation. Further, companies may increase the permitted debt-to-equity ratio if they identify comparable Japanese companies with higher debt-to-equity ratios.

Foreign exchange gains and losses are generally included in the company's taxable income when realized; however, short-term assets and liabilities are subject to revaluation to reflect the current rate.

Exchange Controls

Japan has foreign exchange control laws that affect most cross-border investment transactions.

Business Acquisitions and Dispositions

Capital Contributions into an Existing Local Entity

A capital contribution into a local entity is subject to the registration and license tax when the entity increases its capital. The tax (currently 0.7%) is based on the amount of the capital contribution that is credited to the capital account. To reduce the amount of tax to be imposed, the entity may credit one-half or less of the capital increase to its capital surplus account. Contributions of property require valuation by a court-appointed examiner to ensure accuracy.

The local entity is permitted to continue to use its tax attributes, regardless of the ownership interest held by the foreign entity; however, the additional capital contribution may affect the amount of net worth taxes (e.g., inhabitants tax) that it pays or affect the amount of deductions that can be claimed for certain expense items (e.g., entertainment expenses).

In most cases, both initial and subsequent capital contributions to a Japanese corporation are structured in the form of cash rather than in-kind transfers. This avoids the costs and delays associated with procedural requirements, such as the need for valuations. The contributed cash can then be used to acquire any assets owned by the shareholder, including technology, that will be used in the business.

Purchase or Sale of Shares in a Local Entity

A Japanese non-resident that sells shares in a local entity will be subject to capital gains tax if it owns 25% or more of the shares during the taxable year and if the total shares transferred during the taxable year equal 5% or more of the local entity.

A resident corporation that sells shares in a local entity is subject to corporate income tax, regardless of the amount of its ownership interest. The capital gain is included in the corporation's other income and taxed accordingly. A resident Japanese individual who sells shares in a publicly traded local entity is subject to capital gains tax, regardless of the amount of his or her ownership interest.

The local entity whose shares are sold can continue to use its accumulated net operating losses, regardless of the amount of share ownership change. If the shares are delivered outside of Japan, the securities transaction tax is not assessed.

Purchase or Sale of Assets

In an asset purchase, the acquirer allocates the price paid to the acquired assets based on their fair market value with any excess allocated to goodwill. To the extent that a company pays a premium to acquire assets, any additional depreciation deductions may be allowed to the extent that the premium is allocated to depreciable assets. In contrast, any premium that is paid to acquire stock of a company would not be deductible for Japanese corporate tax purposes. The same allocation applies when purchasing shares of a Japanese company, provided the target company is merged into the purchasing company within a period deemed reasonable by the authorities. The law permits goodwill to be amortized over five years, but shorter periods are possible. If properly structured, the subsequent merger into the purchasing company could be structured tax-free. Any gain that is recognized by the local entity would be included in taxable income and subject to corporate tax. The consequences relating to the purchase and sale of partnership interests would generally be as discussed above.

Start-up Business Issues

Pre-operating Losses and Start-up/Construction Costs

Investors must treat as deferred assets any expenditures having benefit for more than one year. Thus, expenditures used to develop a new market or start a new business are treated as deferred assets, which are amortized on a straight-line basis over the period of the anticipated benefit.

Certain types of deferred expenses can be expensed currently or at the option of the corporation, and can be amortized within a five-year period. These deferred expenses include pre-incorporation expenses and corporate organizational expenses that are incurred prior to commencement of the business.

Customs Duties and VAT

Japan's customs duties laws are consistent with international standards, since Japan is a signatory to the General Agreement on Tariffs and Trade (GATT) and is a member of the WTO. Customs duties can represent a significant cost for most companies importing products into Japan; however, most telecommunications equipment (e.g., switches, cables, cellular stations and cellular phones) are not subject to customs duties. (Japanese consumption tax is discussed under "Value-Added Tax, Sales Tax and/or Other Pertinent Taxes.")

Loss Carryovers

In general, losses may be carried back for one year or carried forward for five years at the option of any company with permission to file a Blue Form tax return. The Blue Form return system was introduced to encourage the use of standardized accounting procedures. Corporations that apply for the privilege of filing a Blue Form and which agree to use a standard bookkeeping system are eligible for certain tax benefits, including the carryback and carryforward of losses. A temporary measure suspends the loss carryback provision for business years ending from April 1, 1992, to March 31, 1998. Losses incurred in the first three fiscal years after incorporation can be carried forward for 10 years.

There are no limitations on the use of loss carryovers following a change in the ownership of a Japanese corporation; however, in structuring mergers, care must be taken so that the loss can be employed effectively. Japan has no consolidated tax return or group tax relief provisions. There are no limitations on the use of losses when a Japanese company changes its business activities.

Operating Considerations

Corporate Income Taxes

The basic income tax rate structure for most Japanese companies and branches is as follows:

Corporate national tax	37.5%
Corporate enterprise tax	12.6
Corporate inhabitants tax	7.8
	57.9%
Less effect of corporate enterprise tax paid for the prior year's taxable income (i.e., 12.6% at 51.4%)	(6.5%)
Approximate effective tax rate	51.4%

The enterprise tax and inhabitants tax are local taxes (see "Local and Provincial Taxes"). Virtually all Japanese corporations and branches file a Blue Form corporate tax return. A newly established corporation or branch must file an application for permission to file this type of return.

The following are some of the differences between the Japanese tax treatment of a branch and a subsidiary:

- A branch is taxable only on Japan-sourced income, whereas a Japanese subsidiary is taxable on worldwide income.

- A subsidiary is subject to an overall effective tax rate greater than the rate for operations through a Japan branch. This is because the remittance of branch profits is not subject to withholding tax, whereas the remittance of a dividend from a Japanese subsidiary to its foreign parent is generally subject to a withholding tax.

- The tax authorities may seek to obtain management and financial data from the head office and may attempt to reallocate income and expense between a Japan branch and a head office. Inter-company transactions between a Japanese subsidiary and its foreign parent must comply with the arm's-length requirements of Japan's inter-company pricing legislation.

- Bonuses paid to a director who represents the Japanese subsidiary are not deductible. Bonuses paid to the general manager of a branch are fully deductible.

Capital Gains Taxes

In general, there are no corporate capital gains taxes in Japan.

Tax Holidays and Exemptions

There are special temporary rules that enable certain foreign-owned corporations to claim tax deductions for developing domestic markets for imported products and that permit specified telecommunications service imports. Although there are conditions that limit the effectiveness and applicability of these incentives, many foreign-owned Japanese corporations receive substantial tax benefits under these provisions.

The MPT provides low-interest special loans to promote the importation of telecommunications equipment and for investments in overseas operations, including the installation of submarine fiber optic cables. Type I telecommunications carriers who deploy subscriber fiber optic networks can apply to obtain reductions in the fixed property tax rate.

Depreciation/Cost-Recovery Conventions/Accelerated Deductions

The Ministry of Finance has formulated detailed rules regarding the applicable useful lives of new depreciable assets and used assets. A Japanese corporation or branch may elect to depreciate assets under the straight-line method (SLM) or the declining-balance method (DBM).

Under the SLM, yearly depreciation expense is calculated by multiplying a prescribed depreciation rate by 90% of the acquisition cost (i.e., the allocated acquisition cost is reduced by a deemed 10% residual value). Under the DBM, yearly depreciation expense is calculated by multiplying a prescribed depreciation rate by the outstanding net book value of the asset. The prescribed depreciation rate reflects an assumed 10% residual value. Under both the SLM and the DBM, 95% of the acquisition cost is recoverable through depreciation deductions; the remaining 5% may be charged to expense when the asset is retired or abandoned.

The amount of depreciation deduction claimed for tax purposes must correspond with the amount of depreciation claimed for Japanese book purposes. If a deduction for depreciation is not reflected in the company's Japanese GAAP books, no deduction is permissible. Assets are usually depreciated from the date they are placed in service. For network equipment used for domestic and international telecommunications business, the effective life is as follows:

Digital switching apparatus	6 years
Analog switching apparatus	10 years
Servers, terminal adaptors	10 years
Fiber optic cables	10 years
Routers	6 years

Type I telecommunications carriers who deploy subscriber fiber optic networks can apply to claim additional depreciation.

If software is installed in telecommunications equipment and if the software value cannot be separated from the hardware value, depreciation is based on the total cost of the equipment, including the bundled software. If software costs can be separated from the apparatus, they are depreciated on a straight-line basis over five years.

Japanese corporations can deduct marketing and advertising expenses. To the extent that the advertising expenses are deemed to be "special expenditures," these costs may need to be capitalized.

Transfer Pricing Rules

Japan's transfer pricing legislation applies to transactions between Japanese corporations, branches and companies that, directly or indirectly, are owned 50% or more by the same interests, or where there is a "special relationship" that suggests such an ownership interest (e.g., the Japanese company is dependent on the foreign company for funding of operating capital, business operations, use of intangibles).

Virtually all types of inter-company transactions must be disclosed, including the sale of tangibles or intangible property, services, financing and licensing arrangements.

The Japanese tax authorities have significantly expanded the size of their special transfer pricing teams, and have engaged in considerable study of transfer pricing methods and practices. Spectacularly large tax assessments have been made against foreign-owned Japanese corporations in recent years. Foreign-owned companies should be prepared for transfer pricing tax audits.

Transfers of Patents, Trademarks and Software

Running royalty payments by Japanese corporations to foreign corporations are normally deductible, provided that the amounts can be supported by reference to the arm's-length criteria and methodologies. Such running royalty payments are subject to Japanese withholding tax at the rate of 20%. Lump-sum payments related to technology transfers, as well as other payments for know-how, are required to be capitalized and amortized over a period of five years.

In contrast, companies that incorporate the intellectual property component of their products into the product price without a separate royalty arrangement are not subject to Japanese income or withholding tax in connection with the sales proceeds. This also applies to the sale of bundled equipment in which the price for software loaded on the equipment is included in the purchase price for the equipment. It should also be possible to structure transactions involving software as sales of software products, rather than as licensing arrangements. If properly structured and implemented, the payments made to the foreign corporation should not be treated as royalties subject to withholding tax.

Service Fees

For a foreign corporation with a Japanese branch, expenses incurred outside of Japan that relate to the Japanese operations may be allocated to the branch and claimed as a deduction.

This includes both direct expenses and allocable overhead expenses. Considerable flexibility is allowed regarding the method of allocation, and it is usually possible to support such deductions in the branch. The transfer of funds from the branch to the foreign head office for these expenses is not subject to withholding taxes. These arrangements are not subject to the requirements of Japan's transfer pricing legislation.

When a Japanese corporation or branch receives services from, and makes payments to, a foreign affiliate for management services, these arrangements are subject to the requirements of transfer pricing legislation. Although such service payments should be tax-deductible and no withholding taxes imposed, supporting these arrangements in tax audits has become increasingly difficult. The tax authorities have successfully challenged these types of arrangements on the basis that the companies have failed to maintain the degree of support or documentation necessary to show that the services had actually been rendered or that they benefited operations in Japan.

Value-Added Tax, Sales Tax and/or Other Pertinent Taxes

The Japanese form of indirect tax is called the consumption tax (CT). The CT has some characteristics of a sales-subtraction form of value-added tax, but also has features similar to the European method, particularly concerning the calculation of CT liability. As of April 1, 1997, the CT was increased to 5% (4% national tax and a 1% local tax) from 3%.

Under the current consumption tax law, a Japanese company is not subject to CT either for its first two years of doing business in Japan or when its annual taxable sales in the two prior years are ¥30 million or less. Taxable sales are those sales realized by the company two years prior to the current business year. A Japanese company can claim a refund for net CT it has paid in excess of CT it has received if it elects to be a CT taxpayer by filing a form with the tax authorities. If this election is not made in the first business year or in the first year of sales that are subject to CT, the company cannot collect its CT refunds from its first taxable year.

If a Japanese importer is a CT taxpayer and pays more CT for assets purchased and services received than it receives for rendering services and making sales, it can receive a refund equal to the difference between the CT paid and received. The refund would be obtained by filing a consumption tax final return to the tax office within two months after the end of the business year. If the amount of CT received exceeds the amount of CT paid, the importer is required to pay the difference to the tax authorities.

Under revisions to the consumption tax law, a new corporation with share capital of ¥10 million or more is not exempt from the consumption tax for its first two accounting years after its establishment. A new corporation is defined under the revised consumption tax law as a corporation that has no base period.

Local and Provincial Taxes

Japanese corporations and branches are fully subject to both the enterprise tax and the inhabitants tax, as described under "Corporate Income Taxes." The enterprise tax is computed on the basis of taxable income and is payable to each prefecture in which a corporation locates its business, with allocations of net income among the different prefectures. The inhabitants tax is payable to both prefectures and municipalities in which a company locates its business, and is computed on the basis of a percentage of the corporate national tax liability. For example, in Tokyo, the inhabitants tax would be computed at 20.7% of the 37.5% corporate national tax.

For Additional Information, Contact:

Al Zencak
Tax Manager
and
Tsutomu Kikuchi
Tax Partner
Kasumigaseki Building, 15F
2-5 Kasumigaseki, 3-chome
Chiyoda-ku, Tokyo 100
Japan
Telephone: 81 (3) 5251 2400
Fax: 81 (3) 5251 2424
E-mail: alfred.zencak@chuo.or.jp
        tsutomu.kikuchi@chuo.or.jp

Korea

Telecommunications Tax Profile
by Yong Kyun Kim, Senior Tax Partner, Seoul
Chun Soo Kim, Tax Partner, Seoul
Kyung Tae Ahn, Consulting Partner, Seoul

Overview of the Telecommunications Market

Historical Background

The telecommunications industry in Korea is administered by the Ministry of Information and Communication (MIC) and governed by the Telecommunications Business Law (TBL). Telecommunications enterprises are broadly classified as either Type I carriers (facilities-based) or Type II carriers (service providers leasing circuits from Type I carriers).

Korea Telecom (KT) has traditionally served as the monopoly telecommunications carrier. In 1982, KT was separated from the government and established as a state-run corporation. The government also established the Data Communications Corporation of Korea (DACOM) to facilitate expansion in that sector.

In 1990, the government established its program of liberalization for the telecommunications sector, which permitted DACOM to compete as a common carrier, and outlined the structure for foreign participation in the market. In 1994, KT's monopoly on international telephone service ended when DACOM began serving that market. In January 1996, DACOM was permitted to begin competing in the long-distance telephone market. SK Telecom (formerly known as Korea Mobile Telecom) held the monopoly in paging services until 1992, when that market was liberalized. SK Telecom's cellular service monopoly ended in 1996, when a duopoly was established with Shinsegi. At that time, both companies initiated digital mobile telephone service based on call division multiple access (CDMA) technology.

Current Status

There are currently 31 Type I carriers and more than 100 Type II carriers active in Korea. The greatest number of Type I competitors provide paging services, although competition exists among providers of cellular, satellite, international and domestic long-distance services.

Korea's telecommunications market is expanding rapidly in a number of industry segments, including fixed-line telephone service, high-speed digital transmission, integrated services digital network (ISDN), Internet access, cellular/mobile/personal communications network (PCN) services, cable TV, broadcasting and telecommunications satellites.

KT monopolizes the local telephone market and dominates the long-distance and international telephone service segments. DACOM currently serves approximately 5% of the long-distance and 30% of the international telephone markets.

Korea's cellular market is expected to grow more than 40% annually over the next few years. Three personal communications service (PCS) providers—Korea Telecom Freetel Co., Ltd. (KT Freetel), LG Telecom Ltd. (LG PCS) and Hansol PCS Co.—initiated services and began competing in the cellular market in October 1997.

Since the end of the paging services monopoly in 1992, many service providers have entered the market. Today, 10 companies compete with SK Telecom in this market, including Naray Mobile Telecom. Approximately 60% of current Korean paging revenues are generated by SK Telecom and 40% are generated by newer regional entrants that commenced operations in late 1993.

In June 1996, the MIC licensed 27 companies to operate in the following Type I service areas:

- CT-2 (cordless telephony generation 2) service: One licensee for nationwide service and nine licensees for regional

- TRS (trunked radio system): One licensee for nationwide service and eight licensees for regional

- PCS (personal communications service): Three licensees for nationwide service, including KT Freetel, LG PCS and Hansol PCS

- Data services: Three licensees for nationwide service

- Paging: One licensee (Happy Telecom Co.) for regional service

- International telephone: One licensee (Onse Telecom Co.) for national service

Current Liberalization Status

Within the scope of its commitments under the World Trade Organization (WTO) negotiations of February 1997, from January 1, 1998 until December 31, 2000, Korea will allow foreign ownership of facilities-based telecommunications service providers (other than KT) up to a maximum of 33%. From January 1, 2000, the Korean government will allow foreign ownership in such service providers up to 49%. No single person will be allowed to own more than 10% of a wireline service provider or 33% of a wireless service provider.

Type of Service	Degree of Liberalization	Key Legislation	Date of Actual or Expected Liberalization	Comments
Local	Medium	Regulation on Foreign Direct Investment (1997)	49% limit for foreigners in 2001	20% limit for KT
Long Distance	High		49% limit for foreigners in 2001	
International	High		49% limit for foreigners in 2001	
Cellular	High		49% limit for foreigners in 2001	
Paging	High		49% limit for foreigners in 2001	
Value-added	High		1998	

Competitive Environment

Type of Service	Entire Market		Top Two Players		
	Market Size* (US$ millions)	Number of Players	Names	Annual Revenue* (US$ millions)	Ownership**
Local	$2,840	1	KT	$2,840	Government***
Long Distance	$3,800	2	KT	$3,603	Government***
			DACOM	$197	Dong-Yang Group, LG Group, Samsung Group
International	$1,330	3	KT	$926	Government***
			DACOM	$308	Dong-Yang Group, LG Group, Samsung Group
Cellular	$2,373	2	SK Telecom	$2,186	SK Group, KT
			Shinsegi	$187	Pohang Iron & Steel (POSCO), Kolon
Paging	$1,328	12	SK Telecom	$855	SK Group
			Naray	$205	TriGem Computer Group
Value-added	$114	578	DACOM	$80	Dong-Yang Group, LG Group, Samsung Group
			Korea PC Telecom	$50	KT

Source: *Korea Infocom Yearbook* issued by *Korea Electronics Newspaper*.
* 1996 figures (in US$ millions at exchange rate of Won 880/$1)
** Refers to major shareholders.
*** 78.6% owned by Korean government with remainder by public companies, including foreign ownership.

Licensing Requirements

Korean telecommunications markets continue to be subject to very stringent regulatory oversight by the MIC, which maintains a pervasive framework of fees, oversees licensing procedures, and provides administrative guidance.

Type I license applicants are required to form a consortium in which no investor holds a greater than one-third equity interest for wireless and one-tenth for fixed-line. Each consortium is allowed one radio frequency. In their license applications, each applicant must propose the amount of license fees to be paid to the MIC to compensate for the use of the radio frequency, ranging from 0.3 to 10 billion Won, depending upon the service scope and the service area.

Potential for Foreign Ownerships/Relationships

Korea's telecommunications markets are generally open to participation by foreign companies. Foreign participation in Type I wireline companies is prohibited; however, foreign companies are permitted to own a share in Type I wireless carriers. For Type I wireless companies, foreign participation is limited to one-third ownership in a licensed consortium. Domestic company participation in wireless is subject to the same ownership limit.

Type II companies have no foreign ownership restrictions. Foreign equipment manufacturers are currently active in many market segments.

Forms of Doing Business

Permanent Establishment

Under the Korean Corporate Income Tax Law, a permanent establishment (PE) is generally defined as "a fixed place of business, through which the business of an enterprise is wholly or partly carried on." Even if a foreign corporation does not have a fixed place of business in Korea, it may be deemed to have a PE if it has an agent in Korea that performs specific business activities on its behalf, such as concluding contracts, and if that agent devotes its business wholly (or almost wholly) to the foreign corporation.

Business Entities

Local Branch of a Foreign Company. Foreign companies may choose to enter the Korean market by establishing a Korean branch. In order to do so, the foreign investor must obtain approval from a local bank under the Foreign Exchange Control Law (FECL).

Type I telecommunications businesses are not open to investment by foreigners under the TBL, although they can participate in Type I wireless companies up to a maximum of one-third ownership. Therefore, a local bank will not approve applications to establish a Korean branch of a foreign corporation for a Type I telecommunications business. However, foreign corporations may establish a Korean branch for a Type II telecommunications business.

In general, the business and tax implications of operating as a branch, including tax rates and filing requirements, are similar to those of operating as a locally incorporated subsidiary of a foreign company (see the discussion below). However, there are several important tax differences that should be noted:

* A Korean branch may be subject to a branch profits tax of 27.5% (or lower, if specified by a tax treaty) in addition to corporate income tax, if applicable under the provisions of a tax treaty. The taxable income of a branch is limited to the Korean-sourced income attributable to the branch.

* Deductible expenses are limited to those that directly or indirectly relate to Korean-sourced income. However, indirect expenses incurred by a foreign head office or other foreign branches in relation to the Korean operation can be deducted from the branch's gross income, as long as they do not exceed the proportion that the Korean revenue bears against worldwide revenue.

Locally Incorporated Subsidiary of a Foreign Company. Foreign companies may choose to enter the Korean market by establishing a Korean company (subsidiary) under the Act on Foreign Direct Investment and Foreign Capital Inducement (the Act on FDI). For Type II telecommunications services, foreign companies may only operate through a Korean subsidiary rather than a Korean branch. Doing business through a Korean subsidiary can convey a more substantive commitment to customers and employees than doing business through a Korean branch.

In almost all cases, the locally incorporated entity would be a joint stock company (chusik hosea), which is the principal type of corporation prescribed under the Korean Commercial Code. As dictated by the Code, a joint stock company is subject to a minimum capitalization requirement of 50 million Won. There is a registration tax imposed on all initial capital, and on subsequent increases, equal to 0.48% of the capital stock amount. A Korean subsidiary is subject to withholding tax of 27.5% (or lower, if specified by a tax treaty) on the distribution of dividends to a foreign parent company. The taxable income of a subsidiary will include its worldwide income, such as any income from its overseas operations. Korean tax laws do not permit the filing of consolidated tax returns.

Joint Venture. Under the Act on FDI, foreign investment can be made in the form of capital into an existing domestic company, the purchase of new stocks, or by jointly establishing a new company with a Korean partner. In the past, foreign investors were only allowed to buy new shares of Korean companies. Now, however, a foreign investor can also buy the outstanding shares held by either another foreign investor or a Korean investor in an existing Korean company that was incorporated jointly between a foreign investor and a Korean investor. Furthermore, it is anticipated that in the near future, a foreign investor will be able to more freely buy the outstanding shares of a Korean company.

Local Funding Alternatives

Debt versus Equity

From a Korean corporate income tax perspective, interest payments are deductible, while dividend payments are not. Korea imposes a withholding tax on interest and dividends paid to foreign shareholders at the rate of 27.5%. This rate can be reduced by tax treaty.

Thin Capitalization Rules. As of January 1, 1997, Korean thin capitalization rules require a 3 to 1 maximum debt-to-equity ratio. These rules apply to foreign-invested companies as well as to the Korean branches of foreign corporations that have interest-bearing foreign-related-party indebtedness. The rules also apply to third-party financing guaranteed by a foreign-related party. Interest expenses incurred on debt that exceeds this ratio will be regarded as a dividend to the related party and will therefore not be deductible. However, if a foreign-invested company can prove that the size, terms and conditions of its borrowings from a controlling shareholder overseas are identical or similar to the normal size, terms and conditions of unrelated third-party borrowings of comparable companies, this rule is not applied.

Exchange Controls

Korea imposes both foreign exchange control laws and a foreign capital investment law, and these should be reviewed when considering cross-border investments or financing transactions involving the receiving or paying of foreign currencies.

Long-Term Loan Treated as Foreign Direct Investment

Under the Act on FDI, long-term loans (with maturities of five years or longer) made to foreign-invested companies by their overseas parent companies, or to enterprises that have capital affiliations with the parent companies, are treated as foreign direct investment, thereby allowing foreign-invested companies access to such loans for certain uses. Foreign-invested companies engaged in the manufacturing industry are allowed access to such borrowings consistent with two uses: financing the import cost of capital goods and materials; and funding their operations. For foreign-invested companies in non-manufacturing

industries, however, such borrowings can be used only for financing the import cost of capital goods and materials.

While permitting foreign-invested companies access to such borrowings, the Act provides borrowing limits as follows:

* If the purpose of the borrowing is to import capital goods or materials, 100% of the amount invested by foreign investors is available.

* If the purpose of the borrowing is to raise operating funds, only 50% of the amount invested by foreign investors or US$10 million—whichever is less—is available.

However, in the case of commercial loans (with maturities of three years or longer), no limitation is imposed in the future.

Business Acquisitions and Dispositions

Capital Contributions into an Existing Local Entity

A Korean subsidiary of a foreign company may make asset acquisitions in Korea. However, if a Korean subsidiary having capital in the amount of 5 billion Won or more, or total assets of 20 billion Won or more, intends to acquire a business, it must first obtain approval from the Ministry of Finance and Economy (MFE).

Purchase or Sale of Shares in a Local Entity

Foreign investors are allowed to buy the issued stock of companies listed on the Korea Stock Exchange up to a certain limit, which is currently 50%. This ratio will be increased in 1998. Restrictions on foreign acquisition of outstanding stock of unlisted companies have been gradually lifted starting in 1997. Foreigners were prohibited from acquiring outstanding stocks of non-listed Korean corporations until the foreign investment law was revised in February 1997. Under the Act on FDI, foreigners are allowed to acquire outstanding stocks or shares of non-listed Korean corporations, although such acquisitions require prior consent from the board of directors of the corporation and must be reported to the MFE.

Given their significant influence over the national economy, foreign access to the acquisition of outstanding stocks of certain large corporations having two trillion Won or more in total assets is restricted. The Act requires the Minister of Finance and Economy to consult other related government ministries before approving foreign acquisition of these large corporations. Notwithstanding these restrictions, however, a foreigner may acquire up to 15% of outstanding shares of such a large corporation.

Under current regulations, foreigners continue to be prohibited from acquiring existing shares of Korean companies engaged in industries where foreign investment is restricted.

When a company purchases shares in a local entity, any existing liabilities, including those that may be undisclosed at the time of purchase, will be transferred to the purchaser. In addition, plant, equipment and inventories will receive no step-up in basis to market value, and an acquisition tax of 2% of the purchase price on the real property of the acquired company will be assessed if 51% or more of the stocks are acquired.

For individuals, capital gains on the sale of shares in an unlisted company are subject to capital gains tax. Conversely, a sale of shares of a listed company would be exempt from capital gains tax. For corporations, capital gains on a sale of shares of both listed and unlisted companies are included in the corporation's non-operating income and subject to regular corporation tax.

Capital gains earned by non-resident investors through dispositions of stocks are exempt from Korean capital gains tax when both of the following two conditions are met:

- A reciprocal exemption for the capital gains tax is granted in the country of the investor.

- The non-resident investor, including any related parties, does not hold more than 25% of outstanding stocks of a listed company during the year in which the stock was transferred and during the previous five years.

Purchase or Sale of Assets

Transactions involving the acquisition of business assets generally have favorable consequences for the purchaser when the amount to be paid exceeds the net book value of the target's assets. By purchasing assets, the buyer can normally avoid assuming any undisclosed liabilities of the company. In an asset purchase, the purchaser may allocate the price paid for the acquired assets based on their fair market value, with any excess allocated to deductible goodwill (the law permits goodwill to be amortized over five years). However, acquisition and registration taxes payable on the purchase of real property may be substantial (i.e., approximately 6% of the purchase price of the real property).

Start-up Business Issues

Pre-operating Losses and Start-up/Construction Costs

Investors must treat expenditures incurred during the pre-operating period as deferred assets. Deferred pre-operating costs are to be amortized on a straight-line basis over three years or less from the year in which the operations commence. Any costs attributable to construction of fixed assets during the pre-operating period must be recorded as construction in progress, separate from general pre-operating costs. These costs must be transferred to the concerned fixed asset accounts after completion.

A foreign company that incurs local costs subject to VAT can recover VAT paid. VAT payments made on the purchase of pre-operating goods or services can be recovered before the operating phase. When the VAT amount paid to suppliers exceeds the VAT amount received from customers, the tax office will refund the excess amount within 30 days from the due date of the final, semi-annual VAT return, or within 15 days from the due date of the quarterly VAT return when early refund conditions are met. Therefore, cash flow issues may arise only for certain periods.

Capital Contributions

In most cases, capital contributions into a Korean corporation, including both initial and subsequent capital contributions, should be in the form of cash rather than in-kind transfers. This will avoid the costs and delays associated with the procedural requirements prescribed by the Korean Commercial Code for in-kind capital contributions, including the need for valuations and court-appointed examiners to confirm such valuations. Contributed cash may then be used to acquire any assets owned by the shareholders, including any technology to be used in the business. Foreign corporations should obtain approval of the capital contribution from the MFE or a local bank, according to the Act on FDI.

Customs Duties and VAT

Customs duties represent a significant cost for companies importing products into Korea. In general, Korea's laws are consistent with international standards, given Korea's membership in the WTO. In the area of telecommunications equipment, most items are subject to customs duty of 8% on the declared value of the goods.

The importation of equipment is subject to VAT. The VAT paid at the time of importation can be recovered by quarterly return or by a final VAT return (semi-annually).

Loss Carryovers

In general, operating losses may be carried forward for five years. There are some limitations that would restrict the availability of a loss carryover following a change in the ownership of a Korean corporation. Under certain conditions, when a profitable Korean corporation is merged into a Korean corporation having loss carryovers, the loss carryovers of the surviving company cannot be used against the profits of the combined business. As Korean tax law contains no group tax-relief provisions, the profits or losses of related legal entities cannot be combined and offset for tax purposes.

Operating Considerations

Corporate Income Taxes

Corporate income tax is charged at a rate of 16% on a company's tax base up to 100 million Won and at a rate of 28% on the tax base in excess of 100 million Won.

Capital Gains Taxes

Capital gains are treated in the same manner as ordinary income (as described above). In addition, there are special surtaxes that may apply to income from the sale of certain real estate, land or buildings. The surtax rate before resident taxes (see "Local and Provincial Taxes") is 20% if the acquisition of the property was registered and 40% if the acquisition of the property was not registered.

Tax Holidays and Exemptions

According to the Act on FDI, various tax exemptions are allowed for foreign investment in certain high-technology businesses if certain conditions are met, as follows:

- The business of the Korean subsidiary is listed in the Korean "List of High-Technology Businesses."

- The main business place (e.g., the plant) of the subsidiary is located in an area other than a metropolitan area.

- The accompanying technology is an advanced technology.

The following tax exemptions are allowed for such qualified foreign investments:

- Corporate income tax of the qualified foreign-invested company shall be fully exempted for five years from the year when taxable income is first generated. If taxable income is not generated within five years from the first fiscal year, the exemption period will start in the fifth fiscal year.

- Taxes on dividends paid from a foreign-invested company to a foreign investor shall be fully exempt for the above-described five years, and 50% shall be exempt for the subsequent three years.

- A 100% exemption will apply on customs duty, special excise tax and VAT for import of capital goods (i.e., facilities and equipment).

- With regard to acquisition tax, property tax and land tax, a 100% exemption for the five-year period from the year of business commencement and a 50% exemption for the subsequent three-year period is available.

When a Korean company pays royalties to a foreign licensor for the high technology used by the Korean company, the royalty shall be exempt from Korean withholding tax for five years from the day when the royalty was first paid under the related royalty agreement if the technology transfer meets certain requirements, which are similar to those covering foreign investment in the high-technology businesses approved under the Act on FDI (see above). For this to occur, the royalty agreement needs to be made under the Act on FDI and an application for tax exemption should be filed.

When a tax-exempt royalty agreement is allowed, a full five-year exemption will also be allowed under the Act on FDI (upon separate application) to expatriate engineers or technicians who carry out the technology transfer under the royalty agreement.

Under the Tax Exemption and Reduction Control Law (TERCL), any foreign technician working for a Ministry of Science and Technology (MOST)-approved engineering services contract or any qualified foreign technician working for a domestic corporation is exempt from individual income taxes on salary and wages for five years from the commencement of service. Also, engineering services rendered by a foreign entity are VAT-exempt when the engineering service agreement is approved by MOST.

A tax credit is available for Type II telecommunications carriers only for qualifying expenses, which are prescribed by the TERCL. According to the TERCL, salaries for a research team, contract fees, educational expenses and so forth fall under the qualified experimental and research expenses, subject to normal documentation requirements. The credit applies if the amount of the qualifying expenses incurred during a business year exceeds the average of such amounts during the preceding two business years. As a general principle, the tax credit is equal to either 50% of the amount in excess of the prior two-year average, or 5% (15% in the case of small- and medium-sized companies) of actual experimental and research expenses incurred in the current business year, whichever is higher. A Type II telecommunications company is considered a small- or medium-sized company if the total employees number fewer than 300 people and the shareholders do not directly participate in the management of the corporation.

A tax credit for qualified investments is available to all Korean companies. The credit is equal to 5% (or 10% for home-made facilities) of the amount invested for foreign-made facilities involved in research and experimentation, or 3% (10% in the case of home-made facilities) of the amount invested for foreign-made facilities other than those for research and experimentation.

Tax credits are also available to Korean corporations for foreign taxes paid, subject to the provisions of Korea's foreign tax credit limitation rules. An indirect foreign tax credit is allowed if it is provided in conjunction with a tax treaty.

Some tax treaties allow for tax-sparing credits whereby credit is allowed for taxes even though no taxes are paid. Most Korean tax treaties, with the exceptions of those with the U.S. and Thailand, incorporate a tax-sparing credit concept.

Depreciation/Cost-Recovery Conventions/Accelerated Deductions

Telecommunications businesses may elect useful lives ranging from four to eight years for depreciation of their business assets. For buildings, they must elect useful lives ranging from 30 to 50 years. For assets used in business administration, useful lives ranging from three to five years may be elected.

Marketing and advertising costs are tax-deductible if they are incurred for business purposes.

Transfer Pricing Rules

The Law for Coordination on International Tax Affairs, enacted in 1995, includes transfer pricing rules that are more systematized and specific than earlier ones. Korean transfer pricing legislation applies to all cross-border transactions between Korean corporations (and Korean branches) and related foreign parties. The rules are applicable to companies that, directly or indirectly, are 50% or more owned by the same interests or where there is a special relationship. If all or some of the business decisions of one party can be influenced by another party due to one of the following reasons, they are deemed to be specially related parties:

- The representative director or one-half or more of the directors of one party are directors or employees of the other party.

- One party indirectly owns 50% or more of voting shares of the other party through a trust partnership.

- One party relies on the other for most of its business.

- One party is financed mostly from the other (either directly, or through guarantee of the other).

- One party heavily relies on intangibles of the other party for its business.

The types of transactions covered by these rules include virtually all related-party transactions, including the sale of tangible or intangible property, services, financing, and licensing arrangements. These transactions must be disclosed in a schedule accompanying the tax return of the Korean corporation or branch.

The Korean tax authorities have progressively become tougher, more experienced, more sophisticated and better trained since the enactment of the new transfer pricing legislation. They have significantly expanded the size and capacity of their special transfer pricing teams and have conducted a considerable amount of study of both transfer pricing methodologies and industry-specific transfer pricing practices. Further, there have recently been some very large tax assessments against foreign-owned Korean corporations. As a result, foreign-owned companies should be prepared for transfer pricing tax audits.

Transfers of Patents, Trademarks and Software

Royalty agreements for payments by Korean corporations to foreign corporations are subject to approval by the Korean government under the Act on FDI. Running royalty payments are normally deductible upon each occurrence for Korean tax purposes if the amount of such royalties can be supported by reference to the arm's-length criteria and the methodologies prescribed by Korea's transfer pricing legislation. Lump-sum payments are required to be capitalized and amortized over the contract period. All payments related to the transfer of know-how are subject to Korean withholding tax at the rate of 27.5%, unless this is reduced under a tax treaty.

Taxation on payments for imported software remains a controversial issue. Payments made by a domestic importer to a foreign supplier as consideration for the use of, or the right to use, information concerning industrial, commercial or scientific knowledge, experience or skills, are subject to withholding tax at the source regardless of the terms and conditions of the payment (e.g., a lump-sum payment or a running royalty payment).

Service Fees

In the case of a foreign corporation having a Korean branch, Korean tax laws and tax treaties provide that expenses incurred by the foreign corporation outside Korea in connection with the Korean operation may be allocated to the Korean branch and claimed as a deduction for tax purposes. This includes both direct expenses and allocable overhead expenses.

When a Korean corporation or Korean branch receives—and makes payment for—management services from a foreign affiliate, those payments are subject to bank approval under the FECL. These types of management service arrangements are subject to Korea's transfer pricing legislation. If such arrangements are acceptable for Korean tax purposes, payments for the services are deductible and payment of withholding tax may depend on the tax treaty provisions.

Value-Added Tax, Sales Tax and/or Other Pertinent Taxes

The Korean form of indirect taxation is VAT. In general, all domestic transactions, including services provided and goods sold in Korea, are subject to VAT at the flat rate of 10% unless a tax exemption is specifically provided in the VAT Law. For goods imported for sale into Korea, VAT is imposed at the time of importation and is generally based on the declared value of the goods for customs purposes. If a service is provided in Korea, the service will generally be subject to VAT unless a specific zero-rated VAT applies (e.g., where the services are performed for a non-resident of Korea). If the services are provided by a non-resident or a foreign corporation having no PE, the buyer is obligated to make VAT payment by proxy in cases where the buyer is a VAT-exempt business.

A Korean company that provides services subject to VAT must collect the tax and remit the amount collected (less any VAT paid by the company for services it receives or goods it purchases in Korea) to the tax authorities, along with a VAT return filing on a quarterly basis.

Enterprises engaged in the telephone business are regarded as VAT-exempt and, accordingly, are exempt from sales VAT and not allowed refunds of VAT paid on purchases. Non-refundable purchase VAT is allowed as a deductible expense for Korean corporate income tax purposes. Other than companies in the telephone business, telecommunications carriers are subject to VAT and may recover the VAT paid on their purchases.

Local and Provincial Taxes

Korean corporations and Korean branches are fully subject to the resident surtax and other relevant local taxes, as follows:

Resident Surtax. A person or a corporation that pays individual income tax or corporate income tax is subject to the resident surtax, which is 10% of the income tax.

Registration Tax. A person who registers the incorporation of a company or ownership of assets, including but not limited to real estate and vehicles, must pay registration tax. The tax rate for the registration of an incorporation is 0.4% of the value of total shares, while the tax rates for registration of the ownership of an asset range from 0.3% to 5% of the value of the asset. If a company is established within certain major cities, these tax rates are increased by five times the normal rate.

Acquisition Tax. When real property, motor vehicles, ships, heavy equipment and mining or fishing rights are acquired, a tax is levied on the asset's declared value at the standard rate of 2%.

Property Tax. A local property tax is assessed annually on buildings, ships and aircraft at rates ranging from 0.3% to 7%. A newly built factory located in a major city is assessed at a rate equal to five times the normal rate for a period of five years from the date of initial payment. Aggregate land tax is assessed annually on land registered under the Land Register Law at progressive rates ranging from 0.2% to 0.5% of the tax base, depending on the value of the land.

For Additional Information, Contact:

Yong Kyun Kim
Senior Tax Partner
Kukje Center Bldg. 21 Fl.,
191, Hankang-ro 2-ka, Yongsan-ku,
Seoul 140-702, Korea
Telephone: 82 (2) 709 0550
Fax: 82 (2) 796 7027
E-mail: YKKim@samil.co.kr

Chun Soo Kim
Tax Partner (Telecommunications Business)
Address: Same as above
Telephone: 82 (2) 709 0697
Fax: 82 (2) 796 7027
E-mail: CSKim@samil.co.kr

Kyung Tae Ahn
Telecommunications Consulting Partner
Address: Same as above
Telephone: 82 (2) 709 0410
Fax: 82 (2) 792 1669
E-mail: KTAhn@samil.co.kr

Malaysia

Telecommunications Tax Profile
by Tay Chong Chim
Tax Partner, Kuala Lumpur
and Eddy Fong Choong Ee
Senior Tax Manager, Kuala Lumpur

Overview of the Telecommunications Market

Historical Background

Jabatan Telekom Malaysia (JTM), the governmental department of telecommunications, was the sole provider of telecommunications services until 1987, when its telecommunications operations were corporatized into Telekom Malaysia Berhad (TMB). TMB was privatized in 1990. Competition was introduced into the telecommunications industry in 1989, when a cellular license was issued to Cellular Communications Network (Malaysia) Sdn. Bhd. (Celcom). In 1992, localized paging services licenses were issued to 18 operators. There are currently 27 paging operators.

The Telecommunications Act 1950 governs the regulation of the telecommunications industry. This act provides for the licensing of telecommunications services as well as the approval process for telecommunications equipment. The national telecommunications policy (NTP), which was issued in 1994, sets forth the government's overall policy direction through the year 2020, and promotes an environment of licensed, open competition for all telecommunications services.

Current Status

TMB has approximately 80% of the telecommunications market in Malaysia, with a virtual monopoly on fixed-line services. Competition is beginning in West Malaysia. In the fixed-line market, Time Telecommunications Sdn. Bhd. is now offering a 100% fiber optic network; and Celcom, in which Deutsche Telekom AG has a 21% interest, is also developing its own 100% fiber optic network. Bina Sat-Com Sdn. Bhd., which is a subsidiary of Binariang Sdn. Bhd., has also commenced fixed-line services. TMB is currently modernizing and expanding its network and expects to have a fully digitized switching and transmission network by the year 2000.

Market penetration in 1996 was 18.4 access lines per 100 people. From 1991 to 1996, the average annual growth rate was 12.3%. The Ministry of Energy, Telecommunication and Posts (METP) projects penetration to reach 30 lines per 100 people by 2005 and 50 lines per 100 people by 2020. New entrants to the fixed-line segment are not expected to seriously challenge TMB until 1999, when equal access is expected to be implemented.

The fastest-growing segment of the telecommunications market is the cellular sector, with a projected growth of 20% per year. Celcom, which operates a GSM-based digital service and an analog service, is the top player with an estimated 60% share of the market in 1996. Celcom's dominance is expected to shrink in the future as a result of intensifying competition from other operators. Currently, there are three operators using the GSM-900 MHz standard, three offering personal communications network (PCN) services using the DCS (digital cellular system)-1800 MHz standard, one with a dual digital/analog mode service using the ETAC (extended total access communication)-900 MHz system, and another using an analog NMT (Nordic mobile telephone)-450 MHz system.

Currently, four operators offer functioning international gateway facilities. These gateways connect a domestic user to the international network. They are operated by TMB, Celcom, Measat Global Telecommunications Sdn. Bhd., which is another subsidiary of Binariang, and Mutiara Telecommunications Sdn. Bhd. Time Telecommunications is expected to make fuller use of its international telecommunications gateway license in the near future. TMB and the Malaysian Institute of Microelectronic Services Bhd. (MIMOS), which is a state-owned company, are the major Internet access providers. There are an estimated 250,000 Internet subscribers in Malaysia, which is approximately 1% of the population. The number of Internet subscribers is expected to increase by 20% to 30% annually in the next few years. There are currently a total of 16 providers of value-added services.

Current Liberalization Status

As outlined in the following table, the telecommunications sector in Malaysia is relatively liberalized.

Type of Service	Degree of Liberalization	Key Legislation	Date of Actual or Expected Liberalization	Comments
Local, Long Distance and International	Liberalized	Telecommunications Act 1950; NTP	1994	Of the five licenses issued, not all have been fully utilized.
Cellular	Liberalized	Telecommunications Act 1950; NTP	1989	Further market growth may be necessary to absorb new entrants.
Paging	Liberalized	Telecommunications Act 1950; NTP	1992	No more new licenses are expected in this congested market.
Value-added	Liberalized	Telecommunications Act 1950; NTP	1992	There is room for innovative services.

Competitive Environment

Malaysia has a highly competitive telecommunications market, as illustrated below.

Type of Service	Entire Market		Top Player(s)		
	Market Size	**Number of Players**	**Names**	**Annual Revenue**	**Ownership**
Local, Long Distance and International	Ringgit (RM) 6 billion*	5 fixed-line; 5 international	TMB	RM6.4 billion**	66% state-controlled
Cellular	RM2.5 billion	8	Celcom	RM950 million	Publicly traded
			Mobikom Sdn. Bhd.	RM250 million	Privately owned

Sources: Telekom Malaysia Berhad 1996 annual report, UBS Research and Sime Securities Research.

* Estimated market size for the fixed-line segment only.

** TMB's revenue from all sources.

Licensing Requirements

The METP regulates the telecommunications sector. While an METP license, which may be local or nationwide, is required to provide telecommunications service in Malaysia, the METP recently called for a consolidation of the telecommunications services market. In this connection, the issuance of new licenses, especially for the fixed-line and cellular segments, would be put on hold. This decision was made to ensure the more orderly development of the telecommunications industry. All telecommunications equipment must receive JTM approval before it can be used or sold in Malaysia.

Potential for Foreign Ownerships/Relationships

The government's general policy is to restrict foreign ownership of Malaysian companies to 30% of equity. This percentage may be increased in certain situations, usually to benefit the Malaysian economy in terms of the transfer of technology and the development of export products. Foreign investors typically gain access to Malaysia's telecommunications market by entering into a joint venture with a current telecommunications license holder.

Potential for Upcoming Liberalization/Investment Opportunities

Malaysia has made a full commitment to the regulatory principles and guidelines of the World Trade Organization (WTO), and further liberalization was expected to occur by January 1, 1998. The form this will take is not yet certain, although there could be a more flexible stance toward licensing approval for foreign service providers, especially in the area of value-added services.

The METP has indicated a desire to see a consolidation resulting in three major players in the fixed-line and cellular sectors. As a result, there may be further acquisitions or mergers among the current operators.

Forms of Doing Business

Permanent Establishment

An entity's business income is taxable in Malaysia if it is derived from Malaysia. Business income is deemed to be derived from Malaysia so far as it is not attributable to operations outside of Malaysia. However under certain conditions, as discussed below, business income may be deemed to be derived from Malaysia even if an entity does not have a permanent establishment (PE) in Malaysia. Malaysia has no special tax provisions covering electronic commerce, which is still in an embryonic development stage.

- The provision of long-distance telephone services to local customers by a foreign company without any local presence or advertising would not be taxable in Malaysia.

- Licensing fees paid to a non-resident by a local company for the use of technology and know-how would be considered as royalty payments and subject to a 10% withholding tax.

- Payments made by a local company to a non-resident for technical assistance or services, including operator services or network management services, would be subject to a 10% withholding tax.

- Payments made by a local company to a non-resident for the lease or rental of telecommunications equipment would generally be subject to a 10% withholding tax.

- Income from a call reorganization/turnaround service attributable to operations conducted outside Malaysia would not be taxable in Malaysia.

- A project consisting of the laying of fiber optic cable or the construction of telecommunications switching equipment (regardless of whether the equipment was meant for sale to a local company or to be operated by a foreign telecommunications company) that took more than 31 days to complete would require that a foreign telecommunications company set up a local branch. The branch would constitute a PE for tax purposes.

Business Entities

Local Branch of a Foreign Company. While a foreign company may invest in Malaysia through a branch, telecommunications service providers are generally required to be locally incorporated companies. Therefore, it would be highly unlikely for a foreign company to be allowed to provide licensed telecommunications services through a branch. However, a branch is an option for equipment contractors undertaking an installation or construction project. A branch of a foreign company is considered to be an extension of the foreign company for corporate tax purposes, and not a separate entity. The foreign company would be taxed on its income from the project on a net basis. A branch is required to prepare audited accounts and file annual tax returns.

Payments to a branch amount to payments to a non-resident, with the associated withholding tax consequences. Payments made on the service portion of a contract are subject to a 15% withholding tax. There is a further 5% withholding tax, which is refundable once Inland Revenue has been satisfied that the branch's expatriate employees have settled their Malaysian tax liabilities.

Locally Incorporated Subsidiary of a Foreign Company. A foreign company may incorporate a local subsidiary to undertake projects in Malaysia. This option is often chosen when the investment in Malaysia is for the long term. A local subsidiary with management and control in Malaysia is considered to be tax-resident in Malaysia. Payments made to resident companies are not subject to Malaysian withholding taxes.

Generally, when foreign ownership of a Malaysian company exceeds 15% of equity, an application must be made to the government's Foreign Investment Committee. For any construction or installation project that involves the Malaysian government, it is usually required that there be at least 30% local ownership in the subsidiary that is undertaking the project. This is an exception to the general policy of restricting foreign ownership of Malaysian companies to 30% of equity. This exception would be allowed when a company was set up to undertake a project in which there was no local expertise and a transfer of technology was required.

Joint Venture. A joint venture with an existing license holder is the typical vehicle for a foreign telecommunications service provider investing in Malaysia. The METP must be notified of any change in interests of the license-holding company or of the ultimate holding company. Generally, foreign ownership of telecommunications service providers is limited to 30% of equity.

When the entity takes the form of a true partnership, such that the responsibilities of the partners overlap and are interdependent, it is required to prepare accounts and file tax returns. The partners, rather than the partnership, pay income tax. When the entity takes the form of an unincorporated joint venture, such as a loose partnership where parties come together for a joint tender, each partner is legally viewed as a separate subcontractor. In this case, it may be possible to apply for a concession from Inland Revenue so that the joint venture does not have to file a tax return.

Local Funding Alternatives

Debt versus Equity

Interest expenses incurred by non-residents are generally tax-deductible. Interest payments made to non-residents are subject to a 15% withholding tax. There are no special tax rules against thin capitalization or that deem interest payments as dividends. There are no restrictions on the payments of interest or dividends to non-residents. Local banking institutions can provide credit of up to RM10 million without any regulatory restrictions.

Malaysian tax law has adopted the full imputation system in relation to the payment of dividends. Under this system, all income taxes paid by a company are available for transfer to shareholders as tax credits attaching to dividend payments (i.e., franking). The tax payments by a company are thus effectively transferred to its shareholders when dividends are paid. The franking rate is the same as the corporate tax rate, which is currently 30%. There is no additional withholding tax on the payment of dividends.

Exchange gains and losses on the loan principal of foreign borrowings are generally capital in nature. These capital transactions are non-events for income tax purposes and thus any resulting exchange gains are not taxable nor are exchange losses deductible. An exchange gain on an interest payment, on the other hand, is taxable, while an exchange loss is deductible if the underlying interest payment is deductible.

Exchange Controls

Malaysia has a generally liberal exchange control regime that is administered by Bank Negara Malaysia, the central bank. A foreign loan to a local company (including a subsidiary of a foreign company) in excess of RM5 million requires Bank Negara's approval, which is readily given when the loan is for investment or productive (i.e., not for consumption or stock speculation) purposes.

Business Acquisitions and Dispositions

Capital Contributions into an Existing Local Entity

A capital contribution in the form of a capital asset qualifying for a capital allowance may have income tax implications. The market value or book value of the asset, whichever is lower at the time the asset is brought into Malaysia, will form the basis for computing the capital allowance. There are no limitations with respect to intangibles that a foreign entity can contribute into an existing local entity. However, in certain cases, government approval may be required for such a contribution.

Purchase or Sale of Shares in a Local Entity

The purchase of shares in a local entity is normally a capital transaction without much income tax implication. Interest incurred

on borrowings obtained to finance the purchase will be tax-deductible against dividends received on a year-to-year basis. Interest expenses not fully utilized in any one year can neither be carried forward nor used to set off income from other sources.

A capital gain from the sale of shares is not subject to income tax. Real property gains tax may be payable if the investee company has real property valued at more than 75% of its total tangible assets. The purchase of shares in a company at a price in excess of the net tangible value of the company cannot be recovered.

Purchase or Sale of Assets

Moveable assets purchased and used in a business usually qualify for capital allowance at annual rates ranging from 6% to 40% on a straight-line basis. The capital allowance is deductible against business income generated. The cost of factories and other industrial buildings qualifies for an industrial building allowance of 2% annually. The cost of land is neither tax-deductible nor tax-depreciable. When assets are paid for in a lump sum, the total sum is allocated to the respective assets for tax purposes. Any excess would be attributed to goodwill. Goodwill is considered capital in nature and its cost is not tax-deductible.

When assets are sold for more than the tax written-down value, the difference is taxable as a balancing charge. However any gain arising from the consideration exceeding the original cost is not taxable. When a lump sum is received for the sale of a group of assets, the sum has to be allocated to the respective assets for tax purposes. Gains arising from the sale of assets that did not qualify for capital allowance are not subject to income tax. Gains from the sale of land and buildings are subject to real property gains tax, ranging from 5% for property that has been held more than four years to 30% for property that has been held for less than two years.

Investing in an existing operation by purchasing shares has no effect on the cost base of the investee company. Shareholding changes are distinct and separate from the operations of a company for tax purposes. Any goodwill for the shares is not recoverable.

The purchase or sale of interests in a continuing partnership is generally considered a capital transaction. The capital gains (including goodwill) are not taxable, while the capital losses are not tax-deductible.

Start-up Business Issues

Pre-operating Losses and Start-up/ Construction Costs

Most expenses (e.g., business investigation costs, fees and other costs to begin a new business) incurred prior to the commencement of business cannot be deducted; neither can they be carried forward. Under special rules, expenses incurred to train employees (including those incurred by a telecommunications business to give employees basic skills training) prior to the commencement of business may be tax-deductible. Once business has commenced, selling, general and administrative expenses incurred are generally deductible. There is no VAT in Malaysia. Service tax, where applicable, is not recoverable.

Customs Duties and VAT

The customs duty on telecommunications equipment ranges from 0% to 30%. Sales tax is payable at the rate of 10%. However, there may be specific equipment (e.g., apparatuses for digital line systems) on which there is no customs duty or sales tax. Sales tax is a one-stage tax and there is no recovery mechanism. Some examples of the customs duty and sales tax rates that apply to different types of telecommunications equipment are given below.

Loss Carryovers

Losses incurred after the commencement of business can be carried forward indefinitely to be set off against future business income. Unabsorbed capital allowances (i.e., a capital allowance in excess of taxable income) can similarly be carried forward. There are no provisions for the carryback of losses. There are no limitations on the use of tax losses due to a change in ownership or a change of business activity of a company. However, unabsorbed capital allowances of one business source cannot be deducted against income from a different business source.

Type of Telecommunications Equipment	Customs Duty	Sales Tax
Telephone sets and videophones		
Line telephone sets with cordless handsets	25%	10%
Other	25%	10%
Facsimile machines and teleprinters		
Facsimile machines	Nil	10%
Teleprinters	Nil	10%
Telephonic switching apparatuses	20%	10%
Other apparatuses for carrier-current or for digital-line systems	Nil	Nil
Telephone and telegraph cables		
Submarine	5%	10%
Other: plastic-insulated	30%	10%

Operating Considerations

Corporate Income Taxes

A local subsidiary or a branch of a foreign company is subject to Malaysian income tax at the rate of 30% on its chargeable income, which is the net taxable income after deductible expenses and capital allowance. Only income derived from Malaysia is subject to Malaysian income tax. Foreign-sourced income, whether remitted or not, is not taxable.

Capital Gains Taxes

Malaysia does not tax capital gains except for capital gains from transactions involving the sale of real property (i.e., land and buildings) or shares in a real-property-based company. The tax rates for real property gains range from 5% when the asset has been held for more than four years, to 30% when the asset has been held for less than two years.

Tax Holidays and Exemptions

In an attempt to develop an information-technology-literate society, the government has created a multimedia supercorridor (MSC) area south of Kuala Lumpur. This area is designed to offer an ideal environment for the development, management and marketing of multimedia products and services. The MSC offers a high-capacity global telecommunications and logistics infrastructure built upon a 2.5–10 gigabit optical fiber backbone. Investment in the MSC is estimated at RM6 billion over the next 10 years. The government has announced a comprehensive set of incentives for companies prepared to set up operations within the MSC or otherwise contribute significantly to the MSC's development. There are no tax incentives specifically for telecommunications companies operating elsewhere in Malaysia.

In order to be granted MSC status, a company must (a) be a provider or heavy user of multimedia products and services (which includes the provision of enabling networks for the distribution of multimedia products); (b) have a substantial number of employees and (c) specify how it will transfer technology and/or knowledge to Malaysia. Once granted MSC status, a company may be eligible for a variety of incentives including (a) a five-year exemption from Malaysian income tax, (b) duty-free importation of multimedia equipment and (c) research and development grants.

Depreciation/Cost-Recovery Conventions/Accelerated Deductions

Capital expenditure is not a tax-deductible expense. Instead, the cost of qualifying plant and machinery and certain industrial buildings is depreciated by way of a capital allowance. Capital allowance rules apply across the board and there are no special rules for the telecommunications industry. The annual capital allowance rates for moveable assets range from 6% to 40% on a straight-line basis. Industrial buildings depreciate at the rate of 2% annually. In addition to the annual allowance rate, an initial allowance is also assessed the first year that an asset is used in a business. The table below gives the rates for selected assets.

Asset	Annual Allowance Rate	Initial Allowance Rates
Telecommunications equipment	10%	20%
Radio and transceiver sets	14%	20%
Information technology equipment	40%	20%
Industrial buildings	2%	10%

In the context of a network, an asset would be considered in use when it is in service, legally and physically, in a continuing business. For a start-up business, the network would be in use when it is in service, legally and physically, after the commencement of the business for tax purposes. Using the equipment for trial runs and simulations prior to commercial service would not generally be considered business use for tax purposes.

For an ongoing business, research and development costs of a revenue nature, such as staff costs, utilities and upkeep expenses, are deductible. For a start-up business, research and development expenditures incurred prior to the commencement of operations may not be deductible. Depending on the specific cost items involved, software development costs incurred by start-up operations may be capitalized into stock-in-trade and deductions claimed when the fully developed products are later sold. Marketing and advertising costs, including payments made directly or indirectly (through sales agents) to attract customers, are tax-deductible.

Transfer Pricing Rules

There are no specific tax rules on acceptable or unacceptable transfer prices between associated companies. The general anti-avoidance legislation is used if there is a suspicion of tax avoidance in the setting of transfer prices. In practice, Inland Revenue would compare transfer prices to open market prices in support of their investigations.

Transfers of Patents, Trademarks, and Software

There is no specific law that restricts the licensing of technology to a local company. However, certain manufacturing companies (those with shareholders' funds exceeding RM2.5 million or employing more than 75 workers) must obtain a license from the Ministry of International Trade and Industry (MITI). As a condition of granting this license, the MITI must approve royalty payments made to foreign companies. Generally, rates ranging from 2% to 5% have been approved by the MITI; higher rates would require justification and would be looked at from the perspective of general anti-avoidance provisions.

Malaysia has no guidelines on the distinction between the sale and licensing of technology. The gain from the sale of technology that is a capital asset of the transferor would not be taxable. However, when the transferor sold technology as part of its regular business, any gains would be viewed as revenue and payments made to non-residents would be subject to a 10% withholding tax. Royalty payments made under a license for the use of technology are similarly subject to a 10% withholding tax.

An Internet access provider bringing access software into the country in physical media such as a compact disk, tape or diskette is considered to be importing goods that are subject to applicable customs duty and sales tax. A payment for Internet access software purchased off-the-shelf is generally not considered as a payment of royalties, but as a payment for goods.

Service Fees

Payments made to a non-resident for technical services are subject to a 10% withholding tax. If the non-resident has a permanent establishment in Malaysia, then this tax applies whether the service is performed inside or outside of Malaysia. If the non-resident does not have a permanent establishment in Malaysia, then this tax only applies when the services are performed in Malaysia.

Payments to a non-resident for services performed in Malaysia through a permanent establishment under a contract are subject to withholding tax of 20%, of which 15% can be used to set off the non-resident's Malaysian tax liability. The remaining 5% is refundable once a company's expatriate employees have settled their Malaysian tax liabilities.

Value-Added Tax, Sales Tax and/or Other Pertinent Taxes

A 5% service tax is leviable on certain services provided in Malaysia including telecommunications services in the form of telephone, facsimile, telemail, paging, cellular telephone and telex. Payments made by Malaysians for services provided from outside of Malaysia are not subject to service tax. There is currently no mechanism for the recovery of service tax. Service tax is not levied on Internet access charges.

Sales tax of 10% is payable on goods imported into and goods manufactured in Malaysia. Sales tax is payable at the point of importation or when the goods leave the local factory. Exemptions from sales tax are available if the goods themselves are to be exported or incorporated into other products that are subsequently exported.

Local and Provincial Taxes

There are no local income taxes.

For Additional Information, Contact:

Eddy Fong Choong Ee
Senior Tax Manager
and
Mohd Afrizan bin Husain
Audit Manager
22nd Floor IGB Plaza
Jalan Kampar
50400 Kuala Lumpur
Malaysia
Telephone: 60 (3) 441 1188
Fax: 60 (3) 441 0880

New Zealand

Telecommunications Tax Profile
by Kevin Best and Stewart McCulloch
Tax Partners, Wellington

Overview of the Telecommunications Market

Historical Background

The New Zealand telecommunications market was first dereg- ulated and opened to competition with the passage of the Telecommunications Act 1987. Since then, this legislation has been amended to further define the competitive environment in New Zealand. All statutory barriers to entering the telecommu- nications market were removed on April 1, 1989. Regulation of the industry was eliminated, with all market entrants subject only to the Commerce Act 1986, which is the general competi- tion law that controls market behavior of competitors and pro- hibits various anti-competitive activities.

Following a government program of corporatization, the telecommunications arm of the New Zealand Post Office was transformed in 1987 into a state-owned enterprise, the Telecom Corporation of New Zealand Limited (Telecom). Telecom re- mained as a state-owned corporation until September 1990, when it was sold to the wholly owned subsidiaries of Bell At- lantic Corporation (Bell Atlantic) and Ameritech. As a condition of the sale, Bell Atlantic and Ameritech were both required to sell down a portion of their investment. Currently, each holds a 24.9% share in Telecom.

In December 1997, Ameritech and Bell Atlantic announced plans to restructure their holdings in Telecom. Ameritech an- nounced that it planned to sell its 24.9% shareholding in Tele- com by a public offering. In February 1998, Bell Atlantic issued approximately US$2.3 billion in notes exchangeable into Tele- com shares from 1999 onwards.

The Kiwi Share, held on behalf of the New Zealand public by the Minister of Finance, is a single-rights-convertible preference share, created in September 1990 as a condition of Telecom's privatization. The consent of the holder of the Kiwi Share is re- quired for the amendment, removal or alteration of the effect of certain provisions of Telecom's constitution. The company's con- stitution also contains provisions that require Telecom to ob- serve certain principles relating to the provision of telephone services and their prices. The holder of the Kiwi Share is not en- titled to vote at any meetings of the company's shareholders nor participate in the capital or profits of the company, except for re- payment of NZ$1 of capital upon a winding up. The Kiwi Share may be converted to an ordinary share at any time by the holder thereof, at which time all rights and powers attaching to the Kiwi Share will cease to have any application.

Current Status

New Zealand is provided with a full range of telecommunications services, covering fixed, mobile, voice, data, value-added and enhanced network services. Enhanced network services include services such as call waiting, call diversion, three-way calling, do not disturb, quick dial and caller display. Network-based call an- swering and messaging services are also available.

Data transport systems that use packet switching technology to accumulate and transmit information in "packets" are also used as a basis for value-added services such as electronic mail, on- line database systems and EFT-POS (electronic funds transfer at the point of sale).

The national network contains relatively advanced technology. More than 99% of customers are served by digital exchanges. Fiber optic cabling provides most intercity links, and is continu- ing to be rolled out through the country. Integrated services dig- ital network (ISDN), frame relay, and asynchronous transfer mode (ATM) services are available.

Currently, the equipment and services sectors of the telecommu- nications market are open to competition, with the exception of residential line rental and local call services. For domestic and in- ternational service, Clear Communications Ltd. (Clear) has been Telecom's most active competitor since the opening of the domestic market in April 1991 and the international outbound call market in December 1991. Telecom began providing Clear customers with non-code access to their network in April 1993. Following disagreements over interconnection prices and terms, a business arrangement between Telecom and Clear was reached in March 1996. Rates have dropped significantly since competition began, and Clear has gained approximately 22% of the market share of all national calls and 21% of all international outward calls.

In 1993, BellSouth New Zealand began providing a cellular service using global system for mobile communications (GSM) digital technology in competition to Telecom's analog cellular service, which is marketed through competing service providers. Telecom's digital cellular service (digital advanced mobile phone service or D-AMPS) was also rolled out in 1993. BellSouth New Zealand's long-term interconnection agreement with Telecom was signed in November 1993, and a new agreement is currently being negotiated. Currently, BellSouth New Zealand has extended its network to provide 91% of the population with coverage, posing serious competition to Telecom.

The New Zealand government sold spectrum management rights to Telstra Corporation Ltd. of Australia (Telstra) in May 1993, enabling Telstra to enter the New Zealand market by establishing New Zealand's third cellular network. In March 1996, Telstra launched its New Zealand operations to provide a range of telecommunications services to business users. Global One has recently extended its international call services to New Zealand. Saturn Communications Limited, a cable TV operator, has signaled plans to extend coverage, and to provide telecommunications services. Telecom has recently abandoned its cable plans in favor of initiatives based on asymmetric digital subscriber line (ADSL) technology. In February 1996, Clear launched frame relay and ATM services in competition with Telecom's offerings.

Telecom has competition from a range of other telecommunications service providers, including suppliers of customer premises equipment and resellers, who acquire bulk transmission capacity from Telecom and resell it in conjunction with offers of network management services.

Current Liberalization Status

The New Zealand telecommunications market currently enjoys a high degree of liberalization. Furthermore, current and recent New Zealand governments have maintained a liberal telecommunications policy. For example, during the World Trade Organization (WTO) negotiations of February 1997, New Zealand committed to a relaxation of foreign ownership limitations, with the exception that no single foreign shareholder may hold more than a 49.9% stake in Telecom.

Type of Service	Degree of Liberalization	Key Legislation	Date of Actual or Expected Liberalization	Comments
Local	Full	Telecommunications Act 1987	April 1, 1989	
Long Distance	Full	Telecommunications Act 1987	April 1, 1989	
International	Full	Telecommunications Act 1987	April 1, 1989	
Cellular	Full	Radio Telecommunications Act 1987	April 1, 1989	Frequency licenses required
Paging	Full		April 1, 1989	
Value-added	Full		April 1, 1989	

Competitive Environment

While the telecommunications market is competitive, Telecom remains the dominant player in most segments of the market.

However, new competitors are starting to gain market share. The cellular and value-added services are currently the fastest-growing market segments.

Type of Service	Entire Market		Top Two Players		
	Market Size	Number of Players	Names	Annual Revenue	Ownership
Local	NZ$913 million	One major player	Telecom	NZ$913 million	*
Long Distance	NZ$700 million	Two major players	Telecom	NZ$555 million	*
			Clear	NZ$140 million	**
International	NZ$650 million	Five switched toll carriers plus a number of call-back operators	Telecom	NZ$514 million	*
			Clear	NZ$130 million	**
Cellular	NZ$396 million	Two major players	Telecom	NZ$316 million	*
			BellSouth	NZ$80 million	BellSouth
Value-added	NZ$320 million	One major player	Telecom	NZ$320 million	*

Sources: Telecom New Zealand Limited's March 31, 1997 annual report; 1997 government estimates.
* 24.9% each held by Bell Atlantic and Ameritech; the remainder publicly traded.
** 25% British Telecom; 25% MCI; the remainder privately held.

Licensing Requirements

The New Zealand government does not require companies to obtain licenses to operate telecommunications services. While no regulatory body for telecommunications exists, the telecommunications market, along with all other markets in New Zealand, is closely monitored by the Ministry of Commerce and the Commerce Commission. For the provision of cellular services, however, an operator is required to hold spectrum management rights as a prerequisite to market entry.

Potential for Foreign Ownerships/Relationships

New Zealand's policy on non-resident investment is administered by the Overseas Investment Commission (OIC), which receives direction from the government as to the criteria for approving non-resident investment proposals. In general, OIC approves the establishment or acquisition of a local enterprise involving less than 25% overseas ownership. Any investment valued at NZ$10 million or less is exempt from this requirement for OIC approval. For overseas participation above 25% and NZ$10 million, applicants must demonstrate the benefits to New Zealand in the form of contributions to national development based on efficient specialization, exports and advanced technology.

Policy statements by government ministers indicate that, although some local participation will be encouraged, approval for a substantial proportion of foreign equity will be granted as long as the criteria are met.

The only specific restriction on foreign ownership of telecommunications companies in New Zealand relates to Telecom. As part of Telecom's privatization, no single non-New Zealand shareholder may own more than 49.9% of the company. In addition, no single person may hold an interest of more than 10% without permission of the Telecom Board and the Minister of Finance.

Potential for Upcoming Liberalization/Investment Opportunities

In accordance with government policy, the New Zealand telecommunications market is already subject to minimal regulation. While the government monitors the emergence of competition and the pricing of services, increased regulation in the current environment is unlikely.

Forms of Doing Business

Permanent Establishment

Under New Zealand's domestic tax law, income derived from any business wholly or partly carried on in New Zealand is deemed to be derived from New Zealand and is therefore prima facie subject to New Zealand income tax. The amount of income attributable to New Zealand is determined by applying arm's-length principles.

This treatment is subject to the double-taxation agreements negotiated by New Zealand with 24 countries. These agreements are based on the OECD Model. In general terms, when a foreign entity is operating in New Zealand through a permanent establishment (PE), the profits attributable to that PE will be subject to tax in New Zealand. When a foreign entity's New Zealand operations do not constitute a PE, the business profits will not be subject to New Zealand income tax. However, withholding tax may be levied on dividends, interest and royalties paid to a non-resident.

While the definition of PE contained in New Zealand's double-taxation agreements generally follows the OECD Model, some variation exists. The examples of telecommunications-related services discussed below are not exhaustive, but merely provide an indication of the wide variety of services to be commonly found in the telecommunications industry. The level of local presence of both assets and personnel required for each of these activities may vary considerably and will critically affect any conclusion as to whether there is a PE.

- The provision of long-distance telephone services by a foreign company to New Zealand customers without any local presence or advertising will generally not constitute a PE.

- The licensing by a foreign company of technology and know-how to a New Zealand company will not generally constitute a PE. Accordingly, the profits derived in New Zealand would not be subject to income tax. However, some or all of the payments received by the foreign telecommunications company would be characterized as a royalty and subject to withholding tax.

- The presence of a foreign telecommunications company's employees as "operators" of a New Zealand-resident company, or as "network managers" including the provision of technical assistance and technology services by the foreign company in exchange for service fees, is likely to be considered a PE. In such cases, service fees would be subject to New Zealand income tax.

- The leasing of telecommunications equipment to a New Zealand company will generally not of itself be considered to constitute a PE. However, the definition of PE in most of New Zealand's double-tax agreements includes a place where a person has, is using, or is installing substantial equipment or substantial machinery. The presence of such equipment may lead to a PE.

- The provision of call reorganization or turnaround services will generally not amount to a PE if the foreign telecommunications company has no substantial equipment in New Zealand.

- The provision of Internet access services would generally not, of itself, constitute a PE, depending upon the extent of the foreign company's operations in New Zealand. If the foreign company's activities are limited to the sale of software (with no presence in New Zealand), then a PE should

not arise. However, if the Internet access server is located in New Zealand, a PE may arise.

- The laying of fiber optic cable and the construction of telecommunications switching equipment for sale to a New Zealand company, or to be operated by a foreign company for a New Zealand company in exchange for a fee, will generally constitute a PE.

- Having a server or switch (but no personnel) located in New Zealand may give rise to a PE.

- Having a website located on a server in New Zealand that is accessible by New Zealand customers may give rise to a PE.

- Having a website located on a server outside New Zealand but accessible to customers in New Zealand is unlikely to constitute a PE.

- Having a website located on a server in New Zealand that is not accessible by New Zealand customers but is accessible by customers in other countries may give rise to a PE.

Business Entities

Local Branch of a Foreign Company. A foreign corporation may operate as a branch in New Zealand and will be taxed on the same basis as a New Zealand-resident company. A branch of an overseas corporation is required to file separate accounts for the business carried on in or from New Zealand and also to file accounts for the overseas corporation with the Registrar of Companies. Accounts filed with the Registrar of Companies are available for public inspection upon the payment of a nominal fee.

Any losses incurred with respect to a New Zealand branch operation may generally be offset against other New Zealand operations, subject to a 66% shareholder commonality test (see below).

Locally Incorporated Subsidiary of a Foreign Company. New Zealand resident corporations are subject to tax at 33% on their worldwide income. Withholding tax is imposed on dividends paid to non-residents up to a rate of 30%, depending on the double-tax agreement (DTA) protection. However, a foreign investor tax credit mechanism can apply to effectively reduce the overall tax rate imposed on a non-resident shareholder to 33% (see "Debt versus Equity"). Accordingly, from an income tax perspective, the tax payable by a branch or a subsidiary will generally be the same. New Zealand-registered corporations with at least 25% foreign ownership are required to file audited accounts with the Registrar of Companies. These accounts are available for public inspection upon payment of a nominal fee.

New Zealand-resident corporations may offset any losses incurred against other New Zealand-resident corporations where the two corporations share common shareholders of at least 66% throughout the year of offset.

Joint Venture. There is no requirement for foreign investors engaging in telecommunications activities in New Zealand to enter into joint ventures. Some local participation in investments by non-residents is encouraged, but it is not mandatory.

New Zealand has no specific tax legislation dealing with joint ventures. When the joint venture is conducted through a New Zealand company, the joint venture company will be treated as a resident company. If the joint venture is unincorporated, no return of income is required to be filed by the joint venture itself, although individual participants are required to return their share of the New Zealand-sourced income. They may claim a deduction for their individual expenditures against this income.

Local Funding Alternatives

Debt versus Equity

Interest paid offshore on debt financing will be subject to non-resident withholding tax (NRWT) of up to 15%, depending on the DTA protection. The cost of NRWT can be eliminated by the borrower's paying an approved issuer levy (AIL) of 2% on the gross interest. AIL is available only for approved unrelated third-party debt.

A comprehensive thin capitalization regime limits the interest deduction in New Zealand where certain thresholds are exceeded. Generally, where the debt-to-assets percentage of a foreign-controlled New Zealand company is less than 75%, or less than 110% of the worldwide group debt-to-assets percentage, an interest deduction will be available.

Unrealized exchange gains or losses on debt denominated in foreign currencies are generally assessable or deductible on an annual basis for income tax purposes. Dividends paid to non-residents on equity investments will be subject to NRWT of up to 30%, depending on the DTA protection. The NRWT cost is effectively eliminated by a foreign investor tax credit mechanism, which applies where imputation credits are attached to that dividend and the company pays a supplementary dividend to the non-resident shareholder. Imputation credits denote that New Zealand income tax has been paid on the underlying income at the corporate level. Provided that the ordinary dividend has sufficient imputation credits attached (reflecting the fact that all of the dividend is in respect of tax-paid income), the NRWT liability on the ordinary and supplementary dividend will be offset by the supplementary dividend. This results in the non-resident shareholder receiving the same cash as a resident shareholder, and limits the New Zealand tax paid on that income to 33%. The company finances the supplementary dividend by receiving an income tax credit for the amount paid. This mechanism is illustrated in the following table:

			NZ $
	NZ company profit		100
Less:	NZ company tax @ 33%		(33)
Plus:	Foreign investor tax credit		12
	Funds available for distribution		$ 79
	Dividend to foreign shareholder		67
Plus:	Supplementary dividend		12
	Total dividend		79
Less:	NRWT @ 15%		(12)
	Net cash to shareholder		$ 67
	Company tax paid		21
	NRWT paid		12
	Overall tax paid		$ 33

Exchange Controls

New Zealand has no exchange controls.

Business Acquisitions and Dispositions

A foreign investor wishing to invest in New Zealand can acquire either the assets or the shares of a company operating a business. The optimum strategy will depend upon the specific investment opportunity being considered. However, the following general comments can be made.

Capital Contributions into an Existing Local Entity

A capital contribution into an existing New Zealand entity would not be subject to any New Zealand tax. A foreign investor may contribute services or technology in exchange for an ownership interest in a New Zealand business. Withholding tax may be payable when the contribution is made by way of licensing an intangible which, therefore, represents a royalty. Changes in ownership of the local entity above 33% as a consequence of a capital contribution may result in the local entity being unable to utilize both its carried-forward tax losses and its imputation credits.

Purchase or Sale of Shares in a Local Entity

The sale of shares in a local entity to a foreign company or by a foreign company would not generally be subject to New Zealand tax (unless the vendor was a dealer or the vendor had acquired the shares for the purpose of disposing of them). As previously mentioned, changes of ownership above 33% may result in the forfeiture of carried-forward tax losses and imputation credits.

If the purchase price of the shares in a local entity exceeds the net book value of the local entity, there is no mechanism that would allow the foreign company to automatically step-up the tax basis in the assets owned by the local company to the extent of the premium paid upon the purchase of the shares.

Purchase or Sale of Assets

Acquirers of assets of an existing telecommunications company are required to allocate the purchase price to individual assets using market value to establish depreciation deductions. Certain intangible property (e.g., copyright, patent rights and rights to use trademarks) with a fixed life may be depreciated by the acquirer over the life of the property. Intangible property with an indefinite life (e.g., goodwill) generally cannot be depreciated.

Capital gains on assets sold to non-associated parties will generally not be taxable (unless the seller is a dealer or acquired the assets for the purpose of disposing of them). However, excess depreciation may be recovered.

Transfer of land may give rise to stamp duty of up to 2% of the value of the land. The purchase of assets within New Zealand will generally be subject to goods and services tax (GST) (see "Value-Added Tax, Sales Tax and/or Other Pertinent Taxes"). However, if the non-resident is registered for GST, the GST paid should be refundable.

The acquisition of a partnership interest is generally treated as a partial acquisition of the underlying partnership assets.

Start-up Business Issues

Pre-operating Losses and Start-up/ Construction Costs

License fees, franchise fees and easements are likely to be capital expenditures and, therefore, non-deductible. These may be amortized depending on the terms of the agreement. Infrastructure costs will also generally be treated as capital expenditures and are not deductible. Assets created for network deployment are likely to be depreciable property, with depreciation calculated based on specific rates for telecommunications assets (see "Depreciation/Cost-Recovery Conventions/Accelerated Deductions").

Capital projects that are not completed before year-end may, in certain cases, be depreciated. The asset must be owned by a New Zealand entity (or be subject to a finance lease) to be depreciated.

During construction of assets, direct costs and direct overhead must be capitalized. However, indirect overhead (such as interest and finance costs) may be expensed. To be deductible or eligible for depreciation, the costs must be borne by the New Zealand operations, rather than a foreign parent. Withholding tax would only be payable on a charge by the overseas parent

to the subsidiary to recover such costs if they represented a royalty.

A foreign company that incurs local costs that are subject to New Zealand GST, which is a value-added tax, will generally be able to recover the GST paid. This GST can be recovered prior to commencing operations.

Customs Duties and VAT

The importation of goods into New Zealand will normally result in GST, which is a value-added tax of 12.5%, payable to New Zealand Customs. Until this tax is paid, New Zealand Customs will normally not release the goods for consumption in New Zealand. Certain exceptions apply: for example, temporary imports of less than 12 months can have tax refunded on export. In addition, certain goods may attract customs duties depending upon the country of origin and the goods that are being imported.

Loss Carryovers

Losses may be carried forward indefinitely, but there must be a minimum level of continuity in the economic ownership of the loss-making corporation. The criteria for a loss carryforward are stringent and a minimum shareholder continuity percentage of 49% must be maintained. The ability to carry forward losses will not be affected by a change in business activities of the corporation. There is a provision for offset or contributions toward losses by corporations within groups where the common holding is at least 66%.

Operating Considerations

Corporate Income Taxes

The income tax rate payable by New Zealand-resident companies and New Zealand branches of foreign companies is 33%. Income tax is assessed on an entity's gross income, taking into account allowable deductions. For a deduction to be allowable, it must be incurred before year-end and be in respect of gaining gross income or carrying on a business to derive gross income.

Specific provisions disallow deductions for certain expenditures: for example, for capital expenditures, interest (except where certain criteria are met), income tax, penalties and certain bad debts.

Capital Gains Taxes

There is currently no capital gains tax in New Zealand. The Income Tax Act, however, includes in gross income certain capital gains derived from real property transactions. Liability is based on factors such as length of ownership, rezoning of property and other business activities of the taxpayer or persons associated with the taxpayer. In addition, all gains, including those of a capital nature, arising from debt transactions are deemed by the Income Tax Act to be on revenue account and therefore subject to income tax.

Tax Holidays and Exemptions

The New Zealand government does not offer any tax holidays or exemptions. This is not expected to change in the future, given the government's policy of maintaining a broad tax base.

Depreciation/Cost-Recovery Conventions/Accelerated Deductions

Depreciation deductions are a benefit and they must be claimed in the year in which the depreciation is allowed or they will be lost. Key features of New Zealand's depreciation regime include the following:

- There are specific depreciation rates for telecommunications equipment that include land-based cables, which are depreciated using the straight-line method at 8% annually; and antennas, networking equipment and telephone switching equipment, which are depreciated using the straight-line method at 10% annually.

- There is a choice between the straight-line and the diminishing-value methods of depreciation. When the diminishing-value method is used, the straight-line rates are uplifted. For example, 8% and 10% using the straight line method will become 12% and 15%, respectively, using the diminishing-value method. The choice of which method to use is up to the taxpayer. Generally, the diminishing-value method is preferred from a cash-flow perspective; however, some taxpayers prefer the straight-line method for consistency with their accounting treatment.

- All assets that cost more than NZ$200 must be capitalized. A pool method of depreciation for assets that cost NZ$2,000 or less is available.

New Zealand has no cost-recovery conventions or accelerated deductions.

Research and Development. Scientific or industrial research expenditures are generally deductible in full in the year they are incurred, subject to general deductibility criteria. The costs of plant or buildings associated with such research must be capitalized and depreciated at the rates applicable to such assets. Expenditures for software development must be capitalized and

depreciated at either 30%, using the straight-line method, or 40%, using the diminishing-value method.

Marketing and Advertising Costs. Investors can deduct marketing and advertising expenses, including payments made directly or indirectly to attract or acquire customer relationships. No special rules exist for these costs.

Leases. Specified (finance) leases of movable property, which is called personal property in New Zealand, are recharacterized for income tax purposes as a vendor-financed sale of the leased asset. As a result, the lessee is deemed to be the owner of the asset and deductions are allowed to the lessee for depreciation of the lease asset and the interest component of the lease payments. Interest income is returned as assessable income by the lessor.

Transfer Pricing Rules

New Zealand has recently introduced transfer pricing rules, based on the OECD arm's-length principles. Given the recent introduction of the regime, its full impact is as yet unknown. The rules allow for a variety of measurement options, including the comparable uncontrolled price method, the resale price method, the cost plus method, the profit split method and the comparable profits method.

Transfers of Patents, Trademarks and Software

The tax implications of the transfer of technology will depend on the nature of the transfer. In general terms, the outright transfer of an entire right would be treated as a capital contribution, with potential depreciation deductions available to the purchaser if certain conditions are met. The mere transfer of a right to use technology would usually be classified as a royalty and would be assessable as ordinary income deductible by the user.

Payments for the right to use patents, trademarks and software are generally treated as capital and, therefore, not deductible upfront. Where the payment is for a fixed term, it can qualify for a depreciation deduction. These payments can be treated as royalties by the New Zealand tax authorities and are subject to withholding tax. The criteria used to treat these payments as capital or royalties are unclear.

Service Fees

Service fees are generally deductible, subject to normal deductibility criteria. Unless a certificate of exemption is obtained from the Inland Revenue, non-resident contractors withholding tax (NRCWT) is required to be deducted by a taxpayer at a rate of up to 30% from payments for work performed by non-residents in New Zealand. NRCWT is a payment-on-account of the non-resident's ultimate liability to New Zealand tax to be determined from returns filed. Notwithstanding the fact that a tax treaty may apply to exempt the non-resident recipient from New Zealand tax, the taxpayer is obliged to make deductions. NRCWT does not normally apply to payments for services performed outside New Zealand.

Value-Added Tax, Sales Tax and/or Other Pertinent Taxes

GST, which is a broadly based consumption tax on goods and services supplied in New Zealand, is imposed on taxable supplies at the rate of 12.5%. Registered persons are able to deduct input tax in calculating the tax payable. GST applies to all goods and services supplied in New Zealand, other than exempt financial services and domestic rental accommodation.

Local and Provincial Taxes

New Zealand has no local or provincial taxes, other than taxes payable to local authorities as a result of the ownership of land.

For Additional Information, Contact:

Kevin Best
Tax Partner
and
Stewart McCulloch
Tax Partner
and
Ross Collins
Telecoms Consulting Partner
P.O. Box 243
Wellington, New Zealand
Telephone: 64 (4) 499 9898
Fax: 64 (4) 499 9696
E-mail: kevin_best@nz.coopers.com
        stewart_mcculloch@nz.coopers.com
        ross_collins@nz.coopers.com

Philippines

Rapidly changing market conditions and/or legislative developments preclude the possibility of offering a comprehensive profile on the Philippines for this edition. Tax and telecommunications specialists in our Makati City office are fully versed in current practices and conditions in the Philippines and can provide assistance to clients regarding investment opportunities and tax requirements. Please contact the representative listed for further information.

For Additional Information, Contact:

Mariano C. Ereso, Jr.
Tax Principal
22/F Antel 1000 Corporate Centre
139 Valero Street, Salcedo Village
Makati City, Metro Manila
Philippines
Telephone: 63 (2) 840 4001
Fax: 63 (2) 816 6595

Singapore

Rapidly changing market conditions and/or legislative developments preclude the possibility of offering a comprehensive profile on Singapore for this edition. Tax and telecommunications specialists in our office are fully versed in current practices and conditions in Singapore and can provide assistance to clients regarding investment opportunities and tax requirements. Please contact the representative listed for further information.

For Additional Information, Contact:

Noris Ong
Tax Partner
9 Penang Road, #12-00
Park Mall
Singapore 238459
Telephone: (65) 3301 218
Fax: (65) 3362 539
E-mail: noris_ong@sg.coopers.com

Taiwan

Rapidly changing market conditions and/or legislative developments preclude the possibility of offering a comprehensive profile on Taiwan for this edition. Tax and telecommunications specialists in our Taipei office are fully versed in current practices and conditions in Taiwan and can provide assistance to clients regarding investment opportunities and tax requirements. Please contact the representatives listed for further information.

For Additional Information, Contact:

Steven Go
Tax Partner
No. 367 Fu Hsing North Road
Taipei, Taiwan R.O.C.
Telephone: 886 (2) 2545 5678
Fax: 886 (2) 2514 0248
E-mail: Steven@ms1.colybrand.com.tw

David Hoffman
Director—Telecoms & Media Practice
Address: same as above
Telephone: 886 (2) 2715 2822
Fax: 886 (2) 2545 1185

Thailand

Rapidly changing market conditions and/or legislative developments preclude the possibility of offering a comprehensive profile on Thailand for this edition. Tax and telecommunications specialists in our Bangkok office are fully versed in current practices and conditions in Thailand and can provide assistance to clients regarding investment opportunities and tax requirements. Please contact the representative listed for further information.

For Additional Information, Contact:

Andrew Jackomos
Tax Partner
Sathorn Thani Building 1
8/F, 90/14-16 North Sathorn Road
Bangkok 10500
Thailand
Telephone: 66 (2) 236 7814
Fax: 66 (2) 236 5226

Vietnam

Telecommunications Tax Profile
by Timothy Thien Chau
Tax and Consulting Partner, Ho Chi Minh City

Overview of the Telecommunications Market

Historical Background

The telecommunications industry is viewed as a national security asset and, as such, is highly regulated. Not only is foreign ownership of a telecommunications business prohibited, local Vietnamese businesses also may not own, operate or provide telecoms services. Therefore, all telecoms service providers are state-owned. The Department General of Posts and Telecommunications (DGPT) had responsibility for both operating and regulating the industry. However, following the international trend of separating the policy arm from the operating arm, in approximately 1990 the Vietnamese government gave DGPT responsibility for establishing telecommunications policy and for regulatory matters, and formed an integrated operating company called the Vietnam National Post and Telecommunications Corporation (VNPT). The VNPT, with its subsidiaries, has essentially dictated and controlled all business aspects of the telecommunications industry. VNPT's total revenue for 1997 was expected to be US$750 million.

In 1994 and 1995, in response to complaints about high costs and inefficiency, the prime minister formed two other telecommunications companies, which are not controlled by the DGPT. The Military Electronics and Telecommunications Company (also known as Vietel), which is under the control of the army, and the Saigon Post and Telecommunications Joint Stock Corporation (Saigon Postel), which is a state-owned enterprise established with other state-owned enterprises as shareholders, have not yet provided telecommunications services. Thus far, they have only engaged in the manufacturing and distribution of telecommunications equipment.

Current Status

The development of the telecommunications infrastructure is a priority for the government. In 1992, there were fewer than 100,000 telephone lines in Vietnam. In early 1997, there were over 1.3 million telephone lines. The government plans to increase this figure to 30 telephones per 1,000 persons in the year 2000. With an expected population of 80 million, this translates into a total of 4 million installed telephone lines by the year 2000. To meet the government's goal, therefore, an additional 2.7 million telephone lines will be needed. Vietnam's telecommunications industry is estimated to be the second-fastest-growing market in the world, and investment has been averaging about US$400 million a year for the past six years.

The VNPT has used a revenue- and cost-sharing agreement called a business cooperation contract (BCC) as a way to accelerate the process of installing wireline systems and has entered into BCCs with several foreign telecoms companies. A BCC is the most common form of foreign investment used in the telecommunications industry. Most of the BCCs to which the VNPT is a party require the foreign entity to provide equipment, training, supervision, financing and technical expertise, while the VNPT provides knowledge and access into the Vietnamese market. (A BCC is a contractual agreement and the terms of what each party will provide are flexible and will be set out in each individual agreement.)

Telstra Corporation Ltd. has been very active in Vietnam and is believed to have signed the first BCC with VNPT in 1988 to install a satellite earth station. Since then, Telstra has been involved in a number of other BCCs: to install a submarine network and a gateway exchange, as well as to provide general training and support to the VNPT.

Telstra is expected to sign another BCC with the VNPT in the near future to take part in a US$1.3 billion project to install telephone lines throughout the country. Cable & Wireless Plc is also expected to sign a BCC as part of this project. At the end of 1997, Nippon Telegraph & Telephone Corporation (NTT) and France Telecom received licenses for separate BCCs to invest US$194 million and US$467 million, respectively, also as part of this project. Korea Telecom is currently fulfilling a separate

US$53.2 million BCC for the installation of 160,000 telephone lines and supporting equipment in several northern provinces.

Digital switching equipment is a key component of the fixed network. However, as Vietnam has moved to build a state-of-the-art network, it has also run into numerous interconnection problems, as a result of the variety of digital switching equipment that has been introduced. Alcatel, Siemens, the LG Group, and Daewoo Telecom have each established a joint venture with the VNPT to assemble digital switches. Alcatel uses an E10 system, has supplied 11 switches and plans to have 2 million lines installed by the year 2000.

Digital microwave systems are used to connect each of the 63 provinces in the national network, as well as the national backbone system that runs from Hanoi to Ho Chi Minh City. There are three mobile cellular systems and four providers, as follows:

- CallLink, which uses an AMPS/D-AMPS (advanced mobile phone service/digital advanced mobile phone service) system, is a BCC between VNPT (through its Ho Chi Minh City Posts and Telecommunications subsidiary) and Singapore Telecom.

- Citynet, which utilizes a two-way CT-2 (cordless telephony generation 2) mobile phone network, is a BCC between the VNPT (also through Ho Chi Minh City Posts and Telecommunications) and Steamers Telecommunications PTR Ltd, a Singapore company.

- VMS (Vietnam Mobile Services)/Mobifone, which uses a GSM-900 (global system for mobile communications-900) network utilizing Ericsson equipment and technology, is a BCC between the DGPT and two Swedish companies—Industriförvaltnings AB Kinnevik and Comvik International Vietnam AB (this BCC had 85,000 subscribers in 1997 and has committed US$341 million over the next four years).

- VinaPhone, which utilizes GSM technology and had 20,000 subscribers in 1997, is a 100%-Vietnamese company owned by the VNPT through Ho Chi Minh City Posts and Telecommunications.

The number of cellular customers is expected to grow to 500,000 by the year 2005. While the VNPT has adopted GSM as its cellular technology, it is now reviewing the possibility of introducing call division multiple access (CDMA).

There are also five paging companies operating throughout the country. In all of the following cases, the VNPT operates through its Ho Chi Minh City Posts and Telecommunications subsidiary. The paging companies are:

- Saigon ABC, a BCC between VNPT and a Hong Kong company called ABC Communications (Holdings) Ltd.

- Phone Link, which is controlled by the VNPT (Phone Link was originally established as a BCC between the Shinawatra Group, a Thai company, and the VNPT through Ho Chi Minh City Posts and Telecommunications; the BCC has expired or been revoked and control has reverted to the VNPT)

- Saigon Epro, a BCC between EPCO Telecom Holdings (a Hong Kong company) and the VNPT

- MCC (Mobile Communication Center), a BCC between Voice International of Australia and the VNPT

- Vietnam Paging Centre, a 100%-Vietnamese company established by Saigon Telecom Co., which is itself a company established by the VNPT

In 1996, there were 70,000 pagers in Vietnam; this number is expected to top 1 million in the year 2000 as prices steadily decrease for both equipment and usage fees.

VNPT has been purchasing and installing very small aperture terminals (VSAT), fiber optic cables, earth stations, trunk mobile radio equipment and submarine fiber optic cables. The market for telecommunications equipment was expected to be US$710 million in 1997 and to grow at an annual rate of 20% per year through the year 2000. In 1997, foreign imports made up 88% of this market, or US$625 million. However, approximately eight joint ventures have been established in 1997 to begin meeting some of this demand. Locally produced equipment will include telecoms equipment such as telephone switchboards, cables and transmission instruments.

The Vietnamese government is now stating that it will require US$4 billion in additional investment by the year 2000 in order to meet its telecoms development objectives. The latest DGPT master plan, which covers 1996 to 2000, continues to emphasize the monopolistic structure of the telecoms industry, as reflected in the following table.

Current Liberalization Status

Type of Service	Degree of Liberalization	Date of Actual or Expected Liberalization	Comments
Local	In transition from monopoly—there will no longer be just one provider; however, all providers will be state-controlled.	The first moves toward liberalization occurred when the prime minister established Vietel and Saigon Postel. It is not known when full liberalization will occur.	Vietel and Saigon Postel were granted licenses in 1994 and 1995, respectively. Neither company has begun to offer telecoms services.
Long Distance	In transition from monopoly	Unknown	The government intends to maintain VNPT's monopoly until at least the year 2000.
International	In transition from monopoly	Unknown	Direct foreign competition is not allowed. Telstra provides services through a BCC.
Cellular	Partially liberalized	In 1992 and 1996, licenses were granted to local tolooo and other common carriers	Direct foreign competition is not allowed. There are currently three mobile phone cellular systems and four providers.
Paging	Partially liberalized	Unknown	Direct foreign competition is not allowed. The paging sector is currently being developed through BCCs with foreign investors.
Value-added	Monopoly	Unknown	VNPT currently offers value-added services such as voice mail, call waiting, call holding and caller ID through its VMS/Mobifone subsidiary.

Source: *Telecom Markets in Southeast Asia*, Pyramid Research, 1996.

Competitive Environment

Editor's note: The Competitive Environment table has been omitted from this chapter because revenue figures were not publicly available.

Licensing Requirements

All foreign investors must apply to the Ministry of Planning and Investment (MPI) for a license to operate in Vietnam (i.e., an investment license). In order for a license to be issued in the telecommunications sector, in addition to the approval from the MPI, additional approvals from the DGPT and the local People's Committee would also be required. Licenses may be nationwide or for specific regions. However, since the telecommunications industry is a strategic industry, all licenses—not just nationwide licenses—would require MPI approval. Licenses issued by the local People's Committee would be limited to a certain area and normally be limited to investment projects of US$5 million or less.

Potential for Foreign Ownerships/Relationships

While foreign investors are not allowed to own, manage or operate telecommunications services, foreign investment can be made in a variety of different forms. See "Business Entities."

Potential for Upcoming Liberalization/Investment Opportunities

Improving the telecommunications infrastructure is a government priority that will require additional foreign investment. Even though Vietnam has applied for membership in the World Trade Organization (WTO), it is not expected to liberalize the industry. It is the policy of the government that no telecommunications business can be owned by a foreign enterprise. Thus far, only state-owned enterprises have been permitted to own telecommunications businesses; private ownership by Vietnamese enterprises has also been prohibited. Opportunities for foreign investors to provide services in cooperation with the government are expected to continue in the future.

Forms of Doing Business

Permanent Establishment

The current tax law does not apply the concept of permanent establishment (PE) except for those countries with whom Vietnam has signed a double-tax treaty. All foreign-invested enterprises (see "Business Entities") are subject to tax.

Currently, foreign entities doing business in Vietnam not in the form of a foreign-invested enterprise are either subject to foreign contractor tax or to royalty tax. Royalty tax is assessed at a rate of either 10% for a contract with a term of less than five years or 15% for a contract with a term of more than five years. Foreign contractor tax is withheld from payments to foreign contractors by the contracting party at rates that range from 3% to 10.3% according to the activity. A foreign contractor is any organization or individual carrying out business activities not in any of the prescribed forms of foreign investment discussed below. In the event that a double-tax treaty exists between Vietnam and the home country of a foreign contractor, an application may be made to exempt the foreign contractor from a portion of the foreign contractor tax if a PE is not deemed to exist under the terms of the double-tax treaty.

The first introduction of PE into the domestic law of Vietnam will occur on January 1, 1999, when new business tax legislation becomes effective. Based on the current understanding of this new legislation, it is expected that a PE will be created when a foreign company carries out business activities either through a fixed place of business or an agent.

Business Entities

All foreign investment into Vietnam must be in one of the following forms. Any foreign investment requires government approval. A potential investor must apply to the MPI for an investment license, which will specify the form, size and other specifics of the investment. Companies established in Vietnam under one of these prescribed forms of investment are referred to collectively as foreign-invested enterprises and subject to Vietnamese taxation as detailed below. (It should be noted that companies established in Vietnam under Vietnamese domestic law with no capital contribution from a foreign company are referred to as either domestic, 100% Vietnamese, Vietnamese or local companies.)

Local Office of a Foreign Company. This option is currently open to foreign banks, tobacco companies and law firms only. A branch of a foreign company is taxed on its Vietnamese-sourced income as the branch office is permitted to undertake activities in Vietnam only. The grouping of profit and losses from other branches would not be possible as other branches would operate under separate licenses.

Joint Venture. In Vietnam, a joint venture is an incorporated limited liability company and, therefore, a legal entity established by at least two parties pursuant to a joint venture contract between at least one enterprise with foreign capital and a Vietnamese (local) enterprise. Each of the joint venture parties is liable only for its share of the contribution to the prescribed capital. The prescribed capital, which is similar to share capital, consists of the contributions of the parties, excluding loans. The prescribed capital cannot be reduced during the term of the joint venture. A foreign party must contribute at least 30% of the invested capital, which can take the form of cash, machinery, buildings or patents, which are valued at international market prices, or technical knowledge, which is usually valued by agreement between the two parties. A joint venture is taxed on an entity basis, therefore, income from all sources is included in its taxable income. Joint ventures are subject to Vietnamese tax and must file tax returns. In the telecommunications industry, a number of joint ventures have been established with foreign investors to manufacture telecommunications equipment.

Wholly Owned Foreign Enterprise. A wholly owned foreign enterprise is a limited liability company established with capital contributed from foreign investor(s) only. The foreign investor assumes full control of the management of the enterprise. In practice, it is more difficult to obtain approval to set up a wholly owned foreign enterprise than a joint venture. Projects in remote areas and those involved in the production of goods for export are more likely to receive approval. To date, this option has not been available in the telecoms industry. A wholly owned foreign enterprise is subject to tax on an entity basis, and therefore, income from all sources must be included in its taxable income.

Business Cooperation Contract. A BCC is an arrangement similar to an unincorporated partnership. Two parties (normally a foreign company and a Vietnamese company) agree to carry out investment activities without creating a legal entity. The BCC sets out the responsibilities of each party. Typically, each party will contribute either technical expertise or other assets to the venture.

The revenues and expenses of the venture are shared by each party in accordance with the BCC. Normally, taxes on the profits of the venture are declared and paid separately by each party. This is due to the difference in profits tax rates for foreign-invested enterprises and Vietnamese companies. The foreign party to the BCC will pay profits tax in accordance with rates for foreign-invested enterprises and the Vietnamese party will pay profits tax in accordance with Vietnamese company rates. (It is expected that under the new business tax legislation that will go into effect on January 1, 1999, the Vietnamese party and the foreign party will be taxed at the same rates.)

This is the most common method of foreign investment in the telecommunications industry. Since no separate legal entity is established, the parties involved assume full liability for the enterprise. The parties decide on the terms of the contract, including the duration of the collaboration. There is normally no limitation or restriction on the withdrawal or repatriation of capital.

Build-Operate-Transfer. A build-operate-transfer (BOT) contract is an agreement between a foreign investor and an authorized Vietnamese state agency to build and commercially operate an infrastructure project. At the end of the contract, the foreign investor will transfer the project without compensation to the Vietnamese government. During the commercial operations of the investment project, the foreign investor will charge a usage fee. Under a BOT contract, a BOT company must be established in Vietnam to hold the investment project. The capital of the BOT company will come from the foreign investor. Only limited licenses have been issued in this format to date, in the areas of water and electricity supply.

Local Funding Alternatives

Debt versus Equity

The law on foreign investment in Vietnam provides that the prescribed capital of joint venture and wholly owned enterprises must be at least 30% of the total invested capital. Therefore, joint ventures and wholly owned enterprises must be capitalized with a minimum of 30% prescribed capital and a maximum of 70% debt.

All offshore loans must be registered and approved by the State Bank of Vietnam. Currently, there is no withholding tax on interest paid to overseas lenders. Interest on loans is deductible as long as the interest rate is within the ceiling established by the State Bank of Vietnam. However, interest on a loan made to an investor for the purpose of meeting its contribution to the prescribed capital of a foreign-invested enterprise is not deductible.

Exchange Controls

Vietnam has stringent exchange controls. All foreign-invested enterprises are required to balance their own foreign currency requirements. (In other words, if a foreign-invested enterprise needs foreign currency, it must generate it within the company and not purchase it from the government.)

All transactions in Vietnam are required to be made in Vietnamese Dong under the current laws. Revenues should be collected and payments should be made in Vietnamese Dong only. However, despite current laws, the U.S. dollar is still in widespread use.

In most cases, foreign currency transactions within Vietnam as well as transfers of foreign currency abroad require the approval of the MPI. However, companies operating in certain strategic areas including telecommunications can obtain a foreign currency conversion license, which allows them to freely convert Vietnamese Dong into foreign currency. Only authorized banks are allowed to buy and sell foreign currency. Foreign investors are permitted to transfer profits abroad in foreign currency.

Business Acquisitions and Dispositions

Capital Contributions into an Existing Local Entity

Currently, foreign investors may only invest in Vietnam through a foreign-invested enterprise. (See "Business Entities.") Foreign investors are not permitted to legally invest into local entities (i.e., companies established with capital from Vietnamese investors only).

Purchase or Sale of Shares in a Local Entity

Vietnam does not currently have a stock market. As such, there is no concept of shares with regard to foreign-invested enterprises. Investors have an interest, which is expressed in percentages rather than in shares. A company is established with capital. Prescribed capital is the equity of the company, which is composed of capital contributions from the investors in the company and which cannot be repatriated. Total invested capital is the total capital of the company, and includes both the prescribed capital and debt of the company.

Few entities exist in Vietnam that possess share capital. The few entities that do exist with share capital are referred to as joint-stock companies. However, unlike in other countries, a share in Vietnam is not currently freely transferable. A local entity would not currently be permitted to sell a part of its interest or shares to a foreign investor, as such a transaction would result in the local entity having foreign capital. (This could happen in the future; such a transaction would most likely require government approval.) A transfer of interest in foreign-invested enterprises is taxed with a capital transfer tax. (See "Capital Gains Taxes.")

Purchase or Sale of Assets

There are currently no restrictions on the purchase or sale of assets by a foreign-invested enterprise from a local entity. Sales of assets are treated as ordinary income and taxed at the normal profits tax rate.

Start-up Business Issues

Pre-operating Losses and Start-up/Construction Costs

Starting from the issued date of an investment license, all pre-operating costs incurred prior to the normal operations of a company must be capitalized. These expenses can be amortized over a period of up to five years starting from the date on which the company commenced its operations. In addition, certain costs incurred prior to the granting of the investment license may be capitalized as pre-operating costs. These costs must be directly attributable to the cost of obtaining the license.

Customs Duties and VAT

Vietnam currently imposes a turnover tax, which is assessed on the sales revenue of an enterprise (including foreign-invested enterprises). The revenues of each enterprise are subject to turnover tax at different rates according to the type of service or product offered by the enterprise. The rate for telecommunications services is currently 6%. The rate for manufacturing telecommunications equipment would depend on the specific type of equipment and components. There is no recovery mechanism available for turnover tax. The turnover tax will be replaced by a value-added tax on January 1, 1999. The VAT rate for telecommunications services is expected to be 10%, and it is likely that the rate for the manufacture of telecommunications equipment will be 10% as well.

Under current legislation, the import of telecommunications equipment and spare parts is subject to normal import duty. Telecommunications equipment falls under the import category of "machines, equipment and parts." Import duties for this category range from 0% to 40%. However, telecommunications equipment will generally have a 0% import rate, reflecting its status as a strategic infrastructure area. Under the new VAT legislation, imported equipment and spare parts will be subject to VAT based on the value of the goods plus their import duties.

Loss Carryovers

Joint-venture enterprises are permitted to carry forward their losses for up to five years. An election must be made to carry forward the entire loss for up to five years, or to amortize the loss in equal parts over a period of five years. Until legislation was passed in November 1996, wholly owned enterprises could also carry forward their losses for up to five years; it is expected that this privilege will be reinstated in legislation to be passed in 1998. Losses may not be carried back. The current tax legislation does not address the question of whether a change in business activity or ownership would have an effect on loss carryovers.

Operating Considerations

Corporate Income Taxes

All foreign-invested enterprises are subject to profits tax. Currently, a foreign-invested enterprise's tax rate depends on the type of activity and is approved at the time the business applies for an investment license. The standard profits-tax rate for all foreign-invested enterprises, with the exception of BOT enterprises, is 25%. This rate applies to all telecommunications busi-

nesses. The current profits-tax rate for BOTs is 10%; BOTs are also subject to different tax incentives than other foreign-invested enterprises.

Under new legislation that becomes effective on January 1, 1999, all foreign-invested enterprises with the exception of BOTs will be subject to business income tax (i.e., corporate income tax); it is expected that the rate will be 32%. Tax reductions and exemptions will be available, as will reduced tax rates for new investment projects in certain economic sectors. It should be noted that no clear "grandfathering" provisions are in place for the transition from the current profits-tax system to the business income tax system. Thus, it is unclear how any incentives, reductions or exemptions from profits-tax rates enjoyed by foreign-invested companies that were licensed prior to January 1, 1999, will be affected by the changeover to the business income tax system.

Capital Gains Taxes

Capital gains arising from the sale of assets are included in regular business income and taxed as part of the profits of the foreign-invested enterprise. There is no special tax on capital gains from the sale of assets.

An interest in a joint venture company or a wholly owned foreign enterprise may be sold to another investor. A gain arising from the sale of an interest in a joint venture or wholly foreign owned enterprise from a foreign investor to another foreign investor is subject to capital transfer tax at the rate of 25%. There is no tax on the sale of an interest from a foreign investor to a state-owned enterprise. A reduced rate of 10% applies on the sale of an interest from a foreign investor to a privately owned Vietnamese enterprise.

Tax Holidays and Exemptions

Currently, businesses that meet certain requirements (for example, those that employ more than 500 Vietnamese workers or use advanced technology) are eligible for reduced profits-tax rates ranging from 10% to 20% for up to eight years. After that period, the standard profits-tax rate applies. In addition, companies that are taxed at the standard profits-tax rate and are engaged in production activities, which would include producing telecoms equipment or providing telecoms services, may be exempt from tax for the first two profit-making years. The first profit-making year is determined as the first year a profit is made prior to the utilization of any loss carryforwards.

Depreciation/Cost-Recovery Conventions/Accelerated Deductions

Foreign-invested enterprises must depreciate their assets in accordance with rates determined by the government for each category of fixed assets. For each category, a minimum and maximum useful life is listed. All assets must be depreciated utilizing a rate within these limits on a straight-line basis.

Transfer Pricing Rules

Vietnam's first transfer pricing legislation went into effect in November 1997. The legislation generally states that when transactions between related parties do not occur on an arm's-length basis, the tax authorities may adjust the results. As this is new legislation, it is unclear by what means or processes it will be enforced or how rigorously.

Transfers of Patents, Trademarks and Software

The law on foreign investment provides that an investor may transfer patents, trademarks or brand names as part of its capital contribution, and that such a transfer is currently not subject to tax. However, royalties received by a foreign entity are subject to a royalty tax at the rate of either 10% for a contract with a term of less than five years or 15% for a contract with a term of more than five years. All transfers of patents, trademarks or technology must be approved by the Ministry of Science, Technology and Environment.

Service Fees

Service fees earned by a foreign-invested enterprise are subject to turnover tax and will be included in the enterprise's taxable income when calculating profits tax. A foreign entity acting as a foreign contractor and receiving a fee for services provided in Vietnam is subject to foreign contractor tax at rates that range from 3% to 10.3%, according to the activity. When the value-added tax system is put into place on January 1, 1999, it is expected that the foreign contractor tax will be modified to a certain extent; however, the exact modifications are not yet known.

Value-Added Tax, Sales Tax and/or Other Pertinent Taxes

Currently, Vietnam has a turnover tax system in place whereby tax is assessed on each sale. This tax applies to all foreign-invested enterprises. The turnover tax rates range from 1% to 30%; the rate for telecommunications services is 6%. The turnover tax system will be replaced with a value-added tax system on January 1, 1999.

Local and Provincial Taxes

There are no local or provincial taxes that apply to foreign-invested enterprises.

For Additional Information, Contact:

Timothy Thien Chau
Tax and Consulting Partner
142 Nguyen Thi Minh Khai Street
District 3, Ho Chi Minh City
Vietnam
Telephone: 84 (8) 829 2389
Fax: 84 (8) 829 2392

Part Two
Europe

Austria
Belgium
Bulgaria
Czech Republic
Denmark
Finland
France
Germany
Hungary
Ireland
Italy
The Netherlands
Norway
Poland
Portugal
Romania
Russia
Slovakia
Spain
Sweden
Switzerland
Turkey
Ukraine
United Kingdom

Austria

Telecommunications Tax Profile
by Helmut Knotzinger
Tax Partner, Vienna

Overview of the Telecommunications Market

Historical Background

Austria's telecommunications services have traditionally been provided by the government through the Post und Telegraphanverwalt (PTT). In the wake of Austria's application to membership in the European Union (EU), the government took action to bring many activities into compliance with EU requirements, including the separation of the PTT's regulatory and operational functions, which occurred in 1992.

In 1994, the Austrian Parliament passed a Telecommunications Act defining the steps to be taken toward liberalization. This law confirmed the PTT's monopoly on basic services until 1998, liberalized the provision of data services and customer premise equipment, and set the schedule for reorganizing the PTT into a state-owned corporation.

In 1995, Austria joined the EU. The government took its first step toward liberalizing the telecommunications sector by licensing Austria's second global system for mobile communications (GSM) cellular network.

In 1996, the PTT was restructured as a limited corporation, Post und Telekom Austria AG (PTA), which is fully owned by the government. Three operational divisions (Postal Services, Post Transport and Telecommunications), plus daughter companies Mobilkom Austria AG (Mobilkom) for GSM and D-Net (900-MHz) services, and Datakom Austria AG (Datakom) for value-added data services, were established. In 1997, 25% of Mobilkom was sold to STET Italy.

In August 1997, the Telecommunication Act BGB1.I Nr. 100/97 was introduced. It provided the basis for full liberalization of the telecommunications market and incorporated EU requirements. At the same time, a license for a third mobile operator was granted to Connect Austria GmbH (Connect), a consortium of Radex-Heraklith International, VIAG Interkom, Telenor A/S, Orange, TeleDanmark A/S and Constantia Privatbank.

Current Status

As of January 1998, new fixed network service providers have entered the market. United Telecom Austria (UTA), City Com Austria Telekommunikation GmbH (City Com) and CyberTron EDV-Netzwerkbetriebs GmbH (Austrian Digital Telecom) are fully licensed. RSLCOM New Telco Telecom AG (Com Austria) and Unisource have received licenses for international telephony. Vorarlberger Kraftwerke AG (VKW) and Stadtwerke Feldkirch hold regional licenses, while Data-Highway Burgenland GmbH has received a license for leased lines. Additional organizations (e.g., Telering Telekom Service GmbH) were preparing their market entry.

Current Liberalization Status

The Telecommunications Act passed in August 1997 brought Austria fully into line with EU directives. This legislation:

- Abolished PTA's monopoly in the provision of fixed telecommunications networks, permitting competition beginning in January 1998.

- Established a regulatory framework that will safeguard fair competition, protect new operators and oblige existing op-erators with a dominant market share (i.e., greater than 25%) to grant access to their networks in return for a fee, and introduced universal service requirements.

- Established a new regulatory body as a limited liability company (Telekom Control GmbH), wholly owned by the government.

- Set up a three-member supervisory board (Telekom Control Kommission), chaired by a judge and working in tandem with Telekom Control GmbH.

Type of Service	Degree of Liberalization	Key Legislation	Date of Actual or Expected Liberalization	Comments
Local	Undergoing deregulation of public voice telephony from monopoly.	Telecommunications Act BGB1.I Nr.100/1997	January 1998	EU regulations 97/33 96/19/EG
Long Distance	Undergoing deregulation of public voice telephony from monopoly.	Telecommunications Act BGB1.I Nr.100/1997	January 1998	RL 90/387 97/33 ONP
International	Undergoing deregulation of public voice telephony from monopoly.	Telecommunications Act BGB1.I Nr.100/1997	January 1998	RL 92/44 97/33 ONP
Cellular	2 GSM, 1 DCS-1800 licenses	Telecommunications Act BGB1.Nr.639/1995 BGB1Nr.313/1996	April 1995	96/2 EG
Paging	Deregulated	Telecommunications Act BGB1.Nr.756/1994	April 1994	96/2 EG
Value-added	Deregulated	Telecommunications Act FG 93	April 1994	RL 90/388

Competitive Environment

Telecommunications services were primarily provided by PTA. The liberalization of public voice telephony in January 1998 re-sulted in license approvals for additional service providers, national organizations and international alliances. Interconnection of new entrants with PTA networks is in preparation. Services of new entrants were expected to start in the first quarter of 1998.

Type of Service	Entire Market		Top Two Players		
	Market Size ATS (1996)	Number of Players	Names	Annual Revenue ATS (1996)	Ownership
Local	9.5 billion	1	PTA	9.5 billion	State-owned
Long Distance	11.1 billion	1	PTA	11.1 billion	State-owned
International	12.1 billion*	Not available	PTA	11.2 billion	State-owned
Cellular	5.9 billion	2	Mobilkom	5.7 billion	75% PTA; 25% STET
			Max Mobil	0.02 billion**	25% DeTeMobil 14.8% Siemens 14.5% BAWAG 10.5% Bayr.LB 10% UTA 9% Krone Verlag 8.1% RZB 8.1% EAGenerali
Value-added	6.3 billion	Not available	Datakom	5.7 billion	100% PTA

Sources: PTA Annual Report 1996

ATS = Austrian Schillings

* Also includes some satellite revenues

** Revenues grew to ATS 1.1 billion in 1997

Licensing Requirements

The Telecommunications Act BGB1.I Nr.100/1997 defined all licensing requirements. These are mainly technical and financial specifications to fulfill quality requirements. License applications will be considered and processed by Telekom Control GmbH. Licenses are valid nationwide or, if requested, in certain regions.

Potential for Foreign Ownerships/Relationships

Licenses for send/receive satellite terminals are granted only to Austrian residents or residents of member states of the European Economic Area (EEA). Otherwise, applicants may receive licenses through an authorized agent that meets these requirements. There are no other restrictions on foreign investment or ownership.

Potential for Upcoming Liberalization/Investment Opportunities

Although Austria has been slow to introduce competition in its telecommunications sector, further market entry of national and multinational telecommunications companies can be expected. PTA is to be privatized at year-end 1999.

Forms of Doing Business

Permanent Establishment

On the basis of most tax treaties to which Austria is a party, a foreign enterprise carrying out business activity in Austria will be taxable only on profits attributable to a permanent establishment (PE) in Austria. Based on the definition in the OECD Model Treaty, a PE will come into existence:

- When there is an office or any other available place for business purposes of a foreign enterprise

- When a person has the power to act on behalf of a foreign enterprise while doing business in Austria

- As a result of a construction project undertaken for a period in excess of 12 months

Telecommunications services can cover a broad range of activities, which may or may not constitute a PE, as the following examples illustrate:

- The provision of long-distance telephone services by a foreign company without any local presence in Austria would generally not be expected to create a PE.

- The licensing by a foreign enterprise of technology and know-how to an Austrian company would generally not be considered to create a PE unless there were some permanent presence in the country.

- The provision of technical assistance and technological services by a foreign enterprise to a local company in exchange for service fees does not necessarily create a PE. However, the extent to which the foreign enterprise has a degree of permanence, either through an office or employees in Austria, will be a relevant factor in determining whether there is a PE.

- The leasing of telecommunications equipment would generally not create a PE unless the leasing activity was itself carried out through a fixed place of business in Austria.

- The provision of call reorganization/turnaround services would generally not be regarded as creating a PE, provided the telephone cards were sold through an independent agent and there was no substantial presence of the foreign enterprise in Austria either by way of equipment or office space occupied by employees.

- The extent to which the provision of Internet access services creates a taxable presence depends on the extent of the foreign enterprise's activities in Austria. For example, when a foreign entity without any presence in the country sells products to Austrian customers, this activity is unlikely to create a taxable presence. However, if the foreign enterprise owns telecommunications equipment through which the service is provided, this may result in a PE.

- Having a server or a switch located in Austria may create a PE, even if no personnel are physically located in Austria. A website on a local server which is accessible by customers in Austria could also constitute a PE. If the server is located outside of Austria, no PE will be deemed to exist.

- The laying of fiber optic cable and the construction of telecommunications switching equipment for sale to a local company or to be operated by a foreign enterprise for a local company will generally be regarded as a taxable presence. However, a construction project does not constitute a PE when the work is completed within 12 months.

Even if there is no PE, there is a withholding tax of 20% on income from royalties and of 25% on income from dividends paid from Austria to a foreign company (except for a company resident in the EU, in which case no withholding tax is imposed). The withholding tax both on royalties and on dividends can be reduced or abolished by a tax treaty.

Business Entities

Local Branch of a Foreign Company. Austrian law basically enables all types of businesses to be carried out in the form of a branch. While this option is available to an investor, this type of arrangement is not commonly used for telecommunications businesses.

A branch is not a legal entity independent of its parent company. Therefore, it can only act on behalf of, and for the account of, its head office. Accordingly, all contracts concluded and all rights and obligations assumed by the branch are effective vis-à-vis the head office. Hence, the latter is liable for any obligations arising from contracts concluded by the branch.

The usual source rules do not apply in the case of an unincorporated Austrian branch of a foreign corporation. Under Austrian tax law, a branch is subject to tax on all income earned by the branch at a 34% corporate tax rate, regardless of the geographical source of the income. Consequently, a branch may be taxed on dividends received from foreign sources. In the case of a non-resident EU corporation that maintains an Austrian branch, dividends are exempted from Austrian corporation tax.

Interest expense and royalty payments to a foreign head office are not tax-deductible. Income is split between a branch and a head office either on the basis of the branch's financial statements or by estimation. In any case, general transfer pricing rules apply. Interest paid by the head office to third parties can only be deductible if the company can prove that interest payments were made on behalf of the branch.

Locally Incorporated Subsidiary of a Foreign Company. This option is available and commonly used in the telecommunications sector. Corporate income tax applies to public corporations, private corporations and certain other entities. The corporate tax rate is set uniformly at 34% of taxable income earned worldwide, or, in the case of limited liability to tax, 34% of taxable income earned within Austria. In this regard, a corporation with its corporate seat in Austria is always subject to an unlimited tax liability, while branches or PEs of foreign corporations are subject to limited tax liability. In general, the computation of profit or loss for tax purposes must follow the financial statements except where there are specific rules for tax purposes. Financial statements have to be prepared according to generally accepted accounting principles.

With one exception, there is no possibility for a tax consolidation within a group of companies. An integrated group of Austrian-operating companies is taxed as one legal entity if a profit-and-loss pooling agreement has been established. This exception applies only for unlimited tax-liable Austrian companies under certain preconditions.

Joint Venture. In practice, joint ventures are preferred for investments in telecommunications companies. Austrian partners and contacts may be helpful in establishing local business. No special approval is required for a joint venture in the telecommunications sector.

Corporate joint ventures consist of an Austrian company with local and foreign shareholders. Partnerships with limited or unlimited liability are transparent for tax purposes (i.e., the partners, rather than the partnership as a whole, pay the income taxes). The most common forms of joint ventures are general partnerships and limited partnerships. In any case, the corporate company has to file tax returns and to pay corporate income tax. Partnerships have to file tax returns, and partners will be assessed for their portion of the total income. The participation of a non-resident company (partner) in a local partnership is subject to limited income taxation similar to that for a branch or PE of a non-resident as provided under treaty.

Local Funding Alternatives

Debt versus Equity

There are no fixed debt-to-equity ratios in force but government discussions about introducing them were being held. Meanwhile, a 5-to-1 debt-to-equity ratio was acceptable. Despite the debt-to-equity ratio, interest on debt to acquire shares is not tax-deductible because dividend income is tax-exempt.

If interest payments are higher than acceptable according to the arm's-length rule, the exceeding amount is qualified as a distribution of dividends and, therefore, not deductible for the Austrian company. If interest is paid to a related company that is seated in a country that is party to a tax treaty with Austria, there will generally be no withholding tax on interest payments. Despite this fact, there will be withholding tax if dividends are distributed, except for dividends received by EU-parent companies that have held a stake of at least 25% in the Austrian subsidiary during the preceding two years from the date of distribution of the profits. The applicable tax rates differ from one treaty country to another; non-treaty countries are subject to a withholding tax of 25%. If an Austrian company buys shares in an Austrian company with debt, the interest payments are not deductible if the tax authority can trace the loan to the acquisition of the shares.

Other Tax Issues Related to Financing. There is a 1% capital (transfer) tax on share capital and shareholders' contributions to a company. There is an 0.8% duty on debt (loans) from shareholders and foreign lenders (without a written loan contract) and from banks and other lending institutions with a written contract. In this context, "loan contract" refers to any kind of written agreement.

Exchange Controls

While Austria does impose exchange controls, these controls do not apply for many countries (e.g., other EU-member countries).

Business Acquisitions and Dispositions

Capital Contributions into an Existing Local Entity

Contributions-in-kind are subject to a 1% capital (transfer) tax. Generally, there is no limitation for contributions-in-kind, but the value of the contributed intangibles must be documented. The actual value of a contribution by a new shareholder and the actual value of the receiving company determine the proportion between new issued shares and existing shares.

Purchase or Sale of Shares in a Local Entity

Foreign investors may purchase shares in a local entity, but it is not possible to obtain a step-up in the basis of the underlying assets in these circumstances. The sale of shares in a local entity to a foreign company will be subject to tax if the earnings exceed the book value of the shares. The book value of the shares is limited by the historic purchase price of the shares. If the earnings of the sale of shares do not meet the requirements of the arm's-length principle, taxation will be based on the difference between the market price of the shares and the book value. There is only one exception to this rule: if an Austrian company holds at least 25% of the shares of a foreign company for at least two years before the previous balance sheet date, the capital gain is tax-exempt in Austria.

Purchase or Sale of Assets

Foreign investors may purchase assets. The purchase of assets allows the investor to allocate the purchase price by reference to market values, as well as to tangible and intangible assets including goodwill, and to depreciate the assets. Goodwill can be depreciated over a period of 15 years. As the asset lives for tangible assets are normally less than 15 years, the purchaser may prefer allocation to tangible assets. A seller will pay tax on the difference between the sale price and the total book value and, therefore, will not be affected by any allocation. If shares are purchased by a foreign company, there are no step-up possibilities to realize amortization of goodwill or intangibles.

Generally, purchasers prefer an asset deal or an acquisition of a participation in a partnership because this structure offers depreciation of assets.

Start-up Business Issues

Pre-operating Losses and Start-up/ Construction Costs

For tax and accounting purposes, capitalization of pre-operating and start-up costs is possible. If capitalized, these costs are de-preciated over five years. While buildings and projects are being constructed, both direct and indirect costs are capitalized. Pre-operating costs have to be borne by the local entity if relief is to be obtained, although the foreign entity may be able to recover VAT in respect of these costs.

Customs Duties and VAT

Most goods imported into Austria from outside the EU are subject to customs duty and import VAT unless exemptions apply. Duty is normally payable on the cost, insurance and freight (CIF) value of the goods. Import VAT is payable on the duty-inclusive value of the goods, although VAT-registered traders can usually obtain a refund of the VAT.

Telecommunications and computing equipment are subject to duty at rates ranging from 1.2% to 10.5%. The rate of duty will depend on the exact description, the tariff classification, and the country of origin of the goods. The current import duty rate for a sample of telecommunications goods originating in non-EU countries (in this example, the United States) are given below. The EU has preferential trade agreements with a number of countries that enable goods to be imported at below those rates indicated or a nil rate of duty.

Line telephone sets with cordless handsets	3.8%
Videophones	7%
Other telephone sets	3.8%
Facsimile machines	3.8%
Teleprinters	3.8%
Telephonic or telegraphic switching apparatus	3.8%
Other apparatus for carrier line systems	2.3%
Other apparatus for digital line systems	3.8%
Building-entry telephone systems	3.8%

Customs duties on some items of equipment were already being reduced under the General Agreement on Tariffs and Trade (GATT). However, over the next few years, duty rates are scheduled to be reduced further still under the Information Technology Agreement (ITA), signed in March 1997.

The ITA also extends the range of goods subject to duty rate reductions. As a signatory to the ITA, the EU has agreed to cut tariffs on imports of computers and computer equipment, software, telecommunications and networking equipment to zero in four equal installments. The first reduction took place on July 1, 1997, and further reductions are to take effect on January 1 each year through 2000. Although the ITA will cut the cost of importing many products, the convergence of technologies in the computing, electronics and telecommunications sectors is likely to lead to disputes over the tariff classification of some equipment and affect the availability and/or phasing of duty reductions under the ITA.

A wide variety of relief from customs duty and import VAT can be claimed in various circumstances (e.g., goods imported for processing and re-export, or goods imported temporarily). There is also relief available for capital goods and equipment, provided the goods are imported by a business on the transfer of its activities to Austria.

Raw materials or components that are not available, or not available in sufficient quantities, within the EU may be eligible for a complete or partial suspension of duty, providing this can be demonstrated to the satisfaction of the Commission of the European Communities in Brussels.

Goods may be subject to antidumping or countervailing duty if, for example, the EU considers they are being imported into the EU at prices substantially lower than their normal values. Antidumping and countervailing duties are chargeable in addition to and independent of any other duty to which the imported goods are liable.

For VAT purposes, there is no distinction between regular telephony and Internet telephony.

Loss Carryovers

Losses do not expire and can be deducted without limit in 1998 and later. A complete change of ownership of a company may restrict the use of loss carryforwards under certain circumstances. The change in activity from wireline to cellular does not reduce loss carryforwards.

Operating Considerations

Corporate Income Taxes

The corporate tax rate is 34%.

Capital Gains Taxes

Capital gains are included in taxable income and are taxed at the corporate income tax rate. As of 1989, capital gains on sales of shares in foreign companies (sales of more than 25% of a foreign company) became exempt from Austrian corporate income tax under certain circumstances.

Tax Holidays and Exemptions

Foreign Tax Relief. In general, taxation of foreign income is based on regulations for avoiding double taxation. A special tax relief called a Schachtelbegünstigung (international participation exemption) applies when a corporation holds at least 25%

of a foreign corporation's shares for more than two years. In this case, dividends from the foreign corporation that are distributed to the company, and any capital gains, are not subject to tax in Austria. To prevent abuse of this exemption, the Austrian Ministry of Finance has issued certain related regulations.

Investment Allowances. In the year of acquisition, an investment allowance of up to 9% of the cost of movable or immovable fixed assets is deductible. In addition, normal depreciation over the estimated useful life amounting to 100% of cost can be applied. If fixed assets (for which the investment allowance has been made) are disposed of within four years, the amount of the allowance relating to the disposed assets must be credited to income. After four years, the investment allowance becomes a free reserve and may be withdrawn without any tax penalty. The investment allowance set up for trucks and intangible assets is limited to 6% of the acquisition cost.

An investment allowance cannot be created for the purchase or lease of passenger cars or for used fixed assets that are transferred within related companies. There are very specific rules about what is considered a passenger car and what is deemed a truck. Generally an investment allowance can be created for typical trucks that cannot be used as passenger cars.

For assets with a useful life of at least eight years, an investment allowance of 12% is deductible if the acquisition or the construction was performed between June 1, 1996 and December 31, 1997. Otherwise, the allowance is 9%.

Tax Credits. A research and development allowance of 12% or, in certain circumstances 18%, of current expenditures for research or for the improvement of fixed assets is available if the research or improvement is declared to be of importance to the national economy by the Ministry of Economics. If patents or know-how are the result of research and development in Austria, the Ministry of Economics may confirm the importance on application. This allowance is mainly granted to industries.

Depreciation/Cost-Recovery Conventions/Accelerated Deductions

Depreciation is mandatory under the commercial law and, for tax purposes, is deductible for all assets used in carrying on a business if experience indicates that the useful life of the assets will exceed one year. Depreciation is allowed only for business assets.

Generally, the basis for depreciation is the original cost. Depreciation must be calculated using the straight-line method; therefore, annual depreciation is a fixed percentage of cost. Modifying the rate of depreciation is possible as a result of fundamental changes affecting the useful life of the asset. For passenger cars, the income tax law provides a fixed depreciation rate of 12.5%.

For buildings, the income tax law provides fixed depreciation rates, ranging from 2% to 4%, depending on the kind of building. Depreciation can begin once a building is completed. Movable assets that cost less than ATS 5,000 may be fully expensed in the year of acquisition.

In the year of acquisition or construction of fixed assets, the full amount of annual depreciation is allowable if the acquisition or construction is completed at least six months before the end of the fiscal year. If the acquisition or construction is completed within six months of the end of the business year, only 50% of the annual depreciation is allowable.

Generally, depreciation rates must be in accordance with the useful life of the assets. Following are some typical yearly depreciation rates:

Machinery	10%–20%
Computer equipment	20%–25%
Trucks	20%
Patents or rights	10%

In general practice, telecommunications equipment do not have a fixed depreciation rate. However, internationally accepted depreciation rates should be applicable in Austria.

Purchased software may be amortized over a life different from the equipment life. The standard software rate is 20%, although in some cases, it may be higher. The cost of self-developed software may not be capitalized under fixed assets.

Transfer Pricing Rules

Generally, the OECD transfer pricing rules are applicable in Austria and the fiscal authorities are increasingly seeking to enforce those rules.

Transfers of Patents, Trademarks and Software

The sale price or royalty paid for an intangible must be made at arm's length, and the intangible itself must benefit the user. Typical royalty rates are up to 5% of sales (turnover) for chemicals, pharmaceuticals and technical patents, and up to 1% of sales (turnover) for trademarks. In the software industry, royalty rates of 30% to 40% are used for services performed by a foreign group supplier.

Royalty payments are tax-deductible. Royalty payments made to countries with which Austria has a tax treaty are normally not subject to withholding tax. For non-treaty countries, a withholding tax of 20% applies.

Service Fees

Service fees are tax-deductible. There is no withholding tax on service fees paid to companies seated in treaty countries. Services performed by companies or individuals from non-treaty countries may be subject to a 20% withholding tax.

Value-Added Tax, Sales Tax and/or Other Pertinent Taxes

As a member of the EU, Austria follows the provisions of the European Community Sixth VAT Directive. Domestic telecommunications services (including those supplied by Austrian-resident foreign businesses) are subject to VAT at the standard rate of 20%. The VAT treatment of international telecommunications services is based on the revised EU VAT model, which took effect in Austria on April 1, 1997.

When supplied to consumers outside Austria, services provided by a telecommunications business located in Austria generally fall outside the scope of VAT. The only exceptions are services supplied to private individuals or unregistered persons located in other member states. Those supplies are subject to Austrian VAT at the standard rate.

Non-resident providers are not liable to register and account for Austrian VAT on supplies used and enjoyed by Austrian customers, providing those customers are taxable persons for VAT purposes. Depending on the VAT status of the customer, these business customers will self-account for VAT under the reverse-charge procedures.

When a non-EU provider makes supplies of services to private individuals to be used and enjoyed in Austria, the provider is required to register and account for Austrian VAT. For an overseas provider, it should be possible to limit Austrian VAT liability to supplies made to Austrian individuals that are effectively used and enjoyed in the EU. However, this may require the overseas provider to be registered for VAT purposes in many different EU member states. Alternatively, an overseas provider may choose to register in a single EU member state (e.g., Austria) in order to contract with all customers that are EU private individuals. The supplies made from the single EU registration to these customers would then be subject to local VAT in the member state of registration.

Access to the Internet is included within the definition of telecommunications, and the principles set out above apply equally to Internet service providers (ISPs).

Local and Provincial Taxes

There are no local income taxes.

For Additional Information, Contact:

Helmut Knotzinger
Tax Partner
Berggasse 31
Postfach 161
1092 Vienna
Austria
Telephone: 43 (1) 313 770
Fax: 43 (1) 313 776
E-mail: helmut_knotzinger@at.coopers.com

Rudolf Gamharter
Telecoms Senior Consultant
Rooseveltplatz 4-5
P.O. Box 60
A-1090 Vienna
Austria
Telephone: 43 (1) 406 61 81
Fax: 43 (1) 408 87 59
E-mail: rudolf_gamharter@at.coopers.com

Belgium

Telecommunications Tax Profile
by Ine Lejeune and Frank Dierckx
Tax Partners, Brussels

Overview of the Telecommunications Market

Historical Background

The Act of March 21, 1991, laid the groundwork for the transformation of the state-owned telecommunications company, the Régie des Télégraphes et des Téléphones (RTT), into an autonomous company, Belgacom. This law gave Belgacom the exclusive right to establish and maintain the public network and to provide basic and leased service.

In accordance with European Union (EU) directives, the provision of terminal equipment in Belgium was liberalized, but Belgacom retained the right to provide each user's first piece of equipment to be connected to the network (e.g., telephones, modems and PBXs). Competition was also authorized for packet-switched data services. In 1994 the markets for mobile telephony and satellite communications were opened. Belgium has scheduled a series of reforms aimed at achieving full competition in all telecommunications sectors by 1998.

Current Status

In 1995 the Belgian telecommunications market was valued at about BEF132 billion. In 1996 it was estimated at BEF162 billion, with an expected annual growth rate of 22%. Growth has been particularly rapid in wireless services. In 1996 the Belgian government sold 50% less one share of Belgacom to ADSB Telecommunications B.V., which is a Dutch company incorporated among Ameritech, TeleDanmark A/S and Singapore Telecom. This transaction, which was qualified by the government as a strategic consolidation, was intended to speed the modernization of Belgacom.

Telenet, a joint venture of U S WEST International, a group of Flemish cable companies and a financing group, was granted a license in March 1997 to provide telephony, Internet access and data services, and began operations later in the year. The partners plan to invest US$1.5 billion in the cable networks of northern Belgium in order to challenge Belgacom for a share of the country's voice telephony market in 1998.

Two new private operators were awarded global system for mobile communications (GSM) licenses in 1996 to build competitive mobile communications networks. Proximus (formerly known as Belgacom Mobile) is a joint venture between Belgacom and AirTouch Belgium, a subsidiary of AirTouch Communications, a U.S. company. The second provider, Mobistar, is a joint venture of France Telecom, Telindus (a Belgian communications equipment manufacturer) and other Belgian partners.

Belgacom has operated national paging networks for several years. In early 1995 RAM Mobile Data (a subsidiary of Bell-South Mobile and France Telecom Mobiles International) became the first competitor to Belgacom in wireless mobile data services. Today Belgacom still holds a monopoly on telex systems, installation and maintenance of state-owned telecommunications equipment, and other activities mentioned in the 1991 telecommunications legislation. All telecoms services not mentioned in that legislation can be provided by private operators.

Copper, coaxial cables and fiber optic cable are all used in transmission. Use of fiber optic is growing (from 5% of the total network in 1992 to 8% in 1996), but still limited, because of costs, to links between central switches. The introduction of synchronous digital hierarchy in the transport network significantly improves the network quality. The Telenet project in northern Belgium will use fiber optics to create a backbone ring of approximately 650 kilometers.

Current Liberalization Status

In the World Trade Organization (WTO) negotiations of February 1997, Belgium committed to full liberalization by 1998 and full adherence to a common set of regulatory principles.

Type of Service	Degree of Liberalization	Key Legislation	Date of Actual or Expected Liberalization
Local, Long Distance and International	Fully liberalized	Ministerial Decree of November 25, 1996 Act of March 21, 1991 European Council: ONP Directive 90/387/EEC European Commission: Directive on competition in telecoms services 90/388/EEC	1998
Cellular	Fully liberalized	Royal Decree of March 7, 1995 Act of March 21, 1991 European Council: ONP Directive 90/387/EEC European Commission: Directive on competition in telecoms services 90/388/EEC European Council resolution of September 14, 1990	1994
Paging	Fully liberalized	Ministerial Decree of November 25, 1996 Act of March 21, 1991	1996
Value-added	Liberalized	Ministerial Decree of November 25, 1996 Act of March 21, 1991 European Council: ONP Directive 90/387/EEC European Commission: Directive on competition in telecoms services 90/388/EEC	1996

Competitive Environment

Type of Service	Entire Market		Top Two Players		
	Market Size	Number of Players	Names	Annual Revenue	Ownership
Local and Long Distance	BEF72.621 billion	1	Belgacom	BEF72.621 billion	Government (49.9%) and private ownership (50.1%)
International	BEF21.620 billion	1	Belgacom	BEF21.620 billion	Government (49.9%) and private ownership (50.1%)
Cellular	BEF16.541 billion	2	Proximus	BEF15.848 billion	Belgacom and AirTouch Belgium
			Mobistar	BEF693 million	France Telecom Mobiles International (57%), and various Belgian investment and holding companies
Paging	BEF1.2 billion	1	Belgacom	BEF1.2 billion	Government (49.9%) and private ownership (50.1%)
Value-added	BEF35.705 billion	11	Belgacom	BEF27.401 billion	Government (49.9%) and private ownership (50.1%)
			British Telecom Belgium	BEF1.5 billion	BT

Sources: Belgian National Bank; European Information Technology Observatory, 1996 report; Belgacom 1996 yearbook; Mobistar 1996 yearbook; annual reports of various providers.

Licensing Requirements

In compliance with EU directives requiring separation of tele-communications operations from regulatory activities, Belgium created a new organization to regulate and control telecommunications, the Belgian Institute of Post and Telecommunications (BIPT). The BIPT's role is to ensure that EU regulations are correctly implemented, to set technical standards and to oversee equipment approvals. Certain services, including those utilizing radio communications frequencies or wirelines, must obtain licenses from the BIPT. All licenses are nationwide, unless otherwise requested by the operator. Other types of operators are not required to obtain licenses; rather they must notify the BIPT of the services they intend to render at least two months before commencing service. Additional licenses are expected to be granted for all types of services.

Potential for Foreign Ownerships/Relationships

As a result of the move toward liberalization of telecommunications services, there is now serious competition among multi-national telecommunications companies to provide service and obtain licenses. There are no limitations on the percentage of a telecommunications business that can be owned by a foreign company.

Potential for Upcoming Liberalization/Investment Opportunities

In line with EU directives, Belgium allows alternative telecoms network operators, including cable companies, to offer non-voice telephony services over their own infrastructure. Telenet plans to install a digital overlay network on top of the existing TV cable infrastructure with the aim of offering interactive entertainment services in northern Belgium. Telenet will pursue a share of the country's voice telephony market in 1998.

Likely targets for investment in the near future include residential service, electronic commerce applications, and Internet access provision.

Forms of Doing Business

Permanent Establishment

In general, a foreign company with a permanent establishment in Belgium will be taxed on the profits that can be attributed to the permanent establishment. Belgian tax law uses a definition of permanent establishment (PE) that broadly corresponds to that used in the OECD Model Convention: a fixed place of business through which the business of an enterprise is wholly or partly carried on. Telecommunications services can cover a broad range of activities, which may or may not constitute PEs. Some examples follow:

- When a foreign company renders long-distance telephone services to local customers, as long as the services are rendered from abroad without any local presence or advertising in Belgium, the foreign company is not taxed on the profits generated by this activity. However, the mere presence of, for instance, a modem through which the services were rendered could trigger taxation in Belgium. Indeed, the mere presence of vending machines and other automated devices could, in certain circumstances, be regarded as a PE.

- The profits generated by the licensing of technology and know-how by a foreign company to a local company or by the leasing of telecommunications equipment to a local company will not be taxed in Belgium, provided the activity is limited to licensing service in the strict sense of the word and that it is not carried on through a fixed place of business.

- A foreign company that renders technical assistance, network management services and technological services, including operator services, to a local company in exchange for service fees constitutes a PE if the employees of the foreign company stay in Belgium for a certain period (usually more than six months per year). Although the foreign company may have no fixed place of business in Belgium, the presence of its employees rendering services to a local company could trigger taxation if the employees are empowered to sign contracts on behalf of the foreign company.

- A foreign company providing call reorganization and turn-around services does not have a PE if certain conditions are met (e.g., the local distributor is not part of the foreign company's group and this distributor acts only as an agent of the company).

- Because of the recent accelerated development of Internet access services, it is still unclear how the authorities will tax the income derived from this activity.

- A construction or installation project will constitute a PE if the work exceeds a fixed period (generally 6 to 12 months), which can vary according to a tax treaty.

- Having a website located on a server outside Belgium to which Belgian customers have access should not give rise to taxation. By contrast, the physical presence of a server in Belgium would probably be regarded as a PE, unless it were used only for preparatory or auxiliary activities.

If a foreign telecommunications company does not have a PE, Belgium is not entitled to levy income tax on the fees paid to the company. However, if the fees are regarded as royalties, they will be subject to withholding tax at a rate of 15%, which may be reduced by a tax treaty.

A foreign company is considered as having a PE for VAT purposes when it has a location in Belgium (e.g., an office or warehouse) that is managed by a person who can legally bind customers or suppliers of the foreign company and when the company performs taxable transactions for VAT in Belgium.

Business Entities

Local Branch and Locally Incorporated Subsidiary of a Foreign Company. Generally, foreign investors can operate through a Belgian company (by purchasing an existing one or by incorporating one), or through a foreign company having a branch in Belgium. Neither a local branch nor a locally incorporated subsidiary of a foreign company may file a consolidated tax return. The table below compares these two types of business entities.

There are several corporate forms possible, in three general categories: limited liability companies, partnerships with legal personality and partnerships without legal personality. The first two categories are taxed at the entity level, and their shareholders have limited liability. The third category differs in that taxation is levied at the partner level and the partners have unlimited liability with respect to the partnership activity.

Joint Venture. A joint venture may be organized as either a company or a partnership. If a joint venture is organized as a company, it is subject to the same tax regulations as any other company. It must, for example, file a resident corporate income tax return. If a joint venture is organized as a partnership without legal personality, it is considered a pass-through entity. As a result, the partners are required to file individual tax returns; foreign partners, because they are considered as having permanent establishment, must file non-resident tax returns. Government approval is not required to create a joint venture in the telecommunications sector; however, the joint venture must inform the BIPT of the services it intends to render.

The taxable basis of branches and subsidiaries is determined according to the same rules. The starting point for determining their taxable basis is their profit as reflected in annual accounts. Some adjustments are nevertheless made in order to bring the accounting figures into line with the tax rules (e.g., some costs are considered non-deductible, such as restaurant and reception costs up to 50% and car costs up to 25%).

If a branch fails to keep probative financial records (for instance, when no turnover is recorded in its accounts because the branch acts as a cost center), the Belgian income tax code provides for a minimum taxable amount, depending on the type of activity carried out by the branch. In practice, the tax authorities often determine the taxable basis as follows: costs + 10% + non-deductible expenses. However, this taxable basis cannot be less than the higher of BEF300,000 per person employed or BEF400,000 as an absolute minimum.

When a foreign company operates in Belgium through several permanent establishments, only one tax return must be filed covering the profits and losses deriving from all the Belgian operations. As a result, profits deriving from a PE are offsettable against the losses incurred by another.

	Locally Incorporated Subsidiary of a Foreign Company	Local Branch of a Foreign Company
Taxation in Belgium	Taxed on its worldwide income	Taxed on both the Belgian-sourced income and the foreign-sourced income that is attributable to the Belgian business
Tax Rate	40.17% There is a 25% withholding tax on dividends distributed to the foreign parent (which can be reduced or voided according to the EC Parent-Subsidiary Directive or a tax treaty).	40.17% There is no withholding tax on after-tax income repatriated by a branch to its head office.
Capital Duty	A 0.5% capital duty is levied on the share capital of the subsidiary.	No capital duty is levied.
Liability	For a limited liability company, liability is limited to the shareholders' contributions.	The net assets of the foreign parent company are at risk.
Other Non-Tax Considerations	A notarial deed incorporates the company. The business's articles of incorporation and annual financial statements must be published.	No notarial deed is needed. The following documents or decisions must be published: —the head office's articles of association —the company's annual accounts —any decision of the board to open a branch

Local Funding Alternatives

Debt versus Equity

The following rules apply when funding a Belgian company:

- A 15% withholding tax is levied on the interest paid by Belgian companies, unless a specific exemption applies.

- If the acquisition of the target is performed with funds obtained from outside the group, it is preferable that these funds come from a Belgian bank, rather than a foreign parent company. Interest paid to Belgian banks is fully exempt from withholding tax, whereas interest paid to a foreign parent company rarely benefits from such an exemption (unless otherwise provided by treaty).

- If a parent company offers a guarantee for a loan granted by a bank, any costs relating to that guarantee that are charged to the Belgian company are tax-deductible insofar as these costs are at arm's length.

- Exchange gains are taxable and exchange losses are tax-deductible. There are no distinctions between shareholder debt or third-party debt. However, the tax authorities have generally not applied this rule to exchange gains or losses realized on a "loan" existing between a foreign head office and its permanent establishment. In such a case, exchange losses are not tax-deductible and exchange gains are not taxable.

Deductibility of Interest Payments. Interest paid on acquisition debt is deductible if it does not exceed the market rate, considering the characteristics of the loan and the debtor's financial situation. However, when interest is paid on a debt due to a member of the board of directors or to another individual shareholder, it is treated as a dividend and, therefore, is not deductible to the extent that (a) the interest rate exceeds the market rate, or (b) the total amount of the loan granted by this director/shareholder exceeds the paid-in capital at the end of the book year increased by retained earnings already taxed at the beginning of the book year (which results in roughly a 1-to-1 debt-to-equity ratio for directors' and shareholders' loans). This debt-to-equity ratio does not apply to interest paid to Belgian resident companies or to most companies with whom Belgium has tax treaties.

Interest is deductible regardless of the source of the funds. The source of debt may be important if the lender is located in a tax-haven country or if it benefits from a tax regime on the interest that is notably more advantageous than the Belgian regime. Interest paid to such lenders is tax-deductible only if the taxpayer can show that (a) the loans are true and sincere and (b) the interest does not exceed an arm's-length rate.

Debt-to-Equity Ratio. With the exception of interest paid to a director or an individual shareholder as discussed above, there are no general debt-to-equity requirements under Belgian law. Highly leveraged investments are preferable because of the tax-deductibility of interest charges and the lack of capital duty on loans (as compared to the 0.5% capital duty on capital contributions). However, interest payments are considered non-deductible expenses when either of the following is true:

- The beneficiary of the interest is not subject to income tax.

- The beneficiary is subject to income tax and it benefits from a notably more advantageous tax regime than the Belgian regime, and the interest relates to the amount of a loan in excess of a certain threshold (seven times the sum of the paid-up capital at the end of the book year and the taxed reserves at the beginning of the book year).

Exchange Controls

There are no exchange controls in Belgium.

Business Acquisitions and Dispositions

Capital Contributions into an Existing Local Entity

A capital contribution into a local entity is subject to a 0.5% capital duty on the company's share capital. Except for contributions in the form of various services, there is no limit on the tangibles and intangibles that can be contributed into the capital of a Belgian company by a foreign or Belgian entity. The use of any of the tax attributes in the local entity (e.g., net operating losses) would not be limited as a consequence of a capital contribution by a foreign company.

Pre-operating goods and services can either be contributed to a Belgian entity or bought by the entity. The tax authorities may not regard the contribution of an intangible as the licensing of an intangible subject to withholding tax.

Purchase or Sale of Shares in a Local Entity

In general, capital gains realized by resident individuals on the sale of shares in a local entity, outside the performance of an occupational activity, are tax-exempt. However, these gains may be taxed if, at any time during the five years preceding the sale, a resident individual owned, directly or indirectly, a share of more than 25% of the company whose shares were being sold. In this case, the capital gains will be subject to tax at the rate of 16.5%, plus municipal tax and an additional crisis contribution tax. Capital gains realized by resident companies on the sale of shares in a local entity are, in principle, fully tax-exempt, even if the shares are sold to foreign entities.

Under Belgium's many tax treaties, capital gains realized by non-resident sellers (both individuals and companies) on the sale of shares in a local company are taxable only in the seller's country. Even if the seller resided in a non-treaty country, the seller would not be subject to tax in Belgium. When a foreign company purchases shares, the basis in the assets remains unchanged. There is no mechanism that would allow a foreign company to consider the purchase of shares as a purchase of assets for local tax purposes. With the exception of the 25% rule for individual shareholders, the tax regime applicable to a minority or majority sale of shares is similar.

Purchase or Sale of Assets

The acquisition of a Belgian company or an existing business in Belgium can also be accomplished by a purchase of its underlying assets. The assets purchased are depreciable on a stepped-up basis. Interest incurred on borrowings to finance the purchase of the assets may generally be deducted from the taxable basis.

The tax attributes of the selling company remain with the seller. Any capital gain realized on the resale of the assets would be taxed in Belgium. A spread taxation applies, under certain conditions, to capital gains realized on tangible and intangible fixed assets that are held for business purposes for more than five years prior to the transfer. VAT (or, for real estate not qualifying for VAT, a registration duty) is levied on the amount paid for the asset acquisition. An exemption may be available in the case of the sale of a department or an entire enterprise.

The price paid is allocated to the acquired assets. Assets must be valued at their acquisition price. If no separation is made between the assets, an objective criterion will have to be made to allocate the price (e.g., fair market value). Tangible assets are generally depreciable over their useful life. Intangible assets, including goodwill, are depreciated over a period of more than five years on a straight-line basis.

Transactions must be negotiated on arm's-length terms. Some anti-avoidance measures are applicable when a resident company grants abnormal benefits to other foreign entities or when one resident company grants such benefits to another resident company that effectively does not pay income tax.

Capital gains realized on the sale of a participation in a partnership (i.e., a transparent entity) are taxable at the level of the seller. Profits and losses deriving from the partnership's activity are considered as immediately realized (and thus taxable) at the level of its partners.

The advantages and disadvantages of purchasing assets versus shares are summarized in the table below.

Asset Acquisition	Share Acquisition
Advantages	**Advantages**
The assets purchased are depreciable.	No VAT or registration duty is levied on the sale of shares.
Interest incurred on borrowings to finance the purchase of assets can generally be deducted from the taxable basis.	Interest incurred on borrowings to finance the purchase of shares can generally be deducted from the taxable basis of the acquiring entity, with some exceptions (e.g., if the shares are held for less than one year).
Future depreciation is on a stepped-up basis.	The capital gain realized on the resale share is, in principle, tax-exempt.
	Beneficial tax attributes can be carried over.
Disadvantages	**Disadvantages**
The capital gain realized on the resale of assets is taxed.	Shares cannot be depreciated.
Capital losses realized on the resale of assets are tax-deductible.	Basis in assets remains unchanged.
Tax attributes of the selling company stay with the seller.	Capital losses realized on the sale of shares are not tax-deductible.
VAT, or registration duty for real estate, is levied on the amount paid for the acquisition of assets (exemption may be available in the case of a transfer of a department or an enterprise).	A stock exchange tax is levied if the shares purchased are listed on the stock exchange.
	Authorization may be required before a company's shares can be purchased (e.g., in a takeover bid).

Start-up Business Issues

Pre-operating Losses and Start-up/ Construction Costs

Only the costs that result in a capital gain can be capitalized. All other costs must be deducted immediately. In general, only costs incurred by Belgian companies are tax-deductible. However, in certain circumstances, foreign research and development (R&D) expenses can be deducted.

A foreign company that effects taxable transactions for VAT purposes in Belgium must register for VAT. If a foreign company has a permanent establishment for VAT purposes, it must apply for a VAT identification number. When a foreign company has no permanent establishment in Belgium, it must generally appoint a tax representative. Consequently, a foreign company can recover the input VAT by reporting it on its Belgian VAT return, if it is a taxable person entitled to recover input VAT.

A foreign company that does not effect any taxable transactions in Belgium can recover the VAT paid on supplies of goods or services it uses for its economic activity. The refund claim must be received by the tax authorities within five years of the date the tax was due.

VAT is either completely or partially not deductible for certain costs (e.g., tobacco products, alcoholic drinks, accommodations, meals and beverages, entertainment and motor vehicles). Only taxable persons carrying out VATable transactions can deduct the VAT paid or claim a refund. If a taxable person does not realize a high turnover at the beginning of the operating phase, and, consequently, the amount of VAT charged is much lower than the amount of VAT deductible, the taxable person can recover the whole amount of the difference between VAT charged and VAT deductible. Thus, VAT paid during that period on the purchase of goods and services used for start-up purposes is recoverable. Even when a company decides not to proceed to the operating phase, the company may have the right to recover the VAT charged on the supply of goods or services relating to the preparations for that economic activity.

No VAT should be charged by a supplier of works of immovable property (this relates mainly to the construction, transformation, demolition, development, repair and maintenance of real estate), owing to a reverse-charge mechanism. This means that if a recipient of services (e.g., a telecommunications company) is registered for VAT purposes and files periodic VAT returns, it must pay the VAT due by reporting it on its Belgian VAT return. VAT can be deducted by reporting it on the same VAT return. This means that no pre-financing of VAT will arise.

Customs Duties and VAT

Most goods imported into Belgium from outside the EU are subject to customs duty and import VAT. Duty is normally payable on the cost, insurance and freight (CIF) value of the goods at the place of importation. Import VAT is payable on the duty-inclusive value of the goods, although VAT-registered traders can usually obtain a refund of the VAT.

The current import duty rates for a sample of telecommunications goods originating in third countries (e.g., the United States) are given below. Preferential import duties may apply to these products when they originate in countries that have passed an association convention with the EU. When they originate in certain developing countries, a zero duty rate may apply.

Line telephone sets with cordless handsets	3.8%
Videophones	7%
Other telephone sets	3.8%
Facsimile machines	3.8%
Teleprinters	3.8%
Telephonic or telegraphic switching apparatus	3.8%
Other apparatus for carrier line systems	2.3%
Other apparatus for digital line systems	3.8%
Building-entry telephone systems	3.8%

Customs duties on some items of equipment were already being reduced under the General Agreement on Tariffs and Trade (GATT). However, over the next few years, duty rates are scheduled to be reduced further under the Information Technology Agreement (ITA) signed in March 1997. The ITA also extends the range of goods subject to duty-rate reductions. As a signatory to the ITA, the EU has agreed to cut tariffs on imports of computers and computer equipment, software, telecommunications and networking equipment to zero in four equal installments. The first reduction took place on July 1, 1997, and further reductions are to take effect on January 1 of each year through 2000. Although the ITA will cut the cost of importing many products, the convergence of technologies in the computing, electronics and telecommunications sectors is likely to lead to disputes over the tariff classification of some equipment and affect the availability and/or phasing of duty reductions under the ITA.

A wide variety of reliefs from customs duty (and import VAT) can be claimed in various circumstances (e.g., goods imported for processing and re-export and goods imported temporarily). There is also a relief available for capital goods and equipment, provided the goods are imported by a business on the transfer of its activities to Belgium.

Raw materials or components that are not available, or not available in sufficient quantities, within the EU may be eligible for a complete or partial suspension of duty, provided the non-availability can be demonstrated to the satisfaction of the Commission of the European Communities in Brussels.

Goods may be subject to anti-dumping or countervailing duty if, for example, the EU considers they are being imported into the EU at prices substantially lower than their normal values. Anti-dumping and countervailing duties are chargeable in addition to, and independent of, any other duty to which the imported goods are liable.

No distinction is made between regular telephony and Internet telephony for the purposes of VAT.

Loss Carryovers

Losses may be offset against taxable income with no limits in time or amount. They may not be carried back. Neither losses nor investment deductions can be carried forward if there is a change in the control of a company unless the change is justified for financial or economic reasons. Such reason is deemed to exist if there is a change of control in a company with even a partial preservation of employment and of the business exercised before the change in control (a change from wireline to cellular should not be regarded as a change of activity). A change in control caused by the transfer of shares or managers within the same consolidated group would not jeopardize the carryforward of losses.

Operating Considerations

Corporate Income Taxes

Resident companies are taxed at the standard corporate tax rate of 39%. Additionally, there is a 3% crisis contribution, which results in a total tax rate of 40.17% (at the time of publication, it was not known for how long this crisis contribution would continue to be levied). Companies whose taxable profits are under BEF13 million may be taxed at a reduced rate.

Non-resident companies are subject to the same standard corporate tax rate as resident companies. However, no deduction may be claimed for interest or royalties paid by a branch to its foreign home office or to another branch of the same company (except when funds used in Belgium are raised by a foreign company or branch from a third-party lender).

Capital Gains Taxes

Capital gains realized on the sale of assets or reflected in a company's accounts are subject to the standard corporate tax rate. A roll-over regime is, however, applicable in some circum-stances. Capital gains on shares are tax-free. Capital losses realized on a sale of assets are tax-deductible. Capital losses or write-offs on shares are generally not deductible.

Tax Holidays and Exemptions

The following tax incentives are provided in Belgian law:

• Under special incentive laws, the costs related to the acquisition of assets (including telecoms assets) may be depreciated at twice the normal depreciation rate for a limited number of years.

• A company may, under certain conditions, claim an investment deduction amounting to a certain percentage of the acquisition or investment value. Incentives such as a lower interest rate, subsidies and accelerated depreciation may be offered to companies located in certain areas.

• Scientific research is encouraged through an exemption from corporate tax equal to BEF440,000 per additional person hired for qualifying work.

Depreciation/Cost-Recovery Conventions/Accelerated Deductions

With the exception of land, most tangible and intangible assets are depreciable. Software must be recorded by a company as an asset in its balance sheet if it contributes to the business and has a future economic use. In this case, the software is depreciated separately from its related equipment. Research and development costs, including software development, can also, under certain conditions, be recorded as assets and be depreciated. Intangible goods must be amortized over a period of at least five years, using the straight-line method. Tangible assets can be depreciated using either the straight-line or the declining-balance methods.

The original acquisition cost is generally the basis for depreciation, and the depreciation rate should be based on the normal useful life of the assets. The tax authorities recommend depreciation rates (e.g., the annual depreciation rate for real estate is generally between 3% to 5% of the real property investment value; for machinery and equipment, the recommended rates are 10%, 25% or 33%). There are no differences in the depreciation rules for different types of telecommunications companies. In the context of a network, assets are considered to be placed in service when they are operational and running.

In general, advertising and marketing costs incurred in order to attract customers are fully tax-deductible, including those paid directly or indirectly through sales agents. However, it should be noted that some costs, such as gifts and restaurant and reception costs, are only 50%-tax-deductible.

Transfer Pricing Rules

Belgium has few specific transfer pricing provisions. In general, arm's-length principles must be followed. If a company established in Belgium is directly or indirectly dependent on a foreign company, all abnormal transfers of profits to the foreign company will be added to the net taxable income of the Belgian company. This rule also applies to abnormal transfers of profits to any other company that receives a significantly more favorable tax treatment than a Belgian company. Interest, royalties and service fees paid to such companies are not deductible as business expenses unless they can be shown to correspond to a real and fair business transaction.

Belgium recently created a fiscal infrastructure for service centers that allows service charges between grouped companies to be pre-approved on an arm's-length basis. For the charges to qualify, the service centers must be active in the field of intellectual services (commercial activities are excluded), such as preparatory or auxiliary activities or the transmission of information to clients. Service centers, which are entities that provide support services to related companies and which often use telecoms services, are subject to the standard corporate income tax, but the taxable basis is determined as a percentage of operating expenses (from 5% to 15% for a cost-plus system) or of sales (5% for a resale-minus system).

In the past, the tax authorities mostly performed consistency controls verifying whether the inter company pricing policy within Belgian companies was in line with the policy applicable to other companies of the group. But the authorities are expected to begin performing more in-depth investigations in the near future.

Transfers of Patents, Trademarks and Software

Patents, trademarks and software licensing fees are tax-deductible as business expenses provided they are directly or closely connected with the conduct of business (i.e., they are borne to obtain or maintain taxable business income). If these payments qualify as royalties, they will be subject to a 15% withholding tax, which may be reduced by a tax treaty. In general, the term "royalty" refers to any payment made for the use of, or the right to use, copyrights, industrial property rights, equipment or know-how.

Belgian law contains anti-avoidance provisions relating to royalties and service fees paid directly or indirectly to foreign companies that are not liable to income tax. Royalties and services fees that are subject to more favorable tax treatment than in Belgium are not tax-deductible, unless the taxpayer shows that the payments correspond to normal business transactions and that the amounts are not abnormally high. There are no restrictions imposed on the licensing of technology to a local company for a royalty fee.

Because of the variety of telecommunications products and services that have developed in recent years (e.g., transmission of information by means of magnetic tape or laser disc), it has become more and more difficult to distinguish a sale from a licensing contract. A transfer of technology is likely to be viewed as a sale if all rights to the underlying asset are transferred. In this case, the payment will be regarded as commercial income in accordance with the OECD Model Convention. On the other hand, a transfer is likely to be seen as a transaction under a license contract if the licensee has limited rights (in the form, for instance, of a contract for a limited period of time or restrictions on the licensee of transferring rights).

Service Fees

If service fees qualify as royalties, they will be subject to a 15% withholding tax, which may be reduced by a tax treaty. This withholding tax is levied when the royalties are paid by a Belgian resident, regardless of where the services are rendered. Service fees are subject to the standard income tax rules as described above, whether the service takes place in or out of Belgium.

Value-Added Tax, Sales Tax and/or Other Pertinent Taxes

VAT legislation in Belgium follows the provisions of the European Community Sixth VAT Directive.

Domestic telecommunications services (including those supplied by Belgian-resident foreign businesses) are subject to VAT at the standard rate of 21%. The VAT treatment of international telecommunications services is based on the revised EU VAT model, which took effect in Belgium on June 1, 1997.

Services supplied internationally by a telecommunications business located in Belgium are generally not subject to Belgian VAT when they are supplied to anyone located outside Belgium. The only exceptions are services supplied to private individuals or unregistered persons located in other member states. Those supplies are subject to Belgian VAT at the standard rate.

Non-resident providers are not liable to register and account for Belgian VAT on supplies used by Belgian customers, provided those customers are taxable persons for VAT purposes. These customers are required to self-account for VAT under reverse-charge procedures.

When a non-resident provider makes supplies of services to private individuals, without taking into account whether the services are to be used in Belgium, the provider is required to register and account for Belgian VAT. For an overseas provider, it should be possible to limit the Belgian VAT liability to supplies made to Belgian individuals for use in the EU. However, this may then require the overseas provider to be registered for VAT purposes in many different EU-member states. Alternatively, an overseas provider may choose to register in a single EU-member state (e.g., Belgium), in order to contract with all customers who are EU private individuals. The supplies made from the single EU registration to these customers will then be subject to local VAT in the member state of registration.

Access to the Internet is included within the definition of telecommunications, and the principles set out above apply equally to Internet service providers.

Local and Provincial Taxes

There are no significant local income taxes.

For Additional Information, Contact:

Frank Dierckx
Tax Partner
and
Ine Lejeune
Tax Partner
and
Eric Van Den Rul
Telecoms Consulting Director
Marcel Thiry Court
Avenue Marcel Thiry 216
B-1200 Brussels
Belgium
Telephone: 32 (2) 774 43 24
Fax: 32 (2) 774 42 99
E-mail: frank_dierckx@be.coopers.com
         ine_lejeune@be.coopers.com
         eric_vandenrul@be.coopers.com

Bulgaria

Rapidly changing market conditions and/or legislative developments preclude the possibility of offering a comprehensive profile on Bulgaria for this edition. Tax and telecommunications specialists in our Sofia office are fully versed in current practices and conditions in Bulgaria and can provide assistance to clients regarding investment opportunities and tax requirements. Please contact the representatives listed for further information.

For Additional Information, Contact:

Irina Tsvetkova
C&L Tax Director
and
Boryana Ventcharska
Lawyer & Tax Advisor
2A, Saborna Street
1000 Sofia
Bulgaria
Telephone: 359 (2) 91003
Fax: 359 (2) 9803 228
E-mail: Irina_Tsvetkova@bg.coopers.com
           Boryana_Ventcharska@bg.coopers.com

Czech Republic

Telecommunications Tax Profile
by Monika Svobodová
Tax Partner, Prague

Overview of the Telecommunications Market

Historical Background

The telecommunications industry operates according to the guidelines set forth in the Telecommunications Act, which was originally passed in 1964 and updated in 1994. A new telecommunications law is expected to be issued in 1998 in response to the liberalization of the telecommunications industry in the European Union (EU). The Czech Republic is an associate member of the EU and has applied for full membership.

SPT Telecom, a.s., which is the main telecommunications provider, was founded on January 1, 1994 when Czech Post and Telecommunications, the state telecommunications and post company, was divided and its telecommunications part was transferred into a joint-stock company. Currently, 51% of all shares are owned by the National Property Fund, which is the government's property administrator. TelSource, which is a Swiss/Dutch consortium composed of PTT Telecom Netherlands and Swisscom (formerly Swiss Telecom PTT), paid US$1.45 billion to acquire a 27% stake in SPT Telecom. The remaining 22% is held by various other investors.

Current Status

SPT Telecom has been granted an exclusive license to provide long-distance and international voice service until December 31, 2000. It is also the main provider of all other telecommunications services, including multimedia network services (e.g., data network for intranet and wide area network (WAN) and Internet access.

The cellular sector was liberalized in 1996. SPT Telecom holds a 51% stake in EuroTel a.s., which operates both global system for mobile communications (GSM) and Nordic mobile telephone (NMT) phone services. Radiomobil, the second GSM operator, began operations in September 1996. As of July 1997, the two firms had a total of about 365,000 subscribers. Radiomobil and EuroTel have achieved about 90% coverage of the Czech Republic and now compete in services and price categories. Call division multiple access (CDMA) and time division multiple access (TDMA) systems are not present in the Czech Republic.

Almost all fixed lines are provided and serviced by SPT Telecom. SPT Telecom currently has 2.13 million fixed lines in place and is planning on investing CZK (Czech Koruna) 136 billion to install 2 million new lines over the next three years. There are currently 34 lines per 100 people. Firms that compete with SPT Telecom including Dattel, a.s., which focuses primarily on Prague with 20,000 lines, and Opatel face substantial difficulties in setting up their own networks. SPT's competitors have thus far mostly received licenses to operate in the less developed areas of the Czech Republic.

SPT Telecom has launched an ambitious program of digitalization and network development to improve the quality of its services. SPT Telecom aims to achieve 80% digitalization by the end of the century. As of September 1996, 13 central and 131 local digital exchanges had been installed or modernized. At the end of 1996, approximately 33% of the telecommunications network was digitalized, which is a significant increase from the end of 1995, when it was only 15%.

SPT Telecom is focusing much of its attention on enhancing value-added services since it faces stiff competition in this area. Value-added services are not regulated, and although SPT Telecom is relatively far ahead of its competitors, the fight for market share could be the first serious test of its competitiveness. Transgas, a gas distributor, gives its customers access to Global One's data services via its private network. Licenses for data services are also held by AliaTel, a.s., a joint venture of several electrical utility companies, and GiTy, a.s. In addition to SPT Telecom, Internet access is being provided by CESNET; EUNet (which is a name used by the company Internet CZ, s.r.o., which has exclusive rights to operate the European Internet network EUNet; PVT, a.s. and Czech On Line, a.s. The size of the Internet market has been estimated at between 300,000 and 450,000 users. The increasing number of competitors in this sector has helped to significantly improve the quality of Internet access.

The only provider of paging services utilizing the RDS (radio data system) standard is Radiokontakt Operator, a.s., a joint venture between Czech Radiocommunications and Télédiffusion de France. A second license was recently issued to Multitone CZ, s.r.o., which planned to begin operations in February 1998. The ERMES (European radio messaging system) paging system was implemented in the fourth quarter of 1997 in Prague by Radiokontakt Operator.

Telecommunications revenues for SPT Telecom, mobile telecommunications providers and Internet providers are growing rapidly. For SPT Telecom, this is the result of network expansion, price increases and monopoly protection that will last until the end of the year 2000. SPT Telecom revenues grew 26% between 1995 and 1996. In 1995, the revenues were CZK 25 billion and in 1996 they were CZK 32 billion. For the first nine months of 1997, SPT revenues were CZK 29 billion, which represented a growth of 24% compared to the same period in the prior year.

Current Liberalization Status

The Czech Republic has made a full commitment to the regulatory principles and guidelines of the World Trade Organization (WTO), and liberalization of a limited range of services is expected to occur between 1998 and 2002.

Type of Service	Degree of Liberalization	Key Legislation	Date of Actual or Expected Liberalization	Comments
Local	Partially liberalized	Telecommunications Act 1964 and 1994	2001	A new telecommunications law is being prepared, and is expected to be issued in 1998.
Long Distance	Monopoly	Telecommunications Act 1964 and 1994	2001	SPT Telecom has a monopoly on long-distance voice service until December 31, 2000.
International	Monopoly	Telecommunications Act 1964 and 1994	2001	SPT Telecom has a monopoly on international voice service until December 31, 2000.
Cellular	Deregulated	Telecommunications Act 1964 and 1994	1994	
Paging	Deregulated	Telecommunications Act 1964 and 1994	1994	
Value-added	Deregulated	Telecommunications Act 1964 and 1994	1994	

Competitive Environment

Competition exists in all sectors of the telecommunications industry except for long distance and international voice communications. While the competitive environment in the other sectors is not fully developed, it is very intense—especially in the cellular sector. In the paging sector, a second competitor has recently received a license. There is also competition among Internet providers.

Type of Service	Entire Market*	Top Two Players		
	Number of Players	Names	Annual Revenue (1996)	Ownership
Local	7	SPT Telecom	CZK 32 billion**	National Property Fund (51%), TelSource (27%) and private investors (22%)
		Dattel	CZK 100 million	CETI CR, a.s. and Nuon International***
Long Distance	1	SPT Telecom	(See above)	National Property Fund (51%), TelSource (27%) and private investors (22%)
International	1	SPT Telecom	(See above)	National Property Fund (51%), TelSource (27%) and private investors (22%)
Cellular	2	EuroTel	Not available****	SPT Telecom (51%), U S WEST Media Group (24.5%) and Bell Atlantic International (24.5%)
		Radiomobil	Not available****	Czech Radiocommunications (51%) and TMobil (49%)
Paging	2 (the second license was just granted recently)	Radiokontakt Operator	CZK 138 million	Czech Radiocommunications (34.02%) and Télédiffusion de France (62.98%)

Sources: Annual reports and publicly issued financial results from *Obchodní vestník*.

* Revenue figures are not available.

** Combined revenues for local, long-distance and international services.

*** Ownership percentages are not available.

**** Mobile communication providers do not announce their financial results.

Licensing Requirements

Until the end of 1997, the provision of any telecommunications service required a license from the Czech Telecommunications Office (Ceský telekomunikaoní úrad, or CTU), which is part of the Ministry of Transport and Communications. Beginning in 1998, licenses to provide Internet access were no longer required. Until December 31, 2000, SPT Telecom has an exclusive license to provide long distance and international voice services. Licenses are granted locally; the only nationwide license belongs to SPT Telecom.

Potential for Foreign Ownerships/Relationships

There are in principle no legal restrictions on foreign ownership in telecommunications. Until December 31, 2000, SPT Telecom has been granted a monopoly for long distance, international and the majority of local telecommunications voice services. Liberalization is expected to begin in the year 2001, but it could happen earlier in response to the liberalization policies of the European Union.

Potential for Upcoming Liberalization/Investment Opportunities

All telecommunications services have already been liberalized with the exception of long distance and international voice services. It is expected that the telecommunications market will be fully liberalized after December 31, 2000, and a wave of new market entrants and heightened competition are expected at that time. There are currently investment opportunities in the areas of paging, data networks, wireless communication and Internet access, as well as the local telecommunications market. A third license for a GSM services supplier is expected to be issued by the year 2000.

Forms of Doing Business

Permanent Establishment

A foreign company has a permanent establishment (PE) if it has a facility (e.g., a workshop or office) located in the territory of the Czech Republic. A construction site is also considered to be a PE as long as the project lasts for more than 6 months in any consecutive 12-calendar-month period. If a foreign company provides services within the territory of the Czech Republic for more than 6 months in any consecutive 12-calendar-month period, a PE is inter alia created. A PE must be registered for corporate income tax purposes and must submit an annual tax return. A PE is taxed on its Czech-sourced income. A PE cannot be registered for VAT purposes nor can it register in the Commercial Register, which means that it cannot engage in entrepreneurial activities. Telecommunications services can cover a broad range of activities, which may or may not constitute a PE. (It should be noted that it is illegal to provide call reorganization/turnaround services in the Czech Republic.) Some examples follow:

- The provision of long distance telephone services by a foreign company to local customers without any local presence or advertising would not create a PE.

- The licensing of technology and know-how by a foreign company to a Czech company would not create a PE.

- The provision of technical assistance and technological services by a foreign company to a Czech company in the Czech Republic would be deemed to create a PE, provided that the duration of these services exceeded 6 months in any consecutive 12-calendar-month period. Such services may be carried out by either employees or independent persons working for or on behalf of the foreign company.

- The leasing of telecommunications equipment without any supporting activities or services being provided by a foreign company to a Czech company would not constitute a PE.

- The provision of Internet access services will most likely constitute a PE if employees and/or equipment are located in the Czech Republic. (It should be noted that an interpretation from the Ministry of Finance distinguishes between various types of software and their respective tax implications. Based upon this interpretation, there could be two different tax consequences for a local person buying Internet access software from a foreign company: (a) if the software were standard software, for which the buyer obtained only usership rights, this software would in principle be considered as a good and, therefore, not subject to withholding tax; (b) however, fees for software to which the purchaser obtained limited rights (regarding, for example, sublicensing) would be considered royalties and would therefore, in principle, be subject to withholding tax.)

- The use in the Czech Republic of software owned by a foreign company rendering Internet access services would normally not result in the creation of a PE.

- Having a server or a switch, but not any personnel, located in the Czech Republic could create a PE.

- A foreign company that has a website located on a server in the Czech Republic that is accessible by customers in the Czech Republic will most likely not result in the creation of a PE.

- Having a website located on a server outside the Czech Republic but accessible from the Czech Republic will normally not result in the creation of a PE.

- Having a website located on a server in the Czech Republic that is *not* accessible by customers in the Czech Republic but *is* accessible by customers in other countries will most likely not lead to the creation of a PE.

- The laying of fiber optic cable and the construction of telecommunications switching equipment by a foreign telecommunications company (a) for sale to a local company or (b) to be operated by a foreign telecommunications company for a local company in exchange for a fee will create a PE if the construction and installation work lasts for more than 6 months in any consecutive 12-month period.

When the provision of services does not create a PE, payments to the foreign company that provides the services are subject to a 25% withholding tax, which may be reduced by a tax treaty.

Business Entities

Local Branch of a Foreign Company. A local branch of a foreign company must be registered in the Czech Commercial Register as a trading branch or non-trading branch. A trading branch can carry out business activities in the Czech Republic without limitations, except that it may not own real estate. A non-trading branch, or representative office, mainly carries out support activities for its foreign parent, and is not allowed to carry on business activities.

A branch is not considered a separate legal entity. A branch must register with the tax authorities for corporate income tax purposes and has the option of registering for VAT purposes. No withholding tax is applicable on profits repatriated from a branch. A branch is taxed on its Czech-sourced income. The profits and losses of a branch may not be grouped with those of other operations.

Locally Incorporated Subsidiary of a Foreign Company. The most common forms of representation used by foreign investors are the limited liability company (s.r.o., or spolecnost s rucením omezeným) and the joint-stock company (a.s., or akciová spolecnost). Locally incorporated subsidiaries are considered as tax-resident in the Czech Republic and, therefore, taxable on their worldwide income. Income already subject to Czech withholding tax and certain other categories of income are not included in the taxable profit. Tax-deductible expenses are defined as the expenses incurred to generate, assure and maintain income. Profits and losses of holding and subsidiary companies may not be consolidated.

Joint Venture. Most joint ventures are structured in the form of either a limited liability company or a joint-stock company, in which both participants hold 50% of the shares. If a joint venture is structured in the form of one legal entity with two equal shareholders, it must file a tax return. A foreign company entering into a joint venture by establishing a limited liability or joint-stock company with a Czech partner will usually not be considered to have a PE in the Czech Republic.

Local Funding Alternatives

Debt versus Equity

Interest is tax-deductible; however, with the exception of newly established taxpayers (i.e., for the year when the company was incorporated and the three years following), the Czech Republic's thin capitalization rules can limit the amount of the deduction. The thin capitalization limits are determined by the ratio of a company's loans to its equity. The total loan amount on which the debt-to-equity ratio is computed does not include loans for acquiring fixed assets or interest-free loans.

The debt-to-equity ratio applies in the case of both domestic and foreign related parties, and foreign unrelated parties. Persons are in this case related if one participates directly or indirectly in the management, control or ownership of the other. (In this case, participation in the control or ownership means ownership of more than 25% of either the share capital or the voting rights.) The interest expense on a loan from a related party is tax-deductible if the loan does not exceed four times the borrower's equity. If the loan is made by a foreign entity to an unrelated local company, then the interest expense is deductible if the loan does not exceed 10 times the borrower's equity. In both cases, the non-deductible interest is considered as a dividend for tax purposes and may be subject to withholding tax at a rate of 25%, which may be reduced by a tax treaty.

Dividends are not tax-deductible. Dividends are subject to withholding tax at the rate of 25%, which may be reduced by a tax treaty.

Exchange Controls

While there are no exchange controls in place, a Czech entity that either makes a payment or receives a payment related to a loan or a credit received from a non-resident must notify the Czech National Bank.

Business Acquisitions and Dispositions

Capital Contributions into an Existing Local Entity

Capital contributions into an existing local entity can be made either in cash or in-kind. Contributions in-kind can be made in two different ways—as a contribution of assets or a contribution of a business. In the first case, the total value is based on the total of the valuations of the individual assets. In the second case, the business as a whole—including potential goodwill—is valued. In all cases, there is no upper limitation on the value of the contribution. The minimum contribution into a limited liability company is CZK 100,000, and CZK 1 million into a joint-stock company. For a limited liability company or a joint-stock company, in-kind contributions must be valued by at least one authorized appraiser. In the case of a contribution of assets, if the accounting values and the real values of these assets differ, it is necessary to record the differences in the relevant accounts of the individual assets. A company to which the assets were contributed will, however, continue with the depreciation scheme started by a contributor. In the case of a contribution of a business, if the accounting and the agreed price of the business differ, this difference should be recorded on one account and may not be depreciated as tax-deductible expense or realized as taxable revenue.

Existing shareholders have pre-emptive rights over any issue of new capital. A capital contribution is not subject to share capital tax or any other tax, except for real estate transfer tax if the shares are held for less than five years.

Purchase or Sale of Shares in a Local Entity

A gain on the sale of stock by a Czech company is taxable, regardless of the period of ownership. If the purchase price for the shares in the local entity were to exceed the net book value of such local company, there is no planning that would allow the buyer to step-up the tax basis in the acquired assets owned by the local company in order to charge the paid goodwill, which is a part of the acquisition price (over a certain period), to the profit and loss account. The purchase price of the shares is, in the case of a subsequent sale, tax-deductible, up to the amount of the sale price.

Purchase or Sale of Assets

An asset sale may take place either as a sale of individually valued (net) assets or as a sale of (net) assets which are valued as a whole. When individual assets are sold, the purchaser must use the price of the individual assets as the basis for depreciation. When a business as a whole is sold, the difference between the accounting and the agreed lump-sum price of a business should be depreciated to tax-deductible expenses (goodwill) or revenues subject to taxation (badwill) on a regular basis over a 15-year period following the sale of the business. A transfer of assets that can be considered as the sale of an enterprise is exempt from VAT when both the buyer and seller are registered for VAT purposes. Except in the case of a merger, a transfer of real estate is in principle subject to a 5% real estate transfer tax.

Differences in the cost basis results of purchasing the assets of an existing telecommunications company as opposed to purchasing the stock of a company arise from timing differences in charging amounts to the profit and loss account. In the first case, this may be done at the sale of the investment (up to the amount of the purchase price); in the second case, this is in principle done during the depreciation period (fixed assets) or sale (inventories). In principle there is no large difference from a tax point of view for a seller. In all cases, the price received is treated as a taxable revenue. However, where there are assets for which an investment deduction has been claimed within three years following the year of acquisition, the seller is obliged to cancel this deduction.

For a partnership, a sale of an ownership interest to a new partner is considered as a sale of assets. If the interest in the partnership is transferred to an existing partner, there is no change in the depreciation basis of the partnership's assets. The buyer accounts for the acquired interest as a capital expenditure, both from an accounting and a tax point of view. In case of a sale, the sale price represents for the seller taxable revenues and the purchase price represents—up to the amount of the purchase price—tax-deductible costs.

Start-up Business Issues

Pre-operating Losses and Start-up/Construction Costs

Business investigation costs and license fees are tax-deductible when incurred to generate, assure and maintain taxable income. Intangible fixed assets are capitalized and depreciated. Intangible fixed assets include assets created by the taxpayer for business purposes; incorporation expenses that exceed CZK 20,000; and know-how, software and other technical or exploitable knowledge whose acquisition cost exceeds CZK 40,000 and whose useful life is of more than one year. Patents are depreciated over 15 years, software over 4 years and other intangible assets, including incorporation costs, over 8 years.

Incorporation costs expended since January 1, 1998 can be depreciated over two to five years. This regime of tax depreciation is also applicable in case of R&D results bought from suppliers (i.e., acquired for a consideration). However, intangible assets contributed into the equity of a company that are acquired by the shareholder without a consideration (i.e., free of charge) cannot be depreciated for tax purposes. Intangible assets purchased abroad may be subject to withholding tax.

Interest paid on assets under construction should be capitalized. When the assets are placed in service, depreciation begins.

A foreign company that incurs local costs that are subject to VAT can, in principle, not recover such VAT unless its local activities are organized in the form of a Czech branch, which is registered for VAT purposes. If the acquisitions made by the branch are charged to the already-incorporated and VAT-registered local legal entity, effective recovery of VAT can, in principle, take place. (VAT paid prior to registration can be recovered in some situations. See "Customs Duties and VAT.")

An investment deduction of, generally, 10% for acquired new tangible fixed assets is in principle granted. The 10% may be deducted from the tax base (the annual tax result decreased by an eventual loss if carried forward). In case of a negative tax base, the taxpayer may deduct the amount in a year in which the taxpayer has a positive tax base.

Customs Duties and VAT

Goods imported into the Czech Republic are subject to customs duties and VAT. The customs rates for telecommunications equipment imported from countries that are not members of the WTO are between 9% and 15%. If an affiliation with the WTO exists, these rates are reduced and range from 1.3% to 8.7%. A reduction of 75% applies on imports from developing countries. There is no customs duty for goods imported from member states of the EU and various other organizations (e.g., the Central European Free Trade Association and the European Free Trade Association).

Imported goods are also subject to VAT at the rate of 22%. There is no distinction drawn between regular and Internet telephony for the purposes of VAT. Only VAT-registered businesses are eligible to receive a VAT refund. In order to register for VAT, a business must be registered in the Commercial Register. This option is not available to permanent establishments; it is available to branches of foreign companies.

A VAT payer is entitled to claim a refund of input VAT for purchases of intangible and tangible fixed assets and stock that are acquired up to 12 months prior to registration. If the respective assets at the time of claiming the refund have a lower tax book value than their purchase price—for example, due to depreciation—then the claim for the refund shall be decreased accordingly.

Loss Carryovers

Tax losses incurred in 1993 or later may be carried forward for no more than seven years immediately following the period in which the losses occurred. Losses cannot be carried back. There are no limitations on the use of losses after a change of business activity.

Operating Considerations

Corporate Income Taxes

Czech legal entities (i.e., a legal entity with its registered seat in the Czech Republic) are taxed on their worldwide income. Branches and permanent establishments are taxed on their Czech-sourced income. The corporate income tax rate for 1997 was 39%; this decreased to 35% on January 1, 1998.

Capital Gains Taxes

Capital gains are taxed as part of ordinary income.

Tax Holidays and Exemptions

There are no tax holidays or exemptions for companies operating in the Czech Republic.

Depreciation/Cost-Recovery Conventions/Accelerated Deductions

Assets can be depreciated using either the straight-line method or the accelerated depreciation method. These methods have an equal period of depreciation but diverge in respect of depreciation charges applied in separate years. Tangible fixed assets with useful lives of more than one year and with a purchase price of at least CZK 20,000 must be capitalized. Only fixed assets that are used for generating taxable income may be depreciated. Low-value assets, which are either fixed assets costing less than CZK 20,000 or intangible assets valued at under CZK 40,000, may be depreciated fully in the year of acquisition. If there are any additional investments exceeding CZK 20,000 in the taxable period relating to fixed assets, the Czech tax legislation considers such investments in most cases as "technical appreciation" of the assets. Technical appreciation has to be capitalized and depreciated. Technical appreciation is specified as expenses incurred for completed extensions, additions, adaptations of buildings or structures, and the reconstruction or modernization of tangible assets. Tangible and intangible assets are divided into five classes as shown in the table below.

Class	Depreciation Period	Type of Assets
1	4 years	Hand-operated tools, computers, switchboards, office machines, measuring instruments, cameras, passenger cars, software, some radiotelephonic instruments, wire telephonic and telegraphic electrical appliances (including faxes)
2	8 years	Most production plant devices, instruments and special devices, trucks, buses, trailers, inventory and most intangible assets, wire products (cables), TV and radio, transmitters and wire radiotelephonic and telegraphic instruments, licenses
3	15 years	Patents
4	30 years	Buildings from wood or light materials, towers, masts, long-distance transmission lines (electrical traction, surface), local transmission lines (electricity mains)
5	45 years	Other buildings

Purchased software with a useful life of more than one year and a purchase price of more than CZK 40,000 is treated as an intangible asset and depreciated over four years. If purchased software forms an integral part of a telecommunications asset costing more than CZK 20,000, it may be depreciated over four years.

Marketing and advertising costs in the form of newspaper advertisements, billboards or advertisements in other media are tax-deductible. All costs relating to sponsorship agreements are also tax-deductible. However, advertising or promotional samples bearing the company's name or trademark can only be deducted if their value does not exceed CZK 200 per item. Research and development costs, including software development costs, may be deducted currently or, in certain cases, deferred and amortized over a number of years.

Transfer Pricing Rules

If there is a difference between the price contracted with a related party and the price that would be contracted with a third party for a comparable transaction and this difference cannot be satisfactorily documented, the tax authority can adjust the company's tax base by this difference. Furthermore, the tax authority may in case of a cross-border payment consider this difference to be deemed a distribution of dividends, which is in general subject to a 25% withholding tax.

Parties are considered to be related when one partly directly or indirectly participates in the management, control or capital of the other party or when the same legal entities or individuals participate directly or indirectly in the management, control or ownership of both entities. (In this case, participation in the control or ownership means ownership of more than 25% of the equity.) Starting in late 1997, the definition of related parties was extended to cover companies that entered into a business relationship mainly for the purpose of reducing their tax base or creating a tax loss.

Transfers of Patents, Trademarks and Software

Payments for the right to use trademarks software, know-how, copyrights and the like are considered as royalty payments. Royalty payments are tax-deductible when incurred to generate, assure or maintain taxable income. Royalty payments made to non-residents are subject to withholding tax at a rate of 25%; however, this rate can be reduced by a tax treaty. License

fees for technology or know-how are subject to a 5% output VAT. There are no restrictions on the license of technology to a local company for royalty fees. When technology is transferred, sales are distinguished from licenses as follows: In the case of a sale, the purchaser acquires all rights related to the technology. In the case of a license, the purchaser obtains only the right to use the technology as agreed with the seller.

Service Fees

Czech companies are obliged to withhold and remit to the tax authorities a 10% tax advance from the gross amount of payment for services provided by a foreign branch or a Czech permanent establishment of a foreign entity. It is possible to apply for an exemption from the requirement to pay such advances (e.g., if the revenues of the branch/permanent establishment will equal its costs, or if there is reasonable certainty that the taxes due will be collected, the tax authority usually confirms the 10% tax advance exemption). Service fees are in principle tax-deductible. Payments for services provided by non-residents to a Czech entity are subject to a withholding tax of 25%, which may be reduced by a tax treaty.

When the services are provided by a foreign entity outside the territory of the Czech Republic, the service fees are not considered Czech-sourced income and, consequently, not subject to withholding tax. When the services are provided within the territory of the Czech Republic by a foreign provider, a withholding tax of 25% applies, which may be reduced by a tax treaty.

Value-Added Tax, Sales Tax and/or Other Pertinent Taxes

VAT is imposed at a rate of 22% on goods and 5% on services. A business whose total revenue for goods or services exceeds CZK 750,000 in three consecutive calendar months must register for VAT. Registration can also take place on a voluntary basis. While most exports of goods and services are exempt from VAT, charges for telecommunications services are subject to output VAT.

Payments to non-residents should not be subject to any VAT. A reverse-charge mechanism does not apply. VAT is in principle recoverable on goods and services acquired to produce goods and services whose sale will be subject to output VAT. It is necessary to register for VAT in order to recover input VAT. Recovering takes place by filing a VAT return form. The Melbourne

Agreement most probably would not apply to exempt payments under the international settlement process from VAT.

If an Internet access provider is a VAT payer, has its seat in the Czech Republic and provides services to Czech customers, VAT is applicable. If the provider has its seat outside the Czech Republic, in most cases no VAT will be charged by the foreign supplier. The import of these services is not subject to Czech VAT. In principle, VAT would apply to payments for the provision of Internet telephony services. Internet access is, in principle, considered telephony.

Local and Provincial Taxes

Road tax is levied on most vehicles that are used for business purposes. The maximum annual amount of possible road tax per vehicle is CZK 50,400. Localities also impose a real estate tax that consists of land taxes and building taxes. The tax rates vary from region to region.

For Additional Information, Contact:

Monika Svobodová
Tax Partner
and
Klára Soukupová
Tax Manager
and
Hans van Capelleveen
Tax Supervisor
Karlovo náměstí 17
120 00 Praha 2
Czech Republic
Telephone: 420 (2) 21 905 111 (Svobodová)
           420 (2) 21 905 249 (Soukupová)
           420 (2) 21 905 312 (van Capelleveen)
Fax: 420 (2) 29 50 74
E-mail: Monika_Svobodova@cz.coopers.com
       Klara_Soukupova@cz.coopers.com
       Johannis_Capelleveen@cz.coopers.com

Denmark

Telecommunications Tax Profile
by Verner Rasmussen
Tax Partner, Copenhagen

Overview of the Telecommunications Market

Historical Background

For the past several years, Denmark has been opening various segments of its telecommunications industry to competition. In 1990 the market for customer premise equipment was liberalized. In 1991 the public limited company, TeleDanmark A/S, achieved the sole concession for telecommunications network facilities and operations, including mobile and international communications. At that time, the Danish government held 51% of the shares in TeleDanmark.

In March 1992 the government allowed a mobile telecommunications provider, SONOFON, to compete against the monopoly's wireless subsidiary, TeleDanmark Mobil. In the autumn of 1997, the American company Ameritech purchased 42% of the shares in TeleDanmark from the government.

Current Status

Denmark implemented the EU Commission's requirement for full liberalization of the telecommunications sector on July 1, 1997. Telia, the Swedish national provider, and Tele2 were planning to establish their own infrastructure in Denmark, which would enable them to compete with TeleDanmark and each other in the local and regional markets.

Over the last two years, Telia has obtained a 17% share of the international telecommunications market in Denmark. Now the competition between the telecoms providers, which also include Mobilix, SONOFON and Tele2, has been extended to national telephony and data transmissions. Global One has obtained a 25% share in the data communications market in Denmark.

Recently, four competitors have been licensed to operate in the global system for mobile communications (GSM)-1800 frequency for mobile telephony, including TeleDanmark, Telia, Mobilix and SONOFON. Licenses for GSM-900 and Nordic mobile telephone (NMT)-450 and 900 are still in use.

Current Liberalization Status

In the World Trade Organization negotiations in February 1997, Denmark committed to full liberalization and to full adherence to a common set of regulatory principles.

Type of Service	Degree of Liberalization	Key Legislation	Date of Actual or Expected Liberalization	Comments
Local	Fully liberalized	Telecommunications Act	July 1, 1997	
Long Distance	Fully liberalized	Telecommunications Act	July 1, 1997	
International	Fully liberalized	Telecommunications Act	July 1, 1997	
Cellular	Regulated	Telecommunications Act	July 1, 1997	The GSM-1800 frequency was expected to be in service as of March 1998.
Paging	Regulated	Telecommunications Act	July 1, 1997	
Value-added	Fully liberalized	Telecommunications Act	July 1, 1997	

Competitive Environment

The market is characterized by strong competition, with providers attempting to offer telephony services at prices lower than Tele-Danmark's.

| Type of Service | Entire Market | | Top Two Players | | |
	Market Size (1996)	Number of Players	Names	Annual Revenue (1996)	Ownership
Local	DKK8 billion	1	TeleDanmark A/S	DKK8 billion	Ameritech 42%, Danish government 9%, other shareholders 49%
Long Distance	Not available	2	Telia	Not available	Swedish government
			TeleDanmark A/S		Ameritech 42%, Danish government 9%, other shareholders 49%
International	DKK3 billion	10	TeleDanmark A/S	DKK2.8 billion	Ameritech 42%, Danish government 9%, other shareholders 49%
			Telia	Not available	Swedish government
Cellular	DKK2.9 billion	2	TeleDanmark A/S	DKK2.6 billion	Ameritech 42%, Danish government 9%, other shareholders 49%
			Telia	DKK300 million	Swedish government
Paging	Not available	2	SONOFON	DKK2.5 billion	GN Great Nordic and BellSouth Corporation
			TeleDanmark A/S	Not available	Ameritech 42%, Danish government 9%, other shareholders 49%
Value-added	DKK3 billion	More than 10	TeleDanmark A/S	DKK2.7 billion	Ameritech 42%, Danish government 9%, other shareholders 49%
			Telia	Not available	Swedish government

Sources: Public reports.

Licensing Requirements

In general, providers of telecommunications services do not need licenses in order to carry out business in Denmark. Providers must meet certain minimum requirements. Providers can now establish their own networks.

A license for the operation of a mobile telecommunications network is granted by the regulatory authority, Telestyrelsen, upon public invitation for tenders. It is unlikely that new licenses will be granted for mobile telephony within the existing frequencies.

Potential for Foreign Ownerships/Relationships

There are no limits to the percentage of a telecommunications business that may be owned by foreign companies. In the autumn of 1997 the Danish government sold 42% of the shares in TeleDanmark A/S to Ameritech.

Potential for Upcoming Liberalization/Investment Opportunities

In mobile telephony, an extension of the transmission routes will make it possible for the authorities to grant a greater number of licenses than in the past.

Forms of Doing Business

Permanent Establishment

A foreign entity that carries out business through a permanent establishment is taxed on the profits that can be related to the permanent establishment (PE). Denmark views a PE in accordance with the definition given in the OECD Model Convention: that a PE is a fixed place of business from which the business of an enterprise is wholly or partly carried on.

According to Danish regulations, building and construction activity is deemed to constitute a PE from the first day of activity.

However, if the activity is being performed by a company domiciled in a country with which Denmark has a double-taxation treaty, there will be a grace period, usually of 12 months, before a PE is deemed to exist.

If the activity is carried out through an agent, a foreign entity may be regarded as having a PE in Denmark. Telecommunications services can cover a broad range of activities, which may or may not constitute a PE, as illustrated in the following examples:

- The provision of long-distance telephone services by a foreign entity to local customers without any local presence would generally not constitute a PE.

- The licensing by a foreign company of technology and know-how to a local company without some permanent presence will generally not constitute a PE. However, payments by a local company to a foreign entity may be considered as a royalty, and the foreign entity will be liable to pay tax on the royalty payment.

- The presence of a foreign telecommunications entity's employees as operators of a Danish-resident telecommunications company and as providers of technical assistance and technology services by a foreign company to a local company in exchange for service fees is likely to constitute a PE. The leasing of telecommunications equipment to a local company without other support activities in Denmark will generally not constitute a PE.

- The provision of call reorganization/turnaround services would generally not constitute a PE if the calling cards were provided through an independent agent and the foreign entity did not have a place of business in Denmark.

- The provision of Internet access services may constitute a PE, depending on the extent of the foreign entity's operations in Denmark. A foreign entity that merely sells or provides software for Internet access to Danish customers without having a presence in Denmark will generally not be characterized as having a PE. However, under certain circumstances, ownership by the foreign company of the access server located in Denmark may be sufficient to constitute a PE.

- Having a website located on a server outside Denmark but accessible by customers in Denmark is not by itself sufficient to constitute a PE.

- Having a website located on a server in Denmark but *not* accessible to customers in Denmark may be sufficient to constitute a PE.

- The laying of fiber optic cable and the construction of telecommunications switching equipment (a) for sale to a local company, or (b) to be operated by a foreign entity for a local company in exchange for fees, generally constitutes a PE. If the activity is covered by a double-tax treaty, there is normally a grace period before a PE will be deemed to exist.

Business Entities

In general, there are no specific legal entities prescribed for suppliers of telecommunications services.

Local Branch of a Foreign Company. A foreign company that carries out business through a branch is taxable in Denmark on the income from the branch if the branch constitutes a PE. The profits of the branch are taxed at a flat rate of 34%. Interest on loans from the foreign company to the branch are generally not deductible from the branch's taxable income. Generally, the profits and losses of a local branch of a foreign company cannot be grouped with those of other operations for tax purposes.

Locally Incorporated Subsidiary of a Foreign Company. Companies registered in Denmark are taxed at a flat rate of 34%. Capital duty is not payable in Denmark, but a small fee is charged in connection with registration of the company. A Danish subsidiary can choose to be jointly taxed with all or some of its Danish as well as foreign subsidiaries, making Denmark one of the few countries that permits the offset of foreign losses against in-country profits.

Joint Venture. Joint ventures are treated as partnerships for tax purposes and each participant is taxed on its part of the income in the joint venture. A joint venture is not in itself subject to tax, and no tax returns must be filed. However, if all the participants are corporations with limited liability, the joint venture has to submit accounts to the Danish Commerce and Companies Agency. If the joint venture constitutes a PE, participation in the joint venture will also be deemed a PE.

Local Funding Alternatives

Debt versus Equity

A public limited company must have a minimum share capital of DKK500,000, and a private limited company must have a minimum share capital of DKK125,000. A subscription for share capital must be registered with the Danish Commerce and Companies Agency. A subscription of new share capital can be made at a premium. If the subscription takes place in connection with an issue of shares, neither the subscription nor the premium will be a tax liability for the company. Share capital can be repaid to the shareholders only in connection with a capital reduction pursuant to legislation. Generally, a repayment of share capital to the shareholder is treated as a dividend. The company must in this situation withhold a tax of 25%. In connection with liquidation of the Danish company, a repayment of share capital may be treated as a capital gain. In this situation, Denmark does not tax the liquidation proceeds.

There are generally no limitations on the deductibility of interest on loans. Foreign lenders can grant unlimited loans to a Danish subsidiary. There are generally no limits to shareholder guarantees. A shareholder's guarantee may in some situations be regarded as a warranty. Exchange gains and gains on debts are taxable for companies, whereas exchange losses and losses on debts are deductible. A gain on a debt to a group company is not taxable if, according to national rules, the group company is not allowed to deduct the corresponding loss on the claim against the Danish company.

Exchange Controls

Capital movements between Denmark and abroad have been fully deregulated. However, amounts exceeding DKK60,000 must be reported to the Central Bank of Denmark.

Business Acquisitions and Dispositions

Capital Contributions into an Existing Local Entity

A contribution of capital or intangible assets into a company without a repayment obligation and without registration of the contribution as share capital will be taxable to the company. A foreign company can contribute capital or assets without limitations into a Danish company. The existing shareholders will generally be taxed only at the time of disposal of the shares.

Purchase or Sale of Shares in a Local Entity

By purchasing shares in a local telecommunications company, a foreign investor will be liable for taxes only on the dividends paid by the telecommunications company. For corporate shareholders resident in Denmark, gains on the sale of shares that have been held less than three years are taxable. Losses can be offset only against gains from other shares sold within three years of acquisition. Losses can be carried forward for five years. Gains on the sale of shares held for more than three years are tax-exempt. Losses cannot be deducted. Non-residents are not taxed on gains or losses on shares.

Gains or losses are computed on the basis of the acquisition price and the sales price. There are no provisions to allow any step-up in basis of the assets of a company whose shares are acquired.

Purchase or Sale of Assets

Foreign investors must receive permission from the Ministry of Justice to acquire real estate in Denmark. The purchase of assets other than real estate (e.g., shares in a Danish company) does not require permission.

When assets are purchased, the purchase price must be allocated over the assets acquired, including intangible assets such as goodwill and licenses. The vendor will be subject to capital gains tax on the excess of the purchase price so allocated and the basis of the assets. It may be possible to allocate the purchase price in a manner that is tax-beneficial for the purchaser.

It is not possible for a foreign company to merge with a Danish company without tax consequences. However, a share-for-share exchange between a foreign company and a Danish company may be made tax-free if permission is obtained from the tax authorities.

A foreign participant in a joint venture is deemed to own an undivided share of the assets in the joint venture. A sale of an interest in a joint venture will therefore be deemed to be a sale of the undivided shares of the assets.

Start-up Business Issues

Pre-operating Losses and Start-up/ Construction Costs

In general, the expenses used to secure a basis of income are considered non-deductible capital expenses. License fees and franchise fees are deductible as operating costs. Infrastructure costs, such as building costs, may be deductible (see "Depreciation/Cost-Recovery Conventions/Accelerated Deductions"). Other infrastructure costs used for the acquisition of assets can be depreciated on a straight-line basis for the duration of the activity (the deemed lifetime of the asset). Costs such as interest, sales and general administration costs are generally deductible. Costs incurred by a foreign company outside Denmark can be amortized by the local entity only if the expenses are incurred by the local entity.

Foreign companies that incur local costs that are subject to VAT can recover the VAT paid if they are registered for VAT purposes in another EU country or if they are registered as legal entities in other countries. VAT payments made on the purchase of pre-operating goods or services can be recovered, even if they are not incurred before the operating phase.

Customs Duties and VAT

Most goods imported into Denmark from outside the EU are subject to customs duty and import VAT. Duty is normally payable on the cost, insurance and freight (CIF) value of the goods. Import VAT is payable on the duty-inclusive value of the goods, although VAT-registered traders can usually obtain a refund of the VAT.

Telecommunications and computing equipment are subject to duty ranging from 1.2% to 10.5%. The rate of duty will depend on the exact description and the tariff classification of the goods and the country of origin of the goods. The current import duty rates for a sample of telecommunications goods originating in non-EU countries (in this example, the United States) are given below. The EU has preferential trade agreements with a number of countries that enable goods to be imported at rates below those indicated or at nil rate of duty.

Line telephone sets with cordless handsets	3.8%
Videophones	7%
Other telephone sets	3.8%
Facsimile machines	3.8%
Teleprinters	3.8%
Telephonic or telegraphic switching apparatus	3.8%
Other apparatus for carrier line systems	2.3%
Other apparatus for digital line systems	3.8%
Building-entry telephone systems	3.8%

Customs duties on some items of equipment were already being reduced under the General Agreement on Tariffs and Trade (GATT). However, over the next few years, duty rates are scheduled to be reduced further still under the Information Technology Agreement (ITA) signed in March 1997. The ITA also extends the range of goods subject to duty rate reductions. As a signatory to the ITA, the EU has agreed to cut tariffs on imports of computers and computer equipment, software, telecommunications and networking equipment to zero in four equal installments. The first reduction took place on July 1, 1997, and further reductions are to take effect on January 1 each year to 2000. Although the ITA will cut the cost of importing many products, the convergence of technologies in the computing, electronics and telecommunications sectors is likely to lead to disputes over the tariff classification of some equipment and affect the availability and/or phasing of duty reductions under the ITA.

A wide variety of reliefs from customs duty (and import VAT) can be claimed in various circumstances (e.g., goods imported for processing and re-export, or goods imported temporarily). There is also a relief available for capital goods and equipment, provided the goods are imported by a business on the transfer of its activities to Denmark.

Raw materials or components that are not available, or not available in sufficient quantities, within the EU may be eligible for a complete or partial suspension of duty, providing this can be demonstrated to the satisfaction of the Commission of the European Communities in Brussels.

Goods may be subject to anti-dumping or countervailing duty if, for example, the EU considers they are being imported into the EU at prices substantially lower than their normal values. Anti-dumping and countervailing duties are chargeable in addition to, and independent of, any other duty to which the imported goods are liable.

Loss Carryovers

Losses may be carried forward for five years. No carryback is permitted. The carryforward of losses may be limited in certain circumstances (e.g., in connection with credit arrangements for the company). If more than 50% of the company's share capital at the end of an income year is owned by shareholders other than those who hold the shares at the start of the previous loss-making income year, the loss carryforward cannot reduce the taxable income to an amount that is lower than the company's net capital receipts. This also applies if, at the end of the loss-making year, the ownership of the company's total voting value has changed more than 50% from the beginning of the year in question. A change of business activity will generally not have any effect on the possibility of carrying losses forward.

Operating Considerations

Corporate Income Taxes

Worldwide income of public and private limited companies is taxed at a rate of 34%. A 34% corporate tax is also levied on the taxable income of a foreign corporation's branch.

Joint ventures are taxed as partnerships in which each member is taxed. Partners that are Danish companies or companies with permanent establishment in Denmark are taxed at the rate of 34%.

A 25% withholding tax is payable on dividends. This rate can be reduced by a tax treaty. No withholding tax is payable on a dividend that a company resident in an EU-member country receives from a company resident in Denmark. This situation occurs when the receiving company has owned at least 25% of the share capital in the subsidiary either for the entire income year in which the dividend is received or for a consecutive period of at least two years before the dividend is received.

Capital Gains Taxes

Most capital gains are added to a company's taxable income and taxed at the regular corporate tax rate of 34%. A tax-free transaction is possible whereby a company resident in Denmark conveys one or more branches of its activity to another company for an allotment of shares in the receiving company. This occurs when the receiving company is resident in an EU-member state and the contributing company is not liquidated.

Assets can be transferred to companies situated both in Denmark and in other EU countries, but different rules apply. The contributing company will not be taxed on a profit or loss on the assets transferred to the receiving company.

Tax Holidays and Exemptions

No tax holidays or special exemptions are available.

Depreciation/Cost-Recovery Conventions/Accelerated Deductions

Depreciation begins when business activity commences, which is generally deemed to be at the time that sale of the entity's products is initiated. There are no rules as to when a network is considered placed in service.

Intangible Assets. Expenses in connection with the acquisition of intangible rights can be depreciated by equal annual amounts over the period in which the right is applicable. A right for an unlimited period can be depreciated by 7% annually over a seven-year period. The purchase price for goodwill can also be amortized over a seven-year period.

Machinery, Plant and Similar Operating Equipment. All production equipment may be depreciated according to the diminishing-balance method. Each year, the taxpayer may write off from 0% to 30% of the balance value. There are no predetermined lives for machinery, plant and similar equipment. Satellites may be depreciated according to these rules. The purchase price for software can be deducted in the year of acquisition.

Buildings. Only buildings used for industrial purposes and adjoining buildings qualify for depreciation allowances. Generally, office and residential buildings do not qualify for depreciation allowances. Buildings and special facilities are depreciated individually on the straight-line basis; no depreciation is allowed on land.

The tax treatment of cellular stations is not dealt with under current legislation, but it can be assumed that cellular stations may be depreciated according to the rules governing the depreciation of buildings or special facilities, since cellular stations are more likely to be grouped with real property than, for example, a working plant. Routers and lines will probably also be depreciated according to these rules.

The taxpayer chooses the depreciation percentage each year, up to a maximum, which is 4%, 6% or 8% for different catego-

ries of buildings or facilities. The taxpayer may continue to apply the initial (maximum) percentages until the accumulated depreciation amounts to 40%, 60% or 80% of the cost of acquisition. For subsequent years, 1%, 2% and 4% of the cost of acquisition are the maximum rates.

Advance Depreciation. Advance depreciation is allowed upon the signing of a binding contract for the contemplated manufacture of machinery and buildings by any percentage up to 30% of the construction price. Advance depreciation for any single investment year cannot exceed 15%. For machinery and buildings, the purchase price must exceed DKK700,000.

Research and Development Costs. Costs related to research and development of new products or systems can generally be deducted either in the year in which the expenses are incurred or depreciated on a straight-line basis over five years.

Marketing and Advertising Costs. Costs related to marketing of products and advertising are generally deductible.

Transfer Pricing Rules

Transactions between closely associated companies must be at arm's length. The rules have so far not been rigorously enforced by the tax authorities, but following the issuance recently of the OECD's report on transfer pricing, the rules in this area have been tightened.

Transfers of Patents, Trademarks and Software

In connection with a sale or transfer of assets, most capital gains or losses are included in the transferor's taxable income, including gains or losses in connection with the sale of intangible rights (e.g., license rights and know-how). Profits are taxed at 34% if the seller or transferor is a company.

Depending on the circumstances, a transfer can be said to exist if the content of the agreement concerning the sharing of experience and expertise implies that intangible assets are transferred between the parties.

The acquisition price for software is fully tax-deductible. Payments of both royalty and software licensing fees are deductible. A 30% withholding tax is levied on a royalty. If Denmark has a double-taxation treaty with the country in which the recipient is resident, the percentage stipulated in the treaty is withheld, up to a maximum of 30%.

Service Fees

Service fees are deductible. In general, a withholding tax is not levied on a service fee if it is a payment for a service and not a payment for a royalty or a dividend. If the entity in Denmark has received a service related to the operation of the Danish entity, the fee paid for the received service will be deductible for the Danish entity.

Value-Added Tax, Sales Tax and/or Other Pertinent Taxes

As a member of the EU, Denmark follows the provisions of the European Community Sixth VAT Directive. Domestic telecommunications services (including those supplied by Danish-resident foreign businesses) are subject to VAT at the standard rate of 25%. The VAT treatment of international telecommunications services is based on the revised EU VAT model, which took effect in Denmark July 1, 1997.

Services supplied internationally by a telecommunications business located in Denmark are generally outside the scope of VAT when supplied to anyone located outside Denmark. The only exceptions are services supplied to private individuals or unregistered persons located in other member states. Those supplies are subject to Danish VAT at the standard rate.

Non-resident providers are not liable to register and account for Danish VAT on supplies used by Danish customers, providing those customers are taxable persons for VAT purposes. These customers are required to self-account for VAT under reverse-charge procedures.

When a non-resident provider makes supplies of services to private individuals, to be used and enjoyed in Denmark, the provider is required to register and account for Danish VAT. For a non-EU provider, it should be possible to limit the Danish VAT liability to supplies made to Danish individuals that are effectively used in the EU. However, this may then require the non-

EU provider to be registered for VAT purposes in many different EU-member states. Alternatively, an overseas provider may choose to register in a single EU-member state (e.g., Denmark) in order to contract with all customers who are EU private individuals. The supplies made from the single EU registration to these customers will then be subject to local VAT in the member state of registration.

Access to the Internet is included within the definition of telecommunications, and the principles set out above apply equally to Internet service providers.

Local and Provincial Taxes

Companies are not subject to local taxes.

For Additional Information, Contact:

Verner Rasmussen
Tax Partner
P.O. Box 2709
DK 2100 Copenhagen 0
Denmark
Telephone: 45 39 27 72 00
Fax: 45 39 27 28 15
E-mail: Verner_Rasmussen@dk.coopers.com

Jens Bisballe
Telecoms Consultant
Skovlytoften 9B
DK 2840 Holte
Denmark
Telephone: 45 42 42 46 11
Fax: 45 42 42 29 46
E-mail: s+b@post4.tele.dk

Finland

Telecommunications Tax Profile
by Ilkka Kajas
Tax Partner, Helsinki

Overview of the Telecommunications Market

Historical Background

Finland was one of the first countries to liberalize its telecommunications industry. In 1987 the Telecommunications Act deregulated the industry, and in 1990 the Finnish PTT made the transition from a government department to a state-owned corporation, Telecom Finland Ltd. Before telecommunications services were opened to competition, metropolitan areas were served by the Finnet Group, a group of 45 private local telephone companies, and other areas were served by Telecom Finland. All providers held exclusive licenses.

On January 1, 1994, Telecom Finland became a limited liability company, and the telecommunications monopoly was abandoned. All of the private telephone companies and Telecom Finland were granted licenses to serve the whole of Finland. International competition commenced later that year. In June 1996 amendments to the Telecommunications Act were implemented to promote further competition in telecommunications

services. The Telecommunications Market Act went into effect in April 1997.

Current Status

Today competition exists in all services. The number of competitors has increased significantly over the past two years. In addition to Telecom Finland, there are several private nationwide telephone companies, such as Telia Finland and the Finnet Group. (Telia Oy bought Telivo Oy in summer 1997.) The number of competitors is expected to grow in the future. Telecom Finland will be privatized within the next two years.

Revenues of the Finnet Group have continued to increase since liberalization. Subsidiaries compete in all aspects of the telecommunications market.

The fixed telecommunications network is fully digitalized. Finland has many different cellular networks, including address resolution protocol (ARP) (150 MHz), Nordic mobile telephone (NMT)-450, NMT-900, global system for mobile communications (GSM)-900 and digital cellular system (DCS)-1800 as well as the digital European cordless telecommunication (DECT) system.

Current Liberalization Status

In the World Trade Organization (WTO) negotiations in February 1997, Finland committed to full liberalization and adherence to a common set of regulatory principles.

Type of Service	Degree of Liberalization	Key Legislation	Date of Actual or Expected Liberalization
Local			January 1, 1994
Long Distance			January 1, 1994
International	Fully liberalized	Telecommunications Act	July 1, 1994
Cellular			January 1, 1994
Paging			January 1, 1994
Value-added			January 1, 1994

Competitive Environment

In May 1997 the long-distance service market was divided between Telecom Finland Oy, with approximately 41% of the market, Kaukoverkko Ysi Oy with 54% and Telivo Oy 5%. In the in-ternational segment, Telecom Finland Oy held approximately 62% of the market, Finnet International 28% and Telivo Oy 10%. At the end of 1996, the Finnet Group held approximately 72% of the local service market.

	Entire Market		Top Two Players		
Type of Service	Market Size (1997)	Number of Players	Names	Annual Revenue (1997)	Ownership
Local	FIM3.15 billion	Finnet Group (45 locals)	Local phone companies	FIM2.13 billion	Private (owned by the users)
		Telecom Finland	Telecom Finland Oy	FIM1.02 billion	Government
Long Distance	FIM450 million	3 main providers	Kaukoverkko Ysi Oy	FIM240 million	Finnet Group
			Telecom Finland Oy	FIM190 million	Government
International	FIM1.08 billion	3 main providers	Telecom Finland Oy	FIM750 million	Government
			Oy Finnet International Ab	FIM250 million	Finnet Group
Cellular and Paging*	FIM3.15 billion	2	Telecom Finland Oy	FIM2.52 billion	Government
			Oy Radiolinja Ab	FIM630 million	Finnet Group
Value-added	FIM1.02 billion	3 main providers	Telecom Finland Oy	FIM615 million	Government
			Finnet Group	FIM400 million	Finnet Group

Source: Televiestintätilasto 1997, the Ministry of Transport and Communications.
* The market for paging is small, with about 50,000 subscribers; its revenues are included in the cellular market.

Licensing Requirements

Licenses are required for most providers of public voice and cellular services, and are granted by the Council of State. Both nationwide and regional licenses are granted. In 1996 the licensing requirements were lightened considerably. Providers of switched-data communications are no longer required to obtain licenses. Only mobile and wireless service providers need licenses. Service providers are free to lease lines from the public network and to engage in resale. Resellers must obtain permits.

Preparation and supervision of telecommunications regulations are the responsibility of the Ministry of Transport and Communications and the Telecommunications Administration Centre (TAC), respectively. TAC enforces regulations, prepares technical standards, approves terminal equipment, manages the radio frequency spectrum and handles international frequency coordination.

Potential for Foreign Ownerships/Relationships

Finland has removed all limitations on foreign ownership, enabling even 100% foreign-owned companies to apply for telecommunications licenses. Most of the Finnet Group is owned by the telephone subscribers themselves, not by outside investors or companies. To gain entry to the Finnish telecommu-nications market, foreign investors may find it necessary to acquire shares of existing Finnish telecommunications companies.

Currently, foreign interest is high, particularly among Swedish companies, in buying shares of Finnish telecommunications companies. The Ministry of Transport and Communications has favored additional deregulation to expand opportunities for competition and investment from foreign companies.

Potential for Upcoming Liberalization/Investment Opportunities

Wireless services are expected to continue their rapid growth and provide the most advantageous investment opportunities. Helsingin Puhelin Oy, the largest local telephone operator in Finland, issued new shares in autumn 1997. No major telecoms mergers or acquisitions are anticipated.

Forms of Doing Business

Permanent Establishment

The Finnish Income Tax Act's definition of permanent establishment (PE) closely follows that of the OECD Model Convention. A PE must have a certain degree of permanency, and operations must be carried out regularly. Therefore, activities carried out in Finland only occasionally and temporarily do not constitute a PE. In addition, when tangible or intangible property is leased to third parties through a fixed place of business maintained by a non-resident, the business is considered a PE. The same applies if capital is made available through a fixed place of business. Conducting only preparatory or auxiliary activities does not constitute a PE.

A business that constitutes a PE will be taxed as a branch. If a non-resident does not have a PE, the only taxes to which it will be subject are Finnish withholding taxes on dividends and royalty payments.

The following activities generally do *not* constitute PEs in Finland:

- The provision of long-distance telephone services to Finnish customers by a foreign company having no local presence or advertising in Finland

- The licensing of technology and know-how to a Finnish company by a foreign company having no permanent presence in Finland

- The provision of Internet access services and the selling of software to Finnish customers; however, if a foreign company owns an access server located in Finland, this may constitute a PE, even if the company has no personnel in Finland

- The provision of call reorganization/turnaround services if the services are provided through an independent agent and the foreign company offering the services does not have a fixed place of business or own equipment located in Finland

The laying of fiber optic cable and construction of telecommunications switching equipment, either for sale to a local company or for operation by a foreign telecommunications company for a local company in exchange for a fee, would constitute a PE.

No rulings have occurred regarding the question of whether websites constitute PEs.

Business Entities

Local Branch of a Foreign Company. Business may be conducted through a branch of a foreign corporation or foundation formed under the laws of a European Economic Area (EEA) member country and which has its statutory residence, administration or main place of business in an EEA country.

A branch of a foreign company is viewed as a separate entity and must pay income tax at a rate of 28% on profits of the foreign company that are attributable to the permanent establishment. This includes income to the PE from third countries. The amount of taxable income of a PE is calculated according to the rules of the Business Income Tax Act (i.e., in the same way as

the taxable income of a limited liability company). In addition, a PE of a foreign company is subject to a wealth tax of 1% on the value of its business assets unless otherwise provided in tax treaties.

A Finnish branch of a foreign company that is resident in the EEA is entitled to the Finnish imputation credit (avoir fiscal) for its dividend-incurring shares that are effectively connected to the branch.

PEs, along with their lines of business, are entered into the Finnish Trade Register. The line of business should be within the line of business of the parent foreign company.

Locally Incorporated Subsidiary of a Foreign Company. Foreign investors can also use a locally incorporated subsidiary, which takes the form of a limited liability company. Limited liability companies were commonly used by foreign investors because the minimum share capital requirement had been quite low, FIM15,000. However, on September 1, 1997, the minimum share capital was raised to FIM50,000 for all limited liability companies established on or after that date. In addition, there is a special rule of transition for limited liability companies already existing on September 1, 1997, with a lower fully paid share capital.

The profits of a subsidiary are taxed at a flat rate of 28%. No grouping of profits or losses is permitted. No wealth tax is imposed on a limited liability company.

Joint Venture. Joint ventures are considered to be partnerships and must have at least two partners. No prior permission is required for a foreigner (an individual or a company) to be a partner in a Finnish partnership. Partnerships may be general or limited. In a general partnership, partners are jointly and severally liable for its obligations. In a limited partnership, one or more (but not all) of the partners can limit their liability to the capital they invest. In practice, partnership structures in Finland are used only by small businesses.

For income tax purposes, a partnership itself is not taxed; rather, its partners are taxed on the partnership's profits. Losses can be deducted only from the partnership's income before the profits are divided.

Local Funding Alternatives

Debt versus Equity

All expenses of acquiring and maintaining business income, including interest payments, are tax-deductible. Interest payments to non-residents are exempt from withholding tax in most cases.

There are no special provisions governing thin capitalization situations; however, both Finnish tax legislation and legal practice provide certain guidelines on these issues. The main rule for thin capitalization cases is that a foreign shareholder loan to a Finnish subsidiary may be considered a capital investment. In these situations, a Finnish subsidiary cannot deduct its interest payments to its foreign shareholder for income tax purposes.

The basis for determining whether a financing is characterized as debt or equity is also contained in the decrees of the Supreme Administrative Court. Factors that have been taken into account are the debt-to-equity ratio, the schedule of partial payments of the debt, and the level of the interest of the debt compared with the common level of dividends for a capital investment. In one of the best-known decrees, the acceptable debt-to-equity ratio was ruled to be 2.25 to 1. As long as the debt-to-equity ratio of the Finnish subsidiary is below this level, the interest payments paid by the subsidiary to its parent company are tax-deductible for income tax purposes. In addition, no withholding taxes are levied on the cross-border interest payments to the parent company.

Foreign-currency exchange losses related to the business of the taxpayer (for instance, on loans from a foreign parent company) are tax-deductible in the year they accrue, or, based on a claim of the taxpayer, presented in his tax return in later years. However, the loss must be deducted no later than the year when the amount corresponding to the exchange loss was paid.

No withholding tax is levied on dividends that are paid from Finland to a foreign company that is (a) located in a country that is a member of the European Union (EU) and that has no right to the Finnish imputation credit and that (b) directly owns at least 25% of the shares in the distributing Finnish company.

In other cases, the rate of the levied withholding tax on dividends is 28%. However, under tax treaties, the applied rates may vary from 0% to 25%. Most treaties include two withholding tax rates, with the lower one granted if the recipient is a company that holds a certain share of ownership, usually 25%, in a Finnish company.

Exchange Controls

The foreign exchange control system is administered by the Bank of Finland. Direct foreign investments in the telecommunications sector do not require the permission of the Bank of Finland, except for direct investments from countries with which Finland maintains payment agreements. A foreign company in a group may grant credit in the form of a direct investment to a Finnish subsidiary or an associate.

For direct investments from countries with which Finland maintains payment agreements, applications to the Bank of Finland must be made in writing. Applications must be submitted even when no capital is transferred.

No permit from the Bank of Finland is required for the remittance of dividends, interest or royalties. Relevant documents are presented to the commercial bank that transfers the payment, which then notifies the Bank of Finland. A permit from the Bank of Finland for the repatriation of capital is required, and is usually granted.

Business Acquisitions and Dispositions

Capital Contributions into an Existing Local Entity

Property given as a capital contribution can include any property, intangible or tangible, that can be entered as an asset on the company's balance sheet. However, as of September 1, 1997, a limited liability company must obtain an auditor's evaluation of the value of the property given.

Finland has implemented the Merger Directive of the EU. Accordingly, international transfers of assets can be carried out without immediate income tax consequences for a company or its shareholders. A transfer tax is payable on a capital contribution from a foreign investor.

When a foreign company transfers a certain part of its activities to a new Finnish subsidiary and the intention is that there be no income tax consequences because of the transfer, only balance sheet values can be used; therefore, depreciation deductions are not affected. The compensation paid to the foreign company must consist only of shares in a Finnish company (cash cannot be used). If the transferred activity has sustained losses, these losses cannot be transferred to the Finnish company.

Purchase or Sale of Shares in a Local Entity

Foreigners are permitted to acquire stock in Finland. If the shares of a company are bought, depreciation continues to be based on the book value of the assets. Goodwill that is included in the acquisition cost of the shares is rarely tax-deductible.

The sale of shares of a Finnish company to a foreign company is subject to income taxation if the selling shareholder is an individual or company resident in Finland; such a taxpayer is liable for Finnish income tax on global income.

If the shares of a Finnish company are sold by a non-resident shareholder (an individual or a company), the capital gain from the sale is considered to be income derived from Finland for income taxation purposes only if more than 50% of the assets of the Finnish company consisted of real estate. In other cases, the income from the sale of shares of a Finnish company is not considered to be income derived from Finland, thus the capital gain is not taxable in Finland. These principles are contained in Finnish law, and tax treaties cannot provide otherwise. A sale of shares of a Finnish company in which both the buyer and the seller of the shares are non-residents is not liable to transfer tax.

The use of a Finnish holding company to acquire the shares of a Finnish target company is not an attractive option: tax-deductible group contributions are not possible because both the receiving and the contributing company must actively carry on business activities in order to make the contribution tax-deductible for the contributing company.

Purchase or Sale of Assets

Foreigners may make asset acquisitions. The Finnish follow-up system for company acquisition by foreigners has been abolished for member countries of both the EEA and the OECD. The follow-up system is still in effect for other countries. It applies to companies that have employed more than 1,000 persons during the previous or current financial period, whose latest accounts show that turnover has exceeded FIM1 billion, or whose latest accounts show a balance sheet exceeding FIM1 billion.

From a buyer's point of view, it is often preferable to buy the assets of the company instead of the shares, as many risks are thus eliminated. If assets are bought, the depreciation is based on the new acquisition cost of the assets, and goodwill is deductible for tax purposes during its useful life. The maximum write-off period for goodwill is 10 years.

From a seller's point of view, the tax consequences of an asset sale depend on the seller's tax position and/or on whether the seller is a company or an individual. Capital gains on shares are treated as normal business income, and subject to a tax rate of 28%. If a target company sells its assets, it will generate taxable income if the fair market value of the assets exceeds their book value. If the company does not continue its business activities, it cannot defer taxation at the shareholder level and, thus, double taxation occurs. However, by following the principles of the Merger Directive (i.e., with a transfer of assets), a sale of assets can be made without immediate income tax consequences.

Start-up Business Issues

Pre-operating Losses and Start-up/Construction Costs

Costs (including business investigation costs) incurred when a company is set up can be deducted as annual expenses, unless they benefit a company over a number of years. In the latter case, the company must amortize these costs over the period during which it benefits, up to a 10-year maximum. Costs for advertising campaigns, improvement costs for rental flats and employee training costs are examples of such costs.

In practice, in many cases, the taxpayer can choose whether to capitalize. Costs must be deducted or amortized by the company that incurred them. Interest payable during construction of a new industrial plant can be capitalized and deducted (based on the claim of the taxpayer) within a period of at least 10 years.

If a foreign company incurs local costs that are subject to VAT, the company can deduct the input VAT if it is registered for VAT in Finland. If a foreign company is not liable for VAT in Finland, it may claim the VAT incurred in the purchase price of goods and services bought in Finland through the refund procedure.

Foreigners are liable for VAT if they are engaged in a type of business subject to VAT and if they have a permanent establishment in Finland. If they do not have a permanent establishment, they can claim the VAT on purchases through the refund procedure.

If no output tax is due in the accounting period, the appropriate repayment will be made by the authorities. If repayment does not exceed FIM10,000, it will be made after the end of the company's financial year.

Customs Duties and VAT

Most goods imported into Finland from outside the EU are subject to customs duty and import VAT. Duty is normally payable on the cost, insurance and freight (CIF) value of the goods. Import VAT is payable on the duty-inclusive value of the goods, although VAT-registered traders can usually obtain a refund of the VAT.

Telecommunications and computing equipment are subject to duty ranging from 1.2% to 7%. The rate of duty depends on the exact description and the tariff classification of the goods and the country of origin of the goods. The current import duty rates for a sample of telecommunications goods originating in non-EU countries (in this example, the United States) are given below. The EU has preferential trade agreements with a number of countries that enable goods to be imported at rates below those indicated or at nil rate of duty.

Line telephone sets with cordless handsets	3.8%
Videophones	7%
Other telephone sets	3.8%
Facsimile machines	3.8%
Teleprinters	3.8%
Telephonic or telegraphic switching apparatus	3.8%
Other apparatus for carrier line systems	2.3%
Other apparatus for digital line systems	3.8%
Building-entry telephone systems	3.8%

Customs duties on some items of equipment were already being reduced under the General Agreement on Tariffs and Trade (GATT). However, over the next few years, duty rates are scheduled to be reduced further still under the Information Technology Agreement (ITA) signed in March 1997. The ITA also extends the range of goods subject to duty rate reductions. As a signatory to the ITA, the EU has agreed to cut tariffs on imports of computers and computer equipment, software, telecommunications and networking equipment to zero in four equal installments. The first reduction took place on July 1, 1997, and further reductions are to take effect on January 1 of each year through 2000. Although the ITA will cut the cost of importing many products, the convergence of technologies in the computing, electronics and telecommunications sectors is likely to lead to disputes over the tariff classification of some equipment and affect the availability and/or phasing of duty reductions under the ITA.

A wide variety of reliefs from customs duty (and import VAT) can be claimed in various circumstances (e.g., goods imported for processing and re-export, or goods imported temporarily). There is also a relief available for capital goods and equipment, provided the goods are imported by a business on the transfer of its activities to Finland.

Raw materials or components that are not available, or not available in sufficient quantities, within the EU may be eligible for a complete or partial suspension of duty, providing this can be demonstrated to the satisfaction of the Commission of the European Communities in Brussels.

Goods may be subject to anti-dumping or countervailing duty if, for example, the EU considers they are being imported into the EU at prices substantially lower than their normal values. Anti-dumping and countervailing duties are chargeable in addition to, and independent of, any other duty to which the imported goods are liable.

Loss Carryovers

Losses may be carried forward and offset against future profits for 10 years. Losses may not be carried back. If the ownership of a company changes by more than 50%, losses from the year in which the ownership changed and from the previous years may not be carried forward. Changes of indirect ownership are also taken into account if a company owns at least a 20% interest in a Finnish company. In this context, only changes of ownership, rather than changes of business activity, prevent the use of the confirmed losses. Based on a written application, a county tax office may grant an exemption and allow the use of the confirmed losses in spite of changes in ownership.

Operating Considerations

Corporate Income Taxes

The flat rate for corporate taxation is 28%. The taxable income of a branch and a limited liability company is basically calculated in the same way; only minor differences exist.

Capital Gains Taxes

Capital gains are taxed as part of the ordinary income of a company. Only realized capital gains are taxed, and no indexation is applied.

Tax Holidays and Exemptions

There are no special tax incentives for telecommunications businesses.

Depreciation/Cost-Recovery Conventions/Accelerated Deductions

The acquisition costs of network deployment or construction must be capitalized as a part of the asset and depreciated. The acquisition costs include the variable costs needed to supply the asset. In addition, certain fixed costs can be allocated to the acquisition cost.

Machines and equipment are depreciated for tax purposes by using the declining-balance method, at a rate of up to 30% of the total book value of all a company's machines and equipment. A company can claim a smaller allowance if it wishes. Short-lived items, such as tools and other assets with useful lives of less than three years, may be expensed in the year of acquisition.

Buildings and other constructions are depreciated using the declining-balance method. Each building is depreciated separately. The rate is 4% if a building is used as a residential building or office and 7% if it is used as a shop, warehouse, factory or workshop.

Development costs of computer programs produced by the taxpayer are tax-deductible as annual costs. Acquisition costs of computer programs bought by the taxpayer must be depreciated over their economic lives from the tax year when they are put into use, the maximum period being 10 years. It is possible for the taxpayer to use a shorter period of depreciation.

The cost of land is never depreciated for tax purposes. The acquisition cost of securities is deducted when they are alienated, but if the taxpayer can show that the current value of the securities at the end of the tax year is substantially lower than its book value, the taxpayer is entitled to an extraordinary depreciation, which reduces the book value to the current value. The costs of patents, other intangibles and long-term expenses may be written off either in equal annual installments over 10 years or over the probable useful life when that is shorter than 10 years.

For 1998, increased depreciation allowances are possible for industrial production investments. The depreciation of investments on fixed assets may be increased by 50% from their original percentages.

There are no special rules governing the deductibility of marketing and advertising costs, which are tax-deductible according to the principal rule of expense deductibility. Research and development (R&D) costs (except for the costs of a building used in a company's R&D activities) can be deducted in the year in which they are incurred. Companies may also elect to deduct R&D costs over a longer period.

Transfer Pricing Rules

Finland's only transfer pricing rule is that intra-group prices must be at arm's length. Few decrees have been made by the Finnish Supreme Administrative Court in regard to transfer pricing issues, thus little guidance exists in this area. OECD transfer pricing principles should be acceptable.

Transfers of Patents, Trademarks and Software

Finnish law does not impose any restrictions on the licensing of technology by a foreign company to a local company for royalty fees. A sale is distinguished from a license by the form of the relevant contract concluded between the parties. Therefore, if the contract provides for an outright transfer of ownership of the assets, the transaction will be considered a sale. If the contract provides only a right to use the assets, the contract will be regarded as a license contract. In this matter, taxation basically follows civil law.

All business income, including gains from domestic or international transfers of intangibles, is taxable. The arm's-length principle must be followed between affiliated companies. Royalty payments paid by a Finnish subsidiary to its foreign parent company at arm's length are generally tax-deductible. For Income tax purposes, the expression "royalty" basically includes payments of any kind paid or received for the use of intangibles.

Royalty fees paid to companies from non-treaty countries are subject to a withholding tax of 28%. For royalties paid to companies from countries with which Finland has tax treaties, the withholding tax rate varies from 0% to 15%, although it can be as high as 25% in exceptional cases. In many treaties, a 5% withholding tax is levied on industrial royalties.

Service Fees

The deductibility of service fees paid to a foreign associated company is extensive, but proof of service is required. In addition, the costs should be shared by using a similar basis throughout the whole group. The fees should be at arm's length. No withholding taxes are levied on services fees paid to a foreign parent company of a Finnish subsidiary.

Value-Added Tax, Sales Tax and/or Other Pertinent Taxes

As a member of the EU, Finland follows the provisions of the European Community Sixth VAT Directive. Domestic telecommunications services (including those supplied by Finnish-resident foreign businesses) are subject to VAT at the standard rate of 22%. The VAT treatment of international telecommunications services is based on the revised EU VAT model, which took effect in Finland July 1, 1997.

Services supplied internationally by a telecommunications business located in Finland are generally outside the scope of VAT when supplied to anyone located outside Finland. The only exceptions are services supplied to private individuals or unregistered persons located in other EU-member states. Those supplies are subject to Finnish VAT at the standard rate.

Non-resident providers are not liable to register and account for Finnish VAT on supplies used by Finnish customers, provided those customers are taxable persons for VAT purposes. These customers are required to self-account for VAT under reverse-charge procedures.

When a non-resident provider makes supplies of services to private individuals to be used in Finland, the provider is required to register and account for Finnish VAT. For a non-EU provider, it should be possible to limit the Finnish VAT liability to supplies made to Finnish individuals that are effectively used in the EU. However, this may then require the overseas provider to be registered for VAT purposes in many different EU-member states. Alternatively, an overseas provider may choose to register in a single EU-member state (e.g., Finland) in order to contract with all customers who are EU private individuals. The supplies made from the single EU registration to these customers will then be subject to local VAT in the member state of registration.

Access to the Internet is included within the definition of telecommunications, and the principles set out above apply equally to Internet service providers.

Local and Provincial Taxes

Neither limited liability companies nor branches are liable for any local or provincial taxes.

France

Telecommunications Tax Profile
by Xavier Rohmer
Tax Partner, Paris
and Jean-Luc Pierre
Tax Partner, Paris

Overview of the Telecommunications Market

Historical Background

In 1990 France Télécom was established as an autonomous public corporation. Since 1990, the French Posts and Telecommunications Code has been amended several times to reflect European Union (EU) directives. In particular, the telecommunications bill of 1996 provided for the full deregulation of the France Télécom monopoly by January 1, 1998. In April 1997 France Télécom was partly privatized. The markets for other telecommunications services, such as cellular, paging and value-added services, were liberalized in 1987.

Current Status

Although France Télécom's monopoly on basic voice service, facsimile transmission services and operation of the public wireline network was ended on January 1, 1998, the company still holds a dominant position in the provision of telecommunications networks and services.

The first authorizations for new licenses for the provision of telecoms services to the public were granted by the Telecommunications Regulatory Authority (Autorité de Régulation des Télécommunications, or ART) to Cegetel, Bouygues-STET Télécom (BS Télécom), Omnicom and SIRIS. Cable television operators are now authorized to provide voice and non-voice telecommunications services.

There are three cellular radio operators: France Télécom, Société Française du Radiotéléphone (SFR) and Bouygues Télécom. France Télécom and SFR operate both analog and digital global system for mobile communications (GSM) networks. Bouygues Télécom operates a digital cellular system (DCS)-1800 network. SFR is 80% held by Cegetel, a subsidiary of Compagnie Générale des Eaux (CGE), with participation from British Telecom. Cable & Wireless Plc, STET and VEBA AG participate in Bouygues Télécom's cellular service.

France Télécom Mobiles Data and Société Française de Transmission de Données par Radio (TDR), a subsidiary of Cegetel, are the only two authorized operators of packet-switched public mobile data networks. Several companies provide regional trunked mobile radio service, including two subsidiaries of France Télécom. Several radio paging service providers compete against France Télécom. The very small aperture terminal (VSAT) market is dominated by France Télécom, but many other VSAT service providers are active.

Several new network operators were authorized in 1995. Société Nationale des Chemins de Fer (SNCF), the French rail company, was authorized to lease capacity on its private network to mobile telephony service providers. SNCF created a telecommunications subsidiary, Télécom Développement (TD), which is allied with Cegetel. MFS Communications was also authorized to construct a fiber optic metropolitan network in Paris. Other network operators have entered this market recently.

Current Liberalization Status

In the World Trade Organization (WTO) negotiations in February 1997, France committed to full liberalization of its telecommunications markets and adherence to a set of common regulatory principles by January 1, 1998. It also retained restrictions on foreign ownership of cellular operations.

Type of Service	Degree of Liberalization	Key Legislation	Date of Actual or Expected Liberalization	Comments
Local, Long Distance and International	Deregulated	Telecommunications bill of July 26, 1996	January 1, 1998	There is no legal distinction between local, long-distance and international services. Voice services were deregulated on January 1, 1998.
Cellular	Limited to three facilities-based carriers	Decree of September 24, 1987	1987	SFR received authorization in 1987; Bouygues Télécom in 1993.
Paging	Deregulated	Decree of September 24, 1987	1987	
Value-added	Fully liberalized		1987	

Competitive Environment

Many new providers are emerging in the market, the largest being Cegetel. The other providers include BS Télécom (Bouygues), SIRIS, Aéroports de Paris, Belgacom Téléport, COLT Télécommunications, EQUANT (owned by SITA-EQUANT Holdings), and WorldCom.

Some providers of alternative infrastructures are trying to position themselves in the opening telecommunications market. These companies include cable operators Lyonnaise Câble and Compagnie Générale de Vidéocommunication (CGV), as well as transportation-sector participants Eurotunnel, Telcité (a part of Régie Autonome des Transports Parisiens, or RATP), Société des Autoroutes du Nord et de l'Est de la France (SANEF), SNCF/Cegetel and Société des Autoroutes Paris-Rhin-Rhône (SAPRR).

Type of Service	Entire Market		Top Two Players		
	Market Size (1996)	Number of Players	Names	Annual Revenue (1996)	Ownership
Local, Long Distance and International	FF102 billion	2	France Télécom	FF151.3 billion*	Government 51%, publicly traded 49%
			Cegetel**	(Launching operations)	Compagnie Générale des Eaux
Cellular	Not available	3	France Télécom Mobiles	FF10.7 billion	France Télécom
			SFR	FF5.2 billion	Cegetel
Paging	Not available	3	France Télécom	FF526 million	Government 51%, publicly traded 49%
			Pager TDR	FF66.7 million	Cegetel
Value-added	Not available	Not available	France Télécom	Not available	Government 51%, publicly traded 49%

Sources: France Télécom, Cegetel/Compagnie Générale des Eaux.
* France Télécom global turnover of FF151.3 billion includes all services.
** Providing only long distance and international in 1998.

Licensing Requirements

Permits and authorizations for services and networks are obtained from the Administration of Posts and Telecommunications (Direction Générale des Postes et Télécommunications, or DGPT), which is part of the Ministry of Telecommunications, or the ART, which is an independent organization. The DGPT and the ART oversee competitive practices and technical standards. Although value-added and data services are open to competition, the DGPT and the ART require that service providers meet certain conditions. In some cases, the DGPT and the ART require only a simple declaration by the service provider; in other cases, formal DGPT and ART authorizations are required.

Licenses for public networks, public telephony services, and telecommunications services using a radio network are granted by the Minister of Telecommunications after an inquiry by the ART. Licenses for independent networks are granted by the ART. No new licenses are likely to be granted in cellular on a nationwide or regional basis. Providers who supply non-telephony telecommunications services to the public over cable networks must make declarations to the ART after informing the local authorities having jurisdiction in the service area. Private networks can be established without formal authorization, unless the network uses radio frequencies.

Potential for Foreign Ownerships/Relationships

Foreign investment restrictions exist only for networks using radio frequencies. For such networks, authorization cannot be granted for companies in which more than 20% of the registered capital or voting rights are held directly or indirectly by non-residents.

Potential for Upcoming Liberalization/Investment Opportunities

On January 1, 1998, the provision of telecoms services and networks was fully deregulated in France. France Télécom was already deregulated for competitors in the most lucrative segments: telecoms services to corporations, long distance and international telephony. Over the next two years, competition will occur in tariffs and quality of services.

Because of the level of investment required, there are still no competitors with their own networks to rival France Télécom in local calling services. The only alternative local loop likely to be available before the year 2000 would be over cable networks, which are partly owned by France Télécom and the "radio local loop" for which an auction should be launched by the ART before the end of 1998.

With penetration in cellular services of less than 5%, the mobile services segment is relatively small compared with other European countries. Strong demand exists among potential business and residential customers, and market revenues are expected to double by 2000. Data services and online information services are also considered areas of strong growth potential.

Forms of Doing Business

Permanent Establishment

If a tax treaty applies, a permanent establishment (PE) is generally defined as a fixed place of business through which a business is wholly or partly carried out, the decisive criterion being whether the activity of this fixed place is an essential part of the activity of the foreign company as a whole. In the absence of a tax treaty, PE may be defined as (1) a fixed place of business having a certain degree of independence and which deals with third parties, (2) activities performed by dependent representatives of a foreign company in France, or (3) a company carrying out a "complete" cycle of transactions in France.

A PE is treated as a taxable entity for the activities it performs in French territory, and all income generated is subject to French corporate income tax. A PE must file a corporate tax return. Its transactions are subject to VAT, and it must file monthly turnover returns. In addition, it pays local taxes and taxes assessed on wages.

Telecommunications services can cover a broad range of activities, which may or may not constitute a PE. Some examples follow:

- The provision of long-distance telephone services does not normally create a PE if no equipment or personnel are located in France.

- The licensing of technology and know-how by a foreign company does not create a PE.

- In the case of an operator agreement, if the employees of a foreign company provide only user-support services or network management assistance to the local company, and these employees do not have the authority to conclude contracts on behalf of the foreign company, it may be argued that the foreign company carries on purely auxiliary activities in France and does not constitute a PE. If personnel of the foreign company are based in France, then any activity of a more substantive nature is likely to constitute a PE.

- The leasing of telecommunications equipment does not create a PE. The provision of call reorganization/turnaround services does not create a PE if the provider has no equipment or personnel located in France.

- The provision of Internet access services does not create a PE if the provider has no equipment or personnel located in France.

- Having a server or a switch located in France does not create a PE if the operator has no other equipment or personnel located in France.

- The PE status and tax treatment of websites are under review by authorities. For the time being, generally, having a website located on a server in France that is accessible by French or foreign customers could create a PE if the website could be used by customers to order merchandise or services. Otherwise, the website would not create a PE if no other equipment or personnel were based in France, even in the absence of an applicable tax treaty. Having a website located on a server outside France but accessible by French customers would not, in principle, create a PE.

- The laying of fiber optic cable and the construction of telecommunications switching equipment (a) for sale to a local company, or (b) to be operated by a foreign telecommunications company on behalf of a local company, generally constitutes a PE. However, most double-taxation treaties provide that construction projects of a defined length (between six months and two years, depending on the treaty) do not constitute PEs.

Business Entities

The choice of an appropriate entity depends mainly on the size of the business. The types of entities are described below:

Local Branch of a Foreign Company. A branch may be defined as a permanent place of business having a certain degree of independence in its operations and dealings with third parties. However, a branch does not have a legal or tax existence separate from its parent company.

From a legal standpoint, it is simpler to establish a branch than a subsidiary in France. From a tax standpoint, when the company creating the branch is a foreign entity, its branch is normally deemed to be a permanent establishment for tax purposes under most tax treaties, and is subject to corporate income tax, VAT, taxes assessed on wages and local taxes. In the absence of a tax treaty, a branch of a foreign company must pay branch withholding tax on all of its net after-tax income. (See "Corporate Income Taxes.")

Locally Incorporated Subsidiary of a Foreign Company. Large business enterprises, in which the capital needs cannot be insured by a limited number of shareholders, commonly choose to operate as joint stock companies (sociétés anonymes, or SAs). Most small and medium-sized enterprises choose to operate as limited liability companies (sociétés à responsabilité limitée, or SARLs).

From a tax standpoint, a subsidiary is subject to the same tax obligations as a French incorporated company (i.e., corporate income tax, VAT, taxes assessed on wages and local taxes). However, it is possible for a parent company and its branches or subsidiaries to be considered as a single entity liable for corporate tax. (See "French Group Tax Relief.")

Joint Venture. From a legal standpoint, a joint venture is an association that does not have a legal existence separate from

its shareholders. It is a legal business relationship with a specific purpose and participants who make contributions and share in the profits and losses.

A joint venture is the appropriate business vehicle for participants who wish to pool their resources and organize their relationships in a flexible and simple manner. It is also the appropriate vehicle for participants who do not wish to disclose to the public that they are working together. A joint venture is usually chosen for temporary, limited projects. If a joint venture is to be formed and controlled by members of non-EU countries, clearance from the French Treasury may have to be secured.

A joint venture is not a taxable entity. Consequently, the participants are subject to income tax on the net taxable income, whether or not it is distributed.

Another option for investors is a simplified joint stock company (société par actions simplifiée, or SAS). A SAS is a limited liability company that may be used by large enterprises (with a minimum share capital of FF1,500,000) as the corporate vehicle for holding companies on both a national and an international level.

Local Funding Alternatives

Debt versus Equity

The tax consequences of using debt are as follows:

- Interest costs are deductible on an accrual basis. However, in certain circumstances, the deductibility of interest is restricted.

- Interest paid in connection with a loan obtained abroad may be subject to withholding tax at a rate of 15%.

- In general, loans from foreign shareholders considered to be managing a French company or from any shareholders with an interest or financial rights in the company of more than 50% may not exceed 150% of the French company's share capital. If they do, the excess interest will be treated as a dividend. (See the discussion of France's thin-capitalization rules below.)

Dividends are not deductible. Dividends paid by a French company to a French-resident shareholder are not subject to withholding tax. However, dividends paid to a company whose residence or headquarters is outside France are subject to withholding tax at a rate of 25% on dividends effectively paid. This may be reduced by a tax treaty.

The thin-capitalization rules applicable to French companies who pay interest to foreign shareholders considered to be managing the French company or owning more than 50% of the financial rights in a company are as follows:

- Interest is not deductible if the French subsidiary capital is not paid in full.

- The maximum rate for deductible interest is equal to the yearly average of the gross yield on bonds at issuance of private company bonds. This rate, which varies on a regular basis, was 5.75% for 1997. Interest is deductible only on loans from all of the shareholders concerned, up to a maximum amount calculated on one and a half times the amount of the company's share capital.

The limitation relating to debt-to-equity ratios does not apply to loans granted to subsidiaries by French companies that qualify as parent companies (i.e., when the parent company owns at least 10% of the share capital of the subsidiary). To avoid thin-capitalization rules, depending on the circumstances, a French company can borrow from a non-shareholder, a sister company or a grandparent company.

There is no withholding tax on interest payments for loans obtained abroad by a French company if a loan agreement is executed prior to the effective cash transfer and if the borrower is a French-registered legal person and the lender is a non-resident. The Ministry of Finance must receive prior notification of loans granted by non-EU controlling shareholders. Although financial operations are included in the general VAT system, interest is not subject to VAT.

Debts and receivables stated in foreign currency are evaluated at market value at the end of each fiscal year; thus, exchange gains are taxable at the standard corporate income tax rate (see "Corporate Income Taxes"), and exchange losses are deductible from taxable income.

Exchange Controls

In principle, all direct investments are exempt from prior administrative declaration or authorization from the Ministry of Finance and are exempt from reporting if they do not exceed FF10 million. A direct investment is considered to be the purchase, creation or expansion of a business in France, or any operation leading to the holding by non-French residents of a controlling interest in a French company (i.e., 20% of its capital or voting rights if the company is listed on the Paris Stock Exchange, or 33.33% of its capital or voting rights if the company is not listed). The concept of controlling interest can also include any other form of control obtained through the grant of substantial loans, advances, warranties and the like.

Certain investments (e.g., the creation of a new branch for an amount exceeding FF10 million) require that a report be sub-mitted to the Ministry of Finance within 20 days following the investment. Other investments (e.g., the granting of a loan to a French company that is controlled by non-residents) are exempt from both the declaration or authorization and from the report requirement.

Business Acquisitions and Dispositions

Capital Contributions into an Existing Local Entity

Transfers made in exchange for an ownership interest in a French company are subject to a fixed capital contribution registration tax of FF1,500. A contribution of land, buildings, goodwill or leasehold rights made by a non-resident contributor who is not liable for corporate tax is subject to registration duties amounting to 8.6% of the contribution plus additional local registration taxes, which vary according to the type of capital contribution, for a global average rate of 13%. The 8.6% rate (plus additional local registration taxes) may, in certain circumstances, be reduced to a flat rate of FF1,500 if the contributor makes a commitment to hold the shares issued as a result of the contribution for at least five years. When a contribution includes liabilities (apports à titre onéreux), registration duties are levied up to the amount of liabilities at the rate applicable to the transfer of assets. There are no specific limitations on the intangibles that a foreign entity can contribute to a local entity, and the contribution should not affect the use of any tax attributes in a local entity (e.g., net operating losses carried forward).

A capital contribution does not normally create any tax consequence for the existing shareholder if the legal and tax status of the company is not modified. Moreover, the financial interest of the existing shareholder is preserved through a share premium device. Thus, the new shareholder must pay to the existing shareholder a premium corresponding to the excess of issue price over par value of stock. The taxation of the share premium is similar to the taxation of the corresponding contribution.

The redemption, in the form of a refund or restitution of the initial contribution to the contributor, is subject to transfer tax of 1%. If the amount of the refund exceeds the initial value of the contribution, the excess of value is subject to registration duties as if it were a sale of goods. The redemption can be subject to corporate tax as a distribution of dividends if the contribution refund exceeds the amount of the initial contribution.

Purchase or Sale of Shares in a Local Entity

A registration tax of 4.8% is imposed on the consideration paid for the transfer of non-negotiable shares of a company that has its registered office in France. However, if the tax administration deems that the market value of the shares or the real value transferred, including goodwill, is greater than the consideration paid, registration tax will be imposed on the market value of the shares. In principle, such a transfer must be made by a written instrument (acte écrit). If such an instrument is not prepared, registration tax is imposed and the parties to the transfer must file a tax return within one month of the date of the transfer with the office of the tax administration in the domicile of one of the parties to the transfer. Registration tax is also imposed on transfers of non-negotiable shares made outside of France.

French law does not lay down any set method for valuing a business or shares. From a practical viewpoint, the parties can use an indicative valuation scale provided by the French Revenue or base the market value on a comparison with similar businesses in the same sector.

A transfer of negotiable shares issued by a company that has its registered office in France is not subject to registration tax unless the transfer is evidenced by a written instrument signed in France. In this case, the transfer is taxed at a rate of 1%, not to exceed FF20,000 per transfer.

Such companies as sociétés en nom collectif (SNCs), sociétés en commandite simple (SCSs) and sociétés à responsabilité limitée (SARLs) issue non-negotiable shares. Joint stock corporations such as sociétés anonymes (SAs), sociétés par actions simplifiée (SAS) and sociétés en commandite par actions (SCA) issue negotiable shares.

Any capital gains realized by a resident individual owning at least 25% of the share capital of a French company liable to corporate tax are subject to capital gains tax at the rate of 26% (16% plus additional contributions such as the prélèvement social, or social levy, which is a 1% exceptional social contribution; the contribution sociale généralisée, or CSG; and the remboursement de la dette sociale, or RDS) on the capital gains arising from the shares disposal. The capital gains arising from the disposal of shares, either in listed or unlisted companies, are subject to a 26% tax if the annual sales proceeds exceed the exemption ceiling of FF50,000 for 1998.

The sale of shares in an undertaking for collective investment in transferable security or in one of the two types of unit trust normally used in France (a SICAV, or société d'investissement à capital variable, and a FCP, or fonds communs de placement), and which are invested in monetary or bond products, subjects the seller to a 26% capital gains tax rate without an exemption ceiling.

Any capital gains realized by a resident company are subject to tax at a rate of 33.33% or, exceptionally, 19% (see "Capital Gains Taxes"). If a non-resident individual or company realizes a capital gain on the sale, exchange or other disposition of shares of a French company in which it held, directly or indirectly, during the preceding five years, an interest entitling it to

at least 25% of the company's profits, the gain is subject to capital gains tax at a flat rate of 16%. Double-taxation treaties usually eliminate this tax liability.

The capital gains tax imposed must be tendered either at the time of the registration of the deed of transfer or, if no registration is required, within one month after the date of sale. A non-resident company must appoint a French tax representative who will be liable for the payment of its capital gains tax.

French law contains no specific provision that would result in a step-up in the basis of the underlying assets. However, it is possible to achieve the same effect when a French holding company merges with a target company. The assets of the target are then deemed to have been disposed of. The special merger regime provides a capital gains rollover relief for the non-depreciable assets and a taxation of the capital gains on the depreciable assets at the same rate as the amortization of the new value of the assets.

Purchase or Sale of Assets

The purchase of a business through the acquisition of its assets has significant tax implications for the buyer, who bears registration duties of 11.4%, which are assessed either on the purchase price of the assets or on their fair market value (whichever is higher). Because the costs are high for both parties, the transfer of assets is unusual, and it is preferable to obtain control of a business through the purchase of the majority or all of the shares in a company.

From a tax standpoint, the sale of assets, which generates a capital gain taxable at the standard corporate income tax rate, is more costly than selling the controlling interests represented by the shares (see "Capital Gains Taxes"). French law does not set out a method for valuing assets for tax purposes.

The sale of partnership interests owned by a company liable to corporate tax is subject to capital gains tax. Moreover, the purchaser is liable for registration duties at the rate of 4.8%.

Start-up Business Issues

Pre-operating Losses and Start-up/ Construction Costs

Start-up expenses, such as legal fees, that are incurred in the creation and organization of a company, must either be amortized over five years or expensed in the first year. Tangible assets, such as network equipment, can be amortized. Intangible assets, such as licenses, cannot.

Pre-operating expenses, such as those incurred through the installation of network equipment or the construction of a building, are capitalized. The two principal methods used to depreciate such expenses are the straight-line method (used for commercial real estate, patents and industrial know-how) and the declining-balance method (used for industrial buildings, plants, certain equipment and vehicles).

In general, the depreciation begins on the date an asset is put into service. When an asset is depreciated under the straight-line method, the first date of service is the date on which it was acquired. When the declining-balance method is used, the first date of service is the date on which it was built. For example, if the construction of a cellular station begins during the 1997 taxable year and takes two years to complete, the company will depreciate construction costs in 1999, when the station will be considered to be placed in service.

Customs Duties and VAT

Most goods imported into France from outside the EU are subject to customs duty and import VAT unless exemptions apply. Duty is normally payable on the cost, insurance and freight (CIF) value of the goods. Import VAT is payable on the duty-inclusive value of the goods, although VAT-registered traders can usually obtain a refund of the VAT.

Telecommunications and computing equipment are subject to duty ranging from 1.2% to 10.5%. The rate of duty depends on the exact description and the tariff classification of the goods, as well as the country of origin of the goods. The current import duty rates for a sample of telecommunications goods originating in non-EU countries (in this example, the United States) are given below. The EU has preferential trade agreements with a number of countries that enable goods to be imported at rates below those indicated or at nil rate of duty.

Line telephone sets with cordless handsets	3.8%
Videophones	7%
Other telephone sets	3.8%
Facsimile machines	3.8%
Teleprinters	3.8%
Telephonic or telegraphic switching apparatus	3.8%
Other apparatus for carrier line systems	2.3%
Other apparatus for digital line systems	3.8%
Building-entry telephone systems	3.8%

Customs duties on some items of equipment were already being reduced under the General Agreement on Tariffs and Trade (GATT). However, over the next few years, duty rates are scheduled to be reduced further under the Information Technology Agreement (ITA) signed in March 1997. The ITA also extends the range of goods subject to duty-rate reductions. As a signatory to the ITA, the EU has agreed to cut tariffs on imports of computers and computer equipment, software, telecommunications and networking equipment to zero in four equal installments. The first reduction took place on July 1, 1997, and further reductions are to take effect on January 1 of each year through 2000. Although the ITA will cut the cost of importing many products, the convergence of technologies in the computing, electronics and telecommunications sectors is likely to lead to disputes over the tariff classification of some equipment and affect the availability and/or phasing of duty reductions under the ITA.

A wide variety of reliefs from customs duty (and import VAT) can be claimed in various circumstances (e.g., goods imported for processing and re-export, or goods imported temporarily). There is also a relief available for capital goods and equipment, provided the goods are imported by a business on the transfer of its activities to France. Raw materials or components that are not available, or not available in sufficient quantities, within the EU may be eligible for a complete or partial suspension of duty, providing this can be demonstrated to the satisfaction of the Commission of the European Communities in Brussels.

Goods may be subject to anti-dumping or countervailing duty if, for example, the EU considers they are being imported into the EU at prices substantially lower than their normal values. Anti-dumping and countervailing duties are chargeable in addition to, and independent of, any other duty to which the imported goods may be liable.

Loss Carryovers

Losses incurred as a result of the operation of the taxpayer's business or as a result of certain events that affect the assets of a taxpayer (for example, debt losses) are deductible in the taxable year during which they were incurred.

For tax purposes, net operating losses can be carried forward or carried backward. The amount of net tax loss will be deducted from a taxpayer's taxable ordinary income realized during the following tax year if the taxpayer does not elect to carry back the loss. A net tax loss can be carried forward for five years following the year in which it was incurred. When a taxpayer realizes a net loss and therefore cannot deduct the depreciation it is entitled to on its fixed assets during a tax year, it may carry forward the unused depreciation deduction indefinitely until the deduction can be used to offset net taxable income.

Loss carryforwards, including one in the form of a depreciation deduction, normally cannot be transferred to another taxpayer. In other words, only the taxpayer who actually incurs the tax loss can benefit from it, and only if the taxpayer does not change its corporate purpose or activity. Accordingly, in the case of a merger or a partial transfer of the taxpayer's business activity, loss carryforwards in the nature of unused depreciation deductions can no longer be carried forward indefinitely but are assimilated into ordinary loss carryforwards, and usage is thus limited to five years. When a taxpayer sells a going concern or substantially changes the nature of its business activity or its corporate purpose, it loses its ordinary loss carryforward. A loss carryforward in the form of a depreciation deduction would be assimilated into an ordinary loss carryforward. A switch from wireline to cellular would not be considered a modification of activity.

French enterprises can elect to carry back losses of a given year and set them against the profits of the three preceding years. This offsetting does not result in an immediate refund, but gives rise to a tax credit, which is calculated by multiplying the deficit actually written off by the normal corporate tax rate that was applicable to the fiscal year when the deficit was recorded. This tax credit may be offset against the corporate income tax for the following five years and, thereafter, any excess can be reimbursed in cash. It can also be discounted with a bank.

Operating Considerations

Corporate Income Taxes

Taxable income deriving from business conducted in France, either through branches or subsidiaries, is subject to corporate tax at the standard rate of 33.33%. A 10% contribution is added, making the total effective rate 36.66%.

Under a new finance bill, taxable income is subject to the standard rate of 33.33% plus the current contribution of 10%, with an additional contribution of 15% of the corporate tax liability. The total effective rate is therefore 41.66% (33.33 + 3.33 + 5). This new rate applies for the fiscal years 1997 and 1998. According to the bill's provisions, it will decrease to 40% (33.33 + 3.33 + 3.33) in 1999 (i.e., the new contribution will decrease to 10% at that time).

Small businesses, with turnover of less than FF50 million, would benefit from the existing lower effective rate of 36.66%. The new contribution of 15% would also not apply to companies that are heads of tax groups, in which at least 75% of share capital is owned by individuals, and which have a total turnover of less than FF50 million (all subsidiaries of the group included).

A minimum annual company tax is due from all entities subject to corporate income tax. It is based on the annual turnover, including VAT. Such a lump-sum corporate tax ranges from FF5,000 to FF100,000.

French Tax Group Relief. Group tax relief allows a parent company and its subsidiaries to be considered as a single en-

tity liable for corporate tax. To be eligible for this option, a parent company and its subsidiaries must be French companies subject to corporate tax at the standard rate and have the same 12-month financial-year opening and closing dates. A French branch of a foreign company is eligible to be a parent for a tax group. The parent company must hold directly or indirectly at least 95% of the share capital of the subsidiaries. The parent company cannot be directly or indirectly a 95%-owned subsidiary of another French company; however, it may be a wholly owned subsidiary of a foreign company. The composition of the group is determined by the parent company, who may choose for which of its eligible subsidiaries group relief will be elected.

Withholding Tax. Dividends paid by a French company to a company whose residence or headquarters is outside of France are subject to withholding tax at a rate of 25% on dividends effectively paid. This rate may be reduced by a tax treaty. In addition, dividends paid by a French company to a parent company located in an EU-member state may be exempt from withholding tax under certain circumstances.

Except for the dividend withholding tax levied on distributions made to non-French residents, company dividend distributions do not give rise to taxation when the distributions can be allocated to after-tax profits, which are taxed at the standard rate. Distributions that cannot be offset against such profits give rise to the dividend equalization tax (précompte), which is levied at 33.33% of the gross amount distributed. This dividend equalization tax (netted from any applicable withholding tax at source) may be reimbursed to shareholders residing in a country with which France has concluded a tax treaty.

Branch Withholding Tax. Net after-tax profits realized by a French permanent establishment (whether a branch or not) of a foreign company are deemed to constitute constructive dividends presumptively distributed at the end of each fiscal year to shareholders of the foreign company. These shareholders are considered to be either individuals domiciled outside of France or non-French operating companies and, therefore, their distributed dividends are subject to a 25% withholding tax. Foreign companies may overcome these presumptions by proving that the profits made in France by their PEs were either not distributed outside of France or were distributed to shareholders having their tax domiciles in France.

Under most tax treaties, the rate of withholding tax imposed on ordinary dividends, or constructive dividends presumptively declared by a PE of a foreign company, is often reduced, or the branch tax liability eliminated. In late 1997, the European Commission found discriminatory the withholding tax provisions of France's regime concerning PE and ordered France to change its legislation. Consequently, the 1997 finance bill was amended so that this branch withholding tax would no longer be applicable to profits made by French branches of companies established in EU-member states. These new provisions were to be in force as of January 1, 1998.

Capital Gains Taxes

The rules governing the determination and taxation of capital gains and losses incurred by companies subject to corporate income tax come into play only in connection with the sale, exchange, transfer or other disposition of fixed assets, both tangible (such as buildings, equipment and real property) and intangible (such as securities and income generated by the sale or licensing of patents). The tax treatment of these gains and losses depends both on the nature of the assets and the period during which they were held. Long-term capital gains are gains on the disposal of assets that are held for at least two years, and also that part of the gain on depreciable fixed assets exceeding the recapture of depreciation deducted on these assets. Short-term capital gains are gains on fixed assets held for less than two years, and also that part of the gain on depreciable fixed assets held for at least two years that corresponds to the recapture of depreciation deducted on these assets.

Long-term capital losses are losses on the disposal of non-depreciable assets held for more than two years. Reserves recorded as a result of depreciation in the value of investment in shares of companies may, under certain conditions, be treated as long-term capital losses. Short-term capital losses are losses incurred on the disposal of all other fixed assets.

Short-term capital gains and losses are set off against each other at the end of the fiscal year. When this results in a net short-term capital gain, the gain is subject to corporate tax at the standard rate. When it results in a net short-term capital loss, the amount is deducted from the taxpayer's taxable ordinary income. Long-term capital gains and losses are set off against each other at the end of each fiscal year. A new provision of the tax law equalized the tax treatment of capital gains and trading income. Long-term capital gains are no longer treated and taxed separately at the low rate of 19%. The low rate provided for long-term capital gains has been abolished, and any capital gains will thus be subject to the standard rate of 33.33% plus additional contributions of 10% or 15% if the companies concerned have a turnover of more than FF50 million (see "Corporate Income Taxes"). This modification is applicable for financial years beginning January 1, 1997.

The low rate of 19% is still applicable to capital gains from the sale of controlling interests and income from specific assets (patents and assimilated industrial properties plus interests in risky capital companies).

Tax Holidays and Exemptions

Tax Credit for Research Expenditures. Through December 31, 1998, companies that increased their research expenditures can elect to use a tax credit to offset their French corporate income tax liability. This credit is equal to 50% of the increase in research expenditures (i.e., the excess of the amount of expenditures incurred during the relevant year over the average amount of those incurred during the two previous years). The credit is limited to an annual maximum of FF5 million, or FF10 million when part of the expenses involved fees paid to approved research centers. The tax credit ceiling is FF40 million for expenses incurred from 1991, with no distinction made between internal and external expenses.

If the tax credit exceeds the tax due, which would be the case if a company was in a loss position, the tax credit may be refunded. A reduction in research expenses does not entail a repayment of any prior credits, but a portion equal to 50% of the negative variation of expenses must be offset against any potential subsequent tax credit. Eligible research expenditures include:

- Depreciation on assets (including buildings purchased or built January 1, 1991, or later) used in scientific and technical research

- Personnel expenses relevant to the research

- Other operating expenses, which are set at 65%, 75% or 100% of the personnel expenses (the 75% rate applies in most of the country)

- The costs of research contracted out to approved research centers

- Expenditures related to acquiring and maintaining patents

- Depreciation charges related to patents acquired

- 50% of the expenses incurred to meet technical standards

- Research expenditures related to the development of new computer software

Tax Credit for Training Expenditures. This tax credit is available through 1998 for companies that increase their training expenditures. It could be used to offset French corporate income tax liability. Excess credits are refundable. The annual tax credit of up to FF1 million is equal to 25% of the increase in expenses incurred for the training of personnel over the preceding year (eligible expenses are those above the minimum legal requirement, which is 1.5% of the gross annual salaries paid).

Training expenses are increased to 40% and the tax credit ceiling is increased to FF5 million when the training expenses are incurred (a) by companies with fewer than 50 employees or for the benefit of employees more than 45 years old, or (b) for the benefit of less-qualified employees.

Other Tax Incentives. The following incentives to promote the relocation of companies may also apply to telecommunications businesses:

- A company with an industrial, scientific or technical research purpose can be granted, under specific conditions, a partial or total minimum five-year period business license tax exemption if it locates its activity in qualifying areas and if it can justify certain minimum levels of investment and employment.

- Companies purchasing real estate or goodwill in certain areas can benefit, with administrative approval, from a reduced rate of transfer duty.

- To promote industrial or service activities, companies making investments in qualifying areas can be granted, under certain conditions, a national planning subsidy (prime d'aménagement du territoire) corresponding to a percentage of their investments.

Depreciation/Cost-Recovery Conventions/Accelerated Deductions

Depreciation must be booked in the accounting records to be deductible for tax purposes. Depreciation of assets is tax-deductible within the limits provided by the practice particular to each business sector concerned. Companies can apply higher rates than the ones normally used if they can demonstrate that specific operating conditions cause greater depreciation. French law does not provide specific rules regarding telecommunications equipment or telecoms businesses.

Straight-Line Method. The straight-line method is the standard depreciation method and can be used for all depreciable fixed assets. The depreciation rate is obtained by dividing 100 by the useful life of the asset. The straight-line depreciation rates range from 2% for buildings to 25% for trucks. The rate is applied to the original cost of the fixed asset every year, with the first and last years of depreciation adjusted on a pro-rata basis.

Declining-Balance Method. Accelerated depreciation using the declining-balance method is expressly authorized by the French tax code for several specific assets, including manufacturing and processing equipment but excluding telecommunications equipment. To qualify for the declining-balance method, assets must be new or reconditioned and have a normal useful life of at least three years.

Expenses for the purchase of computer software can be depreciated totally over 12 months. This includes software embedded in telecommunications equipment. It should be noted that this provision is not applicable for software that is developed by a corporation for its own use.

Depreciation is computed by multiplying the rate corresponding to the straight-line method by the appropriate factor: 1.5, 2 or 2.5, depending on whether the normal useful life of the asset is 3 or 4 years, 5 or 6 years, or more than 6 years, respectively. The rate is applied annually to the net book value of the asset for each year of its useful life. The year of acquisition is counted as a full year.

Exceptional Depreciation. Companies that make specific eligible investments (e.g., equipment used for anti-noise or anti-pollution purposes, or software embedded in telecommunications equipment) are entitled to book a depreciation of 50% of the cost of the qualifying asset within 12 months following its purchase or its construction.

Treatment of Software and Research Expenditures As Operating Expenses or Assets. A company may choose to treat research expenses and expenses incurred in the development of software as (a) operating expenses, which are fully deductible in the year in which they are incurred, or (b) assets, which are depreciable over a maximum period of five years. For accounting purposes, research expenses can be capitalized and depreciated only if they have a reasonable chance of success. A company can depreciate software acquired from third parties over 12 months. Losses corresponding to this depreciation can be carried forward only for five years.

Advertising costs constitute operating expenses and are thus fully deductible in the fiscal year in which they are incurred.

Transfer Pricing Rules

The Economic and Financial Reform Act of 1996 provided for stricter regulation of transfer pricing. The French tax administration was granted power to request information from taxpayers. The administration can assess a fine of FF50,000 for each fiscal year for which a request was made and not answered. This law is applicable to audits of tax years starting April 15, 1996.

To determine whether a transfer of profits has taken place, the French tax authorities set the arm's-length price by referencing the price that would be agreed upon between unrelated parties operating in the market under similar circumstances and conditions.

Transfers of Patents, Trademarks and Software

Royalties paid for the concession of industrial property rights must correspond to bona fide transactions. Case law provides that royalties constitute the cost price of an asset when a company holds rights exclusively, when it has a warranty for the duration of the concession, and when this right can be conveyed to a third person.

Regarding the transfer of technology, there are two important incentives:

- A tax credit is available for companies that increase their research expenditures. Research expenses can be treated as operating expenses that are fully deductible in the year in which they are incurred or as assets that are depreciable over a maximum of five years.

- Income derived from the transfer or licensing of patents and know-how (whether they are exclusive or not) may benefit from a reduced corporate tax rate of 19% (instead of the standard rate of 33.33%).

Services relating to the transfer of technology may be identified as intangible personal property. Unless a tax treaty provides otherwise, the transfer of royalties paid in connection with the licensing of intellectual property rights from France to another country is subject to withholding tax of 33.33%. The services on which such withholding tax is imposed include the maintenance of equipment; the furnishing of technical assistance; the researching or supplying of information of a commercial, industrial or scientific nature; and the leasing of equipment for use in France. The withholding tax on royalties is assessed on the gross amount of the remuneration paid net of VAT or any other indirect tax. This rate is often reduced by a tax treaty.

Service Fees

There are no tax provisions specifically applicable to service fees. French tax authorities follow OECD (Organization for Economic Cooperation and Development) guidelines.

Value-Added Tax, Sales Tax and/or Other Pertinent Taxes

As a member of the EU, France follows the provisions of the European Community Sixth VAT Directive. Domestic telecommunications services (including those supplied by French-resident foreign businesses) are subject to VAT at the standard rate of 20.6%. The VAT treatment of international telecommunications services is based on the revised EU VAT model, which took effect in France on January 1, 1997.

Services supplied internationally by a telecommunications business located in France are generally outside the scope of VAT when supplied to anyone located outside France. The only exceptions are services supplied to private individuals or unregistered persons located in other member states. Those supplies are subject to French VAT at the standard rate.

Non-resident providers are not liable to register and account for French VAT on supplies used by French customers, providing those customers are taxable persons for VAT purposes. These customers are required to self-account for VAT under reverse-charge procedures.

When a non-resident provider makes supplies of services to private individuals, to be used in France, the provider is required to register and account for French VAT. For an overseas provider, it should be possible to limit the French VAT liability to supplies made to French individuals that are used in the EU. However, this may then require the overseas provider to be registered for VAT purposes in many different EU-member states. Alternatively, an overseas provider may choose to register in a single EU-member state (e.g., France) in order to contract with all customers who are EU private individuals. The supplies made from the single EU registration to these customers will then be subject to local VAT in the member state of registration.

Access to the Internet is included within the definition of telecommunications, and the principles set out above apply equally to Internet service providers.

Local and Provincial Taxes

Telecommunications businesses may be subject to real estate tax on the deemed rental value of property, undeveloped land and developed land (buildings). A company will not be liable for this tax if it only rents its premises. However, if the rent paid is not subject to VAT, then the company is liable for lease tax.

Telecommunications businesses may also be subject to business license tax, which is an annual local tax, the rate of which is determined by each local government and which varies from 16% to 30%. This rate is calculated on the basis of the rental value of the premises, the physical assets used by the enterprise and on 18% of its annual salaries.

Germany

Telecommunications Tax Profile
by Stefan Kaufmann
Tax Partner, Frankfurt

Overview of the Telecommunications Market

Historical Background

The German telecommunications sector was long controlled by the federal postal service, Deutsche Bundespost (DBP). In light of technological developments and the growth of the telecommunications market, the government in 1989 cleared the way for competition in the market for services and networks. The Postal Reform One restructured DBP, separating postal services from telecommunications services and creating DBP Telekom. A separate regulatory agency was established. Competition with DBP Telekom in national digital cellular phone services was authorized and further liberalization was planned. After the reunification of Germany in October 1990, DBP Telekom assumed responsibility for telecommunications services and for improvements to the infrastructure in the eastern parts of Germany.

In 1991 the market for telephone equipment was liberalized, and in August 1992 licenses were awarded to private trunk mobile radio operators. In 1993 a third digital cellular operator was authorized.

A July 1993 resolution of the European Union (EU) Council set January 1, 1998, as the deadline to liberalize public voice services. In 1994 the EU Council established procedures for liberalizing the network infrastructure. Germany's Postal Reform Two authorized DBP Telekom's conversion from a federal administration into a private-stock corporation, Deutsche Telekom AG. Legislation granted Deutsche Telekom a monopoly for wire-based telecommunications services through December 31, 1997.

In 1995 competition in satellite services was authorized, and private mobile telephony providers were permitted to use their own infrastructure for interconnection. The liberalization of alternative networks for third-party suppliers became effective in August 1996. Large companies such as Deutsche Bahn AG, VEBA AG, VIAG AG, Mannesmann AG and RWE AG are now permitted to resell network capacity to others.

The Telecommunications Act of July 25, 1996, defined the basic conditions for further liberalization and procedures to ensure fairness for new market entrants as they compete against Deutsche Telekom. Additionally, the law determines the cost-oriented interconnection prices, which are set by the German telecommunications regulatory agency.

Current Status

The German telecommunications market reached more than DM80 billion in revenues in 1996 and is expected to grow by 8% annually for the next several years. Deutsche Telekom holds the competitive advantage in all major voice and data telecommunications services, accounting for approximately 83% of the revenues in the total telecommunications market.

Competition in digital cellular services is limited to four licensees: DeTeMobil, Deutsche Telekom's affiliate; Mannesmann Mobilfunk; E-Plus Mobilfunk, whose investors include o.tel.o, BellSouth Corporation and Vodafone Group Plc; and E2 Mobilfunk, whose investors include British Telecom and VIAG. VIAG was awarded a license in 1997, and the company planned to start digital wireless services in 1998. Several licenses have been granted to trunk radio and paging service providers.

Licensing procedures for new entrants have not yet been established; nevertheless, large diversified companies such as VEBA, Mannesmann, RWE and VIAG have already sent in their tenders for contracts as telephone companies. Large German utilities are planning to enter this capital-intensive business, since they have both the financial power and established networks covering 11,000 kilometers. DBKom, Deutsche Bahn AG's (the German railway) affiliate, also has an extensive network infrastructure, with approximately 40,000 kilometers. Deutsche

Telekom has created one of the most technologically advanced fixed telecommunications networks in the world with approximately 402,000 kilometers in all, including 86,000 kilometers of fiber optic cables. The newly formed company "debitel," owned mainly by the Daimler-Benz Group and the Metro Group, is Germany's largest telephone company that does not own network infrastructure.

Two cellular standards are used in Germany. Deutsche Telekom and Mannesmann use global system for mobile communications (GSM)-900 and E-Plus and E2 have chosen digital cellular system (DCS)-1800.

To compete in the global telecommunications market, the German service providers have entered into domestic and international alliances. Together with France Telecom and Sprint, Deutsche Telekom formed Global One. VIAG, British Telecom and Telenor A/S, the owners of VIAG Interkom, are planning to form a wider alliance with an additional international partner.

RWE and VEBA have formed the alliance o.tel.o; this joint venture lacks an international partner, and at the end of 1997, the companies were still in negotiations to identify a suitable partner.

Deutsche Bahn has contributed its existing cable network in Germany to the newly formed alliance Arcor, which includes global players AT&T, Unisource and AirTouch Communications as well as Mannesmann. Arcor provides cellular as well as fixed network services.

Starting October 1, 1997, Deutsche Telekom was required to adjust charges for its information services based on actual cost. This change in legislation prompted the company almost to double its charges for information services. Its sole competitor in information services is the German company Telegate AG. Deutsche Telekom acquired a minority stake in VocalTec Communications Ltd., an Israeli company that is the world leader in software development for Internet telephony.

Current Liberalization Status

In the World Trade Organization (WTO) negotiations in February 1997, Germany committed to full liberalization and adherence to a common set of regulatory principles. In keeping with EU guidelines, the German Telecommunications Act introduced competition to the market, starting July 1, 1997, for the network, and starting January 1, 1998, for local and long-distance public voice services.

Type of Service	Degree of Liberalization	Key Legislation	Date of Actual or Expected Liberalization	Comments
Telephone equipment	Deregulated	Postal Structural Law	1991	
Public voice services	Monopoly	Telecommunications Law	January 1, 1998	14 licenses have been awarded
Cellular	Deregulated	Postal Structural Law	August 1992	4 digital licenses

Competitive Environment

During 1998 potential competitors to Deutsche Telekom are expected to extend their activities. In digital cellular competition, Deutsche Telekom has already lost its market leadership to Mannesmann Mobilfunk. Analog cellular services are still exclusively provided by Deutsche Telekom; however, their importance in the market is rapidly declining.

Type of Service	Entire Market		Top Two Players		
	Market Size (1996)	Number of Players	Names	Annual Revenue (1996)	Ownership
Local and Long Distance*	DM71.5 billion (for all telecoms services, including DM15 billion for domestic long distance)	Approximately 30 licensees, 4 main competitors	Deutsche Telekom	DM44.5 billion for domestic telephone services	Publicly traded; government is majority shareholder
			Arcor	Not available	Deutsche Bahn, plus consortium of Mannesmann, AT&T, others
International	Not available	3 main players and numerous call-back companies	Deutsche Telekom	DM4 billion (all international services)	Publicly traded; government is majority shareholder
			WorldCom	Not available	Publicly traded

Sources: *Communications Markets Analysis* (Germany), Espicom Business Intelligence, August 1997; *Communications Companies Analysis* (Deutsche Telekom), Espicom Business Intelligence, July 1997; Reuters; *Global Telecoms Business Yearbook 1997; Mobile Telecommunications in Germany,* International Business Strategies, October 1997.

* Domestic services are considered one segment.

Licensing Requirements

The new telecommunications law provides far-reaching market entry options. The only market activities subject to licensing are those that have previously been within the network infrastructure and telephone monopoly, including satellite and mobile radio communications. Private networks and services are not subject to regulation.

On January 1, 1998, the Bundesminister für Post und Telekommunikation (BMPT) was abolished and replaced with a new regulatory agency that is responsible for licensing, the Regulierungsbehörde für Telekommunikation und Post, Bonn. With full liberalization, there is no limit to the number of licenses that can be granted, except where resources, such as radio frequencies, are limited. At the end of 1997, 14 licenses for fixed network telephony were awarded to several companies, to become effective January 1, 1998.

Potential for Foreign Ownerships/Relationships

No limits exist on either the percentage of a telecommunications business that can be owned by a foreign company or on any licensing or service arrangement with foreign parties.

Potential for Upcoming Liberalization/Investment Opportunities

In 1998 several new telephone companies are expected to seek alliances with metropolitan-area fiber-optic carriers to offer basic telephony services. The most likely area for competition and investment in the telecommunications market will be in services to businesses. It is likely that the consumer market will stay with the largest domestic service provider, Deutsche Telekom.

Forms of Doing Business

Permanent Establishment

Permanent establishment (PE) is defined in German tax legislation as a fixed place of business or any other installation that serves the activities of an enterprise, including the place of management and control of enterprises, branches, offices, factories, workshops, warehouses, sales and/or purchase shops, and construction sites that exist longer than six months. Permanent agents, who are persons who regularly pursue the business of an enterprise and are subject to its directions, are treated similarly to PEs.

A similar definition of a PE, which is based on the OECD Model Convention, is found in most double-taxation treaties. However, in general, such definitions limit the cases in which a PE exists both under treaties and German tax legislation. Therefore, the following discussion should be read in the context of relevant treaties, which may modify the results:

- The provision of long-distance telephone services by a foreign company to a local customer without any local presence would, in general, not create a PE.

- The licensing of technology and know-how to a local company does not create a PE, but the license fees are subject to withholding tax at a rate of 25%. When a treaty provides for a reduced withholding tax rate, the creditor of the license fees may apply for an exemption certificate or a partial refund of the withholding tax.

- The provision of technical assistance and technological services, including operator and/or network management services, by a foreign company to a local company in exchange for a service fee usually does not create a PE, unless the foreign company's employees stay in Germany for a considerable period of time to render these services. This presence through permanent agents will be treated similarly to PEs. The use of an agent's own office would constitute a PE.

- Doing business through a German subsidiary that is controlled by a foreign parent company generally does not result in the parent company's being viewed as a PE. However, the local subsidiary might be qualified as a dependent agent and, therefore, constitute a PE if it has, and makes regular use of, the authority to conclude contracts on behalf of the parent company. As long as these services pertain to technical assistance and repairs only, they will not be subject to withholding tax. However, if the services lead to a transfer of know-how, the part of the service fee pertaining to such transfer is subject to a 25% withholding tax.

- When movable telecommunications equipment (i.e., physical objects, not real estate or accessories to real estate) is leased to a local company, the leasing fees are subject to a 25% withholding tax. However, in general, such activities do not create a PE. Leasing fees for real estate and other immobile property are not subject to withholding tax.

- The distributors of telephone cards for call reorganization/turnaround services are seen as permanent agents, and thus their services are treated as PEs under domestic law. Whether the receivables are collected by direct billing, credit card or by prepaid cards is irrelevant. However, most double-tax treaties exclude independent agents. Whether an agent is characterized as independent within the meaning of the applicable treaty depends on the individual case.

- If a foreign corporation's Internet access server is not located inside Germany, the provision of access will not create a PE. However, according to an opinion by Germany's Inland Revenue Office, a 25% withholding tax applies, not only to the lease, but also to the transfer of Internet access software.

- Having a server or a switch located in Germany but not having any personnel there may create a PE. In a recent decision, the Federal Fiscal Court held that a fully automated establishment through which the enterprise operates can create a PE. Whether this is the case under the particular tax treaty is questionable. Having a website located on a third-party server in Germany that is accessible by customers located in Germany does not create a PE. The same is true if the website is accessible only by customers outside Germany.

- Having a website located on a server outside Germany but accessible by customers located in Germany does not create a PE.

- The laying of fiber optic cable and the construction of telecommunications switching equipment for sale to a local company creates a PE if the activity lasts longer than six months.

- The laying of fiber optic cable and the construction of telecommunications switching equipment to be owned and operated by a foreign telecommunications company for a local company in exchange for a fee creates a PE. If the telecommunications network is owned by the local company and is only operated by the foreign company, this would create a PE for the foreign company, if the foreign company uses certain offices in Germany or has employees permanently in Germany.

Business Entities

Local Branch of a Foreign Company. In principle, all types of business can be carried out by a branch. Branch operations of foreign corporations are subject to corporate income tax at a rate of 42%. Additionally, a 5.5% solidarity surcharge of the assessed corporate income tax is imposed (this rate was reduced from 7.5%, as of January 1, 1998). Corporate income tax is levied on the portion of income that is attributable to the German business. Additionally, trade income tax may also be imposed (see "Operating Considerations"). No withholding tax is due on profits remitted to a foreign head office.

Although a branch's results cannot be grouped with the results of other companies, the branch can act as a dominant enterprise within a fiscal unity if it is formally registered and if the shares of German companies are effectively connected with that branch (see "Fiscal Unity").

Locally Founded Partnership of a Foreign Company. A partnership is not a taxable entity for income tax purposes. Federal tax (i.e., income tax and/or corporate income tax) is levied at the level of the partners, who can be either individuals or corporations. Municipal trade tax and VAT are levied at the level of the partnership. The partnership interest of non-resident partners constitutes a PE for tax purposes if the partnership owns a commercial enterprise. Therefore, a non-resident partner's profit is taxable in Germany, and expenses incurred by the partner related to such profit can be deducted. The net profit is subject to corporate tax at a rate of 42% (plus a solidarity surcharge) and trade tax on the income, if a non-resident partner is a corporation. If a non-resident partner is an individual, the tax rate applicable to German residents filing separate returns will apply. The maximum individual tax rate is 47% (plus a solidarity surcharge). Although a partnership cannot act as a dependent enterprise within a fiscal unity, it can act as the dominant enterprise and therefore group the results of its subsidiaries that are not partnerships.

Locally Incorporated Subsidiary of a Foreign Company. There are no restrictions on the establishment of a German corporation by foreign investors. Corporations are subject to corporate income tax, plus a solidarity surcharge and municipal trade income tax (see "Operating Considerations"). A resident corporation is taxed on its worldwide income. A corporation is considered a resident corporation if it maintains its legal seat or place of central management in Germany.

The tax liability of a legal entity amounts to approximately 46% (including trade income tax and solidarity surcharge), assuming the full distribution of the year's profit, whereas the tax burden of a German branch amounts to approximately 56%. These tax rates anticipate a municipal trade tax multiplier of 500% and the solidarity surcharge of 5.5% on the assessed corporate income tax.

Fiscal Unity. Fiscal unity (Organschaft) may be assumed if a resident corporation is integrated into another domestic enterprise (e.g., a corporation, partnership or German branch of a foreign corporation). If the prerequisites of fiscal unity as specified below are met, the consolidation of the results of different companies is possible. Subsequently, the income or losses of the dependent corporations (Organgesellschaften) are attributed to the controlling company (Organträger).

Integration must be fulfilled in financial, economic and organizational respects. Financial integration exists if the dominant enterprise holds more than 50% of the voting rights of the dependent company. Economic integration requires that the dependent corporation support the business of the dominant enterprise. Organizational integration exists if the management of the dominant enterprise is able to enforce its directions and instructions upon the dependent corporation. Organizational integration can, for instance, be ensured by appointing the managing director of the dominant enterprise as the managing director of the dependent corporation or by concluding a domination agreement (Beherrschungsvertrag). To benefit from the tax advantages of fiscal unity for corporate income tax purposes, a profit and loss pooling agreement (Ergebnisabführungsvertrag) is necessary, and it must meet certain formal requirements.

Joint Venture. A foreign investor can form a joint venture by participating in a corporation (a Gesellschaft mit beschränkter Haftung, or GmbH; or an Aktiengesellschaft, or AG) or in a partnership (a Gesellschaft bürgerlichen Rechts, or GbR; a Kommanditgesellschaft, or KG; an Offene Handelsgesellschaft, or OHG; or a Partnerschaft). The preferred alternative depends on how long the business is expected to last, how much flexibility is needed, the specific industry and the tax consequences. Typically, a partnership has been the preferred choice in the telecommunications industry because it permits the investor to benefit from any start-up losses and from a higher degree of flexibility in reducing or increasing the number of partners.

There are no legal or accounting restrictions relating to the formation of a telecommunications joint venture. There are also no important specific tax provisions for joint ventures. A nonincorporated joint venture is normally viewed as a partnership and taxed accordingly.

Local Funding Alternatives

Debt versus Equity

Because interest on loans is generally deductible and triggers no withholding tax, debt financing is the preferred technique for financing an acquisition.

Hybrid Financing Instruments. German law provides for several hybrid financing instruments such as silent partnerships, profit participation loans and usufructuary rights (Genussrechte). However, the thin capitalization regulations discussed below considerably limit the benefits from such instruments. If carefully drafted, all these instruments can be treated as debt financing for tax purposes. Therefore, subject to certain restrictions, payments on these instruments are deductible items in calculating the taxable income of a German entity. In Germany, unlike in many other jurisdictions, any obligations under these instruments are deductible as business expenses on an accrual basis. Payments of normal interest are not subject to withholding tax, whereas payments on usufructuary rights and silent partnerships are subject to a 25% withholding tax (plus a solidarity surcharge). This rate can be reduced by a tax treaty.

Thin Capitalization Rules. Thin capitalization rules went into effect on January 1, 1994, and apply to shareholders owning directly or indirectly more than 25% of a company's shares if the shareholders are not entitled to a corporate tax credit (e.g., foreign residents or German charitable organizations). Interest paid to these shareholders or related parties is regarded as constructive dividends without reclassification of the debt as equity if prescribed debt-to-equity ratios are exceeded. When the relevant interest is calculated as a percentage of the principal amount of the debt (non-profit-related debt), the debt must not exceed three times the relevant equity (a debt-to-equity ratio of 3 to 1). If the amount of the interest would also depend on other factors (e.g., profit or profit-related debt), the debt-to-equity ratio is only 0.5 to 1. The ratio for non-profit-related debt is increased to 9 to 1 for qualified holding companies. The exceeding portion of the interest is not deductible for corporate income tax and can trigger the normal corporate income tax (plus a solidarity surcharge) on distributed profits, even if the company is in a loss position. The related withholding tax (plus a solidarity surcharge) can be reduced by a tax treaty.

These regulations also apply to interest paid to other creditors if a loan is guaranteed by a group company not entitled to a tax credit. However, beyond the tax code, the tax authorities have decided that these guaranteed interest payments should not be subject to the thin capitalization rules when the respective interest income is subject to German taxation (e.g., interest payments to German banks) and the company provides evidence that there is no back-to-back financing.

The use of holding companies may be advantageous in acquisitions with significant debt financing (see "Purchase or Sale of Assets"). Companies can qualify as holding companies if they hold shares of at least two subsidiaries and if (a) the book value of these shares amounts to at least 75% of the company's total assets excluding claims toward the subsidiaries, or if (b) the company's main activity consists of holding and financing subsidiaries. Subsidiaries of qualifying holding companies may not obtain any debt from foreign group members under the safe-haven rules. For companies not qualifying as holding companies, there is limited room for leverage as their equity is reduced by the book value of their subsidiaries. A combination of profit-related and non-profit-related debt does not lead to an accumulation of safe havens.

Exchange Gains and Losses. Any exchange losses of debts in foreign currencies must be recognized on an accrued basis. Corresponding profits can be reported (and taxed) only if realized (i.e., upon redemption).

Exchange Controls

No restrictions exist on the import and export of goods, services, capital, foreign payments or other international commercial transactions. The few existing restrictions are designed to prevent the inflow or outflow of foreign money or capital from disturbing economic equilibrium. Although there are no restrictions in force, a foreign trade ordinance (Außenwirtschaftsverordnung) does require the regular reporting of certain transactions with other countries to the Federal Bank (Deutsche Bundesbank).

Business Acquisitions and Dispositions

An acquisition or purchase/disposition could be structured as any of the following:

- A capital contribution by a foreign company into an existing local telecommunications company or a redemption by the local telecommunications company of the foreign company

- A purchase or sale by a foreign company of shares in a local entity owning the assets

- A purchase or sale by a foreign company of the telecommunications assets owned by an existing local company

Capital Contributions into an Existing Local Entity

Capital contributions of single (tangible and intangible) assets not qualifying as a business division (Teilbetrieb) are possible and must be evaluated with the fair market value of the asset contributed. Generally, these contributions are shareholder-driven and therefore do not trigger income taxes in the recipient company. The capital gains position of the contributing company, which must capitalize the fair market value of the contributed asset upon the shares in its entity, must be considered. When a contribution consists not only of single assets but also constitutes a Teilbetrieb, the regulations of the German Reorganization Tax Act apply, which opens the opportunity for a transfer at book value for EU-legal entities. Such a contribution qualifies as a business division when the assets being contributed are organized as a separate enterprise within the contributing company.

For non-EU-legal entities, this opportunity is given only if the taxation right of capital gains resulting from a future disposal of the shares in the German company is not shifted to the state of residence of the foreign company under the provisions of the applicable tax treaty.

Purchase or Sale of Shares in a Local Entity

The capital gain on a disposal of shares in a local entity is taxable in Germany for both resident and non-resident shareholders. However, for non-residents, a double-taxation treaty may assign the right of taxation exclusively to the country where the non-resident is located.

If the acquisition price of the shares in a corporation exceeds its net equity, a step-up in the book value of the newly acquired corporation's assets can generally be achieved. The corporation must either be converted into a partnership, and thereby preserve its identity, or be merged into a partnership. Investors can now amortize the assets of the remaining partnership in the usual manner, including the portion paid for goodwill. There are certain anti-avoidance rules, especially if the shares are acquired from non-resident vendors.

The acquisition of interest in a partnership leads automatically for tax purposes to an allocation of the purchase price to the tangible and intangible (including goodwill) assets and, therefore, is comparable with an acquisition of assets from the tax point of view.

Purchase or Sale of Assets

The purchase price of assets is allocated based on their fair market value, and a new basis for depreciation is established. The purchase price in excess of the tangible and identified intangible assets must be capitalized as goodwill and, at least for tax purposes, depreciated over 15 years using the straight-line method. (For tax treatment of a sale of assets to a local entity, see "Capital Gains Taxes.")

Recent amendments to commercial and tax law have diminished the traditional contrast between a seller's and a purchaser's views in the acquisition of a corporation. Traditionally, a seller would have preferred to sell shares in the corporation, while a purchaser would have preferred to buy the assets of the corporation in order to use depreciation to offset the earnings of the acquired corporation. Now it is possible to achieve the desired step-up by converting the acquired corporation into a partnership or by simply merging the corporation into a partnership.

A common technique for acquiring a target is formation of a German holding company (usually a GmbH), especially when acquisitions are to be financed significantly by debt. The use of the holding company allows the acquirer to offset the financing costs against the target's profit. Furthermore, using a German holding company as an acquisition vehicle may be necessary for certain post-acquisition structuring. Especially if separate acquisitions take place or are planned in the near future, a German holding company is required to set up a fiscal unity to consolidate positive and negative results within the German group.

For tax purposes, the sale of a partnership interest is deemed to be a sale of the underlying pro-rata portion of the assets and liabilities of the partnership (for tax purposes, the partnership interest includes assets and liabilities owned by the partner that serve the partnership or which support his partnership interest).

Start-up Business Issues

Pre-operating Losses and Start-up/Construction Costs

Pre-operating costs are not deductible if they are not effectively connected with a taxable entity. As long as start-up and construction costs are related to a German corporation, branch or partnership, they are fully deductible for tax purposes. When tangible assets are created through these activities, all costs must be capitalized and depreciated over the useful lives of the assets. The depreciation period begins as soon as construction is finished and the assets are placed in service. A capitalization of self-made intangible assets is not allowed. Therefore, the related expenses are deductible.

Input VAT on pre-operating costs can generally be recovered under German VAT legislation. Even companies that have no sales in Germany may also, upon application, recover invoiced German input VAT. The application must be filed not later than six months after year-end. As of July 31, 1997, this refund is granted only in cases of reciprocity.

Customs Duties and VAT

Most goods imported into Germany from outside the EU are subject to customs duty and import VAT. Duty is normally payable on the cost, insurance and freight (CIF) value of the goods (including costs incurred before the goods arrive at an EU land border). Import VAT is payable on the duty-inclusive value of the goods, although taxable persons can usually obtain a refund of the VAT.

Telecommunications and computing equipment are subject to duty ranging from 1.2% to 10.5%. The rate of duty depends on the exact description, tariff classification, and country of origin of the goods. The current import duty rates for a sample of telecommunications goods originating in non-EU countries (in this example, the United States) are given below. The EU has preferential trade agreements with a number of countries that enable goods to be imported at rates below those indicated or at nil rate of duty.

Line telephone sets with cordless handsets	3.8%
Videophones	7%
Other telephone sets	3.8%
Facsimile machines	3.8%
Teleprinters	3.8%
Telephonic or telegraphic switching apparatus	3.8%
Other apparatus for carrier line systems	2.3%
Other apparatus for digital line systems	3.8%
Building-entry telephone systems	3.8%

Customs duties on some items of equipment were already being reduced under the General Agreement on Tariffs and Trade (GATT). Over the next few years, duty rates are scheduled to be reduced further under the Information Technology Agreement (ITA) signed in March 1997. The ITA also extends the range of goods subject to duty rate reductions. As a signatory to the ITA, the EU has agreed to cut tariffs on imports of computers and computer equipment, software, telecommunications and networking equipment to zero in four equal installments. The first reduction took place on July 1, 1997, and further reductions are to take effect on January 1 of each year through 2000. Although the ITA will cut the cost of importing many products, the convergence of technologies in the computing, electronics and telecommunications sectors is likely to lead to disputes over the tariff classification of some equipment and affect the availability and/or phasing of duty reductions under the ITA.

A wide variety of reliefs from customs duty (and import VAT) can be claimed in various circumstances (e.g., goods imported for processing and re-export, or goods imported temporarily). There is also a relief available for capital goods and equipment, provided the goods are imported by a business on the transfer of its activities to Germany.

Raw materials or components that are not available, or not available in sufficient quantities, within the EU may be eligible for a complete or partial suspension of duty (though not for an exemption from import VAT), providing this can be demonstrated to the satisfaction of the Commission of the European Communities in Brussels.

Goods may be subject to anti-dumping duty if, for example, the EU considers they are being imported into the EU at prices substantially lower than their normal values. Anti-dumping duties are chargeable in addition to, and independent of, any other duty to which the imported goods are liable.

Loss Carryovers

Losses for corporate tax purposes may either be carried back for the last two years, up to a maximum of DM10 million, or carried forward for an indefinite period and in an unlimited amount. However, for a non-resident, such loss treatment requires the losses to be connected with German-sourced income.

Germany has introduced a specific anti-loss trafficking provision by which a corporation loses its entitlement to claim losses incurred in prior years if its economic identity has changed. Economic identity is deemed to have changed if more than half of the shares in a corporation are transferred to new shareholders and if the corporation thereafter continues or resumes its business operations essentially with new assets. The introduction of new assets is not harmful if they serve exclusively the rehabilitation of the business unit that created the remaining losses carried forward and if this business unit continues to exist for the next five years in a comparable dimension. A mere change of business activity (e.g., a change from wireline to cellular) without change of ownership will not affect the use of existing loss carryforwards.

As in the case of corporate income tax, losses for trade tax purposes can be carried forward for an unlimited period. Loss carrybacks, however, are not allowed. Any loss carryforward for trade tax purposes of a partnership will be abolished upon disposal of interests in that partnership proportionally.

Operating Considerations

The following information represents the status of tax rates in effect as of January 1, 1998. Authorities were at that time considering reductions of tax rates.

Corporate Income Taxes

The taxable income earned by a resident corporation is taxed at a rate of 45%. Upon distribution of profits, the tax rate is reduced to 30%. If the corporation has at first retained the income and subsequently distributed it to its shareholders, it may receive a tax refund.

Solidarity Surcharge. To finance German-unification costs, a solidarity surcharge was instituted on January 1, 1995. The rate was reduced to 5.5% (from 7.5%) effective January 1, 1998. The surcharge is based on the assessed corporate income tax after deducting the imputed tax credit for dividends received from German companies, on the assessed income tax, and on withholding taxes.

Withholding Tax. Interest payments are generally not subject to withholding tax, except for a 30% withholding tax on interest paid by a financial institution in Germany. Interest payments to corporations with a foreign seat or place of management are exempt from that withholding. The distribution of dividends generally triggers withholding tax at a rate of 25%. However, under an EU directive, the withholding tax rate is reduced to zero when an EU-resident corporation owns at least one-fourth of the subscribed capital for a 12-month period (the holding requirement can be met even after a dividend payment). Germany's tax treaties with non-EU countries generally reduce the withholding tax to a rate ranging from 5% to 15% when a foreign corporation's share in a German corporation exceeds minority shareholding.

Capital Gains Taxes

Whenever assets of a German branch or a German corporation are disposed of, the capital gain (the difference between the sales price and the book value) realized is subject to income tax at the regular rate. However, under certain circumstances, a rollover relief can be achieved for the disposal of real estate, buildings and movable tangible assets with useful lives of at least 25 years.

Tax Holidays and Exemptions

General Incentives. To encourage the flow of investments to less-industrialized areas of Germany, domestic and foreign companies establishing new business facilities may be eligible for a variety of subsidies and tax incentives. The main criterion for the granting of incentives is the number of jobs expected to be created through the investment project.

Other incentives (either cash subsidies or tax incentives) are offered to individuals and enterprises carrying out investments that serve the public interest (e.g., environmental improvements or research and development). In addition to incentives financed by the government, there are also incentives funded by EU programs and incentives for setting up businesses in East Germany.

Investing in East Germany. Since unification, foreign investors have been able to operate in the former East Germany in the same manner and using the same forms of business organization as in the former West Germany. In some instances, setting up a new company may be preferable to buying an existing East German company because of the traditional overstaffing in East German enterprises. Investment in East Germany is promoted by the EU, the European Recovery Programme and German governmental incentives. Companies investing in East German businesses may be granted tax relief under the Development Area Act (Fördergebietsgesetz). For both domestic and foreign investors, the Investment Subsidy Act (Investitionszulagengesetz) provides tax-free investment subsidies ranging from 5% to 10%, depending on the starting and closing dates of the investment (only for new movable tangible assets) and the type of business. To avoid repayment of the subsidy, the assets must remain in East Germany for at least three years.

There are numerous other incentives. For example, for specified investments in movable and immovable goods acquired or constructed from 1997 forward for a business in East Germany or West Berlin, an additional depreciation of up to 40% can be claimed. Entitlement rules are detailed.

Depreciation/Cost-Recovery Conventions/Accelerated Deductions

Land cannot be depreciated. Assets with a limited useful life are subject to depreciation. This applies to both tangible and intangible assets. Goodwill is depreciated over 15 years. Buildings can be depreciated annually at a rate of 2%, 2.5% or 4%, depending on the date of construction and the date of the application to build. A straight-line depreciation over the useful life is also possible.

Movable tangible assets can be depreciated using the straight-line method over their useful lives. An accelerated depreciation is also possible. This percentage should not be higher than three times the straight-line percentage and should not exceed 30%.

Intangible assets can be depreciated only if their useful lives are limited. Software is generally regarded as an intangible asset, and its useful life is considered to be three years. For custom-made software, the useful life must be estimated. If the software is a non-removable part of telecommunications equipment, or any other hardware, the software must be valued and depreciated with the tangible asset.

German tax authorities often publish rules for depreciation periods of different assets typically used in a certain industry. A depreciation schedule for typical assets used in the telecommunications industry follows:

List of Fixed Assets in the Telecommunications Sector	Useful Life	Depreciation Rate
Transmitting and receiving stations (including carriers)		
Telecommunications towers	25	4
Transmitting/receiving stations for satellite communications (including carriers)	20	5
Antenna arrays		
Stationary	10	10
Mobile	5	20
Telecommunications stations		
Local ends		
Telephone local ends	5	20
Text and data processing terminal equipment	5	20
Multi-service equipment	5	20
Public telecommunications stations	10	10
Telecommunications facilities	5	20
Mobile phones	4	25
Operator facilities	10	10
Transmission facilities	8	12
Radio facilities		
Mobile communications equipment	8	12
Radio link system	8	12
Satellite communications equipment	8	12
Cable line network		
Copper cable	15	7
Glass fiber cable	20	5
Compressed air/high-pressure gas control instruments	15	7
Technical equipment for broadband distribution networks	10	10
Test instruments		
Test vehicles	5	20
Electronic test instruments for mobile communications and radio link systems	5	20

Depreciation is calculated on the purchase costs, including all expenditures incurred to acquire and establish the asset, or, if the asset is self-manufactured, the manufacturing costs. Manufacturing costs do not include research and development costs. Marketing and advertising costs cannot be capitalized.

Transfer Pricing Rules

In general, inter-company transactions must comply with arm's-length principles. This means that the participating corporations must act as if they were unrelated parties using the prudence and diligence of independent business people. Inter-company transactions must meet certain conditions set out by the tax authorities. A payment by a German subsidiary to its foreign parent company that is not in line with arm's-length principles cannot be deducted from the subsidiary's income. Such compensation payment would be viewed as a constructive dividend subject to taxes, even if the subsidiary were in a loss position. The tax authorities have announced that they are generally not implementing the OECD transfer pricing guidelines published in 1995 and, in particular, that they will not accept the profit-related transfer pricing methods. An official review of existing German transfer pricing guidelines by the tax authorities is not expected soon.

Transfers of Patents, Trademarks and Software

When a transfer of technology connected with supplies or services occurs, separate technology payments are disallowed if the price of the supplies or services already includes the transfer of technology. There are no specific rules for differentiating between a license and a sale. Therefore, tax law follows civil law.

Royalty payments or software licensing fees paid by a German telecommunications company are fully deductible when they belong to the business of the German company and they meet arm's-length requirements. Excessive amounts are qualified as constructive dividends. Fees for royalties and licenses that are used within Germany are subject to a 25% withholding tax, which can be reduced by a tax treaty.

Service Fees

Arm's-length service fees are fully deductible and are generally not subject to withholding tax. The main areas for withholding taxation in the telecommunications industry are considerations in the form of license fees, royalties or payments for the transfer of trading, technical or scientific know-how, or for similar experience.

As long as the service provided does not fall under the scope of these regulations, no withholding tax is due. Royalties and license fees in the form of service fees paid to German-related companies are not subject to withholding tax. Pure service fees for services occurring outside of Germany are fully deductible in Germany as long as a double-taxation treaty does not shift the taxation to another country (i.e., a foreign permanent establishment).

Value-Added Tax, Sales Tax and/or Other Pertinent Taxes

As a member of the EU, Germany follows the provisions of the European Community Sixth VAT Directive. Domestic telecommunications services (including those supplied by German-resident foreign businesses) are subject to VAT at the standard rate of 15%, which was to be increased to 16% on April 1, 1998. The VAT treatment of international telecommunications services is based on the revised EU VAT model, which took effect in Germany on January 1, 1997.

Services supplied internationally by a telecommunications business located in Germany generally fall outside the scope of VAT when supplied to anyone located outside Germany. The only exceptions are services supplied to private individuals or unregistered persons located in other member states. Those supplies are subject to German VAT at the standard rate.

Non-resident providers are not liable to register and account for German VAT on supplies rendered to German taxable persons. Depending on the VAT status of the customers (i.e., whether they are able to reclaim all of the VAT incurred on their expenses), one of two procedures will be used. If the customer is able to reclaim in full all VAT incurred on expenses, the Null-regelung applies, and no VAT-payment obligation or VAT deduction right arises. If the customer is not entitled to full recovery of VAT incurred on expenses, the customer must withhold from the funds due to the non-resident provider an amount equivalent to the German VAT (a process known as the Abzugsverfahren). It is important, therefore, for a non-resident provider to understand the VAT status of their business customers in Germany.

Services supplied to private individuals in Germany by non-resident EU-providers are subject to local VAT in the supplier's member state. When a non-EU, non-resident provider supplies services to private individuals to be used in Germany, the provider is required to register and account for German VAT. For an overseas provider, it should be possible to limit the German VAT liability to supplies made for German individuals that are effectively used in Germany. However, when the same type of supplies is made for private individuals in various member states, this may then require the overseas provider to be registered for VAT purposes in many different EU-member states. Alternatively, an overseas provider may choose to register a subsidiary in a single EU-member state (e.g., Germany), in order to contract with all customers who are EU private individuals. The supplies made from the single EU registration in Germany to these customers will then be subject to local German VAT.

Access to the Internet is included within the definition of telecommunications, and the principles set out above apply equally to Internet service providers.

In its decree of April 29, 1997, the German Ministry of Finance defined telecommunications services for VAT purposes as transactions ensuring the emission, transmission and reception of signals, written information, pictures and sounds or information of any kind by wire, radio, optical or other electromagnetic signals as well as the assignment and the granting of a right to use facilities for the emission, transmission or reception. Also covered under this definition are the provision of access to an information network and the granting of the right to use this network as a telecommunications service for VAT purposes.

Germany does not apply a tax exemption to any of these telecommunications services, nor to telecommunications services rendered between providers.

Local and Provincial Taxes

Trade Tax. Until recently, trade tax, which is imposed on all forms of business enterprises, was levied on income and capital. The trade tax on capital (Gewerbekapitalsteuer) was abolished as of January 1, 1998. The basis for computing income for trade tax purposes is the taxable income as determined for corporate-income tax purposes, to which certain additions and deductions must be made. Income is taxed at a basic rate of 5%, multiplied by a municipal multiplication rate (Hebesatz).

Municipal trade tax is laid out in federal tax law, but the municipalities are authorized to determine the municipal multiplication rates, which range from 300% to 515% (i.e., a factor ranging from 3 to 5.15), so that the effective trade tax rate varies between 13% and 20.5%, depending on the municipality. However, because trade tax is deductible in computing a corporation's income tax, the actual tax burden is considerably less than these rates indicate.

When a business is carried out through branches in different municipalities, the trade tax is apportioned among those municipalities based on the amount of wages or salaries paid to employees of these branches.

The most important adjustment to consider when computing a business enterprise's income for trade tax on income purposes is that the interest payable on long-term debt must be added back at 50%. A liability qualifies as long-term debt if it has been

undertaken either in connection with the setting up, acquisition and substantial expansion of a business, or if the term of liability exceeds 12 months.

Net Worth Tax. No net worth tax is levied for assessment periods 1997 and after.

Real Estate Transfer Tax. Upon transfer of real property, a real estate transfer tax (Grunderwerbsteuer) is levied at a rate of 3.5%. The tax basis is either the compensation agreed upon between the contractual parties or an assessed value (minimum: book value; maximum: market value; guideline: 12.5 times the annual rent; all values for developed real estate) if no compensation or an inadequate compensation (e.g., transfer between related parties) is to be paid. In addition, real estate transfer tax is triggered by the transfer (direct or indirect) of all shares of a corporation that owns real property located in Germany. Several anti-abuse regulations exist concerning the transfer of shares/interest in companies that own real estate.

Real Estate Tax. Real estate tax (Grundsteuer) is imposed on the net assessed value of real property and is levied annually by the municipalities. The tax rate ranges from 0.26% to 0.35%, depending on the type of real property. Each municipality applies a multiplying factor to the product of the tax rate and the net assessed value. The net assessed value is, in most cases, significantly lower than the market value of the real property.

For Additional Information, Contact:

Stefan Kaufmann
Tax Partner
Postfach 11 18 42
60053 Frankfurt am Main, Germany
Telephone: 49 (69) 9585 1033
Fax: 49 (69) 9585 4033
E-mail: Stefan_Kaufmann@de.coopers.com

Dr. Ulrich Blaas
Tax Partner
Postfach 10 54 54
40045 Düsseldorf, Germany
Telephone: 49 (211) 7208 345
Fax: 49 (211) 7208 202
E-mail: Ulrich_Blaas@de.coopers.com

Paul Birster
Management Consulting Partner
Am Halberg 4
66121 Saarbrücken, Germany
Telephone: 49 (681) 9814 320
Fax: 49 (681) 9814 321
E-mail: Paul_Birster@de.coopers.com

Hungary

Telecommunications Tax Profile
by Nick Kós
Senior Audit Manager, Budapest
and Sándor Szmicsek
Associate Tax Director, Budapest

Overview of the Telecommunications Market

Historical Background

In 1989, the Ministry of Transport, Communications and Construction was established to oversee the Hungarian PTT, which provided postal and telecommunications services in Hungary. In the same year, the first analog cellular license was issued. In 1990, the Ministry divided the PTT into the Hungarian Telecommunications Company Ltd. (HTC, also known as Magyar Távközlési Részvénytársaság, or MATÁV Rt.), the Hungarian Post Office Ltd., and the Hungarian Broadcasting Company.

The Telecommunications Act of 1992 set the framework for the liberalization of the telecommunications sector in Hungary by providing for the privatization of MATÁV and by structuring the telecommunications market into local, long-distance and international service. This approach was based on the idea that small, independent operators would be the most capable parties to deal with local needs, and that they would use interconnection to create an effective, alternative national network. Hungary was divided into 54 primary service areas. MATÁV received licenses to operate concessions in 29 of these areas. In 1994, tenders for licenses to operate in the remaining 25 local areas were issued, as follows:

- Eighteen licenses were issued to new operators, of which three were MATÁV joint ventures.

- Five licenses were awarded to MATÁV.

- Two licenses reverted to MATÁV because no offers were made to serve those areas.

In 1993, a 30% stake in MATÁV was purchased by Magyar-Com, which is an Ameritech/Deutsche Telekom AG joint venture. In 1995, this stake was increased to 67.4%. In 1993, two global system for mobile communications (GSM) licenses were issued to the MATÁV/U S WEST joint venture and to Pannon GSM, which is a consortium of Hungarian and Scandinavian companies. These licenses were granted for an initial period of 15 years, with a renewal option for a further 7.5 years. MATÁV retained the licenses for all long-distance and international services. In all cases, the fixed-line licenses are for a duration of 25 years, with an eight-year period of exclusive operation. All licenses may be extended by 12.5 years.

Current Status

MATÁV will retain its monopoly on long-distance service until 2001, when its exclusive concession ends. At that time, it will face competition from alternative long distance operators who most likely will be formed by a number of local operators and/or utility companies. Hungarian utility companies have their own telecommunications facilities and are currently making investments with strategic partners in order to be in a position to offer services to third parties with the advent of deregulation.

The tariff (call pricing) policy for fixed-line and wireless communications is dictated by the state. There is a price cap, which was specified in 1994, for the different call types (local, long distance, etc.), with maximum increases tied to the official Producer Price Index (PPI) effective in the middle of the previous year. The structure is based on a particular formula and the service providers have a certain freedom in structuring tariffs within the boundaries of the official caps. The principle of the legislation is also to allow more flexibility in tariff determination and in current tariff restructuring. Currently, the Ministry of Transport, Communications and Water Management must approve all tariff changes. MATÁV is attempting to restructure its tariffs, to bring them broadly in line with those of telecommunications companies in more developed economies, within the limits imposed by the legislation.

MATÁV loses a proportion of its outbound international traffic to "call-back" operators. Although these operations are illegal in Hungary, they have been difficult to monitor and stop. Data transmission operates along free-market lines. Private lines account for most of this traffic, with utilities expanding their operations in this area. At present, the principal competition to the fixed-line service providers comes from mobile operators. MATÁV is cushioned from a negative impact, because it holds 51% of Westel Rádiótelefon Kft. (Westel 450), which is the only analog cellular operator, and effectively controls one of the two GSM operators, Westel 900 GSM Mobil Tóvközlési Rt. (Westel 900 GSM Mobile Telecommunications Company Ltd., or Westel 900).

Hungary has a large mobile market, with over 600,000 users as of June 1997. By the year 2000, it is expected that the number of mobile subscribers will reach 900,000, representing 8.6% penetration. Usage is high and revenues are expected to grow significantly by the end of the century.

All concession licenses awarded were accompanied by certain development targets, including that the number of connected lines be increased by at least 15.5% per year and that the waiting list for telephone lines be reduced in line with the Telecommunications Act of 1992. These requirements, along with others relating to service quality, will direct the strategies of the concession operators over the coming years.

In November 1997, MATÁV made an initial public offering (IPO) of its share capital on the Budapest and New York Stock Exchanges. An Over-allotment Option was exercised and the Hungarian Retail Offering was increased by the state privatization agency Állami Privatizációs és Vagyonkezelô Részvénytársaság (ÁPV) in December. Following the total global offering of 26:31% of the total number of MATÁV shares, MagyarCom now owns approximately 59.58% of MATÁV's outstanding share capital and the ÁPV owns approximately 6.47%.

MATÁV is modernizing its switching architecture, and by consolidating switching platforms into larger centralized switches, the company intends to reduce the number of its switching sites from the current total of approximately 1,100 to 77 within 10 years. In December 1997, MATÁV completed the replacement of all of its manual switches. By June 30, 1997, approximately 66.2% of MATÁV's exchange capacity was digital, as compared to 32.5% on December 31, 1993. MATÁV has also begun to use fiber optic cables in its local loop networks, and has laid 60,000 fiber optic access lines to date. MATÁV plans to install an additional 200,000 fiber optic access lines by December 31, 1999.

The Hungarian Government is actively promoting competition in the provision of public telephony services. State railway operator Magyar Államvasutak Részvénytársaság (MÁV), oil giant MOL Magyar Olaj és Gázipari Részvénytársaság (MOL), state-owned information technology firm KFKI Számítástechnikai Részvénytársaság (KFKI) and Unisource will take 25.1%, 20.9%, 5% and 49% stakes respectively in the newly formed future alternative provider MKM-Tel Távközlési és Kommunikációs Korlátolt Felelösségü Társaság (MKM-Tel). The company, created by the government, may provide data services immediately, and will be allowed to compete in long-distance services when MATÁV's monopoly expires.

On September 5, 1997, the Minister for Transport, Telecommunications and Water Management and the Minister of Finance issued a joint declaration on the basis of the principles of the new telecommunications tariff regime to become effective as of January 1, 1998. The joint declaration sets forth the principles for a new, separate tariff decree concerning subscriber charges and interconnection fees to be prepared jointly by the two Ministers.

Services that require only a license rather than a government-granted concession include all non-voice services, such as leased lines, electronic data interchange, data transmission services and Internet access. These services currently make up a relatively small percentage of the total telecommunications market in Hungary.

Current Liberalization Status

The Telecommunications Act of 1992 set the framework for the liberalization of the telecommunications sector in Hungary by providing for the privatization of the incumbent national telecommunications operator, MATÁV, and by structuring the telecommunications market into local, long-distance and international service sectors. The telecommunications marketplace is also governed by other legislation, including Act XVI of 1991 on Concessions, as amended (the Concessions Act), Act LXXXVII of 1990 on Pricing (the Pricing Act) and Act LVII of 1996 on the Prohibition of Unfair and Restrictive Market Practices (the Competition Act).

In February 1997 Hungary, with 68 other nations, made multilateral commitments as part of the World Trade Organization

(WTO) Telecommunications Agreement to liberalize the telecommunications market. Hungary ratified the agreement, which had an effective date of January 1, 1998, with a dispensation for Hungary to postpone liberalization until 2002. Hungary has adopted the preference paper requiring, for example, regulatory principles supporting competition.

The tariff (call pricing) policy for fixed-line and wireless communications is dictated by the state. There is a price cap, which was specified in 1994, for the different call types. The Ministry of Transport, Communications and Water Management must approve all tariff changes.

Type of Service	Degree of Liberalization	Key Legislation	Date of Actual or Expected Liberalization	Comments
Local	Partially liberalized	The Telecommunications Act of 1992

Act LXXXVII of 1990 on Pricing

Act XVI of 1991 on Concessions as amended

Act LVII of 1996 on the Prohibition of Unfair and Restrictive Market Practices | December 2001 and May 2002 | Service providers have a certain amount of freedom in structuring tariffs within boundaries. Of the 54 local concession areas, MATÁV holds exclusive rights through December 2001 in 31, and through May 2002 in five more. Thirteen other companies hold exclusive rights through May 2002 in the remaining areas. Tariff policy is dictated by the state. |
Long Distance	Monopoly		December 2001	MATÁV has a certain amount of freedom in structuring tariffs within boundaries. MATÁV holds exclusive rights through December 2001. Tariff policy is dictated by the state.
International	Monopoly		December 2001	MATÁV holds exclusive rights through December 2001. Tariff policy is dictated by the state.
Cellular	Partially liberalized			Since January 1, 1998, mobile network subscriber charges are not subject to regulation under the Pricing Act. In 1990, Westel 450 received a license to provide nationwide analog mobile radio-telephone services. Subsequently in 1994, a concession agreement was entered into. In 1993 two concessions to provide nationwide digital/GSM cellular mobile telephone services were awarded to Westel 900 and Pannon GSM. Tariff policy is dictated by the state.
Paging	Partially liberalized	The Telecommunications Act of 1992		Subject to licensing and frequency assignment requirements.
Value-added	Partially liberalized	The Telecommunications Act of 1992		Satellite services, public switched data transmission services, leased line services and other value-added services are open to competition but subject to licensing and frequency assignment requirements.

Competitive Environment

MATÁV currently dominates the market with its monopoly of local service to 75% of the population and its total monopoly of long-distance and international telephony services. The other companies in the market are the two GSM operators, of which the larger, Westel 900, is a subsidiary of MATÁV.

Type of Service	Entire Market		Top Two Players		
	Market Size* (1996)	Number of Players	Names	Annual Revenue* (1996)	Ownership
Local	More than MHUF 88,000	14	MATÁV	MHUF 63,000	MagyarCom 59.4% (Ameritech and Deutsche Telekom), ÁPV 6.1%, others
			UTI Bakonytel Kft.	MHUF 7,000	United Telecom Investment BV 97%, others
Long Distance	MHUF 43,000	1	MATÁV	MHUF 43,000	As above
International	MHUF 30,000	1	MATÁV	MHUF 30,000	As above
Cellular	MHUF 77,000	3	Westel 900	MHUF 44,000	U S WEST Holland BV 42%, Westel 450 9%, MATÁV 44%
			Pannon GSM	MHUF 19,000	PTT Telecom BV 21%, Telecom A/S 21%, Telenor Invest A/S 18%, Telecom Finland 16%, MOL 9%, Wallis 5%, others
Paging	More than MHUF 306	2	Operator Hungária Kft.	MHUF 306	TDF International 49%, Antenna Hungária 51%
			Eurohívó Rt.	Not available	GTS Hungaro VTA, Gerald Aircraft, Microsystem
Value-added	Not available		MATÁV	MHUF 27,000	As above

Sources: *Budapest Business Journal's* Book of Lists; MATÁV's IPO prospectus; public reports.
* MHUF = millions of Hungarian Forints

Licensing Requirements

The Ministry of Transport, Communications and Water Management regulates the telecommunications sector. The services that are required to be operated under a license are the public fixed telephone network, public mobile radiotelephone, public nationwide paging, and national and regional public service broadcast distribution of television programs.

Private networks, special-purpose networks and closed-loop networks, which serve a specified closed group of users, may be established within property limits without any limitations being placed on them, or beyond property limits if they have a license. Services that do not require licenses include construction and operation of proprietary wireline networks; construction and operation of underground telecommunications networks and equipment in deep mines; public address systems; receive-only broadcast services and one-way transmission of satellite signals; the operation of special-purpose networks; and the termination/removal of closed private wireline telecommunications networks.

Potential for Foreign Ownerships/Relationships

Although there are no specific restrictions on foreigners acquiring shares in a Hungarian company, joint ventures between local and foreign investors are common in the telecommunications sector as a result of regulatory requirements that specify a minimum amount of local ownership.

Potential for Upcoming Liberalization/Investment Opportunities

A regulatory framework is currently being developed to define further the rules under which MATÁV and its competitors can operate. In March 1996, at the request of the Hungarian government, the committee for information, computer and communications policy of the Organization for Economic Cooperation and Development (OECD) performed a review of Hungary's telecommunications policy. The report detailed recommendations aimed at enabling telecommunications-sector development in support of an information society in Hungary.

Within Eastern Europe, Hungary's telecommunications sector is far down the road toward liberalization, with local operator and mobile concessions already issued. Investment opportunities will arise in the future with the expiration of the fixed-line licenses in 2001. MATÁV will lose its monopoly over long-distance and international services and competition will be allowed for the first time. Data transmission is also a growth area due to the liberalized nature of the market.

Forms of Doing Business

Permanent Establishment

The Hungarian definition of a permanent establishment (PE) is based broadly on the OECD Model. By definition, a PE is a fixed place of business through which a corporate taxpayer partly or wholly pursues entrepreneurial activities on a durable basis. Apart from the scope of the above-mentioned definition, a commercial representative office could also qualify as a PE if it has the power to negotiate and sign contracts on behalf of the parent company.

With regard to the telecommunications sector, the following examples are considered:

- A PE will not be created when a non-resident company either provides long-distance telephone services or licenses technology.

- Similarly, the licensing by a foreign company of technology and know-how to a local company would not create a PE.

- The provision of technical assistance and technological services could constitute a PE in Hungary.

- The leasing of telecommunications equipment to a local company would not create a PE.

- In Hungary, call reorganization and turnaround services may not be permitted if they are regarded as a telecommunications service for which a license is required.

- The provision of Internet access services without having an office in Hungary would not constitute a PE.

- A PE will be created if a construction site exists for more than three months, although this time period could be adjusted by a tax treaty.

- Insofar as a PE can be any fixed equipment with which the taxpayer performs income-earning activities on a durable basis, having a server or switch located in Hungary would be considered a PE.

- Having a website in or outside Hungary, regardless of who can access it, does not constitute a PE.

- The laying of fiber optic cable and the construction of telecommunications switching equipment could create a PE. Furthermore, it would be immaterial whether these activities were carried out for sale to a Hungarian company or for operation by a foreign telecommunications company.

Business Entities

Local Branch of a Foreign Company. Beginning in 1998, foreign investors may carry on business activities in Hungary by setting up a branch. The branch option is a new legal form. The rules regarding commercial representation offices were also changed.

For Hungarian law purposes, a branch (fióktelep) is an economically separate (independent) unit of a foreign enterprise (legal or non-legal entity having a legal seat outside Hungary and carrying on entrepreneurial activity as a main activity) which is registered as such at the Court of Registration. A branch has no legal personality.

A branch can start its business operation after being registered. The conditions of registration are as follows:

- A branch may be established pursuant to an international agreement (the conditions determining the existence of such an international agreement are detailed in the publications of the relevant Ministries).

- The request for registration and its appendices have to meet the legal requirements defined in a separate law. A stamp duty of HUF 200,000 is payable upon registration.

The branch is to be treated as a domestic business unit, meaning that all relevant regulations and rules apply to the branch in the same way as they do to other companies registered in Hungary. Consequently, for example, if a certain business activity can only be performed by possession of a permit, the branch has to obtain that permit in its own right. The branch cannot perform representative or agent activities on behalf of foreign enterprises or other institutions considered non-resident for foreign exchange purposes.

Locally Incorporated Subsidiary of a Foreign Company. This option is available to a foreign investor. In Hungary, there are two types of company: the limited liability company and the company limited by shares. Under the new legislation entering into force on June 16, 1998, the minimum share capital of a limited liability company will be HUF 3 million, and in the case of a company limited by shares, the minimum will be HUF 20 million.

A locally incorporated subsidiary is taxed in the same way as any other domestic entity. The rate of corporate tax is 18%.

Joint Venture. Joint ventures are more common in the telecommunications sector than in other sectors, partly due to the regulatory requirements for awarding concessions and other licensing requirements that specify a minimum local ownership. A joint venture can take the form of either a partnership (limited liability partnership or unlimited liability partnership) or a limited liability company (limited liability company or joint stock company). Regardless of the form elected, the joint venture must file a tax return as a separate legal entity. The concept of a holding company does not exist in Hungary.

A limited liability partnership is treated as a company for tax purposes. Nevertheless, in a limited liability partnership, at least one of the partners must have unlimited liability. Partnership in a limited liability partnership does not constitute a PE for tax purposes.

Local Funding Alternatives

Debt versus Equity

Because the rate of inflation is comparatively higher in Hungary than in other countries, shareholder debt could be treated as equity financing. Servicing the debt could lead to negative retained earnings. In turn, this could lead to the debt-to-equity ratio exceeding 4 to 1, which is the threshold beyond which thin capitalization rules are triggered. Foreign exchange gains and losses are treated in the same way on shareholder debt and local debt. Further, loans beyond HUF 50 million must be submitted to the Central Bank for approval. If the Central Bank does not raise any objections within thirty days of submission, the loan agreement can then take effect.

When comparing local and shareholder debt, shareholder guarantees are immaterial for tax purposes. There is an 18% withholding tax on interest payments in Hungary, which can be reduced to 0% if a double-taxation agreement applies. In case of the latter, the Hungarian company is required to withhold the 18% tax on interest payments, with the recipient having to submit a reclaim application for the difference between 18% and the applicable tax treaty rate. However, if there is adequate documentation in place as set out by the relevant legislation at the premises of the Hungarian payor (including a residence certificate for the beneficiary), the treaty rates can be applied automatically when the payments are made.

Loans require the approval of the Central Bank when the amount is in excess of HUF 50 million or if the loan is for a period of less than one year. In other cases only a notification is required. Thin capitalization rules apply, but only when the loan is from a shareholder of the Hungarian company and the debt-to-equity ratio exceeds 4 to 1.

Exchange gains and losses are treated the same way for both accounting and tax purposes. Unrealized losses on the principal of a loan may be deducted in full.

Exchange Controls

There are exchange control provisions, although, in practice, these often have no material effect. They can, however, limit the use of offshore Treasury centers.

Business Acquisitions and Dispositions

Capital Contributions into an Existing Local Entity

A capital contribution into a local entity will be subject to stamp duty at a rate of 2% of the amount contributed, subject to a maximum amount payable of HUF 300,000. Such a contribution should not affect the loss-carryforward position in the recipient company.

Contributions-in-kind incur VAT cash-flow cost, though VAT would normally be reclaimable in full in the month following the payment.

Purchase or Sale of Shares in a Local Entity

There are no specific restrictions on foreign investors acquiring shares in a Hungarian company, although consideration must be given where there is a minimum local ownership requirement, normally 25% for telecommunications companies. In addition, almost all telecommunications concessions require the agreement of the authorities for a change in ownership of more than 10%. The sale of shares in a local entity to a foreign company is subject to tax in Hungary unless the vendor is a non-resident.

Intangibles such as goodwill can be capitalized to step-up the tax basis in the acquired assets owned by the local company.

Purchase or Sale of Assets

Purchasing the assets, including the related license, of a telecommunications company is a possible alternative. While an asset acquisition can reduce the risk of hidden liabilities, there are significant cash-flow costs in terms of VAT that must be paid on asset transfers. While this is reclaimable, the amounts involved can lead to delays and, therefore, require significant financing.

Start-up Business Issues

Pre-operating Losses and Start-up/Construction Costs

Under Hungarian accounting law, costs relating to license fees, concession fees and associated costs are capitalized. These costs would then be depreciated over the life of the concession. Intangible capitalized costs would generally be depreciated over 5 to 15 years. Tax relief would be available on the amount depreciated each year.

Interest costs on loans that are specific to a capital project usually have to be capitalized. Interest costs on loans that are not specific to a capital project can be written off through the profit and loss account, although it is still possible to capitalize such interest if the loan is linked to a capital project. In the case of interest that is capitalized for tax purposes, this is added to the cost of the asset and tax relief is given by way of tax depreciation at the rate applicable to the type of asset. Tax relief on interest written off in the profit and loss account is deductible on an accounts basis, subject to thin capitalization provisions.

If pre-operating costs are incurred by a foreign company, they can only be deducted or amortized by the local entity if the costs are re-charged to the local entity by way of a written service agreement. The costs would then be accounted for as if they had been incurred by the local entity, with tax relief being available as set out above. It is important that adequate evidence supporting the costs incurred be available to support the tax relief being claimed. The payment of such service fees is not subject to withholding tax in Hungary.

VAT incurred by a local company for the purchase of pre-operating goods or services or for capital projects can be deducted from the VAT payable by the local company. If the local company is in a VAT-reclaimable position, the refund will only be effected by the tax authorities if the local company has produced revenues from sales of products and provision of services subject to VAT in excess of HUF 2 million. The VAT is repayable within one month of submitting the reclaim, although in practice it may take up to six months to secure a refund.

Customs Duties and VAT

The changes in customs duty regulations that came into effect in 1996 were intended to bring Hungary in line with the EU. The following rates currently apply:

Type of duty	Rate
Customs Duty	14% (average)
Statistical Duty*	0%
Customs Clearance Duty*	0%
Supplementary Duty	Abolished July 1, 1997

* Applicable for GATT (General Agreement on Tariffs and Trade) member states. For non-GATT countries, the rate of statistical duty is 3% and the customs clearance duty is 2%.

Customs duty rates vary considerably for different types of products, and this is likely to continue to be the case. It should also be noted that the importation of certain products may require permission from the relevant authorities. However, permission duty at a rate of 1% is not payable for GATT states.

Hungary has concluded special agreements to reduce customs duty rates with the EU, the Central European Free Trade Association (CEFTA) and the European Free Trade Association (EFTA). The importation of equipment is subject to VAT at a rate of 25%, which can generally be recovered. There is no distinction drawn between regular telephony and Internet telephony for purposes of VAT.

Loss Carryovers

Tax losses incurred in the year of formation and the two subsequent years can be carried forward indefinitely; thereafter, there is a five-year limit. A special provision of the tax law stipulates that, from the third year of operations onwards, a tax loss incurred in a given year can only be automatically utilized by the taxpayer if the revenues exceed 50% of the total costs and expenses accounted for. If the above condition is not met, a permit is needed from the tax authorities to enable the taxpayer to utilize the tax loss. Tax losses cannot be carried back.

Operating Considerations

Corporate Income Taxes

The rate of corporate tax in Hungary is 18%. A withholding tax of 20% is levied on dividends paid to foreign shareholders out of profits earned after January 1, 1997. Broadly speaking, this withholding tax is not levied if the dividend is reinvested in a Hungarian company. The terms of any relevant double-taxation agreement may reduce this rate of withholding tax. However, the tax must be withheld by the Hungarian company and the recipient must make an application to reclaim the difference between 20% and the applicable tax treaty rate. Nevertheless, if there is adequate documentation in place as set out by the relevant legislation at the premises of the Hungarian payor (including a residence certificate for the beneficiary) then the treaty rates can be applied automatically when the payments are made.

The withholding tax rate on interest is 18%, subject to the terms of any double-taxation agreement. The Hungarian company is required to withhold 18% tax on the interest and the recipient must submit an application to reclaim the difference between 18% and the applicable tax treaty rate. However, if there is adequate documentation in place as described in the previous paragraph, the treaty rates can be applied automatically when the payments are made.

Capital Gains Taxes

Capital gains form part of the normal taxable profit of a company, with no adjustment for inflation. In a high-inflation environment such as Hungary's (around 20% annually), it is often the case that shares are not held by a Hungarian holding company but directly from overseas.

Tax Holidays and Exemptions

A number of tax holidays and benefits may be available to companies in Hungary operating in the telecommunications sector. In particular, companies that met certain criteria by December 31, 1993 may qualify for a tax benefit of 100% for five years, followed by an additional tax benefit of up to 60% in the subsequent five years.

For companies that did not meet the relevant criteria by December 31, 1993, only limited benefits and exemptions are available. These benefits fall into the following categories:

- Investment/export-related benefits (i.e., if an investment exceeds a certain size and generates a pre-set minimum increase in export revenues)

- Tax credits for investment in machinery in an area of high unemployment

Certain conditions need to be met in order to qualify for these exemptions.

Depreciation/Cost-Recovery Conventions/Accelerated Deductions

In general, expenditures over HUF 30,000 for assets would be capitalized and then depreciated over the life of the asset. Tax depreciation rates are specified in tax law. Depreciation must be claimed even in loss years. It should be noted that intangible assets can normally be depreciated over 5 to 15 years; the tax treatment follows the treatment for accounting purposes.

Accounting depreciation is deductible for tax purposes provided the rate used in the accounts does not exceed the rate prescribed by the Corporate Tax Law. If the rate does exceed that

provided by the tax law, then the tax law rate is used. A summary of the rates prescribed by the Corporate Tax Law is given below.

If the tax law provides for more depreciation methods, the company can choose the most favorable method. The following specific rules apply:

- For intangible assets, environmental assets, high-technology assets and concession assets, accounting depreciation is tax-deductible.

- Tax depreciation is calculated from the date the assets are brought into use until the date of disposal or write-off. If an asset is acquired or disposed of during a tax year, the depreciable amount must be calculated on a pro-rata basis.

- Depreciation in excess of the set rates is allowed if the taxpayer scraps an asset or if it is destroyed.

The following are the depreciation rates prescribed by the Corporate Tax Law in Hungary:

Buildings	With a long life	2%
	With a medium life	3%
	With a short life	6%
Machinery, Equipment and Installation	Plant, machinery and equipment in general	14.5%
	Computer products and equipment, administration technology equipment, installation and machinery	33%
	Vehicles	20%
	Telecommunications network lines	8%

In the case of experimental development, depreciation write-off in excess of that scheduled may be applied in an amount accounted for on the basis of the Act on Accounting, if the activities to be realized through completed experimental development are restricted, terminated or unsuccessful.

The accounting depreciation of intangibles is accepted for tax purposes. The accounting policy of the company should contain the depreciation rates that may apply for tax purposes as well. Software embedded in telecommunications equipment must be capitalized in order to be depreciated at a higher rate than the hardware.

The treatment of research and development costs depends on whether they lead to a product. If there is no end product, then the costs should be treated as an expense. If there is an end product, then the costs should be capitalized.

Marketing and advertising costs should be treated as an expense.

Transfer Pricing Rules

Broadly speaking, transfer pricing rules apply in cases of a 25% common shareholding. Hungarian law provides that the transfer pricing rules are applicable to contracts between members of an associated enterprise regardless of whether they are Hungarian or non-Hungarian. The law provides the following methods to determine the arm's-length price:

- The comparable uncontrolled pricing method

- The resale minus method

- The cost-plus method

Currently, transfer pricing rules are not rigorously enforced. Nevertheless, these may become an important issue in light of international developments.

Transfers of Patents, Trademarks and Software

Hungarian law does not impose any restriction on the licensing of technology to a local company for royalty fees. The sale and licensing of technology are subject to VAT. Additionally, the sale of technology is subject to corporate tax if the purchaser is a foreign entity.

Any profit or loss on the disposal of licenses, patents, etc., is taxable as part of a company's normal annual income. Royalties paid for patents and trademarks are generally deductible for Hungarian tax purposes.

Under Hungarian domestic law, a Hungarian company must withhold an 18% tax on royalty payments. If a double-taxation treaty provides for a lower rate of withholding tax (which can be as low as 0%), the recipient can reclaim the difference between the tax withheld and the applicable tax treaty rate. However if there is adequate documentation in place as set out by the relevant legislation at the premises of the Hungarian payor (including a residence certificate for the beneficiary), the treaty rates can be applied automatically when the payments are made.

Service Fees

Service fees are not subject to withholding taxes. The place of performance of the services is immaterial for the purposes of withholding taxes.

Service fees payable of less than HUF 200,000 are tax-deductible. Service fees payable in excess of HUF 200,000 are tax-deductible only if both the following conditions are met:

- A written contract is in place for the services.

- Evidence can be provided that the services were received.

Value-Added Tax, Sales Tax and/or Other Pertinent Taxes

Hungary applies an EU-style VAT system, with a relatively high applicable rate of 25%. According to Hungarian domestic law, the sale of products and the provision of services are subject to VAT, if the sale of products and the provision of services are deemed to have been performed by taxpayers in Hungary. Importation is also deemed to be an activity subject to VAT.

In the case of services rendered by non-residents to Hungarian VAT taxpayers, tax shall be paid by the Hungarian VAT taxpayer ordering such services deemed to be performed in Hungary, on his own behalf, if the head office or permanent premises of the non-resident taxpayer providing such services, whichever of the two is most directly involved in performance, is abroad, or, in the absence of such premises, if their permanent residence or usual place of stay is abroad.

If a foreign company incurs local costs that are subject to VAT, it may recover the VAT by making an application for a VAT refund provided the following conditions are met:

- The foreign company is registered as a VAT taxpayer in a country that has a reciprocal agreement with Hungary (currently there are 11 such countries).

- The company has no permanent establishment or headquarters in Hungary and does not supply goods or services in Hungary as a regular Hungarian VAT taxpayer.

- The VAT calculated in the invoice exceeds HUF 10,000.

In the case of a foreign company, VAT shall be reclaimed in the form of an application submitted in writing to the Hungarian tax authority. The company should verify that it is liable to pay VAT in the subject year, with a document issued by the competent authority of the state where it was registered as such a person, and should make a declaration that it has accounted for its expenditures entitling it to tax reclamation as operational business costs. The company should also attach the original invoice issued for its name containing the amount or rate of tax separately.

In addition to the information listed above, the tax authority may require further information for the judgment of the application, about which the tax authority shall notify the taxpayer registered abroad in writing within 30 days after receiving the application.

In Hungary, the Melbourne Agreement applies to exempt payments under the international settlement process from VAT.

According to Hungarian legislation, in the case of the provision of Internet access and Internet telephony services, the place where the permanent establishment of the party providing the services is situated shall be regarded as the place of the performance. VAT applies to payments for those services only when the permanent establishment of the third party providing the above mentioned services is in Hungary.

There were changes made recently in tax rules relating to telecommunications services in EU countries. While the Hungarian legislature has not yet implemented these changes, revisions to the Hungarian tax regulations in connection with telecommunications services were expected to take place during 1998.

Local and Provincial Taxes

Hungary imposes a local business tax, which is a maximum of 1.4% of the adjusted revenue. The adjusted revenue is the net sales revenue of products sold or services provided, reduced by the purchase value of the goods sold, and the value of services provided by subcontractors. Local and provincial taxes are deductible for corporate tax purposes.

For Additional Information, Contact:

Nick Kós
Senior Audit Manager
and
Sándor Szmicsek
Associate Tax Director
P.O. Box 694
1539 Budapest
Hungary
Telephone: 36 (1) 345 1100
Fax: 36 (1) 345 1104
E-mail: nick_kos@hu.coopers.com
        sandor_szmicsek@hu.coopers.com

Ireland

Telecommunications Tax Profile
by Dermot Reilly
Tax Partner, Dublin

Overview of the Telecommunications Market

Historical Background

The 1983 Telecommunications Act converted the telecommunications arm of the Department of Post and Telegraphs into an autonomous government-owned company, Telecom Éireann, and gave it the exclusive right to provide infrastructure and voice telephony, telex, paging and satellite services. There has been no deregulation per se, but rather stages in the introduction of competition. First, in May 1996, mobile telephony and paging services were opened to competition. A second national global system for mobile communications (GSM) license was issued in May 1996.

Recently, the government sold a 20% stake in Telecom Éireann to a consortium of KPN (Koninklijke PTT Nederland NV, a Dutch telecoms holding company) and Telia Oy (the Swedish national carrier), who will act as strategic partners for the company. Further sales of shares are anticipated.

Current Status

The number of telephone lines and cellular users has grown steadily since 1990. It is expected that the number of wireline users will continue to grow at around 6% per year well into the next century, until penetration rates, which are currently 80%, approach European Union (EU) averages.

Telecom Éireann has competition in the international voice market, cellular services, and data and value-added services. Revenues from the provision of these services that utilize the existing public network have been growing annually at an average rate of 11.5% since 1900. Telecom Éireann's recent tariff restructuring and the increased activity by its competitors for international voice services should further stimulate demand and ensure that this growth rate is maintained. Esat Telecom Group Plc, TCL Telecom, British Telecom, MCI and Sprint all compete in Ireland's international voice market.

Mobile phone penetration is running at 9%. A duopoly exists for mobile digital cellular service between Telecom Éireann's wireless mobile subsidiary, Eircell, and Esat Digifone, a consortium that includes Esat Telecom and Telenor A/S. Both providers use GSM technology; two new mobile phone licenses, either for digital cellular system (DCS)-1800 or personal communications network (PCN), were expected to be issued in early 1998. The Department of Public Enterprise has indicated that it may insist a third mobile licensee (expected to be selected in 1998) use a non-GSM, digital network.

Since 1992, approximately 40 value-added service providers have been licensed, including AT&T, British Telecom, France Telecom, MCI, Temanet A/S of Denmark and Cable & Wireless Plc. Since July 1, 1997, providers have been permitted to build their own networks and provide value-added services to business users, prompting further competition.

Recent legislation delegates the telecommunications regulatory functions of the Minister for Public Enterprise to an independent regulator, the Director of Telecommunications Regulation, whose role is to set service standards and to ensure that all competitors have access to the market. Further, the legislation provides for regulating tariffs for certain telecommunications services by means of a price cap. In the case of Telecom Éireann, this remit may extend to its trunk and international charges as part of the efforts to rebalance tariffs by the year 2000.

Current Liberalization Status

Although full liberalization of the voice telephony market is scheduled to occur in most EU countries in 1998, Ireland has received a derogation until January 1, 2000. The government is putting in place a regulatory framework to deal with upcoming liberalization.

In the World Trade Organization (WTO) negotiations in February 1997, Ireland committed to full liberalization and to adherence to a common set of regulatory principles.

Type of Service	Degree of Liberalization	Key Legislation	Date of Actual or Expected Liberalization	Comments
Local and Long Distance	Monopoly	Telecommunications Act created Telecom Éireann, 1983	January 1, 2000	
International	Liberalized	Statutory Instrument 123 of 1996, European Communities Regulations	May 1996	
Cellular	Liberalized	Statutory Instrument 123 of 1996, European Communities Regulations	May 1996	Duopoly, with further competition planned in 1998
Paging	Liberalized*	Statutory Instrument 123 of 1996, European Communities Regulations	May 1996	
Value-added	Liberalized	Statutory Instrument 45 of 1992, European Communities Regulations	1992	

* Paging went through liberalization in stages and was fully liberalized in 1996.

Competitive Environment

The table below describes the players in the Irish telecoms market. Because revenue figures are not generally published, no market or company revenues could be provided.

Type of Service	Entire Market	Top Two Players	
	Number of Players	Names	Ownership
Local	1	Telecom Éireann	Government-owned
International	Approximately 10	Telecom Éireann	Government-owned
		Esat Telecom	Esat Telecom Group Plc
Cellular	2	Eircell	Telecom Éireann
		Esat Digifone	Esat Telecom and Telenor
Paging	1	Eirpage	Telecom Éireann and Motorola
Value-added	More than 40	Telecom Éireann	Government-owned
		PostGEM	

Sources: *Communications Companies Analyses*, Telecom Éireann, September 1997; *Communications Markets Analyses*, Ireland, November 1997; Data Pro, November 1997.

Licensing Requirements

The Minister for Public Enterprise and the Director of Telecommunications Regulation grant licenses and regulate the telecommunications sectors. Value-added service providers must register with the Department of Public Enterprise to obtain licenses. Companies wishing to provide services utilizing the radio frequency spectrum must submit to a more formal licensing process.

The Office of the Director of Telecommunications Regulation was expected to provide at least two new mobile phone licenses in early 1998. It is unlikely that additional licenses will be available for cellular services in the near term.

Potential for Foreign Ownerships/Relationships

There are no restrictions on foreign ownership of telecommunications companies operating in Ireland.

Potential for Upcoming Liberalization/Investment Opportunities

With liberalization occurring over the next two years, many opportunities for investment will arise in the provision of telecommunications services using the existing public network. This will enable new entrants to the market to compete with existing service providers.

KPN and Telia have an option to acquire a further 15% stake in Telecom Éireann before December 20, 1999. The government is also committed to an employee share plan, which will place 15% of the company's shares in the hands of Telecom Éireann's employees. It is envisaged that shares in Telecom Éireann will be offered for sale one year after the KPN/Telia option expiration date, either by means of a trade sale or a public offering.

Forms of Doing Business

Permanent Establishment

The term permanent establishment (PE) is not defined in Irish tax legislation, but arises in the context of double-taxation treaties. When a foreign company that is tax-resident in a country with which Ireland does not have a tax treaty sets up an operation in Ireland, the tax status of the operation must be considered under general Irish taxation principles. For the most part, Ireland's tax treaties use a definition of PE based on the OECD Model Convention, which defines a PE as a fixed place of business through which the business of an enterprise is wholly or partly carried on.

A non-resident company is subject to corporate tax only if it carries on a business in Ireland. The following factors are considered in determining whether a business is being carried on: the items being traded, the frequency of trade, the period of ownership of the items being traded, and the circumstances responsible for the realization and supplementary work on the property realized.

Telecommunications services can cover a broad range of activities, which may or may not constitute a PE. Some examples follow:

- The provision of long distance telephone services by a foreign company to an Irish customer, without any local presence or advertising, usually does not constitute a PE.

- A foreign company that licenses know-how and technology to an Irish customer is generally not regarded as having a PE, unless the foreign company maintains a fixed place of business in Ireland.

- When a foreign company provides technical assistance and technological services to an Irish customer in exchange for service fees, and the company maintains a place of business and a work force in Ireland to carry out its activities, the company is considered to have a PE.

- Operator services provided by a foreign company could be characterized as constituting a PE, as the Irish Revenue authorities could argue that the operator had a fixed place of business.

- Whether the leasing of telecommunications equipment to a company in Ireland constitutes a PE depends on the support facilities used for the leasing activity. If the lessor operates without a fixed place of business, it is unlikely to be regarded as having a PE, even when personnel are supplied by the lessor after installation to operate the equipment. However, if the personnel have wider responsibility, the question of PE may arise if the lease agreement is for more than 12 months.

- Call reorganization and turnaround services provided by a foreign telecommunications company to customers in Ireland are unlikely to constitute a PE if the company does not maintain a fixed place of business wherein it sells telephone cards to customers.

- The provision of Internet access services to Irish customers by a foreign company is unlikely to be regarded as a PE when the company's activities are limited to selling software without a business presence in Ireland. A physical presence to sell the software or locate the access server in Ireland may give rise to a PE.

- The operation of a website, server or switch in Ireland by a foreign company could be considered a PE in certain circumstances. Merely providing information about a business would not normally constitute a PE. However, if the Internet facility offers an interactive service, including the purchase and hire of goods or services, the position is unclear. To date there has been no relevant decision that indicates what Internet facilities are considered to be PEs, nor have the revenue authorities given their view of the tax status of such facilities.

- A foreign telecommunications company that designs, manufactures, installs and tests a fiber optic cable system or constructs switching equipment in Ireland could be treated as having a PE if the system were sold to a local company or if the work were undertaken on behalf of a company under a contract, the duration of which exceeded 12 months.

- Construction and installation projects are regarded as PEs when they last for more than 12 months.

- A foreign company that operates a fiber optic cable system or constructs switching equipment could be characterized as having a PE. Relevant factors would include the presence of any of the foreign company's employees in Ireland and ownership of any of the assets.

If a foreign company has a PE, then it will be treated as though it were operating through a branch for purposes of Irish corporate tax (see "Corporate Income Taxes"). When a PE does not exist, a non-resident company will be subject to Irish withholding tax at 26% on interest, royalties and other annual payments received. The withholding tax rate can be reduced by a tax treaty.

Business Entities

The selection of a corporate structure for an investment in Ireland will be heavily influenced by tax considerations. Tax issues particularly relevant for telecommunications companies are the rates of tax applying to the Irish operations, tax rules applying in the investor's home country, and the investor's long-term plans in relation to the utilization or repatriation of profits generated in Ireland.

Local Branch of a Foreign Company. A non-resident company is subject to Irish corporate tax on profits arising from a business conducted through a branch in Ireland. A branch's taxable profit is determined in the same manner as for resident companies, with a deduction being available for expenses of a foreign head office that can be properly allocated to the activities of the branch. Losses incurred by a branch may be offset against all other profits of the branch in the current or preceding accounting period of equal length, or carried forward for offset against the profits of the same business in subsequent accounting periods.

Locally Incorporated Subsidiary of a Foreign Company. A company that is tax-resident in Ireland is subject to corporate tax on its worldwide income. A company is considered to be tax-resident in Ireland if it is managed and controlled in Ireland, which, in practice, means that meetings of its board of directors are held in Ireland and that major policy decisions are made at these meetings.

There are no provisions for the filing of consolidated tax returns by related companies. In general, however, trading losses incurred by an Irish group company may be offset against the profits of other members of the group for the same accounting period. For this purpose, a group is defined as a parent company together with its 75%-owned subsidiaries that are resident in Ireland. Relief for losses is also available when a company's ordinary share capital is owned by a consortium of Irish-resident companies, none of which owns more than 75% of the ordinary share capital.

Profits would generally be repatriated by way of dividends. A company paying a dividend must pay an amount of advance corporation tax (ACT) equal to the tax credit attaching to the dividend. ACT should not be a real cost to a company if it is profitable, as it can be used to offset the company's corporate tax. (ACT is discussed in more detail under "Operating Considerations.")

Joint Venture. The government has stated that prior to deregulation, the only method of entry into the wireline market is through strategic alliances with existing companies and that such alliances require the approval of the Minister for Public Enterprise. The method of investment would generally take the form of the acquisition of a minority interest from the state. Alternatively, a capital injection could be made by a new investor into an existing company in return for shares. In either of these scenarios, a foreign company would merely be a minority shareholder in an Irish-resident company, and the foreign company would not be considered to have a permanent establishment.

For those sectors not controlled by the state, the selection of a corporate structure would be solely the choice of the investing company. The main types of entities used in Ireland are companies, limited or unlimited (which are separate legal entities for corporate tax purposes), and partnerships (which are tax-transparent, and can also be limited or unlimited). Both companies and partnerships are required to submit tax returns.

The most common form of entity used for doing business in Ireland is a limited liability company.

Local Funding Alternatives

Debt versus Equity

The main consequences of financing a business through debt or equity are as follows:

- Interest on debt is normally deductible if it is incurred wholly and exclusively for business purposes. However, dividends paid on share capital are treated as distributions and are not deductible.

- Interest paid to a non-resident lender that owns 75% or more of the ordinary share capital of an Irish-resident borrower is generally regarded as a distribution, which would not be tax-deductible. However, if the lender is tax-resident in a country with which Ireland has a tax treaty that was in place before April 6, 1976, the Irish Revenue will generally treat such interest as being tax-deductible.

- Subject to certain exceptions, payments of yearly interest (i.e., interest paid on loans lasting more than one year) must be paid net of Irish withholding tax. The standard withholding tax rate of 26% may be reduced under a tax treaty.

- There is no withholding tax on dividends paid by an Irish subsidiary to a non-resident shareholder. However, ACT may be payable on the dividend.

- A capital duty of 1% is imposed on the issue of new shares by an Irish company. No such charge is made on debt financing.

As mentioned above, certain interest payments are treated as distributions for which a tax deduction is not available. These include:

- Interest charged at a rate that exceeds a reasonable commercial rate. Only the excess over reasonable rates will be treated as a distribution.

- Interest charged at a rate that varies according to the company's results. In this case, the entire interest payment is treated as a distribution.

- Under certain circumstances, interest paid to a non-resident associated company (a company under 75% common control).

One advantage of using local debt over shareholder debt is that a deduction is available for the full amount of the interest as long as it is incurred for business purposes. Exchange gains and losses on foreign debt are treated as part of a company's income as long as the underlying debt is used for business purposes. There are no thin capitalization rules or specific tax legislation (except the provision for treatment of certain interest payments as distributions) that relate to the characterization of debt and equity. Therefore, general legal principles apply when determining whether financing is to be regarded as debt or equity. The existence of shareholder guarantees does not affect the application of thin capitalization rules to third-party debt.

Exchange Controls

Exchange controls were abolished on January 1, 1993.

Business Acquisitions and Dispositions

Foreign investors are permitted to make asset or share acquisitions. The purchase of licenses or of companies holding licenses is subject to approval by the Minister of Public Enterprise.

Capital Contributions into an Existing Local Entity

It is possible for a foreign company to acquire an interest in an existing local telecommunications company by a capital injection of cash or assets. When the contribution is made in exchange for shares, a capital duty charge of 1% will be payable. The sale of a minority interest should not affect the company's ability to carry forward existing tax losses, provided there is no major change in the nature of the business carried on by the company.

Expenditure by a resident company for the transfer of inventory and services to it will normally be considered to be of a revenue nature and will be allowable in calculating taxable profits, provided such expenditure is wholly and exclusively incurred for the purpose of the trade. Generally, no deduction is allowed for the acquisition of intangible assets.

The contribution of assets such as a foreign patent or technology will generally not give rise to any tax liability, provided the instrument under which the assets are transferred is executed abroad. When capital expenditure is incurred on patent rights, a write-down allowance is available. The allowance is given on a straight-line basis over the lesser of (1) 17 years, (2) the period for which the patent rights are acquired, or (3) the remaining life of the patent.

Purchase or Sale of Shares in a Local Entity

When an Irish-resident company or individual sells shares in an Irish company, any gain realized, after relief for inflation, will be subject to capital gains tax at a rate of 40%. Non-resident shareholders are subject to Irish capital gains tax on the sale of shares in an Irish company when the greater part of the value of the shares is derived from land, buildings or mineral rights located in Ireland. A stamp duty charge of 1% is payable by the purchaser in a share acquisition.

There is no mechanism to allow a foreign company to step-up the tax base in the assets owned by a local company to the extent of the premium paid on the purchase of shares. Existing trade losses in a company should be available for carryforward post-acquisition, provided there is no major change in the nature of the business.

Purchase or Sale of Assets

With an asset purchase, the seller is charged capital gains tax on any gain on the disposal of assets, including goodwill. The purchaser receives a step-up in the tax base of the assets acquired for tax depreciation purposes. Generally, stamp duty of 6% is levied on all asset purchases. The disadvantage of an asset purchase from the purchaser's perspective is that losses carried forward are generally not transferred with the assets.

All gains (after indexation relief) realized on the disposal of assets used for the purpose of a trade carried on in Ireland are chargeable to capital gains tax at 40%.

Partnerships are transparent for Irish tax purposes. Consequently acquisitions/disposals by or to partnerships are treated as acquisitions/disposals by the partners.

Start-up Business Issues

Pre-operating Losses and Start-up/ Construction Costs

Revenue expenditures (e.g., wages, salaries and rents) incurred three years before a business begins operations are tax-deductible. Capital expenditures incurred on plant or equipment or on the construction of premises prior to the start of business qualify for capital allowances (tax depreciation) once the business commences. (Capital allowances are discussed in more detail under "Operating Considerations.") A company that incurs a capital expenditure on plant and equipment for use in its business will be entitled to capital allowances. Business investigation costs are not deductible in computing a company's taxable profits. However, when an acquisition is made, all costs associated with the acquisition are taken into account when determining a profit or loss arising on a subsequent sale of the business.

Customs Duties and VAT

Most goods imported into Ireland from outside the EU are subject to customs duty and import VAT. Duty is normally payable on the cost, insurance and freight (CIF) value of the goods. Import VAT is payable on the duty-inclusive value of the goods, although VAT-registered traders can usually obtain a refund of the VAT.

Telecommunications and computing equipment are subject to duty ranging from 1.2% to 7%. The rate of duty depends on the exact description, tariff classification and country of origin of the goods. The current import duty rates for a sample of telecommunications goods originating in non-EU countries (in this example, the United States) are given below. The EU has prefer-

ential trade agreements with a number of countries that enable goods to be imported at rates below those indicated or at a nil rate of duty.

Line telephone sets with cordless handsets	3.8%
Videophones	7%
Other telephone sets	3.8%
Facsimile machines	3.8%
Teleprinters	3.8%
Telephonic or telegraphic switching apparatus	3.8%
Other apparatus for carrier line systems	2.3%
Other apparatus for digital line systems	3.8%
Building-entry telephone systems	3.8%

Customs duties on some items of equipment were already being reduced under the General Agreement on Tariffs and Trade (GATT). However, over the next few years, duty rates are scheduled to be reduced further under the Information Technology Agreement (ITA) signed in March 1997. The ITA also extends the range of goods subject to duty rate reductions. As a signatory to the ITA, the EU has agreed to cut tariffs on imports of computers and computer equipment, software, telecommunications and networking equipment to zero in four equal installments. The first reduction took place on July 1, 1997, and further reductions are to take effect on January 1 of each year through 2000. Although the ITA will cut the cost of importing many products, the convergence of technologies in the computing, electronics and telecommunications sectors is likely to lead to disputes over the tariff classification of some equipment and affect the availability and/or phasing of duty reductions under the ITA.

A wide variety of reliefs from customs duty (and import VAT) can be claimed in various circumstances (e.g., goods imported for processing and re-export or goods imported temporarily). There is also a relief available for capital goods and equipment, provided the goods are imported by a business on the transfer of its activities to Ireland. Raw materials or components that are not available, or not available in sufficient quantities, within the EU may be eligible for a complete or partial suspension of duty, providing this can be demonstrated to the satisfaction of the Commission of the European Communities in Brussels.

Goods may be subject to anti-dumping or countervailing duty if, for example, the EU considers they are being imported into the EU at prices substantially lower than their normal values. Anti-dumping and countervailing duties are chargeable in addition to, and independent of, any other duty to which the imported goods are liable.

Loss Carryovers

Losses can be offset against profits of a company in a current or preceding accounting period of equal length. In other words, there is a one-year carryback of the current year's losses, but this is restricted pro rata when the number of months in the current accounting period is less than that in the preceding accounting period. Tax losses generated on transactions that would generally be taxed at the lower effective rate of 10% (see "Operating Considerations") can be used only to offset other profits taxed at the same rate. Any unutilized losses can be carried forward and offset against the profits of the same business in subsequent accounting periods.

If, within a three-year period, there is a significant change in the ownership of a company and the nature of its business, then the company may forfeit the right to carry forward its tax losses. If the business in question is a provider of telephone services, then changing from wireline to cellular will not constitute a change in the nature of the business, and relief for losses forward should be available.

Operating Considerations

Corporate Income Taxes

A company that is tax-resident in Ireland (i.e., managed and controlled in Ireland) is subject to corporate tax on its worldwide income. A non-resident company is subject to Irish corporate tax on the profits arising from business conducted through a branch. A non-resident company that does not have a branch or agency, but has other Irish income, is subject to income tax on such income. The standard corporate tax rate is 36%. However, the government offers various tax incentives that can reduce, or in some cases eliminate, a company's income tax. (See "Tax Holidays and Exemptions.")

Withholding Taxes. Subject to the provisions of double-tax treaties, withholding taxes may apply to interest, royalties and other annual payments. There is no withholding tax on dividends paid by an Irish company to a non-resident shareholder. When an Irish company that is taxable at the standard corporate rate pays a dividend either to a resident or a non-resident shareholder, then it must pay ACT equal to $21/79$ths of the dividend. When a company is taxable at an effective rate of 10%, the rate of ACT is $1/18$th of the dividend.

ACT is available for offset against a company's corporate tax liability on income in the current accounting period or for any accounting period ending in the preceding 12 months. Any balance not utilized may be carried forward indefinitely against future corporate tax liabilities. When a dividend is paid to a non-resident company by a 75%-owned subsidiary and the recipient company is resident in a country with which Ireland has a tax treaty, then no ACT is payable. If there is no tax treaty in place, full ACT is payable.

No withholding tax arises on repatriation of branch profits to a foreign head office.

Capital Gains Taxes

Companies that are tax-resident in Ireland are subject to tax on their worldwide chargeable gains arising from the disposal of capital assets. This gain is determined by deducting from the sales proceeds the cost incurred on acquiring the asset, together with any enhancement expenditure, as indexed upwards for inflation. The resulting gain is taxable at a rate of 40%.

Non-resident companies are taxed on capital gains arising from the disposal of specified assets. Relevant assets include Irish land and buildings. Non-resident companies are also taxed on gains from the realization of assets used for the purposes of carrying on a business in Ireland.

Losses arising from the disposal of capital assets may be used to offset capital gains arising in the corresponding accounting period or carried forward for offset against future capital gains. There is no carryback of capital losses. Capital losses cannot be offset against business income and cannot be surrendered to other group companies.

Tax Holidays and Exemptions

Ireland has long used tax incentives to encourage inward investment and to stimulate investment in specific sectors. The primary incentives available are (a) a reduced tax rate of 10% (whether for a principal or contractor) and (b) incentives for research and development expenditures. Certain activities within the telecommunications industry qualify for a reduced tax rate of 10%, as detailed here.

Manufacture of Goods. The manufacture of telecommunications equipment will qualify for relief. The primary requirement is that the company's income be derived from the sale of products that are manufactured in Ireland. A company claiming this relief must undertake the manufacturing operations directly. Thus, when a company subcontracts all manufacturing work, it will not be entitled to this relief.

Call Center Operations. These include telemarketing and telesales. The effective tax rate of 10% will apply only if income is derived from the provision of the call center services. Call centers are usually operated through a separate legal entity, which provides services and re-charges foreign affiliates.

Incentives for Research and Development. Ireland has introduced a number of tax incentives to encourage industry to undertake research and development. A 100% first-year scientific research allowance is available to companies for capital or revenue expenditures incurred for scientific research. Scientific research is defined as "any activities in the fields of natural or applied science for the extension of knowledge." This term is interpreted very broadly and would, for example, cover work undertaken in the development and modification of telecommunications technology (including software development) or products.

Complete exemption from tax is available to persons who are tax-resident in Ireland on income from registered patents. The patent need not be registered in Ireland, but substantially all the work on the development and testing of the patented process must have been undertaken in Ireland. Tax exemption is available only on income derived from the use of the patent by a manufacturing operation or by an unrelated third party. When the exempt patent income arises to a company, the benefits of the exemption may pass on to any Irish shareholders receiving dividends from that company.

New Industry Program. The government-run New Industry Program provides grants for new projects. Several types of grants are available, including capital grants, rental subsidies, feasibility study grants, product development grants, training grants, employment grants, interest subsidies, loan guarantees and management development grants. All grant claims must be certified by a company's auditors. Among the conditions that will be imposed is a requirement that the investors provide equity equal to the amount of the grant. This condition can be met by a combination of ordinary share capital and loans subordinated to all other creditors, including the grant agency. Of the total capital subscribed by the investor, at least 25% must be in the form of ordinary shares.

Depreciation/Cost-Recovery Conventions/Accelerated Deductions

Generally, in order to qualify as a tax deduction, an expenditure must be wholly and exclusively incurred for the purposes of the business. A tax deduction is not allowed for expenditures on capital assets in computing the adjusted profits of a business for tax purposes. Depreciation charged for book purposes is disallowed for tax purposes. There is, instead, a system of tax depreciation allowances for capital expenditure on industrial buildings plant and equipment and purchased computer software. These allowances are given as deductions in computing taxable income. Capital expenditure qualifying for tax depreciation allowances is reduced by the amount of any grants received in respect of that expenditure.

To qualify for depreciation allowances on plant and equipment, these items must be in use at the end of the accounting period. There is no established precedent on when network assets would be regarded as coming into use, but a view could be taken that assets are placed in service when they form an integral part of the network. This is likely to be a matter of degree.

A depreciation allowance of 15% per year is allowed for plant and machinery. No depreciation allowance is allowed on offices, shops and residential buildings, except in designated areas. Accelerated depreciation rates may be applied in certain locations. Subject to certain restrictions, motor vehicles qualify for wear-and-tear allowances at a rate of 20% per annum on a reducing-value basis.

When an asset is sold or otherwise ceases to be used for business purposes, an adjustment to the allowances already granted is made. This involves comparing the tax written-down value of the asset at the beginning of the accounting period in which the asset is sold with the sale proceeds. If the sale proceeds are less than the written-down value, there is a balancing allowance given in the accounting period of sale. If the sale proceeds exceed the written-down value, there is a clawback of the allowances previously given.

Marketing and advertising costs are generally fully tax-deductible, provided there is no element of capital expenditure or entertainment included.

Transfer Pricing Rules

Transactions between a company qualifying for an effective tax rate of 10% and an associated company taxable at 36% must be conducted on an arm's-length basis. Transactions between non-residents and Irish residents under common control must also be conducted at arm's length. In the absence of such pricing, the Irish Revenue will recalculate the profits associated with the transaction as if it were a transaction between independent parties dealing on an arm's-length basis, and charge tax accordingly.

Transfers of Patents, Trademarks and Software

Business-related royalties paid are fully tax-deductible provided they are calculated on an arm's-length basis. Any excess over the arm's-length rate would not be tax-deductible.

No general ruling has been given as to whether a transfer of technology is viewed as a sale or a license. Each transaction is subject to inspection by the Irish Revenue authorities. When distinguishing a sale from a license, the Irish Revenue would consider what generally happens in the industry.

When a patent right is sold, and the net proceeds consist wholly or partly of a capital sum, the amount receivable is assessed to tax over six years, with one-sixth of the lump sum being assessed in each year. The sale of technology or other such capital items is subject to capital gains tax at a rate of 40%. When a company sells or transfers a license or similar asset, it is subject to Irish stamp duty (at a rate of 6% of sale proceeds) and capital gains tax (proceeds less indexed cost at 40%). Stamp duty is payable on instruments executed in Ireland or instruments dealing with property situated in Ireland. Therefore, it is not possible to avoid stamp duty if the capital asset is situated in Ireland.

Royalties paid for patents are subject to a withholding tax of 26%, which may be reduced by a tax treaty. Royalty payments for the use of software qualify for a tax deduction. Capital payments incurred on the acquisition of software qualify for tax depreciation allowances as plant.

Service Fees

Service fees that are incurred wholly and exclusively for business purposes, no matter where they are rendered, are deductible, and withholding tax does not apply. Inter-company charges of whatever description are generally fully tax-deductible, provided they relate to the Irish business operation and are calculated on a reasonable basis. Such inter-company charges do not attract withholding tax.

Value-Added Tax, Sales Tax and/or Other Pertinent Taxes

As a member of the EU, Ireland follows the provisions of the European Community Sixth VAT Directive. Domestic telecommunications services (including those supplied by Irish-resident foreign businesses) are subject to VAT at the standard rate of 21%. The VAT treatment of international telecommunications services is based on the revised EU VAT model, which took effect in Ireland on July 1, 1997.

Services supplied internationally by a telecommunications business located in Ireland are generally outside the scope of VAT when supplied to anyone located outside Ireland. The only exceptions are services supplied to private individuals or unregistered persons located in other member states. Those supplies are subject to Irish VAT at the standard rate.

Non-resident providers are not liable to register and account for Irish VAT on supplies used by Irish customers, providing those customers are taxable persons for VAT purposes. These customers are required to self-account for VAT under reverse-charge procedures.

When a non-resident provider makes supplies of services to private individuals, to be used in Ireland, the provider is required to register and account for Irish VAT. For a non-EU provider, it should be possible to limit the Irish VAT liability to supplies made to Irish individuals that are effectively used and enjoyed in the EU. However, this may then require the overseas provider to be registered for VAT purposes in many different EU-member states. Alternatively, an overseas provider may choose to register in a single EU-member state in order to contract with all customers who are EU private individuals. The supplies made from the single EU registration to these customers will then be subject to local VAT in the member state of registration.

Under provisions published in the 1998 Finance Bill, the definition of place of supply of telecommunications services supplied to non-business customers from outside the EU was amended. The place of supply is now considered to be the country where the effective use of the service occurs, rather than the country of residence.

Access to the Internet is included within the definition of telecommunications, and the principles set out above apply equally to Internet service providers.

Stamp Duty. Stamp duty is payable on the transfer of assets situated in Ireland when such transfer is effected or evidenced by way of any written document. The rate of duty is 6% when the consideration exceeds IR£60,000, and reduced rates apply below this amount. It is also payable on the transfer of assets located outside Ireland if the document is executed in Ireland. In the absence of a written document, no charge will generally arise.

Stamp duty of 1% arises on the transfer of common stock or marketable securities. Transfers of most other forms of property attract duty at 6% when the amount exceeds IR£60,000. Reduced rates apply when the amount is less than IR£60,000. Stamp duty relief is available for transfers arising from corporate reorganizations and reconstructions. In addition, no duty arises on transfers between associated companies (i.e., 90% affiliates).

Local and Provincial Taxes

Property taxes, known as local rates, are imposed by local authorities (i.e., city corporations, or urban and county councils) on the owners or occupiers of land and buildings used for business purposes. The rates, which change annually, are based on the size (area) of the building. Companies operating in the International Financial Services Center in Dublin or in designated urban renewal areas may be exempt from local rates for 10 years.

For Additional Information, Contact:

Dermot Reilly
Tax Partner
George's Quay
Dublin 2
Ireland
Telephone: 353 (1) 704 8605
Fax: 353 (1) 704 8600
E-mail: dermot_reilly@ie.coopers.com

Italy

Telecommunications Tax Profile
by Dr. Mario Morettini
Tax Partner, Milan

Overview of the Telecommunications Market

Historical Background

Since 1987, Italy's policy makers have broadly followed European Union (EU) directives and guidelines regarding telecommunications. Political uncertainty has often delayed key legislation and rulings.

The Italian telecommunications industry had been operated and regulated as a state monopoly under the provisions of the Postal Code of 1973. A combination of state telecommunications companies was granted concessions for monopolies in individual segments of the marketplace, including basic telecoms services, submarine cable, underground cable, regional international service and satellite service. During the 1990s, these state companies were gradually restructured and consolidated into one primary public service operator, Telecom Italia, which was privatized in 1997.

Real competition in this sector has arrived only recently. Although communications equipment supply has been mostly liberalized since the mid-1980s, the services part of the industry was dominated by Telecom Italia until the introduction of the second global system for mobile communications (GSM) operator in the mid-1990s.

Current Status

On January 1, 1998, Italy, following EU legislation, opened all of its telecommunications services to competition, although a number of critical enabling elements still had not been put in place. One key issue has been the delayed appointment of a telecoms regulator for the sector.

A limited amount of competition has existed since the late 1980s in the value-added-services (VAS) market, where closed-user-group, data-transmission and information-access services were started, using leased circuits from Telecom Italia. A large number of overseas telecoms players established VAS operations, including Unisource, British Telecom, AT&T, IBM, Cable & Wireless Plc, Bell Atlantic Corporation and others.

Several major Italian companies, many of them utilities, have for many years had special concessions to build their own facilities for internal telecommunications, usually based on radio networks. These include ENEL, the state's largest electricity generator and distributor; ENI, the major oil and gas company; and Ferrovie del Stato, the national railway company.

Following EU pressure, the cellular telephony market, hitherto a monopoly of Telecom Italia (Telecom Italia Mobile), was opened in 1994 to a single additional provider, Omnitel Pronto Italia (OPI), a consortium that now includes Olivetti, Bell Atlantic and Mannesmann to offer nationwide GSM services. Further EU legislation has led Italy to follow other European countries in the introduction of cellular competition with digital cellular system (DCS)-1800 services. This latter move had been considerably delayed and was expected in the second quarter of 1998.

A significant number of new groupings have been taking shape over the past year in anticipation of the liberalization of fixed telecoms services. At the local level, some of the established metropolitan cable players, such as MFS Communications and COLT Telecommunications, have been developing and acquiring infrastructure in large cities. Nationally, a number of significant new companies have been formed to roll out full service. Infostrada, owned by Olivetti and others, has already been active in the VAS market and is now planning nationwide telephony offerings. WIND, a joint venture between ENEL, France Telecom and Deutsche Telekom AG, is creating a new nationwide fiber-optic-based network, largely using ENEL electricity networks, and is also targeting DCS-1800 licenses in order to offer nationwide, fully convergent telecoms services. A further joint venture involving British Telecom,

Banca Nazionale del Lavoro (BNL), ENI and others is building out national services and seeking the DCS license. On February 18, 1998, the first fixed licenses were awarded to WIND and Infostrada, with services expected to be rolled out in the second half of 1998.

Telecom Italia has responded to the impending competition with a high-profile series of new technology infrastructure investments, including fiber to the home, joint ventures in Internet and similar advanced services, and the introduction of a digital European cordless telecommunication (DECT)-based service called FIDO.

Current Liberalization Status

Following EU guidelines, all telecommunications services were liberalized in Italy on January 1, 1998. Most of the services are subject to the licensing regime that will come under the management of the new regulatory authority to be established in 1998.

Type of Service	Degree of Liberalization	Key Legislation	Date of Actual or Expected Liberalization	Comments
Local, Long Distance and International	Fully liberalized (subject to license approval)	L. 23/12/1996 n.650 L. 01/07/1997 n.189	January 1, 1998	
Cellular	Multiple licenses	L. 31/07/1997 n.249	January 1, 1998	Second GSM license granted in 1994 (OPI); third DCS-1800/GSM license to be awarded in 1998
Paging	Fully liberalized (subject to license)		January 1, 1998	
Value-added	Fully liberalized		January 1, 1998	

Competitive Environment

Figures given are for 1996.

| Type of Service | Entire Market | | Top Two Players | | |
	Market Size	Number of Players	Names	Annual Revenue	Ownership
Local	Lit3.88 trillion	1	Telecom Italia	Lit3.88 trillion	Publicly traded
Long Distance and International	Lit15.34 trillion (does not include figures for incoming international)	1	Telecom Italia	Lit15.34 trillion	Publicly traded
Cellular	US$4.2 billion	2, with 1 or 2 more to be licensed	Telecom Italia Mobile OPI	US$3.9 billion US$300 million	Telecom Italia Olivetti, Bell Atlantic, Mannesmann, others
Paging	Not available	1	Telecom Italia	Not available	Publicly traded
Value-added Services	Lit6.6 trillion, including data (Lit0.75 trillion), leased circuits (Lit1.28 trillion), telephony access (Lit4.17 trillion) and enhanced voice services (Lit0.4 trillion)	3 main providers plus a few smaller operators	Telecom Italia Albacom	Not available Lit100 billion	Publicly traded British Telecom, BNL, Mediaset, ENI

Sources: Public Reports.

Licensing Requirements

A new regulatory framework has been in place since September 1997, bringing telecoms regulation broadly in line with EU directives. A ministerial decree in November 1997 set out the licensing procedures. A number of secondary measures were being prepared, including a system of licensing fees, a universal service financing scheme and interconnection agreements. An independent regulatory authority, the Autorità per le Garanzie nelle Comunicazioni, was established in 1997. At time of publication this was not yet operational, although a president and various officials had been appointed. In the meantime, the Ministry of Communications continued to act as the regulator.

Licenses for fixed networks were being issued. A third mobile operator and possibly a fourth were expected to be licensed later this year.

Potential for Foreign Ownerships/Relationships

There are no restrictions on foreign ownership of telecommunications businesses in Italy. Because the licensing procedure is difficult, foreign market entrants often seek Italian joint-venture partners who are familiar with the intricacies of the licensing process and have relationships with the authorities. As market liberalization proceeds, an advisor or partner with in-depth knowledge of the industry, its regulations and the Italian market in general, will continue to be beneficial for successful entry.

Potential for Upcoming Liberalization/Investment Opportunities

The Italian telecoms market is one of the most significant in Europe in scale terms, and one of the fastest-growing, particularly in mobile services. Despite bureaucratic difficulties, the local market is improving very rapidly, and the competition and revenue are expected to increase significantly, especially for telecommunications equipment. In addition, the new DCS network operating at 1800 MHz offers new opportunities.

Forms of Doing Business

Permanent Establishment

A foreign company is deemed to have a taxable presence when it has a permanent establishment (PE) in Italy. Generally, a PE exists when a foreign company maintains a fixed place of business in Italy that achieves certain standards of permanency. These standards are contained in Italy's various tax treaties, most of which are based on the OECD Model Convention. Telecommunications services can cover a broad range of activities, which may or may not constitute PEs. Some examples follow:

- The leasing of tangible or intangible property does not constitute a PE if the lessor does not maintain a fixed office or place of business in the country.

- The provision of long-distance telephone services to Italian customers by a foreign company that does not maintain a local office or do any local advertising should not constitute a PE.

- When a foreign company licenses technology or leases equipment to an Italian company, no PE results if the foreign company has no other presence in Italy.

- Whether the provision of services to a local company by a foreign supplier constitutes a PE depends on the nature of the services, the length of time the services are provided, the place at which the services are provided and other factors. For instance, an operator service contract would result in a PE if, under the contract, a foreign company were to provide managerial and technical services through employees located in Italy. Providing call reorganization/turnaround services or Internet access services would generally not result in a PE.

- The laying of fiber optic cable and construction of switching equipment (a) for sale to a local company, or (b) to be operated by a foreign telecommunications company for a local company in exchange for a fee will generally constitute a PE. Most double-taxation treaties provide that construction projects of a certain length do not, in and of themselves, constitute PEs.

- Provided that no local personnel are employed by a foreign company, having a server or switch located in Italy is unlikely to constitute a PE.

- A website owned by a foreign company is considered a PE if the company has personnel in Italy. The location of the website (whether inside or outside Italy) and its accessibility or lack of accessibility to customers in Italy are not factors in determining whether a PE exists. This principle applies for both foreign content and access providers, unless local tax laws and/or international tax treaties provide otherwise.

If a PE is avoided, fees for services generally will not be taxed. Income earned under a license of technology or under an equipment lease are subject to Italian withholding taxes. The statutory rate of withholding on such income is typically 21%, which is frequently reduced by a tax treaty.

Business Entities

Business may be transacted through a representative office, a branch of a foreign corporation or a legal entity. The legal-entity choices include two forms of limited liability corporations and three forms of partnerships.

Representative Office. A representative office performs preliminary and auxiliary functions related to the business of a foreign corporation. A representative office does not result in a taxable presence in Italy.

Local Branch of a Foreign Company. A branch of a foreign corporation is subject to the same tax rules and regulations as an Italian corporation. Earnings distributed by a branch to its foreign home office are not subject to withholding tax. Interest deductible against branch income and paid to a non-resident creditor will be subject to withholding tax at a rate of 15%, which can be reduced by a tax treaty.

Legal Entities. A società per azioni (S.p.A.) is a public limited liability company, and a società per responsabilità limitata (S.r.l.) is a private limited liability company. Shareholders of either a S.p.A. or a S.r.l. enjoy limited liability protection.

A S.p.A. requires a minimum share capital of 200 million Lira. Upon formation of a S.p.A., or upon subsequent additional capital contributions by the shareholders, a registration tax equal to 1% of the amount contributed is generally payable. A S.p.A. may be wholly owned by a foreign shareholder. In order to retain limited liability for a wholly owned subsidiary, it is normal to consider the possibility of a minority interest in the subsidiary being owned by a second company in the group.

Joint Venture. Most joint ventures in the telecommunications industry have been structured as S.p.A.s, with the various joint ventures owning shares in the company. Foreign investors have made significant investments in these joint ventures, typically with significant or even majority interests held by Italian companies.

Partnerships. Three types of partnerships are possible: (1) a società in nome colletivo (S.n.c.), a general partnership in which the liability of the partners is not limited; (2) a società in accomandita semplice (S.a.s.), a partnership in which the liability of certain partners is limited by agreement to the amount of their capital contribution; and (3) a società in accomandita per azioni (S.a.p.a.), an incorporated partnership in which the liability of certain partners is unlimited and which is taxed as a corporation. Only individuals may be partners in a S.n.c. or a S.a.s. Non-residents may be partners in any of these partnerships.

A S.n.c. and a S.a.s. are both required to determine income at the entity level and pay the regional production tax (imposta regionale sulle attivita produttive, or IRAP) on the income. The individual partners declare their share of the income and pay the appropriate national tax.

Local Funding Alternatives

Debt versus Equity

Interest expense is fully deductible for corporate tax purposes, but not for IRAP. There are no thin-capitalization rules or other restrictions or limitations on the use of debt; however, recent legislation restricted the use of back-to-back loans and of shareholder guarantees as means of avoiding Italian withholding taxes.

Gains and losses on foreign currency transactions are taxable in Italy.

Exchange Controls

Italy does not impose any controls on the exchange of currency.

Business Acquisitions and Dispositions

Capital Contributions into an Existing Local Entity

A transfer of assets to an Italian company or partnership is generally treated as a taxable event. A foreign transferor may be subject to Italian corporate tax if the assets transferred are attributable to an Italian permanent establishment or if the transferor is located in a jurisdiction with which Italy does not have a treaty. The recipient takes a fair-market-value basis in the asset, and the contributor realizes a gain or loss on the contribution.

Purchase or Sale of Assets

As of 1998 it is possible to opt to pay a substitutive tax on certain capital gains at the rate of 27%. The option for this tax is available only for transfers of businesses and participating interests that have been owned for at least three years. In this case, the capital gains deriving from the operation can be alternatively subject to:

- Standard taxation (37%), with the possibility of deferring the taxation in equal installments over a five-year accounting period, beginning with the accounting period in which the disposal takes place

- The standard substitutive tax (27%), which can be paid in a maximum of five equal installments, the first installment coming due before the deadline for filing the income tax return for the tax period in which the capital gain is realized, and subsequently thereafter for the four successive accounting periods (a company cannot use its net operating losses to offset a substitutive tax liability)

In general, a company will opt for the substitutive tax, unless it is an Italian corporation with net operating losses it can use to offset the standard tax.

Start-up Business Issues

Pre-operating Losses and Start-up/Construction Costs

The costs of obtaining permits and licenses must be capitalized over the life of the permits or licenses. Business investigation costs can be deducted if they are borne by the Italian entity and if they pertain to the activity performed or to be performed by the same Italian entity.

Costs incurred during the start-up phase (i.e., prior to the realization of revenue) may be deferred and deducted in the fiscal year in which the revenue is earned. Depreciation of fixed assets may similarly be deferred until the revenue is realized. The foreign company can recover VAT applied on the local purchasing through the appointment of a VAT representative.

Customs Duties and VAT

Most goods imported into Italy from outside the EU are subject to customs duty and import VAT unless exemptions apply. Duty is normally payable on the cost, insurance and freight (CIF) value of the goods. Import VAT is payable on the duty-inclusive value of the goods, although VAT-registered traders can usually obtain a refund of the VAT.

Telecommunications and computing equipment are subject to duty ranging from 1.2% to 10.5%. The rate of duty will depend on the exact description, tariff classification, and country of origin of the goods. The current import duty rates for a sample of telecommunications goods originating in non-EU countries (in this example, the United States) are given below. The EU has preferential trade agreements with a number of countries that enable goods to be imported at rates below those indicated or at nil rate of duty.

Line telephone sets with cordless handsets	3.8%
Videophones	7%
Other telephone sets	3.8%
Facsimile machines	3.8%
Teleprinters	3.8%
Telephonic or telegraphic switching apparatus	3.8%
Other apparatus for carrier line systems	2.3%
Other apparatus for digital line systems	3.8%
Building-entry telephone systems	3.8%

Customs duties on some items of equipment were already being reduced under the General Agreement on Tariffs and Trade (GATT). However, over the next few years, duty rates are scheduled to be reduced further under the Information Technology Agreement (ITA) signed in March 1997. The ITA also extends the range of goods subject to duty rate reductions. As a signatory to the ITA, the EU has agreed to cut tariffs on imports of computers and computer equipment, software, telecommunications and networking equipment to zero in four equal installments. The first reduction took place on July 1, 1997, and further reductions are to take effect on January 1 of each year through 2000. Although the ITA will cut the cost of importing many products, the convergence of technologies in the computing, electronics and telecommunications sectors is likely to lead to disputes over the tariff classification of some equipment and affect the availability and/or phasing of duty reductions under the ITA.

A wide variety of relief from customs duty (and import VAT) can be claimed in various circumstances (e.g., goods imported for processing and re-export, or goods imported temporarily). There is also a relief available for capital goods and equipment, provided the goods are imported by a business on the transfer of its activities to Italy.

Raw materials or components that are not available, or not available in sufficient quantities, within the EU may be eligible for a complete or partial suspension of duty, providing this can be demonstrated to the satisfaction of the Commission of the European Communities in Brussels.

Goods may be subject to antidumping or countervailing duty if, for example, the EU considers they are being imported into the EU at prices substantially lower than their normal values. Antidumping and countervailing duties are chargeable in addition to, and independent of, any other duty to which the imported goods are liable.

Loss Carryovers

Losses may be carried forward for five years, but they are usable only against income subject to the national tax (the imposta sul reddito delle persone giuridiche, or IRPEG). This general principle was modified on January 1, 1998, so that any losses incurred in the first three tax periods of the company could now be carried forward without any time limits (subject to special rules relating to dormant companies).

Operating Considerations

Corporate Income Taxes

The corporate income tax (IRPEG) is imposed at a rate of 37%. Italian companies are subject to tax on their worldwide income with potential relief from double taxation provided through a foreign tax-credit mechanism. In addition, starting in 1998, Italian companies are subject to IRAP, the regional production tax. This tax rate will initially be 4.25% of the taxable base (gross operating margin less certain costs, but excluding labor and interest costs). In the future, each Italian region will be able to opt to impose up to an additional 1%. IRAP is not deductible in computing IRPEG.

Non-resident companies with Italian branches are subject to income taxes on the income attributable to their Italian operations. Taxable income is generally determined in accordance with profit or loss for accounting purposes, with certain adjustments allowed.

Withholding Taxes on Dividends, Interest and Royalties. A corporation that pays interest, dividends or royalties to a non-resident must withhold income taxes on the payment. The statutory rates of withholding are 32.4% for dividends, 15% for most interest and 21% for royalties. These rates may be reduced by a tax treaty.

For dividends, the amount of the reduction of the withholding tax is frequently tied to the shareholder's ownership interest in the Italian corporation. Payments of dividends to companies located in other EU countries may generally be made free of withholding taxes under the parent-subsidiary directive.

Dividends paid to Italian shareholders are subject to a withholding tax of 10%. This withholding tax applies even though the corporate tax system is integrated and provides dividend recipients with a tax credit in order to avoid double taxation. Certain tax treaties afford this same treatment to non-resident investors.

Capital Gains Taxes

Capital gains treatment is available for gains on dispositions of property and they are subject to IRPEG of 37%. For the time being, it is uncertain whether capital gains are subject to IRAP. If the property is owned for less than three years, the capital gains may be subject to taxation over a five-year period. Capital gains deriving from the disposal of businesses or of participating interest may be subject to 27% substitutive tax payable in five tax years.

Capital losses are deductible against taxable income. They do not have to offset the capital gains before being deducted from taxable income.

Tax Holidays and Exemptions

Tax holidays are available for new investments located in certain depressed areas of the country. No specific provision exists for telecoms activity.

Depreciation/Cost-Recovery Conventions/Accelerated Deductions

The cost of acquiring or constructing tangible assets with a value of more than Lit1 million must be capitalized and depreciated over the useful life of the assets. Tangible assets are generally depreciated using the straight-line method over the asset's useful life as defined in a decree issued by the Ministry of Finance. Sample depreciation rates for some telecommunications assets follow:

Switching equipment	20%
Undersea cables	12%
Underground cables	5%
Satellites	18%
Transponders	36%
Transmitters/receivers	25%
Fixtures and fittings	12%
Vehicles	25%
Plant and machinery	20%

Depreciation of capitalized costs may begin when the asset begins to generate revenues. An accelerated depreciation method may be adopted for the first three years of an asset's life. The accelerated method essentially provides for a doubling of the otherwise allowable depreciation.

Software is considered an intangible asset and subject to depreciation in an amount not greater than one-third of its cost. Software embedded in telecommunications equipment is amortized over the life of the equipment. Expenses related to research and development (including software) and to advertising and publicity expenses are deductible in the fiscal year in which they are incurred or in five equal installments.

Marketing and promotional expenses are normally deducted in the fiscal year in which they are incurred.

Transfer Pricing Rules

In general, Italy requires that charges between related parties reflect arm's-length prices. Italy generally applies OECD standards in enforcing transfer pricing rules. Sales of products between related parties should occur at the normal value, which is defined as the value at which similar goods would be sold between unrelated parties.

"Normal value" is best determined by reference to other transactions for the same or similar goods under similar circumstances. When such comparables are not available, the related parties may use a cost-plus or a resale-minus approach in determining the appropriate price. These methods are based on the ability to determine a reasonable profit level for one of the parties.

Transfers of Patents, Trademarks and Software

Under Italian transfer pricing rules, marketing intangibles are to be analyzed under rules applicable to related-party charges for services and management fees. In determining the proper charge for technology or other non-marketing intangibles transferred between related parties, the tax law requires that the charges related to the transfer reflect an arm's-length price.

The base methods for determining an arm's-length price for intangible assets are the same as for tangible assets. These methods are based on the ability to identify comparable transactions between the taxpayer and unrelated parties, or between unrelated parties when the information surrounding the transfer and the amounts paid can be determined from public documents. The comparable information is frequently unavailable when technology transfers are at issue because of the uniqueness of the intangible or technology being transferred. Therefore, other evaluation methods must be used. Contributions of technology to the equity of a company may result in the need for an independent appraisal of market value if the value is to be reflected in the shareholder's equity. In such case, the contributing shareholder, if Italian, would be required to reflect the value as the proceeds of the disposition of an asset.

Service Fees

In order to determine whether a charge for services from a parent or related party to an Italian company is deductible, the authorities generally look to the functions performed and the benefit derived by the Italian company from the service. Service fees are not subject to withholding tax under Italian law.

Value-Added Tax, Sales Tax and/or Other Pertinent Taxes

As a member of the EU, Italy follows the provisions of the European Community Sixth VAT Directive. Domestic telecommunications services (including those supplied by Italian-resident foreign businesses) are subject to VAT at the standard rate of 9%. The VAT treatment of international telecommunications services is based on the revised EU VAT model, which took effect in Italy on April 1, 1997.

Services supplied internationally by a telecommunications business located in Italy are generally outside the scope of VAT when supplied to anyone located outside Italy. The only exceptions are services supplied to private individuals or unregistered persons located in other EU-member states. Those supplies are subject to Italian VAT at the special lower rate of 9%.

Non-resident providers are not liable to register and account for Italian VAT on supplies used by Italian customers, providing those customers are taxable persons for VAT purposes. These customers are required to self-account for VAT under reverse-charge procedures.

When a non-resident provider makes supplies of services to private individuals, to be used in Italy, the provider is required to register and account for Italian VAT. For an overseas provider, the Italian authorities will seek to apply Italian VAT to all telecoms services used in Italy both by Italian and non-EU private individuals. Alternatively, an overseas provider may choose to register in a single EU-member state in order to contract with all customers who are EU private individuals. The supplies made from the single EU registration to these customers will then be subject to local VAT in the member state of registration.

Access to the Internet is included within the definition of telecommunications, and the principles set out above apply equally to Internet service providers.

Registration Tax. A registration tax of 1% is generally payable upon share capital increases or other shareholder contributions. Branches are required to pay a 1% registration tax on the amount designated as capital committed to the branch and upon increases to this amount reflected in their annual financial statements. A purchase of a going concern will result in the application of registration taxes ranging from 3% to 8%, depending on the assets being transferred.

Local and Provincial Taxes

Telecommunications businesses are not subject to any local, provincial or regional taxes.

For Additional Information, Contact:

Dr. Mario Morettini
Tax Partner
Via Vittor Pisani 16
20124 Milan
Italy
Telephone: 39 (2) 669 951
Fax: 39 (2) 669 1800
E-mail: Mario_Morettini@IT.Coopers.com

Overview of the Telecommunications Market

Historical Background

The Netherlands has liberalized its telecommunications market in accordance with European Union (EU) directives. In 1989 the government-owned telecommunications monopoly became a public company, PTT Telecom Netherlands (PTT Telecom), a 100% subsidiary of Koninklijke PTT Nederland NV (KPN). Since 1994, the government has gradually reduced its ownership stake in the company through several separate share offers. The government now owns approximately 48% of KPN.

PTT Telecom was given the exclusive right to maintain fixed infrastructure and to supply leased lines and fixed voice services via fixed infrastructure until general market liberalization. The Netherlands opened its telecommunications market to competition in July 1997. PTT Telecom is obliged to provide other providers with interconnection to its networks.

The mobile telecommunications market was liberalized in September 1994 and licensing procedures were introduced. In March 1995 the Ministry of Transport and Public Works granted a global system for mobile communications (GSM) duopoly to PTT Telecom and Libertel.

Current Status

The Dutch authorities implemented the EU's requirement for full liberalization of the telecommunications sector on January 1, 1998. On August 1, 1997, the Dutch authorities appointed an independent regulator, who is responsible for addressing issues such as interconnection and number assignment.

Since July 1, 1997, new operators have offered fixed wire telephony. National licenses for telephony over fixed networks on public lands were granted in 1996; one for the telecommunications infrastructure of Telfort, a joint venture between the Dutch railways and British Telecom, and another for EnerTel Ontwikkelingsmaatchappif BV (EnerTel), a combination of energy and cable companies. The licenses stipulate that the licensees must provide national coverage within five years. Licenses have also been granted to regional telecommunications operators.

Two national and 16 regional licenses for digital cellular system (DCS)-1800 telephony (combined with GSM) in the Netherlands were to be auctioned in early 1998. The Ministry excluded PTT Telecom and Libertel from the auction for the national licenses.

Current Liberalization Status

In the World Trade Organization (WTO) negotiations of February 1997, the Dutch agreed to full liberalization of telecoms by January 1, 1998. Markets were actually opened July 1, 1997.

Type of Service	Degree of Liberalization	Key Legislation	Date of Actual or Expected Liberalization	Comments
Local and Long Distance	Liberalized	Telecommunications Act, 1988 Interim Act consisting of revised Telecoms Act and Fixed Telecommunications Infrastructure Licenses Act, 1996 Telecommunications Act (draft pending)	Liberalization began in 1989 for peripheral equipment and VANS. Fixed-line competition began in 1997.	A revision of the Telecoms Act (Interim Act) was expected to be passed in 1998.
International	Liberalized	Telecommunications Act (draft pending)	1998	Companies offering callback services as well as international alliances were active before July 1, 1997.
Cellular	Liberalized	Telecommunications Act, Auction Act (July 1996) and pending draft	1993 for data; 1994 for public telephony	Nationwide services are offered by several companies. Two additional national and 16 regional licenses (DCS-1800/GSM) were auctioned in February 1998. Telfort and Global One will have national coverage within 3 years.
Paging	Liberalized	Telecommunications Act and pending draft		

Competitive Environment

Competition is becoming widespread and is expected to occur in all types of services. As the following table indicates, new players—both domestic operators and foreign consortia—have entered the market and are aggressively competing against existing service providers for market share.

Type of Service	Entire Market		Top Two Players		
	Market Size (1996)	Number of Players*	Names	Annual Revenue (1996)	Ownership
Local	NLG10 billion to 13.5 billion (estimated)	8 regional telecoms operators**	PTT Telecom	NLG6.513 billion (local and long distance combined)	KPN (45% state-owned, 55% publicly owned)
			A2000	Not available	A2000 Holding
			EnerTel	Not available	Consortium of 11 Dutch cable and utility companies
Long Distance		3 national network operators; 4 long-distance operators	PTT Telecom	NLG6.513 billion (local and long distance combined)	KPN
			Telfort	Not available	British Telecom (50%) and Dutch Railways (NS) (50%)
International	NLG2.6 billion (estimated)	6	PTT Telecom	NLG2.19 billion	KPN
			Unisource	NLG2.432 billion (consolidated revenue)	AT&T, PTT Telecom, Telia and Swisscom

(continued at top of next page)

Type of Service	Entire Market		Top Two Players		
	Market Size (1996)	Number of Players*	Names	Annual Revenue (1996)	Ownership
Cellular	NLG2.1 billion (estimated)	2 established national network operators; 5 regional operators (PTT Telecom, Libertel, TeleDanmark, Orange/VEBA and Telfort)	PTT Telecom	NLG1.886 billion (cellular and paging combined)	KPN
			Libertel	NLG202 million	ING Group (38.5%) and Vodafone Group Plc (61.5%)
Paging	Not available	2	PTT Telecom	NLG1.886 billion (cellular and paging combined)	KPN
			CallMax BV	Not available	EM-Holding, T-Mobil, Telesystem International Wireless Corporation NV (Germany) and Wireless Service (Canada)
Value-added	NLG2 billion (estimated)	25	AT&T-Unisource Communications Services	NLG1.842 billion	AT&T, PTT Telecom, Swisscom and Telia
			PTT Telecom	Not available	KPN

Sources: Annual reports; C&L estimates.

* National operators also operate long-distance, regional and local services.

** Mainly television cable companies.

Licensing Requirements

Licensing, allocation of radio frequencies and technical approvals are carried out by the Ministry of Transport and Public Works. Wireless licenses have in the past been granted through a tender procedure. In early 1998, two national and 16 regional licenses for DCS-1800 (combined with GSM) were auctioned.

Under the proposed Telecommunications Act that was expected to be enacted in early 1998, licenses would be required only for the use of radio frequencies and telephone numbers.

Potential for Foreign Ownerships/Relationships

PTT Telecom and KPN, the parent holding company, have both entered into service and business agreements with foreign PTTs and corporations. There are no limitations on the percentage of a telecommunications business that can be owned by a foreign company. Foreign investors can enter the Dutch telecommunications market by initiating new operations, by co-operating with a Dutch telecommunications company, by taking over or leasing an existing Dutch telecommunications company, or by selling telecommunications equipment to operators on the existing telecommunications network. Typically, foreign companies seek Dutch partners when entering the telecommunications market.

Operators need licenses for the installation and operation of fixed infrastructure. Three national and several regional licenses were granted in 1996.

Potential for Upcoming Liberalization/Investment Opportunities

The Telecommunications Act expected to be enacted in 1998 provides for further regulation and liberalization of the Dutch market. Under the proposed Telecommunications Act, operators will need to register as part of a procedure to ensure that they fulfill their obligations under the Act. For service providers, no formal requirements exist. For operators with a dominant market position, special requirements are in place to allow the development of competition. These mainly concern cost orientation of tariffs. Parties without a dominant market position are not restricted by these rules.

Forms of Doing Business

Permanent Establishment

A non-resident entity is liable for Dutch corporate income tax only if it is deemed to have a taxable presence in the Netherlands (i.e., a permanent establishment). A permanent establishment (PE) is deemed to exist if a physical presence of a permanent character exists. Activities of an auxiliary nature do not, in general, constitute a taxable presence. Also, the mere presence of computer equipment in the Netherlands should not necessarily result in a taxable presence.

A PE is not considered to be a separate legal entity, and its results must be included in the results of a foreign head office. Income received by a foreign company in connection with activities that relate to the Netherlands, but that do not constitute a

PE, is not subject to Dutch taxation. There is no withholding tax on the remittance of profits from a Dutch branch to its foreign head office.

Telecommunications services can cover a broad range of activities, which may or may not constitute PEs. Some examples follow:

- When a foreign company provides technical services and assistance to a Dutch company, this does not constitute a PE. However, if these services are provided from an office in the Netherlands, it is likely that a PE exists, particularly if sales contracts are negotiated and concluded in the office. Even when a foreign company has no office in the Netherlands, the existence of a person authorized to conclude contracts and represent the foreign company (i.e., a permanent representative) can constitute a PE.

- The laying of fiber optic cable and the construction of telecommunications switching equipment can constitute a PE if the activities are carried out for a period exceeding 12 months, even if the equipment is subsequently sold to an operator.

- The provision of long distance telephone services by a foreign company to local customers without any local presence or advertising does not constitute a PE.

- The licensing of technology and know-how by a foreign company to a local Dutch company does not constitute a PE.

- The leasing of telecommunications equipment to a Dutch company by a foreign company does not constitute a PE.

- The provision of call reorganization/turnaround services does not constitute a PE.

- Internet access providers that own or lease servers in the Netherlands, without having their own personnel in the Netherlands, should be able to avoid PE status.

- A content provider that maintains a website on a server located in the Netherlands but provides only product information should not have a PE. However, if transactions occur over the website, it may constitute a PE.

- Having a website on a server located outside the Netherlands but accessible by customers in the Netherlands does not constitute a PE.

- Having a website on a server in the Netherlands that is not accessible by customers in the Netherlands but is accessible by customers in other countries and which provides only product information does not constitute a PE.

Business Entities

Local Branch of a Foreign Company. This is a commonly used option for foreign investors in the telecommunications sector. A foreign company is subject to corporate income tax only on the profits generated by its branch in the Netherlands. There is no withholding tax on the remittance of profits from a Dutch branch to its foreign head office.

Locally Incorporated Subsidiary of a Foreign Company. This option is available to a foreign investor, who could choose to operate as a Dutch limited liability company (a Besloten Vennootschap, or BV) or an unlimited liability company (a Naamloze Vennootschap, or NV).

A corporation's worldwide income is subject to Dutch corporate income tax if the business is incorporated under Dutch law or is effectively managed from the Netherlands. If a Dutch company owns at least 99% of the shares of another Dutch-resident company, the parent company and its Dutch subsidiaries can apply for a fiscal unity status, which permits the filing of a consolidated tax return. Companies included in a fiscal unity are taxed for the fiscal year as one entity (subsidiaries are deemed to be merged into the parent company). Transactions between companies within the same fiscal unity do not result in taxable profits. The losses of one company within a fiscal unity may be offset against the profits of another company that are realized in the same year.

Joint Venture. A foreign company may prefer to enter the telecommunications market through a joint venture with an established Dutch company. This is not a requirement, nor is government approval required. A joint venture can be carried out through either a limited liability company, a general partnership or a limited partnership. For tax purposes, the two latter forms of partnership are in principle not treated as separate legal entities and are, therefore, not required to file corporate income tax returns. Tax returns have to be filed by the individual partners.

BV Company. A joint venture may be carried out through a regular Dutch BV company. The BV company is subject to Dutch corporate income tax for its worldwide income and must file a corporate income tax return.

General Partnership. In a general partnership, or Vennootschap Onder Firma (VOF), each partner is separately liable for the debts of the partnership. For Dutch tax purposes, a general partnership is considered transparent and will thus be treated as a flow-through entity. Each partner is entitled to use his own system of profit allocation. The partners will be taxed for their share in the partnership on an individual basis.

Limited Partnership. In a limited partnership, or Commanditaire Vennootschap (CV), the general, or managing, partner is fully responsible for its debts and each limited partner is liable only up to the amount of his capital contribution. A limited partnership is, in principle, transparent for Dutch tax purposes (closed partnership) only if unanimous consent from all partners is required for the transfer of the partnership interest. The income derived from a transparent limited partnership will be considered income of the partners according to their respective shares. Corporate entities may participate either as general or limited partners in a closed partnership. A foreign corporate limited partner participating in a transparent limited partnership will be taxable in the Netherlands only to the extent that it is considered to have a taxable presence (i.e., a branch) in the Netherlands.

Local Funding Alternatives

Debt versus Equity

In principle, it may be tax-efficient to use debt to finance a Dutch operation. Interest on such debt may be tax-deductible if, among other things, it is calculated on an arm's-length basis. Equity financing could create taxable income in the Netherlands on surplus funds. Equity funding of a Dutch company attracts a 1% capital duty cost. No formal debt-equity ratio requirements exist. A Dutch company must, however, be capable of servicing its debt through interest payments and/or loan principal payments in order to prevent a possible reclassification of debt as equity.

When local third-party debt is used for the funding of a Dutch operation, interest incurred in connection with the debt is deductible for Dutch tax purposes. This in principle also applies when a shareholder guarantee is granted to secure the local debt, unless the local debt should, in fact, be requalified as equity.

Dutch case law has developed certain criteria to determine whether a financing instrument qualifies as debt or equity. The basic rule is that "form controls." However, the Dutch Supreme Court has indicated that the following exceptions exist:

* Situations in which, despite the form, the substance indicates that the parties intend to make a capital contribution (i.e., sham transactions)

* If the funding contributions are such that the creditor becomes, to a certain extent, a participant in the debtor company

* If the parent company or creditor provides a loan to the subsidiary/debtor under such conditions that, from the outset, the debtor will not be able to repay the debt

There are a number of restrictions on the deductibility of interest with respect to intra-group debt. The deductibility on inter-company loans may be limited if group equity is presented in the Netherlands as debt or if a third-party debt is qualified as an intra-group debt (for example, if a shareholder guarantees the debt). In addition, restrictions in offsetting interest expenses may apply if intra-group debt is used by a Dutch company to acquire the shares in a Dutch, non-related target company and if it forms a fiscal unity for corporate tax purposes. Interest expenses incurred on debt used to purchase certain foreign equity interests is not deductible for corporate tax purposes under the participation-exemption provisions.

Foreign exchange results realized on loans granted either by a local company or by a shareholder are fully subject to corporate income tax (i.e., exchange gains are taxable and exchange losses are deductible). Foreign exchange results on loans used to acquire investments in foreign entities which qualify under the Dutch participation-exemption provisions are tax-exempt.

Equity contributed to a Dutch company is subject to a 1% capital duty, which is deductible for tax purposes. However, an exemption from capital duty is possible when a Dutch company issues shares in connection with a share-for-share merger or an asset-for-share merger.

Dividends distributed by a Dutch company to its foreign shareholders are subject to withholding tax at a rate of 25%. However, this rate may be reduced under a tax treaty, or it may be eliminated under the EC Parent/Subsidiary Directive. There is no withholding tax on interest and royalty payments made by a Dutch company.

Exchange Controls

Exchange controls have essentially been abolished. Consequently, there are no exchange control regulations restricting the distribution of profits, dividends, interest or other payments to foreign investors.

Business Acquisitions and Dispositions

Capital Contributions into an Existing Local Entity

Capital contributions in cash or in kind to Dutch companies with capital consisting of shares are subject to a 1% capital duty. However, if a company that has its residence in another EU-member state contributes assets (i.e., goods, services or technology) to a Dutch company in exchange for shares, it may be exempted from this duty. To qualify for this exemption, the assets must be considered an independent part of the contributor's business, or all the assets and liabilities of a company must be contributed to the Dutch company in exchange for shares.

Capital contributions to an existing local company may influence the position of existing shareholders if, after the contribution, their percentage of interest decreases to less than 25% and the existing shareholder is non-Dutch. Under tax treaties, the withholding tax rate on dividends paid by the local company may be higher in such a case.

As of January 1, 1996, it is possible to freely amortize certain intangible assets and goodwill transferred to the Netherlands. The intangible assets should form part of an independent enterprise being transferred to the Netherlands. The acquisition price of the intangible must be less than NLG10 million per enterprise transferred. A request for the application of the free amortization rules should be filed with the tax authorities.

Purchase or Sale of Shares in a Local Entity

If a stock acquisition is made by a Dutch company, the acquired shares should be valued at cost. Any excess value over the net equity value of the subsidiary cannot be reported as a separate asset for tax purposes but should be included in the purchase price of the shares. Therefore, for tax purposes, the purchaser cannot amortize goodwill or classify it as an intangible.

The sale of shares in a Dutch company is exempt from corporation tax if the shares sold represent 5% or more of the paid-up capital of the company and the capital is for the whole or is partly divided into shares. The shares cannot have been held as inventory. If a non-resident company disposes of the shares in a Dutch company, corporate income tax is generally not due.

Losses incurred by the target company become unusable when more than 70% of the stock has been transferred and the acquired company has ceased its business activities.

Purchase or Sale of Assets

When a Dutch company acquires assets, the purchase price should be allocated to the acquired assets based on their fair market value resulting in an increased depreciation base. If the purchase price exceeds the market value of the tangible assets, goodwill can exist. This goodwill can be amortized if it can be shown that the business it relates to will decrease in value over a certain period of time.

If a sale of assets by a Dutch company to a local entity occurs, a taxable event takes place at the level of the disposer. An asset transaction may trigger the recognition of a taxable capital gain for the seller. This gain may be reduced by utilizing any available prior-year losses of the seller. Losses cannot be utilized by the buyer. It may be preferable from the purchaser's perspective to purchase assets, but because tax relief for the assets purchased should be available, sellers generally prefer a sale of shares, which would be exempt from capital gains tax. However, when shares are purchased, the history of the underlying company, including its tax liabilities, forms part of the deal. On the other hand, an asset deal can trigger substantial legal work and related difficulties as the assets and liabilities to be purchased should all be transferred separately.

Under certain circumstances, the disposal of assets to a Dutch company can be free of corporate tax (roll-over) if shares are issued in exchange. Both the purchase and the disposal of an interest in an existing Dutch partnership can be complicated. For example, if a new partner enters into an existing partnership, the existing partners will be deemed to have disposed of their interests, which could result in a taxable step-up in each partner's basis.

Start-up Business Issues

Pre-operating Losses and Start-up/Construction Costs

Dutch tax law does not differentiate between start-up expenses and expenses incurred during the normal course of business. Expenses may be deducted in the year incurred if they closely relate to that period of time. Expenses must be capitalized and amortized if they relate to a period exceeding one year. For example, the costs for placing an ad in a newspaper occasionally should be deducted in the respective year. If, however, the advertising costs apply to an advertising campaign that will run for more than a year, the costs cannot de deducted totally in one year but are, through depreciation, allocated to a number of subsequent years. However, expenses that are deferred in line with generally accepted accounting principles can, for tax purposes, be deducted in the year in which they are incurred.

As mentioned above, expenses that have benefit for more than one year, such as the construction costs of a network, must be capitalized. These capitalized costs can be proportionally amortized during the years the costs are effectively incurred (e.g., the period during which the construction takes place). Amortization of intangibles is allowed only if it can be demonstrated that the intangibles have a limited lifetime.

The costs of research and development (R&D) can be expensed. Costs of self-developed patents can also be expensed. The cost of R&D carried out by another party has to be capitalized unless the benefits of such R&D last only one year.

Direct or indirect pre-operating costs incurred by a foreign company outside the Netherlands can be deducted or amortized, provided the costs are re-charged and it can be demonstrated that the costs are made for the benefit of the Dutch company. A foreign company can, in principle, recover the Dutch VAT related to locally incurred costs in the pre-operating phase.

Customs Duties and VAT

Most goods imported into the Netherlands from outside the EU are subject to customs duty and import VAT. Duty is normally payable on the cost, insurance and freight (CIF) value of the goods. Import VAT is payable on the duty-inclusive value of the goods, although VAT-registered traders can usually obtain a refund of the import VAT.

Telecommunications and computing equipment are subject to duty ranging from 1.2% to 10.5%. The rate of duty will depend on the exact description, tariff classification, and country of origin of the goods. The current import duty rate for a sample of telecommunications goods originating in non-EU countries (in this example, the United States) are shown below. The EU has preferential trade agreements with a number of countries that enable goods to be imported at rates below those indicated or at a nil rate of duty.

Line telephone sets with cordless handsets	3.8%
Videophones	7%
Other telephone sets	3.8%
Facsimile machines	3.8%
Teleprinters	3.8%
Telephonic or telegraphic switching apparatus	3.8%
Other apparatus for carrier line systems	2.3%
Other apparatus for digital line systems	3.8%
Building-entry telephone systems	3.8

Customs duties on some items of equipment were already being reduced under the General Agreement on Tariffs and Trade (GATT). However, over the next few years, duty rates are scheduled to be reduced further under the Information Technology Agreement (ITA) signed in March 1997. The ITA also extends the range of goods subject to duty-rate reductions. As a signatory to the ITA, the EU has agreed to cut tariffs on imports of computers and computer equipment, software, telecommunications and networking equipment to zero in four equal installments. The first reduction took place on July 1, 1997, and further reductions are to take effect on January 1 of each year through 2000. Although the ITA will cut the cost of importing many products, the convergence of technologies in the computing, electronics and telecommunications sectors is likely to lead to disputes over the tariff classification of some equipment and affect the availability and/or phasing of duty reductions under the ITA.

A wide variety of reliefs from customs duty (and import VAT) can be claimed in various circumstances (e.g., goods imported for processing and re-export, or goods imported temporarily). There is also a relief available for capital goods and equipment, provided the goods are imported by a business on the transfer of activities to the Netherlands.

Raw materials or components that are not available, or not available in sufficient quantities, within the EU may be eligible for a complete or partial suspension of duty, providing this can be demonstrated to the satisfaction of the Commission of the European Communities in Brussels.

Goods may be subject to anti-dumping or countervailing duty if, for example, the EU considers they are being imported into the EU at prices substantially lower than their normal values. Anti-dumping and countervailing duties are chargeable in addition to, and independent of, any other duty to which the imported goods are liable.

No distinction is made between regular telephony and Internet telephony for the purposes of VAT.

The Melbourne Agreement applies to exempt payments under the international settlement process from VAT for payments made to and by the Dutch PTT.

Loss Carryovers

Tax losses incurred during a taxable year can be carried back for three years and carried forward without time limit. Special rules apply for the use of tax losses incurred by companies within a fiscal unity. When a company changes ownership, tax losses may not be utilized if more than 70% of the individual shareholders change and the business ceases to exist.

Operating Considerations

Corporate Income Taxes

Companies incorporated under Dutch law or effectively managed in the Netherlands are taxable on their worldwide income. As of January 1, 1998, a flat corporate income tax rate of 35% applies.

Capital Gains Taxes

Capital gains are taxed as part of ordinary income.

Tax Holidays and Exemptions

There are no special tax holidays or exemptions for telecommunications companies. In addition, there are no specific tax credits for R&D activities. However, various government grants and subsidies can be obtained by both foreign and domestic companies for activities carried out in the Netherlands, including R&D and technological projects, among others. Substantial foreign investments may qualify for certain favorable tax treatment that will result in a financial benefit to a foreign investor for a certain period of time. Whether an investment would qualify for these benefits depends on its specific characteristics.

Depreciation/Cost-Recovery Conventions/Accelerated Deductions

Fixed assets that have a limited useful life must be depreciated from the moment the asset is put in use. The depreciation period generally depends on the economic lifetime of the asset. Under the sound-business-practice concept of Dutch tax law, various depreciation methods may be followed, provided that the method is in line with sound business practice and is consistently applied. Usually, the depreciation method used for accounting purposes is adopted for tax purposes. The most commonly applied method is the straight-line method. However, certain environmental investments and investments in economically undeveloped regions may be eligible for accelerated depreciation.

Some typical rates for fixed assets using the straight-line method are given below:

Buildings	2%–5%
Machinery	10%–20%
Transportation vehicles	25%–33.3%
Computers	33.3%

Software embedded in telecommunications equipment can be separately amortized over the useful life of the software. However, if the acquired telecommunications equipment and software have the same useful lifetime, both elements are usually combined as one asset and amortized.

In general, costs related to the research and development of a product (e.g., software) can be capitalized and subsequently amortized over the useful lifetime unless the amount of the costs is considered lost.

The costs of marketing and advertising campaigns should be deducted in the year they are incurred and the campaign is running. If the campaign runs, for example, more than one year, the costs must be capitalized and amortized over those years.

Transfer Pricing Rules

Transactions between related companies should be based on the arm's-length principle. Dutch tax law does not contain specific rules regarding transfer pricing between related parties, but relies on the OECD guidelines for transfer pricing. In general, advance rulings can be sought from the Dutch tax authorities as to the appropriateness of a price in related-party transactions.

Transfers of Patents, Trademarks and Software

There are no restrictions on the licensing of technology to a local company for a royalty fee. A sale is distinguished from a license by the form of the contract. If the contract provides for an outright transfer of ownership of the assets, then a sale has taken place. If the contract provides for a right to use the assets, this is considered a license. Income, whether from a sale or a license, is taxed as part of a company's ordinary income.

Software licensing fees are deductible, provided they are charged at an arm's-length rate. There is no withholding tax payable on software licensing fees.

If a Dutch company owns intangibles and receives license fees in connection with these intangibles, these fees are fully subject to Dutch corporate tax. Disposal of the intangibles, within or outside the country, triggers corporate tax on the proceeds of the disposal. However, a Dutch company that licenses and sub-licenses intangibles from a related foreign company can negotiate a ruling with the tax authorities regarding the taxable spread to be reported. Such a royalty ruling usually requires that the licensing company realize and report for Dutch tax purposes a minimum taxable income of 2% to 7% of the net royalty receipts (the actual percentage depends on the aggregate annual amount of royalties received).

Service Fees

Service fees received by a Dutch company in connection with service activities carried out outside the Netherlands are subject to corporate tax. The Netherlands does not impose withholding tax on services fees, provided the arm's-length principle has been used for the determination of the fees.

Value-Added Tax, Sales Tax and/or Other Pertinent Taxes

As a member of the EU, the Netherlands follows the provisions of the European Community Sixth VAT Directive. Domestic telecommunications services (including those supplied by Dutch-resident foreign businesses) are subject to VAT at the standard rate of 17.5%. The VAT treatment of international telecommunications services is based on the revised EU VAT model, which took effect in the Netherlands on July 1, 1997.

Services supplied internationally by a telecommunications business located in the Netherlands are generally outside the scope of VAT when supplied to anyone located outside of the Netherlands. The only exceptions are services supplied to private individuals or unregistered persons located in other EU-member states. Those supplies are subject to Dutch VAT at the standard rate.

Non-resident providers are not liable to register and account for Dutch VAT on supplies used by customers in the Netherlands, providing those customers are taxable persons for VAT purposes. These customers are required to self-account for VAT under reverse-charge procedures.

When a non-resident provider makes supplies of services to private individuals, to be used in the Netherlands, the provider is required to register and account for Dutch VAT. For an overseas provider, it should be possible to limit Dutch VAT liability to supplies made to Dutch individuals that are used in the EU. However, this may then require the overseas provider to be registered for VAT purposes in many different EU-member states. Alternatively, an overseas provider may choose to register in a single EU-member state (e.g., the Netherlands) in order to contract with all customers who are EU private individuals. The supplies made from the single EU registration to these customers will then be subject to local VAT in the member state of registration.

Access to the Internet is included within the definition of telecommunications, and the principles set out above apply equally to Internet service providers.

Local and Provincial Taxes

Local authorities can impose, at widely varying rates, district and municipality duties on wires, cables and tubes based in or on district/municipality ground. Local authorities can also impose real estate tax, which is levied on the owner and tenant of real estate. The rate of real estate tax depends on the municipality. Real estate tax is based on the property value assessed by the municipality. Currently, wires, cables and tubes in the ground that are used for transport are exempt from real estate tax. However, based on proposed legislation, it is expected that certain municipalities will abolish this exemption.

For Additional Information, Contact:

Paul van Overloop
Tax Partner
P.O. Box 94669
1090 GR Amsterdam
The Netherlands
Telephone: 31 (20) 568 6936
Fax: 31 (20) 568 6900
E-mail: Paul_van_Overloop@nl.coopers.com

Dick van Schoonoveld
Telecoms Consulting Principal
P.O. Box 8283
3503 RG Utrecht
The Netherlands
Telephone: 31 (30) 219 1116
Fax: 31 (30) 219 1195
E-mail: Dick_van_Schooneveld@nl.coopers.com

Norway

Telecommunications Tax Profile
by Rolf H. Nicolaissen
Tax Partner, Oslo

Overview of the Telecommunications Market

Historical Background

In 1987, the Norwegian parliament took the first steps toward liberalizing the telecommunications market. In 1988, the regulatory activities of Post Telephone and Telegraph (PTT) were separated from operations and the market for terminal equipment was liberalized. As Norway is part of the EU's single market created by the European Economic Area (EEA) Agreement, the pace of telecommunications liberalization is following the timetable set by EU directives, and all legislation adopted by the EU within the single market becomes part of the Norwegian telecommunications legislation.

The mobile market was opened to competition in 1993 when two parallel operators were authorized to provide global system for mobile communications (GSM) services. That same year, competition in value-added data services, leased-line resale and data transmission was authorized. Currently, competition exists in satellite communication cable television services, as well as in alternative infrastructures for telecommunications services. The telecommunications market was fully liberalized in January 1998, when voice telephony was opened to competition.

In 1994, the state communications company, Norwegian Telecom, became a limited company. In 1995, it was restructured as Telenor A/S and remains 100% state-owned.

Current Status

Telenor A/S continues to dominate the market through its seven business units, which include international telecommunications services and cable TV. Telenor's telephony revenues are growing at a moderate rate, while fixed-line services revenues are expected to decrease slightly in 1998. With the liberalization of voice telephony earlier this year, new competitors, including Telia Oy, have entered the marketplace and are aggressively pursuing market share.

Last year, Telenor completed the digitalization of all its telephony switches. The network consists of some 250 local switches and approximately 2,500 RSS/RSUs (remote subscriber switch/remote subscriber units). Integrated services digital network (ISDN) subscriptions account for 2% of all new subscriptions, and are growing rapidly.

The analog Nordic mobile telephone (NMT) service market is still a Telenor monopoly. It currently represents 30% of the total mobile market, although that share is decreasing steadily. The GSM service market is a duopoly shared by Telenor Mobil A/S and NetCom A/S, which in 1993 began operations as the first licensed, privately owned telecommunications entity in Norway. NetCom published its first positive results in October 1997.

Three licenses for the digital cellular system (DCS)-1800 were issued in 1997. These licenses do not require full national coverage, which may lead to a first-ever geographic price discrimination in Norway.

Internet usage has been growing rapidly in Norway. It is estimated that 20% of all homes with a telephony subscription also have access to the Internet.

Current Liberalization Status

Under the February 1997 World Trade Organization (WTO) Agreement on Basic Communications, Norway agreed to the complete liberalization of all basic telecommunications services, as well as to the end of the existing duopoly in cellular telephony. As evidenced by the following table, Norway has made significant progress toward that commitment.

Type of Service	Degree of Liberalization	Key Legislation	Date of Actual or Expected Liberalization	Comments
Local	Deregulated	Telecoms Act 1995, with revisions in 1998	January 1, 1998	
Long Distance	Deregulated	Telecoms Act 1995, with revisions in 1998	January 1, 1998	
International	Deregulated	Administrative Act related to public network and public services (December 5, 1997)	1996–1998	Leased-line-based solutions in place for businesses
Cellular	Analog NMT monopoly Digital GSM deregulated	Administrative Act related to public network and public services (December 5, 1997)	Two licenses granted 1991, operations started 1993	
Paging	Deregulated	Parliament decision "Stortingsmelding 38," Administrative Act related to public network and public services (December 5, 1997)	1988–89	
Value-added	Deregulated	Administrative Act related to public network and public services (December 5, 1997)	1989	

Competitive Environment

Competition in the telecommunications sector has increased over the past year, with Telia and Tele2 emerging as the leading new entrants. Electricity companies have formed a number of alliances with well-known international telecommunications operators. This is expected to lead to substantial network investments, though primarily in only a few urban areas, given Norway's sparse population concentration.

	Entire Market		Top Two Players		
Type of Service	Market Size (1996)	Number of Players	Names	Annual Revenue (1996)	Ownership
Local	NOK 4.3 billion	1	Telenor	NOK 3.0 billion in access, NOK 1.3 billion in traffic	Government
Long Distance	NOK 2.3 billion	1	Telenor	NOK 2.3 billion	Government
International	NOK 1.5 billion	5	Telenor (other 4 operators are much smaller)	Not available	Government
Cellular	NOK 5.7 billion	2	Telenor Mobil	NOK 4.5 billion	Government
			NetCom	NOK 1.2 billion	Publicly traded
Paging	NOK 100 million	1	Telenor Mobil	NOK 100 million	Government
Value-added	NOK 400 million	2	Telenor Link	Not available	Government
			Teletopia		

Source: Coopers & Lybrand estimates.

Licensing Requirements

As stipulated in the Telecommunications Act of 1995, public wire-line, leased-line, voice telephony, paging, mobile data and mobile telephony operators must be licensed by Post-og Teletilsynet (PT), formerly Statens Teleforvaltning (STF), which reports to the Ministry of Transport and Telecommunications. As of January 1, 1998, licenses are required only for operators with a "strong market position." Other operators need only complete a simple registration process.

Potential for Foreign Ownerships/Relationships

There is no limit upon foreign ownership. In general, Norwegian antitrust and licensing legislation allow both Norwegian and foreign investors to be telecommunications operators.

Potential for Upcoming Liberalization/Investment Opportunities

Public wireline and leased-line services, which are the most profitable businesses within the telecommunications sector, are currently being liberalized. As previously noted, a number of international competitors are entering the market, building alliances with electricity companies to exploit the opportunities offered by existing networks. Compared to other European markets, this market is small and price levels are low.

Forms of Doing Business

Permanent Establishment

A foreign enterprise carrying out business activity in Norway will, under the respective tax treaty, only be taxable in Norway for profits attributable to a permanent establishment (PE). A PE is normally defined as being "a fixed place of business through which the business of an enterprise is wholly or partly carried on." Telecommunications services can cover a broad range of activities, which may or may not constitute a PE. The following examples are considered:

- The provision of long-distance telephone services by a foreign company to local customers without any local presence would generally not constitute a PE.

- The licensing by a foreign company of technology and know-how to a local company without some permanent presence will generally not constitute a PE.

- The presence of a foreign telecommunications company's employee(s) as an operator of a Norwegian-resident telecommunications company, including the provision of technical assistance and technological services by a foreign company to a local company, in exchange for service fees including operator services and/or network management services, is likely to constitute a PE. Even if no PE is constituted, the employees of the foreign company may be liable for Norwegian income taxes as "hired-in" employees. If the persons providing the operator services and technical support become employees of the local entity, then the foreign entity may not be deemed to have a PE.

- The leasing of telecommunications equipment (without other supporting activities in Norway) to a local company will generally be taxable in Norway under internal legislation. However, the activity will generally not constitute a PE if the leasing business is not carried on through a fixed place of business in Norway.

- The provision of call reorganization/turnaround services will generally not be regarded as a taxable activity in Norway if the telephone cards are provided through an independent agent and the foreign telecommunications company has no substantial equipment or other physical presence in Norway. The existence of an independent agent will not in and of itself constitute a PE.

- Whether the provision of Internet access services may be taxed depends upon the extent of a foreign company's operations in Norway. A foreign entity without a presence in Norway, which merely sells software to Norwegian customers from abroad, will generally not be characterized as carrying on taxable activity in Norway. However, if the foreign entity owns the access server located within Norway, this may result in taxable activity, depending on the circumstances, and might be sufficient to constitute a PE.

- Having a server or a switch located in Norway but not having any other resident personnel will probably constitute a PE.

- Having a website located on a server in Norway that is accessible by customers in Norway will probably constitute a PE.

- Having a website located on a server outside Norway that is accessible by customers in Norway will probably not constitute a PE.

- Having a website located on a server in Norway that is not accessible by customers in Norway but is accessible by customers in other countries will probably constitute a PE.

- The laying of fiber optic cable and the construction of telecommunications switching equipment for sale to a local company or to be operated by a foreign telecommunications company for a local company in exchange for a fee will generally be regarded as a taxable activity in Norway.

Generally, a PE will be deemed to exist if the work lasts for more than one year.

It should also be noted that according to Norwegian internal legislation, a foreign enterprise with no formal presence in Norway may be subject to income tax in Norway for business activity carried on within, or managed from, Norwegian jurisdiction.

Business Entities

Business in Norway can be conducted through various types of entities. The available business entity forms are:

- Private joint-stock company (Aksjeselskap, or AS)

- Public joint-stock company (Almennaksjeselskap, or ASA)

- Partnership with unlimited liability (Ansvarlig selskap, or ANS)

- Partnership with limited liability (Kommandittselskap, or KS)

Business may also be conducted through a local branch of a foreign company. Except for the question of liability of the partners, the main difference between the corporate forms is restrictions on equity. Private joint-stock companies (ASs) must have a minimum share capital of NOK 50,000, and public joint-stock companies (ASAs) a minimum of NOK 1,000,000.

When foreign companies make investments in telecommunications businesses, the most commonly used type of entity is a locally incorporated subsidiary in the form of an AS. However, a local branch of a foreign company may also be used.

Local Branch of a Foreign Company. Telecommunications businesses in Norway can be organized as a branch of a foreign company. There are no restrictions on the distribution of branch profits. A branch is taxed on its Norwegian-sourced income and on foreign-sourced income that is effectively connected with the Norwegian business. Profits and losses of the branch can be grouped with those of other operations within the local branch, but not with other Norwegian subsidiaries of the overseas parent. A positive effect of such organization is that there is no withholding tax on profit distributed from a branch to its foreign parent. A branch is taxed on its income at the corporate tax rate of 28%.

Locally Incorporated Subsidiary of a Foreign Company. A subsidiary will normally be incorporated in the form of a private joint-stock company. Profits can be distributed to the shareholders; however, provisions in the Joint-Stock Companies Act make it necessary to allocate some of the profits to restricted equity (legal reserve), which normally cannot be distributed to the shareholders. A joint-stock company is treated as a separate entity for tax purposes and is subject to tax at the corporate tax rate of 28%. Profits and losses of the local subsidiary can be grouped with those of other operations of another local subsidiary of the overseas parent.

Group relief, by way of a tax group contribution, is permitted between Norwegian joint-stock companies held directly or indirectly by more than 90% of capital and votes by the same ultimate (Norwegian or foreign) parent company. This relief is deductible for the grantor and taxable for the recipient.

Joint Venture. There are no restrictions on the types of entities that are available for joint ventures. Entities commonly used for joint ventures are joint-stock companies and limited or general partnerships, all of which are legal entities. Government approval is not required for a joint venture in the telecommunications sector.

The liability of the shareholders of a joint-stock company is limited to the share capital determined in the founding document unless otherwise agreed with the company or its creditors. A joint-stock company is a separate taxable entity, which files its own tax return. Its shareholders are taxable for distributions from the company. The holding of shares by a foreign shareholder does not constitute a PE.

Participants in a general partnership have joint and several liability for the partnership's debts. For limited partnerships, one or more of the general partners have joint and several liability for the debts of the partnership, and one or more of the limited partners' liability is limited to an amount determined in the partnership agreement. Partnerships are tax-transparent entities: the partners are taxable for their share of the partnership's results, which they include in their own tax returns. Foreign partners are deemed to participate in the business activity of the partnership, and thus to perform business in Norway through a PE.

Local Funding Alternatives

Debt versus Equity

In Norway, financing with debt is normally advantageous because interest costs are deductible. Withholding tax is not levied on interest paid from a Norwegian debtor to a foreign creditor. On the other hand, there are withholding taxes on dividend payments. Where a foreign affiliate company lends money to a Norwegian subsidiary, an interest deduction will be allowed, provided the terms of the loan are the same as those that would have been agreed upon between unrelated parties. Loan guarantees from an affiliate are taken into consideration. As a general rule, a guaranteed debt will be treated as unrelated-party debt. If a Norwegian company is thinly capitalized, a part of the debt might be reclassified as equity. If the debt is not reclassified, an arm's-length guarantee commission, which is paid to the related guarantor, is deductible for a Norwegian company. Excess interest may be taxed as a deemed dividend, and would be subject to Norwegian dividend withholding tax.

A company that is thinly capitalized, with an excessive debt-to-equity ratio, risks having the Norwegian tax authorities recharacterize its debt as equity, which will affect the deductibility of interest. A debt-to-equity ratio of four-to-one should normally be acceptable, provided the debt is not guaranteed by the creditor and the debtor can service its debts without financial support from affiliates.

In principle, there is no difference between shareholder debt and third-party debt. Interest payable to a creditor, including arm's-length interest payable to a shareholder as creditor, is deductible. To the extent that shareholder debt is fully or partly reclassified as equity, exchange gains or losses are not taxable or deductible for a Norwegian company. Ordinary exchange gains or losses on debts are normally taxable or deductible.

Exchange Controls

Norwegian exchange control rules were liberalized in June 1990. If they are not made through an authorized Norwegian bank, cross-border investments and payments must be reported to the Central Bank. There are no regulations concerning foreign currency debts or foreign currency interest or dividend payments. Equity must be in Norwegian Krone, according to company legislation.

Business Acquisitions and Dispositions

Capital Contributions into an Existing Local Entity

Capital contributions from a resident or non-resident company are not taxable income. There are no limitations concerning what types of intangibles can be contributed, provided the intangibles represent material values to the company. The use of any tax attributes in a local entity will not be limited as a consequence of a capital contribution, irrespective of the capital interest achieved by the contributor.

A formal or informal capital contribution from a shareholder to a company is not taxable income for the company. Net operating losses are not limited for tax purposes. Repayment to a foreign shareholder of an informal capital contribution will be treated as a dividend, subject to dividend withholding tax. Repayment of a formal capital contribution made against issuance of shares is not taxable. A contribution of an intangible asset cannot be treated for tax purposes as the licensing of an intangible in exchange for shares in the local entity, and can be subject to local withholding tax.

A capital contribution will not have any tax consequences for existing shareholders.

Purchase or Sale of Shares in a Local Entity

A purchase of shares in an existing telecommunications company will raise few Norwegian tax issues. When shares are acquired, the Ministry of Industry and Energy must be notified within 30 days. A purchase of shares will not affect a company's tax positions and will not result in a step-up in the basis of a company's assets. Generally, carryforward losses will not be affected by such a purchase. However, if the main reason for the purchase is the buyer's intention to exploit losses carried forward, such losses will not be available to the purchaser. If the target company has existing telecommunications activities that are carried on after its acquisition, the losses will probably be available.

There is no capital gains tax for foreign shareholders selling shares in a Norwegian subsidiary. However, if the selling shareholder is Norwegian, any capital gain realized will be taxed. The capital gain is the difference between the buying price, adjusted for the change in the company's taxed equity during the ownership period (known in Norwegian as "RISK"—the adjusted value on taxed capital), and the selling price. The tax rate is 28%.

Purchase or Sale of Assets

A local entity selling assets will be taxed for any capital gain, which is defined as the difference between the asset's historical cost price, reduced by depreciations, and the selling price. If the seller of the assets is foreign, Norwegian tax will be imposed on any gains.

In order to postpone the taxation after selling depreciated assets, the local entity can choose to reduce the remaining balance on the depreciation group by the sales amount, or record the sale as income for the year during which the transaction occurred.

Acquiring the assets of an existing company will result in a stepped-up basis and larger depreciation deductions for the purchaser. Interest incurred on borrowings made to finance an asset purchase are generally deductible. In an asset purchase, carryforward losses are not transferred. As with the purchase of shares, an asset acquisition must be reported to the Ministry of Industry and Energy within 30 days of the agreement.

For both accounting and tax purposes, the total amount paid (cash plus liabilities assumed, plus other capitalized transaction costs) should be allocated to the various tangible and intangible assets included in the acquisition in proportion to the fair market value of these assets. Goodwill is depreciated at a rate of 30%, using the declining-balance method. Other intangible assets such as know-how and patents may be depreciated over the lifetime of the asset on a straight-line basis.

A purchase of assets is more favorable for a buyer if the purchase price is higher than the book value of the assets. Future depreciation deductions are based on this higher purchase price.

Goodwill is depreciated at the rate of 30%. However, if the purchase price is lower than the book value, the buyer should consider purchasing shares, because the basis of assets remains unchanged. In cases where the selling company has net operating losses, tax credits or some other taxation situation, the buyer should consider buying shares in the entity in order to benefit from existing tax statutes.

From a seller's point of view, it may also be more favorable to sell assets rather than shares, unless the seller has a cost basis in the shares that is higher than the equity of the company. In Norway, the taxation of gains from selling assets can be deferred by transferring the gains to a gain and loss account, which annually is taken into income by 20% of the remaining account at year-end. However, if the seller dissolves the company shortly after an asset sale, the tax position will be the same as for a sale of shares.

Unlike a joint-stock company, a partnership is not a separate taxable entity. The individual partners pay tax on the profits and losses. With respect to distributions from a partnership, there are no withholding taxes. Otherwise, there are no significant differences between a joint-stock company and a partnership. Most tax legislation applies to both types of companies. Deductions for depreciation are the same: profits are taxed at a 28% rate and losses are deductible (with certain restrictions for limited partners).

Start-up Business Issues

Pre-operating Losses and Start-up/Construction Costs

Amounts paid to create or to invest in a business before the business begins operations can be classified as start-up expenses, which are deductible in the year of start-up. There are no special restrictions on the length of period prior to start-up within which these expenses can be incurred.

Amounts paid for the construction of new buildings or for the permanent improvement or betterment of any property must be

capitalized. This also applies to machinery and equipment, furniture or any other property that has a useful life of more than three years and costs more than NOK 15,000. The only exception to this rule relates to deductible repairs (e.g., incidental repairs that keep the property in an ordinary, efficient operating condition and which do not add materially to the value of the property), which are made to property held for the production of income. Such repairs may be deducted currently, as can interest on funds used for construction.

Pre-operating costs incurred by a foreign affiliate which are closely connected to the business activity to be performed by and charged at arm's-length terms to the local entity are deductible or must be capitalized, depending on the type of costs. Such payments from the local entity are not subject to withholding tax.

The tax authorities may permit VAT registration before the taxable sales of a business exceed NOK 30,000. Such registration is normally permitted for businesses that make large investments in equipment, which relate to subsequent taxable sales, as long as it is considered highly probable that taxable sales will exceed NOK 30,000 within one to two years after the registration. When such registration is allowed, VAT payments made for the purchase of pre-operating goods or services can be recovered before the operating phase begins.

Customs Duties and VAT

Certain goods imported into Norway may be subject to customs duties. Products relating to telecommunications services that originate in the European Economic Area, the European Union or the European Free Trade Association (EFTA) are normally duty-free. As a signatory to the Information Technology Agreement (ITA) signed in March 1997, information technology equipment imported into Norway is subject to duty reductions. Rates are based upon annual determinations made by the Parliament. Goods produced in countries qualifying under the Norwegian Generalized System of Preferences (GSP) may also be imported free of duty. Rates on telecommunications products vary, as shown in the following table:

Product	Duty
Telephones	Duty-free
Fax machines	Duty-free
Mobile telephones	2.7% of the customs value
Radio transmitters	2.4%–3.6% of the customs value
Radio receivers	15.4% of the customs value
Television sets	17.2% of the customs value
Antennas	Duty-free

VAT must be paid on all imports of goods. Import VAT can only be deducted by businesses registered for VAT. (See "Value-Added Tax, Sales Tax and/or Other Pertinent Taxes.")

Loss Carryovers

Losses can be carried forward for 10 years. In cases where business activity ceases or the enterprise liquidates, losses may be carried back for two years. The ability to carry losses forward will generally not be affected when a company changes ownership.

Operating Considerations

Corporate Income Taxes

Businesses in Norway are subject to tax on their ordinary income, which includes capital gains and losses, at a rate of 28%. This rate includes taxes to the municipality and county. Non-resident shareholders are subject to a dividend withholding tax at a rate of 25%, which may be reduced by a tax treaty.

Capital Gains Taxes

In Norway, capital gains and losses are subject to a 28% tax rate as part of a business's ordinary income. Gains and/or losses are computed as the sales price less historical cost and depreciations. The tax cost base of shares in Norwegian companies is adjusted in accordance with changes in the taxed equity of the company.

Tax Holidays and Exemptions

There are no special tax holidays, exemptions or incentives for telecommunications businesses in Norway. Ordinary tax rates and deductions apply to this sector and there are no anticipated changes in law or policy.

Depreciation/Cost-Recovery Conventions/Accelerated Deductions

The declining-balance system of depreciation is used for physical assets and goodwill. According to the declining-balance system, the assets should be divided into groups, each with its maximum depreciation rate, as shown in the following table. (The higher rates in parentheses may be used in certain geographical areas.)

Depreciation Group	Rate (%)
Office machines	30
Acquired goodwill	30
Trailers, trucks, buses and vehicles for transportation of disabled persons	25
Cars, tractors, other movable machines, other machines, equipment, instruments, fixtures and fittings	20
Buildings, plants, hotels, rooming houses and restaurants	5 (10)
Office buildings	2 (4)

Telecommunications equipment such as switches, routers, cells and lines, will be classified as equipment and depreciated by 20% annually.

Purchased standard software is treated as any other tangible equipment and amortized by 20% or 30% annually, depending on the purpose of the software. Purchased tailor-made software is treated as an intangible asset and the purchase price is subject to amortization when, and to the extent that, the software has been subject to an obvious fall in value. Royalty payments for software are normally deductible when incurred.

Research and development costs, including software development, are deductible. Generally, advertising, marketing and promotional expenses made to attract customers are deductible. However, representation expenses, such as gifts, meals, wine and tobacco, are not deductible.

Transfer Pricing Rules

While Norway has no specific transfer pricing regulations, the General Tax Act contains a general arm's-length provision, which implies that inter-company transactions should be carried out under the same terms and conditions as would have been agreed upon between unrelated parties.

Transfers of Patents, Trademarks and Software

Norwegian law does not differentiate between a sale or a licensing of intangibles such as technology. Generally speaking, a sale occurs when all rights to the intangible are transferred, while licensing takes place when only limited rights are transferred. The tax consequences of a sale or a licensing of intangibles must be determined on a case-by-case basis, in light of relevant legislation.

Local law does not, in general, impose any restrictions on the sale or licensing of technology to a local company for a royalty fee or other kind of payments. Technology, patent, trademark, software and other licensing fees are deductible if they are provided on arm's-length terms. Such payments are not subject to withholding tax. The costs of purchased intangibles are subject to deduction as described above.

Under certain special circumstances, a licensor may be regarded as participating in the business of the licensee, and thus subject to ordinary tax in Norway. Transfers of licenses, expertise and/or technology out of Norway should be carried out on arm's-length terms (i.e., the transferor shall charge the recipient the market price).

For VAT purposes, the legislation does not distinguish sales from licenses. However, from a VAT perspective and according to administrative practice from the authorities, sales of standard software (e.g., off-the-shelf software) is subject to VAT regardless of whether it is sold or licensed. Tailor-made software is not subject to VAT, regardless of whether it is sold or licensed. The transfer and other exploitation of patents, brand marks, production methods and the like are generally subject to VAT.

Service Fees

Service fees are not subject to withholding tax. A provider of services performed outside of Norway is not taxable in Norway. However, if the services are performed through a PE in Norway, the provider will be taxable in Norway.

Value-Added Tax, Sales Tax and/or Other Pertinent Taxes

Since 1970, Norway has had an all-stage, non-cumulative, consumption-type VAT. VAT is imposed at a rate of 23% on imports and domestic sales of goods and on certain services. Telecommunications services, with the exception of broadcasting companies, are subject to VAT. Legislation may be introduced in the near future that would broaden the services that are subject to VAT.

Suppliers of goods and taxable services are obliged to register for VAT when taxable sales exceed NOK 30,000 over a period of 12 months. Only companies registered for VAT can claim credit for input VAT paid on goods and services for use in their business in connection with taxable supplies or imports. Effective July 1, 1996, foreign businesses that do not have sales liable to VAT in Norway are entitled, under certain conditions, to a refund of VAT on goods and services purchased in Norway as well as on the goods they import into Norway. To qualify for a refund, the VAT has to relate to business activities conducted abroad that, had those activities been conducted within Norway, would have been liable to register for VAT, which would have been deductible. This refund system is basically similar to the one that was introduced in the member states of the EU.

Most telecommunications services, including telephone, telegraph, telex, wireline and wireless services are subject to VAT. The transmission of signals through cable networks is also subject to VAT because it is considered to be a taxable telecommunications service. In principle, the legislation does not distinguish between regular telephony or Internet telephony, and VAT authorities have issued no comment or instructions regarding the legislation's position on the topic.

In February 1997, the VAT authorities published an opinion stating that the provision of Internet access services should be considered a taxable supply of telecommunications services and that the provision of advertisements on Internet websites should be considered a taxable advertising service. It is not clear whether other types of services linked to the Internet (for example, providing access to content available on a proprietary subscriber network) should be regarded as telecommunications services or as non-taxable information services.

Information services fall outside the scope of VAT. However, certain non-taxable services may be liable to VAT if they are supplied or mediated by Telenor or similar enterprises through the use of telecommunications and consideration is charged by the provider of the telecommunications service. This rule applies, for example, to certain entertainment services supplied by the use of telecommunications. Supplies of telecommunications services to foreign countries are, under certain conditions, exempt from Norwegian VAT, with full credit for input VAT paid on acquisitions attributable to the exempted supplies.

In January 1998, new legislation took effect regarding the liability to register for and pay VAT on the provision of international telecommunications services. As articulated in a bill passed by the Parliament in December 1997, an entity supplying a telecommunications service to a customer established or resident in Norway must register and pay VAT. If the supplier does not have a fixed place of business in Norway, registrations must be made through a representative entity.

Investment Tax. An investment tax of 7% is levied on any kind of acquisition for use in a business, with exceptions granted for goods for resale, raw materials, semi-finished products and non-permanent plants. The investment tax is payable by VAT-registered persons only, and is chargeable to the extent that input VAT on the acquisition is deductible. A large number of exceptions from the investment tax exist, and it is anticipated that the tax could be abolished when a new VAT system is introduced.

Local and Provincial Taxes

There are no state or local income taxes in Norway. Municipalities can levy a property tax on real estate, up to a maximum rate of 0.7%. This tax is assessed on the basis of a special valuation of the property.

For Additional Information, Contact:

Hans Olav Hemnes
Tax Partner
and
Esben Fiane
Consulting Partner
and
Morten Chr. Stegard
Tax Associate
Havnelageret
N-0150 Oslo
Norway
Telephone: 47 (22) 40 00 00
Fax: 47 (22) 41 17 39
E-mail: esben_fiane@no.coopers.com
          morten_stegard@no.coopers.com

Poland

Telecommunications Tax Profile
by John Ross
Tax Partner, Warsaw

Overview of the Telecommunications Market

Historical Background

In 1991, Poland's Posts and Telecommunications Act went into effect, ending the government's traditional monopoly on telecommunications and separating postal operations from telecommunications. Telekomunikacja Polska S.A. (TP S.A.) was created as a joint stock company with all shares held by the government.

The Polish government has made a concerted effort to encourage foreign participation and investment in this sector. The Act permitted foreign investment in long-distance and local service, but barred foreign operators from the international service market.

Current Status

Poland's telecommunications market has been described as the leader in the region both in terms of the size of its market and the level of services provided. The Polish market for communications services has a significant growth potential as several million people are still waiting to have telephones installed. The new government believes that privatizing TP S.A. will enhance the development of the market and the quality of telecommunications service, as well as secure investment resources for TP S.A. and yield funds for the government's social insurance reforms.

TP S.A. currently holds the monopoly in the long-distance telecommunications sector. All analog and digital mobile network operators are obligated to use the TP S.A. network for long-distance calls. In the local service sector, competition is limited. There are 12 local service providers; however TP S.A. maintains a strong position, serving over 7.4 million customers. The other 11 services providers together serve just over 50,000 customers. The private sector in telecommunications is growing rapidly, with the number of private-sector customers expected to reach 10 million by the year 2000.

Digital data networks are being built by joint ventures of TP S.A. and other investors. These networks include X.25 Telbank (the non-public network for the banking sector), X.25 Polpak (the public packet-switched network) and X.25 Kolpak (the non-public network of Polish railways). The Polpak network will be offered to private customers for Internet access.

In the analog mobile sector, the only operator is Polska Telefonia Komórkowa CENTERTEL Sp. z o.o. (CENTERTEL), jointly owned by TP S.A. (66%) and France Telecom (34%). The current number of subscribers is approximately 151,000 and is projected to reach 300,000 by the year 2000. No other licenses will be awarded.

In the digital mobile sector, two global system for mobile communications (GSM) licenses were granted in 1996 to POLKOMTEL S.A. (Plus GSM) and Polska Telefonia Cyfrowa Sp. z o.o. (ERA GSM). Both companies are jointly owned by Polish and foreign companies, and investments will likely exceed US$1 billion. Operations began in the second half of 1996, and no further licenses will be granted. The anticipated capacity of this sector is 1 million to 1.5 million subscribers by the end of 2000.

On August 1, 1997, analog cellular service provider CENTERTEL, as sole bidder, was awarded the tender for the construction and operation of a digital cellular system (DCS), organized by the Ministry of Telecommunications. CENTERTEL was granted a 15-year license, with the possibility of an extension, to operate on the 1800-MHz frequency in the 10 largest Polish cities.

The local, cable and mobile telecommunications sectors are being opened to private operators, and the terminal equipment market is fully open to private operators.

Current Liberalization Status

Since the Telecom Act in 1990, the generally accepted target structure of the Polish telecommunications market is several service operations competing with each other.

In the World Trade Organization (WTO) negotiations of February 1997, Poland committed to a number of changes in its telecommunications sector. Poland proposed the liberalization of its domestic long distance and international connections. It also affirmed that entities rendering operator services in the Polish telecommunications market must consist of 51% Polish capital.

Type of Service	Degree of Liberalization	Key Legislation	Date of Actual or Expected Liberalization	Comments
Local	Liberalized	Telecom Act of November 1990	November 1990	TP S.A.'s monopoly on inter-city connections is to be eliminated by January 1, 1999. Further invitations to tender for the construction of local telecoms networks are expected. Private operators may bid for licenses to render services in a restricted number of cities (Bydgoszcz, Gdańsk, Gdynia, Sopot, Bialystok, Chelm, Bytom, Sosnowiec, Kraków, Poznañ and Szczecin).
Long Distance	Restricted	Telecom Act of November 1990	1999	Dominant position held by TP S.A., and to be preserved until 1999.
International	Monopoly of TP S.A.	Telecom Act of November 1990	Privatization of TP S.A. planned for 1998	International service is reserved exclusively for TP S.A. Under terms of the WTO Agreement, Poland will liberalize its domestic long distance and international connections after December 31, 2001.
Cellular	Analog: Monopoly Digital: Duopoly	Telecom Act of November 1990	1996	Cellular operators are required to use the network of TP S.A.
Paging	Liberalized	Telecom Act of November 1990	November 1990	POLPAGER held the only license to provide nationwide services.
Value-added	Deregulated	Telecom Act of November 1990	November 1990	Value-added services can be offered by any legal entity or person registered in Poland.

Competitive Environment

The liberalization of telecommunications services in Poland has opened the market to private operators. Their number is growing but their percentage of market share is small. Even if the competition between TP S.A. and the few independent local telephone companies intensifies, TP S.A. should be able to maintain its dominant position in the market.

The mobile phone networks compete on services rather than price, with analog service provider CENTERTEL having greater country-wide coverage but not the roaming features of the GSM networks of Plus GSM and ERA GSM.

	Entire Market	Top Two Players		
Type of Service	Number of Players	Names	Annual Revenue (1997)	Ownership
Local	12	TP S.A.	8,488 million zl (zlotys) *	Government
		Netia Telekom S.A.	Not available	R.P. Telekom (65%), Telia (25%), and EBRD (10%)
Long Distance	Effectively 1	TP S.A.	8,488 million zl *	Government (TP S.A. market dominance protected against competition by Ministry of Telecommunications)
International	1	TP S.A.	8,488 million zl *	Government
Cellular: Analog	1	CENTERTEL	604.6 million zl	TP S.A. (66%), France Telecom (34%)
Cellular: Digital	2	POLKOMTEL S.A. (Plus GSM)	Not available	61.5% Polish, 38.5% foreign
		Polska Telefonia Cyfrowa Sp. z o.o. (ERA GSM)	Not available	61% Polish, 39% foreign
Paging	5	POLPAGER	Not available	Jacek Szymański (100%)
		Easy Call Poland S.A.	20 million zl (1996 figures)	Matrix Europe Ltd. (Matrix Telecommunications of Australia)

Source: *Warsaw Business Journal,* "Telecoms in Focus," February 9–15, 1998.

* Note: TP S.A. does not break out revenue figures for local, long-distance and international services. Figures shown above for those services are total combined revenues.

Licensing Requirements

Concessions are granted by the Ministry of Telecommunications, which also handles technical certification for equipment. Licenses for telecommunications operators are granted through a bidding process. Typically, the license for service to a particular region is granted both to TP S.A. and to another selected private company.

Licenses to build networks are granted by the Ministry of Telecommunications under a simplified procedure. To date, licenses have been granted for local service, wireless telephony, data transmission, other value-added services and paging.

Potential for Foreign Ownerships/Relationships

According to Polish law, Polish shareholders must have a majority stake (i.e., a minimum of 51%) in telecommunications companies.

Potential for Upcoming Liberalization/Investment Opportunities

Work on a new telecommunications law is currently in progress, with plans to end the TP S.A. monopoly in long-distance and international service by the end of the century. In a two-step process, 49% of the company's shares are to be put on sale in a public offering during the second half of 1998. The second step, which is expected to last five years, will involve the privatization of "a stable investor" from the telecommunications business which will contribute "managerial skills and new technology" to the company.

Forms of Doing Business

Permanent Establishment

In practical terms, permanent establishment (PE) issues remain a relatively uncharted area of Polish tax law. This situation arises both from the lack of express domestic legislation and interpretative regulations on the issue of PEs, as well as from the fact that the Polish tax authorities do not currently pursue PE issues. It is expected that in the near future, Polish tax authorities may adopt a more aggressive position on PE matters.

Foreign telecommunications companies may rely on the provisions found in the PE clauses of relevant double-taxation treaties. However, it is clear that the application of the treaty provisions to specific telecommunications situations involves a problematic attempt at interpretation. For example, it is unclear whether the term "installation," as it appears in the treaties, includes certain telecommunications installation services.

To some extent, PE issues also remain unexplored in Poland due to the fact that Polish law requires foreign investors in Poland to operate through a Polish corporation.

Business Entities

Local Branch and Locally Incorporated Subsidiary of a Foreign Company. As mentioned, Polish law generally requires foreign investors to operate in Poland through Polish companies (i.e., either through agreements with Polish companies, or through wholly or partly owned subsidiaries). The establishment of a foreign-owned branch requires a branch permit. Currently, branch permits are not granted for foreign-owned branches seeking to engage in for-profit activities. As a result, foreign-owned branches are limited to representative office functions, such as information gathering, market research, and similar activities. Foreign investors may, however, buy shares in existing Polish companies, or, alternatively, establish new Polish subsidiaries.

Two types of corporate vehicles are available under Polish law: the limited liability company (Sp. z o.o.) and the joint stock company (S.A.). The latter carries more prestige in Poland, and is generally reserved for larger investments and/or if a public subscription is planned.

Repatriation of Profits. Dividends paid by a Polish company are subject to a 20% withholding tax, unless otherwise modified by the terms of an applicable double-taxation treaty. Poland has an extensive network of tax treaties, and the dividend withholding tax rate is generally lowered to 5% in the case of corporate shareholders with 10% to 25% of the shares of the issuing company, and to 15% in other cases. Under certain tax treaties, dividends may be exempted entirely from withholding tax, provided the necessary conditions are met.

Grouping. At the present time, a limited form of tax consolidation is possible for Polish group companies. However, the stringent restrictions required for consolidation have virtually eliminated the application of the consolidation provisions. The new government has expressed a willingness to make amendments

to the law in those instances where the business community believes change is necessary. This issue has been put forward for reform.

Joint Venture. Currently, joint ventures are treated no differently than any other business investment. Previously, foreign investors in Poland had the opportunity to apply for corporate income tax holidays under special legislation relating to companies established with foreign ownership. However, these types of tax holidays are no longer granted, and Polish companies established with partial or total foreign capital are, from a tax perspective, generally treated in the same manner as other domestic companies.

At the present time, foreign investors are not permitted to invest in Polish partnerships.

Local Funding Alternatives

Debt versus Equity

There are no thin capitalization rules in Poland. As a result, debt financing often plays an important role in new investments. Under Polish tax law, interest payments generally form tax-deductible expenses at the time when they are actually paid, and not when they are accrued. No deduction is allowed for dividends. Interest is exempt from withholding tax under many double-taxation treaties to which Poland is a party, while only a few such treaties exempt dividends. The use of hybrid instruments may be possible in certain circumstances.

A 2% stamp duty applies to certain types of loan agreements. Bank loans and loans extended by finance companies are exempt from stamp duty, and shareholder loans may qualify for a 0.1% stamp duty rate. Contributions to capital are subject to a sliding-scale stamp duty rate, which generally amounts to approximately 0.1%. No stamp duty applies to the payment of dividends.

Debt. Accrued foreign currency gains and losses do not constitute a taxable gain or tax-deductible loss until the time they are actually realized. As with other loan instruments, interest on shareholder-guaranteed loans is deductible at the time when actually paid. No special rules apply to loans backed by shareholder guarantees. Domestic loans between corporate entities are not subject to withholding tax.

Exchange Controls

Many transactions in foreign currency are regulated under the Foreign Exchange Law. However, recent changes have eased many restrictions. Loans from foreign shareholders no longer require a National Bank of Poland (NBP) permit, although the NBP must be informed about a foreign-shareholder-issued loan within 20 days after the loan agreement is executed. Non-shareholder loans require NBP approval before the funds enter into Poland if the loans are granted for a period shorter than one year. Approval may depend on the form of the loan agreement and the interest rate charged.

Business Acquisitions and Dispositions

Capital Contributions into an Existing Local Entity

A capital contribution may be made into an existing Polish company by a foreign or a domestic investor. Stamp duty of generally 0.1% will apply on the capital contribution. A domestic or foreign investor may make in-kind contributions of either tangible or intangible assets. No specific limits exist on the types of intangible assets that may be contributed in-kind. However, tax depreciation is not allowed on know-how that is contributed in-kind.

The contribution of intangibles in return for shares in the receiving company will not result in royalty withholding tax for the contributing shareholder under Polish law. Contribution of assets in kind may be made by a shareholder. A Polish company may depreciate tangible assets received, but amortization of contributed intangible assets is, in some cases, not allowed for tax purposes. Shares issued for an in-kind contribution to a joint stock company may not be sold for two years.

Purchase or Sale of Shares in a Local Entity

The sale of shares in a Polish company is subject to 2% stamp duty, based on the market value of the shares. A 2% stamp duty applies regardless of the residency of the buyer or the seller. Shares listed on the Warsaw Stock Exchange are exempt.

Generally, the sale of shares in a Polish company by a Polish-resident person or entity will result in tax liability on any capital gain. A non-resident person or entity will be subject to Polish tax gains from the sale of shares in a Polish company unless such gains are exempt from Polish tax under the terms of an applicable double-taxation treaty.

Individuals (resident or non-resident) are not currently subject to tax liability for gains earned on the sale of shares in companies listed on the Warsaw Stock Exchange. An acquiring shareholder in a limited liability company becomes liable for the unpaid tax obligations of the company.

There is no mechanism in Polish tax law that would allow a foreign company to consider the purchase of shares as a purchase of assets for Polish tax purposes.

Purchase or Sale of Assets

The entity acquiring assets should allocate the purchase price to individual assets using market values, in order to establish the depreciable basis of the assets. The purchase price of an intangible asset is depreciable over the life of the asset, although generally the depreciation schedule for intangibles is at least five years. Accordingly, the purchase of assets will result in a more attractive cost basis than the purchase of the stock of a company. In certain business acquisitions, the buyer of assets will become jointly and severally liable with the seller for liabilities associated with the assets. Asset sales are generally preferred over stock sales by both purchaser and seller.

VAT applies to asset purchases. The standard rate for VAT is 22%. VAT does not apply to asset acquisitions when the business enterprise is acquired. Instead, a stamp duty applies, generally at the rate of 2% of the gross value of assets sold (5% in the case of land). Accordingly, the stamp duty cost for an asset purchase is no different than that for a share purchase.

Restructuring Alternatives

There are no specific rules in relation to mergers and restructuring and each such restructuring should be carefully reviewed to determine the tax consequences. The successor acquires all the tax liabilities of the former owner under the new Tax Code. Losses can be carried forward by the ownership successor following a change in ownership and there are no same-business restrictions either. However, it should be noted that the loss carryforward rules are limited in that, if they are not able to be utilized, one third of a loss carried forward is extinguished in each of the three years following the loss year.

Start-up Business Issues

Pre-operating Losses and Start-up/Construction Costs

Fees incurred in the establishment of a joint stock company may be depreciated for tax purposes over a period of at least five years. This does not apply to a limited liability company, and such costs are neither deductible nor depreciable.

All costs directly related to a construction-type project are capitalized up until the time when the fixed asset is put into use. Interest paid on the construction project during the construction period is also capitalized.

Generally, costs must be incurred by a Polish company (i.e., not by its shareholders or another party) in order for the company to either deduct or amortize such costs.

VAT incurred before company registration is not recoverable. Foreign companies cannot recover Polish VAT incurred. In some cases, VAT refunds (as opposed to credit against output VAT liability) may be available for VAT incurred on investment expenses by an existing company before it begins to issue sales invoices that are subject to VAT.

Customs Duties and VAT

Customs duty rates vary widely according to the specific customs commodity classification of the imported assets and country of origin. Preferential rates apply to items imported from the EU, the European Free Trade Association (EFTA) and the Central European Free Trade Association (CEFTA) countries, with duty exemptions frequently possible for such items. For most industrial goods originating from the EU, the preferential duty rate will be reduced to 0% by January 1, 1999.

In some instances, telecommunications equipment may qualify for customs-exempt status if it is imported as part of the official annual contingent of customs-exempt equipment. An application must be filed by the Polish company seeking to import the equipment under the preferential contingent rules.

Poland is committed under the WTO's Singapore Agreement (Information Technology Agreement, or ITA) to gradually abolish customs duties on most telecommunications equipment and professional information technology components. Poland implemented the first duty reductions on January 1, 1998. The total abolition of customs duties for this sector is presently planned for January 1, 2001, although for certain products the 0% level will be reached sooner.

The import of telecommunications equipment is subject to import VAT. However, this VAT can generally be recovered.

Polish tax regulations do not provide any distinction between regular telephony and Internet telephony.

Loss Carryovers

A tax loss may be carried forward into the three consecutive years immediately following the year in which it was incurred; however, only one-third of the loss may be used in each of those three years. No loss carrybacks are allowed. Tax losses generally will not be affected by changes in ownership. Changes in legal status (e.g., changes in corporate entity form via a transformation or merger), however, may result in the elimination of existing tax losses. Under current interpretation of the law, companies enjoying tax holidays are not allowed to bring forward any tax losses earned during the tax holiday period.

Operating Considerations

Corporate Income Taxes

Corporate taxpayers, including telecommunications companies, are subject in 1998 to a 36% corporate income tax on net profit. Legislation currently provides for the rate to fall each year by 2% until it reaches 32%.

Capital Gains Taxes

Polish tax law does not contain a special capital gains tax regime. Instead, taxable gains earned by a company are added with other forms of revenue in calculating corporate income tax liability, subject to the standard rate of 36% for 1998.

Domestic dividends received are subject to a 20% withholding tax at the source and are not aggregated with other income for corporate income tax purposes. The amount of tax withheld is allowed as a tax credit against the recipient's corporate income tax payable. Unused credits may be carried forward indefinitely.

Tax Holidays and Exemptions

Generally, tax holidays are no longer granted for foreign investors. However, a special corporate tax exemption is available for companies established in the special economic zones located in Mielec and the voivodships (administrative regions) of Katowice, Suwalki, Legnica, Walbrzych, Czestochowa, Kamienna Gora, Mielec, Starachowice, Tarnobrzeg, Tczew, Zarnowiec and Lodz, which are areas with high unemployment. Other economic zones may be established in the future.

New corporate investors, including telecommunications companies, may be eligible for investment relief in the form of accelerated depreciation for investment expenses. Certain conditions apply.

Depreciation/Cost-Recovery Conventions/Accelerated Deductions

Depreciation allowances from fixed assets are treated as tax-deductible costs only to the extent permitted by the January 17, 1997 Ordinance of the Ministry of Finance on Depreciation as amended. Thus, depreciation rates may differ for accounting and tax purposes.

Polish tax law generally requires the use of the straight-line method. The applicable rates vary widely depending on the fixed asset type. In limited instances, the double-declining-balance method may be applied. Accelerated depreciation is available in certain circumstances (e.g., when specific types of fixed assets are to be used in worse-than-average conditions or in cases where the fixed asset relies on state-of-the-art computer components).

Depreciation allowances are taken monthly over the depreciation period, which begins in the month after the month in which the asset was put into use.

As a general guide, telecommunications equipment frequently will be classified in the general-fixed-asset category of telephone equipment, subject to the straight-line depreciation rate. This rate is 8% to 10% per year generally (i.e., a 10- to 12.5-year depreciation schedule) and 4% to 5% in some cases.

However, the depreciation rate can be tripled in areas of high unemployment (i.e., special economic zones). Telecommunications equipment subject to accelerated usage may qualify for a depreciation rate equal to twice the normal rate. This means that, for example, a fixed asset with a standard rate of 10% would instead be entitled to use a 20% rate, and would be depreciable over five years instead of the standard period of 10 years. Note that mobile phones are subject to a depreciation rate of 15% to 20%.

Individual rates may be established for used or modernized fixed assets. These rates will be higher and depreciation schedules accordingly shorter than for new fixed assets, providing that the assets are being booked for the first time.

Marketing and Advertising Costs. Marketing and public advertising costs are tax-deductible. However, expenses on non-public advertising are deductible only up to an amount not exceeding 0.25% of turnover. The tax treatment does not change when payments are made indirectly through sales agents to attract customers.

Transfer Pricing Rules

Polish law includes specific provisions designed to curb transfer pricing abuses. In the event that a taxpayer is related to a foreign person and, as a result of this relationship, shows less income than would otherwise be anticipated, the tax authorities are empowered to estimate the taxpayer's income without regard to any obligations arising from the relationship. Moreover, the tax authorities are further authorized to disregard the price shown in a given contract between related or unrelated parties, if, without justification, the price differs substantially from market prices.

These transfer pricing provisions have been used recently with increasing frequency by the revenue office, and the arm's-length standard should be used for all inter-company payments. An ordinance providing guidelines on estimation rules became effective on November 7, 1997. The ruling provides that the comparable uncontrolled price (CUP) method shall be applied first unless another method more precisely establishes the market value.

Transfers of Patents, Trademarks and Software

Polish law does not contain any specific restrictions on the licensing of technology to Polish companies in return for royalty fees. In the case of a transfer of technology, it is unclear whether existing Polish tax law would allow for a license agree-

ment to be reclassified as a sales agreement (or vice versa). Such reclassification can occur in the area of lease agreements, and, in theory, the tax classification criteria applying to finance and operating leases could apply in the license/sale context as well. This is not the current practice, however. Instead, an agreement that qualifies, for example, as a license agreement for purposes of civil law generally will be respected as a license agreement for tax purposes.

Patents, trademarks and software licensing fees are deductible only if the agreement under which they are paid grants the taxpayer the right to use the intangible assets for a period of one year or less. In other cases, the amount to be paid under the patent, trademark, or software license agreement must be capitalized and depreciated as an intangible asset. The tax depreciation period for most intangibles is at least five years, although a two-year period applies to certain computer-based intangible assets, and a three-year period applies for technological research costs.

Royalties paid to non-residents will be subject to 20% withholding tax, unless otherwise modified under the terms of an applicable double-taxation treaty. Under most double-taxation treaties, royalty withholding tax is reduced to 10%. Under a few treaties, royalties are exempt from withholding tax.

The transfer of licenses, expertise and technology out of Poland could be considered a sale giving rise to capital gain, which would be taxed as ordinary income.

Service Fees

Payments made under service agreements will constitute tax-deductible expenses for the payor, provided the fees represent the arm's-length price for services actually rendered. Service fees are generally not subject to withholding tax.

Services provided to a Polish company by a foreign provider in Poland may result in irrecoverable, self-assessed VAT for the Polish company (see "Value-Added Tax, Sales Tax and/or Other Pertinent Taxes").

Value-Added Tax, Sales Tax and/or Other Pertinent Taxes

Polish VAT arises on the value of most goods and services sold in Poland. The standard rate of VAT is 22%; other rates are 7%, 0% and a few items are exempt from VAT entirely. Telecommunications services, as of February 1, 1998, are generally subject to a 22% VAT rate; previously, a preferential rate of 7% applied.

A particular area of concern for high-tech industries, such as telecommunications, arises in the area of imported services. If a Polish company purchases services from a foreign service supplier and the services are physically performed in Poland, then there is deemed to be an "import of services." In such a case, the Polish service purchaser will be required to self-assess 22% VAT on the value of the imported services. This VAT will not be recoverable, unless the foreign service supplier registers for Polish VAT. Changes are expected in the VAT law in 1998, which may result in VAT incurred on imported services being treated as a recoverable VAT input credit. However, if telecommunications services are imported into Poland, the import of these services is exempt from Polish VAT.

Local and Provincial Taxes

A property tax on real estate applies in certain local governmental regions. Local taxes also apply to vehicle registration.

For Additional Information, Contact:

John Ross
Tax Partner
and
Antoni Turczynowicz
Senior Tax Manager
and
Grzegorz Skrzeszewski
Telecommunications Director
ul. Mokotowska 49
00-950 Warszawa
Poland
Telephone: 48 (22) 821 77 77
Fax: 48 (22) 6211 144 or 48 (22) 6600 573
E-mail: john_ross@pl.coopers.com
          antoni_turczynowicz@pl.coopers.com
          grzegorz_skrzeszewski@pl.coopers.com

Portugal

Telecommunications Tax Profile
by Luis Oliveira
Tax Partner, Lisbon
Teresa S. Gomes and Sofia Claro
Tax Associates, Lisbon

Overview of the Telecommunications Market

Historical Background

Although Portugal's terminal equipment market was opened in 1981, the partial liberalization of the telecommunications sector has occurred only recently. The first laws pertaining to the structuring of liberalization were passed in 1990. In 1991 and 1992, further liberalization laws were passed, Portugal's first private cellular telephony license was granted, and two private paging licenses were granted to companies that compete against the wireless operations of state-controlled Portugal Telecom, S.A. (PT).

PT, the principal company engaged in telecommunications activities, was formed with the merger in May 1994 of Telefones de Lisboa e Porto, S.A. (TLP), Teledifusão de Portugal, S.A. (TDP), and Telecom Portugal, S.A. In 1995 Portugal's monopoly international service provider, Companhia Portuguesa Radio Marconi, S.A. (Marconi), was merged into PT, and 30% of the company was sold to private investors.

Current Status

Compared to other European countries, Portugal is considered to have relatively low telephone penetration, low rates of usage, high international tariffs and medium-quality service. The PT group operates Portugal's basic service, cellular and paging networks, value-added services and international services. PT owns a data transmission business through its associated company, Telepac-Serviços de Telecomunicações, S.A., and a mobile network through its associate Telecomunicações Móveis Nacionais, S.A. (TMN).

In the cellular telephone sector, PT competes with Telecel-Comunicações Pessoais, S.A., a private company whose owners include AirTouch Europe BV. The cellular network covers the entire country and has more than 887,000 subscribers. This represents a market penetration of 8%, which was expected to rise to 10% by the end of 1997. The revenue of the cellular operators is estimated to have reached PTE 100.4 billion in 1996, and the number of subscribers is expected to exceed one million by the year 2000. The companies have experienced revenue growth of 80% and are expected to continue growing.

A public tender for a new cellular license was underway, and the chosen operator is expected to start service by October 1998. TMN and Telecel are currently operating with global system for mobile communications (GSM)-900, but as soon as the third licensee begins operations, all providers are expected to operate on both frequency bands GSM-900 and digital cellular system (DCS)-1800.

In the paging sector, licenses are held by Telemensagem-Chamada de Pessoas, Lda. (TLM), and Contactel-Chamada de Pessoas, Lda. (Contactel), which are both owned by PT; and by Telechamada-Chamada de Pessoas, S.A. (Telechamada), which is owned by Telecel. In early 1997 paging subscribers exceeded 183,000. Total subscription is expected to reach approximately 366,000 subscribers by the year 2000, a market penetration of 3.4%. Of the four paging licenses already granted, one has been withdrawn from the provider (Finacom-Serviços de Mensagens, S.A.), and another will probably be inactive once PT merges Contactel and TLM. The resulting company is expected to dominate the market.

Sixteen companies are authorized to operate as Internet service providers (ISPs), the biggest of which is the state-controlled Telepac. Telepac provides public services, such as videotex, as well as competitive services, such as data transmission with or without switching, electronic mail services and electronic data interchange services. The private companies IP Global-Informática e Telecomunicações, S.A., and Esotérica-Novas Tecnologias de Informação, Lda., are Telepac's leading competitors. The ISP market is said to be growing at a rate of 10% per month and is estimated to be worth approximately PTE 1 million.

Value-added services were regulated in 1990 and experienced remarkable growth in the following years. Thirty-four operators have been licensed, but only 14 are active. Value-added services must abide by a code of conduct and select one or more of the predefined categories of services, such as entertainment or information. Legislation was passed recently requiring wireline customers to request access to these lines from PT. Otherwise the prefix numbers to access these services were blocked. The larger value-added services operators are extending their services to include telemarketing, making use of modern call centers.

Two companies, Radiomóvel-Telecomunicações, S.A, (75% owned by PT) and Repart-Sistemas de Comunicações de Re-

cursos Partilhados, S.A., operate in the trunking sector, which experienced peak growth during 1996, when 8,140 radio terminals were installed. Market size is about 20,000 terminals, and these companies are expected to continue to increase their activities and revenues.

In 1996, Marconi's international network was supported by six digital central office switches. The company has a share in 34 submarine cables, most of which are fiber optic, connecting Portugal to France, Morocco, South Africa, Brazil and the United States. By the end of 1999, Portugal is expected to be connected by fiber optic cables to most countries in Western Europe, the Middle East and Southwest Asia.

Current Liberalization Status

The telecommunications market will be fully liberalized in the beginning of 2000. As a member of the European Union (EU), Portugal must fulfill the schedule set by the EU Commission, as shown in the table below. Portugal has been granted an extension of the term to liberalize wireline telephone services.

As a signatory to the World Trade Organization (WTO) agreements of February 1997, Portugal committed to fully open its telecommunications markets, including satellite services and

facilities, by 2000, as well as to guarantee pro-competitive regulatory principles. The liberalization of the telecoms networks that provide the international connection between wireline and wireless services is scheduled to occur January 1, 1999.

A new framework for liberalization, Law n° 91/97, was enacted in 1997. The law also lifted restrictions on foreign investment. Legislation containing further specifications for services and network operators was expected to be passed soon.

Type of Service	Degree of Liberalization	Key Legislation	Date of Actual or Expected Liberalization	Comments
Local, Long Distance and International	Monopoly	Law 91/97, August 1, 1997 Decree Law n° 240/97, September 18, 1997	January 1, 2000	New legislation expected
Cellular	Fully liberalized (licenses conceded by public tender)	Decree Law n° 346/90, November 3, 1990 Decree Law n° 147/91, April 12, 1991 Decree n° 240/91, March 23, 1991 Decree n° 443-A/97, July 4, 1997 Decree n° 447-A/97, July 7, 1997 Law 91/97, August 1, 1997	March 1991	New legislation expected
Paging	Fully liberalized (licenses conceded by public tender)	Decree Law n° 346/90, November 3, 1990 Decree n° 746/91, August 2, 1991 Decree n° 748/91, August 2, 1991 Law 91/97, August 1, 1997	August 1991	New legislation expected
Value-added	Fully liberalized (free entry with government authorization)	Decree Law n° 329/90, October 23, 1990 Decree n° 160/94, March 22, 1994 Law 91/97, August 1, 1997	October 1990	New legislation expected

Competitive Environment

The number of operators providing telecoms services is relatively low, and few companies from outside the EU have participated. But with the recent lifting of restrictions on foreign investment, far more participation is expected. Wireline telephony services (including local, long distance and international) are still public services rendered by PT.

The consortium Main Road Telecomunicações was formed recently by ETG (EDP, Transgás and Gás de Portugal), Sonae-Tecnologias de Informação, and Maxitel-Serviços e gestão de Telecomunicações, S.A., to bid for the third wireless operator license. This consortium could also be one of the candidates for the wireline license when liberalization occurs.

Type of Service	Entire Market		Top Two Players		
	Market Size (1996)	Number of Players	Names	Annual Revenue (1996)	Ownership
Local	PTE 23.3 billion*	1	Portugal Telecom	PTE 477.8 billion**	Private company controlled by the government
Long Distance	PTE 146 billion*				Private company controlled by the government
International	PTE 72 billion	1	Marconi	PTE 81 billion**	Portugal Telecom
Cellular	PTE 100.4 billion	3, as of December 1997	TMN	PTE 41.6 billion	Portugal Telecom
			Telecel	PTE 58.8 billion	AirTouch Europe 51%, Telepri 10%, publicly traded 39%
Paging	PTE 5.2 billion	3	Telechamada	PTE 2.012 billion	Telecel (100%)
			Contactel	PTE 1.633 billion	Portugal Telecom 61%; Telefónica International Holding BV 15%; Promindustria, S.A. 15%; BPI, S.A. 9%
Value-added	PTE 3.59 billion	34	Televoz-Consultadoria em difusão, Lda.	PTE 1 billion	Televoice-Consultadoria e Comércio Internacional, Lda. 80%, Mr. Manuel Lucas 20%
			Audio-Info Portugal BV	PTE 600 million	Audio-Info BV

* Estimated value based on expected growth rate of 8%.

** Portugal Telecom and Marconi revenues include amounts for other telecoms services.

Sources: Portugal Telecom, Marconi, Portuguese Communications Institute, TMN, Telecel, Telechamada, Contactel, Televoz, Audio-Info.

Licensing Requirements

The Portuguese Communications Institute (Instituto das Comunicações de Portugales, or ICP) oversees the telecommunications sector. All telecommunications operators, except value-added services operators and ISPs, must obtain licenses through a public tender procedure managed by the ICP. ISPs and value-added services operators apply to the ICP for authorization and must meet certain technical requirements. Licenses are usually granted for nationwide service.

Potential for Foreign Ownerships/Relationships

With the lifting of restrictions on foreign ownership and joint ventures, there is abundant potential for foreign companies to operate in Portugal. Several foreign entities, including U S WEST,

British Telecom and MCI (via Concert), Telebrás (which, with PT, has formed the Aliança Atlântica), Telefónica International, AirTouch Europe and France Telecom, have already set up joint ventures and negotiated partnerships.

Potential for Upcoming Liberalization/Investment Opportunities

Between 1995 and 2000, investment in the telecommunications sector is expected to grow by about 50%, and growth in revenues by about 75%. Cellular phone usage is expected to increase threefold. As liberalization occurs, the Portuguese telecommunications market will provide opportunities in several types of services, including wireline (which is still a public service), closed-user-group services and telecommunications networks and facilities.

Further privatization of PT was scheduled to occur before the end of 1997, when more than 26% of the company's shares were to be sold. The government will keep a 25% share until wireline telephone services are completely liberalized, on January 1, 2000.

In the cellular phone sector, a third license tender was underway in 1997, but it is unlikely that additional cellular licenses will be issued in the near future. The government was investigating whether a market exists for digital European cordless telecommunication (DECT)-rule service (a pan-European standard, like GSM or DCS, but more powerful and technologically more advanced).

In the paging sector, competition for a new license for operating in the ERMES pan-European system was to open before the end of 1997. No additional paging licenses are likely to be granted soon thereafter.

The ISP market is growing rapidly, and many business opportunities exist. Several authorized operators are expected to begin providing services soon.

Forms of Doing Business

Permanent Establishment

A permanent establishment (PE) of a foreign company in Portugal is characterized as a fixed installation through which a company carries out its activities. A PE also exists if a company has dependent employees carrying out its activities in Portugal for an aggregate of at least 120 days in a 12-month period. Portugal has entered into several double-tax treaties under the OECD Model Convention, which further defines PE. For example, a company under the OECD Model is also deemed to have a PE where it has a person acting regularly on its behalf, except when the person is an independent agent or his activities are limited to hiring personnel or purchasing merchandise for the enterprise.

Following are some examples of situations that do *not* constitute PE:

- The provision of long-distance telephone service or fax service by a foreign company to a local customer when the foreign supplier has no local presence

- The licensing of technology and know-how to a local company by a foreign company having no permanent presence

- The presence of a foreign telecommunications company's employees operating in a Portuguese resident telecommunications company for less than a total of 120 days in a 12-month period to provide technical services or network management services

- The leasing of telecommunications equipment to a local company by a foreign entity having no other supporting activities in Portugal

- The provision of Internet access service (e.g., selling of enabling software) to Portuguese customers by a foreign company having no other presence in Portugal; the tax authorities have not ruled as to whether the existence of an access server in Portugal owned by a foreign entity who uses it to supply services on a permanent basis should be treated as a PE.

- The use of switches in Portugal without supporting personnel

- The laying of fiber optic cable by a foreign company to a local company, or the construction of telecommunications switching equipment to be operated by a foreign company for a local company in exchange for a price or a fee when the company's employees do not operate in the Portuguese company for more than a total of 12 days in a 12-month period

- Tax authorities have not yet ruled on the PE status of websites located on servers in and out of Portugal and their accessibility by customers in Portugal. Call reorganization and turnaround services are not permitted in Portugal.

A PE is taxed on income directly attributable to the PE in a manner similar to that for other incorporated entities (see "Corporate Income Taxes"). If a telecommunications company is not characterized as a PE, the only taxation to which it is subject is withholding tax on dividends, royalties and interest paid to non-residents.

Business Entities

Foreign companies can carry out foreign direct investment (FDI) operations through a permanent branch or agency, a wholly or partially owned subsidiary, or an acquired share of an existing Portuguese company. Other frequently used investment vehicles include incorporated forms, such as European economic interest groups (EEIGs) and complementary groupings of companies (agrupamentos complementar de empresas, or ACEs), and contractual (non-incorporated) joint ventures, such as consortia. Prior authorization is not required for FDI projects. The investment must be registered with the Foreign Trade Institute (Investimentos, Comércio e Turismo de Portugal, or ICEP) within the 30 days following the closing on the investment operation.

Antitrust law provides that whenever an entity acquires at least 30% of the national market of one product or service, or when the total revenue of the companies involved in the concentration equals or exceeds PTE 30 billion, the operation is required to obtain prior approval from the antitrust authorities (Direcção Geral de Concorrência e Preços).

Local Branch of a Foreign Company. Any foreign company can set up a branch or other form of permanent representation. This is required if it carries on business regularly in Portugal for more than 12 months. Branches are created by translating the foreign company's articles of association into Portuguese and registering them with the Commercial Registry Department.

Because a branch is a PE of a foreign company, it is taxed on income generated in Portugal or attributable to the branch. Taxable income is subject to a 36% basic tax rate, which rises to 39.6% when local municipal tax is included. The determined income is subject to adjustments by the tax authorities whenever it differs from the income that would have been generated by an independent entity carrying out similar activities under similar conditions.

Profits and losses of branches cannot be grouped with those of other operations. No tax consequences arise from transactions made between the head office and the branch; therefore, no interest, royalties or commissions should be charged by the head office to the branch or vice versa. The branch's profits and losses may be transferred to the head office without tax implications.

Locally Incorporated Subsidiary of a Foreign Company. A foreign company can set up a subsidiary, either as a limited liability company (Lda.), with at least two shareholders and minimum share capital of PTE 400,000, or as a joint stock company (S.A.), with at least five shareholders and a minimum share capital of PTE 5 million. The subsidiary's taxable income will be subject to corporate income tax (see "Corporate Income Tax"). The company's losses can be carried over (see "Loss Carryovers"), and its profits can be distributed to its shareholders. Taxation rates on distributed profits or dividends depend on the type of company (if it is a S.A., a special type of inheritance tax of 5% is levied in addition to income tax) and on the characteristics of the shareholders (e.g., whether they are corporations or individuals, residents or non-residents, with or without PE).

Tax consolidation of groups of related companies is possible, with authorization by tax authorities, if the holding company owns, directly or indirectly, 90% of the subsidiaries' shares and if all group companies have their registered head offices and place of effective management in Portugal and are subject to corporate taxes. Thus, profits and losses of a foreign-owned subsidiary cannot be grouped with other operations of the foreign company.

Joint Venture. The most common forms of joint venture are Lda. and S.A. companies, complementary groupings of companies (ACEs) and consortia.

An ACE is regarded for tax purposes as a partnership. The profits or losses of an ACE either flow through to the participating companies, according to the apportionment rules defined in the creation deed, or are divided equally among the participants. The non-resident members of an ACE are regarded as having PE; thus, ACE income attributable to them is taxed accordingly.

A consortium is not regarded as a separate tax entity. Each member of the consortium is taxed independently for its participation in the consortium's income. The consortium's profits are considered capital income for tax purposes. Profits that are distributed by the Portuguese resident leader of the consortium to a non-resident member without PE are subject to 20% withholding at source. The government is clarifying the tax rules applicable to consortia in order to avoid tax evasion and double economic taxation of the deriving income.

Although the income of ACEs and consortia are taxed directly to their members, the joint companies must file tax returns.

Local Funding Alternatives

Debt versus Equity

Interest on shareholder loans is tax-deductible on an accrual basis. Interest paid is subject to withholding tax at the source at a rate of 15% for resident entities and companies with PE in Portugal. The rate may be reduced by double-tax treaties.

Interest on loans from banks or other financial institutions is tax-deductible on an accrual basis. Interest is not subject to withholding tax at the source when these institutions are Portuguese residents. Financing obtained from non-resident banks and shareholders must satisfy Portugal's thin capitalization rules. Interest payments on loans made by non-resident shareholders who have either direct or indirect relations with a Portuguese company should not exceed twice the shareholder's equity, in which case the amount of interest paid on excessive indebtedness is not, in principle, deductible for tax purposes. Additionally, interest payments to the non-resident bank may be disallowed when shareholder guarantees have been given. Any credit facility or loan agreement is subject to stamp tax at 0.5%, based on the total amount granted or loaned. A 4% stamp tax is levied on interest derived from loans made by Portuguese-resident financial institutions or banks (either their permanent establishments or subsidiaries abroad) or non-resident financial institutions or banks.

Equity finance is subject to strict rules and requires the adoption of one of the accepted legal forms:

•   Statutory share capital, which is a company's basic corporate funding and which may be increased either by new share capital contributions, in cash or in kind, or by incorporation

• Supplementary share capital, a non-interest-bearing, supplemental cash contribution to the company by the shareholders

A refund of equity capital through share capital reduction is in itself neither taxed nor subject to capital duties, but the resulting net worth must equal at least share capital plus 20% and be authorized by the competent court. Exchange gains and losses will be included in the taxable profits for corporation tax purposes of resident companies or of non-resident companies with PE in Portugal. If exchange gains occur, they will be subject to a 20% withholding tax.

Dividends paid by a resident corporate entity to non-resident entities without PE in Portugal are subject to the standard 25% withholding tax, unless a double-tax treaty or a Parent-Subsidiary EU Council Directive is in effect.

Exchange Controls

There are no exchange controls in Portugal. Dividends, profits, capital gains and winding-up proceeds are transferable after payment of any taxes due.

Business Acquisitions and Dispositions

Capital Contributions into an Existing Local Entity

The transfer of inventory, intangibles or services from a telecommunications company to another as capital contributions in kind is not subject to taxation in Portugal.

Purchase or Sale of Shares in a Local Entity

Foreign investors may acquire equity holdings in Portugal by foreign direct investment (FDI). There are no restrictions or limits to FDI. Investors must register with the ICEP and abide by antitrust provisions. (See "Business Entities.") The purchaser of shares in a Portuguese company is not subject to taxation on the acquisition unless the purchaser is a Portuguese limited liability company, which attracts transfer tax if the company owns real estate and the investor acquires a participation in at least 75% of its equity. A seller may be subject to capital gains tax on the shares transferred, unless it is a non-resident entity having no PE in Portugal. A step-up in the basis of assets is not possible when acquiring a company's shares.

Purchase or Sale of Assets

From a purchaser's standpoint, no taxation is applicable to the purchase of a company's assets. Only the purchase of real estate is subject to transfer tax, which is calculated on the value of the immovable property acquired. The purchase of assets is subject to VAT at a rate of 17%, which may be recovered (see "Customs Duties and VAT"). No VAT will be levied on the purchase of the assets, or of a part of them if that part is able to run an independent activity and the purchaser is a VAT-taxable person.

From a resident corporate seller's standpoint, capital gains from the sale of fixed assets will be considered part of the overall taxable income subject to standard income tax rates. Companies may benefit from more favorable tax-deferral treatment on capital gains when they reinvest the proceeds from the disposal of qualifying assets.

Goodwill is defined as the difference between the value of the assets acquired and the consideration paid. Goodwill occurs at the shareholder level and is not tax-deductible.

The transfer of a partnership interest produces the same consequences as the transfer of shares.

Start-up Business Issues

Pre-operating Losses and Start-up/ Construction Costs

The following pre-operating and start-up costs are deductible for corporate income tax purposes at a 33.33% rate:

• Start-up costs, including business-investigation costs or research and development (R&D) expenses

• Franchise and license fees

• Infrastructure costs, such as production and purchase of any products, services, materials, labor and energy necessary to the installation of a network and building

• Interest and finance costs incurred from third-party loans for the production of tangible fixed assets incurred by the local entity during the minimum two-year construction period

Customs Duties and VAT

Most goods imported into Portugal from outside the EU are subject to customs duty and import VAT unless exemptions apply. Duty is normally payable on the cost, insurance and freight (CIF) value of the goods. Import VAT is payable on the duty-inclusive value of the goods, although VAT-registered traders can usually obtain a refund of the VAT.

Telecommunications and computing equipment are subject to duty ranging from 1.2% to 7%. The rate of duty will depend on the exact description and the tariff classification of the goods and country of origin of the goods. The current import duty rate for a sample of telecommunications goods originating in non-EU countries (in this example, the United States) are given below. The EU has preferential trade agreements with a number of countries that enable goods to be imported at rates below those indicated or at nil.

Line telephone sets with cordless handsets	3.8%
Video phones	7%
Other telephone sets	3.8%
Facsimile machines	3.8%
Teleprinters	3.8%
Telephonic or telegraphic switching apparatus	3.8%
Other apparatus for carrier line systems	2.3%
Other apparatus for digital line systems	3.8%
Building-entry telephone systems	3.8%

Customs duties on some items of equipment were already being reduced under the General Agreement on Tariffs and Trade (GATT). However, over the next few years, duty rates are scheduled to be reduced further under the Information Technology Agreement (ITA) signed in March 1997. The ITA also extends the range of goods subject to duty rate reductions. As a signatory to the ITA, the EU has agreed to cut tariffs on imports of computers and computer equipment, software, telecommunications and networking equipment to zero in four equal installments. The first reduction took place on July 1, 1997, and further reductions are to take effect on January 1 each year through 2000. Although the ITA will cut the cost of importing many products, the convergence of technologies in the computing, electronics and telecommunications sectors is likely to lead to disputes over the tariff classification of some equipment and affect the availability and/or phasing of duty reductions under the ITA.

A wide variety of reliefs from customs duty (and import VAT) can be claimed in various circumstances (e.g., goods imported for processing and re-export, or goods imported temporarily). There is also a relief available for capital goods and equipment, provided the goods are imported by a business on the transfer of its activities to France.

Raw materials or components that are not available, or not available in sufficient quantities, within the EU may be eligible

for a complete or partial suspension of duty, providing this can be demonstrated to the satisfaction of the Commission of the European Communities in Brussels.

Goods may be subject to anti-dumping or countervailing duty if, for example, the EU considers they are being imported into the EU at prices substantially lower than their normal values. Anti-dumping and countervailing duties are chargeable in addition to, and independent of, any other duty to which the imported goods may be liable.

Loss Carryovers

Tax losses can be offset against taxable profits in the six-year period following the loss, but they cannot be carried back. Changes in the ownership of a company do not affect the deductibility of losses; however, when the nature of a company's business activities is materially changed, the company loses the right to use the accumulated losses in the tax year when these modifications occur. The tax authorities may grant permission to do otherwise. If a telecommunications operator changes its services from wireline to cellular, this would not be deemed a material change in the nature of the business.

Operating Considerations

Corporate Income Taxes

Corporations are subject to a 36% basic tax rate. Dividends, interest and royalties are subject to withholding tax at the standard 25% flat rate (which may be reduced by a treaty), except in the following circumstances:

- Dividends distributed by a Portuguese resident subsidiary to a parent company resident in another EU-member state, with a controlling interest of at least 25% of the Portuguese company's equity capital, for a period of at least two years, are withheld at source at 10% (until December 1999, when the rate drops to 0%).

- Interest incurred is withheld at source at a 20% tax rate.

- Royalties are subject to withholding at source at a 15% rate.

- There is no withholding on capital gains arising from the sale of investment holdings.

Capital Gains Taxes

Capital gains realized by Portuguese resident entities on the disposal of tangible or intangible fixed assets are treated as part of the company's overall taxable income after adjustments to base cost for inflationary effects. Companies benefit from more favorable tax deferral treatment on capital gains when they reinvest the proceeds of the disposal of qualifying assets (i.e., roll-forward relief). For non-resident entities having no PE in Portugal, capital gains deriving from the transfer of shares in Portuguese companies are tax-exempt.

Tax Holidays and Exemptions

Benefits pertaining to corporate income tax, transfer tax, stamp tax and municipal tax on real estate may be available for investment projects of more than PTE 5 billion that benefit the national economy through modernization or internationalization. These benefits are subject to a contract between the investor and the Portuguese government. The following tax credits are available for additional investment:

- 5% of the additional investment expenses incurred with the acquisition of new tangible fixed assets during a tax period are deductible as tax credit up to 15% of the amount of Portuguese corporate income tax due.

- The government may raise the credit rates to 10% for investments made in undeveloped areas and to 30% for those made by small or medium-size enterprises.

Depreciation/Cost-Recovery Conventions/Accelerated Deductions

Depreciation on fixed assets is charged to the profit and loss account, either on a straight-line or declining-balance basis, according to established rates. The law specifies maximum rates to be used for each type of fixed asset and limits the period of depreciation. Intangible fixed assets (except for financial intangibles, goodwill and shareholdings) are also subject to a 33.33% depreciation rate. The following depreciation rates apply to the telecommunications sector:

Telecommunications Assets	Depreciation Rates
Transmission and reception centers	12.5%
Surface and underground cabling	5%
Installation of synchronization and control	14.28%
Public and private wire connections	10%

R&D costs, including software development costs, are accepted as tax costs in the year they are incurred. Nevertheless, the company may choose to subject this cost to the 33.33% depreciation rate. Purchased software is subject to the same depreciation rate. For depreciation purposes, equipment and embedded software should be treated separately.

Marketing and advertising costs incurred to attract customers, directly or indirectly (e.g., through sales agents), are fully accepted as tax costs in the year they are incurred. However, when a marketing or advertising campaign is in effect for longer than one year, these costs should be capitalized and depreciated during the period when returns or results of the campaign are expected. For tax purposes, this period must be at least three years.

Transfer Pricing Rules

Inter-company prices should be established in such a way that local subsidiaries make a reasonable profit in harmony with the arm's-length principle. Tax authorities can adjust the taxable profits of a company or a PE whenever prices or other conditions established diverge from those prevailing in the market between independent parties, or when prices or conditions give rise to abnormally low profits. This has not happened often in recent years.

Transfers of Patents, Trademarks and Software

Royalty payments are deductible for corporate income tax purposes if they are judged to be reasonable (typically less than 5% of revenue). Royalty payments on industrial property, intellectual property, technical assistance and know-how in industrial, commercial and scientific activity provided by non-resident corporate entities are subject to withholding at source at a 15% tax rate.

Capital gains from the sale of licenses or transfer of inventory, services and technology (intangible fixed assets) are taxable. Capital losses from fixed assets or intangible fixed assets acquired reduce taxable income.

Income from know-how or from sharing expertise in industrial, commercial and scientific sectors, even when supported by a contract rather than a license, is considered a royalty and subject to taxation.

Service Fees

Service fees are deductible if the services and the consequent fees paid are reasonable and necessary for a company's activity. There are no withholding taxes on service fees or management fees, regardless of where the services are rendered, except when the services are considered technical assistance. Technical assistance fees, whenever related to intellectual or industrial property held by the company, are taxed as royalties. In principle, VAT is applicable only to service fees rendered by a Portuguese resident entity.

There are no special provisions on cost allocation re-charge schemes; nevertheless, cost-sharing schemes can be employed as long as they are established at arm's length and are necessary to generate the subsidiary's profits. The tax authorities have often rejected the allocation of costs by non-resident parent companies to Portuguese-resident subsidiaries, ruling that the allocations did not meet the arm's-length and necessity criteria.

Value-Added Tax, Sales Tax and/or Other Pertinent Taxes

As a member of the EU, Portugal follows the provisions of the European Union Sixth VAT Directive. Domestic telecommunications services (including those supplied by Portuguese-resident foreign businesses) are subject to VAT at the standard rate of 17%. Reduced VAT rates exist for all the regions of Madeira and Azores. Services supplied internationally by a telecommunications business located in Portugal are generally outside the scope of VAT when they are supplied to anyone located outside Portugal. The only exceptions are services supplied to private individuals or unregistered persons located in other member states. Those supplies are subject to Portuguese VAT at the standard rate.

Non-resident providers are not liable to register and account for Portuguese VAT on supplies used and enjoyed by Portuguese customers, providing those customers are taxable persons for VAT purposes. These customers are required to self-account for VAT under reverse-charge procedures.

When a non-resident provider makes supplies of services to private individuals, to be used in Portugal, the provider is required to register and account for VAT. For an overseas provider, it should be possible to limit the Portuguese VAT liability to supplies made to Portuguese individuals that are used in the EU. However, this may then require the overseas provider to be registered for VAT purposes in many different EU-member states. Alternatively, an overseas provider may choose to register in a single EU-member state in order to contract with all customers who are EU private individuals. The supplies made from the single EU registration to these customers will then be subject to local VAT in the member state of registration.

Internet access services are not considered telephony.

Inheritance Tax. Dividends distributed by a Portuguese-resident joint stock company to shareholders, resident or non-resident, are subject to 5% withholding at source as a substitute inheritance tax. Since this tax is not regarded by the tax authorities as an income tax, it is applicable in addition to income taxes, even when a tax treaty exists.

Local and Provincial Taxes

Municipal Surtax on Corporation Tax. This surtax may be imposed by municipalities that choose to levy it, at a rate of up to 10% of income tax due at the standard rate. Thus, the final corporate tax rate applicable to resident companies and branches may amount to 39.6% [36% + (36% x 10%)].

For companies with taxable income greater than PTE 10 million and having premises located in more than one municipality, the local surtax is levied on profits derived from activities carried out in the territory of each municipality, regardless of whether the premises are a head-office site. In practice, the local surtax is levied on the corporation tax due after apportionment of the tax between municipalities. This is calculated on the percentage of the company's salary costs corresponding to each of the premises or establishments.

Municipal Tax on Real Estate. This is a local tax levied on the officially assessed value of land and buildings at the rate of 0.8% for rural land and ranging from 0.7% to 1.3% for development land and buildings. For companies owning and using land or buildings for their activity, municipal tax paid is considered a deductible cost.

For Additional Information, Contact:

Luis Oliveira
Tax Partner
P.O. Box 1910
1004 Lisbon Codex
Portugal
Telephone: 351 (1) 791 4000
Fax: 351 (1) 791 4001
E-mail: pafisco1@mail.telepac.pt

Romania

Telecommunications Tax Profile
by Rodica Segarceanu
Tax Director, Bucharest
and Nuria Sanchez-Rubio
Tax Consultant/Legal Adviser, Bucharest

Overview of the Telecommunications Market

Historical Background

Telecommunications services in Romania have traditionally been provided by the state and regulated by the Ministry of Communications. In 1991, Rom Post Telecom, the state PTT (Post, Telephone and Telegraph), was divided into three autonomous operating units: Rom Post, Rom Telecom and Rom Radiocom. In September 1997, Rom Telecom was given a monopoly over voice telephony for a duration of five years. Thus, the monopoly will expire in the year 2002; full liberalization is expected on January 1, 2003.

Legislation enacted since 1992 has opened competition in other segments of the telecommunications industry, including value-added services, satellite communications, cellular, paging and the provision of customer premise equipment. In July 1996, Romania adopted the 1996 Telecommunications Law, which outlined the principles of regulation and competition, covering areas such as licensing, authorization, tariffs, interconnection to the public network and wayleaves (i.e., the statutory right over private property and customer protection). This law established a legal framework for the telecommunications industry for the first time.

It is the government's intention to privatize Rom Telecom in 1998. As a first step in this process, in 1997 Rom Telecom was transformed from a regie autonome (i.e., an autonomous body) into a joint-stock company, with the state as the sole shareholder. The State Ownership Fund is then expected to organize a call for bids, in order to sell the majority package of the telecoms company. The intention of the government is to sell at least a 30% equity stake in Rom Telecom.

Current Status

Telecommunications revenue in the fixed-line sector is not growing as rapidly as would be desirable. The government development program for telecommunications in Romania aims to have a fully digital system in place by the year 2005. To that end, telephone exchanges using analog technology are being replaced by digital systems and state-of-the-art equipment. Nearly 40% of all subscribers lines are currently serviced by digital switches.

Rom Telecom is also focusing on introducing fiber optic cable. The first fiber optic cable was installed in Bucharest in 1991. It is expected that Rom Telecom will finish installing a fiber optic cable network throughout Romania by the year 2000.

Increasing the number of lines per customer is also a priority for the government. Currently, there are only about 14 lines per 100 people. In 1997, 500,000 lines were expected to be installed. Rom Telecom needs to update its technology; either the government will invest in Rom Telecom prior to privatization or foreign investors will have to do the necessary restructuring after privatization.

Current Liberalization Status

Romania has made a full commitment to the regulatory principles and guidelines of the World Trade Organization (WTO), and liberalization of a limited range of services is expected to occur by the year 2002 or later. In addition, liberalization of the telecommunications industry is one of the conditions stipulated in Romania's association agreement with the European Union.

Type of Service	Degree of Liberalization	Key Legislation	Date of Actual or Expected Liberalization	Comments
Local, Long Distance and International	Monopoly	1996 Telecommunications Law	2003	Rom Telecom has a monopoly to provide basic telephone services until the year 2003.
Cellular (Analog)	Monopoly	Emergency Ordinance No. 4 (1996)	2002	In 1992, Telefónica Romania was given the exclusive right to provide analog cellular mobile telephony at NMT-450 MHz for 10 years.
Cellular (Digital)	Partially liberalized	Emergency Ordinance No. 4 (1996)	1997	GSM mobile telephony was opened to competition in 1997 when Mobil Rom S.A. and MobiFon S.A. were each given 10-year licenses.
Paging	Partially liberalized	Ministry Order No. 55 (1992)	1992	
Value-added*	Partially liberalized	Ministry Order No. 90 (1992)	1992	There are three main Internet access providers. EUNet Romania SRL started commercial services in 1993 with a UUCP (UNIX-to-UNIX Copy Program) link to Vienna. InterComp SRL provides full Internet services to businesses via VSATs. Kappa Servexim SRL provides services to residential subscribers by cable television network, with a central node connected in Bucharest to the Internet by satellite.

* Internet access providers.

Competitive Environment*

As outlined in the following table, while the voice telephony sector will be under monopoly control for the next few years, competition is opening up in the other sectors of the telecommunications industry.

Type of Service	Entire Market Number of Players	Top Two Players Names	Top Two Players Ownership
Local, Long Distance and International	1	Rom Telecom	Government (through the State Ownership Fund)
Cellular (Analog)	1	Telefónica Romania	Telefónica de España, S.A. (60%), Rom Radiocom (20%) and Rom Telecom (20%)
Cellular (Digital)	2	Mobil Rom	France Telecom Mobiles International (51%), Media Pro (30%), Computer Land (10%), Tomen Telecom Romania (6%) and Alcatel Network Systems Romania (3%)
		MobiFon	Telesystem International Wireless Inc. (39.9%), AirTouch Communications (10%) and four Romanian companies that have a combined stake of 50.1%: Ana Industries SRL, R.A. Posta Romana (the Romanian postal service), Logic Telecom S.A. and ISAF (Societatea de Automatizari si Semnalizari Feroviare)
Paging	11	Page One	Ownership information is not available.
		Radiotel	Ownership information is not available.
Value-added**	100	EUNet Romania	EUNet International BV (100%)
		InterComp SRL	Owners are private citizens: Moisa Trandafir (50%) and Rusu M. Gheorghe (50%)
		Kappa Servexim	Owners are private citizens: Crisan Zara Oana (50%) and Crisan Zara Ioan Ovidiu (50%)

* Revenue figures not available.
** Internet access providers.

Licensing Requirements

No licenses will be issued for voice telephony until Rom Telecom's monopoly expires in 2002. Licenses are required for those sectors of the telecommunications industry where competition is limited. Licenses are issued by the Ministry of Communications and are given only to Romanian companies. Permanent establishments (PEs) and branches may not receive licenses as they are extensions of foreign companies. Licenses may only be granted for a specific type of network or for specific types of telecommunications services and may be limited to a specific region or city. Licenses can also be issued for nationwide service.

For those sectors of the telecommunications industry where competition is open, an authorization from the Ministry of Communications is required. Authorizations are given to Romanian companies and also to PEs and branches. While the provision of customer premise equipment is liberalized, all equipment used in the public network must be type-approved by the Ministry of Communications.

Potential for Foreign Ownerships/Relationships

There are no limitations on the percentage of a telecommunications business that can be owned by a foreign company.

Potential for Upcoming Liberalization/Investment Opportunities

The most important investment opportunity in the near future relates to the privatization of Rom Telecom. Initially, 30% of Rom Telecom will be sold to a foreign strategic investor and between 3% to 5% of Rom Telecom's shares will be made available to its employees. In a second stage of the privatization process, the rest of the shares owned by the state would be sold through a public offering to international and domestic investors, and the state would keep a golden share. (A golden share comes with a veto right, such as the right to prohibit certain decisions from a general meeting of shareholders. The circumstances under which the government would have this share would be limited and of an exceptional nature.)

Forms of Doing Business

Permanent Establishment

A foreign company is typically considered to have a permanent establishment (PE) if it has a fixed place of business through which it carries out business activities, or if it carries out business through a dependent agent. (This general definition may be modified by the provisions of the double-taxation treaties signed by Romania with other countries.) Non-resident legal persons are taxable for the income related to their PEs in Romania. Telecommunications services can include a broad range of activities, which may or may not constitute a PE. Some examples follow:

- The provision of long-distance telephone services by a foreign company to local customers without any local presence or advertising will not create a PE.

- The licensing by a foreign company of technology and know-how to a local company could create a PE only if the license included the provision of surveillance, consulting services or technical assistance for a period exceeding 12 months.

- The provision of technical assistance and technological services, including operator services and/or network management services in exchange for service fees, by a foreign company to a local company (where the foreign company owned equity in the local company) could create a PE if the assistance were provided for more than 12 months.

- The leasing of telecommunications equipment to a local company will not create a PE.

- The provision of call reorganization/turnaround services will not create a PE.

- The provision of Internet access services will not create a PE. Nevertheless, there should be a case-by-case analysis to determine if there is a risk of creating a PE or not.

- If a server or switch is located in Romania without any personnel in the country, this will not create a PE.

- If a website is located on a server in Romania, no PE will be created, regardless of whether the server is accessible by customers in Romania or abroad.

- If a website is located on a server outside Romania, it will not create a PE even if it is accessible to customers in Romania.

- The laying of fiber optic cable and the construction of telecommunications switching equipment (a) for sale to a local company or (b) to be operated by a foreign telecommunications company for a local company in exchange for a fee will create a PE if the project lasts for more than 12 months.

Business Entities

Local Branch of a Foreign Company. A branch is a PE. The foreign company will be taxed on the branch's Romanian-sourced income.

Locally Incorporated Subsidiary of a Foreign Company. If a foreign company sets up a subsidiary in Romania, this company will be considered as a Romanian legal entity and, therefore, taxable as a separate entity from the mother company. There is a 10% withholding tax on dividends, which may be reduced by a tax treaty. Most subsidiaries are established as limited liability companies. The profits and losses of a subsidiary cannot be grouped with those of other operations.

Joint Venture. The most common way for a foreign company to invest in the telecommunications industry is by forming a joint venture with a Romanian company. Joint ventures may be established as either partnerships, limited partnerships, limited partnerships by shares (which is a partnership in which capital is divided in shares), limited liability companies or joint-stock companies. Joint ventures have to file tax returns and pay corporate income tax at the general rate of 38%. No government approval is required for a joint venture in the telecommunications sector. A foreign company entering into a joint venture will not be considered to have a PE; rather the foreign company will be considered to be a shareholder of the joint-venture company.

Local Funding Alternatives

Debt versus Equity

It is more advantageous to finance with debt than with equity since interest is fully deductible. There are no thin capitalization rules in Romania. There is a 10% withholding tax on dividends, which may be reduced by a tax treaty.

A contribution in debts (i.e., a contribution that may be converted into equity) cannot be allowed as consideration for a capital contribution when setting up a joint-stock company by public subscription (i.e., the subscription to the share capital is open to the public), a limited liability company or a limited partnership. When one of these three types of companies is set up or increases its social capital (i.e., share capital), the social capital cannot be a contribution in debts. Realized foreign exchange gains are taxable and realized foreign exchange losses are deductible from the profits tax.

Exchange Controls

The profits earned by non-residents in Romania may be repatriated after payment of the taxes due. However, all payments made in Romania must be in leu, which is the local currency.

Business Acquisitions and Dispositions

Capital Contributions into an Existing Local Entity

Capital contributions are tax-exempt. Which intangibles can be contributed by a foreign entity into an existing local entity is decided upon by a judge from the Romanian Trade Register who approves the capital contribution on the basis of certain criteria. A capital contribution to an existing entity can be made only after the initial capital has been entirely subscribed. (In-kind contributions to the registered capital of a Romanian company are exempt from customs duties and from VAT.)

Purchase or Sale of Shares in a Local Entity

There are no specific restrictions on foreign investors acquiring shares in a Romanian company. If a foreign investor buys shares in a local entity on either the Bucharest Stock Exchange or the RASDAQ market, the investor will be subject to a 1.5% tax on the value of the transaction. (The RASDAQ market is the over-the-counter market. RASDAQ stands for Romanian Association of Securities Dealers Automated Quotation system.) The amounts representing this tax are withheld from the purchaser by the securities company where the transaction is carried out and are paid to the government within a maximum of 10 days from their collection.

Purchase or Sale of Assets

Sales of assets by a local entity will be considered as exceptional revenues and will be included in the revenues of the entity after deducting the related costs (in this case, the undepreciated value of those assets). "Exceptional revenues" are revenues derived by Romanian entities outside their usual business activity. The remaining net value (the difference between the selling price and the undepreciated value of the asset) will be taxed at the normal profits tax rate of 38%.

Start-up Business Issues

Pre-operating Losses and Start-up/Construction Costs

Start-up costs and related fees (such as registration fees, etc.) are tax-deductible. These costs, as well as research and development costs, may be depreciated over a period of up to five years. Other costs, such as license fees, concession fees (i.e., franchise fees) and fees for know-how, trademarks and other similar rights are depreciated over the life of the concession. Tax relief is granted for the amount depreciated each year. Set-up costs, such as registration fees and other fees paid to the Romanian authorities, notarization fees as well as expenses for the issuing and selling of shares that are incurred by a foreign company can be deducted by the local entity provided that the supporting payment documents are in the local entity's name.

VAT charged on domestic supplies to non-resident companies is not recoverable. VAT deductions may be claimed only by registered VAT payers carrying on taxable activities in Romania. VAT incurred in the pre-operating period can only be recovered if the company is a registered VAT payer.

Customs Duties and VAT

Customs duty rates vary considerably for different types of products. Agreements to reduce duty rates have been concluded with the European Union (EU), the European Free Trade Association (EFTA) and the Central European Free Trade Association (CEFTA). The rates for telecommunications equipment range generally between 0% and 20% (normal rate); special rates of between 0% and 15% apply to EU-member states. The current duty rates for different types of telecommunications equipment are given in the table below. There is also a customs commission of 0.5% (0.25% for EU-member states), which is applied on the customs value of the imported/exported goods for the performance of customs services by the customs administration.

Type of Telecoms Equipment	Normal Duty Rate	Special Duty Rate for EU-Member States
Telephone line	20%	8%
Videophones	42%	33.6%
Copying machines	20%	8%
Teleprinters	20%	8%
Other telecoms devices	20%	8%
Interphones	20%	8%
Spare parts for telecoms equipment	20%	8%

The importation of telecoms equipment is subject to VAT at a rate of 18%. VAT paid for goods and services purchased or imported (input VAT) can be offset against VAT invoiced for deliveries of goods or services rendered (output VAT). If output VAT exceeds input VAT, the difference shall be remitted to the government. If the difference results in a VAT refund, the reimbursement shall generally be made only if the company is in a tax credit position for three consecutive months. For purposes of VAT, there is no distinction drawn between regular telephony and Internet telephony.

Loss Carryovers

Losses cannot be carried back. Losses can be carried forward for up to five years. A change in a company's ownership or business activity will not affect its ability to utilize these losses.

Operating Considerations

Corporate Income Taxes

Tax on profits in Romania is 38%. (It is expected that the profits tax rate will decrease from 38% to about 32% sometime during 1998.)

There is a 10% withholding tax on dividends. In addition, the following withholding tax rates apply to various types of income earned by non-residents:

- 10% for the income from interest paid to non-residents

- 15% for the income from commissions paid to non-residents for starting or operating some foreign trade operations

- 10% for income coming from a variety of consulting activities

- 15% for the income paid to non-residents for international transport

- 20% for the income from the due sums paid to non-residents

- 1% on interest payments made by banks in Romania for deposit accounts opened by non-residents

Capital Gains Taxes

Capital gains are taxed as part of ordinary income.

Tax Holidays and Exemptions

All tax holidays were abolished on January 1, 1995. Currently, the Romanian direct investment legislation grants limited tax benefits, which include exemptions from customs duties and VAT for in-kind contributions, use of accelerated depreciation methods and deductibility of advertising and publicity expenses.

Depreciation/Cost-Recovery Conventions/Accelerated Deductions

The accelerated depreciation method can be used for telecommunications equipment. As applied in Romania, 50% of the cost of an asset can be depreciated in the first year and the remaining value depreciated over the useful life of the asset, which is 12 years for most types of telecommunications equipment. The useful life for automatic telephone exchange equipment is 18 years; for digital equipment, it is 10 years. In general, expenditures for assets are capitalized and then depreciated over the useful life of the asset. Software that is embedded in telecommunications equipment can be separately identified and amortized over a life shorter than the useful life of the related equipment. Software can be depreciated over a maximum period of five years. Advertising and publicity expenses are tax-deductible.

Transfer Pricing Rules

According to Romania's transfer pricing rules, transactions between related parties must take place on an arm's-length basis. The tax authorities have the right to verify all such transactions.

Transfers of Patents, Trademarks and Software

Royalties paid for patents, trademarks and software licensing fees are subject to a 20% withholding tax, which may be reduced by a tax treaty. The withholding tax is deductible unless it is paid in addition to the royalty, in which event no deduction is allowed for the tax. There are no restrictions on the licensing of technology to a local company for royalty fees. Patent, trademark and software licensing fees are deductible. Transfers of licenses, expertise and/or technology out of Romania are subject to a 10% withholding tax on payments for technical assistance and a 20% withholding tax on royalty payments.

Service Fees

Management fees and other service fees paid to non-residents are subject to a 20% withholding tax, which may be reduced by a tax treaty. (It is advisable to maintain supporting documents, such as contracts for the supply of services, and physical evidence that the services have actually been performed.) Service fees are taxed at the same rate regardless of where the services are performed.

Value-Added Tax, Sales Tax and/or Other Pertinent Taxes

Payments to non-residents for services whose place of supply is deemed to be in Romania are subject to VAT. However in these cases, a reverse-charge mechanism applies. The place of supply for telecommunications services is deemed to be the place where the supplier has its business. The VAT rate of 18% applies to payments for the provision of Internet access and to payments for the provision of Internet telephony services. For purposes of VAT, Internet access is considered telephony.

In order to recover VAT, a customer must be a registered VAT payer in Romania and carrying on taxable transactions in Romania. The recovery mechanism for VAT is as follows: All transactions involving the supply of goods or the performance of services are subject to VAT. The person liable for the tax is the one carrying out such activities on a regular or temporary basis.

The VAT paid for goods and services purchased (input VAT) can be offset against VAT invoiced for deliveries of goods or services rendered (output VAT).

Local and Provincial Taxes

Telecommunications businesses are not subject to any local, provincial, or regional taxes.

For Additional Information, Contact:

Corina Arcus
Tax Consultant
and
Cezar Boleac
Tax Consultant
Hristo Botev 28
70472 Bucharest
Romania
Telephone: 40 (1) 312 09 79
Fax: 40 (1) 312 09 78
E-mail: Corina_Arcus@ro.coopers.com
       Cezar_Boleac@ro.coopers.com

Russia

Telecommunications Tax Profile
by Lioudmila Mamet
Tax Partner, Moscow
and Gennady Kamyshnikov
Tax Manager, Moscow

Overview of the Telecommunications Market

Editor's note: A draft tax code was under consideration by the Russian Duma in 1997 and was expected to be enacted in 1998. Substantial changes were expected in tax laws applicable to telecommunications. The descriptions of tax rules presented here are based on laws that were in effect on July 31, 1997.

Historical Background

Sovtelecom was the owner and operator of the domestic network in the Soviet Union. The quality of service was poor, penetration was low, and placing long distance and international calls was very difficult. When the Soviet Union broke apart in 1991, Sovtelecom was renamed Intertelecom; in 1993 Intertelecom was replaced by Rostelecom as the sole owner and operator of international and inter-city, long-distance service. In 1994 Sviazinvest, a holding company, was established and became a major shareholder of Rostelecom and 88 local operating companies throughout the Russian Federation.

In 1992 the Ministry of Communications (MOC) authorized the first foreign joint venture to build a cellular communications network. In 1993 Russia's regional telecommunications operators were privatized. Although the state remains the majority owner in many of these companies, the responsibility for managing them has moved substantially away from the state ministries to local management and owners.

Russia's communications law, which went into effect in February 1995, encourages entrepreneurial activities by foreign companies, restricts monopoly, expands international cooperation, and sets the framework for regulation. The MOC has established a plan to develop the local, cellular, inter-city and international telecommunications infrastructure by 2020.

Current Status

Telecommunications is one of the fastest growing industries in Russia. Nearly 100 local telephone companies provide service today. Large and small American, European and Asian telecommunications companies and manufacturers have actively pursued joint ventures with Russian partners. Many ventures are building digital overlay networks in large cities across Russia.

Infrastructure improvements have permitted higher volumes of international traffic and made it easier to place and receive international calls. Inter-city digital links using fiber optics, microwave and satellite transmission are being built across Russia. Participants include Rostelecom, the group of local companies serving 50 of Russia's largest cities, U S WEST International, Deutsche Telekom AG and France Telecom. Nippon Telegraph & Telephone Corporation (NTT) and others are expected to participate in the future. Other joint ventures are developing cellular technology, paging, data transmission and videoconferencing services.

Russia has 500,000 inter-city and 51,000 international channels, providing significant capacity for the next 10 to 15 years. By the middle of 1997 there were 26 million telephone numbers in Russia, including 1.5 million operated by automatic exchanges. A network of switches also allows for significant redundancy. The total number of exchanges was 34,000, including 100 automatic international exchanges. More than 2 million lines were installed in 1996. Nonetheless, the number of telephone lines remains insufficient to handle demand. The average teledensity is 17.3 lines per 100 persons. In Moscow the density is almost 45, but in some regions it hovers around 10 per 100 persons. Outstanding applications for telephone installation number more than 11 million.

Cellular networks operate in more than 50 Russian cities. The number of cellular subscribers reached 250,000 in April 1997.

Federally approved cellular technologies include Nordic mobile telephone (NMT)-450 (64,000 subscribers) and global system for mobile communications (GSM)-900 (40,000 subscribers), but cellular companies are allowed to operate other technologies as well, including GSM-1800, AMT, advanced mobile phone system (AMPS), digital advanced mobile phone system (D-AMPS), call division multiple access (CDMA) and others. The fastest-expanding standard is GSM-900.

Paging subscribers numbered 250,000; five inter-regional paging networks were in operation. By 2000 the number of paging subscribers is expected to reach 1.5 million, including 750,000 in Moscow. Paging companies use such standards as European radio messaging system (ERMES), Post Office code standard advisory group (POCSAG) and flexible high speed coding (FLEX). About 60% to 70% of cellular and paging services are concentrated in Moscow and St. Petersburg.

Current Liberalization Status

The largest telecommunications companies are still owned by the government, but shares of these companies may be sold to investors, including foreign companies. Tariffs for wireline services provided by state-owned companies are regulated. However, independent companies providing wireline services set their own tariffs.

The government holding company, Sviazinvest, owns controlling stakes in all the local telecommunications operating companies. Sviazinvest was majority state-owned, but in July 1997, 25% plus one of Sviazinvest's shares were sold for $1.875 billion at an auction open to Russian and foreign investors. Another 24% of shares were to be sold to private investors later in 1997. A license for long distance and international service has been granted to Sviazinvest.

At the time of publication, Russia was negotiating its membership in the World Trade Organization (WTO).

Type of Service	Degree of Liberalization	Key Legislation	Date of Actual or Expected Liberalization	Comments
Local, Long Distance and International	Partially liberalized	Telecommunications Law of 1995	Law "on privatization of statutory and municipal enterprises" of 1991	The state is a major shareholder. Tariffs for services are regulated by the state. Licenses are required.
Cellular	Fully liberalized		Services did not exist before privatization.	Licenses are required. Only one license may be issued to operate a specific standard in a region.
Paging	Fully liberalized		Services did not exist before privatization.	Licenses are required.
Value-added	Fully liberalized		Services did not exist before privatization.	Licenses are required.

Competitive Environment

A high level of competition exists within cellular and paging sectors in the largest cities of Russia, but in other regions, these types of business are not yet developed. In these areas, state-owned companies providing local, long distance and international services compete with private companies that provide services of the same type, but of higher quality and at higher prices. Total 1996 revenues from all types of telecommunications services were 39.46 trillion rubles.

| Type of Service | Entire Market | | Top Two Players | | |
	Market Size*	Number of Players	Names	Annual Revenue*	Ownership
Local	R10.73 trillion	About 100 local companies	Moscow Telephone (MGTS)	R2.09 trillion	Open joint stock company with major state participation
Long Distance	R13.63 trillion	One state-owned company and several much smaller private operators	Rostelecom	R10.42 trillion (including international)	Open joint stock company with major state participation
International	R2.97 trillion	One state-owned company and several much smaller private operators	Rostelecom	R10.42 trillion (including long distance)	Open joint stock company with major state participation
			TELMOS Communications	R125 billion	Closed joint stock company (Joint venture of AT&T, MGTS and Rostelecom)
Cellular	Not available	270 licensed companies, only 100 operating companies	VimpelCom	R1.37 trillion	Joint stock company, privately owned
			Moscow Cellular Communications (MCC)	Not available	Joint stock company, privately owned
Paging	Not available	390 licensed companies, 250 operating companies in 52 regions	Mobile Telekom	Not available	Joint stock company, privately owned
			Inform-Excom	Not available	Joint stock company, privately owned
Value-added**	Not available				

Sources: The Statistical Committee of Russia; media reports.

* Revenues for 1996 (net of VAT).

** Companies' filings do not contain separate information regarding different types of services provided; therefore it is impossible to determine revenue figures for value-added services alone.

Licensing Requirements

Licenses are required for all providers of telecommunications services, and separate licenses should be obtained for different types of services. One entity is allowed to hold several licenses. Usually regional licenses are provided, but it is possible to obtain a nationwide license. Licenses are not required for installation of a communications network for internal purposes of an enterprise or for provision of services to the government and the military.

Licenses are granted by the MOC for periods ranging from three to ten years. Prior to obtaining a license, a company should get spectrum authorization, which is provided by the State Radio Frequency Commission (Gosudarstvennaya Komissia Radiochastot, or GKRcH) for the frequencies to be used. Several hundred telecommunications companies have applied for licenses to build networks and operate services.

Usually licenses are awarded through a tender process; however, individual license applications have also gained approval.

At this stage in the development of the nation's infrastructure, new licenses are likely to be granted in all sectors. In cellular, only one license is granted for a particular technology in one area.

Potential for Foreign Ownerships/Relationships

The 1995 telecommunications law encourages foreign investment and participation in the telecommunications sector. The lifting of many legal and economic constraints has led to a high degree of activity in the industry, spurring the initiation of many joint ventures between Russian companies and foreign investors. There are no special restrictions on foreign investment.

Potential for Upcoming Liberalization/Investment Opportunities

Upgrading the telecommunications infrastructure will require a huge investment, and abundant opportunities exist for foreign investors. Investors will want assurances regarding the reliability and stability of the companies in which they might invest, and local operators will likely have to improve the comparability, consistency and transparency of their financial statements, provide more complete performance data, and develop business plans. Information systems must be upgraded to improve management and maximize returns on investment in the emerging competitive environment.

The MOC has planned for wireless service deployment in 60 cities and regions. Licenses to operate NMT and GSM networks will be granted through public tender.

Forms of Doing Business

Permanent Establishment

Permanent establishment (PE) is defined in tax legislation as either (a) a permanent (fixed) place of business in the Russian Federation through which regular activity is conducted or (b) an agent authorized to conclude contracts on behalf of the foreign legal entity. Types of telecommunications activity mentioned in the legislation include contracts to build, modify and service equipment, to render services, and to perform other activities to generate income in Russia or abroad. A permanent place of business is understood to be an affiliate, branch, bureau, office or agency. Telecoms services can cover a broad range of activities, which may or may not constitute a PE. Some examples follow:

- The provision of long distance telephone services to local customers by a foreign company having no local presence generally does not constitute a PE.

- A foreign company that licenses technology and know-how to an unrelated, independent local company generally does not constitute a PE.

- A foreign company that owns an equity interest in the local company and charges the local company a fee to provide technical assistance, including operator services, may create a PE, depending on the types of activities conducted in Russia.

- The leasing of telecommunications equipment (without other supporting activities in Russia) to the local company generally does not constitute a PE.

- The provision of call reorganization/turnaround services using debit cards generally does not constitute a PE if the cards are provided through an independent agent that is not authorized to conclude contracts or represent interests of the foreign entity. An independent agent could buy cards on its own behalf and then sell them to the general public, or it could provide cards as part of its regular business activity.

- The provision of Internet access services generally does not constitute a PE if the foreign entity has no permanent place of business in Russia. Payments for the use of software are treated as payment for imported goods (not subject to income-tax withholding) or as royalty payments (subject to income-tax withholding), depending on the specific provisions of the agreement between the provider of software and its customers. Local use of an intangible owned by the foreign company does not lead to a PE if the entity has no permanent place of business in Russia.

- Having a server or a switch located in Russia without having any other personnel in the country is unlikely to create a PE.

- Having a website located on a server in Russia that is accessible by customers in Russia is unlikely to create a PE. Having a website located on a server outside Russia that is accessible by customers in Russia is unlikely to create a PE. Having a website located on a server in Russia that is not accessible by customers in Russia but is accessible by customers in other countries is unlikely to create a PE.

- The laying of fiber optic cable and the constructing of telecommunications switching equipment, either for sale to a local company or for operation by a foreign company for a fee on behalf of a local company, generally constitute a PE. A building site forms a separate PE commencing with the beginning of work; however, many double-tax treaties override this by identifying a period of time (generally from 12 to 36 months) during which a building site does not constitute a PE.

When a foreign entity organizes a branch or representative office that constitutes a PE, it is subject to profits tax at a rate of up to 35%, property tax at a maximum rate of 2%, and other taxes, including wage taxes, expense taxes, and turnover taxes. Profits tax is applicable to the company's turnover (proceeds from the sale of goods and services, net of VAT) decreased by specified deductible expenses related to provision of goods and services. Turnover taxes consist of the road-users tax (2.5% maximum) and housing tax (1.5% maximum) applicable to a company's turnover. Trading companies apply turnover taxes to their trading margin, determined as the difference between sale proceeds and expenses incurred by the company and related to the sale of the goods.

If a PE is not created, the foreign entity is subject to withholding tax at a rate of 20%, which may be reduced by double-tax treaties. A separate VAT withholding tax also applies; double-tax treaty relief does not apply to VAT withholding tax.

Business Entities

Representative Office or Local Branch of a Foreign Company. Although it has been possible to establish a branch of a foreign legal entity since September 1991, few have been established. Representative offices are more commonly used. Although this form was intended to be used primarily for the completion of preparatory and auxiliary activities, many foreign companies conduct ongoing activities through representative offices. Representative offices and branches of foreign companies are taxed similarly.

A branch is generally subject to corporate profits tax at 35% (or 38% for intermediary activities, and 43% for banks and insurance companies) on Russian profits. Rates may be lower in some regions. Taxable profits may be calculated using either the direct method (revenues minus deductible expenses) or a notional method (25% of expenses or 20% of revenues). A branch may be non-taxable if protected by a double-tax treaty.

A branch is subject to payroll taxes at 40.5% of the gross salary fund of Russian employees and to 1% transport tax on gross salaries of expatriate staff. A branch should pay property tax at a maximum rate of 2%, unless it is protected by a double-tax treaty or (in rare cases) exempt under regional legislation. Local authorities can decrease the property tax rate and provide exemptions from the tax. If a branch conducts sales in Russia, it is subject to 20% VAT and at least 2.5% turnover taxes. If a branch does not have output VAT, input VAT is not recoverable. A branch may also be subject to a number of minor federal and local taxes.

Under a "sales below cost" rule, a branch generally cannot have a loss. If a company's sales are lower than expenses, for the purposes of VAT and turnover taxes, the company should use market prices or be prepared to prove that it cannot sell at a market price. Losses from sales of assets do not decrease the profits tax base. A foreign entity cannot carry over losses.

Locally Incorporated Subsidiary of a Foreign Company. A subsidiary is a separate legal entity and can be established with or without a local company's participation. Many foreign investors seek the participation of a local partner to leverage its local knowledge, expertise and connections when entering the market, as well as to use the local company's licenses to provide telecoms services. Russian legal entities can obtain licenses more easily than can branches and representative offices, but the procedure of state registration of a Russian company is more complicated.

A subsidiary generally has limited liability and owns its own assets and liabilities. To open an offshore hard-currency account, it must receive authorization from the Central Bank of Russia (CBR). A subsidiary is taxed as a separate entity at a maximum combined federal and local profits tax rate of 35% (38% for intermediary activities, 43% for banks and insurance companies), chargeable on worldwide income. Consolidation of separate legal entities is not permissible. These rules may be adjusted upon the redrafting of the tax code. After-tax profits can be repatriated to foreign investors through payment of non-deductible dividends, which are subject to a 15% withholding tax, unless reduced by a double-tax treaty.

Other taxes include VAT (20% on telecommunications services, payable as the difference between output VAT and input VAT), property tax (2% of the annual average book value of assets), road-users' tax (2.5% from sales of goods and services or from the margin), payroll taxes (40.5% from gross salaries of employees) and several minor taxes. Most of these taxes (e.g., property tax and payroll taxes) are profits-tax deductible, whereas minor local taxes are payable from after-tax profits.

Profits and losses are generally treated the same way for locally incorporated subsidiaries as they are for branches and representative offices. However, a subsidiary can carry forward certain losses up to five years, subject to limitations.

Joint Venture. Joint ventures may be established in the form of simple partnerships (i.e., joint-activity agreements) that are tax-transparent, or full partnerships. A simple partnership has no separate legal identity; a full partnership does.

A full partnership is taxed in the same way as other Russian legal entities (including subsidiaries of foreign companies). Companies participating in a simple partnership should choose a managing company to represent the interests of the partnership. The managing company should allocate profits and property gained as a result of joint activity and inform other participants of the simple partnership who are responsible for payments of profits and property taxes. The managing company should pay and file reports on all other taxes due.

A foreign company entering into a joint venture does not necessarily create a PE. The degree of its presence and the issue of whether it must file tax returns depend upon the activity performed by the foreign company (see "Permanent Establishment").

Local Funding Alternatives

Debt versus Equity

Debt financing generates potential repatriation opportunities through debt service payments, but the profits-tax benefit is severely limited. Interest paid to banks and for commercial supplier credits is generally deductible, but interest for fixed-asset financing is not. In certain cases, a special capital-expenditure deduction is allowed for interest on fixed-asset and intangibles financing, but this is subject to complicated limits, including a provision by which this and other special tax concessions in combination may not reduce a taxpayer's profits-tax liability by more than 50% a year.

Interest that exceeds statutory limits (currently 15% for foreign currency loans, and the CBR rate plus three points for ruble-denominated loans) is not deductible. Double-tax treaties can reduce these limits.

Interest on non-bank, inter-company loans is generally not deductible. These types of arrangements traditionally have been discouraged by exposure to VAT on the loan principal received; however, the latest VAT amendment exempts valid debt obligations from the taxable base.

In both debt and equity financing, withholding taxes apply to payment of interest or dividends, subject to reduction in withholding rates by double-tax treaties. Also, foreign exchange gains arising since January 1997 on hard-currency debts are subject to profits-tax. Losses are profits-tax-deductible.

Exchange Controls

A license must be obtained from the CBR for financing in hard currency via debt instruments extending for more than 180 days or hard-currency investments in equity by a foreign investor, since the movement of capital is involved. Carrying out the administrative requirements for the license may take several months. License-free transactions are limited in number and scope, and exchange-control issues should always be considered when entering into any commercial transaction.

Business Acquisitions and Dispositions

Capital Contributions into an Existing Local Entity

Authorized charter contributions are not subject to tax in Russia; however, if an existing Russian company issues new shares or bonds, tax on the securities issued is paid at a rate of 0.8% of the nominal value of the securities issued. If a Russian company issues securities to a foreign company for hard currency, it must obtain a license from the CBR.

There are few limitations on assets that may be contributed to charter capital of a Russian entity, and even intangible assets may be contributed; however, the value of contributed non-monetary assets, when higher than a nominal statutory limit, may require an independent appraisal.

Services cannot be contributed as charter capital to a Russian legal entity. Such transfers are subject to VAT and to profits tax. However, contributions of qualified assets by shareholders to the authorized charter capital of a Russian legal entity, whether tangible or intangible, are not subject to VAT or profits tax.

If a foreign entity with no presence in Russia contributes an intangible asset (such as a trademark, patent, software or know-how) that is treated as a license, then any royalty payment or license fee paid for the use of the asset is subject to withholding tax. The tax rate, based on a default rate of 20%, depends on tax treaties. Russian entities are subject to VAT withholding on payments made to foreign entities having no PE for intangibles consumed in Russia.

Capital contributions made by a foreign company do not influence the tax liabilities of the company receiving these investments, although it may be possible to reduce withholding rates provided by tax treaties when dividend payments, share redemptions or capital gains occur in the future.

Purchase or Sale of Shares in a Local Entity

Sellers of shares are subject to income or withholding taxes depending on their tax status. If the purchase price for shares exceeds the net book value of the local company, no mechanism exists to allow the company to step up the tax basis in the assets owned by the local company to the extent of the premium paid on the purchase of shares.

The purchase of shares of a Russian company in an amount exceeding 20% of the company's charter capital would usually require the permission of the Antimonopoly Committee (a government body that controls monopolies and regulates competition).

Purchase or Sale of Assets

A sale of assets by a local company is subject to VAT and income tax. VAT is calculated on the sales price. Taxable profit is considered to be the difference between sales price and net book value of the assets, multiplied by an inflation index. Losses from sales of assets do not decrease the taxable profit of a seller.

Acquired assets, including intangibles, are booked at their purchase price, which reflects the fair market value of the assets on the date of acquisition. The value of fixed assets is depreciated using statutory norms, and the value of intangible assets (excluding trademarks and expenses associated with the establishment of a company) is amortized during the period of their use, not to exceed 10 years. The net book value of purchased assets is subject to property tax up to 2% per annum, which is profits-tax deductible. The purchase of assets is subject to VAT, and VAT paid for assets used for the purposes of production can be offset against VAT charged to customers.

Purchase or sale of stock is not subject to VAT, although sale of stock may be subject to profits tax if it is sold with gain. Russian legislation does not provide any tax-free structuring alternatives for dispositions.

Purchase or sale of stock requires re-registration of charter documents of a local company and may require the permission of the Antimonopoly Committee. There may be other legal implications related to the change of shareholders. The purchase of stock or immovable property in hard currency by a non-resident requires a license from the CBR. The sale of interest in entities such as limited liability companies and partnerships may result in VAT and profits tax on gains.

Start-up Business Issues

Pre-operating Losses and Start-up/Construction Costs

Start-up expenses such as license fees, franchise fees and easements are capitalized and amortized as intangible assets over their useful lives. Infrastructure costs, such as network deployment or construction costs, are capitalized as tangible assets and depreciated according to statutory asset lives. Depreciation may not begin until an asset has been placed in service. Infrastructure costs in international areas, such as satellites or undersea cable, are subject to the same profits-tax rules as Russian start-up and construction costs when they are attributable to activities of a foreign company in Russia.

Purchases of or lease payments for movable property located in Russia are subject to VAT. After it is paid, input VAT is offset by a foreign company against its output VAT if the company is registered with the tax authorities and the costs of property acquisition are deductible or amortizable for profits-tax purposes. If the current input VAT exceeds the output, the excess carries forward to future periods. Refunds are difficult to obtain.

Costs relating to immovable property in Russia are subject to VAT, regardless of where they are incurred. For example, architectural or engineering design services provided entirely outside Russia are subject to Russian VAT. VAT associated with the construction or installation of an asset is accounted as part of the cost of the asset and, as such, does not qualify as creditable input VAT. It can be recovered only as part of the deductible depreciation.

Customs Duties and VAT

Import duties and customs tariffs vary, depending on the type of asset. Typically, import tariffs for telecommunications equipment range from 0% to 5%.

In-kind charter capital contributions to Russian companies with foreign investment may qualify for an exemption from customs duties and VAT. The exemption is granted in respect of non-excisable fixed assets (e.g., telecommunications equipment) that are to be used for the purposes of production (e.g., rendering telecommunications services) and imported within a period set by charter. The rules for granting such an exemption were tightened recently.

A temporary import regime is also available to accredited representative offices of qualified foreign entities that import assets for non-production use. Special rules apply to the importation of automobiles. Customs VAT paid on assets usable for production is recoverable against output VAT after the equipment has been accounted for by the recipient.

Loss Carryovers

Foreign companies with branch losses are not able to carry forward or carry back such losses to other taxable periods. Losses incurred by Russian companies in a reporting year may be carried forward in equal parts for the succeeding five years, subject to certain restrictions. For instance, this deduction together with other incentives must not lower the profits-tax liability by more than 50%. Losses may not be carried back to prior tax years. No restrictions exist on the use of losses after a change of ownership or business activity of a company.

Operating Considerations

Corporate Income Taxes

When federal and local rates are taken into account, a company's profits tax may result in a maximum current rate of 35%, or higher in certain cases.

Capital Gains Taxes

Capital gains of a Russian legal entity are taxed at the same rate as other types of business income, generally at a combined maximum federal and local profits tax rate of 35%, or higher for certain types of income.

Capital gains of a foreign entity having a PE are also subject to taxation at the normal profits tax rate. Capital gains not associated with a PE are subject to withholding tax. The default withholding rate is 20%, which can be reduced by double-tax treaties.

Tax Holidays and Exemptions

A Russian company with foreign investment enjoys access to several tax advantages, including, in certain circumstances, the elimination of VAT and customs duties on imported in-kind contributions for the authorized charter fund. Other exemptions may be available in local jurisdictions.

Companies can use capital investment allowances and research and development expenditures to reduce the taxable base for profits tax. However, a company is limited in its use of these types of incentives. It may not use them to reduce its tax liability by more than 50%; research and development expenditures may not reduce the tax base by more than 10%. Some tax concessions previously granted have been repealed or abolished.

Depreciation/Cost-Recovery Conventions/Accelerated Deductions

Russia permits eventual recovery of costs for a company's assets. Depreciation deductions are calculated on the basis of annual statutory asset lives that are published in a detailed register (Regulation No.1072 of October 22, 1990). In general, asset lives for Russian profits-tax purposes are longer than asset lives in other tax systems, with the straight-line method of cost recovery applicable. The depreciation rates for telecommunications equipment vary from 3.3% (for some types of automatic exchanges) to 20% (on telephone equipment for public use), the most commonly applicable rate being 8%.

Purchased software is treated as an intangible asset and depreciated during its useful life (not exceeding 10 years). There are no special rules for software embedded in telecommunications equipment and, accordingly, such software can be depreciated separately from equipment.

Deductibility is limited for certain expenses, including advertising, business trips, entertainment, insurance, training and other expenses. Limits are set in the form of statutory norms or percentages of a company's revenue. The limits on deductions were expected to be liberalized in the new tax code.

Russian legislation distinguishes research and development costs of a current nature from those of an investment nature, the latter being distinguished by the acquisition of licenses guaranteeing the right to use the results of the research. Current research and development costs are included in the costs of production directly, whereas investment research and development costs may qualify for a profits-tax deduction (which cannot exceed 10% of taxable profit).

Transfer Pricing Rules

There are no sophisticated transfer pricing rules. The tax authorities apply a sales-below/at-cost rule to trigger revaluation of the consideration between related parties. In general, when parties to a transaction are covering their costs and earning a profit, the consideration of a transaction is not challenged.

Transfers of Patents, Trademarks and Software

Lump-sum payments for patents and software are not deductible, but they are capitalized and depreciated as intangible assets. Periodic payments for royalties or licensing fees are deductible against profits tax as long as relevant agreements are properly worded and registered. Only payments for certain Russian-registered patents and certain royalties are exempt from VAT. A company making these types of payments to a foreign company having no presence in Russia must withhold income tax and VAT at source. The withholding income tax rate, based on a default rate of 20%, depends on the provisions of double-tax treaties. VAT withholding is not influenced by double-tax treaties.

The provision of rights to use technology during a certain period of time for a royalty fee can be treated either as a sale of an intangible or as a license agreement. Such a right may be granted by a foreign company to a Russian company and vice versa without restrictions, if:

- The country where the foreign company is incorporated does not impose any restriction (or if there is a relevant international agreement).

- The license or sale agreement is properly worded and registered with the Russian patent authorities.

Another difference in tax consequences of sales versus licenses is in the applicability of property tax. An intangible purchased by a Russian company is subject to property tax of up to 2% per annum, whereas royalty fees do not increase a user's taxable base.

Service Fees

Service fees are deductible for profits-tax purposes, subject to certain restrictions on management, advertising, training, entertainment, business-trip expenses and insurance. Services performed entirely outside Russia are not subject to withholding tax on income in Russia, provided proper documentation exists. Recent VAT legislation introduced new sourcing rules for service provision. If the economic activity of the service recipient is in Russia, the service will be subject to VAT, regardless of where the service is rendered.

Value-Added Tax, Sales Tax and/or Other Pertinent Taxes

VAT is assessed at 20% on the proceeds of the sale of goods and the provision of services. Russian VAT law does not specifically determine a place of provision of telecommunications services, but these may be covered by one or more of the following conditions:

- Telecommunications services are considered to be provided at the place of location of immovable property when such services relate to the construction of telecommunications lines and other equipment.

- Telecommunications services are considered to be provided at the place of actual provision of services when the services are connected with immovable property (e.g., repair of telecommunications equipment).

- In all other cases, telecommunications services are considered to be provided at the place of economic activity of the supplier of services.

Therefore, the provision of services associated with both incoming and outgoing traffic is generally subject to Russian VAT. Exported telecommunications services, defined by the VAT law as international telecommunications services partially provided outside of the Commonwealth of Independent States (CIS), are exempt from Russian VAT. A company's revenue from international telecommunications services that is subject to VAT should be calculated as total revenue from these services, decreased by amounts of payments to foreign telecommunications companies involved in the provision of services. In practice, telecommunications companies face difficulties in applying the allowance.

No specific provisions exist regarding Internet services. It is likely, therefore, that the principles applying to other telecommunications services will also apply to Internet services, and that VAT will apply to payments for Internet services when the supplier has its place of economic activity in Russia. Internet telephony services would likely be taxed on the same basis as regular telephony. Russian legislation does not treat Internet access as telephony.

Local and Provincial Taxes

Various taxes are charged by local communities, with little uniformity. These taxes include:

- A turnover tax, the rate of which is established locally. For example, the aggregate rate of turnover taxes in Moscow, including the federal road users' tax, is 4% from the revenue of sale of goods or from the gross amount of service fees received by a taxpayer, less VAT.

- Property tax of up to 2% of the net book value of assets. The property tax rate is determined locally but capped by federal legislation.

- Advertising tax of up to 5% of advertising expenses.

Usually, other local taxes do not create a material burden for taxpayers. For telecommunications companies, many local taxes are subject to local exemption.

For Additional Information, Contact:

Lioudmila Mamet
Tax Partner
and
Gennady Kamyshnikov
Tax Manager
and
Richard Adams
Senior Audit Manager
5 Nikitskiy Pereulok, 6th Floor
Moscow, 103009
Russia
Telephone: 7 (503) 232 5511
Fax: 7 (503) 232 5522
E-mail: Lioudmila_Mamet@RU.Coopers.com
        Gennady_Kamyshnikov@RU.Coopers.com
        Richard_Adams@RU.Coopers.com

Slovakia

Telecommunications Tax Profile
by Miroslav Mrázik
Tax Advisor, Bratislava
and Viera Kučerová
Senior Tax Consultant, Bratislava

Overview of the Telecommunications Market

Historical Background

Since the separation of the Slovak Republic from the Czech Republic in 1993, the Ministry of Transport, Post and Telecommunications has been responsible for development of the telecommunications sector. In 1993 the government agreed to bring telecommunications in line with European Union (EU) guidelines for liberalization, with the intent of eventually establishing Slovak Telecom, the state-owned monopoly, as an independent corporation. In accordance with the Association Agreement that Slovakia signed with the EU, full liberalization of the telecommunications market is expected by the end of 2003.

Fixed-line telecommunications services are provided by Slovak Telecom. Slovak Telecom provides telephone services as well as telex, telegraph, leased circuits and data networks. Slovak Telecom is a joint venture partner in EuroTel a.s., the operator of Nordic mobile telephone (NMT)-450 and global system for mobile communications (GSM)-900 telephony and packet-switched data networks. A second license to operate a GSM-900 network in the Slovak Republic was awarded to Globtel a.s.

(a consortium in which France Telecom Mobiles International holds a 35% share).

Current Status

Telecommunications revenues are growing dramatically in Slovakia. In 1996 Slovak Telecom and EuroTel together generated SK14.826 billion in revenue, compared with SK11.045 billion in revenue in 1995 and SK9.297 billion in 1994. Slovak Telecom has gradually improved its network technology by introducing digital transmission, adding access lines and making other key upgrades. Slovak Telecom has installed more than 207 kilometers of fiber optic cable and has deployed synchronous digital hierarchy (SDH) switching technology. Approximately 23 main stations are in place for every 100 inhabitants.

Basic voice service will remain the monopoly of Slovak Telecom until 2003. Liberalization of other telecommunications services commenced in 1996. Customer premise equipment supply and installation is provided by a number of companies.

Mobile communications subscribers using the NMT standard totaled 80,000, and GSM users numbered 60,000 as of October 31, 1997.

Current Liberalization Status

In the World Trade Organization (WTO) negotiations of February 1997, Slovakia committed to full liberalization of its telecommunications markets by January 1, 2003. Since January 1, 1998, Slovakia has allowed business entities to create their own telecommunications infrastructures and use them for commercial purposes. Business entities are also allowed to lease their telecommunications infrastructures for voice telephony

purposes. The leasing of telecommunications infrastructures is permitted only for closed-user-group services that have no possibility of connecting with Slovak Telecom's network.

The liberalization of construction and commercial use of alternative telecommunications networks was enabled by Government Decree No. 813, dated November 1997. At the time of publication, the Ministry of Transport, Post and Telecommunications was preparing a new version of the Telecommunications Act.

Type of Service	Degree of Liberalization	Key Legislation	Date of Actual or Expected Liberalization
Local, Long Distance and International	Monopoly	Telecommunications Act 110/1964	2003
Cellular	Duopoly		
Paging	Deregulated		
Value-added	Deregulated		

Competitive Environment

Type of Service	Entire Market		Top Two Players		
	Market Size (1996)	Number of Players	Names	Annual Revenue (1996)	Ownership
Local, Long Distance and International	US$330 million (estimate)	1	Slovak Telecom	US$330 million (estimate)	Government
Cellular*	US$40 million	2	EuroTel	Not available*	Slovak Telecom, Atlantic West BV
			Globtel	Not available*	France Telecom Mobiles International and others
Paging	**	1	Slovak Telecom	**	Government
Value-added	US$30 million	Not available			

Sources: Datapro, TREND Top 100.
* Globtel and EuroTel began GSM operations at the beginning of 1997.
** Included in local, long distance and international revenues.

Licensing Requirements

The Ministry of Transport, Post and Telecommunications regulates the telecoms industry, issues licenses for non-basic lines and services, and allocates frequencies from the spectrum. To achieve a standardized telecommunications environment comparable to others' in the EU, subsequent amendments to the Telecommunications Act are required, particularly regarding the establishment of a standard licensing system. Amendments are still being negotiated in the Parliament. The provision of telecommunications equipment requires certification from the Telecommunications Authority.

Potential for Foreign Ownerships/Relationships

Under legislation designed to secure the state's interest in the privatization process, Slovak Telecom was included within the category of strategically important companies. Thus, the first stage of privatization for the government monopoly will be the transformation of Slovak Telecom into a joint-stock company with 100% property participation of the state. In 1996 an "Analysis of the Possibilities of Foreign Capital Entry to Slovak Telecom" was submitted to a conference of economy ministers.

Potential for Upcoming Liberalization/Investment Opportunities

The Slovak Republic will gradually liberalize the telecoms industry and encourage open competition in the service market. The potential privatization of Slovak Telecom presents the most immediate opportunity for investment by a foreign company.

Forms of Doing Business

Permanent Establishment

In general, a foreign telecommunications company with no formal presence in Slovakia is deemed to have a permanent establishment (PE) in Slovakia if its employees or persons operating on its behalf provide services in Slovakia for more than six months (regardless of the term of the fiscal year). Duration for a PE shall be calculated in calendar days of the foreign company's employees' presence in Slovakia, but it shall be discontinued if activity is interrupted for more than 12 successive calendar months.

Telecommunications services can cover a broad range of activities, which may or may not constitute a PE, as the following examples demonstrate:

- The provision of long distance telephone services by a foreign company to local customers without any local presence or advertising does not create a PE.

- The licensing of technology and know-how by a foreign company to a Slovak company does not create a PE.

- The provision of technical assistance and technological services by a foreign company to a Slovak company in exchange for service fees, including operator services and/or network management services, are deemed to be a PE when the total time spent in Slovakia by employees or other persons working on behalf of the foreign company exceeds six months.

- The leasing of telecommunications equipment by a foreign company to a Slovak company without provision of any supporting activities or services does not constitute a PE.

- The provision of call reorganization/turnaround services constitutes a PE if a local distributor working on behalf of a foreign company performs its activities in Slovakia for more than six months. However, no PE is created under these circumstances if the local distributor is independent and is acting in the ordinary course of its business.

- The provision of Internet access services constitutes a PE in Slovakia if personnel and/or equipment are located in Slovakia.

- A server or a switch of a foreign company located in Slovakia constitutes a PE even if the foreign company has no personnel in Slovakia.

- A website of a foreign company on a server located in Slovakia does not constitute a PE.

- A website located on a server outside Slovakia but accessible by customers in Slovakia does not constitute a PE.

- A website located on a server in Slovakia that is not accessible by customers in Slovakia generally is not deemed to be a PE.

- The laying of fiber optic cable and the construction of telecommunications switching equipment by a foreign telecommunications company creates a PE if the construction and installation work last for more than six months. This period can be extended by a tax treaty.

- A PE exists if telecommunications equipment is constructed over a period of more than six months in Slovakia and is either (a) sold to a local company or (b) operated by a foreign telecommunications company for a local company in exchange for a fee.

When the provision of services does not create a PE, payments to a foreign entity for services provided in the Slovak Republic may be subject to withholding tax. When a PE is created, the company must register with tax authorities in Slovakia for tax purposes and must submit a tax return. A PE of a foreign entity is taxed as a branch.

Business Entities

Foreign entities in Slovakia can open a branch office, establish a subsidiary with 100% or less participation of foreign capital (e.g., a limited liability company or a joint-stock company) or participate in an existing Slovak legal entity (e.g., an equity joint venture). To conduct business in Slovakia, foreign entities must register in accordance with the Slovak Commercial Code.

Local Branch of a Foreign Company. A branch is liable for corporate income tax at the rate of 40% on its taxable profits from Slovak sources. If there is no income declared in the accounts, the tax authorities can use a special taxation method to determine the taxable profit of the branch. A percentage of turnover/sales made by the foreign entity that is attributable to the branch is the method commonly used.

When registering a branch, no minimum capital injection is required. A branch can also be registered for Slovak VAT purposes. In accordance with the Commercial Code, a registered branch must use double-entry accounting.

Locally Incorporated Subsidiary of a Foreign Company. As previously noted, a locally incorporated subsidiary of a foreign company can take the form of a limited liability company or a joint-stock company. Once the company is incorporated, it is considered to be a Slovak tax resident and is taxable on its worldwide income. Slovak tax residents are subject to corporate income tax at a rate of 40%, which is calculated on their taxable profits. The taxable base of a Slovak company is determined as the difference between its taxable income and the expenses incurred to achieve, maintain and sustain its taxable income.

Joint Venture. The term "joint venture" is commonly used to describe the participation of foreign entities in an existing Slovak legal entity. Generally, a joint venture takes the form of a limited liability company or joint-stock company. Incorporated joint ventures are taxed at the corporate tax rate of 40%.

Unincorporated joint ventures can be created on the basis of an agreement for carrying out activities in pursuit of a common purpose. An unincorporated joint venture is not a legal entity, and all liabilities and rights of the joint venture are borne by its founders. An unincorporated joint venture is not required to file a tax return. Income generated by the joint venture is shared between the participants, who then include the proceeds as income on their own tax returns. If the activities of an unincorporated joint venture are sufficient to constitute a PE, then a foreign participant in the joint venture is deemed to have a PE.

If the foreign participant in a joint venture provides business, technical or other consultancy services, management and intermediary activities, or similar services in Slovakia, or has employees who spend more than six months in Slovakia, a PE of any foreign participant could arise (see the discussion above), irrespective of whether the joint venture activities in and of themselves would have caused the foreign participant to have a PE.

Local Funding Alternatives

Debt versus Equity

According to Slovak tax legislation, both interest and dividends are subject to withholding tax. Interest paid to entities that are not resident or do not have a PE in Slovakia is subject to withholding tax at a rate of 25% of the gross sum of the interest payment. This rate may be reduced by a tax treaty. No withholding tax is due when interest is paid on debt that is incurred locally.

The deductibility of interest paid on a financial loan or a borrowing is limited when the loan or borrowing is provided by a company that is directly or indirectly participating in the management, control or assets of the recipient company. In accordance with the thin capitalization rules, when a loan exceeds four times (six times for bank loans) the equity of the recipient company, the interest on the excess is not deductible for tax purposes. When the loan is provided by a non-related company, the full amount of interest is tax-deductible. Unrealized exchange gains or losses should not be considered when calculating the taxable profits.

Dividends are subject to withholding tax at a rate of 15% of the gross sum of dividends, regardless of whether the recipient of the dividend is a foreign entity or a local company. This rate can be reduced by a tax treaty. Dividends are paid out of the profit after tax and are, therefore, not deductible for tax purposes.

Exchange Controls

As stipulated by the Slovak Foreign Exchange Act, there are foreign exchange limitations regarding the provision of financial loans, purchasing and selling of foreign currency and acquisition of real estate by a foreign company in Slovakia. When a Slovak entity (other than a bank) provides a financial loan to a foreign entity or vice versa, a foreign exchange permit must be obtained from the National Bank of Slovakia. A foreign exchange permit is not required when a Slovak entity provides a financial loan payable within five or more years to a foreign entity seated in an OECD-member state or if a loan is provided for settlement of goods or services sent to that foreign entity. A foreign exchange permit is also not required if a foreign entity provides a financial loan payable within three or more years to a Slovak entity or if a foreign entity seated in an OECD-member state provides a loan to a Slovak entity for settlement of goods and services received from that foreign entity.

There are also foreign exchange regulations stipulated in the Foreign Exchange Act under which only banks and entities with foreign exchange licenses are entitled to purchase and sell foreign currency.

A foreign entity is not generally allowed to purchase real estate in Slovakia.

Business Acquisitions and Dispositions

Capital Contributions into an Existing Local Entity

A capital contribution into a Slovak entity would not be subject to any tax. There are no limits to the value of intangibles that a foreign entity can contribute into an existing Slovak entity. Intangibles contributed by the shareholders to the registered capital of a company cannot be depreciated if the intangibles were acquired without consideration. Capital contributions to a Slovak entity have no tax consequences to existing shareholders at the time the capital contributions take place.

Purchase or Sale of Shares in a Local Entity

When a Slovak individual sells shares in a joint-stock company to a foreign company, the proceeds generated will not be taxable in Slovakia if the time between the acquisition and the sale of the shares by Slovak individuals exceeds one year. If the period between the acquisition and the sale of the shares is less than one year, the proceeds from the sale of shares in a joint-stock company should be included in the taxable base of the Slovak individual. Proceeds from the sale of shares in a limited liability company or any other kind of commercial company are not taxable in Slovakia for individuals if the time between the acquisition and the sale of the shares exceeds five years.

When shares are sold by a Slovak company to a foreign company, the proceeds from the sale of the shares are considered to be part of the taxable income of the Slovak company, irrespective of the period of ownership. If shares are sold between two foreign companies, no Slovak tax is imposed. The same tax treatments apply in a minority sale of shares. There are no provisions in Slovakia that affect the tax basis of assets on a share purchase.

Purchase or Sale of Assets

If a Slovak company sells an asset, the capital gain from the sale is included in the tax base of the company and is taxed at a 40% corporate income tax rate. If the tax net book value is higher than the selling price of the asset, the tax net book value is a tax-deductible cost for the company up to the amount of the proceeds of the sale.

When a foreign company purchases the assets of a Slovak company and the purchase price exceeds the net book value of the assets of the Slovak company, the purchase price can be allocated to the assets acquired based on their fair market value. Any excess purchase price can create goodwill, which can be depreciated over 15 years. There are no tax-free alternatives available for dispositions.

When a company acquires an interest in a partnership from another company, the vendor company is treated as disposing of its interest in the assets of the partnership with the purchasing company acquiring an interest in the assets of the partnership. There is no step-up in the basis of the partnership assets for tax-depreciation purposes. The assets continue to be held by the partnership at the original tax basis, and attract tax depreciation on that amount. The incoming partner's cost of acquisition will be deductible only against a future disposal of the partnership interest.

Start-up Business Issues

Pre-operating Losses and Start-up/ Construction Costs

Business investigation costs, including license and franchise fees, incurred by an existing company to derive taxable income are tax-deductible. License and franchise fees that exceed SK20,000 and license and franchise rights that last more than one year are considered intangible assets and are subject to depreciation. Patents are depreciated over 15 years and software is depreciated over four years. Other intangible assets are depreciated over eight years.

Interest on loans obtained during construction should be capitalized. After construction is completed, interest incurred during construction is deductible as part of the cost of the asset being constructed. If the tangible assets are constructed or manufactured by the company itself, all direct or indirect costs relating to the construction of the assets are capitalized and depreciated. Intangibles manufactured by the company itself may be depreciated if they are used for trade purposes.

When pre-operating costs are incurred by a foreign company outside Slovakia, these costs can be deducted or amortized by the local company only if the foreign company re-charges them to the local company and if the pre-operating costs are incurred to derive taxable income for the Slovak company.

If the pre-operating costs relate to the intangible assets contributed by a foreign founder to a local company, such costs and intangible assets cannot be depreciated by the Slovak company. If the intangible assets are purchased from a foreign company by a Slovak company, the withholding tax applicable on royalties will apply when the Slovak company pays for the assets.

A foreign company that incurs local costs that are subject to VAT cannot recover such VAT paid unless the foreign company is registered for VAT purposes in Slovakia. A VAT refund is available only for registered VAT payers when certain conditions are met. The only way to recover the VAT paid by a foreign company is to re-charge the costs, including VAT, to a Slovak company.

A Slovak company is entitled to a refund of VAT on payments for the purchase of pre-operating tangible and intangible assets and stock that are acquired within 12 months prior to the registration of the Slovak company as a VAT payer. This does not apply to the purchase of cars. The refund is available in the first taxable period after registration. When assets or stock have been depreciated or otherwise written down to a book value below the purchase price, the VAT refund is available only by reference to the net book value of the assets or stock.

If the amount of the VAT refund exceeds the VAT received from customers, Slovakia will refund the VAT within 30 days after the submission of a VAT return.

Customs Duties and VAT

Telecommunications equipment imported into Slovakia is subject to customs duty and VAT. The average customs duty rate on imported telecommunications equipment is 15%. The VAT rate is 23%.

Under certain conditions, telecommunications equipment imported as a non-monetary contribution by a foreign founder for the production activities of a Slovak company may be exempted from customs duty and VAT. This exemption applies to telecommunications equipment imported before December 31, 1999.

The VAT paid on imported telecommunications equipment can be refunded if the importer is registered for VAT purposes in Slovakia. There is no special VAT treatment for Internet telephony.

Loss Carryovers

Under Slovak law, losses may be carried forward and offset against taxable profit during five tax periods immediately following the tax period in which the loss was incurred. The loss shall be carried forward in five equal portions. If another loss is incurred during this five-year period, this loss cannot be offset against the taxable profit.

A loss incurred in the previous tax period can be deducted only to the extent it exceeds the reserve fund, a legally required non-distributable accounting reserve that is created out of the company's net profit and which equals a minimum of 10% of the share capital of a limited liability company or 20% of the share capital of a joint-stock company.

The possibility of carrying forward losses does not apply to state companies and entities with majority shareholding by the state. There is no specific legislation in Slovakia that deals with the restriction of loss carryforwards when there is a change in ownership of a company. Generally, it is understood that a change of ownership of a company that incurred a tax loss should not influence its deductibility. The same applies for a change in the activity of a company. When losses are incurred by a state company or by entities with majority state shareholding, these cannot be deducted even if the entity was privatized.

Operating Considerations

Corporate Income Taxes

The corporate income tax rate in Slovakia is 40%. Taxable income is the accounting profit adjusted for tax purposes. Legal entities incorporated in Slovakia are liable for taxation on their worldwide income. Legal entities not incorporated in Slovakia are taxed only on their Slovak-sourced income.

Withholding tax is imposed on interest, dividends and royalties paid to non-residents. The rate of withholding tax on Slovak-sourced income is generally 25% of the gross amount of the royalty. This rate may be reduced by a tax treaty.

Capital Gains Taxes

There are no special rules for the treatment of capital gains. Capital gains and losses are subject to corporate income tax in the same way as are all other income and expenses.

Tax Holidays and Exemptions

No special tax incentives exist for telecommunications businesses in Slovakia, and none are expected.

Depreciation/Cost-Recovery Conventions/Accelerated Deductions

Depreciation is an allowable deduction over the useful life of an asset. Both the straight-line and reducing-balance methods are acceptable for tax purposes, and the taxpayer may elect which method to use. Fixed assets are classified as assets with a cost of more than SK10,000 and with useful lives exceeding one year. Intangible assets are classified as industrial know-how and similar rights, software, and technical or other exploitable knowledge with a cost of more than SK20,000 and with useful lives exceeding one year.

Fixed assets and intangible assets are divided into five groups for tax-depreciation purposes. The depreciation groups, depreciation periods and examples of assets are shown in the table at the top of page 2–161.

Depreciation Group	Depreciation Period	Type of Assets
1	4 years	Computers, office equipment, TV cameras, photocopiers, printers, passenger and light-commercial cars, buses, computer software and know-how, telephone equipment, facsimile transmission equipment and trucks.
2	8 years	Trailers, semi-trailers, aircraft and equipment, fixtures and fittings, furniture and intangible assets excluding patents and software, fixed network telephones.
3	15 years	Patents, most power plants and devices, energy-generating equipment.
4	30 years	Buildings constructed of wood or light materials.
5	40 years	All other buildings.

Expenditures for telecommunications networks are likely to fall mainly in the first two groups. Depreciation may be on a straight-line or a reducing-balance basis, as shown below.

Depreciation Group	Depreciation Rates for the Straight-Line Method	
	First Year	Subsequent Years
1	14.2%	28.6%
2	6.2%	13.4%
3	3.4%	6.9%
4	1.4%	3.4%
5	1.5%	2.5%

Depreciation Group	Coefficient for the Reducing-Balance Method	
	First Year	Subsequent Years
1	4	5
2	8	9
3	15	16
4	30	31
5	40	41

The reducing-balance method of depreciation is calculated as follows:

$$\text{In the first year, depreciation} = \frac{\text{purchase price}}{\text{first-year coefficient}}$$

$$\text{In subsequent years, depreciation} = \frac{2 \times \text{tax net book value}}{\text{current year's coefficient} - \text{number of years the asset has already been depreciated}}$$

Software. Purchased software is treated as an intangible asset if its value is more than SK20,000 and its useful life is more than one year. In such a case, it will be classified as a Depreciation Group 1 purchase, and may be depreciated over four years.

If software (other than "off the shelf" software) is purchased from a foreign company, 25% tax must be withheld from the payment to the foreign company. Tax treaties may reduce the rate of withholding tax. When "off the shelf" software is purchased from a foreign entity, it is treated as a good, and VAT and customs duty apply. In such cases, withholding tax does not apply.

Research and Development Costs. There is no special treatment of research and development costs in Slovak tax legislation. Generally, the tax treatment follows the accounting standards under which the research and development costs are capitalized and, in most cases, depreciated over five years. If a patent is a result of research and development, it is classified in Depreciation Group 3, and depreciated over 15 years.

Marketing and Advertising Costs. Investors can deduct marketing and advertising expenses (i.e., newspaper advertising, posters, billboards, television and radio) that relate to the promotion of the taxpayer's activity in full. Other advertising costs can be deducted up to 1% of the taxable profit per annum. State-owned companies, companies whose only member or shareholder is in Slovakia, and investment funds or investment companies may deduct advertising costs up to 3% of their taxable profit per annum.

Transfer Pricing Rules

Transactions between related parties must be carried out at arm's length. If contracted prices between individuals or legal entities differ from market prices and the difference cannot be satisfactorily documented, the tax authorities will use the market prices. The market value provisions of the Income Tax Act apply if the same individuals or legal entities participate, directly or indirectly, in the management, control or ownership of companies that are contracting with each other.

Transfers of Patents, Trademarks and Software

Slovakia imposes no restrictions on the licensing of technology to a local company for royalty fees. Unless royalty payments and software licensing fees are of a capital nature, they are deductible. Whether a contract constitutes a sale or a license is determined by the terms of the contract. It is necessary to determine whether the agreed-to terms are for the right to use the technology, in which case the contract would be characterized as a license, or for a transfer of the entire right, in which case the contract would be characterized as a sale.

Payments made to a foreign telecommunications company for the licensing of technology, know-how or any economically usable knowledge or for the provision of technical assistance and technological service would be treated as royalties, and withholding tax would be imposed. In addition, leasing fees paid for telecommunications equipment would also be subject to withholding tax.

Service Fees

Payments to foreign individuals or companies for services that are provided in Slovakia are subject to withholding tax. The rate of withholding tax on Slovak-sourced income is generally 25%. However, this rate may be reduced by a tax treaty.

As discussed previously, the provision of services in Slovakia can lead to the creation of a PE. Once the PE has been registered, it becomes subject to corporate income tax. When services of the PE are provided outside Slovakia, the payments are not subject to withholding tax. The tax authorities may try to have some of these activities classified as the provision of know-how. When a company provides know-how to another company, it does not matter where the know-how is provided; withholding tax must be deducted.

Value-Added Tax, Sales Tax and/or Other Pertinent Taxes

A VAT rate of 23% is applied to telecommunications services. Exportation services and transfers of rights to foreign countries are VAT-exempt, meaning that the registered VAT payer shall not charge output VAT.

Reverse-charge mechanisms do not apply in Slovakia. Only VAT-registered payers in Slovakia are entitled to deduct input VAT.

In Slovak tax legislation, there is no special treatment for the provision of Internet access. The provision of Internet access is considered to be a service and, if it is provided within Slovakia by the registered VAT payer to a foreign company, VAT must be charged. If it is provided outside Slovakia, it is considered an exportation of services, which is VAT-exempt. The same rules apply to the provision of Internet telephone services.

Local and Provincial Taxes

Real Estate Tax. Real estate tax is paid by the owners of land and buildings at rates ranging from 4% to 20% per annum on the value of the real estate.

Road Tax. Road tax is charged on motor vehicles, wheeled tractors and trailers and semi-trailers when they are registered and used for business purposes. There are various exceptions. The tax is paid by the owner of the vehicle as recorded in the registration document. The amount ranges from SK1,200 to SK54,000 per annum for cars and trucks, depending on the engine size of the vehicle.

For Additional Information, Contact:

Miroslav Mrázik
Registered Tax Advisor
and
Viera Kučerová
Senior Tax Consultant
Hviezdoslavovo nám. 20
815 32 Bratislava
Slovak Republic
Telephone: 421 (7) 531 41 01
Fax: 421 (7) 531 41 02

Spain

Telecommunications Tax Profile
by Carmen García de Andrés
Tax Director, Madrid

Overview of the Telecommunications Market

Historical Background

The Telecommunications Law of 1987 established guidelines for liberalization, authorizing competition in the market for terminal equipment and value-added network services. Telecommunications services are classified as carrier (leased and packet-switched circuits), fixed telephone (including local, long distance and international), value-added and cellular. All telecommunications services in Spain were traditionally provided by Telefónica de España, S.A. (Telefónica), which is a private company.

In 1992 the National Plan for Telecommunications provided goals for infrastructure enhancement and competition. In 1993 carrier services were opened to competition. In 1994 pay telephone services were partially liberalized, and Airtel Móvil, S.A., was granted a license to establish a global system for mobile communications (GSM) digital service in competition with Telefónica. In 1995 Telefónica's monopoly on leased circuits ended when Retevisión, which distributes television signals for TV companies in Spain, was granted a license. In June 1996 the Spanish government adopted a royal decree that established the framework for a second competitor in basic telephony and for third-party access to the public network. It also established the Telecommunications Market Commission, an independent regulatory body, to ensure that competitive rules are applied fairly.

In 1997 a consortium made up of STET Italy, Grupo Endesa and Banco Central Hispano (BCH) acquired a majority percentage of Retevisión, which was granted a license to establish a global operation providing fixed telephony, data transmission and value-added services in competition with Telefónica.

Current Status

Basic telephony (local, long distance, international voice and value-added services) has been a duopoly, but starting in 1998, cable TV operators can also provide local telephony services. Other operators were to gain entry December 1, 1998, in accordance with the timetable accepted for Spain by the European Union (EU). Some restrictions on competition are in effect for leased circuits and packet-switched services. Competition in e-mail and other services is fully open.

Telefónica Servicios Móviles, S.A., has long operated its analog mobile service throughout Spain. Mobile telephony revenues increased sharply in 1995, when both Telefónica and Airtel Móvil began service. Airtel Móvil consortium members include leading Spanish banks, utilities, British Telecom (BT) and AirTouch Communications. Paging services are provided by Telefónica's subsidiary and two other service providers.

Current Liberalization Status

In the World Trade Organization (WTO) negotiations in February 1997, Spain committed to full liberalization and adherence to a common set of regulatory principles as of January 1, 1998. In fact, Spain will not fully liberalize the sector until the end of 1998.

Type of Service	Degree of Liberalization	Key Legislation	Date of Actual or Expected Liberalization	Comments
Local	Fully liberalized	Telecommunications Law 1997	1998	Licenses for local cable operators granted in 1997
Long Distance	Duopoly	Telecommunications Law 1997	1998	Second operator authorized from January 1, 1998
International	Duopoly	Telecommunications Law 1997	1998	Second operator authorized from January 1, 1998
Cellular	One licensed analog service; duopoly for digital GSM	Telecommunications Law 1997	1998	Three new licenses for DCS-1800 to be granted by end of 1998
Paging	Deregulated	Telecommunications Law 1987	1987	
Value-added	Fully liberalized, deregulated	Telecommunications Law 1987	1987	

Competitive Environment

The Spanish market for telecommunications services came to nearly US$12.7 billion in 1996, representing 13% growth over revenues in the previous year; 72% of the total was from basic telephony, 17% was from mobile telephony (which experienced remarkable growth, with penetration increasing from 2.5% in 1995 to 7.4% at the end of 1996, when Airtel entered the market), and 11% was generated by pay TV and data services (including X.25, frame relay, Internet services and leased lines).

| Type of Service | Entire Market | | Top Two Players | | |
	Market Size (1996)	Number of Players	Names	Annual Revenue (1996)	Ownership
Local and Long Distance	Ptas1.223 trillion	2	Telefónica	Ptas1.223 trillion	Banco Bilbao Vizcaya (BBV), Argentaria, Banco Santander, others
			Retevisión	Launching its operation	STET Italy, Grupo Endesa, BCH, Spanish government, others
International	Ptas136.1 billion	2	Telefónica	Ptas136.1 billion	BBV, Argentaria, Banco Santander, others
			Retevisión	Launching its operation	STET, Grupo Endesa, BCH, Spanish government, others
Cellular	Ptas366 billion*	2	Telefónica Móviles	Ptas256.4 billion*	Telefónica
			Airtel Móvil	Ptas110 billion**	AirTouch, British Telecom, BCH, Unión Fenosa, others
Paging	Not available	3 national, 27 regional	MensaTel	Not available	Telefónica, CERSA
			Radiobip	Not available	
Value-added	Ptas43 billion	More than 10	Internet: Servicom, CompuServe, Telefónica	Not available	
			Database access: BT, EFE (Agency Press), IBM		
			Fax: Cable & Wireless, Global One, Sprint		

Sources: Communications Companies Analysis report, August 1997; Communication Market Analysis, December 1997; Datapro, July 1997

* Estimates for 1997.

** Actual revenues for 1997.

Licensing Requirements

The Ministry of Public Works and Transport is responsible for granting concessions (through public tenders), authorizations and licenses. Each of the telecommunications industry segments has its own specific regulations and licensing procedures. Although licenses are usually nationwide, for local fixed telephony services rendered by cable operators, one license is granted per territorial zone.

A licensee must be a company resident in Spain. In some cases, telecommunications companies must provide a minimum amount of capital. For example, the Cable Telecommunications Act requires the licensee to be a Spanish limited company (sociedad anónima, or S.A.) with a minimum share capital of 100 million pesetas (Ptas) to 1 billion Ptas, depending on the surface and population of the area in which the licensee operates.

A guarantee may be required after the license has been awarded. The amount varies depending on the sector and is set in the tendering process. For example, for a license to render data, packet or circuit-switching services, a guarantee of 30 million Ptas is required. Licenses are granted for a maximum of 30 years and are, in general, unassignable.

Potential for Foreign Ownerships/Relationships

Limitations on foreign investment remain. Clearance by the Directorate General for Foreign Transactions is required for any direct foreign investment in Spain exceeding 500 million Ptas and exceeding 50% of a Spanish company's share capital. Cabinet authorization is required for any foreign investment in final services or telecommunications carriers. In general, however, foreign shareholdings of up to 25% of the share capital of Spanish corporations are deregulated. This percentage may be altered by the government in accordance with the reciprocity principle.

Capital investments in cable telecommunications by companies resident in EU-member countries are fully deregulated; non-EU capital cannot exceed 25% of the company's share capital unless a higher percentage is approved by the cabinet.

Potential for Upcoming Liberalization/Investment Opportunities

Spain's telecommunications sector is expected to be fully deregulated by December 1, 1998, in accordance with EU directives. Data switching, paging and provision of virtual networks for voice and data are all likely to become fully liberalized. Retevisión has transferred all of its network to a new private company, and 51% of its shares have been awarded under a limited tender to a new consortium of owners (see "His-

torical Background"). Retevisión was to have started fixed telephony operations by January 1, 1998.

A significant number of licenses was granted in 1997 for local fixed telephony services provided by cable TV operators, and these were expected to begin operations in 1998. By mid-1998, a license for a third fixed telephony operator will be granted. Local licenses for cable operators are also likely targets for foreign investment.

A new national license for digital cellular system (DCS-1800) is to be granted to a third mobile operator by mid-1998.

Forms of Doing Business

Permanent Establishment

A company operates through a permanent establishment (PE) in Spain when it has a regular installation or place at which it carries out part or all of its activities, or when it operates through an agent who enters into contracts on behalf of the non-resident company on a regular basis. Places of management, branches, offices, factories, workshops, warehouses and places where construction, installation and assembly work are conducted for more than 12 months are considered PEs. The definition of a PE in Spain's double-taxation treaties is consistent with the OECD Model Convention. When a tax treaty is in place, the following examples of telecommunications services are considered:

- The provision of long distance telephone services by a foreign company to local customers without any local presence is not deemed a PE.

- The licensing by a foreign company of technology and know-how to a local company, without a permanent presence, is generally not deemed a PE. Income from these activities, however, is regarded as royalties earned in Spain and taxed accordingly.

- The presence of a foreign company's employees to operate a Spanish telecommunications company or to provide technical assistance or network management services in exchange for service fees is likely to be deemed a PE. If these persons become employees of the local entity, there is no PE.

- The leasing of telecommunications equipment to a local company (without other personnel or activities in Spain) is not deemed a PE. Revenues from the leasing, however, may be regarded as royalties earned in Spain and taxed accordingly.

- The provision of call reorganization/turnaround services is generally not deemed a PE if the telephone cards are provided through an independent agent and the foreign telecommunications company has no substantial equipment in Spain.

- The provision of Internet access services is not deemed a PE. If the foreign entity merely sells access software to Spanish customers without a presence in Spain, it is generally not deemed a PE. In general, payments for software transfers are regarded as royalties and taxed in accordance with provisions of a relevant treaty.

- Having a server or a switch located in Spain may be sufficient to constitute a PE, even without the presence of any personnel, although actual circumstances should be considered.

- A website located on a server in Spain and accessible to customers in Spain without any other presence in Spain is not likely to be deemed a PE.

- A website located on a server outside Spain but accessible by customers in Spain is not a PE.

- A website located on a server in Spain that is not accessible by customers in Spain is not a PE.

- Although the OECD Model Convention includes in its definition of PE building sites, construction and installation projects lasting more than 12 months, Spain is allowed to tax installation or assembly work having a duration of less than 12 months when there is a degree of permanence to the work. Companies that carry on supervisory activities for more than 12 months in connection with construction work or installation projects of the same duration are deemed to have PE.

If any service described above creates a PE, the foreign company is taxed as a branch (see "Local Branch of a Foreign Company").

Business Entities

The most common form of business organization in telecommunications is a public limited company (sociedad anónima, or S.A.).

Local Branch of a Foreign Company. For services that are not subject to foreign ownership restriction, a branch may be a possible structure, but it is not often used in telecoms services. A branch may be used in the case of construction works (e.g., laying of cable) or other temporary activities. From a tax viewpoint, a branch of a foreign company is subject to virtually the same tax treatment as a Spanish company when a double-

taxation treaty applies. If a treaty does not exist, the tax burden is higher for branches than for companies because of the non-deductibility of an additional 25% tax on net profits transferred and income paid to the head office or PE (i.e., royalties, interest and commissions paid for technical assistance or for the use of other goods or rights).

Spanish law prohibits the combining of profits and losses by a foreign company with multiple branches in Spain that carry out different activities (i.e., telecoms and others) and which are managed separately. However, the grouping of profits and losses may be defended on the basis of the non-discrimination clause in most double-tax treaties.

Locally Incorporated Subsidiary of a Foreign Company. The Cable Telecommunications Act and other legislation require the use of public limited companies (S.A.) in telecommunications rather than private limited companies (sociedad de responsibilidad limitada, or SRL). A public limited company offers certain advantages: It may be listed on stock exchanges; it can incur greater debt; non-voting shares may be issued; and, in principle, no restrictions are placed on the transfer of its shares. A minimum share capital of 10 million Ptas is required. A peculiarity of this sector is that share capital must consist of registered shares.

Transfer tax (on corporate operations) of 1% is payable on the nominal amount of share capital plus the share premium, if any, when a company is incorporated. Subsequent capital increases are also subject to a 1% transfer tax.

There is no restriction on the grouping of profits and losses of a subsidiary with those of other operations.

Joint Venture. Spanish law does not contain any specific regulations on joint-venture contracts. There are regulations governing several forms of associations that may be used to carry out this type of contract, including trading companies, temporary consortia and joint-venture accounts.

In general, in the telecoms sector, concessions are granted to Spanish companies. Therefore, irrespective of the existence of a joint-venture contract that clearly specifies relationships between shareholders, in practice, the joint venture would be a trading company. For this reason, in this sector, the application of the restrictions on the foreign investment would not be avoided through a joint venture. (See "Potential for Foreign Ownerships/Relationships" and "Locally Incorporated Subsidiary of a Foreign Company.")

Temporary consortia are used only for preparatory activities and do not have legal identities separate from their shareholders.

Local Funding Alternatives

Debt versus Equity

The Corporation Tax Act specifies that when the net direct or indirect interest-bearing borrowings of a Spanish company from a non-resident related company are greater than three times the borrower's net worth, the interest paid on the excess is treated as a dividend; thus, it is not deductible, and could be subject to withholding tax in some cases. If there is a double-taxation treaty and reciprocity agreement, the taxpayer can propose the application of a different ratio, based on the borrowing that would be obtained at arm's length.

Participating loans have a variable interest rate linked to the borrower's net income, turnover, net worth or other agreed-upon criterion. Additionally, they may have a fixed interest. Advance repayment occurs only if the borrower's capital and reserves are increased by an amount equal to the paid-off loan balance. Participating loans are regarded as net worth in terms of commercial legislation and as loans for tax purposes. In general, interest accrued is tax-deductible.

Shareholder debt and local debt can be denominated in a foreign currency. Any gains on exchange are considered taxable income, and losses on exchange are considered deductible expenses.

Exchange Controls

If a non-resident company grants a long-term loan (i.e., for more than five years) to a Spanish company, the loan may be regarded as direct investment in Spain subject to exchange control regulations (see "Potential for Foreign Ownerships/Relationships"). Any resident company obtaining financial loans from a non-resident company must inform the Bank of Spain.

Business Acquisitions and Dispositions

Capital Contributions into an Existing Local Entity

Capital contributions into an existing Spanish company are subject to the exchange control restrictions described above and to a 1% transfer tax on corporate operations. In addition, prior cabinet authorization is often required before foreign capital can be invested in telecommunications companies. For contributions of intangible assets valued in monetary terms, the transfer can be made in the form of a non-cash contribution. Non-cash contributions to a sociedad anónima must be valued by one or more independent specialists appointed by the Spanish Mercantile Registry. In general, assets received will be valued at the value share capital increase plus premium, if any.

The transferee will need to recognize income for the difference between the value of the shares received and the book value of the assets contributed.

However, if the assets contributed constitute a branch of activity (an independent business unit capable of operating using its own means) or if they represent at least 5% of the new net worth of the receiving entity, the contributions can be carried out without the transferee recognizing any income. The special regime governing mergers, spin-offs, contributions of assets and exchange of shares can be applied. In either of these cases, the receiving entity values the assets at their original value (on the transferee's books) for tax purposes (i.e., depreciation and income or loss on disposal). Transfer tax (on corporate operations) at 1% is not payable in this case. If the contribution of assets does not constitute a branch activity, the special regime may be applicable if, after the contribution, the contributing entity owns at least 5% of the transferee company.

There are no tax implications for existing shareholders.

Purchase or Sale of Shares in a Local Entity

From a tax viewpoint, a Spanish company that acquires shares at a premium may step-up the assets owned by the acquired company. If the premium is related to goodwill, under certain conditions it may be written off if the shares of the local company were acquired through another local company and both entities are subsequently merged. It should be noted that anti-abuse rules are applicable to tax-free mergers. Financial goodwill is not deductible for corporate income tax, except in certain regional territories (e.g., the Basque Country).

The transfer of listed or unlisted shares is exempt from transfer tax. This exemption is not applicable to the transfer of shares in companies with at least 50% of assets consisting of real property located in Spain. In this case, 6% transfer tax is payable. The capital gains arising from such a sale are taxable (see "Capital Gains Taxes").

Purchase or Sale of Assets

Concessions are generally unassignable, but there are certain segments (e.g., cable telecommunications) in which this restriction is not applicable. In such cases, where licenses are granted to specific persons, transfer is possible, provided that the acquiring party possesses the technical capacity to provide the service. There are no restrictions, in principle, on transferring the remainder of a company's assets, which is subject to 16% VAT paid by the acquirer. When the acquirer engages in a business activity in which input VAT may be deducted, the VAT paid in the transfer of the assets may be deducted. The seller will be taxed on any capital gain arising from the sale (see

"Capital Gains Taxes"). The purchaser may depreciate the sale value for tax purposes.

The prices paid are allocated according to the actual value of each transferred asset, based on its fair market value. The goodwill value is the difference between the market prices of the tangible and other intangibles assets and the total price paid. Depreciation of goodwill, trademarks, transfer rights and other intangible assets may be tax-deductible up to an annual limit of one-tenth of the relevant acquisition price.

Depreciation of goodwill acquired from non-resident entities or resident entities that form part of the same group for accounting purposes is, in principle, not deductible for tax purposes. For accounting purposes, goodwill must be written off over a five-year period, which can be extended to 10 years in certain cases.

Within the scope of group reorganizations, there are structuring alternatives that allow for the tax-free disposition of assets. If the assets contributed constitute a branch of activity or if the value of the assets represents at least 5% of the new net worth of the receiving entity, these contributions can be carried out without the transferee recognizing any income. Additionally, the sale of assets between companies forming part of a tax-consolidated group are not taxable unless the assets are later sold to a third party. A deferral of the tax due on any capital gain exists for capital gains reinvestment (see "Capital Gains Taxes").

From the seller's point of view, any capital gain obtained on the sale of stock will be taxable, although a 100% tax credit is allowed for the portion of the capital gain related to retained earnings generated by the transferred entity during the holding period. Deferral of tax due on the remaining capital gain upon reinvestment is also applicable.

From the buyer's view, buying assets allows the step-up of the assets (up to price paid) and the relevant depreciation, whereas acquisition of shares does not allow step-up of the value of the assets in the acquired company.

Start-up Business Issues

Pre-operating Losses and Start-up/Construction Costs

Start-up expenses include fees, traveling expenses and expenses for technical and financial studies; initial advertising costs; and staff recruitment, staff training and formation costs. These expenses must be written off systematically over a maximum period of five years.

Expenses relating to infrastructure (e.g., network deployment, construction and building) are generally capitalized and written off (see "Depreciation/Cost Recovery Conventions/Accelerated Deductions"). Depreciation of fixed assets constructed by a company for its own use may commence once the assets have been placed in service.

Costs incurred by a non-resident company may be attributed to the Spanish company and amortized or deducted as current expenditures for the year, provided that the non-resident's costs were incurred for the Spanish company's benefit.

VAT paid in Spain by a company that is resident in an EU-member state may be recovered through the system governing refunds. This refund procedure is also applicable to non-EU residents, provided that reciprocal treatment exists in favor of Spanish businesses and professionals. Refunds must be effected within six months, but in practice this takes longer.

If VAT is paid on the purchase of pre-operating goods or services by the non-resident company, VAT may be refundable. If VAT is paid by a PE or a company residing in Spain, a special procedure applies whereby input VAT paid prior to the commencement of the business activity is refundable. The taxpayer may apply to use this procedure, which is available during the year between the time an application is submitted and the commencement of the business activity. If the nature of the activity requires that the start-up period last for more than one year, the period may be extended at the taxpayer's request. VAT paid on the acquisition of land does not qualify for this treatment and may not be deducted by the taxpayer until the business activity effectively commences.

Customs Duties and VAT

Most goods imported into Spain from outside the EU are subject to customs duty and import VAT. Duty is normally payable on the cost, insurance and freight (CIF) value of the goods. Import VAT is payable on the duty-inclusive value of the goods, although VAT-registered traders can usually obtain a refund of the VAT.

Telecommunications and computing equipment are subject to duties ranging from 1.2% to 10.5%. The rate of duty depends on the exact description and the tariff classification and country of origin of the goods. The current import duty rates for a sample of telecommunications goods originating in non-EU countries (in this example, the United States) are given below. The EU has preferential trade agreements with a number of countries that enable goods to be imported at rates below those indicated or at a nil rate of duty.

Line telephone sets with cordless handsets	3.8%
Videophones	7%
Other telephone sets	3.8%
Facsimile machines	3.8%
Teleprinters	3.8%
Telephonic or telegraphic switching apparatus	3.8%
Other apparatus for carrier line systems	2.3%
Other apparatus for digital line systems	3.8%
Building-entry telephone systems	3.8%

Customs duties on some items of equipment were already being reduced under General Agreement on Tariffs and Trade (GATT). However, over the next few years, duty rates are scheduled to be reduced further still under the Information Technology Agreement (ITA) signed in March 1997. The ITA also extends the range of goods subject to duty rate reductions. As a signatory to the ITA, the EU has agreed to cut tariffs on imports of computers and computer equipment, software, telecommunications and networking equipment to zero in four equal installments. The first reduction took place on July 1, 1997, and further reductions are to take effect on January 1 of each year through 2000. Although the ITA will cut the cost of importing many products, the convergence of technologies in the computing, electronics and telecommunications sectors is likely to lead to disputes over the tariff classification of some equipment and affect the availability and/or phasing of duty reductions under the ITA.

A wide variety of reliefs from customs duty (and import VAT) can be claimed in various circumstances (e.g., goods imported for processing and re-export, or goods imported temporarily). There is also a relief available for capital goods and equipment, provided the goods are imported by a business on the transfer of its activities to Spain.

Raw materials or components that are not available, or not available in sufficient quantities, within the EU may be eligible for a complete or partial suspension of duty, providing this non-availability can be demonstrated to the satisfaction of the Commission of the European Communities in Brussels.

Goods may be subject to anti-dumping or countervailing duty if, for example, the EU considers they are being imported into the EU at prices substantially lower than their normal values. Anti-dumping and countervailing duties are chargeable in addition to, and independent of, any other duty to which the imported goods are liable.

No distinction is made between regular telephony and Internet telephony for the purposes of VAT.

Loss Carryovers

Tax losses may be offset against profits earned in the seven years following the year of the loss. No carryback of losses is allowed. Newly created entities may compute the seven-year period from the first tax period in which taxable income is obtained (i.e., losses generated until the year in which the company first achieves a positive taxable income).

There are no limitations on offsetting tax-loss carryforwards in cases in which only the business activity changes. There are, however, limits in cases in which ownership has changed by more than 50% in a dormant company (for these purposes, dormant companies are those that have not carried out any activity during six months prior to the acquisition of the majority shareholding). In a merger, tax-loss carryforwards of the absorbed company can also be used by the resulting entity, although there are also certain restrictions.

Operating Considerations

Corporate Income Taxes

The general corporate income tax rate is 35%. Taxable income is calculated by adjusting the accounting results (as determined by accounting legislation) to the relevant taxable provisions. The assessment period of an entity coincides with its financial year. Corporation taxpayers are required to file returns and pay taxes within 25 calendar days after the six-month period following the closing date. Taxpayers are required to make advanced tax payments during the tax year.

Special Royalties in the Telecommunications Industry. Telecommunications companies are often required to pay to the authorities annual royalties, which are calculated on the percentage of gross revenue from a company's operations, not to exceed 0.1%. If telecommunications service delivery requires the use of local public domain (e.g., land, subsoil or areas bordering municipal thoroughfares), an additional royalty of 1.5% of the gross annual income obtained in each municipality must be paid.

The authorities required a fee of 85 billion Ptas for granting the second cellular license to Airtel. This practice has recently been rejected by the EU as discriminatory because it was payable only by the second operator. The government has recently recognized an equivalent credit in favor of Airtel. This credit is to take the form of a license to operate a DCS-1800 service, a reduction in the price for connection with the public network owned by Telefónica, and access to a wider range of frequency.

The initial fee for the three licenses for the DCS-1800 service has been fixed at 26 billion Ptas, and it will be payable by the licensees (Telefónica, Airtel and a third). Airtel will offset this fee with the above-mentioned credit.

Withholding Taxes. In general, dividends, interest and royalty payments made to non-residents on their Spanish-sourced income are subject to withholding tax at the rate of 25%, which can be reduced by a tax treaty. Interest paid to residents in another EU-member state is not subject to withholding tax.

Dividends transferred from a subsidiary to a parent company resident in another EU-member country are not subject to withholding tax if the amount of direct holding of the recipient company in the Spanish company is at least 25%, if this holding has been maintained during the year prior to the date on which dividends are paid, and if other requirements are met. Dividends paid to foreign shareholders in non-EU-member countries are not affected by the shareholders' percentage interest in the company, unless an applicable tax treaty provides otherwise.

Capital Gains Taxes

No special tax is assessed on capital gains; they are included within the company's other taxable income and taxed at the corporate income tax rate of 35%. Capital gains are reduced by the monetary depreciation calculated under corporate tax rules.

A tax deferral does exist for capital gains reinvestment. The capital gain obtained, after adjustment for monetary depreciation, from the transfer of assets or corporate shares (representing not less than a 5% stake in the participating entity) that have been held for at least one year may be deferred if the proceeds are reinvested in similar assets. A four-year period is allowed for making the reinvestment.

Tax Holidays and Exemptions

There are no tax holidays, special exemptions or reduced rates applicable specifically to telecommunications businesses. Lower corporate tax rates, higher deductions for investments and accelerated depreciation are generally available in the Basque Country and the Canary Islands. Telecoms businesses may also benefit from other general tax incentives.

Research and Development Tax Credits. A 20% tax credit is allowed for expenses incurred in research and development (R&D) during a tax period. If the expenses incurred for R&D activities in the tax period are higher than the average incurred in the two preceding years, 20% is applied up to the average and 40% to any surplus. The amount of the R&D deduction is reduced by 65% of any R&D taxable grants received. R&D expenses relating to activities carried out abroad also qualify for

deduction, provided the main R&D activity is carried out in Spain and those expenses do not exceed 25% of the total amount invested.

Other Tax Credits. Professional training expenses less 65% of any grants received could also qualify for an annual tax deduction of 5%. For this credit, any excess amounts could be carried forward for five years.

Depreciation/Cost-Recovery Conventions/Accelerated Deductions

Fixed-asset depreciation is deductible for tax purposes if the depreciation is recorded in the accounts using one of the officially approved methods, which include the straight-line, constant-percentage and sum-of-the-year's-digits methods.

In the straight-line method, rates by type of asset are defined by the tax authorities. These rates must be used unless it can be shown that higher rates correspond to the actual decline in value. Examples of rates applicable to the telecommunications industry are shown below:

Types of Assets	Maximum Rate	Maximum Number of Years
Land infrastructure	3% to 5%	68 to 40
Technical installations (including switches*)	8% to 15%	25 to 14
Cellular stations	15%	14
Cables	7%	30
Other installations	12% to 20%	18 to 10
Computer equipment	25%	8
Software	33%	6

* For analog and digitals witches, the maximum depreciation rate is 12% and the maximum depreciation period is 18 years.

The constant-percentage method uses a percentage determined by multiplying the straight-line depreciation rate, calculated on the basis of the depreciation period on the officially approved tables, by 1.5, 2 or 2.5, depending on the depreciation period of the assets. Buildings, furniture and fittings may not be depreciated using a constant percentage.

The sum-of-the-year's-digits method is based on the depreciation period set in the officially approved tables, but it provides a higher depreciation for the first years. Buildings, furniture and fittings may not be depreciated using this method. Companies may depreciate their fixed assets according to special depreciation plans that they design if approval is first obtained from the tax authorities.

Depreciation of tangible fixed assets commences when they become operational. There are no specific rules for starting up a network.

Tangible and intangible fixed assets, excluding buildings, that are used for R&D activities can be freely depreciated. Buildings used for R&D activities may be depreciated on a straight-line basis over 10 years.

Marketing and advertising costs are recorded under the general accrued method for income and expenses, irrespective of whether they are carried out directly by the company or indirectly through external agents. If these expenses are to accrue over a period exceeding one year, they can be treated as deferred expenses, to be amortized over a maximum of five years.

Purchased software can be depreciated at a maximum rate of 33%. If software is embedded in telecommunications equipment but has a useful life that differs from that of the equipment (i.e., if it can be updated or modified), it may be amortized separately from the equipment, using the specific rates for software. In other cases, the software may be amortized together with the equipment.

Transfer Pricing Rules

The Tax Administration may value operations performed between related entities at their normal market value when the agreed valuation would otherwise lead either to lower-than-normal taxation in Spain or to a deferral of such taxation. To determine the normal market value, the tax authorities can apply any of several methods, including the comparable uncontrolled price method, the cost-plus method and the resale-price method. When none of these is applicable, the profit-split method is used; that is, the price is derived from the distribution of the overall result of the operation.

Taxpayers may submit a proposal (based on the normal market value) for the valuation of operations carried out between related entities to the tax authorities prior to performing them. The advance price agreements are valid for three years.

For contributions made to R&D activities by a related entity to be deductible, there must be a written contract signed beforehand that identifies the projects and grants the right to use their results. The distribution criteria for the expenses incurred must reasonably relate to the rights to use the results.

These transfer pricing rules were effective on January 1, 1996. The authorities are showing an increasing interest in this area as Spain's economy becomes more international.

Transfers of Patents, Trademarks and Software

Royalty payments and software licensing fees are deductible, provided that the Spanish company obtains a true advantage and that the agreed-upon price complies with the arm's-length principle. Royalty fees paid to a non-resident company are subject to a 25% withholding tax, unless a treaty provides a reduced rate.

Service Fees

These expenses are deductible when related to income generated during a tax period. Expenses relating to management services between related companies qualify for tax deductions when the following requirements are met:

• The amount is specified in a prior, written contract that establishes distribution criteria for expenses incurred by the service provider.

• The nature of the services to be supplied is stated in the contract.

• The distribution method for the expenses complies with the principles of continuity and rationality.

Service fees paid to a non-resident entity are subject to a 25% withholding tax in Spain, unless a double-taxation treaty provides otherwise.

Value-Added Tax, Sales Tax and/or Other Pertinent Taxes

As a member of the EU, Spain follows the provisions of the European Community Sixth VAT Directive. Domestic telecommunications services (including those supplied by Spanish-resident foreign businesses) are subject to VAT at the standard rate of 16%. The VAT treatment of international telecommunications services is based on the revised EU VAT model, which took effect in Spain on September 1, 1997.

Services supplied internationally by a telecommunications business located in Spain are generally outside the scope of VAT when supplied to anyone located outside Spain. The only exceptions are services supplied to private individuals or unregistered persons located in other member states and in Canarias, Ceuta and Melilla. Those supplies are subject to Spanish VAT at the standard rate.

Non-resident providers are not liable to register and account for Spanish VAT on supplies used and enjoyed by Spanish customers, providing those customers are taxable persons for VAT purposes. These customers are required to self-account for VAT under reverse-charge procedures.

When a non-resident provider makes supplies of services to private individuals, to be used in Spain, the provider is required to register and account for Spanish VAT. For an overseas provider, it should be possible to limit the Spanish VAT liability to supplies made to Spanish individuals that are effectively used in the EU. However, this may then require the overseas provider to be registered for VAT purposes in many different EU-member states. Alternatively, an overseas provider may choose to register in a single EU-member state (e.g., Spain) in order to contract with all customers who are EU private individuals. The supplies made from the single EU registration to these customers will then be subject to local VAT in the member state of registration.

Access to the Internet is included within the definition of telecommunications, and the principles set out above apply equally to Internet service providers (ISPs).

Transfer Tax. The transfer of land and/or buildings will normally be subject to VAT of 16%. Where VAT is not applicable to the transfer of land and/or buildings (e.g., exempt second supplies of buildings), transfer tax is applied at the general rate of 6%. Administrative concessions are subject to a 4% transfer tax on the value of the concessions.

Local and Provincial Taxes

The most important local taxes are as follows:

Tax on Business and Professional Activities. This is an annual municipal tax levied on the performance of professional and business activities by individuals and companies. For telecommunications services, this tax is based on the number of subscribers and the area served. For every 1,000 subscribers or fraction thereof in 1997, the tax ranged from 24,000 Ptas to 36,000 Ptas, plus an additional 50 Ptas for each square meter of area served.

Property Tax. The basis of the assessment is determined using the official values set by each municipality and is based on the market value of the property. Depending on the size of the municipality, the rate may vary from 0.3% to 1%.

Municipal Capital Gains Tax. This tax is payable only on the transfer of urban land. The basis of assessment is calculated by each municipality and varies from 2% to 3.7% of the ratable value of the land (depending on the number of years since it was last sold). Tax rates vary from 20% to 30%.

For Additional Information, Contact:

Carmen García de Andrés
Tax Director
and
Antonio Rodríguez Roldán
Global Telecoms Director
C/ Ulises, 18
28043 Madrid
Spain
Telephone: 34 (1) 301 95 00
Fax: 34 (1) 300 17 58
E-mail: cgarcia@colybrand.es
        arodriguez@colybrand.es

Sweden

Telecommunications Tax Profile
by Stefan Carlsson
Tax Partner, Stockholm

Overview of the Telecommunications Market

Historical Background

Sweden's first direct legislation in this sector was the 1993 Telecommunications Act, which established the framework for competition, regulatory oversight and price regulation. At that time, the Swedish public telecommunications carrier was restructured as a state-owned limited liability company, Telia AB.

Sweden joined the European Union (EU) in 1995, and the amended Telecoms Act that came into force on July 1, 1997, complies with all proposed EU telecommunications liberalization directives. Much of Sweden's liberalization of telecommunications occurred in advance of the pan-European initiatives.

Current Status

All sectors of the Swedish telecommunications market are liberalized and open to competition. Telia competes in nearly all telecommunications businesses and dominates in local and long distance. For several years, it has been subject to intense competition in international service from domestic and foreign carriers.

Further legislative changes are expected with the implementation of number portability. The preliminary schedule for the implementation of number portability is July 1, 1999, for fixed operators. No date has yet been set for number portability for mobile operators.

Open markets also exist for terminal equipment, value-added services, very small aperture terminals (VSATs) and other data networks, and the carriage of third-party data and voice traffic.

Construction of terrestrial networks is also liberalized. Thus, service providers may either build their own networks or lease lines from Telia or other providers.

The number of competitors has grown rapidly in the market for public switched telephony in all sections of the value chain. Five international operators competed in international and long distance in 1997, and others were ready to enter the market. There are also several national service providers with operations in Sweden and abroad. In infrastructure, there are three fixed-link suppliers and one radio-link supplier with national coverage, and numerous local government networks using owned cables and leased lines. There are also several regional networks reserved mainly, but not only, for the use of local government.

While international traffic volume has increased, total revenues generated by this segment have not risen at the same rate because of vigorous competition and call-price cuts by the operators.

Three operators have been licensed to compete in the global system for mobile communications (GSM) market: Telia Mobitel, Europolitan and Comviq. These three and a fourth, Tele 8, have also obtained licenses for digital cellular system (DCS) services in the 1800 band. Because of the growth in the number of subscribers, total revenues on the GSM market increased very rapidly in 1996.

Ninety-six percent of the fixed subscribers were connected to digital switches at the end of 1996, and Telia plans to have all subscribers connected to AXE switches by the end of 1997. The Telia network consists of about 13 trunk switches, some 250 local switches and more than 6,000 RSSs (remote subscriber subsystems).

Current Liberalization Status

In the World Trade Organization (WTO) negotiations in February 1997, Sweden pledged to adhere to a common set of regulatory principles.

Type of Service	Degree of Liberalization	Key Legislation	Date of Actual or Expected Liberalization	Comments
Local, Long Distance and International	Full liberalization	Telecommunications Act	July 1, 1993	There was never a formal monopoly in Sweden.
Cellular	Full liberalization	Telecommunications Act and Radiocommunications Act	July 1, 1993	
Paging	Full liberalization	Telecommunications Act and Radiocommunications Act	July 1, 1993	
Value-added	Full liberalization	Telecommunications Act	July 1, 1993	

Competitive Environment

Since 1993, competition has emerged in all segments of the market. Telia still holds a dominant position in the fixed local and long distance segments, but competitors are becoming established in these markets. Tariffs for mobile services are still between five and ten times higher than the average price for a fixed national call. With an expected convergence of fixed and mobile tariffs, a greater substitution effect will be seen.

	Entire Market		Top Two Players		
Type of Service	Market Size (1996)	Number of Players	Names	Annual Revenue (1996)	Ownership
Local	SEK4.1 billion	2	Telia	SEK4 billion	Government
			Tele2	SEK100 million	NetCom Systems AB (owned by Kinnevik)
Long Distance	SEK3.1 billion	5	Telia	SEK2.8 billion	Government
			Tele2	SEK300 million	NetCom Systems AB
International	SEK3.2 billion	+20*	Telia	SEK2.3 billion	Government
			Tele2	SEK700 million	NetCom Systems AB
Cellular	SEK10.1 billion	4	Telia Mobitel	SEK7.2 billion	Telia
			Comviq GSM	SEK1.6 billion	NetCom Systems AB
Paging	SEK200 million	1**	Telia Mobitel	SEK200 million	Government
Value-added	Not available	100	Telia	Not available	Government
			Tele2	Not available	NetCom Systems AB

Source: Stelacon-report; Marknaden för telekommunikation i Sverige, 1996.

* Including resellers and call-back operators.

** One other operator is licensed but had not begun service.

Licensing Requirements

According to the amended Telecommunications Act, a new operator is obligated only to notify the regulator of its intention to supply telecoms services. Regulators may impose special requirements on operators with significant market power, following the requirements in EU directives. The national regulator, Post-och Telestyrelsen, has yet to decide whether the new rules will mean that small operators that currently hold licenses will lose them and/or no longer need them.

Potential for Foreign Ownerships/Relationships

There are no limitations on the percentage of foreign ownership permitted in Swedish telecommunications companies.

Potential for Upcoming Liberalization/Investment Opportunities

Mobile operators are building new infrastructure for nationwide DCS-1800 networks. None of these networks were yet operating in 1997, and considerable investment was needed.

Discussions were underway regarding privatization of Telia, but as of August 1997, the government had given no indication of its intent.

Forms of Doing Business

Permanent Establishment

A foreign entity is subject to tax if it carries on a business from a permanent establishment (PE) in Sweden or if it owns real property located in Sweden. Swedish tax law uses a definition of PE that broadly corresponds to the definition in the OECD Model Convention, which states that a PE is a fixed place from which the business of an enterprise is wholly or partly carried on. However, the domestic definition does not include all exceptions noted in the OECD document. Thus, performing preparatory and auxiliary services will, in the absence of a tax treaty based on the OECD Model Convention, give rise to a PE. Given the large number of tax treaties entered into by Sweden, the OECD definition of PE applies to most developed countries.

A non-resident recipient of lease payments or license fees for the use of intangible rights (e.g., patents or trademarks) or know-how is deemed to have a PE if the lease or fee is an expense in a Swedish business of a domestic or a foreign entity. Subject to tax treaty provisions, Sweden has in many cases wholly waived this liability for a foreign licensor to pay income tax on the Swedish fee. Notable exceptions to this waiver are Italy, Japan and Spain. A lessor in any of these countries is liable to pay Swedish income tax on leasing income or fees for the use of intangible rights.

Telecommunications services can cover a broad range of activities, which may or may not constitute a permanent establishment. Some examples follow:

- Typically, call reorganization/turnaround services, which require no presence in Sweden other than a rented line and a local phone subscription, do not result in a PE. The same is true for the provision of Internet access services.

- A long-term commitment by a foreign company to provide services may require sufficient infrastructure to constitute a PE. This means, for example, that operator/network management services could result in a PE if the provider of such services has staff located in Sweden for a period of time.

- The laying of cable and the construction of switching equipment for sale to a local company constitutes a PE because this falls within the scope of an installation project. Normally, tax treaties require that a project last for at least 12 months to be considered a PE.

- The laying of cable and the construction of switching equipment to be leased to and operated by a local company is more complicated. If the transaction is regarded as a lease, tax liability will arise, and this is subject to relief under certain tax treaty provisions. In the case of a lease of an asset, such as a fiber optic cable, the lease contract may be reclassified as an installment sale after an analysis of the terms of the contract to determine whether the parties intended to conclude a sales or a lease agreement.

- The licensing of technology or the leasing of equipment to a local company may constitute a PE for the licensor. However, a tax treaty may provide for a full or partial exemption of income tax. A routing of a royalty or a lease through a treaty country has, in some cases, been challenged by the Swedish Revenue.

- The periodic payment for the use of software might be regarded as a royalty and therefore be subject to income tax unless tax treaty provisions apply.

- A server or switch located in Sweden without staff to service the equipment or make it accessible to customers does not normally constitute a PE. If it is used to provide services to local customers, a PE could occur, depending on the specific circumstances.

- No laws specifically address website issues, and no cases have been tested. The location of a website server or its accessibility by local or other customers is unlikely to be decisive in determining whether a company has a PE. A fixed place of business will occur only in cases of physical presence of staff and/or equipment. A website cannot constitute such a presence.

It should be noted that even in the absence of a PE, if the particular type of income is governed by the royalty provisions of the OECD Model Convention (rather than the provision pertaining to business income), Sweden may have the right to impose income tax at a rate stipulated (i.e., normally 5% to 10% of the gross rental or license fee, as stipulated in a tax treaty).

Business Entities

Local Branch of a Foreign Company. This option is available to an investor. The tax consequences are as follows:

- Income attributable to the branch is taxed.

- There is no withholding tax on remittances of branch capital.

- The branch's profits and losses may not be grouped with those of other operations.

- Liability exists to the extent of the net assets of the foreign corporation.

- There is no minimum capital requirement.

A Swedish branch of a foreign corporation is required to have separate accounts and to appoint a certified public auditor.

Locally Incorporated Subsidiary of a Foreign Company. This option is available to an investor. The tax consequences are as follows:

- A Swedish subsidiary of a foreign corporation is taxed on its worldwide income.

- Group relief may be claimed if the subsidiary is a member of a Swedish group of companies.

- Liability is limited to the investment of capital in the Swedish company.

- There is a minimum capital requirement of SEK100,000, and measures must be taken if losses erode shareholders' equity.

The filing of a consolidated tax return is not possible, but it is possible to transfer the profits between companies in a more than 90%-owned group by using a special dividend (group contribution) that is taxable for the payee and deductible for the payor. Certain limitations do exist; for instance, the qualifying ownership must have prevailed for the whole financial year for both companies.

A locally incorporated subsidiary of a foreign company is required to have separate accounts and to appoint a certified public auditor.

Joint Venture. There are two forms of joint ventures: corporate and non-corporate. A corporate joint venture will take the form of a Swedish corporation, owned by the partners. It is subject to the same taxation as a Swedish subsidiary of a foreign corporation. Non-corporate joint ventures are rare. Other available legal forms are a general or limited partnership, which are used very rarely, and a consortium, in which the parties act on their own vis-à-vis the customer but cooperate in terms of preparatory work and completion of a project.

A joint venture is a commercial, rather than a legal, concept. Therefore, the tax implications for a joint venture depend on its legal form. A Swedish corporation pays tax and files a tax return. A partnership is a transparent entity. The partners pay tax on their individual shares of the partnership income; however, the partnership also files a master tax return.

A consortium is not a legal entity. The partners in a consortium each pay tax based on their individual income and file their own tax returns. Partnership joint ventures and consortia formed for the completion of contracts in Sweden are likely to constitute PEs.

Local Funding Alternatives

Debt versus Equity

The use of debt is normally advantageous because interest costs are deductible, with few limitations. Even for a company that has an excessive debt-to-equity ratio (thinly capitalized), there is only a minimal risk that the tax authorities will recharacterize its debt as equity. The debt financing of a subsidiary would more likely raise legal issues, such as the issue of compulsory winding-up when half the share capital has been consumed. The lower the equity, the more attention should be devoted to the balance sheet of the subsidiary.

Sweden does not impose a withholding tax on outbound interest remittances, and it has no special rules for exchange gains and losses or shareholder guarantees. Subject to tax treaty provisions, a 30% withholding tax is imposed on dividends paid to the foreign parent.

The tax treatment of exchange gains and losses on both local and shareholder debt is the same as the accounting treatment. Gains and losses on short-term receivables and liabilities are recognized when accrued. For long-term receivables and liabilities, losses, but not gains, are recognized when accrued. The non-recognition of gains is deemed to provide a tax deferral, which is an undesired consequence for the company. To eliminate this consequence, an imputed income has to be included in the company's tax return. The resulting tax largely corresponds to the economic benefit of the tax deferral.

Exchange Controls

Sweden does not have any exchange controls.

Business Acquisitions and Dispositions

Capital Contributions into an Existing Local Entity

A contribution of capital into a local subsidiary is not taxable. No stamp duties or capital duties are imposed. A contribution can be made either in the form of cash or assets. If assets are contributed, the valuation of the assets is critical from both an accounting and a tax perspective. The value attributed to an asset for accounting purposes—which is also the basis for income tax purposes—must not exceed its fair market value. For tax purposes, there is no limit on the intangibles that a foreign entity can contribute to an existing entity; as long as the value of the intangible can be assessed, it can be contributed to the Swedish company and be depreciated. It is advisable, however, to contribute the assets at a share issue in order to support the value.

An issue of shares by a local entity will not have any direct tax consequences for the existing shareholders.

Purchase or Sale of Shares in a Local Entity

In a share transaction, there are no tax consequences for the underlying business other than a potential limitation on the use of loss carryforwards. The financing of the purchase is organized by—and will, at least initially, be the responsibility of—the purchasing entity. When a local company buys more than 90% of the shares in a Swedish subsidiary, it may be able, from the year following the year of acquisition, to cover the financing expenses of the Swedish parent company with the pre-tax profits of the target company. The profits from the subsidiary are transferred to the parent by issuing a special dividend (group contribution), which is taxable for the recipient and deductible for the subsidiary.

Any goodwill arising from consolidation of a Swedish subgroup is not deductible, since the consolidated accounts are not taxed. Only the separate companies pay tax. A step-up in basis to obtain tax deductibility for such goodwill in a Swedish company cannot be made tax-free.

A sale of shares in a Swedish company is taxable only if the seller is a Swedish company, an individual resident in Sweden, or an individual who has been a resident of Sweden but has moved abroad within the last 11 years (or a shorter period, as stipulated by a tax treaty).

Purchase or Sale of Assets

A sale of assets is taxed at the normal 28% rate if the seller is a company or a partnership with corporate partners, or at applicable personal tax rates (30% to 57%) if the seller is an individual or a partnership with individual partners. The gain to tax is the difference between the price paid by the buyer and the cost (normally, book value) of the assets.

In an asset transaction, the financing of the purchase is the responsibility of the acquiring company. The revenue from the business and the financing expenses are offset without any special mechanism, since they arise within the same company.

A sales contract attributes a value to certain classes of assets and to goodwill that cannot be attributed to any particular asset. Goodwill is deductible for tax purposes in the same way as tangible assets. For this reason, and because all machinery and equipment are depreciated in the same way, there is no strong need for rules on the allocation of the purchase price to various classes of assets, even if such allocation normally would be made in the sales contract.

A buyer would usually prefer an asset purchase because of the deduction available for goodwill. For a seller, a share transaction is usually preferable because it provides the opportunity for tax planning or the use of a high cost basis, which cannot be used in an asset sale. Similarly, the personal income tax for an individual seller in a sale of shares is considerably lower than the aggregate taxes imposed on his company in an asset sale and upon him as a shareholder at the payment of a dividend or at the liquidation of the company.

If the consideration for the shares to be acquired is new stock issued by the buyer, a rollover provision may allow for a deferral of the taxation of a capital gain. Such rollover relief will generally be applicable at the purchase of all shares in a publicly traded company, but restrictions may apply to transactions in other contexts.

A sale of a partnership interest is regarded as a sale of a share in a legal entity, not as a sale of a corresponding portion of the partnership's assets, and is taxed accordingly. For the purchaser of all interests in a partnership, a step-up in the basis of the assets, including goodwill, can be achieved tax-free through an appropriate post-acquisition restructuring.

Start-up Business Issues

Pre-operating Losses and Start-up/Construction Costs

Start-up expenses (other than investments) are charged to the profit and loss account and deducted when accrued. Companies can amortize and deduct start-up expenditures over a period of 60 months if this is acceptable for accounting purposes. Licenses may be amortized ratably over five years. Interest expenses and overhead costs incurred during a construction period are normally not capitalized.

VAT during a construction period is normally recovered. However, VAT recovery can be granted after a special application in cases in which substantial investments were made in the start-up phase of a new business. In all cases, interest expenses are deductible as incurred, on an accrual basis.

If start-up expenses have been incurred by another company and re-charged to a local entity, these should be treated as if the local entity had incurred the same expenses directly. No withholding tax issues will arise because Sweden does not generally impose withholding taxes on payments other than dividend distributions.

Customs Duties and VAT

Most goods imported into Sweden from outside the EU are subject to customs duty and import VAT. Duty is normally payable on the cost, insurance and freight (CIF) value of the goods. Import VAT is payable on the duty-inclusive value of the goods, although VAT-registered traders can usually obtain a refund of the VAT.

Telecommunications and computing equipment are subject to duty ranging from 1.2% to 10.5%. The rate of duty will depend on the exact description, tariff classification, and country of origin of the goods. The current import duty rates for a sample of telecommunications goods originating in non-EU countries (in this example, the United States) are given below. The EU has preferential trade agreements with a number of countries that enable goods to be imported at rates below these or at nil rate of duty.

Line telephone sets with cordless handsets	3.8%
Videophones	7%
Other telephone sets	3.8%
Facsimile machines	3.8%
Teleprinters	3.8%
Telephonic or telegraphic switching apparatus	3.8%
Other apparatus for carrier line systems	2.3%
Other apparatus for digital line systems	3.8%
Building-entry telephone systems	3.8%

Customs duties on some items of equipment were already being reduced under GATT (General Agreement on Tariffs and Trade). However, over the next few years, duty rates are scheduled to be reduced further still under the Information Technology Agreement (ITA) signed in March 1997. The ITA also extends the range of goods subject to duty rate reductions. As a signatory to the ITA, the EU has agreed to cut tariffs on imports of computers and computer equipment, software, telecommunications and networking equipment to zero, in four equal installments. The first reduction took place on July 1, 1997, and further reductions are to take effect on January 1 of each year through 2000. Although the ITA will cut the cost of importing many products, the convergence of technologies in the computing, electronics and telecommunications sectors is likely to lead to disputes over the tariff classification of some equipment and affect the availability and/or phasing of duty reductions under the ITA.

A wide variety of reliefs from customs duty (and import VAT) can be claimed in various circumstances (e.g., goods imported for processing and re-export, or goods imported temporarily). There is also a relief available for capital goods and equipment, provided the goods are imported by a business on the transfer of its activities to Sweden.

Raw materials or components that are not available, or not available in sufficient quantities, within the EU may be eligible for complete or partial suspension of duty, providing the insufficiency or lack can be demonstrated to the satisfaction of the Commission of the European Communities in Brussels. Goods may be subject to anti-dumping or countervailing duty if, for example, the EU considers they are being imported into the EU at prices substantially lower than their normal values. Anti-dumping and countervailing duties are chargeable in addition to, and independent of, any other duty to which the imported goods may be liable.

Import duties are calculated on the customs value, which is the transaction value (i.e., the price actually paid for the goods when they are sold for export to the EU).

The importation of equipment is subject to Swedish VAT, which can be recovered if the importer is a taxable person entitled to recover input VAT. Provided the equipment will be used to carry on an economic activity, and that, as a result, the foreign company has to appoint a tax representative in Sweden, a refund of the VAT paid can be claimed through the filing of a VAT return. For a Swedish company, the VAT paid will, in principle, be deducted in a VAT return.

No distinction is made between regular telephony and Internet telephony for the purposes of VAT.

Loss Carryovers

Companies cannot carry back net operating losses, but the use of an untaxed reserve (see "Tax Holidays and Exemptions") has the effect of a partial loss carryback. A corporation that experiences more than a 50% change in ownership over a five-year period may be limited in its use of net operating losses in the post-change period. A change in the business activity will not affect a company's ability to utilize losses carried forward.

Operating Considerations

Corporate Income Taxes

Sweden imposes national income tax on the net income of a company or a branch at the rate of 28%. Generally, the statutory accounts form the basis for the computation of taxable income. Only a few adjustments are necessary and these are mainly timing differences.

A Swedish corporation or a Swedish branch of a foreign company can defer the taxation of up to one-fifth of its taxable income in a particular year by setting up special reserves in its balance sheet (see "Tax Holidays and Exemptions").

Sweden withholds tax on remittances of dividends to recipients in countries with which Sweden does not have tax treaties. The tax imposed on royalties is not a withholding tax, but is based on a tax return submitted by the licensor. Royalties can be paid gross. No withholding tax is imposed on interest.

As a member of the EU, Sweden also grants unilateral relief for withholding taxes under the parent-subsidiary directive.

Capital Gains Taxes

Sweden does not differentiate between capital transactions and other transactions. However, certain special rules apply to transactions of a capital nature, such as disposals of securities. Taxpayers may not deduct losses from transactions between certain related persons.

Tax Holidays and Exemptions

As a way to enable businesses to retain funds free of tax, various regimes for untaxed reserves have been put into effect. Corporations and individuals conducting business are allowed to set up tax-free reserves on their balance sheets. These reserves can be released for taxation under certain circumstances.

The regime for untaxed reserves allows a taxpayer to allocate up to one-fifth of its taxable income (before allocation) to a tax-free reserve. This reserve can be reversed and added to taxable income in a later year—for example, to offset a loss in that year—but not later than in the fifth year after it was established. In the absence of an open carryback of losses, this regime can provide a similar effect.

Swedish tax policy does not favor tax-based incentives, thus there are no special tax holidays or exemptions available for any industry other than a partial exemption from social security charges for specific businesses located in certain areas where employment is low.

Depreciation/Cost-Recovery Conventions/Accelerated Deductions

For tax purposes, a company may amortize machinery and equipment (M&E) over five years, irrespective of the useful life of the asset. This makes it necessary to charge the same annual depreciation to the profit and loss account. Equipment with a short useful life and equipment with a low cost may be expensed. Buildings are depreciated over their useful lives, between 20 and 50 years. Land cannot be depreciated, but certain land improvements, such as roads, parking lots and walls, can be amortized over 20 years. Telecommunications equipment such as switches, routers, cell networks, lines and satellites are M&E for depreciation purposes.

It should be noted that the classification of a particular asset is based on its function rather than on whether it is fixed or movable. Assets that are used mainly in an enterprise as M&E may be amortized as M&E. Expenses for research and development, including the development of software, are deductible when incurred.

Generally, advertising and promotion expenses are deductible. Institutional or goodwill advertising is also deductible. Advertising that is only remotely connected to the business will be challenged by the Swedish Revenue. The treatment of commissions paid to phone retailers for selling subscriptions to cell networks has not been a subject for debate in terms of tax treatment. The GSM service providers, who pay these commissions, either expense them or capitalize and amortize them over a few years.

Purchased software is normally expensed but may in some cases be capitalized and amortized. Software embedded in other products will be treated in the same way as the hardware, which normally is depreciated over five years.

Transfer Pricing Rules

The Swedish Revenue can adjust income to reflect income among businesses owned or controlled by the same interest. For this purpose, an arm's-length standard is used. The rules apply to all commercial transactions that give rise to a transfer of profit to a non-resident entity related to a local enterprise.

The Swedish Revenue has historically been unsuccessful in applying the transfer pricing rules. Several cases brought before the Supreme Fiscal Court have all been won by taxpayers. The Swedish Revenue is, however, quite active in this area and is pursuing a number of cases, which have not yet been tried by the Supreme Fiscal Court.

Transfers of Patents, Trademarks and Software

Outbound transfers or inbound licensing of intangible assets can be made without any restrictions, provided that license charges are at arm's length. For tax purposes, acquired intangible assets can be depreciated over five years.

Unless a tax treaty provides otherwise, royalties are taxed as Swedish-sourced income, at ordinary income tax rates. No withholding at source is required.

Service Fees

No withholding tax is due on service fees. A Swedish company that pays a service fee can deduct this fee as long as it can prove that it receives a service that benefits the business, and can provide supporting documentation. Inbound, as well as outbound, service fees frequently have VAT implications.

Value-Added Tax, Sales Tax and/or Other Pertinent Taxes

Sweden follows the provisions of the European Community Sixth VAT Directive. Domestic telecommunications services, including those supplied by Swedish-resident foreign businesses, are subject to VAT at the standard rate of 25%. The VAT treatment of international telecommunications services is based on the revised EU VAT model.

Services supplied internationally by a telecommunications business located in Sweden are generally outside the scope of VAT when supplied to anyone located outside Sweden. The only exceptions are services supplied to private individuals or unregistered persons located in other member states. Those supplies are subject to Swedish VAT at the standard rate.

Non-resident providers are not liable to register and account for Swedish VAT on supplies used by Swedish customers, provided those customers are taxable persons for VAT purposes. These customers are required to self-account for VAT under reverse-charge procedures.

When a non-resident provider supplies services to private individuals, to be used in Sweden, the provider is required to register and account for Swedish VAT. For an overseas provider, it should be possible to limit Swedish VAT liability to supplies made to Swedish individuals for use in the EU. However, this may then require the overseas provider to be registered for VAT purposes in many different EU-member states. Alternatively, an overseas provider may choose to register in a single EU-member state in order to contract with all customers who are EU private individuals. The supplies made from the single EU registration to these customers will then be subject to local VAT in the member state of registration.

Access to the Internet is included within the definition of telecommunications, and the principles set out above apply equally to Internet service providers (ISPs).

Settlements under the Melbourne Agreement can, in principle, be made tax-free. Since the introduction of rules on the place of supply for telecommunications services, on July 1, 1997, the Melbourne rules have had less practical impact.

Local and Provincial Taxes

Local taxes are paid only by individuals, not by corporations.

For Additional Information, Contact:

Stefan Carlsson
Tax Partner
and
Peter Lynél
Telecoms Consulting Manager
S-113 97 Stockholm
Sweden
Telephone: 46 (8) 690 30 00 (Carlsson)
            46 (8) 690 30 76 (Lynél)
Fax: 46 (8) 31 39 90 (Carlsson)
      46 (8) 690 35 00 (Lynél)
E-mail: Stefan_Carlsson@se.coopers.com
         Peter_Lynel@se.coopers.com

Switzerland

Telecommunications Tax Profile
by Charles Hermann
Senior Tax Manager, Zurich

Overview of the Telecommunications Market

Historical Background

Traditionally, the government-owned Swiss Telecom PTT has benefited from a large-scale monopoly in various areas of the telecommunications business, including wireline, wireless and the customer equipment business. During the last 10 years, the monopoly has been reduced, with the first wave of liberalization opening the customer premise equipment market.

In 1992 the Telecommunications Act defined the PTT's role and established regulatory guidelines for telecommunications. In 1994 the telecommunications and postal activities of the PTT were officially separated, and in 1998 they were to become independent companies. The postal service was to be owned by the government, and Swiss Telecom PTT (renamed Swisscom) was to be partially privatized, with government retaining at least 51% ownership.

Current Status

In mid-1997 a comprehensive telecommunications act, the Fernmeldegesetz, was passed, laying the groundwork for full liberalization of telecommunications activities as of January 1, 1998. Specific issues such as interconnection and number portability have been clarified in subsequent ordinances. Fixed network competition was to begin immediately. Additional mobile licenses were expected to be issued in mid-1998. Although Switzerland is not a member of the European Union (EU), the regulations are essentially in accordance with pan-European liberalization of this sector.

Switzerland has a high penetration of fixed telephony, at 64 lines per hundred population. Revenue in 1996 totaled approximately CHF 10.5 billion, with a profit margin of more than 12%

before restructuring costs. More than 90% of the local exchange has been digitized, and the remainder should be fully digitized by the end of 1998.

The international wireline business was to be legally liberalized on January 1, 1998, but competition has existed for some time. Some of the major players in the long-distance sector, such as British Telecom and Global One, already provide services in Switzerland for both consumers and businesses.

Swisscom took aggressive steps to prepare for a competitive market, reducing tariffs for local and national calls and introducing new peak/off-peak rates. Growth rates varied in 1996, with local calls increasing 1.8%, long distance 4.6%, and international 8.9% in terms of paid minutes.

New entrants into the Swiss mobile market will face a well-established incumbent. Swisscom's mobile arm, Natel, operates two networks, one analog and one digital. The Natel C network, which is for local purposes, has achieved about 97% coverage of Switzerland. By the end of 1995 the Natel D GSM network, which is primarily for international purposes, had 95% national coverage. To further its reach, Swisscom has concluded roaming agreements with more than 100 countries. The mobile licensing process may be slowed by a shortage of available frequencies resulting from the previous allocation to Swisscom and the military, and the absorption of spectrum by neighboring countries. However, there should be considerable room for increasing the penetration of mobile phones given the high standard of living in Switzerland and the relatively low penetration of mobile phones (as of 1996, there were 9 subscribers per 100 people).

The customer premise equipment sector is almost completely liberalized. Today the key players in the sector hold a significant share of the Swiss market, and the number of competitors is not likely to increase significantly in the future.

Current Liberalization Status

In the World Trade Organization (WTO) negotiations in February 1997, Switzerland pledged full liberalization of telecommunications between 1998 and 2002 and also committed to adhere to a full set of common regulatory principles.

Type of Service	Degree of Liberalization	Key Legislation	Date of Actual or Expected Liberalization	Comments
Local	Fully liberalized	Fernmeldegesetz April 1997	1998	Universal service to be provided by Swisscom until 2003
Long Distance				
International				
Cellular				One, possibly two additional licenses to be issued
Paging				At least one independent paging firm has been active in Switzerland since the early 1970s
Value-added				

Competitive Environment

Because of the nascent stage of competition in Swiss telecoms, no revenue information is available.

Licensing Requirements

Telecommunications regulations are the responsibility of the Office Fédéral de la Communication (OFCOM), which was formulating new licensing procedures following passage of the Fernmeldegesetz. Telecoms service providers will be required to have a license if they control transmission capabilities. All other providers are required to be registered. Wireless licenses will be limited because of the scarcity of frequencies. The key area for intervention by the regulator will be in interconnection. The regulator will act as an arbitrator in interconnection disputes.

Universal service is a major political issue in Switzerland because of the high cost of access to the rural population in mountainous regions. Swisscom agreed to ensure basic, universal service for five years following liberalization. After that, licenses will be issued for universal service provision. Where the costs of provision could not be covered, a subsidy would be paid to the operator, or a "negative auction" could be held.

Potential for Foreign Ownerships/Relationships

There are no limitations on the percentage of a telecommunications business that can be owned by a foreign company.

Potential for Upcoming Liberalization/Investment Opportunities

New competitors in national service were to begin operations January 1, 1998. Major groups who were preparing to enter the market included: Newtelco/Sunrise, a joint venture between British Telecom, SBB (Swiss Railways), Migros (a large Swiss retailer) and UBS (Union Bank of Switzerland); Diax, a joint venture including SBC Communications, TeleDanmark A/S, and several large Swiss electricity companies; WorldCom; COLT Telecommunications; Global One; and possibly some smaller electrical companies.

Utilization of local cable television networks for telecommunications services is also expected. Competitors will have to form alliances in order to use the cable companies to provide an alternative local loop throughout Switzerland. Additional investments will be necessary to gain access to business areas.

The following segments of the telecommunications business are likely to be important targets for investment in the next two years:

- Private networks for individual companies

- Networking, network management and other operational support systems

- Wireless and mobile telecommunications, including cellular phone businesses

- Customer support

Forms of Doing Business

Permanent Establishment

There are no special rules applicable for the taxation of a permanent establishment (PE) in the telecommunications industry. Swiss tax authorities have not yet addressed the tax implications related to the drastic restructuring of the industry.

Swiss tax laws and most Swiss treaties follow the OECD Model Convention. Swiss tax is imposed on the actual or assumed profit and capital attributable to a branch. Profits are remittable abroad without deduction of withholding taxes. Branches of foreign corporations are treated for income tax purposes in the same way as those of local corporations. The tax rates are basically the same as for subsidiaries. However, the income used for the determination of the applicable tax rates is always the foreign company's total income.

Telecommunications services can cover a broad range of activities, which may or may not constitute a PE. Some examples follow:

- When long-distance telephone services and any advertising pertaining to them are provided without any local presence, a foreign company will not be treated as having a PE in Switzerland. The licensing of technology and know-how does not constitute a PE. Even if the licensing of technology and know-how exceeds 12 months, a foreign company will not be considered to have a PE.

- The provision of technical assistance and services to a local company in exchange for service fees, including operator services, may generate a place of business if premises, facilities or installations are at the disposal of a foreign company. However, as long as this activity is temporary or is not carried out in a fixed place, the provision of technical assistance and services to a local company in exchange for service fees does not qualify as a fixed place of business, and a foreign company will not be treated as having a PE.

- The leasing of telecommunications equipment to a local company does not constitute a PE as long as the contract is limited to the leasing of equipment.

- For call reorganization and turnaround services, there is no local presence or fixed place of business and thus no PE. (A few foreign companies already provide long distance telephone services to Swiss local customers without any local presence.)

- Internet access services purchased from a foreign company will be treated as the licensing of intangibles. Royalty payments are not subject to withholding tax. Thus, the mere provision of these services will not trigger any tax consequences. However, the local use of an intangible will increase the chances of a foreign company creating a PE.

- The tax authorities have not yet published any specific guidelines on the tax treatment related to the location of a server, a switch or a website in Switzerland. Therefore, general tax principles apply. According to general principles, the location of a server, a switch or a website in Switzerland does not constitute a PE.

- The laying of fiber optic cable and construction of switching equipment by a foreign company in Switzerland is treated as an installation project. If the project lasts more than 12 months, it will constitute a PE. If the fiber optic cable system is later sold to a Swiss company and the foreign company does not maintain any interest in the system, then the foreign company will not have a PE.

- If a foreign company acts as a contractor, undertakes activities in Switzerland and has personnel in Switzerland for a period exceeding one year, then it will be considered as having a PE. If the presence of employees of the foreign company in Switzerland lasts less than 12 months and the foreign company does not undertake activities in the planning or supervision of the fiber optic cable system, then the foreign company will not have a PE.

Business Entities

Local Branch and Locally Incorporated Subsidiary of a Foreign Company. Foreign investors in the telecommunications industry may choose either option, but a locally incorporated subsidiary may be preferable. There are no tax consolidation rules in Switzerland. Each company is assessed separately. These two types of business entities are compared in the table on page 2-184.

Joint Venture. Joint ventures may be established in the form of equity investments in corporations or as ordinary partnerships. No legislation applies specifically to joint ventures. Joint venture corporations are taxed as regular corporations.

Ordinary partnerships are regarded as transparent conduits, with partners being taxed on their share of income and net assets. A foreign venture may or may not have a permanent establishment in Switzerland, depending on the circumstances of each case. If there is no PE, no Swiss tax liability will arise.

	Local Subsidiary of a Foreign Company	Local Branch of a Foreign Company
Basis of Taxation	Taxed on its worldwide income	Either the direct method, based on branch accounts, or the indirect method, based on an allocation of a company's total profit
Withholding Tax	35% withholding tax on dividend distributions (which may be refunded under a double-tax treaty)	No withholding tax on the transfer of branch profits to its foreign headquarters
Stamp Duty	1% on paid-in capital	No stamp duty
Tax Losses	Can be carried forward for 7 years; cannot be carried back	Depends on the allocation method
Audit	Statutory requirement for all companies	No statutory audit requirement
Publication of Accounts	Accounts do not have to be made available to the public	Not applicable
Capital Taxes	Levied at the federal and cantonal levels on total equity	Normally based on branch equity, as for branch accounts
Tax Rate	Progressive rates (maximum rate is approximately 35%)	Progressive rates (maximum rate is approximately 35%)
Number of Directors	A majority of Swiss directors living in Switzerland; there is a minimum of one director	Not applicable

Local Funding Alternatives

Debt versus Equity

Federal and cantonal tax laws may treat as equity part of the interest-bearing debt from related parties. If the amount of a loan is considered excessive, then part of it may be reclassified as equity and the interest on that part of the loan as a dividend distribution. The level of acceptable debt is that which a company could obtain from a bank with no parent guarantee. In general, however, the ratio of interest-bearing debt to equity should not exceed 5 to 1, as provided in the 1997 guidelines issued by the tax administration. Any interest paid on loans from related parties in excess of this ratio may be treated as a hidden distribution. Excessive interest payments (i.e., remunerations that do not comply with the arm's-length principle) may also be treated as a hidden distribution. The interest will be added back to the taxable income of the company and will be subject to a 35% withholding tax. The recipient of the hidden distribution may claim a partial refund of the withholding tax, if it is entitled to treaty protection.

Only realized foreign exchange gains may be taken up in the account, whereas unrealized foreign exchange losses need to be accounted for. Provided the gains and losses have been recorded according to these rules, they are recognized for tax purposes in the same way. If unrealized losses have not been reflected in the books, they will also not be deductible for tax purposes, and unrealized gains will be taxable if recorded.

Exchange Controls

Switzerland does not impose any exchange controls.

Business Acquisitions and Dispositions

Capital Contributions into an Existing Local Entity

A capital issue duty of 1% is levied on the issue of shares by a local company upon its formation or upon a subsequent share-capital increase. It is also levied on capital contributions either in kind or in cash made by the shareholders without formal increase of the company's capital. If the shares are issued other than for cash, the tax is calculated on the basis of the greater of the issued shares' face value or the fair market value of the asset received.

No stamp tax is levied on the issue of, or an increase in, the nominal value of shares on the occasion of qualifying reorganization transactions, such as a merger, a merger-like transaction or a division. The contribution of business assets constituting an enterprise may be considered as a division.

A capital contribution into a general partnership does not raise any capital duty issues.

For tax purposes, there is no limitation on the contribution of intangibles by a foreign company into a Swiss entity. From a legal point of view, the intangibles cannot be contributed at a value exceeding their fair market value. If the intangibles are contributed at a value above the fair market value, the part exceeding this amount will be treated as a hidden distribution and will be subject to Swiss withholding tax at a rate of 35%.

Any capital contribution made by a Swiss or foreign company into a Swiss entity will not modify the tax status of the local company.

Purchase or Sale of Shares in a Local Entity

Capital gains realized by individual shareholders on the disposal of shares are tax-exempt if the shares were held for private purposes. Capital gains realized by Swiss operating companies, Swiss partnerships and foreign entities having permanent establishments in Switzerland are taxed on the disposal of shares as ordinary income if the shares are part of the assets of the PE. However, as of January 1, 1998, capital gains realized by companies on the disposal of equity investment of more than 20% of the capital of the subsidiary acquired after January 1, 1997, and held for a period of more than one year, will benefit from the participation reduction system at the federal tax level. In practice, this participation reduction system leads to a 95% federal tax exemption. Nevertheless, such capital gains remain taxable at the cantonal and communal levels. Capital gains realized by holding companies from the disposal of investments are free of taxes at the cantonal and communal level. In addition they benefit from the participation reduction system at the federal level, provided (1) the investment has been acquired after January 1, 1997, (2) the investment is an equity investment of more than 20% of the capital of the subsidiary, and (3) the investment has been held for a period of more than one year.

If the purchase price for shares in a local entity exceeds the net book value, there is no mechanism that would allow a foreign company to step-up the tax basis in the assets.

Generally, the interest paid by a purchaser for financing a share acquisition is outside the scope of the local entity and must be borne by the shareholder. After the acquisition, it may be possible to merge the acquisition vehicle with the local company. Then the interest costs incurred as a result of acquiring the company may be offset against the income of the local company.

Purchase or Sale of Assets

There are no restrictions on foreign corporations making asset or share acquisitions in Switzerland. However, in certain circumstances, if the business assets include Swiss real estate or if the acquired company owns Swiss real estate, permission must be obtained from the cantonal authority. The sale of assets by a local entity triggers a capital gain tax on the difference between the book value and the disposal price of the assets.

There are no tax-free alternatives available for dispositions. If the assets are transferred within a qualified reorganization (merger, spin-off, or merger-like transaction), the dispositions of assets may be carried out tax-free.

A step-up in the tax basis of the assets is possible if the market value exceeds the current basis. Goodwill can normally be depreciated over five years. The interest on loans taken in order to

finance the acquisition is deductible. No stamp taxes are payable.

Generally, tax losses cannot be carried forward. The seller may realize taxable gains (e.g., goodwill). The transfer of assets constituting an enterprise does not trigger any VAT consequences.

Asset or Share Deal

A purchaser will generally prefer to acquire assets rather than shares in order to be able to offset the acquisition costs (goodwill amortization and interest expenses) against the taxable profits generated by the assets. A seller, however, will normally prefer to dispose of the shares rather than the assets in order to trigger a capital gain. A share disposal is generally tax-free if the seller is a Swiss individual, is almost tax-exempt if the seller is a holding company, and is taxed at a reduced rate if the seller is an operating company. Thus, the decision whether to acquire shares or assets depends on the specific circumstances.

Start-up Business Issues

Pre-operating Losses and Start-up/Construction Costs

The tax treatment of pre-operating losses and start-up/construction costs generally follows the account treatment, provided it is in line with the Swiss GAAP (generally accepted accounting principles). The costs of establishing a local company may be capitalized and must be written off on the straight-line basis over a period of five years or less. According to the prudence principle, costs that do not correspond to anticipated revenues cannot be capitalized. Costs related to marketable products may be capitalized up to the amount of reasonable anticipated future earnings. If these costs are capitalized, they must be written off over a period of no more than five years or when the corresponding revenue materializes. The goodwill of a business does not constitute an asset. However, the acquirer of the assets and liabilities of an existing business may capitalize the goodwill paid for and properly identified. Goodwill should be written off over a period of three to five years (in certain cases, this may be extended to seven years).

Pre-operating costs incurred by a foreign company outside Switzerland cannot be capitalized or deducted from the income of the local company. VAT paid by a foreign company in connection with pre-operating costs cannot be recovered.

Customs Duties and VAT

Apart from a few items, customs duties are generally based on the weight rather than the value of the goods imported. Currently, 100 kg. of telecommunications equipment costs about CHF 120 to import. No changes were expected to result from the WTO commitments. In addition to customs duty, a VAT of 6.5% must be paid on imports to Switzerland (see "Value-Added Tax, Sales Tax and/or Other Pertinent Taxes").

Loss Carryovers

Operating losses can only be carried forward. On the federal level, losses may be carried forward for a maximum of seven years. The cantons normally provide for loss carryforward periods of three to seven years. Only the canton of Thurgau provides for a one-year loss-carryback possibility.

Losses from one activity can offset profits of other activities. There is no distinction among income derived from active businesses, passive income, capital gains, or exchange gains or losses. A change of ownership does not affect the loss carryforward opportunities of an active local company. Swiss tax laws do not provide for the consolidation of profitable and unprofitable group companies.

Operating Considerations

Corporate Income Taxes

Taxes are paid at three levels: federal, cantonal and communal. The federal tax law and the tax laws of the 26 cantons are being harmonized so that all cantonal laws are similar. Communal taxes follow the cantonal tax laws.

Aggregate tax rates (including federal, cantonal and communal tax rates) are generally progressive and are based on the ratio of taxable income to net taxable equity. Minimum and maximum tax rates apply. The federal statutory tax rate amounts to 8.5% of the profit after tax. The cantonal and communal statutory tax rates vary from about 7% to about 30% of after-tax profit. The overall effective tax rate on the profit before tax ranges from approximately 12% to 33%.

Withholding tax is deducted at the rate of 35% from dividends and similar distributions paid to both residents and non-residents. Non-resident shareholders may obtain relief under a tax treaty. No withholding tax is levied on interest payments made on inter-company loans. Withholding tax is levied on interest from bonds and bond-like loans from Swiss debtors.

Capital Gains Taxes

For the most part, capital gains are taxed as part of ordinary business income. Certain cantons have a special tax treatment for capital gains generated by the sale of real estate. In addition, gains on the disposal of certain fixed assets can be used against the base cost of replacements. Capital gains realized by companies on the disposal of equity investment acquired after January 1, 1997, and representing more than 20% of the capital of the subsidiary benefit from the participation reduction

system at the federal tax level, provided the investment has been held for a period of more than one year (see "Purchase or Sale of Shares in a Local Entity").

Tax Holidays and Exemptions

Tax incentives, in the form of relief or complete exemption from income tax, are granted by a canton or the federal government on a case-by-case basis. The extent and duration depend largely on the size of the investment and the importance attributed to the economic development. The maximum tax holiday is 10 years, but the typical duration is five to seven years. Telecommunications companies have already obtained such tax holidays.

Depreciation/Cost-Recovery Conventions/Accelerated Deductions

Depreciation of both tangible and intangible fixed assets is allowed where commercially justified and recorded in a company's financial statements. Both the straight-line and the declining-balance methods may be used. Accelerated rates of depreciation may be allowed for assets used only for short periods or for assets that are used intensively. There are no special rules for different types of telecoms businesses, or for software embedded in telecommunications equipment, or for research and development costs, including software development costs.

The following rates are commonly used:

	Declining-balance	Straight-line
Amortization of intangible assets (e.g., goodwill and know-how)	40%	20%
Computer hardware and software	40%	20%
Telecoms infrastructure (cables, etc.)	20%	10%
Cars, fixtures and fittings	40%	20%
Operating buildings	8%	4%

According to the new federal tax law, deductible provisions for future research and development costs can be made. However, the maximum deductible amount is the lower of 10% of taxable income or CHF 1 million. Marketing and advertising costs (including payments made directly or indirectly to attract customers) are generally tax-deductible.

Transfer Pricing Rules

Transfer pricing rules in Switzerland are based on the arm's-length principle. There is no specific transfer pricing tax legislation and no standard rules that may be generalized. If transfers of goods and services between related companies are not conducted at arm's-length prices, the difference between the market price and the transfer price is considered a hidden profit distribution with income-tax and withholding-tax consequences. Rulings can often be obtained for service companies to be taxed on a cost-plus basis.

Transfers of Patents, Trademarks and Software

License fees and royalties are generally tax-deductible and not subject to withholding tax, as long as they are paid on an arm's-length basis. In the telecommunications business, a license fee of 5% of sales is basically accepted as a tax-deductible item by the local tax authorities. Local law does not impose any restriction on the licensing of technology to a local company for a royalty.

Service Fees

Service fees are generally tax-deductible and not subject to withholding tax if they comply with the arm's-length principle.

Value-Added Tax, Sales Tax and/or Other Pertinent Taxes

Swiss VAT of 6.5% (standard rate) is charged on the supply of services and goods within Switzerland and the principality of Liechtenstein. According to the current practice of the VAT authorities, the supply of cross-border telecommunications services is zero-rated as long as these services are used or exploited abroad. The supply of telephone services provided and invoiced by Swiss Telecom PTT (renamed Swisscom) must be taxed according to the Swiss VAT ordinance, which provides that telecommunications services supplied to Swiss territory from foreign territory or from foreign territory across Swiss territory to foreign territory (transit) are zero-rated. Other telecommunications services, however, are taxable, even if they are supplied from Swiss to foreign territory.

In general, payments to individual and/or business entities that are not resident for tax purposes in Switzerland are not subject to Swiss VAT. No reverse-charge mechanism applies for such transactions. According to the Swiss VAT ordinance, a reverse-charge mechanism applies only to business entities that are tax-resident in Switzerland and liable to Swiss VAT, and which receive VATable services from abroad that are used in Switzerland. Any Swiss-resident individual who receives VATable services from abroad exceeding CHF 10,000 on a yearly basis has to declare and pay the VAT to the Swiss VAT authorities.

Generally, any foreign entrepreneur who is liable for VAT is entitled to recover Swiss VAT if certain criteria are fulfilled. The re-

fund application has to be filed with the VAT authorities by a fiscal representative who is resident in Switzerland no later than June 30 of the year following the year for which the refund is requested. Recovery of VAT can take place without having to register for VAT in Switzerland.

The Melbourne Agreement applies currently, but only for services supplied by Swiss PTT Telecom.

According to the current practice of the Swiss VAT authorities, the domicile principle applies to cross-border telecommunications services; thus, the provision of Internet access by a Swiss provider to a recipient abroad is zero-rated. The provision of Internet access by a Swiss provider to a recipient within Switzerland and the principality of Liechtenstein is VATable at 6.5%. There is currently no distinction between regular telephony and Internet telephony for VAT purposes.

Stamp Duty. Stamp duty of 1% is levied on any capital increase in a Swiss corporation and on the formation of a company. However, the first CHF 250,000 equity contribution is exempt, regardless of the size of the issue.

Local and Provincial Taxes

Net Wealth Tax. Corporations are subject to annual net wealth tax at the cantonal and communal levels on their equity (paid-in capital, reserves and taxed hidden reserves). The tax rates vary from approximately 0.1% to 0.4% of the equity. No such tax is levied on debt financing unless it is reclassified as equity (see "Debt versus Equity").

For Additional Information, Contact:

Charles Hermann
Senior Tax Manager
and
Stephan Hürlimann
Tax Partner
Stampfenbachstrasse 73
Zurich
Switzerland
Telephone: 41 (1) 365 8365
Fax: 41 (1) 365 8773

Rune Aresvik
Senior Telecoms Consultant
Address: same as above
Telephone: 41 (1) 365 8658
Fax: 41 (1) 365 8686
E-mail: Rune_Aresvik@ch.coopers.com

Turkey

Telecommunications Tax Profile
by Adnan Nas
Senior Tax Partner, Istanbul

Overview of the Telecommunications Market

Historical Background

All telecommunications services are provided by the national telecommunications company, Türk Telekomünikasyon A.S. (Türk Telekom), either directly or, for some value-added services, through revenue-sharing agreements with independent operators. As part of initiatives to reform the economy, the government is planning to privatize Türk Telekom. While the concept has been approved by the Parliament, the actual implementation has been delayed for a number of years by legal challenges and the lack of a regulatory framework. There is no legislation allowing direct competition with Türk Telekom.

Current Status

Over the last 15 years, the number of telephone lines has increased from 3.5 lines to more than 20 lines per 100 people. The recent growth in the network means that a high proportion of switching is digital. Industry developments have included the establishment of paging services, one Nordic mobile telephone (NMT) and two global system for mobile communications (GSM) networks, and the launching of three Türksat satellites.

The GSM networks were developed by two private consortia, and operated under revenue-sharing agreements with Türk Telekom. In 1997, the consortia negotiated with Türk Telekom for the outright acquisition of full operating licenses. These licensing agreements are currently awaiting approval. There are now more than 1.2 million cellular subscribers, and this number is growing rapidly, which may result in the creation of a third GSM or personal communications (PCN) network in the next two to three years.

Internet backbone services are also provided under a revenue-sharing agreement with the national Internet network, or Turnet, which is a joint venture with Deutsche Telekom AG, Satko and Sprint. There are a growing number of Internet access service providers.

There are three main laws relating to the telecommunications industry. Law No. 4000, which went into effect in June 1994, established Türk Telekom and allowed the transfer of the telecommunications business from the state-owned Post Telegraph and Telephone (PTT) to Türk Telekom. Law No. 4046, which is also known as the privatization law, contained the basic provisions for selling up to 49% of the shares of Türk Telekom. Law No. 4107 authorized the licensing of private companies to operate and provide such telecommunications services as mobile telephone, paging, data network, intelligent network, pay telephones, satellite systems, directory publishing and other value-added services.

Current Liberalization Status

Turkey has made a limited commitment to the regulatory principles and guidelines of the World Trade Organization (WTO), and partial liberalization of a limited range of services is now taking place.

Type of Service	Degree of Liberalization	Key Legislation	Date of Actual or Expected Liberalization	Comments
Local, Long Distance and International	Monopoly	Law No. 4000 Law No. 4046 Law No. 4107	Unknown	The regulatory framework for privatization is under discussion. It will need to be consistent with EU initiatives on competition and allow alternative service providers. This is not likely to happen in the short or medium term.
Cellular	Partially liberalized	Law No. 4000 Law No. 4046 Law No. 4107	1994	The two GSM service providers operated under revenue-sharing agreements with Türk Telekom, which were converted into licensing agreements. Both licenses were granted in 1997 and are pending approval.
Paging	Monopoly	Law No. 4000 Law No. 4046 Law No. 4107	Unknown	
Value-added	Partially liberalized	Law No. 4107	1994	Consists of services other than the main telecommunications services of Türk Telekom. Typically, these are provided through revenue-sharing agreements and there is one provider per value-added service.

Competitive Environment*

At the moment, Turkey does not have a very competitive environment in the telecommunications industry, as the following table reflects.

Type of Service	Entire Market	Top Two Players	
	Number of Players	Names	Ownership
Local, Long Distance and International	1	Türk Telekom	State-owned
Cellular	2 (GSM)	Türkcell	Telecom Finland Ltd., Ericsson Telekomunikasyon A.S., Cukurova Group, Bilka and MV Komunikasyon
		Telsim Mobil Telekomunikasyon Hizmeretleri AS (Telsim)	Rumeli Holding, Siemens and Alcatel Bell
Paging	1	Türk Telekom	State-owned
Value-added	1	Türk Telekom	State-owned

* Revenue figures are not available.

Licensing Requirements

It is expected that once the telecommunications industry is liberalized, both new and existing telecommunications operators will require licenses. It is not yet known who the regulator of the industry will be or whether licenses will be granted to compete with Türk Telekom's main wireline business. Currently, the only telecommunications services for which licenses are allowed are value-added services (VAS). Law No. 4107 describes VAS as services other than the main telecommunications services of Türk Telekom, including mobile phone, paging, data networks, intelligent networks, cable TV, satellite systems and pay phones. Licenses for VAS are given through competitive bids and they may be local, regional or national. In order to apply for a license:

- The bidder or at least one of the consortium partners must have been previously engaged in telecommunications activities and services.

- At least one of the shareholders holding 20% or more of the capital and/or other properties of the company must be experienced in telecommunications services.

- The bidder must be a company or a person or a legal entity undertaking and committing to establish a Turkish company.

- The company must be established exclusively for the purpose of the specified VAS and at least 51% of its shares must be held by Turkish individuals or entities.

Potential for Foreign Ownerships/Relationships

Foreign ownership of VAS is limited to 49%. When Türk Telekom is eventually privatized, it is expected that 49% of the company will be sold, of which a total of 15% will be held by the postal service and by employees of Türk Telekom. The balance of 34% will be available for sale to the public and/or a potential strategic investor; although the form the sale will take has not yet been decided.

Potential for Upcoming Liberalization/Investment Opportunities

Currently, the only segments of the telecommunications industry that present opportunities for investment are VAS and the likely creation of a third cellular network. Liberalization of the rest of the industry has been slowed by the delay in privatizing Türk Telekom. Until a regulatory framework is developed and approved, it is unclear as to what level of competition will be permitted. However, the initial preparation for the privatization of Türk Telekom is now taking place and the sale of the first group of shares may occur in 1998.

Forms of Doing Business

Permanent Establishment

In order for a non-resident to be deemed to have a permanent establishment (PE), the non-resident must obtain its business income through either a fixed place of business (e.g., any place either designated for business, agricultural or independent professional activities or used in these activities such as a shop, an office, a branch, a warehouse or a construction site) or a permanent representative (i.e., a person or entity with a contract carrying out continuous business activity, a person whose expenses are partly or wholly regularly paid by the entity being represented, or a person continuously holding consignee goods for sale purposes on behalf of the entity represented). A

PE is subject to all Turkish direct and indirect taxes on its attributable profits and transactions. Telecommunications services can cover a broad range of activities, which may or may not constitute a PE. Some examples follow:

- The provision of long distance telephone services by a foreign company to local customers without any local presence or advertising would not create a PE.

- The licensing of technology and know-how to a Turkish company by a foreign company that does not have a fixed place of business or a permanent representative would not constitute a PE.

- The leasing of telecommunications equipment to a Turkish company would not create a PE.

- The provision of technical assistance and technological services by a foreign company to a Turkish company in exchange for services fees, including operator services and/or network management services, would not constitute a PE, regardless of whether the foreign company owned an equity interest in the local company.

- The provision of call reorganization/turnaround services would not create a PE unless the telephone cards were provided through a fixed place of business or a permanent representative.

- The provision of Internet access services would not create a PE. The software would have to be sold directly from abroad or through an independent agent in Turkey, and not through a permanent representative.

- Having a server or a switch located in Turkey without any personnel in Turkey may create a PE.

- Having a website located on a server outside Turkey but accessible by customers in Turkey would not create a PE.

- Having a website located on a server in Turkey that is not accessible by customers in Turkey but is accessible by customers in other countries may create a PE.

- The laying of fiber optic cable and construction of telecommunications switching equipment either for sale to a local company or to be operated by a foreign telecommunications company for a local company in exchange for a fee would constitute a PE.

Business Entities

Local Branch of a Foreign Company. Foreign companies may operate through a branch office. The income of a Turkish branch of a foreign company is taxed in the same way as a resident corporation. Turkish branches of foreign companies are subject to tax on an annual return basis on income received from the PE in Turkey. The profits and losses of the branch cannot be grouped with those of other operations.

Locally Incorporated Subsidiary of a Foreign Company. A foreign investor in the telecommunications industry can operate either as a joint-stock company (anonim sirket), which is the most common type of business entity used by foreign investors, or a limited liability company (limited sirket). Both are separate legal entities and offer their shareholders limited liability. In either case, a company is subject to corporate income tax at the rate of 27.5% and withholding tax at the rate of 22% including a "fund," which is a surcharge on the tax. The effective tax rate is 44%. The withholding tax rate applied to dividends may be reduced to 10% by a tax treaty. The profits and losses of the subsidiary cannot be grouped with those of other operations.

Joint Venture. A foreign company entering into a joint venture with a local or foreign partner would be deemed to have a PE in Turkey. While a joint venture is not a separate legal entity, it is a separate taxable entity and must file a tax return. A joint venture is taxed at the effective corporate tax rate of 44%. The dividends derived by the joint-venture partners are exempt from both corporate and withholding taxes. From a tax viewpoint, a joint venture cannot be created in the telecommunications industry. In Turkey, the joint venture was created essentially as a vehicle for long-term infrastructure projects.

Local Funding Alternatives

Debt versus Equity

Interest payments on loans not related to fixed assets are tax-deductible during the year in which they are accrued. When a loan is granted by a shareholder to a corporation, it should be on an arm's-length basis. If the terms of a loan agreement between related parties is not on an arm's-length basis, the interest on the loan is regarded as a disguised profit distribution and the amount of interest over market interest rates is not tax-deductible. Dividends are taxable at the corporate level regardless of distribution. At the time of the actual dividend distribution to both resident and non-resident shareholders, there would be no further taxation. Any advance payment (e.g., prior to a general board meeting) made to a shareholder during the year is considered as a loan and subject to an interest charge. However, if the loan remained as a long-term liability on the balance sheet and the company's debt-to-equity ratio was higher than for similar companies' in the same industry, neither interest expenses nor exchange differences related to the loan would be tax-deductible since the loan would be considered as hidden capital. Interest on hidden capital is not deductible. For a loan to be considered as hidden capital, one of the following conditions must be met:

- The loan must be provided by a related party, which is defined as a party having a direct, indirect or economic relationship with the company.

- The loan must be used continuously by the company (in general, for more than one year).

- The ratio of the loan to the equity of the company must be greater than the same ratio in other similar companies.

A loan from a non-resident bank or company must be registered with the Foreign Investment Directorate (FID). The FID is the authority overseeing all foreign investments in Turkey. All operations involving foreign capital must first apply to the FID for approval. Foreign currency transactions over US$50,000 must be reported to the Central Bank. As of January 1, 1998, transactions of TL (Turkish Lira) 5 billion or more, or the equivalent in foreign currency, must be reported to the Board of Money Laundering. If its maturity period exceeds 365 days, a foreign loan must also be registered with the Undersecretariat of the Treasury. Generally, foreign exchange gains on both shareholder and local debts are taxable and foreign exchange losses are tax-deductible. However, foreign exchange losses on shareholder loans that are regarded as hidden capital are not tax-deductible (see the discussion above).

When a local company obtains a loan from a non-resident bank, shareholder or company, interest paid on the loan is not subject to withholding tax or banking and insurance transactions tax (BITT). The interest on debt provided by non-financial companies or resident shareholders would be subject to VAT at the rate of 15%. However, a reverse-charge mechanism would also be applicable, which would result in a zero tax burden for the non-resident. VAT would be paid to a tax office on behalf of a non-resident by the local company using the loan, who would also deduct the VAT paid from its output VAT. The interest on debt obtained from a local financial institution is subject to BITT at the rate of 5%.

In general, loans obtained from local and foreign financial institutions are subject to the resource utilization support fund (RUSF) at rates ranging from 4% to 10%. The RUSF rate on foreign currency bank loans from local and foreign banks is 6%. A foreign currency loan obtained by a local company or a branch with an average maturity of two years is not subject to RUSF. When a local firm or a branch of a foreign company with an investment incentive certificate (which is a Treasury document that must be obtained by the investor in order to benefit from the incentives) borrows from overseas, it is exempt from paying RUSF.

Exchange Controls

There are no exchange controls in Turkey. However, in the case of certain large or significant transactions, the repatriation of funds requires the permission of the Undersecretariat of the Treasury and the Council of Ministers.

Business Acquisitions and Dispositions

Capital Contributions into an Existing Local Entity

A contribution of capital, which may be either in the form of cash or assets, by non-residents into an existing company must be approved by the FID. Intangibles cannot be contributed. When the contribution is in the form of assets, the FID determines the value of the assets being contributed. The amount of a cash contribution cannot be less than US$50,000 for each foreign shareholder; however, the total amount of the cash contribution can be shared among shareholders. A capital contribution is subject to both stamp tax, which is progressive, and to consumer protection fund tax, at a rate of .02%.

Purchase or Sale of Shares in a Local Entity

In general, a purchase of shares in a Turkish entity by a non-resident is subject to FID approval. Such approval is not required for a transfer of shares between non-residents. There is no mechanism that would allow the purchase of shares to be considered as a purchase of assets for local tax purposes.

A gain derived from a sale of shares in a local company by either a foreign company or a local company is taxable. There is no VAT on a sale of stock. A sale made to a non-resident by a non-resident results in no taxation. There is no difference between a majority and a minority sale with respect to tax treatment. The amount of capital gains to be taxable from the sale of shares in a local entity by a resident company and/or a branch in Turkey can be reduced provided that the shares are held for over two years (this is the cost value increase fund).

Purchase or Sale of Assets

If an asset is bought and sold in Turkey, the gains are taxable. For the seller, capital gains will be calculated based on the net book value (i.e., after deduction of accumulated depreciation and the revaluation fund). A fixed asset and its accumulated depreciation are increased by the revaluation rate. The revaluation rate, which is determined by the ministry of finance, is generally in line with the inflation rate. The difference between the increase in the fixed asset and its depreciation is recorded as the revaluation fund, which cannot be transferred to any account except the capital account.

The capital gains obtained by a resident company or a branch of a foreign company from a sale of assets can be reduced through the cost value increase fund mechanism and the cor-porate tax exemption. The corporate tax exemption and reduced withholding tax rate apply to the gains obtained by the resident companies and the branches of foreign companies from the sale of immovable assets such as buildings and land.

When any asset is purchased from an existing telecommunications company, the purchase is subject to VAT. The disposition of immovable assets is also subject to a registration fee at the rate of 4.8% of the sale price for both the buyer and the seller. When immovable assets are disposed of, those transactions that are exempt from corporate income tax are also exempt from VAT and registration fees. The only tax-free structuring available for the disposition of fixed assets is the full exemption that applies when production facilities are fully or partly subscribed as capital in-kind for companies possessing incentive certificates or for joint-stock companies that are established with a foreign investor.

Start-up Business Issues

Pre-operating Losses and Start-up/Construction Costs

Start-up costs are deductible for all type of business entities once the company is established. These costs can either be capitalized as organization costs or expensed in the initial year of establishment. Some of the more common categories of start-up costs include market research and the preparation of feasibility reports, expenses incurred during the preparation of articles of association, travel expenses relating to the business, legal and professional fees, expenses relating to the issuance of stock, employee training, advertising expenses, and general and administrative expenses.

Pre-operating costs incurred by a foreign company outside of Turkey cannot be deducted or amortized by the Turkish entity. In order for these costs to be deductible or amortized, they must be incurred by a local entity. Those costs incurred by a local company may be subject to withholding tax, which may be eliminated or reduced by a tax treaty.

License fees, franchise fees and fees for easements are considered to be intangible assets, rather than start-up costs, and must be amortized. Legal fees and organization costs incurred in the start-up period can either be expensed or amortized. Intangible assets cannot be revalued. (See "Purchase or Sale of Assets.") Fixed assets, such as office equipment, computers or automobiles, that are independent of the construction activity and have an economic life of more than a year, have to be capitalized during the pre-operating period.

For a foreign company, VAT paid for goods and services consumed in Turkey is not recoverable. However, for a local company, VAT paid during the pre-operating phase is recoverable as long as the company has transactions that result in output VAT. VAT paid in the pre-operating period cannot be revalued. It creates a financial burden on the companies due to Turkey's high rate of inflation.

Customs Duties and VAT

As a result of the Customs Union Agreement it has signed with the European Union (EU), Turkey does not impose customs duties on manufactured goods imported from EU-member states. Manufactured goods imported from non-EU states are subject to customs duties. Customs duty rates for imported telecommunications equipment range from 3% to 14%, depending on the nature of the equipment. The importation of telecommunications equipment is subject to VAT. The general VAT rate is 15%. VAT paid upon the importation of equipment is deductible as input VAT. There is no distinction drawn between regular telephony and Internet telephony for the purposes of VAT.

Loss Carryovers

Losses may be carried forward for up to five years, but they cannot be carried back. The use of a loss carryover can be limited after a change of ownership of a company. In a merger, because a new company is formed, no loss carryovers from either company prior to the merger can be brought forward into the new company. In an acquisition, the losses of the target company cannot be carried forward. However, the losses of the acquiring company can be carried forward. A change of business activity would not affect a company's ability to use its losses.

Operating Considerations

Corporate Income Taxes

Corporations resident in Turkey are subject to tax on their worldwide income. Branches of foreign corporations are subject to tax only on their Turkish-sourced income. The effective corporate tax rate is 27.5%, which includes the basic corporate income tax rate of 25% and supplemental levies ("fund") of 10%. For private companies, there is an additional withholding tax of 20% plus supplemental levies of 10%. For public companies (i.e., companies with at least 250 shareholders and 15% or more of their shares held by the public), the withholding tax rate is reduced to 10%. Fund is also applicable to withholding taxes. Public companies are subject to supplemental levies of 10% as well. Even when allowances or incentives reduce the effective tax rate, the corporate tax law stipulates a minimum corporate income tax of 20% with supplemental levies increasing this to 22%. Dividends from resident corporations and companies and certain types of investment income are excluded from the computation of taxable profit. The current corporate income tax rates can be summarized in the following table:

	Combined Income Tax	
	Private Company	Public Company
Corporate income tax	27.5%	27.5%
Withholding tax (on income after corporate income tax)	22%	11%
Total taxes on corporate income	44%	35.75%
Minimum corporate income tax	22%	22%

Capital Gains Tax

Capital gains are taxed as part of ordinary income.

Tax Holidays and Exemptions

There are no specific incentives for the telecommunications industry. To encourage investment in certain areas of the country, the government provides investment incentives. Incentives vary according to the location, scale and subject of the investment. Turkey is divided into three regions for investment purposes. To qualify for these incentives, new investments must be over TL 18 billion. All eligible projects must receive an incentive certificate from the Undersecretariat of the Treasury. Investment incentives include exemption from customs duties and VAT on imported machinery and equipment; investment allowances of up to 100% for approved projects; low-interest loans; exemption from taxes, duties and fees on long-term credit; a subsidy for 25% of the electricity consumption, and a deferral of 25% of taxable income. Payment of 20% of the corporate tax may be deferred if it relates to research and development expenses made in relation to new technology. Such deferred taxes become payable in nine equal installments over three years, starting in the following tax year.

Depreciation/Cost-Recovery Conventions/Accelerated Deductions

Maximum rates of depreciation are set by the Ministry of Finance. The two common methods of depreciation are the straight-line method and the double-declining-balance method; either method can be used for telecommunications equipment. The maximum rate is currently 20% per year for the straight-line method and 40% per year for the double-declining-balance method. Assets may not be written off in less than five years. Generally, assets are considered to be placed in service when they are capitalized and ready for use. In the context of a network, this would occur when the network was ready to begin operation.

With the exception of land, all tangible and intangible assets are depreciable over a minimum of five years. Buildings are depreciated at a rate of between 2% and 10% per year, over a minimum of 10 or 25 years depending on the type of building. Property, plant and equipment held throughout the year and the related accumulated depreciation may be revalued in accordance with the regulations of the Ministry of Finance. The Ministry sets a rate annually that is in line with the official inflation rate. The surplus is credited to reserves as revaluation fund. (See "Purchase or Sale of Assets.") The fixed assets except buildings are depreciated over their revalued costs. Buildings, even if revalued, are depreciated on the basis of original cost.

Leasehold improvements are amortized over the lease term. Leasehold improvements, intangible assets and capitalized start-up costs cannot be revalued. Software is generally treated as an intangible asset and is depreciated over five years. It cannot be revalued. The tax treatment of the software embedded in telecommunications equipment depends upon whether it can be separated from the equipment and used in other equipment or for different purposes. Software that can be separated will be capitalized as an intangible asset independently of the equipment. Software that cannot be separated will be treated as part of the telecommunications equipment and will be depreciated as the equipment would.

Research and development costs, including software development costs, relating to the business of the company are tax-deductible on an accrual basis. Marketing and advertising costs are tax-deductible provided they are incurred wholly and exclusively for the purposes of the business.

Transfer Pricing Rules

All transactions between related parties must be on an arm's-length basis. Purchases made at high prices or sales made at low prices between related parties, when compared with similar transactions in the market, could be considered as disguised profit distributions. The difference between the normal price and the high or low price would then be added to the company's taxable base.

Transfers of Patents, Trademarks and Software

All sales of intangible assets are taxable and are subject to VAT. When two parties agree to share their experience and expertise without an actual license or technology transfer, there are no tax implications since interests are simply shared.

Royalty agreements, including know-how and patent licenses, must be registered with the FID. Patents and trademark and software licensing fees are tax-deductible. They are generally subject to a 22% withholding tax, which can be reduced to 10% by a tax treaty. The transfer of technology would be regarded as a license rather than a sale when the transferor retained ownership of the intangible. The export of licenses, expertise and technology is subject to income tax.

Service Fees

Royalty, management and technical assistance agreements are subject to approval of the FID. Fees payable under approved agreements are tax-deductible; fees paid under disapproved agreements are not.

All consultancy fees are subject to a 22% withholding tax and to a 15% VAT. Generally, under many tax treaties, services rendered outside of Turkey may avoid withholding tax. A reverse-charge mechanism applies to VAT imposed on the transaction.

Value-Added Tax, Sales Tax and/or Other Pertinent Taxes

Value-Added Tax. Deliveries of goods and services are subject to VAT at rates varying from 1% to 40%. The general rate applied is 15%. Banking and insurance company transactions are exempt from VAT. Inter-company interest charges are subject to VAT at 15%. The Melbourne Agreement is not applicable to transactions that are subject to Turkish VAT law.

VAT paid is recoverable by being deducted from output VAT. It is necessary to register in a tax office for this recovery to take place. This option is not available to non-residents and, therefore, VAT paid by non-residents to Turkish sellers is not recoverable.

There are three different kinds of payments for Internet access: software, telephony and access services. A payment for software is likely to be regarded as a sale. If the company has a PE in Turkey, then the payment will be subject to VAT. Internet access is unlikely to be considered telephony. The access is provided by an Internet service provider (ISP) together with the software. The use of a telephone line may be regarded as an auxiliary service to Internet access and it is charged separately by a telephone company.

Stamp Tax. Stamp tax applies to a wide range of documents, including but not limited to contracts, agreements, notes payable, capital contributions, letters of credit, letters of guarantee, financial statements and payrolls. Stamp duty is levied as a percentage of the value of the document at rates ranging from 0.12% to 0.6%.

Property Tax. Property taxes are paid annually on the tax values of land and buildings at rates ranging from 0.3% to 0.6%. In the case of the sale of a property, a 4.8% registration fee is paid on the sale value by both the buyer and the seller. The rate is reduced to 2.4% if the property is contributed as capital-in-kind.

Local and Provincial Taxes

There are no provincial or municipal income taxes.

For Additional Information, Contact:

Adnan Nas
Senior Tax Partner
and
Faruk Sabuncu
Senior Tax Manager
Buyukdere Caddessi No. 111
Kat: 2-3-4
Gayrettepe 80300
Istanbul
Turkey
Telephone: 90 (212) 275 2840
Fax: 90 (212) 273 0493

Ukraine

Telecommunications Tax Profile
by Gerry Parfitt
Partner-in-Charge, Kiev

Overview of the Telecommunications Market

Historical Background

Utel, the first joint venture in the telecommunications industry, was established in 1992 by the government, AT&T, Deutsche Bundespost Telekom and PTT Telecom Netherlands to provide international and long-distance telecommunications services. Utel is one of the two major providers of international service. In 1993, the Ministry of Communications consolidated all government-owned telecommunications enterprises into the Ukrainian State Telecommunications Corporation (Ukrtelecom). Ukrtelecom is the other major provider of international calls and provides international service between Ukraine and the other members of the Commonwealth of Independent States (CIS). Ukrtelecom receives approximately 85% of its revenue from long-distance communications.

Ukrtelecom is responsible for implementing the government's telecommunications strategy and administering the national wireline infrastructure. By establishing a number of joint ventures, Ukrtelecom introduced foreign investment capital into the telecommunications industry. According to the Ministry of Communications, the total volume of foreign investment in the telecommunications industry reached more than US$200 million, or UAH 377 million, by the end of 1996, and, additionally, about US$90 million was received in loans.

Since 1992, more than 950 licenses have been issued to 680 different operators, many of whom are government-owned enterprises, for different types of telecommunications activities. In 1993, the first mobile cellular operator, Ukrainian Mobile Communications (UMC), was established. UMC offered service using the Nordic mobile telephone (NMT)-450i standard and had a monopoly in this sector until 1996, when Digital Cellular Communication (DCC) and Golden Telecom (which is a trademark of the Bankomsvyaz telecommunications company) were established. DCC operates a digital advanced mobile phone service (D-AMPS) network in Donetsk and Kiev, and Golden Telecom operates a global system for mobile communications (GSM)-1800 network in Kiev and Boryspil. Licenses to provide cellular service using the GSM-900 standard were received in March 1997 by UMC, Kyivstar and Ukrainian Radio Systems (URS). In September 1997, UMC began operating its GSM network in Kiev. Kyivstar started its operations in December 1997. It is not yet known when URS will begin operating. In December 1997, Ukrtelecom signed an agreement with Qualcomm, Inc., to develop services using the call division multiple access (CDMA) standard; these operations have not yet begun.

The State Committee on Communications, formerly the Ministry of Communications, is the main government body regulating the industry. The Telecommunications Act of 1995 is the main legislation affecting the telecommunications industry. This document set the framework for the liberalization of the telecommunications industry—only primary telecommunications networks and satellite services were to be retained as monopolies of the state. In December 1996, the Telecommunications Act was amended so that satellite telecommunications were no longer a state monopoly. This amendment was made to allow Globalstar to develop its program of satellite communications in Ukraine by the end of 1998. The Globalstar system will use a gateway built in Ukrainian territory and Ukrainian rocket-carriers to launch the majority of its satellites. At the end of 1997, the government announced its plan to begin privatizing the telecommunications industry in January 1998. Further amendments to the Telecommunications Act are expected in order to privatize Ukrtelecom.

Current Status

The Ukrainian Enterprise for International and Interurban Telecommunications and Broadcasting (UKRTEC) is the major provider of services for the construction and maintenance of communications networks. (UKRTEC was formerly a part of Ukrtelecom; it is now a separate legal entity.) Ukraine is in the process of establishing a unified telecommunications system and plans to build 7,500 kilometers of fiber optic cable by the year 2002. Three fiber optic lines have already been built as a part of the Trans-European Line project. These lines run from Lviv to Krakow, Poland; from Uzhgorod to Kisvarda, Hungary; and from Uzhgorod to Mihaylovce, Slovakia. In the fall of 1997, Ukrtelecom completed construction of a 750-kilometer fiber optic line from Kiev to Lviv, which uses the synchronous transport module (STM)-16 transmission system. These projects, in combination with other international projects such as the Trans-Asia Line and ITUR, which is the "optical highway" linking Italy, Turkey, Ukraine and Russia, will provide Ukraine with access to the digital telecommunications networks of southern Europe and the Middle East as well as to the Fiber-optic Link Around the Globe (FLAG) system.

Although fixed-line penetration in Ukraine is relatively high compared to that of other countries in the region (as of December 1997, it was 18.6 lines per 100 persons), the quality of the lines is poor—less than 10% of traffic is served by digital exchanges (these are mainly in Kiev and a few other major cities); the remainder is served by antiquated analog exchanges.

The major provider of fixed-line services is Ukrtelecom, which expects to make a substantial investment in this sector to improve the current network. Ukrtelecom plans to increase the number of lines to 17 million by the year 2006, which would increase the penetration rate to 35%. According to government estimates, the development of the fixed-line infrastructure will require about US$500 million to US$1 billion of investment per year.

The local telecommunications segment is the most liberalized part of the fixed-line market, with approximately 180 providers. However, out of 321,500 new telephone lines installed in 1996, only 65,000 (20.2%) were installed by private enterprises. A number of independent operators have begun providing local

service through their own digital exchanges. Although the quality of their services is higher than Ukrtelecom's, they serve fewer than 70,000 lines (or less than 1% of the total traffic). At the end of 1996, Ukrtelecom began providing digital telecommunications with ISDN (integrated services digital network) services in Kiev; this service is currently being introduced in other regions of Ukraine.

Paging and trunking telecommunications services are quickly developing in Ukraine. Licenses have been issued to over 40 providers of paging services, four of whom are actively developing operations in Kiev. Some of the operators use the same frequencies as operators in other regions of Ukraine to increase the areas covered. The UkrPage company uses satellites for communication with other cities in Ukraine. Currently, the total number of paging communication users in Ukraine is 30,000.

UMC, which has about 50,000 subscribers, has the most developed cellular network in Ukraine, covering about 100 cities and 4,500 km of highway with the NMT-450i standard, and the city of Kiev and Boryspil international airport with the GSM-900 standard. UMC provides automatic roaming with Moscow and St. Petersburg in Russia, and Germany and Switzerland, and plans to introduce roaming with Lithuania, Bulgaria and Poland. The total amount of UMC's investment in Ukraine is about US$90 million.

Value-added services are not yet developed. Currently, 90% of the telephone system is serviced by outdated and worn-out telephone switches; and most telephones use rotary dialing rather than tone dialing. In 1997, modern electronic switches were introduced in certain districts of Kiev and state-owned telecommunications enterprises began providing value-added services. In addition, a number of Internet providers offer data transferring services throughout Ukraine. Ukrpak runs an X.25 data transferring network.

Current Liberalization Status

The Ukrainian telecommunications market may be described as being in transition from monopoly. It is expected that after the privatization of some state-owned telecommunications enterprises, which may begin in 1998, the resulting competition will give new impetus for the industry's development. Details of the current liberalization status are given in the table below. It should also be noted that Ukraine is not part of the World Trade Organization (WTO), and therefore is not required to liberalize its market in order to meet provisions of WTO agreements.

Type of Service	Degree of Liberalization	Key Legislation	Date of Actual or Expected Liberalization	Comments
Local	Partially Liberalized			More than 350 licenses have been granted to provide local service.
Long Distance	Duopoly	Telecommunications Act of 1995	1999	
International	Duopoly			
Cellular	Liberalized			
Paging	Liberalized			

Competitive Environment*

The overall level of competition in the telecommunications industry continues to increase. The most competitive sector is that of local service, with the paging sector ranking second and cellular ranking third.

Type of Service	Entire Market Number of Players	Top Two Players	
		Names	Ownership
Local	180	Ukrtelecom	Government
		Regional Telephone Company Intersvyaz Ltd	Not available
Long Distance	3**	Ukrtelecom	Government
		Utel	Ukrtelecom (51%), AT&T (19.5%), Deutsche Telekom (19.5%), and PTT Telecom Netherlands (10%)
International	2	Ukrtelecom (CIS countries)	Government
		Utel (non-CIS countries)	Ukrtelecom (51%), AT&T (19.5%), Deutsche Telekom (19.5%) and PTT Telecom Netherlands (10%)
Cellular	4	UMC	Ukrtelecom (51%), PTT Telecom Netherlands (16.33%), TeleDanmark (16.33%) and Deutsche Telekom (16.33%)
		Bankomsvyaz (Golden Telecom)	Bancomservice (51%) and Global TeleSystems Group (49%)
Paging	44	Radiocom	Closed joint-stock company
		Deepei	Closed joint-stock company

* Revenue figures are not available.

** Kyivstar has a license to provide long-distance services, but does not currently operate in this sector.

Licensing Requirements

A new entrant to the telecommunications market must obtain a license. With the exception of telecommunications equipment providers, all telecommunications activities require licenses. State-owned telecommunications companies must purchase locally manufactured equipment unless no domestic manufacture capabilities exist. Licenses are issued by the State Committee on Communications. There is no limit to the number of licenses that can be issued; however, the number of licenses for operating radio frequencies can be limited. An application for a license must include the region where the activities will be conducted; however it is also possible to apply for a single license to operate on a nationwide basis. When two or more entities agree to enter into a joint activity in the telecommunications industry, it is possible for only one party to hold the relevant license.

Potential for Foreign Ownerships/Relationships

Foreign ownership of telecommunications companies is limited to 49%. In addition, the maintenance and operation of primary telecommunications networks and satellite services, with the exception of Globalstar, can be provided only by state-owned companies.

Potential for Upcoming Liberalization/Investment Opportunities

Ukraine represents one of the largest markets in Eastern Europe, with tremendous growth prospects for foreign investment. The most important targets for investment in the telecommunications industry are the cellular and paging sectors, as there is both an immediate demand for these services and an acceptance that the government does not have the resources to develop these sectors without significant assistance from foreign investors. As part of the privatization process, Ukrtelecom will be transformed into a state-owned joint-stock company sometime during 1999–2000. According to estimates, privatization of the telecommunications industry may generate more than US$2.5 billion.

Forms of Doing Business

Permanent Establishment

A foreign company is considered to have a permanent establishment (PE) if it (a) carries out business through a fixed place (e.g., an office or place of management, a branch, a factory or a workshop); or (b) is represented by a dependent agent who has and habitually exercises the authority to act on behalf of the foreign company. Telecommunications services can include a broad range of activities, which may or may not constitute a PE. Some examples follow:

- The provision of long-distance telephone service by a foreign company to local customers without any local presence or advertising will not create a PE.

- The licensing by a foreign company of technology and know-how to a local company will not create a PE.

- The provision of technical assistance and technological services—including operator and/or network management services—by a foreign company to a local company in exchange for service fees, when the foreign company owns an equity interest in the local company, will not create a PE.

- The leasing of telecommunications equipment to a local company will not create a PE.

- The provision of call reorganization/turnaround services will not create a PE.

- The provision of Internet access services will not create a PE.

- Having a server or a switch located in Ukraine but without any personnel in the country will not create a PE.

- Having a website located on a server in Ukraine that is accessible by customers in the country will not create a PE.

- Having a website located on a server outside Ukraine but accessible by customers in the country will not create a PE.

- Having a website located on a server in Ukraine that is not accessible by customers in the country but is accessible by customers in other countries will not create a PE.

- The laying of fiber optic cable and the construction of telecommunications switching equipment (a) for sale to a local company or (b) to be operated by a foreign telecommunications company for a local company in exchange for a fee may create a PE unless the relevant double-taxation agreements provide otherwise.

If a PE did not exist, then a non-resident would be subject to a withholding tax of 15% on its Ukrainian-sourced income. However, income related to international communications or international exchange of information is not subject to withholding tax. If a PE does exist, then profits earned by the PE are taxed at the rate of 30%. Withholding tax would not apply to the income of a PE of a telecommunications company.

Business Entities

Local Branch of a Foreign Company. A foreign company can set up a representative office in Ukraine, which is similar to an unincorporated branch. While the representative office must be registered with the state authorities, it does not constitute a legal entity. A non-resident company operating a representative office is deemed to be conducting business activity in Ukraine through a PE and may be subject to corporate profits tax unless protected by a double-taxation treaty. The profits and losses of the representative office may not be grouped with those of other operations.

Locally Incorporated Subsidiary of a Foreign Company. While this option is available to a foreign investor, it should be noted that due to the 49% limitation on foreign ownership of telecommunications companies, a subsidiary company cannot, by itself, engage in telecommunications operations. A local subsidiary of a foreign company is subject to corporate profits tax at the rate of 30%. The profits and losses of the subsidiary cannot be grouped with those of other operations.

Joint Venture. A joint venture can take the form of an incorporated entity, which has a distinct legal personality, or an unincorporated entity, which does not. An unincorporated joint venture agreement between a resident entity and a non-resident entity must be registered with the Ministry of Foreign Economic Relations and Trade. An unincorporated joint venture does not have the status of a separate legal entity; however, it is treated separately for tax purposes and the joint venture must file tax returns. A joint venture's profits are subject to 30% profits tax, and a distribution of profits is treated as a dividend payment for Ukrainian tax purposes.

Local Funding Alternatives

Debt versus Equity

Shareholder debt and equity financing are not included in a local entity's taxable gross income. For tax purposes, there is no difference between shareholder debt and local debt.

When there are no restrictions on the deductibility of interest, it is more advantageous to use shareholder debt rather than equity financing because of the lower withholding tax rate. Interest is subject to a 15% withholding tax; dividends are subject to a 30% withholding tax. There are restrictions on the deductibility of interest when at least 50% of the capital of a local entity is controlled by a non-resident. In that case, the deductibility of interest is limited to (i) the total interest income received during the period, plus (ii) 50% of the amount calculated as the company's gross income exclusive of interest received less gross expenses exclusive of interest paid. Any interest that is not included in gross expenses for the relevant reporting period as a result of these restrictions can be carried forward indefinitely to future reporting periods.

Exchange gains and losses on any loans should be included in either gross income or gross expenses for the relevant reporting period. Foreign loans must be registered with the National Bank of Ukraine.

Exchange Controls

The key requirements of Ukrainian currency control regulations are as follows:

- Funds in a foreign currency received by a Ukrainian company are not subject to a mandatory conversion requirement.

- Generally, payments under foreign trade contracts between a resident and a non-resident entity should be made in foreign currency only.

- Payments in foreign currencies between residents on the territory of Ukraine are prohibited.

- Settlements under foreign trade contracts must be made within a statutory 90-day period. Failure to satisfy this requirement attracts a penalty at 0.3% of the amount of goods or money due, accrued on a daily basis.

Business Acquisitions and Dispositions

Capital Contributions into an Existing Local Entity

A capital contribution into a local entity would not be subject to any local tax. In-kind contributions are exempt from customs duty. In accordance with the VAT law that went into effect on October 1, 1997, assets contributed by a foreign investor into an existing local entity in return for corporate rights are not subject to VAT. (However, regulations for customs clearance of such assets without paying VAT have yet to be adopted.) Disposal of such assets within three years of their contribution will result in

the local entity's paying all import duties. This requirement, however, does not apply to the repatriation of assets imported into Ukraine as an in-kind contribution by a non-resident.

There is no limitation with respect to intangibles that a foreign entity can contribute into an existing local entity. However, the value of intellectual property (e.g., copyrights, trademarks, know-how) must be confirmed both by valuation authorities in the Ukraine and in the foreign investor's home country.

Purchase or Sale of Shares in a Local Entity

VAT does not apply to the purchase or sale of shares; however, stamp duty at a rate of 0.2% would apply to such transactions. Goodwill is not deductible and not subject to depreciation. No planning exists that would consider the purchase of shares as a purchase of assets for local tax purposes.

Purchase or Sale of Assets

Capital gains arising from a sale of assets by a local entity should be included in the entity's taxable gross income, which can be reduced by current allowable expenses and any losses carried forward. A sale of assets will be subject to VAT at the rate of 20%.

Start-up Business Issues

Pre-operating Losses and Start-up/ Construction Costs

Business investigation costs, fees (such as license fees, franchise fees and easements) or similar costs that might be incurred in the start-up phase are not deductible. If pre-operating costs (direct or indirect) are incurred by a foreign company outside Ukraine, they cannot be deducted or amortized by the local entity. Compensation for pre-operating expenses made to a foreign company may be subject to a 15% withholding tax.

VAT incurred by a foreign company on local purchases is not recoverable. VAT payments made on the purchase of pre-operating goods or services cannot be recovered before the operating phase.

Customs Duties and VAT

The importation of telecommunications equipment attracts customs duty ranging from 0% for certain components to 20% for radio telephones. However, exemption from customs duty is available when the equipment either is contributed by a foreign investor into an existing local entity or originates from a country that has a free-trade agreement with Ukraine. Currently, Ukraine has signed free-trade agreements only with the members of the CIS. While Ukraine is not yet a member of the WTO, it has applied for membership and is moving rapidly to harmonize its customs system with that of the WTO.

The importation of telecommunications equipment is subject to VAT at a rate of 20%. Import VAT would be recoverable provided the assets were used in the taxpayer's business. Goods that are deemed to be critical imports (i.e., goods to be used in a Ukrainian importer's business) may be exempt from VAT until January 1, 1999. There is no distinction between regular telephony and Internet telephony for purposes of VAT.

Loss Carryovers

Losses cannot be carried back. Losses can be carried forward for up to five years, commencing from the quarter following the one where the loss occurred. There are no other specific limitations upon the carryover of losses. Losses may continue to be used after a change of ownership of a company or a change of business activity.

Operating Considerations

Corporate Income Taxes

Corporate profits tax is levied at the rate of 30% for both PEs and companies. Income earned by non-residents from Ukrainian sources is subject to withholding tax. Income in respect of international communications or international exchange of information is not subject to withholding tax.

Capital Gains Taxes

Capital gains are taxed as part of ordinary income.

Tax Holidays and Exemptions

Currently, no tax holidays or exemptions are available for telecommunications businesses.

Depreciation/Cost-Recovery Conventions/Accelerated Deductions

There are no specific differences in the rules for different types of telecommunications businesses. Fixed assets are divided into three groups and depreciated quarterly using the reducing-balance method at the rates shown below. Telecommunications equipment will be included in Group 2 or Group 3, depending upon the type of equipment.

- Group 1 (buildings) — 1.25%

- Group 2 (transport vehicles, furniture, office equipment, electrical appliances, information networks systems including computers, and telephone sets) — 6.25%

- Group 3 (all other assets) — 3.75%

A company can elect to depreciate newly purchased Group 3 assets using accelerated depreciation over a seven-year period. Intangible assets are depreciated over their expected useful life using the straight-line method. The estimated useful life is limited to a maximum of 10 years. For 1998, a reducing coefficient of 0.6 is applied to the standard depreciation rates. Software is treated as an intangible asset. No special rules exist for depreciating software embedded in telecommunications equipment.

Research and development costs are deductible for tax purposes. Marketing and advertising costs are fully deductible provided they are incurred as part of the taxpayer's business.

Transfer Pricing Rules

A transaction between related parties must be based on the usual market price, which is defined as the price that can be obtained by a seller for the sale of goods, works or services to non-related entities in the normal course of the seller's business. Related parties include a legal person that exercises control over the taxpayer, is controlled by the taxpayer, or is under common control with such taxpayer. The exercise of control over a taxpayer means holding, directly or indirectly through a number of related entities, the largest participating interest (shares) in a charter fund of the taxpayer, or control of the majority of votes in the governing body of such a taxpayer, or possession of participatory interests amounting to at least 20% of the charter fund of the taxpayer. When the tax authorities have grounds for challenging the prices charged or paid by a taxpayer as the result of an audit of the taxpayer's records, the taxpayer has the burden of justifying the price, if so requested by the tax authorities.

Transfers of Patents, Trademarks and Software

There are no restrictions on the license of technology to a local company for royalty fees. Patent, trademark and software licensing fees are deductible. Patent, trademark and software licensing fees are subject to a 15% withholding tax, which may be reduced by a double-taxation agreement. No export taxes apply to the transfer of licenses, expertise and/or technology out of Ukraine.

Service Fees

Service fees are not subject to withholding tax. Service fees are deductible as long as (a) the services received relate to the taxpayer's business activity; and (b) supporting documents in respect of payment for the services are available. If a service fee is paid to a related party, it is tax-deductible only if there is documentary evidence that the fee was paid for the services actually rendered.

Value-Added Tax, Sales Tax and/or Other Pertinent Taxes

VAT payers must register with the local tax authorities. Domestic or foreign legal entities will qualify as VAT payers when either:

- The entity's monthly volume of transactions that are subject to VAT is in excess of 600 non-taxable allowances (a non-taxable allowance is the amount of income that is not subject to individual income tax; at the time of publication, it was UAH 17) for any month within the last 12 months of operations; or

- The entity imports goods to Ukraine or receives from a non-resident contractor works or services for use or consumption in the territory of Ukraine.

The following transactions are subject to 20% VAT:

- The sale of goods, works or services in the customs territory of Ukraine.

- The import of goods or the receipt of works or services rendered by non-residents for use or consumption in the customs territory of Ukraine.

- The export of goods, works or services from Ukraine.

VAT can be recovered on costs included in the taxpayer's gross expenses or assets subject to depreciation. Debit VAT amounts shown in a taxpayer's VAT return for the relevant reporting period should be refunded to the taxpayer within the month following the reporting period.

VAT would apply to payments for the provision of Internet services (including the provision of Internet access and Internet telephony services). Internet access is not considered telephony.

Local and Provincial Taxes

There are 16 local taxes and charges that can be imposed at the discretion of the local authorities. Taxes relevant to the telecommunications sector include advertisement tax, which is calculated as a maximum of 0.5% of the advertisement services value; and municipal tax, which is calculated as follows: 10% multiplied by UAH 17 (non-taxable allowance) multiplied by the number of employees. Accordingly, the monthly tax is UAH 1.7 per employee.

For Additional Information, Contact:

Gerry Parfitt
Partner-in-Charge
and
Igor Dankov
Senior Tax Consultant
and
Vladimir Tomash
Telecoms Consultant
38 Turgenevska Street
Kiev, Ukraine
Telephone: 380 (44) 216 85 85
Fax: 380 (44) 216 45 58
E-mail: gerry_parfitt@ua.coopers.com
 igor_dankov@ua.coopers.com
 vladimir_tomash@ua.coopers.com

Telecommunications Tax Profile
by Barry J. Marshall
Tax Partner, London
and John K. Steveni
Tax Director, London

United Kingdom

Overview of the Telecommunications Market

Historical Background

The telecommunications market in the United Kingdom (UK) was one of the first in the world to undergo privatization and liberalization. Local, national and international infrastructure are fully liberalized and all market segments are open to competition.

Liberalization and deregulation of telecommunications began with the Telecommunications Bill of 1981, which split the General Post Office into two organizations, the Post Office and British Telecom (BT), and introduced competition in basic services. In 1982 Mercury Communications Limited (MCL) received a license to build and operate an independent network to compete across the full range of fixed-link network services. In the same year, MCL became a wholly owned subsidiary of Cable & Wireless Plc. In 1984, as a prelude to privatization, another telecommunications bill established BT as a public limited company, wholly owned by the government. The government sold 51% of BT shares to the public, raising £3.9 billion. The remaining government shares were sold in two tranches, in 1991 and 1993, reducing the government's shareholding to zero.

The initial approach to liberalization was cautious, with "managed competition" implemented through a duopoly policy that limited the number of long-distance fixed-link operators to two for a period of seven years through 1991. This enabled MCL, the new entrant, to construct its network and establish itself in the market. In 1989 competition was extended by allowing simple resale for national traffic.

The major change in the industry occurred in 1991, when the duopoly policy was ended and the market fully liberalized with a pro-competitive regulatory environment in which all restrictions on the number of public fixed-linked operators were removed. Restrictions on international simple resale (ISR) were also removed in 1991.

In 1983 the first cellular licenses were awarded for national cellular networks (total access communications system, or TACS-900), to Cellnet, a subsidiary of BT, and to Vodafone Group Plc, an independent company. The same companies were awarded global system for mobile communications (GSM) licenses in 1994 and 1992, respectively.

In 1989 four telepoint cordless telephony generation 2 (CT-2) licenses and three personal communications network (PCN) digital cellular system (DCS)-1800 licenses were awarded. However, because of their limited mobility, none of the CT-2 operations were successful, and there are none currently in operation. Of the three PCN licensees, two remain following the merger of two of the original holders (MCL and Unitel) to form Mercury One 2 One in 1992. The other licensee is Orange.

The last restriction on infrastructure provision in the UK was the BT/MCL duopoly on international facilities, which was removed in June 1996. Since then, more than 40 international facilities licenses have been granted.

The number of UK telecommunications licenses has increased from one in 1982 to more than 1,000, including more than 150 licensed domestic public telephony operators (PTOs) plus a wide range of other operators with individual telecommunications licenses. These include ISR operators, 44 international facilities operators, and operators providing wireless local-loop (WLL) services (e.g., Ionica, which was granted a nationwide public telecommunications license to provide short-wave digital microwave links for local access in 1993), satellite services, mobile telephony, public access mobile radio and private networks.

Despite the highly liberalized and competitive marketplace in the UK, regulation remains a major influence. The stated overall goal of the Office of Telecommunications (OFTEL), the industry regulator, is "to obtain the best possible deal for the consumer in terms of quality, choice and value for money." As liberalization unfolds in the European Union (EU), the UK market enters a new phase of competitive development and, increasingly, a different approach to regulatory control: moving away from detailed regulation and intervention toward general competition regulation.

Since liberalization, BT's retail prices have been regulated by a price-cap formula for a basket of basic services. The initial price cap was set at retail price index (RPI)-3% in 1983 and was subsequently adjusted to RPI-4.5% in 1988, RPI-6.25% in 1991 and RPI-7.5% in 1993. The latest retail price cap of RPI-4.5%, effective from August 1, 1997, to July 31, 2001, is generally expected to be the last retail price cap imposed by OFTEL because competition should be sufficiently developed in all market segments by 2001 to eliminate the need for a cap.

The current reduced cap reflects OFTEL's position that competition in the UK is now fully developed in relation to business customers and the highest-spending 20% of retail customers. Consequently, the price cap now covers only services supplied to low-usage residential customers (80% of all residential customers) and small businesses with usage patterns similar to those of the low-usage residential customers. Only 26% of BT's revenues derive from price-capped services under the current price cap, compared to 64% under the last cap.

BT has much greater freedom in determining wholesale prices as a result of a major change in the regulation of BT interconnect charges, from twice-yearly determinations by OFTEL to a network price cap set at RPI-8%. The change covers only those services currently regarded as non-competitive. In line with this shift in regulatory style, a number of clauses have been removed from BT's license, enabling increased commercial freedom, counterbalanced by the introduction of the Fair Trading Condition. This condition prohibits BT, when providing telecoms services or running a telecoms system, from engaging in any activity that prevents, restricts or distorts competition. The Fair Trading Condition is intended to prevent both the abuse of a dominant position and collusion between companies that could have a detrimental effect on competition. Similar conditions are being included in all public telecommunications operator licenses.

Current Status

There is now competition in all market segments, but BT remains dominant in most market sectors. OFTEL reported BT's share of the overall fixed public switched telephony network (PSTN) market at the end of September 1996 to be 81.5% of all call revenues, 90.5% of all connection revenues, 92.3% of all rental revenues and 91.4% of total subscribers.

Competition has developed faster in some segments of the market, including the provision of international and long-distance services, and services to business customers. Where competition is most developed, BT's market share is much lower. For example, OFTEL reported BT's share of the PSTN market for international call revenues at the end of September 1996 to be 63.8% of all international calls, 80.6% of all residential international calls and 48% of all business international calls (down from 57.3% in December 1995).

Competition is beginning to have a significant impact in the local loop: cable TV operators have recently begun to gain a significant share of the residential telephony market (increasing from 2.6% of residential subscribers in 1994 to 8.1% in 1996, according to OFTEL); wireless local-loop operators, such as Ionica, have launched services in certain regions of the UK; and direct access to business customers is provided by a number of competitors, including metropolitan area network operators, such as MFS Communications and COLT Telecommunications, and by regional network operators, such as Torch Telecom.

Liberalization and competition continue to stimulate growth in the UK market: for the year ended September 1996, the total value of the UK retail telecommunications market (fixed and mobile) was reported to be £12.45 billion, which represented growth of 3.5% in value and 10.5% in volume over the preceding year.

In the World Trade Organization (WTO) negotiations in February 1997, the EU, on behalf of member states, committed to liberalization and to a full set of common regulatory principles, and agreed that it would impose no restrictions on foreign ownership. In practice, this will have no significant implications for the UK market as there are no restrictions on foreign ownership and the market is already fully liberalized.

Current Liberalization Status

In general, UK policy toward liberalization has led the way in Europe. The major exception to this trend has been in the area of equal access. The EU proposes to introduce equal access to local networks by long-distance providers by having subscribers pre-select providers. UK regulations do not require equal access; rather they rely on indirect access, whereby long-distance or international traffic is routed to the chosen network by the use of a short-code prefix (usually automatically). If no alternative carrier is selected, the default is to route traffic to BT.

OFTEL and the British government have opposed the proposed EU directive. The UK recently voted in favor of the EU numbering policy proposals, which embody the equal-access approach, only after an agreement was reached that equal access would be made obligatory only "where necessary."

The UK government is expected to continue to resist the introduction of equal access on the grounds that it is unnecessary in the UK market and may undermine operators who have their own infrastructure. If the EU directive is passed, the UK could be forced into line.

Type of Service	Degree of Liberalization	Key Legislation	Date of Actual or Expected Liberalization	Comments
Local	Deregulated	Telecommunications Bill 1984; Duopoly Review 1991	BT/MCL duopoly, 1984–1992 Full liberalization, 1992	
Long Distance	Deregulated Resale allowed	Telecommunications Bill 1984; Duopoly Review 1991	BT/MCL duopoly, 1984–1992 Simple resale, 1989 Full liberalization, 1992	
International	Deregulated Resale allowed	Telecommunications Bill 1984	BT/MCL duopoly, 1984–1996 International resale, limited, 1991 Full liberalization for facilities and resale, 1996	ISR only with reciprocating countries, 1991-1996
Cellular	Competitive	Telecommunications Bill 1984	Duopoly 1984–1989 Liberalized 1989 with the awarding of 3 PCN licenses; 6 national licensees currently in operation	No additional licenses expected in the short term
Paging	Deregulated	Telecommunications Bill 1984	1984	
Value-added	Deregulated	Telecommunications Bill 1981	1981	

Competitive Environment

Type of Service	Entire Market		Top Two Players		
	Market Size*	Number of Players	Names	Annual Revenue	Ownership
Local	£5.387 billion (£2.207 billion from call revenues; £3.18 billion from access revenues)	National: 19 PTO licensees	BT	£4.904 billion (£1.978 billion for calls; £2.926 billion for access)	BT: Publicly traded
		Regional: More than 140 CATV operators providing telephony	MCL (now Cable & Wireless Communications (CWC))	£105 million: (£51 million for calls; £54 million for access)	MCL: Cable & Wireless Communications, NYNEX CableComms, Bell Canada International, publicly traded shares
Long Distance	£1.955 billion	Same as local, plus 46 licensed resellers	BT MCL (now CWC)	£1.544 billion £218 million	
International	£1.479 billion	Same as local, plus 46 licensed resellers	BT MCL (now CWC)	£907 million £213 million	
Cellular	£1.986 billion	6 national licensees	Vodafone Cellnet	£878 million £751 million	Publicly traded Securicor, BT
Paging	Not available	7 national licensees	BT Vodafone	Not available Not available	Publicly traded Publicly traded
Value-added	Not available	46 facilities-based licensees, plus several providers using leased lines	Not available		

* Market revenue figures are for 1997.

Sources: OFTEL market information; *Yearbook of European Telecommunications, 1998*.

Licensing Requirements

Licenses are required for all telecommunications activities; they may be nationwide or regional. Except where there are restrictions associated with the availability of frequency, there is no pre-set maximum number for any type of license. Licenses are likely to be granted within months to applicants able to meet requirements. License applications are made to the Department of Trade and Industry. The only category of service in which no additional licenses are expected to be granted is cellular telephony.

Potential for Foreign Ownerships/Relationships

There are no restrictions on foreign ownership of telecommunications license holders.

Potential for Upcoming Liberalization/Investment Opportunities

As competition intensifies, the industry is beginning to consolidate, illustrated by the recent merger of Mercury with three cable television (CATV) operators (Bell CableMedia, Videotron and NYNEX CableComms) to form Cable & Wireless Communications (CWC). Competitive pressures are expected to continue to grow as a result of continued industry consolidation and domestic and global alliances. Provision of services to major and multinational businesses is increasingly being targeted by global alliances, such as Concert (the BT-MCI joint venture), Uniworld (an alliance between Europe's Unisource and AT&T's World Partners consortium) and Global One (Sprint, France Telecom and Deutsche Telekom AG).

Forms of Doing Business

Permanent Establishment

A non-UK resident company is not subject to tax in the UK unless it carries on a trade through a branch or agency. Notwithstanding a liability to tax under domestic law, in most double-taxation treaties to which the UK is a party, a non-resident company will be subject to UK tax only if it has a permanent establishment (PE). A PE is subject to UK tax on its attributable profits. Although most double-taxation treaties give general guidance as to what constitutes a PE, the test itself is based on the facts and circumstances of the operation. Factors to be considered are the location of key assets and personnel and the territory in which sales contracts are negotiated and concluded.

Telecommunications services can include a broad range of activities, which may or may not constitute PEs. Some examples follow:

- The provision of long-distance telephone services by a foreign company without any local presence to local customers is unlikely to constitute a PE.

- The licensing by a foreign company, without any local presence, of technology and know-how to a local company is unlikely to constitute a PE.

- The provision of technical assistance and technological services by a foreign company to a local company in exchange for service fees, including operator services and/or network management services, when the foreign company's personnel are based in the UK, is likely to constitute a PE.

- The activity of leasing telecommunications equipment to a local company is not likely to constitute a PE. However, if personnel employed by the foreign company operate and maintain the equipment in the UK, then the whole activity may constitute a PE.

- Provided that no personnel employed by a foreign company offering call reorganization/turnaround services are located in the UK, and that the equipment it uses to provide this service is not located in the UK, this type of activity is unlikely to constitute a PE if the calling cards are marketed and sold through independent agents.

- The laying of fiber optic cable and construction of telecommunications switching equipment (a) for sale to a local company or (b) to be operated by the foreign telecommunications company on behalf of a local company will generally constitute a PE. However, most double-taxation treaties provide that construction projects of a certain duration (between six months and two years, depending on the treaty) do not, in and of themselves, constitute a PE.

The provision of Internet access services and the carrying out of commerce via websites represent a relatively new area of telecommunications activity, and the concept of PE in relation to these activities has not been developed. Some examples are considered below:

- A server or switch located in the UK and owned by a foreign Internet access provider not having any personnel in the UK may constitute a PE of the foreign Internet access provider.

- A website advertising goods or services of a foreign company located on a server in the UK that is accessible by UK customers is unlikely to constitute a PE of that foreign company if (a) the website is provided by a third-party Internet access provider and (b) there is no interactivity (i.e., ability to process orders). If there is interactivity, the situation is more complex, but a double-tax treaty may provide some protection. The same should be true for a foreign company's website located on a server *outside* of the UK but accessible by UK customers.

- A website advertising goods or services of a foreign company located on a server in the UK that is not accessible by UK customers, but is accessible by customers in other countries, should be treated in the same way as a website accessible by UK customers.

The examples of telecommunications-related services discussed above are not exhaustive, but provide an indication of the wide variety of services possible. Clearly, the level of local presence of both assets and personnel required for each of these activities may vary considerably and will critically affect any conclusion as to whether there is a PE.

If sales contracts are negotiated and concluded in the UK, then the Inland Revenue views the profits derived from these contracts as taxable in the UK, irrespective of whether the foreign company has a fixed place of business, assets or personnel in the UK. The impact of this is usually mitigated by a double-taxation treaty.

When no PE exists, activities can be subject to UK tax as a result of withholding tax requirements on, for example, royalty payments.

Business Entities

The business entities that an overseas investor can use to make an investment in the UK telecommunications industry are:

- A non-UK-resident company that operates in the UK through a branch

- A UK-resident subsidiary company of an overseas incorporated company

- A joint venture vehicle, either a partnership or a jointly owned entity of one of the two types of businesses mentioned above

The distinction drawn between UK-resident and non-UK-resident companies is important; any company incorporated in the UK or incorporated in another jurisdiction that is centrally managed and controlled in the UK is considered to be resident for tax purposes. The only exceptions to these rules are found in certain double-taxation treaties, in which a company that would otherwise be UK-resident is deemed to be resident solely in another territory and thus becomes non-UK-resident for tax purposes.

Local Branch of a Foreign Company. A non-UK-resident company operating through a branch is taxed on trading income or capital gains arising directly or indirectly from the branch activity as reduced for appropriate costs. Under most treaties, this is recharacterized as attributable profit and allows for an allocation of head-office costs, including overhead costs and interest, to the extent these are attributable to the branch. However, loans between the foreign head office and the branch are normally ignored for tax purposes.

A branch cannot be grouped with another UK branch or a UK-resident company for the purposes of transferring losses or assets. There is no withholding tax or liability to account for ACT on remittances from a UK branch. UK branches can be incorporated into UK-subsidiary companies without incurring tax.

Locally Incorporated Subsidiary of a Foreign Company. UK-resident companies are subject to corporate tax on their worldwide income and gains. Companies in a tax group consisting of a UK-resident holding company and one or more 75%-owned UK-resident subsidiaries may transfer current tax trading losses (including interest costs) to one another, and the transfer of assets between such companies takes place at no gain/no loss for capital gains tax purposes. There are restrictions on the transfer of losses from dual-resident companies (entities that are treated as resident for tax purposes in more than one territory) to other group companies.

There is no withholding tax on dividends paid by UK-resident companies to residents and non-residents. When a UK-resident company pays a dividend, it is required to pay advance corporation tax (ACT) on the dividend. For dividends paid from April 6, 1994, the rate of ACT is 25% of the dividend paid. Subject to certain limits, ACT is set off against the company's corporate tax liability for the period in which the dividend is paid. To the extent that the ACT cannot be set off in the period in which the dividend is paid, it can be carried forward (without limit) or carried back (for up to six years) for relief. Dividends paid by a 51%-owned UK-resident subsidiary company to its UK-resident parent may, by election, be paid without having to account for ACT.

UK dividends received by UK companies carry a tax credit (unless paid without ACT under election) that can be used to frank dividends paid by the receiving company to its own shareholders. UK-resident individuals can use the tax credit against any tax liability arising on a dividend from a UK-resident company.

Under certain double-taxation treaties, a tax credit repayment may be available to a non-resident shareholder. Legislation enacted in 1997 contains significant revisions to the ACT system, including substantial reductions or elimination of tax credit repayments.

Joint Venture. A joint venture can take the form of a partnership or of a company with split shareholdings. If a UK-resident company is formed, the tax considerations are as set out above. If a partnership structure is used by corporate investors then, generally, the partnership results are calculated as for a UK company, and the partners are taxed on their shares of the partnership results. If the partner is a foreign investor, then the investor is taxed on its partnership share as if the foreign investor had a UK branch, provided the UK partnership activity constituted a taxable presence for the investor. As with branches, partnership distributions are not subject to withholding taxes.

Partnerships are not treated as separate legal entities; the partnership itself does not hold the assets—rather, each partner has a share in the assets and the partners will be jointly and severally liable for the debts of the partnership. Whether the joint venture is carried on through a UK-resident company or a partnership, a tax return must be filed annually. In addition, foreign partners in a partnership that constitutes a PE are required to file annual tax returns.

Local Funding Alternatives

Debt versus Equity

In general terms, debt financing results in a tax deduction, whereas equity financing does not. Interest paid to non-residents is subject to a 20% withholding tax unless reduced or eliminated under a double-taxation treaty, in which case there is an advance clearance procedure. There is no capital duty or stamp duty payable on the issue of equity or debt.

Taxation of Corporate Debt. The rules regarding taxation of corporate debt were substantially reformed in the Finance Act of 1996, and the new rules are complex. The underlying principle is that interest will be taxable and deductible on an accrual basis, rather than on a receipt/payment basis, and the same treatment applies to discounts, premiums and other profits and losses. However, there are many exceptions and specific transitional rules. For example, an interest deduction may be deferred to the time when the interest is actually paid if the recipient is a related party not subject to UK tax and the interest is not paid within 12 months of the end of the accounting period in which the interest is accrued.

Shareholder Debt versus Third-Party Debt. Generally speaking, shareholder debt and third-party debt are treated in the same manner, providing the thin capitalization rules do not apply to the debt. The thin capitalization rules were amended in 1995 to incorporate an arm's-length principle for borrowings between related parties (parties with a 75% relationship).

Arm's-length is determined according to the rate of interest and the level of indebtedness. If the borrowing satisfies the arm's-length test, interest will be deductible. If the borrowing does not meet the arm's-length test, then that part of the interest that would not otherwise have been payable under an arm's-length borrowing is reclassified as a distribution, which is not deductible. Furthermore, if the payor of the interest is a UK-resident company, it would be required to account for ACT on that portion of the interest that was reclassified as a distribution. The thin capitalization provisions do not apply when the recipient of the interest is subject to UK corporate tax on the interest receipt.

The Inland Revenue's view of arm's-length has not been set down in statute, but a 1-to-1 debt-to-equity ratio and a 3-to-1 interest cover have been used for some time as indicators of appropriate levels of debt. These are only guidelines, and it is open to the taxpayer and the Inland Revenue to argue what would be arm's-length given a specific set of facts.

There is no specific provision allowing the Inland Revenue to consider parent company guarantees when judging whether third-party debt is arm's-length. The thin capitalization rules are restricted to related-party borrowings, and it has been possible to introduce guaranteed debt to a UK company without falling afoul of the thin capitalization rules. However, the Inland Revenue continues to monitor the use of parent-company guarantees and back-to-back loans.

Exchange Gains or Losses on Foreign Currency Borrowings. Detailed rules govern the taxation of foreign exchange differences. In general, exchange gains are taxed and exchange losses are deductible as they accrue, irrespective of realization. There are provisions for the deferral of taxation of unrealized exchange gains in certain cases.

Exchange Controls

There are no restrictions on the currency in which loans are denominated.

Business Acquisitions and Dispositions

Capital Contributions into an Existing Local Entity

Capital contributions to a UK company without an issue of shares, or to a partnership without an increase in the partner's capital account, in exchange for the capital contributed, may result in a zero-tax basis for a UK-resident contributor and can, in certain circumstances, constitute a taxable receipt for the recipient company or partnership. No taxable receipt arises if shares are issued as consideration for the capital contribution, and, in most cases, a UK taxpayer will obtain a tax basis in the new shares.

Purchase or Sale of Shares in a Local Entity

When shares are purchased, there is no potential for a basis step-up in the target company's assets. A seller may prefer a share disposal if the tax basis in her shares is higher than the target's asset tax basis. An asset disposal may require a distribution by the target, which could result in a further shareholder tax.

Purchasers of shares in UK companies are normally subject to a .5% stamp duty based on the transfer price. Subject to certain conditions, relief from stamp duty is available on transfers between companies with 75% or more common ownership, and also on qualifying corporate reorganizations.

The disposal of shares will be subject to tax if the shares are effectively connected with a branch of a foreign company. Disposals by non-residents will not be subject to tax. The capital gain will be the difference between the sales price and the tax-base cost of the shares. For VAT purposes, the disposal of shares is likely to result in a degree of irrecoverable VAT cost for the vendor.

Purchase or Sale of Assets

An asset transaction will usually cause the recognition of a capital gain or loss or a reclaim of tax depreciation (on assets that qualify for tax depreciation) in the hands of the seller, which will be subject to tax at the relevant corporate tax rate unless the capital gain can be sheltered by rollover relief. Rollover relief is available on the disposal of certain types of assets when the proceeds are reinvested in similar types of assets within the appropriate time frame.

Generally, the purchase price may be allocated, on a reasonable basis, between the assets being purchased. It may be possible to allocate more of the purchase price to depreciable assets than to goodwill, which is not amortizable. A purchase price allocation agreed upon between unrelated parties should be respected unless the Inland Revenue could show that the allocation grossly misstated the fair value of the purchased assets.

A seller of assets may prefer to allocate the purchase price to capital assets rather than trading assets or tax-depreciable fixed assets, since capital assets are subject to an indexation adjustment when capital gains are computed. Additionally, the seller may have capital losses available, which are available only for offset against capital gains.

Purchasers of assets will be liable to stamp duty. Stamp duty on certain other assets, including real estate, is charged as follows:

More than £60,000 and less than £250,000	1%
More than £250,000 and less than £500,000	1.5%
More than £500,000	2%

Under certain conditions, relief from stamp duty is available on transfers between companies with 75% or more common ownership and on qualifying corporate reorganizations.

The disposal of assets will be subject to tax if the disposor is a UK-tax-resident company or a UK branch of a foreign company. Disposals of assets owned by non-residents that are not connected to a UK branch will not be subject to tax. The capital gain is the difference between the sales price and the tax-base cost of the shares.

Acquisition of Partnership Interests. When a company acquires a partnership interest from a partner in a company, the vendor company is treated as disposing of its share of partnership assets. However, there is no step-up in the basis of the partnership asset for tax purposes, as there would be in a straightforward asset purchase. The incoming partner's cost of acquisition will be deductible only against a future disposal of the partnership interest.

Start-up Business Issues

Pre-operating Losses and Start-up/ Construction Costs

Costs that are incurred in a period of up to seven years prior to trade commencing, and which would otherwise have been deductible for the purposes of computing the taxable profits of the trade if a trade had commenced, are usually "rolled up" and treated as a trade loss incurred on the day trade commences. The key issue, therefore, is whether the costs incurred in the pre-trading period would otherwise have been deductible if trade had commenced.

Costs are deductible for the purposes of calculating the profits of a trade if they are incurred wholly and exclusively for the purposes of the trade, providing the costs are revenue, as opposed to capital, in nature. The revenue vs. capital distinction has been the subject of numerous court cases. Broadly speaking, an item is capital in nature if it provides an enduring benefit to the business.

There are specific items of expenditure that are not deductible for tax purposes, whether revenue in nature or not (e.g., non-staff entertainment expenditure). However, such items are not deductible in all circumstances, and the pre-operating distinction has no impact on this analysis.

The treatment of pre-trading expenditure on capital assets, which would be eligible for tax depreciation if incurred in a trading period, is discussed below. (See "Depreciation/Cost-Recovery Conventions/Accelerated Deductions.")

Business Investigation Costs/License and Franchise Fees. The statutes do not specify whether business investigation costs are deductible in a pre-operating period. The Inland Revenue takes the position that if business has not commenced and costs are incurred while the company is considering whether to commence a business, then these costs are not deductible. Items such as license fees and franchise fees have also been debated with the Inland Revenue. The key factors in the classification of these costs are whether the fees are one-time or recurring (for example, an annual license fee may be more revenue in nature than a one-time, up-front fee) and whether the payment of the fee brings into existence a new asset (for example, a license that can be sold separately from any other asset is likely to be capital in nature).

Pre-Operating Interest Expense. If interest expense is incurred in relation to a loan used for business purposes, then such interest expense incurred in the seven years prior to the date operations began is included in the rolled-up trade loss. This loss is deductible on the first day of operations. However, if interest is incurred in relation to a loan that would have been for non-trade purposes even if operations had commenced when the interest was incurred, then this non-trade, pre-operating interest expense will be available to offset against future non-trade profits, such as capital gains or investment income.

No relief for pre-trading interest is available when the company has no source of taxable income. This situation can be avoided by ensuring that a company has, for example, an interest-earning deposit account in pre-trading periods when interest expense is being incurred.

Customs Duties and VAT

Most goods imported into the UK from outside the European Union are subject to customs duty and import VAT. Duty is normally payable on the cost, insurance and freight (CIF) value of the goods. Import VAT is payable on the duty-inclusive value of the goods, although VAT-registered traders can usually obtain a refund of the VAT.

Telecommunications and computing equipment are subject to duty ranging from 1.2% to 10.5%. The rate of duty will depend on the exact description and the tariff classification of the goods and the country of origin of the goods. The EU has preferential trade agreements with a number of countries that enable goods to be imported at a reduced or nil rate of duty.

Customs duties on some items of equipment were already being reduced under the General Agreement on Tariffs and Trade (GATT). Over the next few years, duty rates are scheduled to be reduced further still under the Information Technology Agreement (ITA) signed in March 1997. The ITA extends the range of goods subject to duty rate reductions. As a signatory to the ITA, the EU has agreed to cut tariffs on imports of computers and computer equipment, software, telecommunications and networking equipment to zero in four equal installments. The first reduction took place on July 1, 1997, and fur-

ther reductions are to take effect on January 1 of each year through 2000. Although the ITA will cut the cost of importing many products, the convergence of technologies in the computing, electronics and telecommunications sectors is likely to lead to disputes over the tariff classification of some equipment and affect the availability and/or phasing of duty reductions under the ITA.

A wide variety of reliefs from customs duty and import VAT can be claimed in various circumstances (e.g., goods imported for processing and re-export, or goods imported temporarily). There is also a relief available for capital goods and equipment, provided the goods are imported by a business on the transfer of its activities to the UK. Raw materials or components that are not available, or not available in sufficient quantity, within the EU may be eligible for a complete or partial suspension of duty, provided this can be demonstrated to the satisfaction of the Commission of the European Communities in Brussels.

Goods may be subject to anti-dumping or countervailing duty if, for example, the EU considers they are being imported into the EU at prices substantially lower than their normal value. Anti-dumping and countervailing duties are chargeable in addition to, and independent of, any other duty to which the imported goods may be liable.

Loss Carryovers

Losses in either a UK-resident company or a UK branch may be carried forward indefinitely against future profits of the same business and are available for carryback for one year against any profits (three years for losses incurred before July 2, 1997). Capital losses may be carried forward indefinitely against future capital gains, but restrictions exist on the set-off of losses following a change in ownership.

If there has been a change in ownership of a company with trading losses, there are restrictions on the availability of the carryforward losses when there has also been a major change in the nature or conduct of the business.

Operating Considerations

Corporate Income Taxes

The corporate tax rate applied to income and capital gains of UK-resident companies or UK branches of foreign companies is 31%. This is reduced to 21% in the case of UK-resident companies with taxable income of less than £300,000, and a marginal rate calculation applies to taxable income between £300,000 and £1,500,000. These limits are reduced pro rata by reference to the number of active worldwide associated companies. These rates also apply to UK branches of foreign companies when the foreign company is resident in a territory with which the UK has a double-taxation treaty with an appropriately worded non-discrimination clause.

Capital Gains Taxes

Capital gains (as reduced by available capital losses) are included in a UK-resident company's taxable profits and are subject to corporate tax at the rates set out above. A UK branch of a foreign company is subject to UK capital gains tax only on gains realized on chargeable assets used or held by the branch. As with UK-resident companies, branches are subject to capital gains tax when there is a relevant chargeable gain, at the corporate tax rates set out above.

Chargeable assets are generally all capital assets of the company, including intangible assets. When tax-depreciable assets are sold for less than or equal to their original cost, the gain is taxed by way of a recapture of tax depreciation. Any excess of proceeds over the original cost of tax-depreciable assets is treated as a capital gain. The capital gain is calculated by reference to the proceeds received for the disposal of an asset less the base cost of the asset, which is the original cost of the asset as adjusted for enhancement expenditure.

An inflation-related adjustment is indexed on the base cost of the asset, thus reducing the chargeable gain. When the proceeds received are less than the base cost, a capital loss arises. In these circumstances, no indexation allowance is available to enhance the loss.

There are provisions within the UK statutes deeming market value acquisition cost or sale consideration in place of actual cost or consideration when a transaction is between connected parties. However, as mentioned above, there are provisions allowing a tax-free transfer of assets between UK group companies. Additionally, there are numerous relieving and anti-avoidance provisions covering areas such as share reorganizations, business transfers, part disposals and restriction of artificially generated capital losses. Finally, except for the provisions regarding taxation of assets used by a UK branch set out above, the UK has no provisions for the taxation of capital gains on non-residents. Thus, for example, the sale of shares in a UK company by a non-UK resident is not subject to capital gains tax.

Tax Holidays and Exemptions

There are no tax holidays or exemptions specific to the telecommunications industry. Depending on the nature and location of operations, grants may be available to assist companies in capital expenditure projects or in setting up businesses that result in employment growth in a specific region. The tax treatment of these grants depends on the source and nature of the grant.

Depreciation/Cost-Recovery Conventions/Accelerated Deductions

A depreciation deduction is generally available on items of plant and machinery, which are capital assets employed in the trade. The case law surrounding expenditures that qualify as plant and machinery is voluminous but, in general, "plant" can be defined as "apparatus kept for permanent employment in a trade" and includes such items as fixture and fittings. The costs of digging trenches and laying cable for a telecommunications network generally qualify as plant and machinery expenditures.

Where capital assets qualify as items of plant and machinery, tax depreciation is calculated by reference to the cost of the asset on a 25% reducing-balance basis. This results in approximately 90% of the cost of the asset being deducted for tax purposes over a period of eight years. Recently the rate was reduced to 6% for long-life assets, which are defined as assets with an economic useful life of at least 25 years. Although general guidance as to the definition of useful economic life has been issued, and the authorities have indicated that potential economic and technological obsolescence will be taken into account, the specific applicability to telecoms network expenditures is unclear.

Generally, no tax depreciation is available for expenditures on buildings, unless the building is an "industrial building" or is located in an "enterprise zone." Relief is given on expenditures for industrial buildings over 25 years on the straight-line basis (i.e., 4% per annum). Expenditures on buildings usually qualify for industrial building allowances if the expenditures are for structures used for manufacturing or processing in the course of the business. Relief is given at 100% in the first year for buildings in an enterprise zone.

Generally, tax depreciation is available on qualifying assets and industrial buildings from the date the expenditure was incurred. When capital expenditure is incurred in a pre-operating period on an asset that would qualify for tax depreciation if business had commenced, the capital expenditure is deemed to occur on the first day operations begin.

Purchased software is treated in the same way as other items of plant and machinery, regardless of whether it is embedded in telecommunications equipment.

It is possible to elect not to claim tax depreciation and to defer depreciation to a later period if the deduction in a later period may provide a preferential tax result. When assets that have been depreciated for tax purposes are disposed of, the difference between the proceeds and the tax-depreciated value (if greater, a balancing charge; if less, a balancing allowance) may be realized as part of the trading result for the period in which the disposal is made.

However, assets are generally held in a single "pool" (the exceptions to this rule being motor cars and assets elected out of the pool), such that, when an asset is disposed out of the pool and other assets remain in the pool, the proceeds reduce the total pool value and no balancing adjustment is made; rather, tax depreciation is calculated on the reduced pool value.

Research and Development Costs. These costs can generally be deducted in calculating profits or losses when they are of a revenue nature and incurred wholly and exclusively for the purposes of the business. When they are considered to be of a capital nature, there is no relief unless the expenditure is on equipment or buildings that qualify for tax depreciation.

Marketing and Advertising Costs. These are generally deductible in calculating profits or losses, provided the costs are revenue and not capital in nature and they are incurred wholly and exclusively for the purposes of the business. There is no difference in principle whether these expenditures are incurred directly or through an agent. However, if the costs involve the provision of hospitality to any person who is not an employee, then these costs are non-deductible. Hospitality is not defined in the statutes, and the case law on the subject is complex and unclear. However, for example, the provision of food, drink and entertainment at a marketing or advertising reception is generally accepted as hospitality. In addition, expenditures for the provision of gifts are not deductible unless the gifts have minimal value and carry conspicuous advertisements for the taxpayer, and the gifts are not food, drink or tobacco.

Expenditures made to attract customers need to be considered on a case-by-case basis. If they are treated as hospitality, as described above, they are unlikely to be deductible. Payments that are treated as discounts on invoices for services provided are likely to be deductible.

Transfer Pricing Rules

The UK's transfer pricing rules allow the Inland Revenue to adjust prices on transactions between associated parties when these have not been arrived at on an arm's-length basis. The UK is revising its transfer pricing law to put the onus of proof on the taxpayer to show that transactions have occurred on an arm's-length basis. A documentation requirement is likely to be introduced, and the taxpayer will be obliged to file a tax return that adjusts any non-arm's-length prices.

The transfer pricing rules apply to UK branches of foreign companies as well as to UK-resident companies. In appropriate cases, a markup of costs may be agreed upon as a taxable profit calculation for a branch (for example, when there are no valuable intangibles in the UK).

Normally, no prior authorization or ruling on inter-company prices can be obtained. However, the Inland Revenue may be willing to advise on acceptable policy in specific cases. For capital gains transactions, the deemed market value acquisition cost or sale consideration provisions between connected parties effectively applies transfer pricing.

Transfers of Patents, Trademarks and Software

There is no restriction on the license of technology to a UK-resident company. The general transfer pricing rules (see "Transfer Pricing Rules") will apply where the transfer is from a related party. In addition, withholding taxes may be levied on the payment of royalties.

In cases in which royalties or software license fees are paid periodically to a non-UK-resident owner of a copyright to which a royalty or license fee attaches, there may be a requirement to deduct withholding tax at the rate of 23%. This rate may be reduced, in most cases to nil, by double-taxation treaties.

Service Fees

The general rules regarding expenditure being wholly and exclusively for business purposes apply to items such as service fees, central research fees, central administration fees and the like. There are no withholding taxes on service fees, irrespective of whether the service is provided in the UK.

Value-Added Tax, Sales Tax and/or Other Pertinent Taxes

VAT is a multi-stage consumption tax imposed on most goods and services sold in the UK. The VAT legislation follows the provisions of the European Community Sixth VAT Directive and, therefore, is the same model used throughout the EU.

The standard 17.5% rate of VAT is charged on all goods and services unless the item is specifically listed as being exempt from VAT (for example, health care, education and financial services) or taxable at another rate (e.g., 5%, which applies to domestic fuel and power, or the zero VAT rate that applies to the most essential items, such as foods and the sale of new domestic housing). Businesses engaged in supplying goods or services that are taxable (at any rate) are allowed full credit for VAT paid on their purchases or expenses (input tax). Businesses that supply taxable goods or services plus exempt services are subject to a restriction of the VAT paid on their purchases and expenses. A business that provides only exempt services cannot obtain a refund for VAT purposes; thus, all VAT paid on its purchases or expenses becomes an absolute cost to the business.

Domestic telecommunications services (including those supplied by UK-resident foreign businesses) are subject to the standard rate of VAT. The VAT treatment of international services is based on the revised EU VAT model, which took effect in the UK on July 1, 1997.

Services supplied internationally by a telecommunications business located in the UK are generally outside the scope of VAT when supplied to anyone located outside the UK. The only exceptions are services supplied to private individuals or un-registered persons located in other EU-member states. Those services are subject to UK VAT at the standard rate.

In some circumstances, the UK VAT authorities may argue that VAT is due on services billed internationally. This might apply if the services were effectively used and enjoyed in the UK by a business resident in the UK (e.g., services used and enjoyed by a UK branch of a United States bank, to which services are billed). International contractual arrangements should take this issue into account.

Non-resident providers are not liable to register and account for UK VAT on supplies used and enjoyed by UK customers, pro-viding those customers are taxable persons for VAT purposes. These customers are required to self-account for VAT under reverse-charge procedures. (Previously, UK businesses could import telecoms services free of VAT.)

When a non-resident provider makes supplies of services to pri-vate individuals, to be used and enjoyed in the UK, the provider is required to register and account for UK VAT. For an overseas provider, it should be possible to limit VAT liability to supplies made to UK individuals that are effectively used and enjoyed in the EU. However, this may then require the overseas provider to be registered for VAT purposes in many different EU-member states. Alternatively, an overseas provider may choose to register in a single EU-member state (e.g., the UK) in order to contract with all customers who are EU private individuals. The supplies made from the single EU registration to these customers will then be subject to local VAT in the member state of registration.

UK telecoms providers receiving international services from other telecoms providers are not required to apply the UK VAT reverse-charge procedures. This change reflects the provisions of the Melbourne Agreement (Final Acts of the World Adminis-trative Telegraph and Telephone Conference, Melbourne 1988).

Access to the Internet is included within the definition of telecommunications, and the principles set out above apply equally to Internet service providers (ISPs). However, there are clearly more complex issues to consider in determining where an ISP belongs for VAT purposes in respect of the services it supplies. If an ISP provides services from outside the UK that are used and enjoyed in the UK by private indi-viduals, it may be liable to register and account for UK VAT. This depends on the range of services it provides and the basis of charging for those services. Businesses supplying services to private individuals are likely to use the Internet to deliver VAT-free services from overseas locations to UK pri-vate individuals.

Local and Provincial Taxes

Property, whether freehold or leasehold in nature, that is used in a business is subject to a business property rate, which is calculated by reference to the value of the building.

For Additional Information, Contact:

Barry J. Marshall
Tax Partner
1 Embankment Place
London WC2N 6NN, United Kingdom
Telephone: 44 (171) 213 4764
Fax: 44 (171) 213 2414
E-mail: barry_j_marshall@gb.coopers.com

John K. Steveni
Tax Director
Address: Same as above
Telephone: 44 (171) 213 3388
Fax: 44 (171) 213 2404
E-mail: john_k_steveni@gb.coopers.com

John M. Dowson
Telecoms Consulting Partner
Address: Same as above
Telephone: 44 (171) 213 4823
Fax: 44 (171) 213 2454
E-mail: john_m_dowson@gb.coopers.com

Part Three
Middle East and Africa

Israel
South Africa

Israel

Telecommunications Tax Profile
by Avidor Avni
Senior Tax Partner, Tel Aviv

Overview of the Telecommunications Market

Historical Background

Prior to 1984, all telecommunications services in Israel were provided exclusively by the Israeli government through the Ministry of Communications (MOC) and its predecessors. As a first step in the gradual liberalization of the telecommunications sector, in 1984 MOC transferred direct ownership and control of the national communications system to Bezeq—The Israel Telecommunications Corp. Ltd. (Bezeq), which was then wholly owned by the State of Israel and which replaced MOC as the sole provider of telecommunications services in Israel.

In the mid-1980s, the Israeli government began to introduce competition in several telecommunications services and to create new markets. Special licenses were awarded to a number of private companies pursuant to which such companies were authorized to provide customer premises equipment and certain data and value-added services, effectively opening these areas to competition. In 1986, Pele-Phone Communications, Ltd. (a joint venture owned by Bezeq and Motorola Israel Ltd.) began providing cellular telephone services in Israel.

In 1990, the Israeli government began to implement a privatization policy with respect to Bezeq that has resulted in a reduction of the Israeli government's current ownership interest to approximately 63.6% of Bezeq's outstanding ordinary shares. The balance of Bezeq's outstanding ordinary shares is currently owned by an affiliate of Merrill Lynch & Co. (approximately 9.99%), which has an option to require the Israeli government to repurchase such shares; Cable & Wireless Plc (approximately 10.0%); and the public (approximately 16.5%).

In 1994, MOC awarded a second license to provide cellular services in Israel to Cellcom Israel Ltd. (Cellcom). In March 1994, the Israeli government amended Bezeq's existing license, in order to specify the services that Bezeq may provide as a regulated monopoly (including basic domestic telephone service) and to require that Bezeq establish independent subsidiaries to provide, in markets to be opened to competition, services previously offered exclusively by Bezeq.

As a result, in 1996 Bezeq formed Bezeq International and transferred all of its operations as an international telecommunications service provider to the new entity. In mid-1997, MOC issued a tender for a third operator of cellular telephone services in Israel based on global system for mobile communications (GSM) technology. Bids in response to this tender were submitted to MOC on October 28, 1997, and the winner is expected to start operations by the end of 1998. The Israeli government has also announced its intention to introduce competition in the domestic telecommunications sector by 1999.

Current Status

In February 1997, Israel joined 68 other World Trade Organization (WTO) members in committing to the liberalization of its basic telecommunications services, such as telephone, fax and telex services. The WTO Agreement has been ratified by the government. Under the Israeli schedule submitted pursuant to the agreement, the government has committed to ending Bezeq's monopoly position in the domestic telecommunications market by the year 2001.

The government's recent trend toward liberalization of the Israeli telecommunications industry has in the past few years brought open competition in the provision of international long-distance calls, mobile telephony, value-added services, customer premises equipment and wiring. Open competition in the supply of domestic nationwide telephony and infrastructure services is expected in the next few years, thus ending the last vestiges of Bezeq's monopoly over the provision of telecommunications services.

Israel is one of the most developed and fastest growing telecommunications markets in the world. Telecommunications revenues are growing rapidly. The licensing of two additional international operators, while creating serious competition for Bezeq International in the provision of unrestricted two-way international telephone services, has stimulated demand through dramatically reduced consumer prices. The volume of international calls is significant and increasing. According to estimates published by MOC, the Israeli market in 1996 had 2.5 million fixed telephone lines representing nearly 100% of all households and 45% per-capita penetration, as well as 1.6 million cellular telephones, representing 28% per-capita penetration.

The public-switched telephone network is completely digital. There is a thriving Israeli equipment manufacture and service provision sector, a vibrant and competitive paging market, and a competitive mobile radio services market. The recent launching of Israel's first satellite is expected to expand the range of available telecommunications services (e.g., digital business services, high-speed transfer of data via satellite, and satellite TV broadcasting).

Current Liberalization Status

The following table summarizes the progress toward liberalization and the introduction of competition into the telecommunications sector in Israel. Given Israel's relatively small geographic size, all calls within the country are local and domestic. The term "long-distance service," as it is used in other countries, does not apply.

Type of Service	Degree of Liberalization	Key Legislation	Date of Actual or Expected Liberalization	Comments
Local and Domestic National	Monopoly	1982—Bezeq Act 1984—Incorporation of Bezeq 1994—new General License issued to Bezeq	1999	1999 is the target date for liberalization as recommended by the Rosen Committee report published in 10/97. The WTO Agreement schedule specifies 2001.
International	Partially liberalized	1982—Telecommunications Law 1995—publication of tender process for second and third operators	2002	Three licenses have been granted in transition stage from monopoly to oligopoly. Additional licenses will be granted in 2002.
Cellular	Partially liberalized	1982—Telecommunications Law 1994—second operator licensed 1997—publication of tender process for third operator	2002	Two licenses have been granted; third operator tender process initiated. Additional frequencies to be allotted in 2002; Pele-Phone Communications Ltd. uses NAMPS standard; Cellcom uses TDMA standard; the third operator will use GSM standard.
Paging	Deregulated			Mostly alpha-numeric services; some numeric services.
Value-added	Deregulated			

Competitive Environment

The Israeli telecommunications market is opening up to competition after many years of statutory monopoly.

Type of Service	Entire Market		Top Players		
	Market Size*	Number of Players	Names	Annual Revenue*	Ownership
Local and Domestic National	US$1.76 billion (est.)	1	Bezeq	US$1.76 billion (est.)	Government; Cable & Wireless
International	In excess of US$680 million (est.)	3	Bezeq	US$680 million (est.)	Bezeq
			Golden Lines	Not available (started operations in 1997)	Aurec Ltd., Southwestern Bell, STET, Globoscom Ltd.
			Barak ITC	Not available (started operations in 1997)	Clalcom, MATÁV, Sprint, Deutsche Telekom, France Câbloo ot Radio
Cellular	US$465 million	2	Cellcom	US$380 million	BellSouth Corporation; Safra Brothers; Israel Economic Corporation
			Pele-Phone	US$85 million	Joint venture of Motorola Israel and Bezeq
Paging		2	Beeper Communications Israel Ltd.	Not available	Joint venture of Motorola Communications Israel and Beeper Pagecall
			Bip-a-Call	US$2.5 million	Tadiran Telecommunications Ltd.

* 1996 figures issued by Ministry of Communications. At that time, Bezeq was sole local and long-distance service provider.

Licensing Requirements

Providers of telecommunications services and importers of telecommunications equipment are required to obtain a license from MOC. The licensing procedures have recently been streamlined, and there is a governmental recommendation to approve requests for telecommunications licenses, subject to satisfying basic threshold conditions concerning financial stability and technical standards.

Potential for Foreign Ownerships/Relationships

The acquisition of stock by non-resident corporations that provide vital services, including telecommunications services, may be limited. To date, however, only Bezeq has been declared a "vital service" and is subject to certain ownership restrictions. Any acquisition of 5% or more of Bezeq stock requires ministerial permission. Control of Bezeq may only be by a person who is a citizen and resident of Israel, including a corporation registered in Israel and controlled by citizens and residents of Israel. Furthermore, the government has imposed certain other restrictions on foreign ownership; for example, foreign companies can own only up to 49% of cable television companies and Israeli Second Channel broadcasters, 80% of cellular companies and 75% of international operators.

Potential for Upcoming Liberalization/Investment Opportunities

As part of its plan to reduce its stake in Bezeq to 51%, the government intends to carry out a public sale of shares during 1998 and, by means of a public tender offer at a later stage, is considering the transfer of effective control of Bezeq to a strategic investor. It has recently agreed to allow Cable & Wireless to increase its share in Bezeq to 13% with the possibility of a maximum share of 20% within the next 18 months.

The liberalization trend in telecommunications markets is reflected in reports issued by various committees over the past few years:

- In March 1996, the government accepted the recommendation of a committee, appointed by MOC, to examine the role and functioning of MOC as a regulator of telecommunications services. One of its principal recommendations was the establishment of an independent apolitical regulatory body with broad powers of enforcement.

- In December 1996, the Wachs-Brodett Committee recommended to the government that infrastructures, telephony and data transmission in the local telecommunications market be opened to competition no later than January 1999.

- In June 1997, the Peled Committee Report reinforced the combined recommendations of the two earlier committees.

- In October 1997, the Rosen Committee made detailed suggestions on how to implement the Wachs-Brodett recommendations, the adoption of which will open the entire telecommunications market to competition and eliminate the Bezeq monopoly.

Forms of Doing Business

Permanent Establishment

Under Israeli domestic tax law, Israel imposes tax on income accrued from or derived in Israel, and on other income received in Israel from abroad. With respect to foreign investors, an Israeli tax presence will generally arise where an activity constitutes doing business *in* Israel (as opposed to just *with* Israel). In this regard, there are no formal rules, and the permanent establishment (PE) criteria of the OECD Model Treaty are often used as a general and loose guideline.

In general, the Israeli taxation principles applicable to several sectors of the telecommunications industry are still being crystallized as the industry experiences rapid growth and the constant introduction of new services and products. Israeli tax law states that a non-resident that carries on the business of transmission of messages by cable or wireless telegraphy shall be taxed as if the non-resident were a non-resident ship owner. The implications of this could include either of the following:

- The non-resident will be exempt from Israeli taxation, where stipulated in a relevant treaty, since most of Israel's treaties provide that profits of ship owners will be taxed only in the country in which the effective management of the shipping enterprises is located.

- Only the proportional part of activity arising from having a terminal in Israel will be taxable in Israel.

Nevertheless, it is unclear for two reasons how far-reaching this provision would be for a telecommunications enterprise:

- The above-mentioned exemption is viewed as relating solely to profits from the actual transmission, and not from any other activities that might be connected to such transmission.

- It is difficult to obtain this exemption where the transmission operation is not akin to the operations of a ship owner that solely calls in and departs from Israeli ports (i.e., no operations of any degree of permanence, such as the leasing of space, or a wide range of activities that require investments of time and effort).

Based on the above, telecommunications services can cover a broad range of activities, which may or may not constitute a PE. Some examples follow:

- The provision of long-distance telephone services by a foreign company to local customers with no local presence or advertising by the foreign company should generally not, by itself, create a PE.

- The provision of call reorganization or turnaround services would generally not create a PE, provided the foreign company had no equipment or other presence, including that of a dependent agent, in Israel.

- The provision of Internet access services is a relatively new area of telecommunications activity and its Israeli tax consequences are still in the developmental stage. The provision of such services may not create a PE, depending upon the entire scope of the foreign company's operations in Israel. The presence of a server or modem links in Israel might be regarded as a fixed place of business, resulting in a PE, whereas the mere sale of software with no other presence may be regarded as a sale or royalty, depending on the circumstances of the transaction.

- The physical presence of a server or switches in Israel might constitute a PE even if no personnel are located in Israel. Factors that may increase the PE exposure include: whether the server is used for more than merely providing information or if it is also used as a medium for accepting customer orders, and whether a dependent agent in Israel maintains the equipment and/or accepts subscriptions to the Internet access service.

- A website located on a server in Israel that is accessible by customers in Israel may not constitute a PE where an independent access provider is used and the website does not have the ability to process customer orders. If the website does have sales activity, tax treaty protection may be available depending on the overall scope of the foreign company's presence in Israel.

- A website located outside of Israel but accessible to customers in Israel is unlikely to constitute a PE.

- A website located on a server in Israel that is not accessible by customers in Israel but is accessible by customers in other countries will most likely not constitute a PE.

- The mere licensing by a foreign company of technology and know-how to a local company would generally create Israeli-sourced royalties subject to Israeli withholding tax at a rate of 25%, which may be reduced by a tax treaty.

- The provision of technical assistance and technological services by a foreign company to a local company may constitute a PE, depending on the extent of the services and the presence of company employees in Israel to perform such services. The existence of a PE is likely in the case of operator services and/or network management services due to the presence in Israel of the foreign company's employees. Because technology is involved, even if the operation is not a PE, some of the payments being made to the foreign company could be characterized as royalties and be subject to withholding. In such a case, it would be important to bifurcate the arrangement between services and royalties.

- When a foreign company provides technical assistance by "seconding" its employees to a local company and the foreign company has no further responsibility or control over these employees, then it can be contended that a manpower-type "placing fee" is non-Israeli-derived income and not subject to Israeli tax. On the other hand, if the foreign company still has to exert its knowledge and know-how in the services and has responsibility and participation in the services being rendered, this may create a PE.

- The leasing of telecommunications equipment in Israel is generally considered Israeli-sourced income and subject to Israeli tax. Even under many tax treaties, the presence and use of a company's equipment may create a PE in Israel. Some treaties view equipment rentals as royalties, subject to withholding tax. In the case of a finance lease, the foreign company would be deemed to have sold assets on a financed basis to the customer. The portion of the payment representing the finance element would be subject to Israeli withholding tax (25% or lower based on the applicable treaty rate for interest income remittances).

- The laying of fiber optic cable and the construction of telecommunications switching equipment for sale to a local company or to be operated by a foreign company in exchange for a fee would generally be subject to Israeli taxation. However, most double-taxation treaties provide that construction projects, or supervisory activity connected thereto, of a defined length (generally less than 6 or 12 months, depending upon the treaty) do not, in and of themselves, constitute a PE. It should be noted that Israel's territory for this purpose would generally be considered to extend to the Continental Shelf, which is often far beyond the standard six nautical miles employed for the definition of territorial waters in the context of international law.

Business Entities

Local Branch and Locally Incorporated Subsidiary of a Foreign Company. Foreign investors can invest and undertake business operations in the telecommunications industry in Israel by means of a registered branch of a foreign company or through an Israeli company. Experience has shown that the Israeli MOC, in its granting of the prerequisite license, may require that the actual license-holder authorized by the Ministry be an Israeli company, which would necessitate that a foreign investor establish, at some point, such a company for its intended Israeli telecommunications activity.

Some tax consequences of a branch and a subsidiary are discussed below. Branches and subsidiaries are subject to the same 36% rate of income tax.

When the same foreign company that operates a branch and conducts business *in* Israel also conducts business *with* Israel from abroad, there is an increased risk that profits arising from the business activity *with* Israel may also be exposed to Israeli tax (whereas, under a local subsidiary structure, it would not be). In such cases, the incorporation of a separate foreign-based company (in the country of residency of the head office or elsewhere) for the purpose of carrying on business *in* Israel by its branch (an "earmarked company") may help to minimize such tax exposure.

There is no branch tax on regular (i.e., non-approved enterprise) profits, while dividends, subject to the provisions of an applicable treaty, are generally subject to a 25% withholding tax. The Israeli Investment Center grants the status of approved enterprise (AE) to productive-type plans of investment that meet certain economic criteria. Where the profits are from AE income, a 15% withholding or branch tax rate generally applies whether a branch or subsidiary structure is utilized. However, the branch tax may be waived if the profits are reinvested in the AE. Certain treaty provisions may provide that both the dividend withholding tax and the underlying Israeli company taxes on profits out of which a dividend was paid may be creditable by the foreign company recipient of the dividend.

Capital gains arising from the disposition of non-traded shares in an Israeli company (i.e., a subsidiary) are taxable in Israel, subject to the provisions of an applicable treaty, but the tax may be creditable against the foreign country tax. If a foreign company is established whose sole activity is its Israeli branch, then the sale of its shares might be taxable in Israel, subject to the provisions of the applicable treaty.

If an initial public offering on the Tel Aviv Stock Exchange were to be contemplated, it should be noted that there is an exemption for capital gains arising from the sale of *Israeli* shares that are traded on the Tel Aviv Stock Exchange; however, shares of a *foreign* company that are traded on the Tel Aviv Stock Exchange could be taxed at the rate of 35%.

Generally, losses of one branch of an Israeli company can be used to offset income of another Israeli branch if they are part of the same company (i.e., divisional branches); losses cannot be used in this way for different companies of a group.

Joint Venture. A joint venture is not, in itself, a legal entity, but, rather, an economic concept that may be defined and organized in a number of ways, including: (a) an agreement establishing a contractual relationship between the participants; (b) a company in which the participants in the joint venture are shareholders; or (c) a formal partnership.

Joint ventures are generally subject to the same PE considerations described above. Each joint venture participant would generally be taxable in Israel only to the extent of its participation in the venture. Partnerships are recognized under Israeli law as separate registrable entities and can be established with either full or limited liability for partners. Israeli tax law does not tax partnerships as such, but generally taxes each partner on a current basis on its share of the income of the partnership and in accordance with its particular status (e.g., local or foreign company, or individual). Where a joint venture is structured as a company, as opposed to a partnership, it must file a tax return.

Local Funding Alternatives

Debt versus Equity

Interest and dividends are generally subject to a 25% withholding tax upon remittance (subject to the provisions of a relevant tax treaty). However, interest is generally deductible when computing Israeli taxable income, provided that it is incurred wholly and exclusively in the production of taxable income. Therefore, a corporation may find it beneficial to meet its financing needs by the use of debt rather than equity. The circumstances of the payor company should also be considered (for example, when a company is expected to incur future losses and would not benefit from the use of an interest deduction).

Generally, shareholder debt and third-party debt are treated in the same manner for Israeli tax purposes. Under certain tax treaties, a lower rate of withholding tax may apply in the case of interest paid to a financial institution resident in a treaty country.

Under the Israeli Companies Ordinance, there is no statutory minimum capital requirement and the issued share capital may be minimal, subject to the provisions of the company's founding charter and bylaws. Moreover, Israeli tax law does not contain thin capitalization rules per se and, with the exception of an AE, there are generally no restrictions regarding debt-to-equity ratios. For an AE, there is generally a 30% equity requirement.

Although the terms debt and equity are not specifically defined under Israeli tax law, in practice, the tax authorities often will look at several criteria in their determination of whether an arrangement is of a debt or an equity nature. Particularly, an outlay may be regarded as a bona fide loan, where it is characterized by the existence of a loan agreement with specific loan terms (e.g., a fixed or ascertainable maturity date, or a stated percentage of interest).

A payment made to a non-resident is deductible in a tax year only either when effected during the tax year or when applicable withholding tax is deducted within three months after the tax year-end and remitted to the authorities within seven days after such deduction, together with linkage differences (i.e., indexation to the rate of Israeli inflation) and interest accrued since year-end.

There are no formal tax rules that limit the use of shareholder guarantees and, accordingly, certain back-to-back loan structures might be acceptable from an Israeli tax perspective and, thereby, be a viable means of financing a local operation.

Exchange differences on a loan granted by a non-resident are generally exempt from Israeli taxation, except where attributable to a loan granted by a PE of a non-resident.

Exchange Controls

In general, loans can be provided by non-residents to Israeli residents if the Israeli commercial bank, acting on behalf of the Bank of Israel, is satisfied as to the terms thereof and that the foreign currency is transferred from overseas to an Israeli resident's bank account.

Under the Israeli Currency Control Law of 1978 and its regulations, a foreign resident is generally permitted to invest in any class of shares of public and private Israeli companies. However, in order to repatriate in foreign currency dividends from the company, or the proceeds from a sale of shares in the Israeli company or from a liquidation of the company, after payment of all taxes due, Israel's currency regulations require that the purchase of shares be made in foreign currency, or its equivalent, and be recorded as such.

Business Acquisitions and Dispositions

Capital Contributions into an Existing Local Entity

When a foreign investor is involved, a transfer of assets (e.g., a capital contribution) to an Israeli corporation should generally not be an Israeli tax event for the contributor or for the existing shareholders where shares are issued in consideration for the capital contribution.

There are no limitations with respect to intangibles that a foreign entity can contribute to an existing local entity, provided the transaction adheres to arm's-length principles. When technology is made available to a local entity, the transfer might be regarded as a licensing arrangement and not as a sale. The determination of whether a licensing arrangement is involved would generally depend upon the nature of the rights transferred.

Capital contributions should not restrict the use of tax attributes in a local entity. However, proposed legislation has been considered which would curtail loss relief claims by companies in which control is considered to have changed over a 12-month period.

Purchase or Sale of Shares in a Local Entity

Both residents and non-residents are taxable in Israel on capital gains arising from the sale of non-traded securities issued by Israeli companies. However, many of Israel's tax treaties provide an exemption from Israeli tax on Israeli-sourced capital gains subject to certain conditions.

The purchaser's basis in the acquired shares will generally be equal to the price paid by the purchaser for the shares plus the expenses of the acquisition, and the basis of the underlying assets and the acquired company's tax attributes would carry over. When shares are purchased, there is generally no potential for a basis step-up in the acquired company's assets.

Purchase or Sale of Assets

In a taxable sale of assets, the seller recognizes ordinary income to the extent of its gain on the sale of inventory: the remaining gain is generally considered a capital gain. Capital gains tax may be deferred where new depreciable assets (except for a building) are acquired to replace depreciable assets that are sold, provided the new assets are acquired within 12 months after or four months prior to the sale. The amount of the sales consideration that exceeds the cost of the acquired assets remains subject to capital gains tax.

The purchaser will obtain a step-up in the basis of the seller's assets equal to the amount paid for the assets plus any liabilities assumed by the purchaser. The purchaser's ability to depreciate or amortize the purchase price of the acquired assets will depend upon the allocated fair market value of the individual assets purchased. The portion of the purchase price allocated to an intangible (e.g., customer lists, current contracts or patents) may be amortized over its useful life where a limited useful life can be proven. The seller's tax attributes (e.g., net operating loss carryforwards) remain with the seller and do not carry over to the purchaser.

A purchaser's basis in a partnership will generally be equal to the purchase price paid. A disposition of a partnership interest by a partner is generally treated by the Israeli tax authorities as a sale of the partner's share of the underlying partnership as-

sets. However, under a court decision, such a sale may be regarded as the sale of a separate intangible asset comparable to a shareholding in a company. The authorities have contested this decision.

Start-up Business Issues

Pre-operating Losses and Start-up/ Construction Costs

Costs incurred in the start-up phase of forming a business, such as legal fees, underwriters' fees and promotional expenditures, must be capitalized and are not amortizable. A franchise, license or easement acquired with an indefinite life generally must also be capitalized. In certain cases, the cost of a franchise, license or easement with a limited life may be amortized as an operating expense over the life of the franchise.

Operating losses incurred in the start-up of a business generally are not capitalized, but may be carried forward. Property, plant and equipment costs of building a telecommunications business are allocated to future periods by means of the depreciation process (see "Depreciation/Cost-Recovery Conventions/Accelerated Deductions"). Expenditures made to acquire and develop land to ready it for use, such as digging and installation, are considered as part of the cost of the land and are not depreciable.

In general, interest costs incurred to finance the construction, building, installation, manufacture, development or improvement of real or personal property must be capitalized.

Customs Duties and VAT

The importation of telecommunications equipment is subject to customs duty, purchase tax and VAT. Rates of tax (excluding VAT) vary between 0% to 50% depending on the origin of the equipment and the specific item imported. VAT is chargeable at the rate of 17% on all imports regardless of their origin and is recoverable in the normal course of operating a VAT file. A foreign entity doing business in Israel must register for VAT and appoint an Israeli-resident representative within 60 days of commencing Israeli operations.

Importers of telecommunications equipment into Israel will also require approval from MOC before such equipment will be released from the port of entry. Such approval may involve the obtaining of a type-approval license or, for wireless equipment, a license for the installation and maintenance of transmission stations.

Pursuant to the WTO Agreement, Israel has committed itself to reducing customs tariffs on importation of a variety of telecommunications equipment. The reductions are to be carried out in stages, ending with a complete phaseout of tariffs on all equipment covered by the year 2000. With respect to certain items, the phaseout will be completed in 2005.

The first of four reduction stages was implemented in July 1997. The agreement guarantees parallel reductions for importation of Israeli products into all other signatory countries, which represent 92.5% of global trade in information technology products.

Loss Carryovers

Losses arising in the course of a business activity may be set off by the taxpayer against income from other sources earned during the same year. The balance of such losses cannot be carried back, but they may be carried forward indefinitely and may offset both ordinary business income and capital gains of the business. Generally, there are no limitations on the carryover of losses after a change of ownership or a change in business activity, although legislation on the matter has been discussed.

Operating Considerations

Corporate Income Taxes

Israeli taxable income less attributable expenses are taxable at a corporate tax rate of 36%. In general, taxpayers are required to report their taxable income on a calendar-year basis. Companies whose shares are publicly traded on the Tel Aviv Stock Exchange, or which are associated with such companies, or which are subsidiaries of companies publicly traded on a foreign stock exchange, are permitted to apply for a different tax year. In practice, however, such permission is rarely granted to companies whose shares are traded on the Tel Aviv Stock Exchange.

Israeli tax laws provide for adjustments in the determination of taxable income that aim to neutralize the erosion of capital invested in a business by inflation (as measured by the Israeli consumer price index), and, conversely, undue benefits that emanate from the deduction of certain inflationary financial expenses for tax purposes. The provisions of the law generally apply in determining the income of corporations and other entities, partnerships and individuals.

Certain taxpayers may elect to submit tax returns based on books of account maintained in U.S. dollars, in accordance with rules of translation as prescribed in the tax regulations, or to adjust their taxable income based on changes in the exchange rate of the shekel to the U.S. dollar.

With the exception of industrial holding companies (a status that is generally inapplicable to companies in the telecommunications industry), companies may not file consolidated returns.

Capital Gains Taxes

In general, Israeli residents are subject to tax on capital gains on a worldwide basis. Subject to the provisions of an applicable treaty, non-residents are taxable in Israel on capital gains arising from the sale of assets located in Israel or on the sale of direct or indirect rights to such assets, including securities issued by Israeli companies.

Israeli capital gains tax is generally calculated in local currency, and the taxable gain is segregated for Israeli tax purposes into its real and inflationary components. The inflationary amount is exempt to the extent that it accrued after January 1, 1994, and is generally subject to tax at a rate of 10% for the portion accrued before then. The real gain, if any, is taxable at the regular Israeli rate, which is currently 36% for a company.

In the case of a disposal of shares, an amount of gain equal to the investor's share of the retained profits (as defined in the law) of the company is treated not as a real gain but as an additional inflationary amount and is taxable at 10%, irrespective of when the profits accrued.

Capital gains derived by private individual investors and non-residents on the sale of publicly traded securities on the Tel Aviv Stock Exchange are, in principle, exempt from Israeli tax. Certain businesses that hold listed (publicly traded) securities may be taxable on revaluation gains in the year of acquisition, and afterward upon disposition. Registration of shares on the Tel Aviv Stock Exchange is considered a taxable sale event, but there is an election to defer the tax payment.

Capital losses (with respect to stock losses, in historic or non-inflationary-indexed terms only) may offset capital gains realized in the current year or in the following seven years. Capital losses from business equipment replaced in the same tax year may, as an alternative, be expensed up to the cost of replacement. Generally, sales of network assets are regarded as capital in nature; therefore, losses on the sale of such assets are treated as capital in the manner described above.

A non-resident who invests in taxable assets with foreign currency generally may elect to pay tax effectively at the regular rate on the real gain calculated in terms of the foreign currency originally invested. Under this election, the inflationary amount attributable to exchange differences on the investment is completely exempt from Israeli tax when the investment was in shares of an Israeli company, but is taxable as above for most other assets.

Tax Holidays and Exemptions

Companies with approved-enterprise (AE) status are entitled to receive certain benefits. However, these benefits are expected to be modified and reduced. The following are some highlights of the current benefits:

- A 10% to 25% tax rate on AE income generally for 7-10 years, depending on the percentage of foreign ownership

- A 15% withholding tax rate on dividends paid from AE profits

- A tax holiday alternative of up to 10 years, where any entitlement to government grants is foregone. As applicable, the reduced tax rates noted above will apply for the remaining benefit period, if any. Certain dividend limitations apply under this option.

Depreciation/Cost-Recovery Conventions/Accelerated Deductions

The straight-line method is used when computing depreciation. The annual rates for some typical assets used in telecommunications enterprises are as follows:

- 4% for buildings, depending on the building type

- 15% for electronic and computerized equipment

- 20% for radio-based equipment

- 20%– 33% for computers and peripheral equipment, depending on the purchase date and the type of system

An AE is entitled to claim accelerated depreciation for machinery and equipment forming part of the approved program of investments in fixed assets at double the standard depreciation rates during the first five years in which the assets are operated. Where it can be demonstrated that there is unusual wear and tear on machinery and equipment due to their being operated on additional shifts or under extremely difficult conditions, the tax authorities may grant depreciation of 250% of the standard depreciation rates. For buildings of an enterprise approved after July 30, 1978, depreciation of 400% of the regular rate may be claimed, but the rate is not to exceed 20% per annum.

The annual depreciation for purchased software is generally in accordance with the depreciation rate for the computer using the software (20%– 33% per annum).

Research and development capital expenditures relating to scientific research that have been approved by the appropriate government department are generally deductible, upon meeting certain additional conditions, in the tax year in which they are paid. Other capital expenditures for scientific research incurred for the advancement or development of an enterprise may be amortized in three equal annual installments beginning with the tax year in which they were paid.

Marketing and advertising costs, including payments made directly or indirectly (through sales agents) to attract customers, are normally deductible. However, in certain cases, advertising costs may have to be treated as a capital non-deductible expenditure where the costs are incurred not for the promotion of immediate sales but, rather, to develop goodwill (e.g., in the initial phases of business), which would be regarded as resulting in long-term benefits.

Transfer Pricing Rules

Transactions between related parties must adhere to arm's-length principles. Although there are no regulations setting forth detailed transfer pricing guidelines, the tax authorities can disregard a pricing arrangement and substitute the price that would have been expected if the transaction had occurred between independent, non-related parties. When technology is transferred exclusively to related parties, the tax authorities may consider the consistency of the treatment worldwide, the general industry practice and the value of the technology to the business.

Transfers of Patents, Trademarks and Software

An outright sale of technology is generally treated as the sale of a capital asset. A license or transfer of technology that constitutes a transfer of all substantial rights in the technology may, under certain circumstances, be deemed a sale of a capital asset. When the technology sold or transferred is inventory or property held by the taxpayer primarily for sale to customers in the ordinary course of business, the sale or transfer will generally be taxable as part of ordinary business income. When all substantial rights are not transferred or where the amount realized on the sale, license or transfer of technology is contingent on its productivity or use, the arrangement will generally be treated as royalty income for the recipient. Transfers of technology that have received benefits from the Israeli Office of the Chief Scientist are subject to certain restrictions.

When payments for the use of know-how, patents or trademarks are expressed as a percentage of production, turnover or profits, such payments will be deductible. A lump-sum payment normally indicates that the expenditure is of a capital nature.

The Israeli tax authorities are still developing their position on whether a payment for a software product should be viewed as a sale or a royalty payment. Payments for lower-priced, mass-marketed, shrink-wrapped software may generally be regarded as a sale, while payments for low-volume specialized software may be treated as a license. Royalty remittances are generally subject to Israeli withholding tax at a rate of 25%, which may be reduced by a tax treaty.

Service Fees

The portion of fees that relate to services rendered in Israel is taxable (subject to the provisions of an applicable tax treaty). Under Israeli tax operating guidelines, Israeli commercial banks generally are required to withhold tax from income remittances to non-residents at a rate of 25%. The Israeli tax authorities may confirm a lower rate of tax or an exemption (e.g., for non-Israeli-sourced income or pursuant to the provisions of a tax treaty). In practice, the imposition of withholding tax on the gross remittance abroad is normally the final tax requested, provided that the non-resident is not deemed to have a taxable presence in Israel.

Service fees incurred wholly and exclusively in the production of taxable income are deductible for tax purposes.

Value-Added Tax, Sales Tax and/or Other Pertinent Taxes

The standard rate of Israeli VAT is 17%. Persons doing business in Israel (including non-residents) are required to register and operate as authorized VAT dealers. Non-residents performing services in Israel are additionally required to appoint an Israeli representative to act on their behalf. VAT inputs incurred by authorized dealers registered in Israel are recoverable as an offset against output VAT, and the excess will be refunded.

If an Israeli resident is charged for imported services or intangible assets provided by a foreign resident who does not maintain an Israeli VAT file, the Israeli resident is required to account for VAT under a self-billing mechanism on behalf of the foreign resident.

Upon meeting certain conditions, certain transactions may be zero-rated for VAT. These include:

- The export of goods (such as the sale or licensing of technology)

- The supply of services to a person resident abroad (except if such services were effectively rendered to an Israeli or foreign resident in Israel)

- The supply of services in connection with an asset in Israel where the consideration for such services was included in the price of the asset for customs purposes

In 1994, when guidelines were issued in anticipation of the opening of the international telecommunications sector to pri-

vately owned providers, the VAT authorities took the position that international carriers are required to open VAT files in Israel and to appoint a local representative for VAT purposes.

Under these guidelines, VAT would be imposed on all calls made by Israeli residents in Israel. Service charges from an Israeli subsidiary or an Israeli representative of such international carriers would also be subject to VAT as being indirectly related to the provision of services to the Israeli customers. The guiding intent was to impose VAT on the basis of the location of the source of the call.

Recently, however, the VAT authorities have expressed the viewpoint in certain discussions that VAT should be imposed on the full amount charged to Israeli customers with respect to international telecommunications, regardless of the location from which the phone call was initiated or the residency of the service provider.

The significance of this policy change for imposition of VAT is that it has a direct impact on individual consumers, financial institutions and not-for-profit institutions that are not "dealers": unlike dealers, individual consumers, financial institutions and not-for-profit institutions cannot recover VAT charges incurred.

Local and Provincial Taxes

There are no local taxes applicable to foreign telecommunications enterprises operating in Israel except for a municipal real property tax, which has widely varying rates.

For Additional Information, Contact:

Avidor Avni
Senior Tax Partner
and
Gerry Seligman
Senior International Tax Manager
and
Zeev Katz
International Tax Manager
37 Montefiore Street
Tel-Aviv 65201
Israel
Telephone: 972 (3) 564 8612 (Avni)
            972 (3) 564 8616 (Seligman)
            972 (3) 564 8620 (Katz)
Fax: 972 (3) 564 8556
E-mail: Avidor_Avni@il.coopers.com
        Gerry_Seligman@il.coopers.com
        Zeev_Katz@il.coopers.co

South Africa

Telecommunications Tax Profile
by Eric S. Louw
Tax Partner, Johannesburg

Overview of the Telecommunications Market

Historical Background

In 1991 the telecommunications arm of the government was separated from postal activities and transformed into an unlisted public company, Telkom SA Limited (Telkom), which today has a statutory monopoly to provide all telecommunications services to the public. The Minister of Posts, Telecommunications and Broadcasting represents the state as shareholder in Telkom. Telkom's tariffs are subject to approval by the Minister.

In 1994 South Africa signed several agreements intended to lower barriers to international trade, including the Uruguay Round of the General Agreement on Tariffs and Trade (GATT) and the associated Trade Related Investment Measures (TRIMs) and Agreement on Technical Barriers to Trade (TBT Agreement). Consequently, the South African terminal equipment market is now open to new entrants, who can compete on favorable terms with South African companies. During the same year, the cellular services industry was liberalized with the award of licenses to two companies.

Current Status

In early 1996 Parliament passed the Telecommunications Act, setting out the liberalization policies for the industry. In 1997 three licenses were issued to Telkom, giving it a five-year period of exclusivity in public switched telecommunications services (PSTS), with the prospect of a sixth year if performance exceeds the targets set. The licenses also provide a framework for the company's service quality and line roll-out commitments and set out time periods in which to fulfill them. Telkom faced immediate competition in the value-added network service market.

In March 1997, 30% of the equity in Telkom was sold to the consortium of SBC Communications Inc. and Telekom Malaysia, which have formed a limited liability company called Thintana Communications LLC. The Minister can make future share transfers of up to 10% of the total issued shares (or greater with the equity partner's consent) for the purpose of empowering disadvantaged groups and/or for the benefit of present and future employees of Telkom and its subsidiaries.

The main suppliers of telecommunications services and equipment in South Africa are:

- Telkom, which installs, maintains and operates voice and non-voice telecommunications networks. Telkom also controls and manages telecommunications number schemes for voice and non-voice services.

- Two licensed cellular operators, Vodacom (Pty) Ltd and Mobile Telephone Networks (Pty) Ltd (MTN), which both operate global system for mobile communications (GSM) networks that, combined, serve approximately 1.2 million subscribers. Vodacom, which holds roughly 66% of the market, also operates the analog C450 "motorphone" cellular telephone system formerly operated by Telkom. The cellular network operators provide capacity to 14 retail cellular providers, including the two major exclusive Vodacom service providers, Teljoy Holdings Limited and Vodac, serving approximately 100,000 and 205,000 subscribers, respectively. M-Tel serves approximately 200,000 MTN subscribers exclusively. Proposals were under discussion regarding a third cellular operator. If a third license is granted, the government will likely require that a substantial portion of the shareholding be in the hands of the disadvantaged community.

- Two licensed radio trunking operators, Fleetcall (Pty) Ltd and Q-Trunk (Pty) Ltd (which is owned by Telkom), several radio paging operators, and several suppliers of customer premises equipment

- Two utilities that provide extensive in-house telecommunications networks to support their core activities—Transtel, a business of Transnet Limited, the national transport utility, and Eskom, the electricity utility

- Several suppliers of value-added network services that operate under licenses issued by the South African Telecommunications Regulatory Authority (SATRA)

- Telkom is committed to having a fully digital network by the year 2001-02. Currently, 74% of automatic working lines are connected to digital exchanges. Fiber optic cable is being used as new lines are installed and older lines are replaced. Telkom added 256,000 working lines during the past financial year to bring the total number of working lines to 4.3 million. Telkom's PSTS license sets forth future service targets split between six categories. This license provides for approximately 4.5 million new lines to be installed within its exclusive five-year license period.

Current Liberalization Status

In the World Trade Organization negotiations in February 1997, South Africa committed to limited liberalization by the year 2002 and pledged to adhere to a common set of regulatory principles. It retained certain restrictions on foreign ownership (see "Potential for Foreign Ownerships/Relationships").

Type of Service	Degree of Liberalization	Key Legislation	Date of Actual or Expected Liberalization	Comments
Local, Long Distance and International	Monopoly	Section 36 of the Telecommunications Act	2002	An additional one year of exclusivity will be granted if Telkom meets the license agreement service targets. The license is valid for 25 years and can be transferred to another party only with written consent from the authorities.
Cellular	Duopoly	Section 37 of the Telecommunications Act	1994	The government was considering licensing a third provider before the end of 1997.
Paging	Fully liberalized			
Value-added	Fully liberalized	Section 40 of the Telecommunications Act	1997	License is valid for 25 years.

Competitive Environment

The new regulatory framework contained in the Telecommunications Act provides for a phased progression to a competitive telecoms marketplace while policy makers pursue much-needed infrastructure improvements.

Type of Service	Entire Market		Top Two Players		
	Market Size (1997)	Number of Players	Names	Annual Revenue (1997)	Ownership
Local	R3.64 billion	1	Telkom	R3.64 billion	Government 70%, Thintana 30%
Long Distance	R7.46 billion	1	Telkom	R7.46 billion	Government 70%, Thintana 30%
International	R2.79 billion	1	Telkom	R2.79 billion	Government 70%, Thintana 30%
Cellular	R4.1 billion	2 network operators, plus 14 retail service providers	Vodacom	Not available	Telkom, Vodafone Holdings, Rembrandt Group, Descarte Investment
			MTN	Not available	SBC, M-Cell Ltd., Cable & Wireless
Value-added	Not available	Approximately 20	Not available		

Source: Annual financial statements for 1997.

Licensing Requirements

The South African Telecommunications Regulatory Authority was established in 1997 to assume responsibility for issuing licenses and monitoring compliance. To operate the following services, licenses are issued for regional use:

- Frequency spectrum services

- Station license

- Public switched telecommunications service

- Mobile cellular telecommunications service

- National long-distance telecommunications service

- International telecommunications service

- Local access telecommunications service and public pay-telephone services

- Value-added network services

- Private telecommunications network services

There are no sectors in which it is likely that new licenses will be issued in the near term.

Potential for Foreign Ownerships/Relationships

For fixed-line and cellular operations, licensing agreements require that shareholding for formally disadvantaged groups must be provided for. Foreign investment is not specifically restricted, however.

Potential for Upcoming Liberalization/Investment Opportunities

Value-added services will be opened to competition. There is a possibility of a license being granted to a third cellular provider. Opportunities also exist for Internet service providers in South Africa.

Forms of Doing Business

Permanent Establishment

If a foreign enterprise generates profits from a real or deemed South African source, it will be liable for normal tax (income tax) on those profits if there is no double-tax treaty between the foreign enterprise's country of residence and South Africa. If a tax treaty is in effect, a foreign enterprise will be exempt from tax if it has no permanent establishment (PE) in South Africa to which the profits are attributable.

A PE is usually described in double-taxation agreements as a fixed place of business through which the business of the enterprise is wholly or partly carried on. It usually includes a place of management, branch, office, factory and workshop. The definition also includes a dependent agent who has the authority to contract on behalf of a non-resident principal, and who habitually exercises that authority. Following are examples of situations that do and do not constitute PEs for telecommunications providers:

- The provision of long-distance telephone services by a foreign company without any local presence or advertising would not amount to a PE. A dependent agent might cause it to have a PE.

- The licensing of technology and know-how to a local company by a foreign company would not be seen as a PE. The license fees would, however, be regarded as royalties, which would be subject to a withholding tax.

- The provision of technical services and assistance, including operator services, by a foreign enterprise to a local company in exchange for service fees, including cases in which the foreign enterprise owned equity in the local company, would constitute a PE if the foreign enterprise that received fees for its services provided the services from a fixed place of business in South Africa.

- The leasing of telecommunications equipment to a local company would not qualify as a PE unless operation and maintenance services were provided as part of the leasing arrangements. Certain double-tax treaties would require the rentals to be treated as royalties. In the absence of double-tax treaties, the source of the income would probably be considered South African and subject to withholding tax.

- Call reorganization/turnaround services would not amount to a PE if the foreign provider owned no switches related to these services in South Africa.

- An Internet access service provided to South African residents would be unlikely to create a PE in South Africa if the server were not in South Africa. The sale or provision of software by an access provider to a local customer would probably not constitute a PE.

- Content providers selling goods and services via an Internet service are not likely to have a PE in South Africa merely by virtue of being on the Internet, irrespective of whether a server is located within South Africa.

• The laying of cable and construction of telecommunications switching equipment would amount to a PE; however, there is usually a cut-off period (usually 12 months) under which construction activities would not constitute a PE.

If the provision of services does not constitute a PE (in the case of services provided by an enterprise of a treaty country) or if the provision of services is not made within South Africa, then withholding taxes on royalty and know-how payments will be the only relevant taxes for the foreign enterprise.

Business Entities

Local Branch of a Foreign Company. This option is available to an investor and is known as an external company. The company is not incorporated in South Africa, but establishes a place of business in South Africa. The main corporate taxes are income tax and the secondary tax on companies (STC). An external company will pay income tax at the rate of 40% on taxable income in financial years ending on or after April 1, 1997. This tax cannot be deferred in any significant manner. Taxable profits, or tax losses, of the branch of a non-resident company will be grouped with that company's other South African-sourced or deemed-sourced taxable income (or tax losses, if any) in arriving at total South African taxable income. STC is not levied on external companies.

Locally Incorporated Subsidiary of a Foreign Company. This option is available to an investor. Income tax on South African companies is levied at a flat rate of 35% on taxable income. Taxable income, or tax losses, of a subsidiary will be grouped with that subsidiary's other South African-sourced or deemed-sourced taxable income (or tax losses, if any) in arriving at total South African taxable income. STC is levied at a rate of 12.5% on net dividends that are declared by locally incorporated subsidiaries. Thus, a South African incorporated company will be subject to an effective tax rate of 42.22%, but 7.22% of that can be deferred by not declaring dividends. These percentages are arrived at as shown in the following table:

	Amount (R)	Effective Tax Rate (%)
Profit before tax	100.00	
Less: income tax	(35.00)	35.00
Available for distribution	65.00	
Less: STC (12.5% of distribution of 57.78)	(7.22)	7.22*
Distribution	57.78	
Effective tax rate		42.22

*Can be deferred by not making distributions or deemed distributions

Joint Venture. A non-resident company may invest in or carry on business in South Africa in partnership with a resident company. Although legally distinguishable from a partnership, a joint venture is generally taken to mean a partnership for a particular period or for a particular undertaking.

A joint venture may be a suitable vehicle for investing in South Africa when the non-resident partner is reluctant to invest cash capital, but has goodwill, expertise, intellectual property or other tangible property that may be profitably employed in South Africa, with the cash being provided by the resident partner.

A partnership generally is required to incorporate as a company if it has more than 20 partners. The main disadvantage of a partnership is that, unlike a company, it does not afford its partners limited liability. Partners are taxed separately on their allocations of the partnership income, since a partnership is not a legal or taxable entity. Partners must file their own tax returns. A non-resident partner will be taxed on its allocation of the partnership profits derived from a source within or deemed to be within South Africa. The remittance of the non-resident's profit share is not subject to withholding taxes.

A foreign company entering into a joint venture with a local or foreign partner would not by itself be deemed to have a PE. However, if the joint venture creates a PE in South Africa, that PE will effectively act as a PE of the foreign company.

Local Funding Alternatives

Debt versus Equity

In terms of shareholder equity, the local company would receive no tax deduction for dividend payments. Dividends attract 12.5% STC, which is paid by the local company. The investor incurs no further South African tax or withholding tax on such dividends.

The use of shareholder debt can result in a tax deduction for interest payments. The recipient of the interest will not be subject to any tax if it is managed and controlled outside of South Africa and does not carry on business in South Africa.

For tax purposes, no formal substance-over-form rules exist for determining whether shareholder advances are debt or equity. Equity is invariably taken to be investment, which is recorded as share capital and share premium with the Registrar of Companies.

When there is cross-border shareholder funding, interest rates must be on an arm's-length basis, and thin capitalization rules become relevant. Excess interest cannot be taken as a deduction, and it is treated as a distribution for STC.

The offshore funding of a local company must be done on a maximum debt-to-equity ratio of 3 to 1. Any Rand-denominated loan may carry a maximum interest at the prime South African overdraft rate plus 2%. Loans denominated in foreign currency are capped at the relevant London Interbank Offered Rate (LIBOR) plus 4% maximum. However, for exchange-control purposes (see "Exchange Controls"), the rates are restricted further, to prime plus 1% for Rand-denominated loans and LIBOR plus 2% for loans of foreign currency. There are no limitations on non-related foreign party or local loans, but exchange-control approvals are required for all non-resident loans, whether related-party or not.

Exchange gains and losses on non-resident debt are tax-deductible on translation and/or realization.

Exchange Controls

There are exchange-control restrictions on local borrowings, such as overdrafts, letters of credit, discounting and/or factoring and capital equipment leases. Limits are placed on the degree of local financial assistance that may be acquired by entities operating in South Africa that are 50%-or-more-owned or -controlled by non-residents.

The level of local financial assistance available to a wholly non-resident-owned subsidiary company is limited to 100% of the subsidiary's total effective capital. This limit is increased, depending on the degree of local participation, to 200% of total effective capital when the non-resident participation is 50%. When the non-resident participation is less than 50%, there are no restrictions on local borrowings.

There are no limitations on foreign borrowings made by South African-resident entities, provided that prior permission from the Exchange Control division of the South African Reserve Bank has been obtained. Capital is repayable on pre-agreed bases, and interest can be freely transferred abroad if approval has been obtained.

No exchange-control restrictions exist on the investment into or withdrawal out of South Africa of equity capital. Dividends may be freely transferred out of earned profits, provided that local borrowing limits have not been, or will not as a result of the distribution be, exceeded.

Business Acquisitions and Dispositions

Capital Contributions into an Existing Local Entity

A capital contribution into a local entity—for example, through the issuance of shares, with or without a premium—does not normally give rise to any income tax liability, either in the hands of the company, the existing shareholders or the incoming shareholders. There is no limitation on intangibles that a foreign entity can contribute to an existing local entity. The intangibles should be valued at arm's length, preferably by a professional valuator.

Non-residents may invest in the equity of private or public companies without restriction. Any share transfers are subject to stamp duty of 0.25% of the consideration for the shares or their value, whichever is higher. Duty of 0.25% is also imposed on the issue of shares and is applied to the total issue price of the shares, including share premium. A capital duty is also imposed, at the rate of 0.5%, on the par value of any increase in the authorized share capital of a company.

Purchase or Sale of Shares in a Local Entity

With the purchase of shares, there is no allocation of cost to assets. The assets retain their original tax basis. However, it may be possible, in certain circumstances, to structure the purchase in a way that allows the buyer to attribute any excess of the purchase price for the shares over the net asset value acquired to the tax-deductible cost of intellectual property.

Purchase or Sale of Assets

If assets are bought and some of the excess cost over net asset value is allocated to intangibles, the allocation should be based on the market value of the intangibles acquired. Allocations of purchase consideration to intangibles should be supported by independent professional valuation.

Surpluses arising on the sale of assets are allocated first to recoupment or recapture of previously allowed deductions (usually by way of tax depreciation or amortization). Any surpluses above such recoupments are regarded as either capital or revenue gains. Capital gains usually arise on the disposal of capital assets such as intangibles and other fixed assets, whereas revenue gains arise on disposal of non-capital assets such as inventory. Capital gains are not subject to tax in South Africa.

Buyers prefer the allocation of the majority of costs to tax-deductible or depreciable assets, including intangibles other than goodwill. Sellers prefer the major cost allocation to assets where no taxable recoupments can arise (for example, with a goodwill sale). It is virtually unheard-of for buyers and sellers to take different positions on the allocation of the price for a business. There is thus no public precedent for how the tax authorities would react to this practice.

The same principles of purchasing assets apply to buying partnership interests, except that the purchase is limited to the extent of the partnership interest.

Start-up Business Issues

Pre-operating Losses and Start-up/ Construction Costs

Costs incurred in producing income can be deducted in the year incurred, even if the income is generated in subsequent years, unless the deduction is postponed by law. Preproduction interest, for instance, is not deductible until operations begin.

Infrastructure costs, including business investigation costs (e.g., licenses and franchise acquisition costs) are capital in nature and may be allowed in the form of tax depreciation or amortization. The depreciation or amortization is calculated on a straight-line basis over periods to be agreed upon with the revenue authorities. There are no specific rules for the telecommunications industry.

Expenditures on fixed assets such as machinery or plant, computer hardware and vehicles qualify for depreciation deductions, and the allowance is first claimed when the asset is brought into use. The depreciation is calculated, usually on the straight-line basis, over standard periods published by the revenue authorities or over periods agreed with the revenue authorities when standard periods are not published for specific asset types.

A foreign company registered for VAT and conducting an enterprise can recover VAT paid. VAT payments made on the purchase of pre-operating goods and enduring services (e.g., legal costs for setting up a company) for the start-up phase of an existing company registered for VAT can be recovered when the costs are first incurred. VAT payments on pre-incorporation costs are recoverable, but recoveries are limited to VAT on costs incurred six months prior to incorporation.

Customs Duties and VAT

Customs duty rates vary from 0% to more than 100%. The majority of items are dutiable at rates ranging from 5% to 25%. With regard to telecommunications equipment, the main units and equipment are subject to 5% duty, but most other parts are free from duty.

The importation of equipment is subject to VAT. A registered vendor submits VAT returns and can claim VAT refunds.

A distinction is drawn between regular telephony and Internet telephony in relation, broadly speaking, to computer equipment. Generally, computer equipment for Internet telephony would attract a 10% ad valorem duty.

Loss Carryovers

A loss may be carried forward and set off against taxable income in future years, provided that the company continues in business. There is no carryback of losses to prior years. Anti-avoidance provisions prevent the set-off of losses when:

- There is an agreement affecting any company or affecting a change in shareholding of the company with the loss carryover.

- Income has been received by or accrued to the company as a direct or indirect result of the agreement.

- The agreement was entered into, or the change of shareholding was effected solely or mainly, to utilize the loss carryover to avoid or reduce the liability for any tax, duty or levy on income.

Operating Considerations

Corporate Income Taxes

Only amounts received or accrued from a source within South Africa are subject to income tax. Because there is no definition of source, a company must conduct its own analysis to determine the originating cause for the receipt or accrual and the geographic location of the originating cause. Certain receipts or accruals that have a real source outside South Africa are deemed to be from a source within South Africa.

Although source is the basis of taxable income, residence is sometimes relevant. The residence of a company is determined by reference to where it is managed or controlled or by reference to the terms of a double-tax agreement.

Receipts and accruals of a capital nature are generally not subject to tax. Taxable income is determined by deducting exempt income and qualifying expenditure, losses and allowances from gross income. Dividends accrued or received are exempt from all income tax.

Companies, including locally incorporated subsidiaries, are taxed at a rate of 35% of taxable income. External companies or local branches are taxed at a rate of 40% of taxable income. Partners in a partnership are taxed separately, as a partnership is not a legal entity.

STC is levied at 12.5% of net dividends declared (i.e., dividends declared less dividends accrued) during a dividend cycle. A dividend cycle runs from the date of declaration of a dividend to the date of declaration of the next dividend. STC is a tax on the company, but it is not regarded by some foreign tax regimes as a tax on income, which leads to problems in obtaining credit for the tax in those countries. In any event, a credit for STC may be academic where the foreign tax rate is equal to or less than the South African tax rate of 35% and where facilities for mixing tax rates do not exist.

Capital Gains Taxes

No such tax exists in South Africa.

Tax Holidays and Exemptions

The Manufacturing Development Programme, introduced in October 1996, consists of a tax holiday in relation to new projects with an investment in land, buildings, plant and machinery exceeding R3 million; a development program for projects with an investment in land, buildings, plant and machinery not exceeding R3 million; and a foreign-investment grant.

Tax Holiday. The tax holiday varies between two and six years, depending on which elements of the program the project qualifies for. The first two years apply to the so-called spatial component, which is dictated by the geographical location of the project. The second two-year period applies to the industry component, which is dictated by the type of manufacturing activity undertaken, qualifying activities having been identified on the basis of those that will contribute most significantly to sustained economic growth and employment creation. The third two-year period is in respect of the human resources component available for projects that achieve a ratio of human resources remuneration to "value added" (as defined in the relevant legislation) in excess of 55%.

Small/Medium Manufacturing Development Programme. The incentives consist of an establishment grant payable for three years, a profit output incentive payable for one year, and a further profit output incentive payable for an additional two years if the investor meets certain human resources requirements.

Foreign Investment Grant. This is available to reimburse foreign investors for expenditure incurred on shipping new machinery and plant to South Africa. The grant covers the cost of overseas insurance, freight (including relocating of personnel and commissioning technicians), wharfage, handling, customs duty, local transport in South Africa, off-loading and packing, local insurance and agency fees. The grant is limited to US$250,000 for companies qualifying for the tax holiday scheme and US$55,000 for entities that qualify under the Small/Medium Manufacturing Development Programme.

Depreciation/Cost-Recovery Conventions/Accelerated Deductions

Wear-and-tear and depreciation allowances are granted at varying rates on plant, machinery and other business assets, including purchased software, telecommunications equipment (with or without embedded software), switches, routers, cells, lines and satellites. Network assets are considered placed in service when the network is available for use by customers.

Research and development costs of a revenue nature are deductible in the years incurred. This usually includes a company's internally developed software. Capital expenditure on research and development is subject to wear-and-tear and depreciation allowances at varying rates, as with other capital assets.

Marketing and advertising costs, including payments made indirectly through sales agents to attract customers, are allowed as a deduction if they are incurred in the production of income and are not of a capital nature. Certain forms of advertising may be of a capital nature and not deductible, as in the case of an advertising campaign launched to introduce a new product name to create long-term customer awareness. A second example would be the production and air-time costs of television and radio commercials to be used over a long period of time.

Transfer Pricing Rules

Transfer pricing rules have only recently been enacted, therefore it is uncertain how they will be applied. It is likely these rules will be rigorously enforced eventually. Generally, the tax authorities may adjust the consideration to reflect an arm's-length price in cases in which (a) goods and services are supplied in a cross-border agreement (i.e., between a company managed and controlled in South Africa and a company managed and controlled elsewhere), (b) the agreement is between connected persons, and (c) the price of goods or services is higher or lower than it would have been in an arm's-length transaction. When a South African company has benefited its foreign shareholders by means of transfer pricing, any amount adjusted by the tax authorities will be treated as a deemed dividend subject to STC. It will be disallowed as an income tax deduction.

Transfers of Patents, Trademarks and Software

Non-resident companies that receive royalties for the use of intellectual property in South Africa are subject to a withholding tax of 12%. The withholding tax can be reduced or eliminated by double-tax treaties. Of this, 1.5% will be refunded if the recipient company files a tax return disclosing the gross royalties accrued or received. If there is an outright acquisition of intellectual property from a non-resident, the amount received by the transferor will often be a capital amount; thus, no withholding tax would be payable.

A taxpayer is allowed a deduction for an expenditure actually incurred in devising, developing, obtaining and acquiring from another person any knowledge or right to the knowledge from a patent, trademark, software, design or similar property.

Transfers of intangible property in exchange for ownership interests can be made free of tax provided the assets transferred are capital assets. Intangible property is usually regarded as a capital asset when the intention of the taxpayer in acquiring or developing the property is one of investment in order to earn revenue by way of royalties, license fees or the like.

Service Fees

Service fees are generally deductible by the entity incurring them. Fees paid to non-residents for imparting know-how or providing support connected to the know-how for use in South Africa are subject to withholding taxes.

Value-Added Tax, Sales Tax and/or Other Pertinent Taxes

Supplies of telecommunications for use in South Africa are subject to VAT at the standard rate (currently 14%). Non-resident suppliers may be required to register for VAT if they have a branch or equipment located in South Africa (from a date to be announced, probably in 1998, all non-residents supplying telecommunications services that are used in South Africa will be obliged to register and account for VAT in South Africa). When the supplier is not registered in South Africa, imported telecommunications services are subject to VAT using a reverse-charge-type procedure. This is applicable to the extent that the services will not be used in the course of providing taxable supplies. VAT incurred on telecommunications is recoverable as an input credit by registered VAT vendors, to the extent that the services are acquired in the course of providing taxable supplies.

International settlements for telecommunications are not currently subject to VAT. The provision of Internet access is generally subject to VAT at the standard rate. All imported services that would be standard-rated if supplied in South Africa are subject to VAT under the imported service provisions noted above.

Payments for Internet telephony, to the extent that the service is used in South Africa, are subject to VAT at the standard rate, either via a direct VAT charge (if provided by a VAT vendor), or via the reverse charge on imported services (if provided by a non-resident, non-VAT vendor). The question of whether Internet access is telephony has not yet been formally considered by the revenue authorities.

Other taxes include donations tax, stamp duty and transfer duty. Donations tax is levied at the rate of 25% on the value of property disposed of under donation or deemed donation (subject to certain exceptions) by a South African resident or company incorporated or managed and controlled in South Africa. Transfer duty is levied on the acquisition of real estate at rates varying from 0% to 10% of the value of property acquired. There are exemptions from transfer duty, particularly if the acquisition is subject to VAT.

Local and Provincial Taxes

The Regional Services Councils (RSCs), which serve as the local governing bodies, levy two types of impost:

*   The regional establishment levy, which is based on turnover (i.e., the consideration, excluding VAT, earned by an enterprise within a region from leviable transactions)

*   The regional services levy, which is based on wages and salaries, including drawings of partners, paid or payable by an employer to an employee

The rates of the levies are determined by the RSCs concerned and vary from region to region. Currently, the average rate for the establishment levy is 0.129%, and 0.3058% for services.

For Additional Information, Contact:

Eric S. Louw
Tax Partner
12th Floor, Ten Sixty Six
35 Pritchard Street
Johannesburg, 2000
South Africa
Telephone: 27 (11) 498 4264
Fax: 27 (11) 836 6720
E-mail: eric_louw@za.coopers.com

J. Nic Campbell
Audit Partner
4th Floor, Leopont
451 Church Street
Pretoria, 0002
South Africa
Telephone: 27 (12) 322 1211
Fax: 27 (12) 322 2413
E-mail: nic_campbell@za.coopers.com

Part Four
North and South America

Argentina
Brazil
Canada
Chile
Colombia
Mexico
Peru
United States
Venezuela

Argentina

Telecommunications Tax Profile
by Esteban G. Macek
Tax Partner, Buenos Aires
and Eduardo O. Meloni
Tax Manager, Buenos Aires

Overview of the Telecommunications Market

Historical Background

Until privatization occurred in 1990, basic voice transmission service between fixed points for local and long-distance calls throughout Argentina was provided by the government through Empresa Nacional de Telecomunicaciones (ENTEL). In 1990, two private companies were granted seven-year monopolies for basic service in distinct areas. The southern half of Argentina is served by Telefónica de Argentina (Telefónica), whose owners include Telefónica de España, S.A. The northern half is served by Telecom Argentina (Telecom), whose owners include France Telecom and STET. Both companies jointly own Telintar, which provides the international service, and Startel S.A., which provides packet-switched data and other value-added services.

In 1989, Compañía de Radiocomunicaciones Móviles (Movicom), a private consortium that includes BellSouth Corporation, Motorola, Socma S.A. and BGH S.A., received the first cellular license to serve Buenos Aires. In 1992, a second cellular license for Buenos Aires was awarded to a Telecom Argentina and Telefónica de Argentina joint venture called Miniphone. In 1994, a license to serve the rest of the country was awarded to Compañía de Teléfonos del Interior (CTI), a consortium that includes GTE, AT&T, and other Argentine investors. A second license for cellular service in the interior of the country was granted to Telefónica for the northern region (Unifon) and to Telecom for the southern region (Personal).

In 1993, the license to build and operate Argentina's first domestic satellite system was granted to a private international telecommunications and aerospace consortium, led by DASA, a subsidiary of Daimler-Benz. NahuelSat commenced operations in 1997. There are two other satellite companies: PanAmSat and INTELSAT.

Current Status

Argentine telecommunications sector revenues are estimated to be growing at 7% annually. Licenses have been granted for a variety of telecommunications services including wireless, data, videoconferencing, alarm, trunking, message transmission, vehicle location, rural messaging, and others. There has been a dramatic improvement in the quality and penetration of telephone service since privatization began in 1990. It is estimated that 95% of the network utilizes fiber optics and is digitalized. Submarine cable projects involving Telintar and international telecommunications companies are underway to significantly expand Argentina's international traffic capacity. These improvements are intended to strengthen the position of these service providers as the liberalization of this market nears.

A personal communications service (PCS) provider was in the process of starting activities. The PCS licensing will probably be finished during 1998.

At the end of 1997, the estimated number of cellular users was nearly 2 million, with continued growth expected. The calling-party-pays system has dramatically increased penetration of the cellular services.

Although paging services have existed since the early 1970s, the market has only begun to expand in the last few years. Paging companies serve an estimated 200,000 customers. Five companies lead the market, including Mtel International, whose SkyTel service provides coverage throughout the country.

Very small aperture terminals (VSATs) have proliferated in the last few years as a way to provide data transmission capacity for private networks. IMPSAT, a service provider in many South American countries, is the dominant VSAT supplier in Argentina, although other competitors are active (e.g., Comsat and Startel).

Argentina's new domestic satellite system commenced operations in 1996. Telecommunications equipment is provided by subsidiaries of leading U.S., German, Japanese, Swedish and Italian suppliers.

Current Liberalization Status

As part of the February 1997 World Trade Organization (WTO) Agreement on Basic Telecommunications Services, Argentina committed to phase in liberalization of voice telephony by November 2000 and eliminate any remaining barriers to foreign ownership within the Argentine telecommunications sector. Full competition without phase-in for other basic telecommunications and a most-favored-nation (MFN) exemption on the supply of fixed satellite services by geostationary satellites was also promised. It remains to be seen whether Argentina will be able to honor all of the commitments it made as scheduled. At press time, the current monopolies (Telefónica and Telecom) in the Argentine telecommunications market, which were expected to end at the close of 1997, had been extended through 1999. However, ownership limitations with respect to investments made by foreigners in Argentina within the telecommunications sector no longer exist. Accordingly, provided that foreign investors obtain the appropriate license, up to 100% ownership is allowed.

Type of Service	Degree of Liberalization	Key Legislation	Date of Actual or Expected Liberalization	Comments
Local, Long Distance and International	Regional monopolies	1989 privatization of telephone services rules	December 2000	
Cellular and PCS	Regional monopolies	1989 privatization of telephone services rules and 1996/1997 CNC regulations ND 1996/1989		First PCS license for Buenos Aires area was in the process of being granted.
Paging	Deregulated			
Value-added	Telex and other international record services are deregulated			

Competitive Environment

The telecommunications sector is the most dynamic sector of Argentina's national economy in terms of generating new investments. Many projects have already been announced, with expansion expected to continue over the next several years. The level of investment by domestic and foreign companies in these projects is estimated to be US$10 billion.

Type of Service	Entire Market		Top Two Players		
	Market Size*	Number of Players*	Names	Annual Revenue*	Ownership
Local, Long Distance and International	US$5 billion	2	Telecom Argentina	US$5 billion (top two players combined)	STET, France Telecom
			Telefónica de Argentina		Telefónica de España, others
Cellular	US$1 billion	5	Miniphone	US$600 million (top two players combined)	Telecom Argentina and Telefónica de Argentina
			Movicom		BellSouth, Motorola, Socma S.A., BGH S.A.

* Estimates based on information gathered from industry publications. Annual revenue figures were calculated based on available interim 1997 financial statements. Actual annual 1997 financial results are not currently available.

Licensing Requirements

The Comisión Nacional de Comunicaciones (CNC) is the regulatory body responsible for the oversight of the telecommunications market. The CNC allocates frequencies, sets technical standards, approves equipment, and establishes service goals. In order to provide service, telecommunications system service operators must register with and obtain a license from the CNC. Licenses are granted upon the applicant's fulfillment of certain technical requirements for system operation.

At present, the only exclusive licenses that exist in the telecommunications sector are for basic telephony and international services. While these licenses were initially scheduled to expire in 1997, a two-year extension was recently granted by the Justice Department.

Potential for Foreign Ownerships/Relationships

With the exception of the broadcast television sector, there are no limitations on the involvement of foreign companies in the telecommunications market. All eligible sectors of the market are currently receiving major investments from domestic and foreign companies.

Potential for Upcoming Liberalization/Investment Opportunities

The monopoly on basic service, which is currently held by Telefónica and Telecom, was scheduled to be opened to competition in 1997. However, this liberalization may be postponed until 2000 if a three-year extension that was incorporated within the original franchise agreement is implemented. The extension is subject to a Justice decision that did not take place until early 1998. Meanwhile, the monopoly is maintained. When this liberalization occurs, the carriers will be free to compete for any service throughout the country and other carriers will be free to enter the basic telephony market.

Domestic satellite communications service will be liberalized in 2005.

Forms of Doing Business

Permanent Establishment

While Argentina does not formally follow the OECD Model Convention definition of a permanent establishment (PE), the provisions under local law are quite similar to those prescribed by the OECD. A foreign company will generally be deemed to have a PE in Argentina when it has a domicile, is organized as a business enterprise (with a management, organization structure and assets) and engages in business activities in Ar-

gentina. When a foreign company has a PE in Argentina, it must set up a business entity, keep separate accounting records and report its own taxes. A PE will not exist when isolated business acts are conducted in Argentina or when repeated business acts are conducted through independent agents that do business on their own.

Telecommunications services can cover a broad range of activities, which may or may not constitute a PE. Some examples follow:

- The provision of long-distance telephone services by a foreign company to local customers without any local presence or advertising, or call reorganization services or turnaround services, will usually not constitute a PE. However, there are very few regulations in this area and, depending on how the services are rendered, there might be cases where a PE could be deemed to exist.

- The licensing by a foreign company of technology and know-how to a local company will usually not constitute a PE.

- The leasing of telecommunications equipment to a local company will usually not constitute a PE.

- When technical assistance and technological services are provided by a foreign company to a local company in exchange for service fees, and the foreign company owns an equity interest in the local company, a PE may or may not be deemed to exist, depending on the circumstances. Operator services will usually constitute a PE, although, as previously mentioned, there are no specific provisions in this respect.

- The provision of Internet access services when there is a server, switch or website located in Argentina could be viewed as generating Argentine-sourced income, and would thus be subject to Argentine tax. However, due to the lack of legal provisions, the existence of a PE depends on the circumstances. A website located on a server outside the country is not considered as a PE.

- The laying of fiber optic cable, and the construction of telecommunications switching equipment or other building activities will generally constitute a PE.

Business Entities

Local Branch of a Foreign Company. Foreign corporations may operate as a branch in Argentina and are taxed on the same basis as an Argentine-resident company. Profits remitted to a foreign head office are not taxed. In general, no limitations are imposed on the types of activities that a branch may carry out.

In order to set up a branch in Argentina, a foreign company must prove its existence under the laws of its country, establish a domicile in Argentina, appoint a manager or legal representative, keep separate accounting records, and submit annual financial statements. There is no maximum or minimum limitation for assigned capital. The parent company is responsible for all debts incurred by the branch.

Contracts signed with a foreign head office or another branch are deemed to have been made on an arm's-length basis, provided their terms and conditions conform to normal business practice among unrelated parties. If they do not conform to market conditions, the amounts paid by the branch to the head office are treated as profit remittances, which are currently not subject to tax, but which may not be deducted as expenses by the branch for tax purposes.

Locally Incorporated Subsidiary of a Foreign Company. Foreign corporations may operate as a locally incorporated subsidiary in Argentina and are taxed on the same basis as an Argentine-resident company. Dividends distributed by the subsidiary are not taxed.

In order to set up a subsidiary in Argentina, a foreign company must establish a domicile in Argentina and register as a shareholder. A subsidiary must have at least two shareholders, is required to file annual financial statements and certain other documents, and must comply with various requirements relating to its board of directors, the frequency of meetings for both the board and the shareholders, and the maintenance of rubricated legal and accounting records.

The parent company's responsibility is limited to paying the shares subscribed. The minimum capital required is 12,000 pesos. In general, no limitations are imposed on the types of activities that a subsidiary may carry out.

All taxed operations of a branch or a subsidiary are jointly computed for income tax purposes, and losses stemming from any operations are deductible from profits arising from other taxed operations.

Joint Venture. Joint ventures, which are called temporary unions of companies (UTEs) constitute another vehicle available for a foreign investor doing business in Argentina. In order to be a member of a joint venture, a foreign company must set up a domicile in Argentina and appoint a legal representative of the company. Subsidiaries, branches or sole proprietorships domiciled in Argentina can also be members of a joint venture. It is necessary to have a PE in Argentina in order to be able to enter into a joint venture.

A joint venture is not a legal entity in its own right. Its transactions are, in effect, transactions of the companies that have formed it.

Joint venture transactions are financed with a common operating fund formed with the members' contributions. Third parties acquire rights and undertake obligations toward the managing member or members, rather than with the joint venture.

The members of the joint venture, subject to certain limitations, are free to divide the responsibilities of the joint venture among themselves. This division will be described in the joint venture agreement. No state approval is required in order to form a joint venture, but the UTE contract must be recorded with the Public Register of Commerce. Income tax is levied on the partners, not on the joint venture. However, a joint venture must pay VAT, gross revenue and social security taxes, and file a tax return.

Local Funding Alternatives

Debt versus Equity

The interest paid by a borrower to a local or foreign lender is deductible from the borrower's income for income tax purposes when the loan is related to a borrower's operation from which could arise taxed income. From a VAT point of view, the borrower receives a fiscal credit for the VAT paid to the lender, which could be offset against VAT obligations.

When financing is obtained abroad, the lender is subject to a 13.2% withholding tax on the interest on the loan or the securities. If the tax is to be borne by the local borrower, the tax rate has to be grossed up and rises to 15.2074%. Interest on negotiable bonds is exempt when the bonds fulfill certain requirements.

When interest is paid to a foreign related company, it must conform to the arm's-length business practice between unrelated companies in order to be taken as a deduction for income tax purposes. Otherwise it is treated as a dividend distribution or a remittance of profits, which are not deductible. Subject to the arm's-length principle, there are no limitations on foreign lenders and no special provisions for debt services, including any restrictions on the deductibility of interest.

Corporations are required to appropriate at least 5% of their net annual realized profits for a legal reserve, until the reserve reaches 20% of the subscribed capital of the corporation. The reserve does not generate interest and is not taxable. It may not be distributed to the shareholders until the corporation has been formally liquidated.

In many cases, debt financing is used instead of equity financing. Exchange gains are taxable and exchange losses are deductible.

Exchange Controls

Exchange controls were abolished in Argentina in December 1989. There is now a single exchange market, where the rate of the peso fluctuates based on supply and demand. There is also a forward exchange market.

On April 1, 1991, the national government enacted the Convertibility Law, establishing among other things a fixed exchange rate between the peso and the U.S. dollar. One peso was made equivalent to one U.S. dollar effective January 1, 1992. The Argentine Central Bank maintains gold and foreign currency assets to guarantee this exchange rate.

The Argentine Central Bank is responsible for all matters involving foreign exchange. Under existing regulations, all exchange transactions must be channeled through duly authorized banks, financial entities or exchange houses.

Business Acquisitions and Dispositions

Capital Contributions into an Existing Local Entity

In some provinces, incorporation of local companies or increases in their capital are subject to stamp duty at a rate of about 1%. Capital contributed in cash is not taxed. Capital contributions consisting of movable assets are subject to VAT at the rate of 21%.

In order for services and technology to be contributed as capital, they must have a specific value (i.e., a fair market value) assigned to them. Therefore, it is required that the intangible being contributed have either a patent or trademark protection.

Purchase or Sale of Shares in a Local Entity

Foreign investors can acquire shares without any restrictions. The acquisition of a company through the acquisition of its shares is not taxable. The sale of shares is taxed for companies doing business in Argentina, although not for foreign beneficiaries. Argentina does not have a mechanism that would allow a foreign company to step-up the tax basis.

Purchase or Sale of Assets

Foreign investors can acquire assets without any restrictions. The purchase and sale of assets is taxable to the seller, and their depreciation is deductible by the acquirer.

The acquisition of a company through the acquisition of its business assets is taxable to the seller. There are exemptions when it is accomplished within the framework of a business reorganization that fulfills certain requirements. The basic requirements are that the transfer must take place among companies of the same business group, that the line of business acquired must continue operating for a period of at least two years, and that

the investment made in the assets acquired should also be maintained for that same period.

Start-up Business Issues

Pre-operating Losses and Start-up/ Construction Costs

At the election of the taxpayer, expenses incurred in organizing a company may either be fully deducted in the first fiscal year or amortized using the straight-line method over a maximum of five years.

Construction costs are capitalizable, and their depreciation for tax purposes will begin when the assets are put into service. Assets are considered to have been placed into service when they start being used for the purpose for which they are intended. Depreciation charges are based on the probable useful lives of the assets, which may be up to 50 years for buildings.

Expenses incurred abroad are presumed to be related to foreign-sourced income and, unless proven otherwise, are not considered to be deductible for Argentine tax purposes. A foreign company that incurs local costs that are subject to VAT may recover the VAT paid only if the company is formally registered as a VAT payer.

A system is currently being implemented whereby a taxpayer who is registered for VAT purposes will be able to obtain an immediate credit for the VAT paid upon the importation of capital assets to be utilized in the export sector. In such instances, instead of having to wait for the completion of export operations, the taxpayer will be allowed to obtain a loan from an authorized bank for the total amount of the VAT credit due and the government will make the interest payments associated with the loan contracted by the taxpayer.

Customs Duties and VAT

As a result of Mercosur, which is a trade agreement between Brazil, Argentina, Uruguay and Paraguay, there are common customs duties applicable to most of the traded goods. For telecommunications equipment, there is a movement toward standardizing these duties at a maximum of 16% by the year 2006. At the present time, the maximum customs duty is 30%, but most rates range from 8% to 20%, depending on the product.

The definitive importation of telecommunications equipment into Argentina is subject to variable import duty, which ranges between 3% and 30% depending on the type of equipment, as well as to VAT at the general rate of 21%. Recovery of the VAT paid is accomplished through offsetting against the VAT charges that have to be paid to the tax authority. If telecommunications equipment is imported on a temporary basis, it is only necessary to post a bond for the duty. In this case, VAT is not applicable. With the exception of transportation, insurance and sales commissions, which are included in the taxable price of the product, there are no customs duties on services.

Software importation will not be subject to customs duty if it arrives through the Internet or if it arrives on material media (diskettes, CD-ROM, etc.) and is invoiced separately.

Loss Carryovers

Net operating losses may be carried forward to offset future years' taxable income, subject to a five-year statute of limitations. Losses may not be carried back. Losses stemming from the sale or other divestment of shares or from activities carried out abroad may only be used to offset profits from a similar source.

Tax credits stemming from loss carryforwards cannot be transferred to another taxpayer, except in the case of a tax-free business reorganization such as a merger, a spin-off or a sale within the same business group. A change in ownership or in the business activity of a company does not affect the use of loss carryforwards.

Operating Considerations

Corporate Income Taxes

Argentine-resident companies and Argentine branches of foreign companies are subject to corporate income tax at a rate of 33%. Argentine residents must report their income on a worldwide basis for Argentine income tax purposes. Non-residents, however, are taxed in Argentina solely on the basis of their Argentine-sourced income.

Payments made by a local company or user to a foreign company for the provision of long-distance telephone, call reorganization or turnaround services will be subject to a 16.5% withholding tax. When Internet access services are rendered from abroad, payments for them will also be subject to a 16.5% withholding tax. There are no withholding taxes applicable to payments made by local users to local companies rendering public telephony services.

Special Tax on Telephony. As soon as an entity starts providing wireline (local and long-distance) and wireless (cellular and pager) communications services or receives a license, whichever occurs first, it will be assessed a 0.5% tax on the monthly revenue stemming from these services.

Capital Gains Tax

There is no specific capital gains tax for corporations or branches. Instead, corporate capital gains are considered as part of a business' taxable income for income tax purposes.

Tax Holidays and Exemptions

There are no exemptions or other tax incentives for wireline or wireless communications service providers.

Depreciation/Cost-Recovery Conventions/Accelerated Deductions

Depreciation for tax purposes is normally determined using the straight-line method. The rates vary according to the asset classification and their probable useful life. Other depreciation systems may be used provided they can be justified. Marketing and advertising costs incurred to obtain taxable income are deductible, without limitations.

Transfer Pricing Rules

Payments made as consideration for licensing arrangements to transfer technology from one business unit of a company to another are deductible on an arm's-length basis.

Non-resident exporters' income, which is obtained by exporting their products to Argentina, is not subject to Argentine income tax. The Argentine importer is subject to customs duties and VAT. The importer is also subject to income tax and VAT advance payments (provided the goods qualify as inventories of the importer) which may be offset against the definitive tax of the period. The subsequent sale of the imported goods is taxable.

In the case of exports made by foreign exporters, when the selling price to the Argentine importer is higher than the wholesale price in the country of origin plus transportation and insurance expenses to Argentina, there is deemed to be a link between the exporter and the importer (even if the taxpayer provides evidence that he does not control and is not controlled by the foreign exporter). In this case the price difference is considered Argentine-sourced income of the foreign exporter, and taxed in Argentina.

Transfers of Patents, Trademarks and Software

The distinction between a sale and a transfer of technology is made based on the retention of rights. When the transferor retains rights to the technology, the transaction is deemed a transfer. If all the rights are transferred, a sale is deemed to have occurred. Sales of technological products are not subject to any withholding provided they are completed outside of Argentina. Transfers of technology and know-how from abroad are exempt from VAT.

When technical assistance and technological services are provided by a foreign company that does not have a PE in Argentina, payments for technology transfers will be subject to withholding tax at a rate of either 29.7%, 26.4% or 19.8%, depending on the circumstances. Payments made to a foreign company for the licensing of technology, know-how, patents or trademarks to a local company will be subject to a 29.7% withholding tax. However, if the contract is registered with the appropriate authority, the withholding tax will be reduced to 26.4%. If the technology is not available in Argentina, the rate is 19.8%.

The acquisition of the copyright or a perpetual-use license for software already developed from a foreign entity is not subject to withholding tax if it is treated as the sale of an asset, carried out outside Argentina. Software development done to order, followed by the transfer of the copyright by a non-resident party, is not taxable if it can be considered to involve the construction of a product or the rendering of a service outside Argentina.

Payments for the license to exploit or use software are taxed at an effective withholding rate of 29.7%. If a software use license is granted for the provision of Internet access services and there is no PE in Argentina, the payments for the license will also be subject to a 29.7% withholding tax. Payments made to a foreign company for the leasing of telecommunications equipment are subject to a 13.2% income tax withholding. All these payments, when necessary to obtain taxable income, are tax-deductible.

Argentine corporations and branches of foreign companies may take a credit against Argentine income tax for foreign taxes paid. The amount of the credit is the amount of foreign taxes paid limited to the additional Argentine income tax generated by the foreign-sourced income.

Service Fees

Under the special provisions covering payments to non-resident beneficiaries, royalties covering technical assistance, engineering or consulting services rendered to be used in Argentina but not otherwise available in Argentina are subject to an effective withholding tax rate of 19.8%, provided the underlying contracts fulfill the requirements of the Technological Transfer Law. Royalties for operating patents and other types of consideration covered by contracts fulfilling the requirements of this law are subject to an effective withholding tax rate of 26.4%.

Fees for technical, financial, and other advisory services not covered by contracts for the transfer of technology, which have been registered in line with the requirements of the Technological Transfer Law, are subject to a 29.7% withholding.

Technical assistance fees are deductible as long as the services are rendered on an arm's-length basis. However, the de-

ductibility of technical service fees is limited to one of the following:

- Up to 3% of the sales or revenues generated as a result of the technical services provided

- Up to 5% of the investment made by the taxpayer in connection with the technical services provided (e.g., purchase of computers or high-tech equipment)

Services rendered from abroad are not subject to VAT. Services rendered in Argentina whose effective utilization is made abroad are considered as service exports and are not subject to VAT rate. The exporter can recover the VAT paid for the goods and services included in the exported services.

Value-Added Tax, Sales Tax and/or Other Pertinent Taxes

Telecommunications services rendered in Argentina are taxed at a rate of 27%, except for household wireline services, which are taxed at a rate of 21%. International communications are taxed at the same rates when the payments are allocable to services rendered in Argentina.

Local and Provincial Taxes

Tax on Gross Revenues. This tax is levied by the provinces and the city of Buenos Aires on the gross receipts from primary production, manufacturing, business, and services carried out within their respective jurisdictions. The standard rate is generally 3%.

Stamp Duty. This tax is levied by the provinces on documents supporting legal transactions, such as deeds, mortgages, contracts or letters of intent. The rates and rules for assessment are determined by each jurisdiction. Usual rates range from 0.5% to 1.5%, and there are many exemptions in the city of Buenos Aires.

For Additional Information, Contact:

Nico del Castillo
Tax Partner
and
Paulo Espindula
Tax Senior Associate
1301 Avenue of the Americas
New York, NY 10019
Telephone: 1 (212) 259 2563 (del Castillo)
            1 (212) 259 1288 (Espindula)
Fax: 1 (212) 259 1301
E-mail: Nicasio.delCastillo@us.coopers.com
        Paulo.Espindula@us.coopers.com

Brazil

Rapidly changing market conditions and/or legislative developments preclude the possibility of offering a comprehensive profile on Brazil for this edition. Our tax and telecommunications specialists are fully versed in current practices and conditions in Brazil and can provide assistance to clients regarding investment opportunities and tax requirements. Please contact the representatives listed for further information.

For Additional Information, Contact:

Nico del Castillo
Tax Partner
and
Paulo Espindula
Tax Senior Associate
1301 Avenue of the Americas
New York, NY 10019
Telephone: 1 (212) 259 2563 (del Castillo)
1 (212) 259 1288 (Espindula)
Fax: 1 (212) 259 1301
E-mail: Nicasio.delCastillo@us.coopers.com
Paulo.Espindula@us.coopers.com

Telecommunications Tax Profile
by Paul Glover
Tax Partner, Toronto

Overview of the Telecommunications Market

Historical Background

Historically, the Canadian telecommunications market has been dominated by nine major regional telephone companies (Bell Canada, BC Telecom Inc., TELUS Corporation, SaskTel, Manitoba Telecom Services, New Brunswick Tel, Maritime Telegraph and Telephone Company Ltd., NewTel Communications Ltd., and The Island Telephone Company Ltd.) providing integrated local and long-distance services on a monopoly basis. Overseas telecommunications and satellite services have been provided respectively by Teleglobe Canada Inc. and Telesat Canada, also on a monopoly basis.

The Canadian government has long been committed to a policy of increased liberalization in the telecommunications sector and, during the past two decades, competition has gradually been introduced. Competition started with private line and data services in 1979, terminal equipment in 1980, then selected toll resale and sharing provisions and the introduction of cellular mobile radio services (CMRS) in 1984. Public long-distance voice services competition was introduced in 1992 and the further licensing of wireless services with personal communications services (PCS) and local multipoint communications systems (LMCS) was authorized in 1996. On May 1, 1997, the regulatory framework for competition in basic local telephone services was announced, with competition expected to begin in 1998.

Current Status

The telephone market in Canada today is highly competitive, with rapidly growing revenues exceeding C$20 billion in 1996.

In competition with the Stentor Alliance (an association of the aforementioned major regionally based telephone companies) and the established Independent Telephone companies, four top alternative toll service providers have emerged. These include AT&T Canada Long Distance Services Company, Sprint Canada, fONOROLA and ACC TelEnterprises. In addition, over 400 resellers and other small alternative service providers are represented in the Canadian telecommunications marketplace.

The wireless communications market in Canada is also highly competitive, with revenue growth rates of almost 20% per year. Although Rogers Cantel Mobile Communications Inc. and Mobility Canada are the main wireless service providers in Canada, there are also hundreds of small carriers associated with the distribution of cellular and paging wireless services. Rogers Cantel, which is licensed to operate in all provinces, is a subsidiary of the communications and broadcasting holding company, Rogers Communications Inc. (RCI), and Mobility Canada is an association of the regional companies affiliated with the Stentor companies providing wireless service. Each Mobility Canada member is limited to providing cellular service to the territory in which its associated telephone company operates. In 1997, newly licensed PCS operators, Clearnet PCS Inc. and MicroCell Network Inc., established service and began actively and successfully competing in the digital mobile communications market.

In 1996, three applicants were awarded LMCS licenses for wireless broadband distribution systems—WIC Connexus Ltd., MaxLink Communications Inc. and RegionalVision Inc. Business plans for new LMCS-based services are under development, for implementation in the 1998-1999 timeframe.

Current Liberalization Status

Currently, 96% of the telecommunications services market in which telecommunications carriers operate in Canada is open to competition. The only exceptions remain the facilities-based overseas services provided by Teleglobe Canada Inc. and domestic fixed satellite services provided by Telesat Canada. The monopoly delivery of these services, in accordance with the 1997 World Trade Organization (WTO) Agreement on trade in basic telecommunications services, will end in 1998 and 2000, respectively. At that time, foreign satellites will be able to provide telecommunications services to Canadians and the special foreign ownership restrictions in the areas of global mobile satellite services and ownership of submarine cable landings will be removed.

Type of Service	Degree of Liberalization	Key Legislation	Date of Actual or Expected Liberalization	Comments
Local	Partially liberalized, in transition from monopoly	Telecom Decision 97-8	May 1, 1997	Competitors expected to emerge in 1998 following implementation of interconnection access and local number portability arrangements.
Long Distance	Fully liberalized, resale permitted	Decision 92-12	June 1992	Limited resale and sharing of toll services permitted since 1984.
International	Monopoly	Public Notice 97-34	1998–2000, in accordance with WTO Agreement	
Cellular	Partially liberalized	Decision 94-15 Public Notice 96-7	Duopoly since inception in 1984. Cellular resale under consideration by CRTC.	Regional licenses granted to each of the major incumbent telcos and one national license granted to Cantel.
PCS			PCS competitors licensed since February 1996.	PCS licenses granted to existing cellular providers as well as to two new competitors, Clearnet and MicroCell.
Paging	Deregulated			
Value-added	Deregulated	Enhanced services decision 1979	Public data network competition since 1979	CRTC forbearance from regulation of most data services effective December 1997.

Competitive Environment

The following table illustrates the relative size of the telecommunications market segments in Canada and identifies the top two service providers in each market segment based on annual revenue.

Type of Service	Entire Market		Top Two Players		
	Market Size (C$ 1996)	Number of Players	Names	Annual Revenue (C$ 1996)	Ownership
Local	$7.8 billion	12 major, 50 + minor	Bell Canada	$3.9 billion	BCE Inc.
			BC Telecom	$1.2 billion	GTE
Long Distance	$8.3 billion	16 facilities-based, 400+ resellers	Bell Canada	$3.0 billion	BCE Inc.
			BC Telecom	$0.8 billion	GTE
International	$1.5 billion	1	Teleglobe	$1.5 billion	Teleglobe
Cellular	$2.76 billion	16	Cantel	$935 million	RCI
			BCE Mobile	$775 million	BCE Inc.
Paging	Not available	90 +	BCE Mobile	$68 million	BCE Inc.
			Cantel	$53 million	RCI

Source: "The Telecommunications Service Industry 1990–1996," *Industry Canada Report*, 1996/1997 edition.

Licensing Requirements

Although somewhat fragmented in the past, Canada's new Telecommunications Act passed by the Federal Parliament in 1993 consolidated and updated the laws governing Canadian telecommunications and established a new legislative framework for all federally regulated common carriers.

The Act provides for the supervision and, where required, the regulation of telecommunications common carriers under federal jurisdiction that own or operate transmission facilities. Resellers that lease facilities to provide services to the public are not subject to direct regulation under the Act. All carriers that require use of the radio spectrum are also subject to licensing and regulation under the Radiocommunication Act.

Responsibility for telecommunications policy and spectrum management rests with Industry Canada, the federal government industry department. Radio authorizations are assigned by Industry Canada under a non-competitive, first-come-first-served (FCFS) process or through a competitive process such as comparative hearings and, in the near future, spectrum auctions.

The Canadian Radio-television and Telecommunications Commission (CRTC) is the independent federal agency responsible for the supervision and regulation of telecommunications in Canada. Under the terms of the Telecommunications Act, the CRTC has broad powers to regulate rates and conditions of service, approve interconnection agreements, establish quality of service standards and to choose to exempt carriers from the Act or forbear from regulation where it finds that competition is sufficient to protect the interests of users.

Potential for Foreign Ownerships/Relationships

The Canadian Telecommunications Common Carrier Ownership and Control Regulations describe the Canadian ownership rules for facilities-based telecommunications carriers under the Telecommunications Act. These restrictions do not apply for resellers or enhanced service providers. Canadians must own a minimum of 80% of voting shares in facilities-based carriers, and at least 80% of the board of directors must be Canadian. Investor companies in such carriers are treated as Canadian if at least 66$\frac{2}{3}$% of their voting shares are held by Canadians. In combination, this allows a total of 46.7% foreign ownership of voting shares. There are no limits on non-voting shares.

Potential for Upcoming Liberalization/Investment Opportunities

Generally, all telecommunications sectors are important targets for investment and liberalization in Canada as demonstrated by

the increased investments being made by Canadian and foreign companies in all sectors of the Canadian market.

U.S. telecommunications providers are leading the wave of foreign investment, although foreign ownership limitations have been somewhat of an impediment, as the Canadian government attempts to reconcile the need for Canadian control over its infrastructure with the need to encourage competition and financing of new competitive alternatives.

Forms of Doing Business

Permanent Establishment

Canada taxes income of a foreign entity only to the extent the income is earned by its permanent establishment (PE) doing business in Canada. Canada's tax treaties generally define a PE as a fixed place through which the business of the non-resident is wholly or partly carried on, including a management location, branch, office, factory or workshop. The definition of PE also includes a person exercising authority in Canada to conclude contracts on behalf of a non-resident, other than an independent agent.

Non-Canadian investors may, therefore, carry on business in Canada either through:

- *An independent Canadian agent.* In this instance, sales commissions paid to the independent Canadian agent would be taxed as the agent's Canadian income and the non-Canadian investor would not have a PE in Canada. Any fees paid by the ultimate customer to the non-Canadian investor for services, intangibles, or other purposes may be subject to Canadian withholding tax depending on the destination country and its treaty status with Canada.

- *A dependent agent that has the ability to conclude contracts.* In this instance, a PE clearly exists, resulting in the non-resident having taxable branch operations in Canada.

Some examples specific to the telecommunications sector follow:

- The provision of long-distance telephone services to local customers by a foreign company without a presence in Canada would normally not be considered a PE, on the assumption that the services were being provided outside Canada.

- The licensing of technology and know-how from a foreign company to a local customer is not normally considered sufficient to constitute a PE in Canada unless the foreign entity has a significant presence in Canada. Canada collects a withholding tax on royalty payments to most countries for the use of technology and know-how in Canada. The Department of Finance has taken action in recent years to eliminate withholding tax on this type of payment as it negotiates Canada's recent tax treaties, such as its treaty with the United States.

- To the extent a foreign company sends employees to Canada to provide operator services, the foreign company's presence via the employees will be considered a PE, depending on the degree of control exerted by the employees and by the foreign company over the Canadian operation. If an employee made sales and service decisions while in Canada on behalf of a foreign employer, it is likely such activities would constitute a PE. The foreign employees may also be subject to Canadian personal tax depending on existing residential ties to Canada, the number of days spent in Canada on business and the particular tax treaty that applies to the employees.

- The leasing of telecommunications equipment to a company in Canada is generally not considered a PE under Canadian domestic rules unless the foreign company uses substantial machinery or equipment in a particular place in Canada to carry out its business. Although there is little guidance on the issue, Revenue Canada usually interprets "substantial" in monetary and relative terms. Canada's tax treaties may override the domestic law in this area, since treaties often exclude the presence of substantial equipment (other than real property) as a test for determining PE.

- The provision of call reorganization/turnaround services generally does not constitute a PE because customer telephone cards are offered through a local independent distributor. This interpretation assumes the foreign entity providing the service has no fixed or formal place of business in Canada and does not have substantial equipment being used for the business in Canada.

- Providing Internet access service to customers in Canada may be considered a PE if the foreign entity actually owns the access server and locates it in Canada. Generally, simply selling software to a Canadian user does not constitute a PE in Canada.

- The laying of fiber optic cable and the construction of telecommunications switching equipment either for sale to a local customer in Canada or for operation by the foreign entity on behalf of the local customer are likely to be considered a PE of the foreign entity. As discussed above, the use of substantial equipment in Canada or the presence of a construction or installation site generally constitutes a PE; however, this varies depending on the particular tax treaty in effect.

Business Entities

Local Branch of a Foreign Company. A foreign corporation operating directly in Canada will be taxed on the Canadian-sourced income and the foreign-sourced income that is earned by a Canadian PE. A reasonable portion of head office administration, management and financial expenses are allocable to the Canadian branch and deductible in computing branch income. In addition to income tax, a branch must pay a 25% branch tax each year on its net Canadian business profits after deducting federal and provincial income taxes and an allowance for reinvestment into Canada. The percentage of branch tax is subject to treaty reduction (e.g., 5% for branches of U.S. companies).

The principal tax advantages of a foreign company's operating a branch in Canada are as follows:

- Certain Canadian tax treaties provide an exemption from branch tax on the initial earnings of a new branch (e.g., C$500,000 for the United States and £250,000 for the United Kingdom).

- Canadian thin capitalization rules do not apply to branches (see "Local Funding Alternatives").

- A branch may be incorporated on a tax-free basis after it has become profitable, provided that it maintains the appropriate amount of capital invested in Canada.

The principal tax disadvantages of a branch operation are as follows:

- The foreign corporation has unlimited liability for the branch's obligations.

- Once the branch becomes profitable, the branch tax could, in effect, accelerate the payment of withholding tax that a subsidiary must pay if dividends are paid.

- Canadian-sourced branch income must be reported for both Canadian and home country tax purposes. Where the computation of taxable income differs between the foreign party and the Canadian branch (for example, due to different rates of tax depreciation of fixed assets or inventory valuation methods), the foreign corporation may not be able to fully utilize foreign tax credits.

- The structure does not lend itself to joint venture investment with Canadian partners or to raising public funds on the Canadian stock markets.

Locally Incorporated Subsidiary of a Foreign Company. Foreign-owned Canadian corporations are subject to tax in

Canada on their worldwide income at combined federal and provincial income tax rates ranging from 38% to 46%, depending on the province in which the income is earned.

Withholding tax paid to a foreign parent is charged at varying rates on dividends (generally 5% to 10%), royalties (generally 10%) and interest (generally 10% to 15%), depending on applicable tax treaties. If no treaty applies, the withholding rate is 25%. Certain treaties, such as that with the United States, provide withholding tax exemptions for some royalty and technology payments.

Each taxable entity in a related group must file its own tax return. Consolidated tax filings are not permitted.

The advantages of using a subsidiary structure are:

* Limitation of a shareholder's liability to the financial investment in the subsidiary

* Possible increased market acceptance in Canada

* Restricted disclosure of information on tax filings and financial statements that pertain only to the Canadian subsidiary

* The ability of federally incorporated Canadian subsidiaries to carry on business anywhere in Canada without the need to obtain extra provincial licenses

* The possibility of structuring joint venture corporations and public company vehicles

A subsidiary's principal disadvantage is that a Canadian subsidiary's losses generally cannot be used to reduce the income of its foreign parent. In some circumstances, however, it may be possible to structure the Canadian company to have pass-through characteristics that enable the Canadian losses to be included in the parent company's consolidated tax filings. An additional requirement is that the majority of directors of a Canadian corporation must be Canadian residents, a requirement that does not apply to a branch.

Joint Venture. Partnerships are the primary type of entity through which telecommunications companies participate in joint ventures in Canada. A partnership can either be a general or a limited partnership. For Canadian income tax purposes, partnerships are not taxable entities but rather flow-through entities that allocate income computed at the partnership level to the partners for inclusion in their taxable income in proportion to their respective partnership interests. The tax advantages of this structure are that the allocation of the partnership income to a non-resident partner is not subject to Canadian withholding tax, and losses of the partnership flow through to the partners.

In addition, a limited partnership partner's liability is generally restricted to its capital contribution.

However, a partnership is not likely to be the most favored structure for non-residents investing in the telecommunications industry for several reasons:

* Although a limited partner is technically a passive investor with limited liability, such liability can become unlimited if the limited partner regularly takes an active part in the management and control of the partnership's business.

* A Canadian partnership is defined as having only Canadian residents as partners. Certain tax provisions that permit tax-free reorganizations are available only to Canadian partnerships; therefore, Canadian-resident partners prefer not to invest in a partnership where non-residents are direct partners. To avoid this problem, many non-resident investors incorporate a Canadian subsidiary that enters into the partnership; however, this prevents the partnership's activity from flowing through directly to the non-residents.

Local Funding Alternatives

Debt versus Equity

The cost of financing investments in Canada can be reduced by the tax deduction for interest paid on funds borrowed to invest in income-earning property and (within limits) the repatriation of capital in priority to accumulated earnings. Since withholding tax does not apply on the return of capital, a foreign investor has the flexibility of returning capital or distributing earnings, depending on cash flow considerations and the foreign tax credit position in the foreign jurisdiction.

Interest Expense. Interest is generally regarded as a non-deductible capital expenditure. Specific provisions governing its deductibility are as follows:

* Interest must be paid or payable pursuant to a legal obligation, and the rate must be reasonable (i.e., comparable to a commercial rate).

* Interest must be paid on debt borrowed to earn business or property income or to acquire income-producing assets.

* Interest on funds borrowed to pay dividends or repatriate capital is generally deductible, provided the dividend or repatriation of capital funded by debt does not exceed equity.

Withholding Tax on Interest. Interest paid in respect of non-resident loans is subject to withholding tax. The Canadian statutory rate of 25% may be reduced by tax treaty to the 10% to 15% range, depending on the applicable treaty.

Exemption from withholding tax may apply. The most common exemption applies in cases where the lender is at arm's length to the Canadian-resident borrower and where 25% or less of the debt principal is required to be repaid within five years from the issue date of the loan.

Thin Capitalization Rules. Canadian income tax law contains regulations that prevent non-residents of Canada who own a significant percentage of the voting shares (generally over 25%) in Canadian-resident corporations from withdrawing the profits of the corporation in the form of deductible interest payments.

When interest-bearing debt is owed by a Canadian corporation to its controlling non-resident shareholders and affiliates, a portion of the interest expense may not be deductible. If at any time during the year the greatest amount of interest-bearing debt to specified non-residents exceeds three times the equity from these non-residents of the Canadian-resident corporation, a prorated portion of the interest paid or payable in the year to the non-residents is not allowed as a deduction in computing the taxable income of the Canadian-resident corporation.

Branch operations and partnerships are not subject to the thin capitalization provisions.

Exchange Controls

There are no foreign exchange controls on inbound or outbound transfers of Canadian or foreign currencies.

Business Acquisitions and Dispositions

Capital Contributions into an Existing Local Entity

In addition to interest expense, expenses incurred in the course of borrowing money or incurring indebtedness for certain purposes may be deducted. These financing cost deductions are limited in any one year to 20% of the expense incurred, thereby spreading expenses incurred in a taxation year over a five-year period. If a taxpayer repays the debt obligations for these expenses within the year, the entire balance of such expenses may be deducted in that year, providing the repayment was not part of a refinancing and was not satisfied by issuing a further unit, interest, share or debt obligation.

Under this provision, many expenses incurred in the course of issuing units, partnership interests or shares, or borrowing money would not be deductible in any manner, because they would not be used to earn income from a business or property.

Purchase or Sale of Shares in a Local Entity

The advantages of purchasing shares are as follows:

• Recognizable trade names, leases, contracts and other intangibles may be acquired along with the shares.

• Beneficial tax attributes of the acquired company (e.g., operating loss carryovers, tax credit carryovers and research and development, or R&D, pools) can be transferred to the purchaser. Some restrictions may apply on an acquisition of control.

• Interest accrued on borrowings to finance the purchase of the corporation's shares (i.e., a leveraged buyout) can be structured to be deductible from the earnings of the acquiring company. A non-resident investor can structure the acquisition by first investing nominal capital in a new Canadian holding company that borrows the remaining funds required to make the acquisition. After the target shares are acquired, the acquiring company can be merged on a tax-deferred basis with the target, so that the interest expense incurred to buy the target shares is deductible from the Canadian income of the acquired company.

• Techniques are available to ensure that the cost of the acquisition takes the form of capital invested in Canada, which can subsequently be withdrawn from Canada as a tax-free return of capital without exposure to withholding tax.

• A share acquisition can sometimes be structured so that the tax basis of certain non-depreciable capital assets may be increased if the purchase price of the shares exceeds the tax cost of the target corporation's underlying assets.

• A lower purchase price may be possible where the vendor pays less tax as a result of realizing capital gains on a share sale as opposed to income from the recapture of tax depreciation or sale of inventory in an asset sale.

• A share acquisition might be structured as a share exchange, enabling the vendors to defer tax in Canada until the shares are taken back by the vendor.

There are also several disadvantages to the purchase of shares in an existing local entity:

• The tax basis of the company's assets remains unchanged and does not normally reflect the higher purchase price paid for the shares. An increase in cost basis, due to the excess share purchase price, is only available for certain non-depreciable capital property.

- Limits on the use of operating losses and certain tax credits may result from an acquisition of control if the acquired company does not continue the same or similar business to that carried on prior to the control change.

- Capital losses are generally terminated on a change in control.

Purchase or Sale of Assets

In an asset acquisition, the purchase price of the assets is the total value of the consideration paid by the buyer, including cash, assumed liabilities and other capitalized transaction costs. Generally, the total purchase price must be allocated to tangible assets based on their fair market values. Any difference between the total amount paid and the aggregate of fair market values of the tangible assets is assigned to intangible assets (e.g., goodwill).

Specific Canadian tax provisions require that the purchase price of a bundle of assets be allocated on a reasonable basis to each particular asset acquired. As a general rule, where adverse parties are dealing at arm's length, the allocation specified in the asset purchase agreement will be considered reasonable; however, this allocation may not be accepted as reasonable if there is no evidence of hard bargaining between the parties, as might be the case where one of the negotiating parties was indifferent to the allocation of the purchase price.

The tax advantages of purchasing assets of an existing entity in Canada are as follows:

- Only desired assets need be purchased. Due diligence procedures are not complicated by the need to review existing legal and tax history, as is the case when shares of an existing corporation are acquired.

- The cost basis of the assets acquired will equal the purchase price, subject to allocation.

- Future depreciation deductions will be based on the purchase price of the assets.

- Generally, interest accrued on borrowings used to finance an asset purchase may be deducted.

There are two primary disadvantages to this approach. Attractive corporate tax attributes of the vendor (e.g., loss carryovers, R&D pools and tax credit carryovers) may not be transferred. Also, the vendor may set a higher selling price to compensate for the higher tax cost of an asset sale that is caused, for example, by recaptured tax depreciation.

Start-up Business Issues

Pre-operating Losses and Start-up/ Construction Costs

Start-up costs, including amounts paid for incorporation costs, goodwill, customer lists, certain legal fees and other intangibles, are included in a pool to the extent of 75% of their cost. The pool can be deducted at the rate of 7% of the declining balance per annum. Dispositions of such items are credited to the pool to the extent of 75% of the proceeds received. A credit balance in the pool at year-end is included in taxable income.

Generally, amounts paid out for the construction of new buildings, including financing costs during construction or for permanent improvements to increase the property value, are treated as capital expenditures. These must be added to the cost of the building and depreciated for tax purposes, instead of being taken as deductions in the current year.

Customs Duties and VAT

Foreign companies that carry on business and supply goods or services in Canada are required to register for and collect the Goods and Services Tax (GST), which is a value-added tax, under the same rules as a domestic business. GST registration is required in order for a foreign business to recover the GST paid on purchases related to its commercial activities in Canada. Foreign businesses that do not carry on business in Canada and do not have a PE in Canada may still be entitled to register voluntarily, although some amount of security may need to be posted in order to effect voluntary registration. Security requirements are calculated as 50% of net tax for the year, subject to a minimum of C$5,000 and a maximum of C$1 million. In some cases, GST payments made on the purchase of pre-operating goods and services can be recovered. It is not necessary that the registered entity be fully operational, provided the entity is involved in commercial activity in Canada.

Currently, telecommunications equipment imported into Canada is generally subject to customs duties at various rates. For example, duties for telecommunications apparatus for carrier-current line systems or for digital line systems typically range from 0% to 8.5%. This telecommunications apparatus will also be subject to GST at the time of importation, based on its duty-paid value. However, if the importer is a GST registrant, it is possible to recover this tax on importation if the apparatus is to be used in commercial activities in Canada.

On January 1, 1994, Canada, the United States and Mexico adopted the North American Free Trade Agreement (NAFTA), which reduced and will eventually eliminate tariffs on goods imported into the free trade territory.

Beneficial rates on importation may also be available under the new Canada Chile Free Trade Agreement and the Canada Israel Free Trade Agreement, both implemented in 1997.

Loss Carryovers

Non-capital or operating losses incurred in a taxation year may be carried back for deduction from income earned in the prior three taxation years, and carried forward for deduction in the following seven taxation years. When control of a corporation is acquired, undeducted capital losses expire and the deduction of operating loss claims becomes restricted. Pre-acquisition-of-control operating losses are deductible from income earned in the post-acquisition-of-control period and vice-versa, provided the same business that generated the loss is carried on throughout the year that the loss is to be used, with a reasonable expectation of profit.

Operating Considerations

Corporate Income Taxes

Canada imposes federal corporate income taxes on the worldwide income of resident corporations, and on the Canadian-based income of non-resident corporations that carry on business in Canada through a PE. Canada's provinces and territories also impose income taxes on corporations and branches of non-resident corporations. Most provinces also impose capital tax on corporations and branch operations. The basis for income taxation for federal and provincial purposes is usually very similar.

The overall combined federal and provincial tax rates for non-resident-controlled corporations in Canada range from 38% to 46%, depending on the province in which the income is earned. Effective tax rates can be reduced by various federal and provincial tax credits and accelerated tax depreciation.

When a company is first incorporated, it is free to choose any fiscal year-end, provided the fiscal year does not exceed 53 weeks. Approval from Canadian taxation authorities is required to change a year-end. Each corporation must file federal and provincial returns within six months of its year-end to avoid penalties for late-filed returns. Extensions are not permitted.

Capital Gains Taxes

Capital gains or losses are realized on the disposition of capital property. Capital property is defined to include both depreciable and non-depreciable capital assets, but to exclude "eligible capital property" (generally intangible property that will benefit future periods and hence has an estimated useful life that exceeds one year, such as goodwill). The "current vs. capital" treatment for accounting purposes is often indicative of the tax

treatment. Only three-quarters of such gains are included in Canadian taxable income. Capital losses can only be used to offset capital gains; however, they can be carried forward indefinitely and carried back three taxation years.

Tax Holidays and Exemptions

Various incentives and tax credits are available that are intended to encourage manufacturing and processing (M&P) activity. For example, qualifying M&P assets other than buildings are permitted an accelerated deduction for tax depreciation. Also, qualifying M&P activity, based on capital invested and labor, can reduce the effective federal and provincial tax rate by up to 9%.

Canada's tax rules, both provincial and federal, provide generous tax incentives to encourage scientific research and experimental development activity. Revenue authorities have historically taken a broad view of the interpretation of R&D, including costs associated with the development of software. In the 1996 budget, the Department of Finance indicated that information technology, specifically software costs, will generally qualify for tax incentives provided the software otherwise meets the R&D criteria (i.e., scientific or technological advancement, uncertainty or content).

Some or all of qualifying R&D expenditures can be deducted in the year incurred. Undeducted amounts can be carried forward indefinitely without limitation, except on acquisition of control. Qualifying R&D expenditures incurred in Canada may result in a 20% to 35% federal tax credit. The credit may be available even though the Canadian resident is fully reimbursed for the expenditures by a related non-resident on a contract basis. In this case, the Canadian resident must be entitled to exploit the results of the R&D. As a consequence of the tax deduction and tax credits, the 1997 after-tax cost of C$1.00 of R&D expenditures in Ontario is approximately C$0.40.

Depreciation/Cost-Recovery Conventions/Accelerated Deductions

Accounting depreciation is not deductible; however, the Canadian tax system permits the cost of depreciable fixed assets to be deducted at rates from 4% to 100%, depending on the classification of the asset.

New acquisitions are added to the classes only when they are put into use. Generally only half of the new acquisition's cost is available for capital cost allowance in the first year. Disposals of assets are removed from the class at the lower of their cost or proceeds. If this results in a negative balance in the class and no assets remain, the resulting negative amount is added to income as recaptured depreciation. If a positive balance remains when no assets remain in a particular class, the amount is deducted as a terminal loss.

Deduction of capital cost allowance is discretionary. A taxpayer may choose not to deduct the maximum available capital cost allowance in a year in which the corporation is otherwise in a net loss position. (Loss carryforwards have a limited life, whereas undepreciated amounts can be carried forward indefinitely.) A catch-up deduction, however, is not permitted.

Canada encourages investment in certain sectors by accelerating the capital cost rates. Examples include rapidly depreciating electronic equipment, manufacturing and processing equipment, and some computer software.

The chart at page bottom illustrates the tax depreciation rates of typical assets that may be acquired for a telecommunications business.

Depreciation is generally computed on a declining-balance basis of the balance of the pool at year-end. Note that only one-half the cost of newly acquired assets is eligible for depreciation in the year of acquisition, and that the depreciable cost of automobiles is capped at C$25,000 plus applicable sales tax.

Marketing and advertising costs are generally deductible on a current basis as incurred. An exception to this general rule could apply for significant upfront costs that are capitalized under generally accepted accounting principles and amortized over time. Amortization for tax purposes may then parallel the accounting treatment. Only 50% of meals and entertainment expenses are deductible. Also, advertising expenses directed primarily to a market in Canada but through a non-Canadian newspaper or periodical are not deductible.

Transfer Pricing Rules

Canadian tax rules require that "reasonable" pricing be applied in non-arm's-length transactions. Activities and goods to which these rules apply include:

- Inter-company purchases and sales of goods and property

- Transfers of technology, rights, patents and intangibles

- Use of intellectual property and provision of technical assistance

- Management fees and similar payments for services

- Royalties

- Payments resulting from research and development

- Transfers of know-how

- Allocations of expenses

"Reasonableness" is determined by reference to a price to which an unrelated, informed buyer and seller could agree upon for similar goods or services.

Canadian tax authorities closely monitor transfer pricing issues and require Canadian companies to use Form T106 of their annual tax filing to report such transactions. Consequently, transfer prices must be carefully documented and documentation must be kept current.

Canadian tax authorities have participated in the advanced pricing agreement (APA) program permitted by the United States tax system. Canada will also accept the comparable uncontrolled price, cost-plus and resale price methodologies in determining acceptable transfer pricing.

It was announced in the 1997 federal budget that all the transfer pricing methods set out in the 1995 OECD guidelines will be available to Canadian taxpayers, in addition to the traditionally accepted comparable uncontrolled price method. These changes

Asset	Class	Tax Depreciation
Electrical generating equipment and new buildings	1	4%
Telephone, telegraph or data communication equipment for wireline or cable systems	3	5%
Office furniture, electric generators, and radio communication equipment in general	8	20%
Automobiles, systems software, satellites and cable TV system interface equipment (e.g., decoders)	10	30%
Applications software	12	100%
Leaseholds	13	Term of lease plus one renewal period (minimum: five years)
Telephone, telegraph or data communication switching equipment	17	8%
Fiber optic cable	42	12%

will ensure that such profit-based methods as the profit split and the transactional net margin will be available.

Also announced, for years beginning after 1997, was a contemporaneous documentation requirement to ensure that taxpayers can provide information supporting their transfer prices on a timely basis.

Canada's tax treaties generally provide a competent authority provision that permits the tax authorities of Canada and of the non-resident's country to negotiate a settlement of tax adjustments resulting from disputed transfer prices.

Transfers of Patents, Trademarks and Software

Canada is currently revising its treaty network. In the amended treaties with the U.S. and the Netherlands, the Department of Finance has shown its intent to reduce withholding tax to non-residents from 10% to 0% on royalty payments for the use of, or the right to use, computer software, patents or any information concerning industrial, commercial or scientific experience. Other treaties will likely be modified in the same manner as they are renegotiated.

In addition, this exemption was extended to include know-how royalty payments. Know-how is defined as "undivulged technical information, whether capable of being patented or not, that is necessary for the industrial reproduction of a product or process, directly and under the same conditions; in as much as it is derived from experience, know-how represents what a manufacturer cannot know from mere examination of the product and mere knowledge of the progress or technique."

Service Fees

Management or administrative-type payments to non-residents are generally deductible in Canada, provided the charges are reasonable and represent arm's-length transactions. Assuming the fees are reasonable and to the extent they are in lieu of, or in satisfaction of, specific expenses incurred by the non-resident for the performance of services for the benefit of the Canadian payor, tax withholding does not apply. In addition, many tax treaties negotiated by Canada provide exemption from withholding taxes to the extent of business profits earned by the non-resident. In this case, less emphasis need be placed on establishing that the expenses represent a reimbursement of specific expenses, since the treaty provisions override the domestic rules.

Value-Added Tax, Sales Tax and/or Other Pertinent Taxes

Goods and Services Tax. Under the GST value-added tax, a business collects GST from its customers on the basis of the consideration paid or payable for taxable goods or services at a rate of 7%. However, the business is entitled to claim a refund or credit for any tax paid on the purchase of goods and services used in its commercial activities. This credit (i.e., the input tax credit) is available to each entity in the production and distribution chain, except to the final non-business consumer of the good or service, who bears the full burden of the tax.

Telecommunications Services and Commodity Tax. Both the GST and the provincial sales tax (PST) are levied on the supply of various types of telecommunications services. Internet services may generally be regarded as telecommunications services. The tax treatment of these services will vary according to federal and provincial jurisdiction. Therefore, the specific rules relating to Internet services should be reviewed in detail.

Many jurisdictions adopt a policy of taxing telecommunications services based on a two-out-of-three rule. Under this rule, tax applies if two out of three of the following are located in a particular taxing jurisdiction: the origin, termination, or billing of a telecommunications service. Special rules apply for private or dedicated lines. While the GST/PST policies in this area are evolving in an attempt to keep up with rapid changes within the industry, there remain many unresolved interpretation issues relating to the method of collecting tax, the jurisdiction entitled to collect, and the types of services considered to be taxable in each of the provinces.

Large Corporation Tax. A federal large corporation tax of 0.225% is imposed on taxable capital employed in Canada in excess of C$10 million. This tax is not deductible in computing income for income tax purposes, and it is reduced to the extent of federal corporate surtax payable. To the extent that a corporation's surtax exceeds its large corporation tax, the excess is available for a three-year carryback and a seven-year carryforward period.

Local and Provincial Taxes

The provinces of Quebec, Ontario, Manitoba, Saskatchewan and British Columbia impose a capital tax on taxable capital employed in Canada. The rate varies from 0.3% to 0.64%, depending on the province. This tax is a deductible expense for income tax purposes.

The provinces of British Columbia, Saskatchewan, Manitoba, Ontario and Prince Edward Island impose a retail sales tax on a wide range of tangible personal property used in the provinces and on the purchase of selected services, including telecommunications. The tax is generally based on the sale price or fair market value of the goods or services, with rates ranging from 7% in British Columbia to 10% in Prince Edward Island. No provincial sales tax is payable in the provinces of Alberta, the Yukon, or Northwest Territories.

The province of Quebec imposes a value-added tax similar to the GST, with refunds or credits available for tax paid on the purchase of goods and services used in commercial activities. The tax was previously levied at the rate of 6.5%. Effective January 1, 1998, the QST (Quebec sales tax) rate was increased to 7.5%.

Effective April 1, 1997, the provinces of Newfoundland, Nova Scotia and New Brunswick harmonized their respective provincial sales taxes with the federal GST. The new harmonized sales tax (HST) is a value-added tax, similar to the GST, which applies to the same base of goods and services taxable under the GST. The HST applies, at a rate of 15%, to all goods and services that are considered to be made in the provinces of Newfoundland, Nova Scotia and New Brunswick.

For Additional Information, Contact:

Paul Glover
Tax Partner
201 City Centre Drive
Suite 900
Mississauga, Ontario L5B 2T4
Canada
Telephone: 1 (905) 897 4505
Fax: 1 (905) 897 4550
E-mail: paul.glover@ca.coopers.com

Tom Grandy
Principal & Director of Telecom & IT
99 Banks Street
Suite 800
Ottawa, Ontario K1P 1E4
Canada
Telephone: 1 (613) 237 3702
Fax: 1 (613) 237 3963
E-mail: tom.grandy@ca.coopers.com

Chile

Telecommunications Tax Profile
by Rodrigo Valenzuela
Tax Partner, Santiago

Overview of the Telecommunications Market

Historical Background

Prior to 1989, Empresa Nacional de Telecomunicaciones (ENTEL) had a monopoly on providing long-distance and international services. Local service throughout the 12 regions into which Chile is politically and administratively divided was provided exclusively by Compañía de Telecomunicaciones de Chile S.A. (CTC). In 1989, both ENTEL and CTC were privatized, and the first license for wireless service was granted to CTC Celular. Additional licenses were granted in 1991. The Telecommunications Law of 1982 (Law 18.168), which is the principle regulatory legislation for the telecommunications industry, established the framework that made competition possible in value-added services. This legislation has been revised several times in order to foster a more competitive environment within the industry. Value-added telecommunications services are currently open to competition. As a result of the enactment of the Multicarrier Law in 1994, which amended and broadened the scope of the Telecommunications Law of 1982, CTC, ENTEL and several other companies have expanded in the areas of local, long-distance and international services. These companies have invested heavily in new technologies in order to increase their market share. Consumers now have the choice of routing calls through their preferred domestic long-distance or international long distance carrier by simply dialing a carrier-specific code number.

Current Status

The telecommunications industry plays an important role within Chile's overall economy. From 1989 through 1996, it sustained an annual growth rate of approximately 14% and it currently accounts for approximately 2% of the country's gross national product. CTC and ENTEL, although privatized, remain the two largest telecommunications companies.

Despite its relatively small size, the Chilean telecommunications market is intensely competitive. CTC faces competition in basic service and has fought back by expanding into other sectors, improving productivity and increasing the number of access lines.

Although it is estimated that only 8,000 homes and businesses currently use international telecommunications services, it is anticipated that this segment of the market will grow at an annual rate of at least 25% in the coming years. ENTEL, CTC-Mundo, Chilesat S.A., VTR Telecomunicaciones S.A., BellSouth Chile S.A., Telefónica del Sur Carrier S.A., Transam Comunicaciones and IUSATEL Chile S.A. (which is partially owned by the Bell Atlantic Corporation) all compete vigorously in the long-distance and the international marketplace by om phasizing service quality, and by offering discounts and other types of incentives in order to increase their customer base. Three competitors—CTC, ENTEL and Chilesat—have installed parallel, fiber-optic trunk lines to link major business centers. These lines run from Arica, a city in northeastern Chile, to Punta Arenas in southeastern Chile.

As a result of the considerable competition that exists among the cellular carriers, it is relatively inexpensive to buy a cellular phone and to make a cellular telephone call in Chile. There are 18 cellular switches in Chile. The leading wireless service providers include Startel S.A. (which resulted from a merger between CTC Celular and VTR Celular), BellSouth Celular and Telecom Celular (which is owned jointly by ENTEL and Motorola).

Substantial investment is being made by several telecoms companies in personal communications service (PCS) technologies (i.e., developing a fully digital cellular telephone with fax transmission, data transmission, paging and voice-mail capabilities). So far, the government has granted three PCS licenses (one to Chilesat and two others to ENTEL). PCS services were scheduled to begin in January 1998 and to use both call division multiple access (CDMA) and time division multiple access (TDMA). Paging is a relatively small area of the telecommunications industry. The number of Internet users has skyrocketed in the past few years, increasing from 2,000 in 1995 to 30,000 in 1996. By the end of 1997, the number of Internet users was expected to reach 100,000.

Current Liberalization Status

As illustrated in the following table, the telecommunications industry is almost completely liberalized. Although the industry is still highly regulated, the main rules which all telecoms providers must follow are grouped in a single statute (i.e., the Telecommunications Law of 1982). Licenses are still restricted for some services, but this is mainly due to perceived technical obstacles that make it impractical to have more than a limited number of participants and thus prevent the government from issuing li-

censes to all interested companies. Prices are generally established by market forces, unless the Resolutory Commission, an entity with jurisdiction over antitrust issues, determines that the degree of existing competition is insufficient to allow free and fair price determination. In such a case, prices are subject to tariff regulation. In fact, the following services are currently subject to tariff regulation: local service, public telephones, dedicated lines, line connections, as well as long-distance and international access charges and interconnection fees charged to carriers for the operation of the multicarrier system.

Type of Service	Degree of Liberalization	Key Legislation	Date of Actual or Expected Liberalization
Local	Fully liberalized. Licenses are required.	Telecommunications Law of 1982 and Administrative Rule 425-97	1982
Long Distance	Fully liberalized. Licenses are required.	Telecommunications Law of 1982 and Administrative Rule 189-94	1994
International	Fully liberalized. Licenses are required.	Telecommunications Law of 1982 and Administrative Rule 189-94	1994
Cellular	Partially liberalized. Licenses are restricted.	Telecommunications Law of 1982	1994
Paging	Partially liberalized. Licenses are restricted.	Telecommunications Law of 1982	1994
Value-added	Fully liberalized. Administrative authorization from the Subsecretariat of Telecommunications (SUBTEL) is required.	Telecommunications Law of 1982	1994

Competitive Environment

It is expected that in the future there will be even fewer competitors in the telecommunications industry. This consolidation

is expected to occur as the implementation of new technologies increases the need for substantial capital investment in Chile's telecommunications infrastructure.

Type of Service	Entire Market* Number of Players	Top Two Players Names	Annual Revenue (1996)	Ownership
Local	7	CTC	CLP (Chilean pesos) 266 billion	Telefónica Internacional Chile S.A. (42.78%), publicly traded
		Conatel	CLP 24.1 billion	VTR (73.5%), publicly traded
Long Distance	9	ENTEL	CLP 72.6 billion	Depósito Central de Valores S.A. (26.05%); STET International Netherlands N.V. (19.99%); Chilquinta S.A. (19.99%); Samsung Chile Holding Ltda. (12.47%); publicly traded
		CTC-Mundo	CLP 46.1 billion	CTC (99.15%), publicly traded
International	9	ENTEL	CLP 63 billion	Depósito Central de Valores S.A. (26.05%); STET International Netherlands N.V. (19.99%); Chilquinta S.A. (19.99%); Samsung Chile Holding Ltda. (12.47%); publicly traded
		CTC-Mundo	CLP 46.1 billion	CTC (99.15%), publicly traded
Cellular	3	Startel	CLP 57.8 billion	CTC Celular (55%) and VTR Celular (45%)
		BellSouth Celular	CLP 41.2 billion	BellSouth Corporation (99.9%)
Value-added	**	CTC	CLP 12.1 billion	Telefónica Internacional Chile S.A. (42.78%), publicly traded

Sources: Records of the Superintendencia de Valores y Seguros (Chilean SEC), reports of Santander Investments, and other private publications.
* Revenue figures are not available.
** This information is not available, since most of the companies that provide this service do not have to register.

Licensing Requirements

To obtain a license, a new market entrant must apply to the SUBTEL, the regulatory arm of the Ministry of Transportation and Communications that is responsible for supervising competition, allocating frequencies among service providers and establishing technical standards. Licenses are required for the provision of public services, which are services provided for the needs of the community (e.g., local, long-distance and international service), and intermediate services, which are services provided by and between companies that are holders of telecommunications licenses and long-distance and international services provided through the multicarrier system. (The multicarrier system is the system that allows for multiple providers of long-distance and international services and enables telecoms customers to choose which company will carry their calls.) Licenses are granted for each of the 24 geographic areas into which Chile is divided for telecommunications purposes. A company may apply for and obtain licenses in all 24 areas.

An administrative authorization from SUBTEL is required for providers of value-added services. The authorization process is less regulated than the license process and only requires the submission of information to SUBTEL and the registration of the company in SUBTEL's records.

Potential for Foreign Ownerships/Relationships

There are no restrictions on foreign ownership of a telecommunications company.

Potential for Upcoming Liberalization/Investment Opportunities

In the coming years, substantial investment is expected in the local service sector. Line penetration for local service is expected to rise from 16.1 per 100 inhabitants in 1996 to 26.9 by the year 2000. Chile already has one of the most open, liberalized telecommunications markets in Latin America and it has made a full commitment to the regulatory principles and guidelines of the World Trade Organization (WTO).

Forms of Doing Business

Permanent Establishment

Telecommunications services can cover a broad range of activities, which may or may not create a permanent establishment (PE). To determine whether a PE exists, the specific facts and circumstances of each case must be thoroughly analyzed. Some general examples follow:

- The provision of long-distance telephone services by a foreign company to local customers without any local presence or advertising should not constitute a PE.

- The licensing by a foreign company of technology and know-how to a local company should not create a PE. However, licensing fees are subject to withholding tax at a rate of 30%.

- The provision of technical assistance, technological services and network management services by a foreign company to a local company will not create a PE. However if the company maintains assets such as equipment, the risk of creating a PE increases, although there are no clear guidelines. The conclusion as to whether or not there is a PE will depend on the degree of presence of a foreign company in Chile to provide these services. The presence in Chile of technicians of a foreign company for more than six months would require some analysis to determine whether it gives rise to a PE. If no PE is deemed to exist, the withholding tax on technical assistance is 20%.

- The leasing of telecommunications equipment to a local company should not create a PE. However, in some cases, lease payments for capital assets made to non-residents are subject to a reduced withholding tax of 1.75%.

- A non-resident entity that renders call reorganization or turnaround services should not have a PE.

- The provision of Internet access services should not create a PE.

- The laying of fiber optic cable and the construction of telecommunications switching equipment, either (a) for sale to a local company or (b) to be operated by a foreign company on behalf of a local company in exchange for a fee, should give rise to a PE. This determination would depend on several factors, including how long the foreign company's employees were in Chile. A presence of more than six months could create a PE. If these activities did not give rise to a PE, then fees for the provision of technical assistance would be subject to a 20% withholding tax; fees for other services rendered in Chile would be subject to a 30% withholding tax; and fees for services rendered outside of Chile would be subject to a 35% withholding tax.

- A foreign entity carrying out activities through a dependent agent would be considered to have a PE.

- A non-resident entity that has a server or a switch in Chile may be considered to have a PE depending on the nature of the services rendered and whether personnel were present in the country to service such equipment. For example, if the equipment were used exclusively to code or decode, it would probably not be considered to give rise to a PE. On the other hand, if the equipment were used in activities of a more complex nature, a PE might exist.

- Having a website located on a server inside or outside of Chile should not create a PE regardless of whether the website was accessible by customers in Chile or abroad.

Business Entities

Local Branch and Locally Incorporated Subsidiary of a Foreign Company. There is basically no difference in the tax treatment of a branch or a subsidiary. Both options are available to a foreign investor. The Chilean-sourced income of these kinds of organizations will be based on their net earnings for their activities in the country. Generally, profits and losses can only be grouped if they are generated in the same company.

Joint Venture. While it is legally possible to operate with third parties using a joint venture structure, the use of a joint venture is usually not recommended in the telecommunications industry because resolving VAT- and invoicing-related issues, which are typically observed in joint ventures, requires a special ruling from the tax authorities. According to Chilean law, a joint venture is not an entity distinct from its shareholders. As a consequence, a joint venture is not considered a taxpayer and does not file a tax return. Instead, each partner in the joint venture is taxed on its own income and is liable for filing its own tax return.

Government approval is not required for a joint venture in the telecommunications industry. A foreign company entering into a joint venture with a local or foreign partner may or may not be considered to have a PE. The degree of presence of the foreign company as a result of the activities to be undertaken by the joint venture would be a key determining factor.

Local Funding Alternatives

Debt versus Equity

All foreign investment into Chile, whether it be equity or debt, must enter through one of two legal vehicles—Decreto Ley, or Law Decree 600 (DL 600) or Chapter 14 of the Compendium of International Exchange Regulations of the Central Bank of Chile (Chapter 14). Foreign investors can freely choose between either vehicle for each investment they make into Chile, and may also combine them as desired.

Chapter 14 only applies to capital brought into Chile in the form of foreign currency. Chapter 14 investments must be registered

with the Central Bank and are not subject to thin capitalization rules. Registered investors may repatriate capital and profits under the terms and conditions provided by the specific Central Bank regulations in force at the time the foreign exchange is converted into local currency. At the present time, one year must elapse from the time of the initial investment before capital may be repatriated. There are no limitations with respect to the timing or amount of repatriation of profits.

Under DL 600, foreign investors must enter into an investment agreement with the government. The Foreign Investment Committee is the administrative entity that represents Chile in the acceptance of foreign investment. The signed contract guarantees foreign investors access to foreign currency for repatriation of capital and profits. It also grants them special benefits such as an exemption from VAT on the importation of certain fixed assets and an overall income tax rate of 42% for 10 years (or 20 years for certain manufacturing investments).

DL 600 covers in-kind investment contributions, including contributions of intangibles. This type of investment requires the authorization of the Foreign Investment Committee. With the exception of tangible assets and technology contributions, the minimum amount of capital that can qualify as a DL 600 investment is US$1 million. There is a minimum of US$25,000 for tangible assets and technology contributions. At the present time, DL 600 status requires a minimum of 50% equity of the total investment.

Foreign loans may be brought into Chile either under the Chapter 14 regulations or in conjunction with a DL 600 investment project. Registration with the Central Bank is required. With proper tax planning, the withholding tax on interest payments made abroad can be reduced to 4%. As long as the debt is established on an arm's-length basis, the interest expense should be fully deductible for the local entity.

Interest paid on shareholder loans is generally deductible for income tax purposes. Chile does not currently have any thin capitalization rules. (Thin capitalization rules, however, do exist for investments made through DL 600. In such cases, the maximum capitalization allowed is 50% debt and 50% equity.) Borrowers must recognize exchange gains or losses on the repayment of loans denominated in foreign currencies. In that respect, foreign-currency-denominated loans must be adjusted at the end of the year using the exchange rate as of December 31st. As a result of this adjustment, either a taxable gain or a deductible loss may be generated.

A stamp tax is assessed on a monthly basis on debt financing at a rate of 0.1% of the value of the debt. It is imposed over a maximum 12-month period. Therefore, the maximum stamp tax rate that would apply to a loan with a maturity of more than one year would be 1.2%. Chilean borrowers are required to keep on deposit at the Central Bank for one year an amount equal to 30% of the total value of a foreign currency loan. Alternatively, the borrower may elect to pay the Central Bank an amount equal to the London Interbank Offered Rate (LIBOR) plus 4% on 30% of the loan proceeds.

Exchange Controls

While there are currently no exchange controls, the formal exchange market (i.e., the Chilean banks) must be used to convert foreign currency investments coming into Chile, as well as profit or capital remittances leaving the country. Capital repatriations are allowed after the initial year of an investment. Available profits can be remitted abroad at any time.

Business Acquisitions and Dispositions

Capital Contributions into an Existing Local Entity

A capital contribution into a local entity is generally not subject to any local tax. While, in theory, intangibles can be contributed into a Chilean entity, the Foreign Investment Committee rarely approves such requests.

Purchase or Sale of Shares in a Local Entity

If the purchase price of the shares exceeds the book value of the target company, a step-up in the tax basis of the assets cannot be achieved unless the acquired company is legally dissolved and the total purchase price paid for the shares is reallocated among the existing non-monetary assets of the target. For tax purposes, the difference between the price paid for the shares and their book value does not create goodwill. The price paid for the shares constitutes their tax cost.

Generally, to the extent that the seller is treated as habitually trading in securities, capital gains derived by a Chilean-resident company from the sale of shares in Chilean corporations are subject to a 15% First Category Tax when accrued and an additional 35% tax at the time such gains are distributed. (With respect to the 35% additional tax at the time of distribution, a 15% credit is available for the 15% First Category Tax previously paid.) However, capital gains on the sale of shares may be subject to a reduced 15% capital gains tax if (a) the seller is not considered to be a habitual seller, (b) the buyer is a not a related party and (c) the shares are sold at least one year after the original purchase. (A company is considered a habitual seller if (a) the company's by-laws state that one of its purposes is to buy and sell shares or (b) the company usually buys and sells shares.)

Purchase or Sale of Assets

A sale of assets is taxed at the general corporate rate of 15%. Compared to a stock purchase, an asset purchase has the following characteristics:

- The tax attributes (e.g., loss carryforwards or VAT credits) of the local company are lost.

- The purchase price paid can be distributed reasonably among the amortizable assets.

- Capital gains realized by a non-habitual seller on a sale of stock may be subject to capital gains tax at a rate of 15%. Gains realized upon the sale of assets are subject to corporate tax and withholding tax at a total rate of 35%.

- Certain asset sales carried out as part of a business restructuring may qualify for tax-free treatment. As a general rule, sales or contributions must be made at an arm's-length price. Recent regulations have allowed asset contributions at tax cost, which is generally lower than the arm's-length price. This technique, which is only allowed in the event of a business restructuring, can make it possible to transfer assets from one company to another without tax effects.

Purchase or Sale of Partnership Interests. Capital gains realized on the sale of partnership interests are subject to tax at the general corporate rate of 15%, plus an effective 20% withholding tax when the profits are remitted abroad. The tax cost of partnership interests will be determined in one of two ways: (a) if the partnership interests are sold to a third company in which the seller is a direct or indirect owner, the cost will be the purchase value of the interests adjusted by inflation; or (b) if the sale is not made to a company in which the seller is a direct or indirect owner, then the tax cost is equal to the book value of the respective interests. For tax purposes, the difference between the price and the book value of the partnership interest does not create goodwill. The price paid for the partnership interest constitutes its tax cost.

Start-up Business Issues

Pre-operating Losses and Start-up/ Construction Costs

Taxpayers may amortize business investigation costs and other start-up expenses over any period between one and six years. During the pre-operating period, interest can either be capitalized or deducted as an expense. If pre-operating costs are incurred by a foreign company outside of Chile, these costs can only be deducted by a local company if they are either charged back or contributed to the local company. A charge-back will be subject to withholding tax at the time it is paid. The withholding rate will depend on what is being charged back. Rates range from 0% to 35%.

A foreign company cannot recover VAT that it incurs on local costs. VAT payments made on the purchase of fixed assets during the pre-operating phase that have not been recovered from the VAT on sales to customers can be recovered by way of a cash reimbursement from the Treasury Department after six months have elapsed from the first month the company incurred a VAT credit excess.

Customs Duties and VAT

The importation of all types of telecommunications equipment is generally subject to an 11% customs duty rate. The customs duty rate may be lower if the equipment is imported from a country with which Chile has signed a free-trade agreement (e.g., Canada, Mexico or members of Mercosur, which is the Common Market of the South). The importation of telecommunications equipment is also subject to VAT at an 18% rate. However, equipment imported as part of an in-kind equity contribution in a DL-600 investment is not subject to VAT. In general, any VAT paid (i.e., a VAT credit) can be recovered against the VAT charged to customers (i.e., a VAT debit). VAT refunds are only available in the case of a VAT credit excess on the purchase or importation of fixed assets or in the case of exporters. There is no distinction between regular telephony and Internet telephony for VAT purposes.

Loss Carryovers

Tax losses can be carried forward or carried back indefinitely. They are adjusted for inflation. A change in the ownership of a business or a change of business activity would not affect the right to use a loss carryforward. A loss carryback allows a company to recover in cash the 15% corporate income tax on accrued but undistributed income indefinitely. (See "Corporate Income Taxes.")

Operating Considerations

Corporate Income Taxes

The income generated by companies in Chile is taxed in two stages. First, when income is accrued it is subject to a 15% corporate tax, which is called the First Category Tax. A second tax is imposed when profits are distributed to shareholders or partners. In the case of resident individuals, distributed profits are subject to a personal progressive tax, which is called a Global Complementary Tax. In the case of non-resident individuals or legal entities, distributions made abroad are subject to a 35% withholding tax at the source, which is called an Additional Tax. Partners and shareholders are entitled to a credit against their

tax liability on distributions, provided the distributed profits have been subject to the First Category Tax at the corporate level. The credit corresponds to the First Category Tax, and is treated as taxable income for the purposes of assessing the tax on distributions or withdrawals. For illustrative purposes, the following is an example of the computation of the Chilean tax payable by Chilean companies on their income, assuming that income is remitted to their foreign interest-holders:

Net taxable income	100
Corporate income tax (First Category Tax) at 15%	(15)
After-tax distributable income	85
Profit remitted	85
Plus credit (First Category Tax paid)	15
Taxable basis subject to additional tax	100
Additional tax at 35%	35
Less credit (First Category Tax paid by the company)	(15)
Effective withholding tax	20
Overall tax burden	**35**

Capital Gains Taxes

No separate capital gains tax exists in Chile.

Tax Holidays and Exemptions

The government has been gradually phasing out tax incentives for foreign investors. There are currently no tax incentives available for investors in the telecommunications industry.

Depreciation/Cost-Recovery Conventions/Accelerated Deductions

For tax purposes, assets are generally depreciated on a straight-line basis, with no residual value, over their useful lives, which are determined by the tax authorities. Taxpayers may request formal authorization from the tax authorities to use alternative depreciation methods. The tax authorities have not issued general rules about useful lives for telecommunications equipment. In responding to specific inquiries made by telecommunications companies, the tax authorities have stated that most items of telecommunications equipment have useful lives of 10 years. Some telecommunications equipment with different useful lives include: (i) user equipment, 5 years; (ii) aerial cables, 15 years; and (iii) subterranean cables, 25 years. However, taxpayers are allowed to depreciate certain imported or new assets at higher rates by reducing the useful life of the depreciable assets by a third. This benefit is only available for assets with useful lives of at least five years. Moreover, if an asset becomes obsolete for technological reasons, the taxpayer is generally entitled to accelerate its depreciation by reducing its remaining useful life by half.

Marketing and advertising costs are generally expensed in the year incurred. There are no limitations on the deductibility of these costs as long as they follow arm's-length principles and are considered necessary to generate taxable income. Software development costs and research and development costs can be amortized over one to six years. The length of time is determined by the taxpayer.

Software purchases are generally amortized over a 10-year period. The taxpayer, however, may elect to increase the amortization rate at any point in time by reducing the remaining useful life of the software by one-third. Should the software become obsolete, the taxpayer may also accelerate its amortization by reducing its remaining useful life by half. In certain cases, the tax authorities have permitted embedded software in telecommunications equipment to qualify as technical assistance.

Transfer Pricing Rules

The tax authorities may, upon audit, challenge the pricing of transactions carried out between related parties by comparing such transactions to similar ones carried out by unrelated parties or by using prices in the international market as a benchmark.

Transfers of Patents, Trademarks and Software

For tax purposes, there is no distinction between a license and a sale of technology. Payments made to non-residents for either the licensing or the purchase of technology are subject to withholding tax at a rate of 30%. Payments made to non-residents for the provision of technical assistance are subject to withholding tax at a reduced rate of 20%, and payments for fees regarding transfers of expertise or technology received outside of Chile are also subject to withholding tax at the rate of 20%. On a case-by-case basis, it may be important to determine whether the transaction is a sale of technology (i.e., information) or technical assistance (i.e., services). No VAT is applicable. Local law imposes no restrictions on the licensing of technology to a local company in exchange for a royalty fee.

Licensing fees are deductible provided they are within market values and are necessary for the payor to produce taxable income. Licensing fees paid to related parties abroad are tax-deductible up to a maximum of 4% of operational sales. This limitation is not applicable if the licensor is subject to an income tax rate of 30% or higher in its own country.

Service Fees

Fees paid to non-residents for international telecommunications services rendered abroad are not taxable. Fees paid to non-residents without a permanent establishment in Chile for the provision of technical assistance are subject to withholding tax at a rate of 20%. Fees paid to non-residents for other types of services (e.g., management services) are generally subject to withholding tax at a rate of 30% if the services are rendered in Chile. Fees paid for services rendered outside of Chile are generally subject to withholding tax at a rate of 35%.

Value-Added Tax, Sales Tax and/or Other Pertinent Taxes

There are no sales taxes other than VAT. Telecommunications services provided or used in Chile are generally subject to VAT at a rate of 18%. The provision of Internet access and Internet telephony services is also subject to VAT at this same rate. International telecommunications services rendered abroad by a non-resident entity without a Chilean permanent establishment are exempt from VAT. VAT can only be recovered by a foreign entity if it is registered as a Chilean VAT taxpayer.

Local and Provincial Taxes

Municipalities may impose a business license tax (patente municipal), which is assessed based on each taxpayer's equity. Companies are only taxed by the municipality in which they are physically located. When companies have establishments in more than one municipality, their tax payment is distributed among them. The rates vary by municipality and range from 0.25% to 0.5%; however, the maximum business license tax for each company cannot exceed CLP 97.7 million per year. This amount is adjusted monthly for inflation.

For Additional Information, Contact:

Nico del Castillo
Tax Partner
and
Paulo Espindula
Tax Senior Associate
1301 Avenue of the Americas
New York, NY 10019
Telephone: 1 (212) 259 2563 (del Castillo)
          1 (212) 259 1288 (Espindula)
Fax: 1 (212) 259 1301
E-mail: Nicasio.delCastillo@us.coopers.com
        Paulo.Espindula@us.coopers.com

Telecommunications Tax Profile
by Terry Pearson
Tax Partner, Bogotá
and Christian Vargas
Senior Tax Attorney, Bogotá

Overview of the Telecommunications Market

Historical Background

Telecommunications services have traditionally been a monopoly operated by the Colombian government. During the early 1990s, the Ministry of Communications worked toward encouraging development of and investment in this sector through greater private participation and liberalization initiatives.

In 1990, the Colombian Congress passed Decree 1900, which provided a structure for this transition. The following year, value-added services were liberalized, enabling private companies to establish very small aperture terminal (VSAT) and data networks. In 1992, the government transformed the largest of the state-owned telecommunications companies, Empresa Nacional de Telecomunicaciones de Colombia (TELECOM) into a public service entity, which in Colombia is known as an empresa de servicios públicos (ESP). The same year, the Congress authorized foreign investment in certain telecommunications ventures, such as value-added services, satellite transmission and wireless services. In 1994, the Colombian government started issuing concessions for private cellular telephone services in each of three geographic regions: Central Zone, West Zone and Caribbean Coast Zone.

In 1994, a new law on residential utility services enabled public companies to become mixed-ownership companies—that is, to take on private sector partners and benefit from their capital investment for telecommunications projects. Two organizations, the Regulatory Commission for Telecommunications (Comisión Reguladora de Telecomunicaciones, or CRT) and the Superintendency of Residential Utility Service, were created to ensure proper compliance with and implementation of this law. Since then, the Ministry of Communications has issued a series of resolutions to establish competition in Colombia's long-distance telecommunications sector.

In 1995, the CRT defined the services and established the tariffs for competition in the provision of long-distance services. As originally proposed, the long-distance sector would be opened to allow three private enterprises to compete with TELECOM. Subsequently, the government decided to open the market to any qualified entity. To date, Empresa de Teléfonos de Bogotá (ETB) has been assigned a license, and it is expected that additional licenses will be granted to Empresas Públicas de Medellín (EPM) and Empresas Municipales de Cali (EMCALI).

In 1995, the number of long-distance circuits reached a total of 88,000, representing an increase of 76%. In order to reach its goal of installing 46,000 additional long-distance circuits in 1996, TELECOM entered into significant contracts for the construction and installation of fiber optic lines in Colombia. These fiber optic lines increased the capacity for other telephony-related services, such as video communications, and multimedia and high-speed data transmissions.

Current Status

The telecommunications sector in Colombia has been one of the most dynamic sectors of the country's economy. In 1995, as cellular and satellite communications expanded, the sector grew at a rate of approximately 4% over the previous year. In 1996, the growth rate was estimated to be 16.1%. Based on demand projections, it was expected that in 1998 there would be 18 telephone lines per 100 individuals and a total of 7 million telephone lines. The latest available data showed that there were approximately 9.49 telephone lines for each 100 individuals.

Colombia currently receives satellite services via INTELSAT from providers in other countries including connections with the United States, Venezuela and Chile. Satellite services are primarily limited to providing corporate communications applications, such as voice, videoconferencing, digital video transmission, electronic mail, and Internet access. TELECOM has extended its underwater fiber optic cables for connection with the United States, Central and South America, and Europe.

In 1997, the CRT issued Resolution 086/97, which stated that long-distance services may be provided by private enterprises in competition with TELECOM. Initially, it was provided that there would be only three private operators and TELECOM, but the government later decided to open the market to any private enterprise. However, TELECOM will continue to operate as the public operator.

Current Liberalization Status

In Colombia, telecommunications services (other than cellular telephony and value-added services) are considered public domiciliary services, and may be provided either by the State or by private enterprises, subject to the regulation and control of the Colombian government. The electromagnetic spectrum is also considered a public good.

As stipulated by the national Constitution of 1991 and the subsequent issuance of Law 142 of 1994, a gradual process of liberalization has been introduced with the objective of increasing the level of services while decreasing their price to consumers. The provision of such services by private enterprises requires the conclusion of a concession contract with the Colombian government and the granting of a license. For these reasons, to date, the market is neither completely free nor liberalized.

The CRT regulates telecommunications monopolies and encourages free market competition in Colombia and is charged with ensuring quality and efficiency in the provision of such services. It is also responsible for curbing abuses in the market that may result from enterprises in positions of dominance. The CRT also fixes rate structures and, in appropriate circumstances, can reduce and fix the tariff established by each operator.

In general terms, the rate structure regime contemplates two possibilities: the system of subsidies, and the system of free-market rate structures. With respect to the latter, there are three types of free-market rate regulations:

- Regulated free market rates (Libertad Regulada): The CRT fixes the criteria and methodology, with the enterprises determining the maximum rates.

- Observed free market rates (Libertad Vigilada): The enterprises determine their rates but must inform the CRT, which may intervene if it considers the pricing to be an abuse of market dominance.

- Free market rates (Libertad Total): Enterprises determine their rates and no single enterprise is in a position of dominance in the market.

It is important to note that in Colombia the process of privatization has resulted in large opposition by the labor unions, which at times has led to delays in the privatization process. The tables that follow are based on information received from the CRT and the Ministry of Communications.

Type of Service	Degree of Liberalization	Key Legislation	Date of Actual or Expected Liberalization	Comments
Local	Open to competition	Law 142, 1994	1998	Some rate structure regulation
Long Distance	In period of transition	Law 142, 1994, Resolution 028/95, Resolutions 033, 034, 035, 036, 038, 039, 040, 041, and 044/96; Resolutions 086, 087/97	1998	Although liberalized, TELECOM continues to participate in the market.
International	In period of transition	Same as above	1998	Same as above
Cellular	Five operators in concession	Law 37/93, Decree 741 and 2061/93	1993	Open-market rate structures
Value-added	Free competition (42 operators)	Not available	1993	

Competitive Environment

Currently, telecommunications services are provided by publicly held companies that have been investing heavily in infrastructure in order to better manage increased competition.

Type of Service	Entire Market		Top Two Players		
	Market Size* (US$)	Number of Players	Names	Annual Revenue* (US$)	Ownership
Local	930 million	33	ETB	330 million	Local public entities
			EPM	160 million	
Long Distance	586 million	1	TELECOM	586 million	Government
International	617 million	1	TELECOM	617 million	Government
Cellular	984 million	6	Comcell	Not available	ETB
			Celumovil		Santodomingo Group
Value-added	158 million	60	Not available		

* Market size and annual revenue data were derived from published financial statements for public and private companies in the telecommunications sector for 1996 or, where these were not available, 1995. An average exchange rate of US$1 to Col$1,000 was used. International vs. national long distance revenues were estimated by prorating 1996 revenue for TELECOM using available data for 1994.

Licensing Requirements

The Ministry of Communications issues all telecommunications licenses in Colombia and is supported by the CRT in setting policy, regulating, and allocating radio frequencies. All companies offering telecommunications services must be licensed by the Ministry. The Ministry has granted 10-year concessions for operating cellular telephony services in specific regions. Long-distance services may now be provided by private enterprises.

The requirements for participating in the long-distance market include, among others:

- An operating license must be obtained from the Ministry of Communications, at a cost of approximately US$170 million to US$200 million. The license is for ten years, but may be renewed automatically once for the same term. TELECOM is the only enterprise not required to pay for the license.

- The operator must be established as an empresa de servicios públicos domiciliarios (public household services company) according to Law 142, 1994, Law 286/96 and the Code of Commerce.

- The operator must demonstrate that it owns fewer than 35% of the telephone lines installed in Colombia and has at least 150,000 telephone lines installed in Colombia. These requirements must be certified by its legal representative.

- Foreign investors in the long-distance service market are required to associate with a local partner. There cannot be

100% foreign ownership of a long distance carrier in Colombia, due to the fact that the requirements described above make a local partner mandatory.

If the license is obtained, the beneficiary must obtain an insurance policy for US$30 million, 20 days after the license is issued. After two years of operation, companies receiving governmental licenses must tender at least 10% of their shares to the public. Each operator is required to pay 5% of its gross income to the Colombian government annually.

Potential for Foreign Ownerships/Relationships

Generally, there are few restrictions on foreign capital investments in telecommunications companies in Colombia. However, as described above, long-distance carriers in Colombia must operate through a public services household company and may not be 100% foreign-owned.

Potential for Upcoming Liberalization/Investment Opportunities

The procedures for the liberalization of long-distance telephone services were issued in September of 1997, which should bring competition to TELECOM in 1998. Currently, only ETB has received a license. Additional licenses were expected to be issued in 1998. The authorization for private companies to operate long distance services was granted by Resolution 086 in September 1997.

Forms of Doing Business

Permanent Establishment

There are no special rules governing the treatment of telecommunications services, such as long distance. As such, there is a risk that such services may be considered technical services rendered outside or inside of Colombia. Under those circumstances, the income could be subject to withholding tax at a rate of 10% for services performed outside of Colombia, or 35% for services performed in Colombia. Colombian tax law considers the telecommunications service to be performed in Colombia if the first contact impulse made by the final customer originated in Colombia and a portion of the equipment and network used by the service provider is located in Colombia.

Telecommunications services can cover a broad range of activities, which may or may not constitute a taxable presence or permanent establishment (PE) in Colombia, as illustrated in the following examples:

- Long-distance telephone services provided by foreign companies from abroad do not constitute a PE in Colombia; however, these activities may be subject to withholding tax as technical services at a rate of 10%.

- The licensing of technology and know-how by a foreign company to a Colombian company does not constitute a PE, but is subject to a 35% withholding tax plus a 7% remittance tax, resulting in an effective withholding tax rate of 39.55%.

- The provision of technical assistance services by a foreign company located outside of Colombia owning a percentage of a local company and without any other presence in Colombia does not constitute a PE of the foreign company in Colombia; however, it is subject to a single 10% Colombian withholding tax on the technical services.

- A foreign telecommunications services provider that offers call reorganization/turnaround services is not considered to have a PE, and thus is not subject to Colombian tax on a net basis. However, such a provider may be subject to withholding tax if the provided services are deemed to be performed in Colombia or if the services can be viewed as technical in nature.

- A foreign company that lays fiber optic cable or constructs telecommunications switching equipment for sale to a Colombian company should not be considered a Colombian PE. On the other hand, the operation of such equipment by a foreign service provider would likely give rise to a PE. The services are taxed only when they are rendered within the country; they are subject to 35% withholding plus a 7% remittance tax, unless they are viewed as technical services. In such cases, a withholding tax would apply regardless of whether the services were performed inside or outside of Colombia.

- Any Internet service rendered through the relevant software should nonetheless be treated as a service provided to the Colombian user. If Internet access services are being rendered from abroad, no PE should arise. However, rendering Internet access services from a site within Colombia would likely constitute a PE.

The purchase of software products from a non-resident would likely be treated as an acquisition of a license or right to use the software. The purchase price of the software would be subject to a withholding tax at the rate of 35% on 80% of the purchase price (an effective 28% rate), plus a 7% remittance tax, which is imposed on the net amount resulting after deducting the withholding tax.

There are no rules that address the treatment of Internet services and whether the equipment necessary to provide such services gives rise to a taxable presence in Colombia. Unlike the United States and other countries that may have begun to develop a framework for analyzing Internet commerce and its tax implications, the Colombian tax authorities have not expressed their views on the matter. Nevertheless, applying general principles to Internet commerce, the following observations may be made:

- The presence of a switch or server may be sufficient to give rise to a PE in Colombia.

- Having a website located on a server in Colombia accessible by Colombian users may give rise to a PE.

- Having a website located on a server in Colombia but not accessible to Colombian users may also give rise to a PE.

- Having a website on a server located outside Colombia and accessible by Colombian users probably does not give rise to a PE.

Note that it is the location of the server—not the location of the users—that may be considered significant by the Colombian tax authorities.

It should be noted that contracting with governmental entities requires a PE in Colombia.

Business Entities

Local Branch of a Foreign Company. This structural option is available to an investor that desires to pursue permanent activities in Colombia. Under Colombian law, a branch is a wholly owned company of a foreign company and is considered the local presence of the foreign company in Colombia. Colombian branches are subject to a corporate income tax rate of 35% on a net basis.

Locally Incorporated Subsidiary of a Foreign Company. This structural option is also available to an investor in Colombia. Taxation of subsidiaries is the same as described above for branches. Two types of subsidiaries are available: a sociedad anónima (S.A.), which is classified as a corporation for U.S. tax purposes, and a sociedad de responsibilidad limitada (S.R.L.), which may be structured as either a corporation or a pass-through entity for U.S. tax purposes. Both are taxed as corporations for Colombian purposes and provide limited liability to the investors in such entities.

Joint Venture. Under Colombian law, a joint venture can be formed either between a private and a governmental entity or between two private entities. Contracting with the government must be made through a joint venture. Joint ventures are not subject to taxation and do not file tax returns. Members declare their share of income on their separate tax returns. Joint ventures do serve, however, as withholding tax agents in that they charge income withholding tax on vendor payments, file monthly withholding tax returns and make payments to the tax authorities.

Joint ventures are not considered separate legal entities. They take one of two forms—a consortium, or a temporary association (known as a unión temporal, or UT). In a consortium, partners share the responsibility for the liabilities in the same ratio as their interest participation. In a temporary association, the relative liabilities are agreed upon by the parties in the joint venture contract. The contract also states which of the partners is in charge of the joint venture's accounting. A non-resident's participation in a Colombian joint venture would cause the non-resident to have a PE in Colombia if the activities of the joint venture were intended to be pursued on a permanent or indefinite basis in Colombia.

Local Funding Alternatives

Debt versus Equity

Investors weighing the choice of financing using debt versus equity must carefully consider restrictions on the deductibility of interest paid to foreign entities (particularly related parties), the cost of local financing sources and the indirect tax effect of capital (see "Operating Considerations"). Regulations affecting the length, terms and conditions of foreign loans must also be considered in light of Central Bank regulations regarding the inflow of foreign currencies into Colombia in the form of debt.

Interest is deductible when it is necessary for the development of an income-producing activity. Interest paid to local banks under government supervision is fully deductible. Interest paid to all other persons is deductible up to the highest authorized rate of bank interest. This limit also applies to interest paid to non-resident creditors that is subject to withholding tax. In cases where interest is paid to non-residents who are exempt from withholding tax, the deduction of interest may be limited to 15% of net income as determined before the deduction of such interest. The limitation would not apply if the debt financing qualified as a debt that did not give rise to interest (financial earnings) from Colombian source under Article 25 of the tax statute. Similar treatment applies to other expenses paid abroad that are not subject to withholding tax.

The following interest payments are exempt from both withholding tax and the deduction limit of 15% of net income, which was discussed above:

(a) Short-term import loans, and loans for financing or pre-financing exports.

(b) Foreign credit granted by banks or financial institutions, and credits for foreign trade transactions made through banks and financial institutions.

(c) Foreign credit obtained by national, foreign and mixed enterprises established in Colombia for activities that are considered of national interest for economic and social development. Eligible activities have been broadly defined and, in general, include telecommunications services.

Generally, interest paid to broadly defined foreign-related persons is not deductible. However, interest paid to a foreign-related person who is acting in the capacity of a direct supplier of, for example, short-term import loans or loans for financing or pre-financing exports, as in (a) above, is deductible. Interest payments made by Colombian borrowers to non-resident lenders are subject to a 35% final withholding tax plus a 7% remittance tax, resulting in an effective 39.55% withholding tax.

Exchange gains and losses realized by Colombian enterprises in respect to non-Colombian-Pesos-denominated borrowings generally constitute income or loss for Colombian income tax purposes.

Exchange Controls

Exchange control regulations require that all international loans be made through financial institutions. With proper planning, cross-border leasing financing structures can provide significant tax savings.

The Colombian government has established controls over currency remittances to foreign countries. Under these controls, company stockholders are required to register their capital investment with the exchange authorities to convert dividends/profits into another currency. Since 1992, foreign stockholders have been allowed to receive dividends of up to 100% of their duly registered foreign investment base. As discussed above, there are a number of limitations in respect to certain foreign borrowings, such as the requirement to make an interest-free deposit with the Central Bank in an amount equal to a percentage of the borrowing for a pre-determined length of time. Because these rules are constantly changing, it is important to seek counsel prior to infusing foreign debt into Colombia.

Business Acquisitions and Dispositions

The acquisition or disposition of a business in Colombia could be structured as: a capital contribution by a foreign company into an existing local telecommunications company or a redemption by the local telecommunications company of the foreign company; a purchase or sale by a foreign company of shares in a local entity owning the assets; or a purchase or sale by a foreign company of the telecommunications assets owned by an existing local company.

Capital Contributions into an Existing Local Entity

Capital contributions are not subject to local income taxes. There are no restrictions on the intangibles that a foreign entity may contribute into an existing local entity. Similarly, there are no tax consequences to existing shareholders for contributions to the capital of a company by a new shareholder.

Purchase or Sale of Shares in a Local Entity

Both local and foreign investors are subject to tax on a gain from a sale of shares of a local company. When calculating the taxable gain, the tax cost of the shares must include inflation adjustments on such shares while they were held by the taxpayer. The tax authorities are required to accept as valid a sale price contracted by private parties that is within 25% of the commercial value. The tax authorities normally presume that the accounting capital of a company, divided by the number of shares outstanding, is a strong indication of per-share commercial value. Note that Colombian GAAP (generally accepted accounting principles) require that fixed assets and investments be carried at their commercial value and thus included in net worth. The tax attributes of the purchased company (e.g., losses or tax basis in assets) are not affected by the purchase of shares. A purchase by a foreign investor requires registration of the foreign investment. Notwithstanding the above, a gain

from the sale of stock listed on the Colombian Stock Exchange is exempt from tax.

Purchase or Sale of Assets

A gain on a sale of assets is taxed as part of ordinary income and can be offset by operating losses. Asset purchases must, in general, be made at their commercial value (see "Transfer Pricing Rules"). In practice, the tax authorities normally have not challenged a sale price that was equal to or greater than the tax cost of the asset. The tax cost of an asset also includes inflation adjustments made during the tax holding period. (There were optional inflation adjustments made prior to 1992, at which time the adjustments became mandatory.)

The purchase of an asset results in a new tax cost for the asset and a new cadastral value (real estate appraisal value) for real estate tax purposes (impuesto predial). Tax attributes, such as losses, remain with the selling company. Various tax planning techniques that should be considered are available for both stock and asset sales. For example, it is possible to effect asset spin-offs and other similar transactions to effectively dispose of assets on a tax-free basis. When purchasing partnership interests, special attention should be given to issues such as debts, tax liabilities and labor liabilities.

Start-up Business Issues

Pre-operating Losses and Start-up/ Construction Costs

Start-up costs may be amortized over a period of five years or more. However, when such costs are affected by the nature or duration of the business, a company can make the case that amortization should be made over a shorter period. During the construction period and until the company becomes operational, any interest, fees, exchange differences and acquisition costs must be capitalized.

Pre-operating costs incurred outside of Colombia and re-billed to a local company are capitalized and amortized. If such re-billed costs are of a nature that they are not required to be capitalized, then they are deductible subject to the normal limit for expenses incurred abroad. (Expenses incurred abroad that are not subject to withholding tax are generally deductible up to a limit of 15% of net income, which is calculated before the deduction of such expenses incurred abroad.)

VAT paid by a local company for the purchase of fixed assets can be offset against VAT received. The net VAT paid can then be deducted from the income tax payable by the local company. After operations begin, VAT paid on pre-operating purchases of goods and services can be recovered either by means of a VAT return for expenses or an income tax return for fixed assets. (See "Operating Considerations.")

Customs Duties and VAT

The customs duty rates for the importation of telecommunications equipment vary between 5% to 15%. Certain imported goods are assessed using a list of international prices. The importation of equipment is subject to VAT at a rate of 16%. The VAT paid upon importation of telecommunications equipment can be offset against a company's income tax.

There is no distinction between regular telephony services and Internet telephony for VAT purposes.

Loss Carryovers

Losses can be carried forward for five years. Net operating losses are deducted after any inflation adjustments are applied. Losses cannot be carried back.

Operating Considerations

Corporate Income Taxes

Colombian corporations are subject to a 35% income tax. A remittance tax of 7% is imposed on profits sourced in Colombia and remitted abroad. A branch profits tax of 7% also applies to after-tax accounting profits of branches of foreign companies operating in Colombia. If the profits of the branch are reinvested in Colombia, the payment of the tax can be deferred. Moreover, if the branch profits are reinvested in Colombia for a minimum of five years, the branch profits tax is no longer applicable to the reinvested profits. Utility companies rendering services such as public switched telephony or rural mobile telephony may receive special tax treatment. (See "Tax Holidays and Exemptions.")

Calculation of Taxable Income. In Colombia, costs may be deducted if they are necessary, reasonable in proportion to the income produced, and have a causal relation to the production of income. Expenses incurred abroad are deductible if the proper withholding tax is withheld. For expenses not subject to withholding tax, the deduction of all such expenses for the year is limited to 15% of net taxable income, calculated before the deduction of expenses paid abroad.

Inflation accounting rules have been applied since 1992, which result in a net inflation gain or loss to be included in taxable income. As of January 1, 1998, tax credits may not reduce income tax liability below 75% of the tax liability that would arise under the presumed income tax regime described below. As such, it functions as an additional effective minimum tax.

Capital Taxes and Presumed Income Taxes. Currently, there are no direct taxes on the capital or net worth of corporations. However, the amount of a company's capital can have some indirect effect on its taxes and other obligations.

Colombia has a system of presumptive income tax that operates similarly to the United States' alternative minimum tax system. On an annual basis, companies are subject to income tax at the normal rates on the higher of either their actual taxable income or their presumed income. Presumed income for a year is the higher of either 5% of their net worth on the last day of the prior tax year or 1.5% of their total assets on the last day of the prior tax year. The excess of presumed-over-actual taxable income is allowed as a carryforward to reduce a company's presumed income for the five subsequent years.

Capital Gains Taxes

In general terms, capital gains are considered to be ordinary income and are taxed at the normal rate of 35%. Certain transactions are classified as "occasional gains and losses." Under current law, this classification no longer affects corporate taxpayers.

Tax Holidays and Exemptions

Effective January 1, 1996, companies rendering public household services were excluded from the presumptive income system. Income derived from public household services, such as local telephony and rural mobile telephony operated by governmental entities, or from mixed capital companies, is exempt from income tax for an eight-year period. This exemption applies to the profits that these companies capitalize or set aside as reserves for system overhauling, expansion or replacement. Generally speaking, qualifying service providers can expect:

- In Year 1, a 100% tax exemption, followed by a 10% decrease in the exemption annually for Years 2 through 5 (i.e., in effect, a 60% tax exemption for Year 5).

- In Years 6 and 7, a 20% further reduction in the exemption.

- No tax exemption in Year 8 or thereafter.

- No other tax exemptions are granted to the sector and no further changes in policies are expected.

However, the tax authorities have interpreted this exemption in a manner designed to eliminate the intended tax benefit. The position of the authorities is that, although the company rendering public household services enjoys the exemption, its domestic and foreign shareholders are subject to Colombian tax on their share of the company's taxable income. The tax authorities have applied this position in rulings.

As stated above, the privatization procedures issued with respect to long-distance services require that public household services companies be established to operate long-distance concessions in Colombia. As of January 1, 1998, the benefits described above would apply to the earnings that were subsequently distributed by such companies to the national government.

Depreciation/Cost-Recovery Conventions/Accelerated Deductions

Colombian tax law allows the use of accelerated depreciation methods based on additional wear of the assets for their use in additional daily eight-hour shifts. The same depreciation method must be used for tax and accounting purposes. Depreciation is computed using either the straight-line method, the declining-balance method or any other technically acknowledged method, provided that the method chosen has been authorized by the tax authorities. The assets of a telecommunications business are considered to be placed in service when they become operational.

Marketing and advertising costs may be deducted if they are necessary, reasonable in proportion to the income produced, and have a causal relation to the production of income.

There are no special rules regarding the depreciation or cost-recovery treatment of purchased software or software embedded in telecommunications equipment.

Transfer Pricing Rules

Generally, assets must be transferred or sold at their commercial (arm's-length) value, taking into account their nature and condition at the time of the transaction. The commercial value of most classes of assets as specified by the parties to the transaction is normally accepted by the tax authorities if the actual market value does not differ from the contracted value by more than 25%. Notwithstanding the above, the transfer of real estate cannot be at less than its cadastral value, or 50% of its commercial value.

From a practical perspective, Colombia's transfer pricing rules are still at a very early stage of development as compared to the United States, Europe and most OECD (Organization for Economic Cooperation and Development) member countries. Consequently, transfer pricing audits are not common in Colombia. Nevertheless, upon an examination or audit by the Colombian tax authorities, there is always a risk that a transaction could be challenged under the rules described above.

Transfers of Patents, Trademarks and Software

Patents, trademarks and software license fees are all deductible. If the fees are paid abroad, the withholding tax rate is an effective 39.55%. In cases where fees are paid for intangibles purchased in Colombia, the withholding tax rate is 3%. In

Colombia, all transfers of licenses and/or technology must be specified in a contract and approved by the Committee of Science and Technology. In addition, the contract must be registered with the Colombian Institute of Foreign Commerce (Instituto Colombiano de Comercio Exterior, or INCOMEX).

Service Fees

The withholding tax rate for ordinary service fees rendered inside Colombia by a non-resident is effectively 39.55%. Service fees for ordinary services provided outside Colombia are not subject to withholding tax in Colombia.

Fees for technical assistance and technical services rendered outside of Colombia are subject to withholding tax at a single rate of 10%. Fees for technical assistance and technical services rendered inside Colombia are subject to a single 35% withholding tax rate. Technical assistance generally means the provision of services such as a transfer of technology, know-how or other intangibles to the service recipient. Technical services involves the application of technology, know-how or other intangibles without their actual transfer to the service recipient.

Value-Added Tax, Sales Tax, and/or Other Pertinent Taxes

Value-Added Tax. Selling or importing goods and rendering services are activities that are subject to VAT, while the sale of real estate is not. The general VAT rate of 16% applies to most telecommunications products and services. VAT payers must register with the national tax offices, issue invoices, keep special records for sales, purchases and sales tax liabilities, and file a sales tax return bi-monthly.

VAT paid on qualifying purchases of goods and services can be claimed as a credit against VAT on a company's sales, services and imports. VAT paid for the acquisition of fixed assets, including telecommunications assets, can be credited against a company's income tax payable. Refunds of VAT are permitted only in limited circumstances for Colombian VAT taxpayers; to date, none of these cases has been applicable to the telecommunications sector. VAT is refundable for export sales, certain exempt products in Colombia and certain exports and other services.

Payments to non-residents are subject to VAT only if they relate to services deemed provided or goods sold in Colombia. In this regard, a service is deemed provided at the location of the service provider's principal place of business. However, the tax reforms introduced in 1997 provide a number of exceptions, which were generally intended to subject to Colombian VAT the services provided by non-residents to Colombian residents. Most significantly, the following services are deemed performed at the service recipient's or beneficiary's principal place of business:

(i) The licensing of intangible property for use or commercialization in Colombia.

(ii) Professional consulting, advisory and auditing services.

(iii) The leasing of tangible property by leasing companies, excluding ships, aircraft and other assets used in international transportation.

(iv) Insurance, reinsurance and coinsurance services.

(v) Services performed on tangible property, except those related to international transportation.

In addition, services performed on real property are deemed performed where the real property is located. Such VAT should be self-assessed by the Colombian taxpayer and remitted to the Colombian tax authorities under the general VAT return procedures.

If VAT is incurred by a Colombian VAT taxpayer, such VAT may be recovered through the VAT tax return mechanism. Also, VAT incurred in the importation of capital assets may be used as a credit against the Colombian taxpayer's income tax return. However, if a non-resident incurs VAT in Colombia, no recovery mechanism exists.

VAT could apply to the provision of Internet services (including access and telephony services), depending on whether the service were viewed as performed in Colombia. In this respect, if the Internet service provider's principal place of business were outside Colombia, the service would not be deemed provided in Colombia for VAT purposes.

Stamp Taxes. Stamp taxes apply to a wide variety of public and private documents, contracts and securities. Taxable documents are those that are either issued in Colombia, executed in Colombia or produce effects in Colombia. The tax is normally 1% of the contract value or the face amount of the document above 36 million Pesos as annually adjusted for inflation.

Real Estate Taxes. A unified property tax (impuesto predial unificado) is levied on the cadastral or appraised value of each plot of real estate. The tax rates range from 0.1% to 2%, depending on the use and location of the land. In addition, municipalities are permitted to impose a surcharge of 10% of the property tax. Transactions involving the transfer of real estate can result in an increase in the cadastral value, thus increasing the tax in subsequent years.

Local and Provincial Taxes

The industry and commerce tax is a municipal tax that is applied to many industrial, commercial, and service and financial activities, including those in telecommunications. This tax must be paid to the municipality every two months or annually depending on the municipality, and the rate varies between 0.2% and 1% of gross revenue or net revenue, depending upon the municipality from which the company's revenues are obtained.

In the case of public household services (such as telephony), the industry and commerce tax must be paid to the municipality where the end-user of the service is located. The tax is imposed on the monthly average of gross revenues if the tax is paid on a bi-monthly basis, or on the previous year's average monthly gross revenues.

For Additional Information, Contact:

Terry Pearson
Tax Partner
and
Juan Guillermo Villa
Telecoms Consultant
and
María Cristina Tellez
Telecoms Consultant
Apartado Aereo 251697
Bogotá, Colombia
Telephone: 57 (1) 622 3999
Fax: 57 (1) 622 5250
E-mail: colybbog@openway.com.co

Mexico

Telecommunications Tax Profile
by Manuel F. Solano
Tax Partner, New York
on Secondment at C&L Mexico City

Overview of the Telecommunications Market

Historical Background

Until recently, most telecommunications facilities were owned and operated by the government of Mexico. In 1989 the government established cellular duopolies in nine regions to allow private companies to compete against the cellular subsidiary of Teléfonos de México (Telmex), which until then had held the telecommunications monopoly.

In 1991 Telmex was privatized, with the government reducing its ownership interest to 3% of the total capital in the company. Telmex was given a five-year monopoly on local and long-distance service in exchange for expanding its network capacity, quality, penetration and geographic coverage. In June 1995 the federal telecommunications law (Ley Federal de Telecomunicaciones) went into effect, regulating the use and development of networks and establishing the framework for fair competition. In August 1996 Telmex's monopoly on local and long-distance service ended.

Between 1994 and 1997, Mexico's telecommunications sector accounted for approximately 1% of Mexico's GNP. The telecommunications market currently has an estimated value of between US$7 billion and US$11 billion.

Current Liberalization Status

Mexico is opening its telecommunications markets to competition. Most basic and enhanced services are now open. In the World Trade Organization (WTO) negotiations in February 1997, Mexico committed to full liberalization by 1998 and to full compliance with a common set of regulatory principles.

Current Status

Telmex has dramatically improved its infrastructure, adding lines, deploying wireless-in-the-local-loop technology, and digitizing its network. Many domestic and foreign investors have formed alliances to compete against Telmex in the long-distance service market.

The cellular service sector is dominated by Teléfonos Celulares de México (TelCel), the Telmex cellular subsidiary, and by Grupo Iusacell S.A. de C.V. (Iusacell), which competes in four of the nine service regions and is partially owned by Bell Atlantic Corporation. Baja Celular is another key service provider. Motorola is in partnership with service providers in several regions.

Satellites operated by Satélites Mexicanos (Satmex), which is a government-owned entity, provide telephone, fax, radio, TV and data services to businesses and homes in more than 10,000 isolated towns.

On October 24, 1997, a consortium formed by Telefónica Autrey and Loral Space & Communications, Ltd., bought a 75% stake in Satmex in an auction sponsored by the Secretaria de Comunicaciones y Transportes (Secretary of Communications and Transport, or SCT). This transaction gives the consortium the right to operate Mexican satellites. Satmex revenues for 1996 were approximately US$100 million. The government retains the right to use 7% of the satellite capacity of Satmex. Production of telecommunications equipment is concentrated among a few large manufacturers, such as Lucent and Motorola.

Competition in long-distance service, including national and international calling, was expected to extend to 100 cities by February 1998. Local service is also open, with regional and national concessions granted to several companies.

A spectrum auction for point-to-point and point-to-multipoint wireless local loops was held in 1997, and local service rules were published in October 1997, thus allowing concessionaires to start deploying their networks early in 1998.

With privatization, the market for satellite services has become highly competitive.

Type of Service	Degree of Liberalization	Key Legislation	Date of Actual or Expected Liberalization	Comments
Local	Partially liberalized	Ley Federal de Telecomunicaciones (Federal Telecommunications Law)	1998	
Long Distance	Fully liberalized in 100 cities		1997	Up to 49% foreign ownership permitted
International	Fully liberalized in 100 cities		1997	Up to 49% foreign ownership permitted
Cellular	Fully liberalized		1990	100% foreign ownership permitted
Paging	Fully liberalized		1991	100% foreign ownership permitted
Value-added	Fully liberalized		1989	100% foreign ownership permitted

Competitive Environment

Telmex, with 9 million lines, is the only local telephone operator. In long-distance and international services, Alestra, a joint venture of AT&T and the Alfa Group, began competing in April 1997. In the period before service commenced, Alestra gathered subscriptions from 16% of all long-distance users; however, it is estimated that approximately 50% of these subscribers actually remained with Telmex. As a result, Alestra is estimated to have 8% of the long distance subscribers and revenues of the long-distance market. Avantel, a joint venture between MCI Communications and Grupo Financiero Banamex-Accival, is just behind Alestra in number of long-distance service subscribers and revenues.

Type of Service	Entire Market		Top Two Players		
	Market Size (1996)	Number of Players	Names	Annual Revenue (1996)	Ownership
Local	US$2.8 billion	3	TELNOR*	US$2.8 billion	Telmex
			Telinor*	Not available	Tomas Milmo and Heartland Wireless
Long Distance	US$2 billion	10	Telmex	US$1.97 billion	Grupo Carso, France Telecom, SBC Communications, government, plus publicly traded shares
			Alestra	Not available (1997 first year of operation)	AT&T and Alfa Group
International	US$1.8 billion	10	Telmex	US$1.8 billion	Grupo Carso, France Telecom, SBC Communications, government, publicly traded shares
			Alestra	Not available (1997 first year of operation)	AT&T and Alfa Group
Cellular	US$815 million	10	TelCel	US$481 million	Telmex
			Iusacell	US$233 million	Bell Atlantic and Peralta Family
Paging	US$96 million	72	SkyTel	US$5 million	Bell Atlantic and Peralta Family
			Iusacell	US$365,000	Televisa de México and Bell Atlantic
Value-added	US$38 million	5 players dominate 90% of the market	GE Information Services	US$27 million	General Electric

Sources: Telmex statements and historical records; Instituto Nacional de Estadística, Geografía e Informática.

* TELNOR is Telmex's arm in northwest Mexico. Telinor is another player in the local market. Telinor and TELNOR are engaged in a trade suit over name confusion.

Licensing Requirements

The SCT grants concessions, licenses and permits for use of radio frequencies and for the installation and operation of public networks. It also regulates the operations of satellite service providers, third-party resellers (comercializadoras de servicios de telecomunicaciones), VSATs and other types of private networks. The Federal Telecommunications Commission (Comisión Federal de Telecomunicaciones, or Cofetel) regulates and promotes the telecommunications industry under the direct supervision of the SCT.

Additional permits will be granted in all sectors. Telecommunications network concessions are granted for a maximum of 30 years, with the possibility of extension for an additional 30 years. Licenses are required in all sectors, except value-added services, for which only registration with the Cofetel is required.

Potential for Foreign Ownerships/Relationships

Concessions and licenses are granted to Mexican individuals and entities, which are permitted to have up to 49% foreign investment. Up to 100% foreign investment is allowed in the cellular service sector with permission from the Foreign Investment Commission (Comisión Nacional de Inversiones Extranjeras, or CIE). The Foreign Investment Law defines foreign investment as the participation of foreign investors, regardless of the percentage, in the capital stock of Mexican entities, or indirect foreign ownership through a Mexican entity.

All foreign companies investing in Mexico must register with the CIE. In addition, all telecommunications providers must register with the SCT and request approval for foreign ownership. Any changes subsequent to the awarding of the initial concession must be reported.

Potential for Upcoming Liberalization/Investment Opportunities

The SCT permits an unlimited number of competitors in local and long-distance telephone service markets. All providers were required to permit interconnection with other networks by January 1997.

The Mexican market requires a substantial injection of capital investment and technology. Investment opportunities exist in cellular telephone services, rural networks, satellite communications and value-added services.

The Mexican government has already liberalized the satellite sector by selling shares in Satmex, allowing direct investment in satellite systems and permitting Satmex to outsource satellite transponders to be sold to third parties.

Forms of Doing Business

Permanent Establishment

If a foreign company is deemed to have a permanent establishment (PE), revenues derived from its Mexican operations will be subject to income tax on a net basis at a rate of 34%. Under the Mexican income tax law (Ley del Impuesto Sobre la Renta, or LISR), a PE is considered to be a fixed place of business through which the business of an enterprise is wholly or partially carried out. Activities such as marketing and sales could give rise to a PE; however, if the activities are performed through an independent agent, it is less likely that the business will be viewed as a PE. Following are examples of circumstances that do and do not constitute PEs:

- A foreign telecommunications company providing long-distance services to local customers without any local presence or local advertising is generally not treated as having a PE if it does not maintain a fixed place of business in Mexico (i.e., there is no telephone systems installation) or if its relationship with the local telephone company does not cause it to be viewed as operating in Mexico. To be viewed as operating in Mexico, the relationship with the local telephone company would either be that of a dependent agent acting on behalf of the foreign corporation or an independent agent habitually exercising the authority to bind the foreign company to contracts in Mexico.

- The licensing of technology and know-how to a local company generally does not constitute a PE for a foreign company. This type of activity is treated as a royalty and taxed at a rate of 10% under most tax treaties or 15% under domestic law. The domestic rate may be increased to 35% if the royalty relates to the license of a specific patent, invention or trademark. The 35% rate also applies to payments for all types of royalties paid to countries that have been identified by the tax authorities as tax havens.

- When a foreign company is contracted to operate or run a local telecommunications company, a PE is likely to exist. If the foreign company has employees in Mexico, a fixed base may be considered to exist. In addition to the tax on the foreign company, the Mexico-based employees may be taxed on income earned from their Mexican activities.

- Leasing telecommunications equipment to a local company does not constitute a PE.

- A foreign company that provides call reorganization or turnaround services with a local distributor who advertises and markets its telephone debit card services may be considered to have a PE if the local distributor is perceived to be contracting or acting on behalf of the foreign company. If the services rendered by the distributor are part of the normal business and are provided in exchange for an arm's-length service fee, it is less likely that the foreign company will be viewed as a PE, provided that the distributor does not have the power to contract on behalf of the foreign company.

- The installation of fiber optic cables and the construction of telecommunications switching equipment would most likely give rise to a PE, particularly if the activity lasts more than six months. The tax authorities (Secretaría de Hacienda y Crédito Publico, or SHCP) have taken the position that when a non-resident subcontracts substantially all of the construction work, the activities and the time related to the subcontract agreement will be attributed to the primary contractor and used to evaluate whether a PE exists.

- Having a server or switch equipment located in Mexico that is operated by a third party may or may not create a PE, depending on the terms of the agreement between the third party and the non-resident entity. Even if there are no in-country personnel, a PE may be deemed to exist based on the equipment and the activities that are performed on behalf of the non-resident entity. The issues surrounding these types of transactions are not specifically addressed in the laws. The interpretation of relevant laws must be applied to the individual facts and circumstances surrounding the transactions.

Mexican tax law currently does not address the question of whether a PE exists in the case of a website located on a server either inside or outside Mexico.

Business Entities

Local Branch of a Foreign Company. Because foreign ownership is generally limited to 49%, foreign investors must enter into some type of joint ownership arrangement with Mexican partners. Therefore, no possibility exists for local branches of foreign companies to operate in most segments of the telecommunications industry. If a branch is deemed to exist, based on limited activities not directly related to owning concessions to provide services to a Mexican company, the branch is taxed on a net basis as a separate business. All income of a foreign company related to the activities of its branch will be subject to tax, whether the income is of Mexican or foreign source.

Locally Incorporated Subsidiary of a Foreign Company. A locally incorporated subsidiary may be used to invest in the telecommunications industry. The most common type of investment vehicle is a Mexican corporation (sociedad anónima de capital variable, or S.A. de C.V.). A foreign investor may invest directly in up to 49% of an existing local operating subsidiary; alternatively, the foreign entity may establish a Mexican subsidiary to hold its 49% investment in the telecommunications

subsidiary. The structure chosen generally depends on the overall activities of the foreign investor in Mexico. If there are no other current or planned investments in Mexico, then the foreign investor will generally invest directly in the operating subsidiary. If the foreign investor has other activities in Mexico, it may be beneficial for it to establish a holding company in Mexico.

Mexico's integrated tax system does not tax dividend distributions at the shareholder level. To the extent that dividends result from previously taxed earnings, the distribution is not taxed. A Mexican corporation must maintain an accumulated after-tax earnings account, or CUFIN (cuenta de utilidad fiscal neta) account, that is increased annually for taxable income less income taxes, profit sharing and certain non-deductible expenses, and is decreased for dividends paid. If a dividend distribution is made in excess of the CUFIN balance, a tax is imposed on the distributing company on the amount of the excess distribution grossed for the amount of the tax, resulting in an effective tax rate of 51.5% at the distributing company level.

Joint Venture. Joint ventures are commonly entered into through a joint venture contract (asociación en participación, or AenP), a limited liability company (sociedad de responsibilidad limitada, or SRL) or a jointly owned S.A. de C.V. An AenP is a contractual arrangement and not a separate legal entity. Under an AenP, a general partner is identified and held responsible to third parties and the tax authorities. The liability of the limited partners is limited to the amount they actually contribute to the venture. Both the SRL and the S.A. de C.V. provide limited liability to the shareholders and both are separate legal entities.

In each of these forms, the joint venture entity calculates its income tax liability separately. Under an AenP arrangement, however, the partners are allocated a portion of the income or loss of the AenP, based on percentages defined in the AenP agreement. This profit or loss is taxed on a current flow-through basis to the partners. To the extent that a foreign entity enters directly into an AenP, the foreign partner is considered to have a permanent establishment and under domestic law must become a Mexican resident taxpayer. This position is based on domestic law and may be challenged in certain transactions with partners that are resident in a treaty jurisdiction. Foreign investment through a joint venture would also require registration with the CIE and SCT.

Local Funding Alternatives

Debt versus Equity

Financing an acquisition through debt is usually preferred, since interest may be deductible, whereas dividends are not. Dividends received from previously taxed income are not subject to taxation at the shareholder level; however, in arranging investment financing, consideration must be given to the income tax treatment of interest expense to determine whether the tax benefit of the interest expense is likely to be eroded either by inflation or by withholding taxes, which may apply in the case of cross-border financing.

In general, the LISR requires taxpayers to recognize as taxable income the effects of inflation as well as foreign currency gains or losses on borrowings, which, respectively, increase or decrease taxable or deductible interest.

With regard to debt financing, the inflationary component would affect the amount of the deduction for interest expense incurred each year on the debt. This is because the inflationary gain attributable to the debt for each month it is outstanding would be deducted from the interest expense accrued thereon during each month. If, after subtracting the total monthly inflationary components for a given year from the total monthly interest expense accrued during that year, the resulting amount is positive, then that amount constitutes the interest expense deduction for the year. If the resulting amount is negative, then it constitutes inflationary gain, which is included in taxable income.

If the debt of a Mexican corporation is denominated in a foreign currency, the exchange gains or losses attributable to a devaluation/appreciation of the peso are treated for tax purposes as interest, which is recognized on an accrual basis. Such debts are also subject to the inflationary adjustments described above. Thus, a company can claim an interest deduction only to the extent that the sum of the interest and the exchange loss exceeds the inflationary component attributable to the loan. When inflation and devaluation rates are similar, the inflationary gains should be offset by the exchange losses on debt. In Mexico, however, economic conditions do not always enable such matching. In 1994 the peso devalued by approximately 40% while inflation reached only 7.2%, causing many companies to recognize significant exchange losses for the year. In 1995 inflation reached 52%, while the peso devalued approximately 50%, and in 1996 inflation totaled 27% compared to a devaluation of approximately 3%. In the event that inflation exceeds the devaluation of the peso for the period in which debt is outstanding, companies will recognize a net inflationary gain for the period. Consequently, if it is anticipated that inflation will exceed devaluation, there may be a tax disadvantage to financing an investment with debt.

If debt is to be used in financing a telecommunications venture, it is possible to structure a hybrid financial instrument that would be treated as debt for Mexican tax purposes and equity for tax purposes in another country. Taxpayers must be careful in structuring such instruments, as the tax authorities can recharacterize interest payments as non-deductible dividends in certain instances. At this time, Mexico does not have any thin capitalization rules to reclassify debt as equity.

On funds borrowed from foreign lenders, the interest is subject to withholding tax, the rate of which depends on the nature of the company that provides the financing, as well as the country in which the lender resides. Interest paid to qualifying financial institutions resident in countries with which Mexico has entered into tax treaties is subject to withholding tax at a rate of 4.9%; otherwise, the applicable withholding tax rate is 15%. The withholding tax requirement for other types of financing arrangements is usually 15% under the terms of tax treaties and 35% under domestic law. A reduced domestic rate of 21% (which may be further reduced by a tax treaty) can also be obtained for certain transactions related to asset acquisition.

Exchange Controls

Mexico has no exchange controls. The value of the peso is based on market conditions. Since December 1994 the peso has been allowed to float against foreign currencies with practically no government support. As a result, the peso was devalued by more than 100% from December 20, 1994, through 1995. However, the peso remained relatively stable for most of 1996 and 1997, with an exchange rate against the U.S. dollar of 7.68 on December 31, 1995, and 7.7 on September 17, 1997.

Business Acquisitions and Dispositions

Investors may enter the telecommunications market either by purchasing shares of an existing telecommunications company, thereby acquiring a percentage of the existing business, or by creating a new company that can be used to acquire certain assets and operations of a target company.

Capital Contributions into an Existing Local Entity

Investment in an existing company may be made through a capital contribution to the company in exchange for newly issued shares. Capital contributions in exchange for equity of a company are not taxable to the recipient corporation. Such contributions are not subject to transaction, stamp or value-added tax at the recipient company. Contributions may be made in the form of assets or cash. The contribution of assets would be recorded at the fair market value of the contributed assets, including intangibles. In-kind contributions, however, could result in a gain at the contributing company level. In-kind contributions by a non-resident will generally not result in taxation as long as the contribution is not considered to be Mexican property. Under corporate law, shares issued in exchange for assets must be held by a company for a period of two years. During this two-year period, if the fair market value of the contributed assets is at least 25% less than the value at which the shares were issued, an additional contribution must be made by the shareholder. If the additional contribution is not made, the company will not release the shares for the full amount to the shareholder at the end of the two-year period. Issuing additional shares either to a foreign or Mexican owner does not affect the tax attributes of the operating company.

Purchase or Sale of Shares in a Local Entity

When shares of a Mexican corporation are acquired directly from an existing shareholder, the transaction is usually taxable to the seller. Proper tax planning can minimize the tax in these transactions. Certain tax treaties provide for the tax-free transfer of shares in certain transactions (e.g., with respect to shareholders with an interest of 25% or less). Domestic law, however, does not differentiate the capital gains treatment for minority interests. The purchaser of shares of a Mexican company does not obtain an increased basis in the assets of the company. The tax attributes of the company do not change unless the assets are acquired by a separate company.

Purchase or Sale of Assets

An asset acquisition is sometimes preferred because it limits responsibility for past contingent liabilities of an existing company. However, from a tax perspective, the acquisition of assets may be considered as the acquisition of a going concern, which results in the assumption of past tax liabilities for the business. The acquisition of assets of a pre-existing business allows a step-up in the basis of the assets, which permits increased depreciation deductions. The purchase price is allocated based on the fair market value of the acquired assets with any excess purchase allocated to goodwill, which is not deductible.

The acquisition of assets is subject to VAT at a rate of 15%, which is applied to the fair market value of the assets acquired, including goodwill. The tax is applied to the gross value of most acquired assets, and not to the value of the assets less the liabilities assumed. VAT is not charged on the acquisition of accounts receivable or land. In most instances, VAT may be recovered through credits against VAT collected in the operations of the company. This ability to recover VAT, however, does not apply to the VAT allocated to goodwill, which represents an absolute cost related to the acquisition.

A Mexican seller generally prefers a sale of shares rather than a sale of assets, since the sale of shares is taxed at the shareholder level at a lower rate than the sale of assets. The sale of assets is subject to tax on the excess of the purchase price over the tax basis at 34% and profit sharing at a rate of 10%. Because the only way to increase the tax basis of the assets is to acquire the assets, buyers generally prefer this approach.

Generally, the sale of a partnership or joint venture interest will also be a taxable transaction. With proper planning, it may be possible to dispose of an interest on a tax-free basis.

Start-up Business Issues

Pre-operating Losses and Start-up/Construction Costs

The LISR requires that pre-operating costs be capitalized and amortized over a 10-year period using the straight-line method. Taxpayers may elect a longer period for amortization. The pre-operating period for tax purposes ends when a company begins selling products or providing services on a continuous basis. The LISR definition of pre-operating expenses includes:

> . . . research and development expenses relating to the design, elaboration, improvement, packaging or distribution of a product as well as the rendering of services as long as these expenses are incurred prior to the time when the taxpayer sells its products or renders its services on a continuous basis.

Accordingly, there are important costs a taxpayer could expense during the pre-operating period, such as interest and general administrative expenses.

Any costs related to the construction of the infrastructure must be capitalized as part of the fixed asset costs and amortized over the life of the facility. Costs incurred by the foreign company outside of Mexico are deductible in Mexico only if they are actually charged to the local entity through an invoice. Limitations exist on the deductibility of indirect costs that are allocated to the Mexican company on a pro-rata basis. These costs may be subject to withholding tax depending on the nature of the expenditure; however, general services that do not include the transfer of know-how or technical assistance and purchases of materials may be exempt from withholding tax.

Costs incurred by a foreign company locally are likely to be subject to VAT. Unless the foreign company is deemed to have VAT activities in Mexico and registers as a VAT taxpayer, this VAT is not recoverable and represents an additional cost of the project. In practice, it is difficult to register exclusively as a VAT taxpayer in Mexico and a ruling should be obtained from the SHCP to allow such registration. Such a ruling could be issued if the foreign company has activities that are subject to VAT, but these activities do not create a PE for income tax purposes.

During the pre-operating stages of a Mexican telecommunications company, VAT is incurred on most costs and expenses and can be recovered either through credits against future collected VAT or through a refund. A pre-operating company can obtain a refund of the excess VAT by providing certain documentation to the tax authorities. This can create a cash-flow issue, since the refund process takes at least 60 days. It should be noted that the refund amount is adjusted for inflation from the date that the return is filed through the date of its payment by the SHCP. The SHCP is required to pay interest on the amounts to be refunded after 50 working days have elapsed from the date a return was filed.

Customs Duties and VAT

Importation of equipment into Mexico is generally subject to customs duties. The rate of duty depends on the type of equipment and its country of origin. As a result of the North American Free Trade Agreement (NAFTA) and other trade agreements, imports from the United States, Canada, Costa Rica, Bolivia, Chile and Venezuela are generally subject to reduced duty rates. NAFTA-country duty rates range from 5% to 20% and are subject to annual reductions until the year 2000.

All equipment imported into Mexico on a permanent basis is generally subject to VAT at a rate of 15%. This tax is generally credited against VAT collected from customers. It should be noted that NAFTA and other trade treaties do not affect VAT that is imposed on imports. Additionally, NAFTA establishes that access to networks and public services must be under reasonable terms and conditions that are transparent and non-discriminatory for the execution of business. In this case, non-discriminatory means that terms and conditions less favorable than those granted to other clients or users of the telecommunications network or public service cannot be enforced.

Loss Carryovers

Companies that incur net operating losses for income tax purposes may use these losses against future taxable income in the following 10 years. These losses are adjusted for the effects of inflation through the year in which they are utilized. Not operating losses cannot be carried back. Net operating losses carried forward cannot be used for purposes of determining a taxpayer's profit-sharing liability.

Operating Considerations

Corporate Income Taxes

A company operating in Mexico is subject to income tax on a net basis at a corporate rate of 34%. In determining taxable income, generally all expenses that are intrinsically related to the business and necessary to the operation are deductible. Costs that must be capitalized and amortized over a period of time are adjusted for inflation. A company is also subject to mandatory profit-sharing with employees at a rate of 10% of its adjusted taxable income. In practice, this profit-sharing expense is not deductible for income-tax purposes. A calendar year is used for income-tax and profit-sharing purposes.

Mexico also has a business assets tax, which serves as a type of alternative minimum tax. This tax is computed on the adjusted tax basis of the assets of a company at a rate of 1.8%. The assets tax is calculated on the value of assets, with limited deductions allowed for balances payable to Mexican suppliers. Financing obtained from financial institutions and foreign enti-

ties is not deductible in determining the tax base of a company's assets.

The amount of tax payable will be the greater of the assets tax liability or the income tax liability. During a given tax year, taxpayers are allowed to credit their income tax against their assets tax liability. Thus, if a company has an income tax liability greater than its assets tax liability, it will have to pay only the former. If the assets tax liability exceeds the income tax liability, then the taxpayer would pay an amount of tax equal to the assets tax liability but would receive a credit against such tax equal to the income tax liability for that year. A company may credit against its current year's assets tax the income tax paid in excess of its assets tax liability during the prior three years. In addition to the credit mechanism, a Mexican company can also claim in the current tax year a refund for assets tax paid in excess of the income tax in the prior 10 years. This refund is limited to the amount by which its income tax liability exceeded its assets tax liability during the current tax year. Companies are generally exempt from assets tax during their pre-operating periods, the initial year of operations and the two subsequent periods.

Capital Gains Taxes

The sale of shares in a Mexican company constitutes a taxable event. A non-resident that sells shares of a Mexican company is subject to tax at a rate of either 20% of the gross proceeds or 30% of the net gain. To elect to be taxed on a net basis, the seller must appoint a legal representative in Mexico prior to the sale and cannot be resident in a country that is considered a tax haven under Mexican law. A list of these countries has been published by the tax authorities. Additionally, the sale of shares must be audited by a public accountant in Mexico, who will issue a tax opinion (dictamen fiscal) to be filed with tax authorities.

For a resident company, capital gains derived from a sale of shares are taxed at the corporate rate of 34%. A loss on the sale of shares in a Mexican company may be used only to offset gains realized on the sale of other shares and other non-debt instruments. This loss may be carried forward for five years and is adjusted for inflation. The gain on the sale of shares in a Mexican company is calculated as the difference between the tax basis of the shares and the proceeds on the transaction. In broad terms, the tax basis is calculated on the original investment in the shares adjusted for inflation and for the inflation-adjusted change in the CUFIN from the date of acquisition through the date of sale. Sales of fixed assets are taxed at the corporate rate of 34%, and losses generally can be used to offset other taxable income for the year.

Tax Holidays and Exemptions

The income tax system does not provide for special tax incentives for any industry. However, general tax incentives for taxpayers that fulfill certain requirements include immediate depreciation deduction of investments in fixed assets.

Depreciation/Cost-Recovery Conventions/Accelerated Deductions

Most infrastructure costs must be capitalized and amortized over a prescribed period. In general, these types of costs fall into one of three investment categories: fixed assets, pre-operating costs and deferred expenses (concessions). For costs that are capitalized and depreciated over a period of time, the annual deduction is adjusted for inflation. The inflation adjustment is based on the change in the consumer price index from the date on which the cost was incurred.

Fixed Assets. Taxpayers may elect to depreciate fixed assets annually, using the straight-line method, or immediately if the equipment is used permanently outside of Mexico's major metropolitan areas, provided that certain requirements are met. In the latter case, the entire depreciable amount is deducted in a single tax year.

Depreciation for income tax purposes begins when the asset is placed into service, unless the taxpayer elects to depreciate the present value of the future depreciation deductions immediately, in which case the asset may be depreciated in the year of investment, the year the asset is put into service or the following year. These immediate deductions cannot be elected for profit-sharing or assets tax purposes.

Depreciation rates are based on the classification of the assets, as shown below. These statutory rates represent the maximum allowable rates of depreciation. The taxpayer can elect the applicable depreciation rates, provided that they do not exceed the maximum allowable rates established by the LISR. Once such election is made, the depreciation rate cannot usually be changed for at least five years. The recovery periods for certain classes of assets are as follows:

Types of Assets	Straight-Line Recovery Method Years of Useful Life	Immediate Deduction Method Percentage of Deduction
Construction	20	74%
Office machinery and equipment	10	Not applicable
Computer equipment	3.3	94%
Other equipment not otherwise defined	10	85%

The rates included in the income tax law are provided in broad categories, which do not specifically address most telecommu-

nications equipment. This type of equipment would have to be included as either computer equipment, which is depreciated based on a 3.3-year useful life, or other equipment, which is subject to a 10-year depreciation period.

Since the LISR does not include depreciation rates for all types of equipment or costs related to the telecommunications industry, there is some flexibility in determining their classification for depreciation purposes. The depreciation rate depends on the type of equipment in use and not the industry of the taxpayer.

Deferred Expenses—Concessions. The LISR does not make clear whether a payment for a concession to provide telecommunications services falls within the strict definition of a deferred expense. Accordingly, such payment may be treated as a normal and necessary business expense and expensed in the year incurred. Alternatively, the cost could be treated as a deferred expense, in which case the initial payment would be amortizable at an annual rate of 15%. Most companies treat concession payments as deferred expenses and amortize them at an annual rate of 15%.

Marketing costs are generally expensed as they are incurred and are not capitalized. There is no requirement to capitalize marketing costs unless these fall within the definition of a deferred expense. Most costs paid through sales agents would be considered deductible expenses.

The income tax law does not specifically provide for the tax treatment of software costs or costs of software embedded in telecommunications equipment. If the cost is joint and not specifically separated, the software cost would be capitalized and depreciated along with the overall cost of the telecommunications equipment. Software costs, unless acquired as part of the computer equipment, are generally expensed in the year of acquisition.

Research and development costs, including those related to software development, are generally deductible expenses. The law also provides for the possibility of establishing research and development trusts to which deductible contributions can be made for future research activity. With respect to costs to produce software, all costs related to the production of a product for sale would be considered inventory-related and would be deductible in the year in which the cost was incurred.

Transfer Pricing Rules

Mexico adopted new transfer pricing guidelines in 1997. The law now requires that transactions between related parties be carried out at arm's-length prices. This applies to all related-party transactions, including loans, service fees and royalties. The burden of showing compliance with transfer pricing criteria has been extended to all companies entering into transactions with related parties, and specific transfer pricing criteria have been set forth. Two or more parties are deemed to be related when one participates directly or indirectly in the administration, control or capital structure of the other, or when one individual or group of individuals participates directly or indirectly in the administration, control or capital structure of the others.

Companies that enter into cross-border related-party transactions must conserve specific records showing that the pricing methods used are those that would have been used if the transaction had been carried out between unrelated parties. These include documentation that demonstrates the arm's-length nature of the transaction. The acceptable methods for establishing the arm's-length price are: (1) the comparable-price method; (2) the retail method; (3) the cost-plus method; (4) the profit-split method; (5) the residual profit-split method; and (6) the transaction-margin method.

Although such transfer pricing studies do not have to be submitted and approved, evidence of advance approval may be requested from the Mexican tax authorities at any time. An advance pricing study approved by the Mexican tax authorities would provide confirmation that the company is transacting at prices that will not be questioned by the tax authorities. Such approval would be effective for four years after the approval was issued. Upon request, the approval can be extended for the previous four-year period. If a formal transfer price study is not obtained, the taxpayer must still maintain information to support the arm's-length nature of the transaction.

Transfers of Patents, Trademarks and Software

Payments made to non-residents for patents, trademarks or software licensing are generally subject to withholding tax. Withholding tax rates for royalties under domestic law is either 15% or 35%, depending on the type of agreement; whereas, under the terms of the negotiated treaties, this rate is generally limited to 10%. However, all payments made to residents of a low-tax jurisdiction for patents, trademarks or software licensing would be subject to withholding tax at a rate of 35%. No restrictions exist on the transfer or licensing of these types of intangible assets.

When there is a transfer of technology, sales are distinguished from payments for licenses through the terms of the agreement. Mexican law usually looks to the intent of the agreement itself. In a license agreement, withholding tax is applied to the total of the payments. In the case of a sale agreement, the purchase price would be subject to withholding tax if the sale were contingent upon use or productivity of the assets or rights being sold. The acquisition of the intangible requires that the asset be recorded and amortized over a period of time, usually 6.6 years.

Service Fees

Fees related to services are deductible by a Mexican company in most circumstances. The main restriction on service fees charged by non-residents is that the amount of the charge should not be determined on a pro-rata basis. In addition, the service must be necessary to the business of the company. Documentation must exist to show that the services were actually performed.

If the services do not include any transfer of know-how or technical assistance, it is possible to design a service fee agreement in which there is no withholding tax requirement for the payments made to non-residents. Service agreements that include the transfer of know-how or technical assistance would be subject to withholding at a rate of either 10% or 15%, depending on whether the payment was covered by a tax treaty.

Value-Added Tax, Sales Tax and/or Other Pertinent Taxes

VAT is applicable to most telecommunications transactions at a rate of 15%. A company also pays VAT for most goods and services acquired in Mexico. Although not specifically listed as taxable activities, the provision of Internet access and Internet telephony are also generally considered services subject to VAT. The VAT paid to suppliers is creditable against VAT collected from customers so that the amount paid to the government is the excess collected over payments made to suppliers. VAT may be credited and recovered only by registered VAT taxpayers. Thus, non-residents that do not have taxable activities in Mexico are not able to recover VAT.

VAT is also imposed on the importation of goods and services; consequently, a new business within the telecommunications sector can be expected to pay a significant amount of VAT while it is establishing itself. This excess VAT may be carried forward and credited against future collections. In certain circumstances, a company can obtain a refund. A reduced VAT rate of 10% may be available for a company that is domiciled in the border zones of the country.

Imported services are also subject to VAT at the general rate of 15%. In this respect, a Mexican importer is required to self-assess the VAT so that the foreign provider is not required to register for VAT. The Mexican acquirer of such services would also be able to take a credit for the self-assessed VAT, and generally there is no actual cash outlay for these transactions.

A 0% rate of VAT is provided for the exportation of goods and certain specific services. The VAT law, however, does not list telecommunications services as qualifying for this 0% rate of VAT. Consequently, a Mexican telecommunications provider is generally required to charge VAT on all telecommunications services provided to both resident and non-resident customers.

Local and Provincial Taxes

Individual states in Mexico do not impose corporate income taxes; however, the states are responsible for administering and collecting real estate transfer taxes, annual real property taxes and certain payroll taxes.

The real estate transfer tax is applied to the fair value of real estate transferred. The rate applied to the transfer depends on the state in which the property is located. For transactions that occur in Mexico City, the rate ranges from 2.3% to 3.3%, depending on the value of the property. Most states impose a 2% rate on the transfer of real property, which includes the value of land and any structures on it.

In addition, the states impose an annual real property tax, which is applied to the assessed or appraised value of the property. The rate of real property tax depends on the state in which the property is located and generally ranges from 0.5% to 3% of the value of the property.

The state payroll tax is assessed as a percentage of the salaries paid by the employer. The tax generally ranges from 1% to 2% of the total payroll. In most instances, there is no maximum salary base for applying this tax.

For Additional Information, Contact:

Manuel F. Solano
Tax Partner
and
Terri Grosselin
Tax Manager
and
Rogerio Casas Alatriste Urquiza
Consulting Partner
Telephone: 52 (5) 229 8093 (Solano)
            52 (5) 229 8032 (Grosselin)
            52 (5) 229 8063 (Casas Alatriste)
Fax: 52 (5) 229 8045
Apartado Postal 24-348
Col. Roma
06700 Mexico, D. F.

Peru

Telecommunications Tax Profile
by Rudolf M. Röder
Tax Partner, New York
and Orlando Marchesi
Tax Manager, Lima

Overview of the Telecommunications Market

Historical Background

In 1970, Peru's private operating companies were nationalized and the government became the sole provider of telecommunications services for nearly a quarter of a century. Compañía Peruana de Teléfonos Limitada (CPT) provided fixed-line services in Lima and Empresa Nacional de Telecomunicaciones del Perú S.A. (ENTEL PERU) provided these services for the rest of the country. In 1994, as part of the government's privatization initiative, controlling stakes in CPT and ENTEL PERU were sold to Telefónica de España, S.A. for approximately US$2 billion. The operations of CPT and ENTEL PERU were subsequently combined and they currently operate as a single entity under the name of Telefónica del Perú S.A.

As part of the privatization strategy, on May 16, 1994, Telefónica del Perú was granted a monopoly to provide fixed-line services until June 28, 1999. While Telefónica de España owns a minority stake of 30% in Telefónica del Perú, it is effectively responsible for that company's operation and management. The government still owns approximately 35% of Telefónica del Perú. Shares of Telefónica del Perú are also traded on the Lima Stock Exchange.

In order to foster fair competition as Peru privatizes its telecommunications industry and to protect the interests of end-users, on May 6, 1993, the government created OSIPTEL (Organismo Supervisor de Inversión Privada en Telecomunicaciones) to promote and supervise private investment in telecommunications. OSIPTEL regulates licensees' operations, supervises the quality of services provided to end-users, guarantees the fairness of tariffs charged, resolves disputes between licensees and determines the maximum tariff rates for services provided.

Current Status

While Telefónica del Perú has a monopoly in the fixed-line sector, the government has made substantial strides in liberalizing the rest of the telecommunications industry and in fostering free-market-oriented policies among participants. Telefónica del Perú and Tele 2000 currently compete for cellular customers in Lima. The government was expected to start licensing providers of the cellular B band in the other provinces by December 1997.

Peru has a fairly reliable telecommunications infrastructure, which provides international direct dialing capabilities, mobile telephone services, telex and Internet access. Most pay phones still use coins, but they are being updated to accept phone cards. Currently, there are approximately 604,000 telephone lines, which works out to 2.6 telephone lines per 100 inhabitants. This rate is quite low even for Latin American standards and underscores the market's growth potential.

While the range of services to be opened under the World Trade Organization (WTO) Agreement on Basic Telecommunications Services is limited, Peru has made a full commitment to the regulatory principles and guidelines of the WTO and liberalization is expected to occur between 1998 and 2002.

Current Liberalization Status

Type of Service	Degree of Liberalization	Key Legislation	Date of Actual or Expected Liberalization	Comments
Local, Long Distance and International	Limited	D.S. 11-94-TC*	June 28, 1999	Telefónica del Perú has a monopoly until June 28, 1999, when the market will be opened.
Cellular	Free competition	D.S. 13-93-TC	Already liberalized	Licenses have been awarded for Lima (the cellular A band) and bids for the other provinces (the cellular B band) were to be accepted by December 1997.
Paging	Free competition	D.S. 13-93-TC	Already liberalized	
Value-added	Free competition	D.S. 13-93-TC	Already liberalized	

* D.S. stands for Decreto Supremo or Supreme Decree, which contains rules passed by the executive branch. TC stands for Ministry of Transportation and Communications, the entity responsible for enacting the Decretos Supremos.

Competitive Environment

At the moment, Peru does not have a very competitive environment in the telecommunications industry, as is reflected in the following table.

Type of Service	Entire Market		Top Two Players	
	Market Size* (NS = Nuevos Soles)	Number of Players	Names	Annual Revenue* (NS = Nuevos Soles)
Local	NS 1.3 billion	1	Telefónica del Perú	NS 1.3 billion
Long Distance	NS 370 million (1997)	1	Telefónica del Perú	NS 370 million (1997)
International	NS 596 million	1	Telefónica del Perú	NS 596 million
Cellular	NS 423 million	2	Telefónica del Perú	NS 316 million
			Tele 2000	NS 107 million
Paging	Not available	27	Telefónica del Perú	NS 223 million**
			Tele 2000	NS 42 million
Value-added	Data not available	2	Peruvian Scientific Network***	Not available
			Telefónica del Perú	NS 223,883**

Sources: Telefónica del Perú 1996 Annual Report; Tele 2000 1996 Annual Report.

* Except where otherwise noted, figures are as of December 31, 1996.

** This is an aggregate figure for paging and value-added.

*** The Peruvian Scientific Network is a major player only for Internet access service.

Licensing Requirements

The provision of any telecommunications service requires a license from the Ministry of Transportation and Communications. However, because of Telefónica del Perú's monopoly, licenses for the fixed-line sector will not be available until June 28, 1999.

Potential for Foreign Ownerships/Relationships

There are no limitations on the participation of foreign investors in a telecommunications business except for the fixed-line sec-

tor as a result of Telefónica del Perú's monopoly until June 28, 1999. Legislation currently in force provides equal treatment for both domestic and foreign investors. However, in many instances, there are still sizable barriers to entry in the telecommunications market. For instance, licenses must be obtained from the government and imported telecommunications services are subject to substantial import duties. These barriers to entry generally apply to basic telephone services, such as telephone line installation, and to local and long-distance calls (either national or international connections). Services subject to import barriers include telex, pay phones, cellular telephones, paging and radio-communications systems. Barriers to entry do not exist for entities interested in providing value-added services such as data storage and transmission, videotex, teletext and e-mail. There are also no restrictions on supplying telecommunications equipment.

Potential for Upcoming Liberalization/Investment Opportunities

Clearly, once Telefónica del Perú's monopoly to provide fixed-line services expires on June 28, 1999, this will create significant investment opportunities. In addition, a law has recently been enacted to liberalize radio communications trunking systems, which should help develop this area of the telecommunications industry. Cellular service outside of Lima is another area with investment opportunities. Licenses for provinces outside the capital city were expected to be offered to private investors by the end of 1997. There are no anticipated major developments in terms of mergers and acquisitions in the telecommunications industry.

Forms of Doing Business

Permanent Establishment

A foreign company is considered to have a permanent establishment (PE) if it (a) has a fixed place of business through which it carries out business activities, or (b) carries out business in Peru through an agent who has and habitually exercises the authority to sign contracts on behalf of the foreign company or (c) maintains an agent in Peru who habitually keeps an inventory of merchandise to be sold in Peru on behalf of the foreign company. Telecommunications services can include a broad range of activities, which may or may not constitute a PE. Some examples follow:

- The provision of long-distance telephone services by a foreign company to local customers without any local presence or advertising would most likely not qualify as a PE.

- The licensing of technology and know-how by a foreign company to a local company would not create a PE.

- The provision of technical assistance and technological services by a foreign company to a local company in exchange for service fees, including operator services and/or network management services, when the foreign company owns an equity interest in the local company, will not create a PE as long as it is not an ongoing service. If ongoing technical assistance is provided in Peru with staff assigned for that purpose on a temporary or permanent basis, a PE may be created.

- The leasing of telecommunications equipment to a local company will not create a PE. However, if the leased equipment is operated directly or indirectly by a foreign company, then this may create a PE.

- The provision of call reorganization/turnaround services will not create a PE if the equipment is not located in Peru. However, if the equipment is located in Peru and is operated either automatically or manually by an individual located in Peru, then a PE may exist.

- The provision of Internet access service may create a PE if there is heavy equipment located in Peru and especially if the equipment is operated automatically or by the foreign company through an agent in Peru.

- Having a server or a switch located in Peru without any other personnel may create a PE if there is heavy equipment located in Peru and if the equipment is operated automatically.

- Having a website located on a server in Peru that is accessible by local customers may create a PE; however, this is highly unlikely.

- Having a website located on a server outside of Peru but that is accessible by customers in Peru will not create a PE.

- Having a website located on a server in Peru that is not accessible by customers in Peru but is accessible by customers in other countries may create a PE; however, this is highly unlikely.

- The laying of fiber optic cable and the construction of telecommunications switching equipment (a) for sale to a local company or (b) to be operated by a foreign telecommunications company for a local company in exchange for a fee might create a PE.

Business Entities

Local Branch of a Foreign Company. A branch (sucursal) of a foreign company may conduct business in Peru, provided that it is properly registered with the government, which involves the filing of a variety of documents. Branches are taxed on their Peruvian-sourced income. Branches may group the profit and losses derived from all of their operations when determining their income tax liability.

Locally Incorporated Subsidiary of a Foreign Company. A subsidiary of a foreign company is usually established either as a corporation (sociedad anónima) or a limited liability company (sociedad de responsabilidad limitada). A corporation, which may be either privately held or publicly traded, is the most common form of business organization. In order to establish a corporation in Peru, a public deed must be signed and the entity's articles of incorporation and bylaws must be registered. Corporations are also subject to substantial information disclosure requirements. Subsidiaries of foreign companies are regarded as independent entities in relation to their head offices, and hence, are taxed on their worldwide income. However, they are also entitled to group their profits and losses derived from different operations when determining their income tax liability.

Joint Venture. With the exception of mining joint ventures and some income tax provisions, there is no legal definition or regulation for joint ventures. Therefore, as a general rule, parties entering into a joint venture may freely agree to whatever conditions they consider appropriate for their business purposes. Joint ventures can take the form of incorporated general partnerships (sociedad colectiva), incorporated limited partnerships (sociedad en comandita) or an asociación en participación, which is an entity that is similar to a joint venture in structure but without its legal entity status. While a joint venture contract has to be notarized and the joint venture itself registered with the tax authorities, the individual parties entering into the joint venture do not have to be registered as business entities. Government approval is not required for a joint venture in the telecommunications industry. Joint ventures would generally file tax returns. A foreign company entering into a joint venture with a local partner would not automatically create a permanent establishment.

Local Funding Alternatives

Debt versus Equity

The decision as to whether a local company should be funded through debt or equity is directly related to the fluctuation in the value of the Peruvian currency and the inflationary pressure within the Peruvian economy. Foreign currency debt may give rise to a taxable profit or a deductible loss as a consequence of exchange rate gains and losses, whereas equity financing is accounted for in local currency and is not affected by such exchange rate variations. However, local currency is subject to the effects of inflation, which can also result in a gain or a loss.

Expenses are deductible as long as they are necessary to generate taxable income or to maintain the source of such income. Therefore, accrued interest is deductible as long as the financing obtained was necessary to fund a company's operations. (There are no thin capitalization rules.) Interest from loans is subject to withholding tax depending on its source. Interest will be subject to a 1% withholding tax rate if the lender is an unrelated party. If the lender is a related party, a 30% withholding tax applies. Parties are related when one party owns directly or indirectly at least 30% of the other party's share capital. An interest-bearing loan from a shareholder would be considered to be a loan from a related party. No withholding tax is imposed on dividends paid; however, they are not tax-deductible.

Exchange Controls

There are currently no exchange controls in Peru.

Business Acquisitions and Dispositions

Capital Contributions into an Existing Local Entity

Capital contributions of cash to a new or existing local entity are not taxable. If a contribution is made in kind—which may include the contribution of intangibles—the difference between the fair market value of the property transferred and its adjusted basis would constitute a gain or loss to the transferor. Such gain or loss must be recognized on a current basis. If the transferor is a foreign entity with no local presence, any resulting gain would be foreign-sourced and would not be taxable. Contributions of services are not allowed under Peruvian law.

Purchase or Sale of Shares in a Local Entity

The tax treatment of a sale of shares in a local entity to a foreign company varies depending on who the seller is. If the seller is a domestic company, the gain or loss will be treated as part of ordinary taxable income. If the seller is a foreign company, the gain or loss will only be taxable if the company qualifies as a frequent buyer and seller of stock. Under Peruvian law, an entity is considered a frequent buyer and seller of stock if, during the calendar year, it has placed more than 10 orders on the Lima Stock Exchange to purchase stock and more than 10 orders to sell stock. It should be noted that under a special exemption that is in effect until December 31, 2000, gains derived from the sale of stock on the Lima Stock Exchange are tax-exempt.

The tax basis of the shares in a domestic company is equal to the original acquisition cost adjusted for inflation. The tax basis of the assets in the acquired company is generally not affected by the sale of the company's shares.

Purchase or Sale of Assets

Unlike a sale of stock, a sale of assets by a local company is subject to value-added tax (impuesto general a las ventas) at a rate of 18%. However, the transfer may be exempt from VAT if it encompasses all assets and liabilities connected with a particular line of business. For example, if a transfer occurs as a result of a merger or if an entire production line is transferred to a different company, there will be no VAT on the transaction.

Gains realized by domestic companies on the sale of assets are taxable at the ordinary corporate income tax rate of 30%. The taxable gain is equal to the difference between the final sale price and the inflation-adjusted tax basis of the asset. For the purchaser, the acquired assets would have a tax basis equal to the fair market value, which is usually the acquisition cost.

An interest in a partnership (e.g., an unincorporated joint venture, an asociación en participación or a consortium) should be sold at market value. This value is determined based on the balance sheet of the partnership, business projections and other pertinent factors. Income tax is imposed on the difference between the book value at which the seller has registered its participating interest and the final sale price.

Start-up Business Issues

Pre-operating Losses and Start-up/ Construction Costs

An expense is deductible from gross income if it is necessary to produce or maintain said income. If the company is not yet producing any operating revenues, it is generally not allowed to deduct operating expenses. However, non-operating gains and losses, such as exchange rate gains and losses, may be taxable or deductible.

Generally, organization expenses, pre-operating expenses—including initial operations and further expansion of operations—and interest accrued during the pre-operating period may be expensed in the first year of operation or amortized over a period of 2 to 10 years using the straight-line method. Once the amortization period has been elected, it may only be changed if prior approval has been obtained from the tax authorities.

Value-added tax is imposed on the purchase of goods and services, as well as on the importation of goods. This essentially increases the initial capital requirements of a start-up business, although the VAT can later be recovered over the normal course of operations. To reduce the up-front capital cost, VAT paid on the importation and the local acquisition of capital goods may be recovered by the business prior to starting operations. However, the following limitations apply:

- No VAT credit will be refunded until six months after the purchase.

- Taxpayers can only apply for a VAT refund twice a year.

- Only businesses that have not commenced operations can apply for a VAT refund.

- Only new machinery or equipment that qualify as capital goods and are recorded as fixed assets are eligible for this VAT benefit.

- Capital goods have to be earmarked for the production of goods or services that will either be subject to VAT or exported.

- Capital goods must be included in the CUODE (classification according to usage or economic destination) list. (The CUODE classification was developed by the Economic Commission for Latin America and the Caribbean.)

- Assets must be owned by the company and subject to depreciation.

- The value of VAT charged upon the purchase of any single good must be at least equivalent to two tax units. (A tax unit [unidad impositiva tributaria, or UIT] is a standard reference in Peruvian tax legislation. Its value is determined by the Ministry of Economics and Finance, and is adjusted periodically. At the time of publication, the approximate value of a UIT was US$900.)

- The total amount of VAT involved must be at least equivalent to four tax units (approximately US$3,600).

- The purchase must have been made on or after April 14, 1996.

Customs Duties and VAT

Tariffs, or custom duties, are levied at rates ranging from 12% to 25% of the CIF (cost, insurance and freight) value. The customs duty rate for most telecommunications equipment is 12%. Purchases of telecommunications equipment are also subject to VAT. As discussed below, Peru has a variety of regimes in effect that can reduce the amount of customs duty imposed.

Temporal Admission Regime. Under this regime, certain goods, raw materials and intermediate goods can be introduced into the country free of tariffs and other taxes levied on imports, provided that they are re-exported within a maximum period of 24 months, after being processed or transformed in Peru. This regime would be beneficial if telecommunications equipment were to be manufactured in Peru.

Drawback Regime. Under this regime, an exporter can obtain a refund of the import duties paid on the importation of raw material and parts originally brought in to Peru but which were either consumed in the manufacturing process or included in a final product that was subsequently exported. If the final product is sold in Peru, the drawback regime does not apply. This regime would also be beneficial if telecommunications equipment were to be manufactured in Peru.

Duty-Free Replacement Goods Regime. This regime lets companies that export products that contain imported parts to import such parts free of duty. However, if the final product is sold in Peru rather than exported, the exemption expires and the applicable duties must be paid.

Temporary Entry Regime. This regime allows capital goods such as machinery and equipment to be imported under a duty-free status for a period of 12 months. This regime is particularly useful when performing construction or similar activities that require the use of specialized machinery for a relatively short period of time. The imported machinery can be owned by either a foreign parent company or a third party. Upon expiration of this period, the capital goods must be returned to the foreign supplier. If the capital goods are not returned, then the importer must pay the applicable duties.

Temporal Export Regime. This regime applies when goods are sent abroad for repair and/or improvement and they are returned to Peru within 12 months. Customs duties in this case will only be applied on the value, if any, that was added to the original goods after the repairs or improvements.

Loss Carryovers

Tax losses may be carried forward indefinitely during the pre-operating stage. However, starting with the first fiscal year in which the company derives a profit, any previously accumulated losses may be carried forward only for a maximum period of four years. Subsequent losses may be carried forward until the next profitable year, and from then for a maximum of four years. (This period may be extended by the tax authorities.) Tax losses may not be carried back. Tax losses are not adjusted for inflation. Tax losses can be used regardless of whether a company changes ownership or business activity.

Operating Considerations

Corporate Income Taxes

Peruvian companies are taxed on their worldwide income. Branches and permanent establishments are taxed on their Peruvian-sourced income. Dividends or profit distributions are not taxable. The general corporate income tax rate is 30%.

Non-resident entities with no permanent establishments in Peru are subject only to withholding tax, as follows:

- 1% on interest income derived from foreign loans, provided that the proceeds of the loan actually came into Peru and the interest rate on the related loan did not exceed either the prime interest rate plus six points, or London Interbank Offered Rate (LIBOR) plus seven points

- 12% on income attributable to technical services rendered partially within and partially outside of Peru

- 30% on royalty income

- 30% on other income, including interest income on foreign loans granted to related parties

Capital Gains Taxes

Capital gains are taxed as part of a company's ordinary income.

Tax Holidays and Exemptions

There are currently no tax incentives that are specific to the telecommunications industry, nor is there any proposal to implement such incentives in the near future.

Depreciation/Cost-Recovery Conventions/Accelerated Deductions

As a general rule, fixed assets used to generate taxable income are depreciable. The depreciation basis is the purchase price or production value of the asset, including any costs incurred as a consequence of the purchase, such as insurance, custom duties, transportation, etc. The depreciable basis is also adjusted to reflect the effects of inflation. Usually, tax depreciation follows the straight-line method, although other methods are acceptable if the prior approval of the tax authorities is obtained. The average depreciation rate for telecommunications equipment is 20% per year. However, the tax authorities may allow different rates.

Software is treated as an intangible asset of limited duration, and as such, can be amortized on a straight-line basis over a period of between 1 and 10 years. No special rules exist for software that is embedded in telecommunications equipment. There are no differences in the rules for different types of telecommunications businesses.

Depreciation of assets will commence from the moment they are used to generate taxable income, and not from the moment in which they are registered as assets of the company. In this sense, the moment in which an asset is considered to be used to generate taxable income (i.e., placed in service) may depend upon the nature of the asset. In the context of a network, assets may be depreciated from the moment any service, which is to be later invoiced, is rendered through the network to end-users.

Research and development costs are considered to form part of the acquisition cost of assets related to them. Therefore, for software, once research and development is over and the final product is ready for use, the amortization basis will include all such research and development costs.

Marketing and advertising costs, including payments made to sales agents, are deductible expenses as long as they are connected to the generation of taxable income or to the maintenance of its source.

Transfer Pricing Rules

Transfers must be carried out at fair market value. In the case of transfers between related companies (i.e., when one company owns directly or indirectly 30% or more of the share capital of another company), market value will be considered to be what is normally charged in similar operations with third parties. The tax authorities have the power to adjust the value of said transaction for both the transferor and the transferee.

Transfers of Patents, Trademarks and Software

There are no restrictions on the licensing of technology to a local company in exchange for royalty fees. Although not frequently done so, technology transfers are sometimes treated as property transfers, if the property attributes vested to the purchaser are significant. Neither the tax authorities nor the courts have issued any relevant rulings or guidelines regarding this particular issue.

Patent, trademarks and licensing fees are deductible provided they are related to maintaining or generating taxable income. Patents, trademarks and software licensing fees are all subject to VAT at a rate of 18%, in addition to the 30% withholding tax applicable to royalty payments made to non-residents.

Service Fees

Service fees are taxed depending on the nature of the service rendered. Technical services rendered completely from abroad are not subject to withholding taxes since the income related to these services is not considered to be of Peruvian source. Technical services rendered partly within Peru and partly from abroad are subject to a 12% withholding tax. In addition, fees paid to non-residents for non-technical services performed in Peru are subject to a 30% withholding tax. Fees for technical assistance services, which include the transfer of know-how, are classified as royalties.

Value-Added Tax, Sales Tax and/or Other Pertinent Taxes

VAT must be paid on a monthly basis and is levied on the following transactions, among others: (a) the sale of goods, (b) the supply or use of services (including Internet access and Internet telephony services), (c) construction contracts, (d) the first sale of real estate performed by the builder and (e) the importation of goods. The applicable VAT rate is 16%, but after adding the Municipal Promotion Tax of 2%, the effective VAT rate is equal to 18%. The total 18% generates a tax credit for the tax-payer. As discussed above under "Pre-operating Losses and Start-up/Construction Costs," VAT can be recovered under certain circumstances.

VAT functions as a tax on revenue. VAT paid by a company is, generally, creditable against VAT charged by the company on other activities that are also subject to VAT. Certain activities, such as the exportation of goods and services, are exempt from VAT. Payments to non-residents will be subject to VAT if they are made in connection with the sale of movable goods situated inside Peru or the rendering or use of services within the country. In addition to VAT, a selective consumption tax ranging from 10% to 25% is also levied on the importation and sale of certain non-essential or luxury goods such as spirits, cigarettes and limousines.

Local and Provincial Taxes

Telecommunications companies may be subject to the following municipal taxes:

Real Estate Equity Tax. This is a municipal tax levied on the value of real estate. The tax rates are progressive and the highest marginal rate is 1%. The tax basis is determined by the province and is usually lower than the market value of the property.

Real Estate Transfer Tax. This tax is levied on the transfer of real estate property as a gift or in consideration of a payment (in cash or in kind) at a rate of 3%.

Vehicle Tax. This tax is levied on the value of new cars at a rate of 1% during the first three years after manufacturing.

For Additional Information, Contact:

Rudolf M. Röder
Tax Partner
1301 Avenue of the Americas
New York, NY 10019
U.S.A.
Telephone: 1 (212) 259 1832
Fax: 1 (212) 259 1616
E-mail: Rudolf.Roder@us.coopers.com

Orlando Marchesi
Tax Manager
Juan de Arona 830, 11th floor
San Isidro, Lima, Peru
Telephone: 51 (1) 442 4248
Fax: 51 (1) 442 2073
E-mail: orlmar@clpe.com.pe

United States

Telecommunications Tax Profile
by Dennis J. McCarthy
Tax Partner, New York

Overview of the Telecommunications Market

Historical Background

The telecommunications sector in the United States (U.S.) has a long history as being one of the most open, competitive markets in the world. Regulatory and court rulings over three decades have resulted in open markets in long-distance service, customer premises equipment, and private voice and data networks, and most recently, in local telephone services. Markets for common-carrier wireless and electronic services have always been competitive. Wireless has always been subject to a licensing process.

For more than a decade, the U.S. telecommunications market has been made up of separate local and long-distance providers, a result of the Modified Final Judgment (MFJ), the court ruling that set the terms for the 1984 breakup of the AT&T Bell System. The MFJ split the Bell System between AT&T, which continued to provide nationwide long-distance service, and the seven regional Bell operating companies (RBOCs), which were created to provide local services and access for long-distance carriers. The local market also included more than 1,100 smaller companies, which generally served the less-populated areas of the U.S. In addition to restructuring the telecommunications industry, the MFJ prohibited the RBOCs (and their associated operating companies, or BOCs) from entering the long-distance telephone market and the manufacturing and electronic publishing markets.

The Telecommunications Act of 1996 set the ground rules for freeing some of the former Bell System local telephone companies from restrictions contained in the MFJ. The Act established rules for opening competition in local wireline services, which was the last portion of the U.S. telecoms market to have functioned essentially as a monopoly. All local telcos, not just the BOCs, were affected. The intent of the legislation was to spur investment in the next-generation telecommunications infra-structure and to stimulate competition among many types of communications service providers.

Current Status

Details of how competition will be implemented continue to be defined by the Federal Communications Commission (FCC), the regulatory bodies in each state (public utilities commissions, or PUCs), and the federal courts. The FCC has issued numerous decisions on the interconnection obligations of the incumbent local telcos and has set rigorous requirements for RBOC entry into the long-distance market. Legal challenges to the FCC rules have been mounted by local telcos, interexchange carriers (IXCs), competitive local exchange carriers (CLECs) and PUCs. The principle objections have centered on the FCC's jurisdiction to set prices, terms and conditions for interconnection. The lower courts have generally decided these challenges in favor of the local telcos and PUCs, although the Supreme Court has agreed to review the decisions. The final outcome of the cases will probably not be known until 1999. In the meantime, the state PUCs are setting their own rules on interconnection.

The RBOCs (of which there are now five, after two separate mergers) have also challenged the constitutionality of certain provisions of the Telecommunications Act of 1996, arguing that they were unfairly singled out to satisfy in advance conditions placed on their entry into long distance and other lines of business. The case has been heard in federal court and was decided in favor of the RBOCs. At press time, the FCC and IXCs had appealed the decision.

All segments of the telecommunications market are showing healthy growth, investment and activity, as illustrated below. Mergers, joint ventures and new alliances have been announced frequently since the Telecommunications Act was passed in February 1996.

- Domestic and international long-distance revenues have steadily increased in a market that was worth more than

US$100 billion in 1996, according to the FCC. AT&T, MCI, Sprint and a handful of other facilities-based carriers are the market leaders, but hundreds of resellers are actively marketing long-distance services to businesses and consumers. The reseller share of the long-distance market was almost $7 billion.

- The FCC reported that the market for fixed local telephone service in the U.S. was worth more than US$61 billion in 1996, with an additional US$36 billion for interstate and intrastate access service. Local service has traditionally been provided by local telephone operators serving specific geographic regions. The RBOCs and the largest two independent telcos serve more than 93% of the total access lines in the U.S., with more than 1,100 smaller independent telcos serving the rest. In the last few years, the incumbent telcos have faced growing competition. The Telecommunications Act of 1996 requires incumbent local telcos to interconnect with facilities-based competitors and also requires them to make all of their retail services available to resellers at discounted prices. In most larger cities, CLECs have been authorized to provide switched and dedicated services in competition with the incumbent local telephone providers. Most CLECs concentrate on the business market segment, although there has been recent growth in high-density residential areas. The FCC reported that in 1996 CLECs and local resellers had more than $1 billion in revenues.

- Subscribers to cellular, paging, personal communications service (PCS) and mobile data services continue to grow. According to the FCC, total wireless revenues grew 39% in 1996 to US$26 billion. Price and promotional competition in the cellular market have been heated. Many players are moving toward consolidation, mainly through acquisitions, in order to gain nationwide markets. Bell Atlantic Corporation, AT&T, GTE Wireless and SBC Communications lead the market in numbers of cellular subscribers.

- PCS frequencies have been auctioned to new service providers in a series of competitions, some open to all qualified participants and others reserved for small businesses. The first round of auctions generated some US$7.7 billion in revenue for the federal government; licensees include BellSouth Corporation, SBC and Sprint PCS. A second round of licenses was auctioned to "entrepreneurs" (small businesses with revenues and assets below certain caps) and generated bids totaling $10 billion; however, the total expected to be paid for these licenses over 10 years is expected to fall short of the bid amount. A subsequent auction for smaller bands of radio spectrum was completed in January 1997 and resulted in a net revenue of $2.5 billion.

- Data and other value-added services are generating growing revenues, with tremendous growth and interest in the use of the Internet by businesses and consumers. Four commercial on-line services lead the U.S. consumer market: America Online, CompuServe, the Microsoft Network and Prodigy (America Online recently acquired CompuServe but announced that both would continue to operate as separate services). Other major players and hundreds of regional and local Internet access service providers are joining the market.

- Several carriers, including Qwest Communications International, Inc., and Level 3 Communications, Inc., have announced plans to offer Internet protocol-based telephony services to residential and/or business subscribers. Such carriers may put additional pressure on prices.

A shift to digital technologies and equipment is underway in both wireline and wireless, helping to account for a 15.9% increase in industry spending on network equipment and facilities in 1997. Deployment of fiber optic cable has also been a factor, with the number of kilometers installed rising to nearly 1.8 million in 1997 (compared with 541,000 in 1995). Much of the recent growth reflected buildout by new long-distance carriers and former regional operators. Although RBOCs are expected to increase their fiber optic installations over the rest of the decade, installations by IXCs and other providers can be expected to slow as they complete current rollouts, according to the *MultiMedia Telecommunications Market Review and Forecast*. In cellular, time division multiple access (TDMA) technology has been deployed in many metropolitan areas throughout the U.S. Call division multiple access (CDMA) is in use in some areas.

Current Liberalization Status

In February 1997 members of the World Trade Organization (WTO) signed an agreement intended to open the worldwide telecommunications market. The U.S. was among 69 signatory countries, which make up 85% of the global market (see "Potential for Foreign Ownerships/Relationships").

Type of Service	Degree of Liberalization*	Key Legislation**	Date of Actual or Expected Liberalization	Comments
Local	Both facilities-based and resale competition are permitted in every state, subject to a "finding of public interest and necessity" by the state PUC and the FCC. In most cases, authorizations are routinely granted.	Telecommunications Act of 1996 Authorization by PUCs	Leased-line: 1985, beginning in New York City Local switched: 1995, beginning in Rochester, New York	The opening of the local-exchange market to competition is required under the Telecommunications Act of 1996. As of January 1998, incumbent telcos had signed more than 2,400 interconnection agreements and were processing more than 8,000 orders for service per day from competing carriers.
Long Distance	Regulated under "non-dominant carrier" rules under which rates and conditions are presumed lawful and pro-competitive; resale allowed	FCC Specialized Common Carrier Decision (1971) FCC Execunet Decision (1973) FCC Resale and Shared Use Decision (1976) Telecommunications Act of 1996 permits RBOC entry after they open their networks to interconnection with competitors.	Leased line: 1996 Switched service: 1973	The market was opened after MCI successfully sued AT&T in the 1960s. Because of pending court challenges to the Telecoms Act, full-scale long-distance competition from RBOCs is unlikely before 1999.
International		International Record Carrier Act of 1981 FCC Foreign Participation Order (1997)	Telex and other international record services: 1960s International voice: 1985	Applications from carriers from WTO countries are usually approved. Applicants from non-WTO countries must demonstrate equivalent competitive opportunities for U.S. carriers in their home countries.
Cellular	Duopoly for facilities-based carriers; resale allowed	In 1977, the FCC licensed Illinois Bell Telephone Co. (Chicago) and a Motorola subsidiary (Washington, D.C./Baltimore) to provide cellular services.	First license awarded: 1977 Duopolies established in top 50 markets: 1961	Spectrum is split into separate blocks for wireline and non-wireline competitors.
Paging	Fully liberalized; operators must be licensed	FCC allocation of frequencies for General Mobile Radio Service (1949)	Bell System granted experimental license: 1946 Wider commercial applications: 1965	Widescale deployment followed technical advances in the 1960s.
Value-added***	Fully liberalized	FCC Computer I Inquiry (1971) FCC Second Computer Inquiry (1980)	1971	Subsequent FCC actions set rules for telco entry.

* Telecommunications in the United States has always existed as a private enterprise and has been regulated since 1934 by the FCC and state PUCs.

** FCC actions that triggered competition are listed because most markets were opened to competition prior to the enactment of the Telecommunications Act of 1996. However, new rules were written to provide detailed instructions on implementation issues under the Act. A number of these new rules are under challenge in the federal courts.

*** Definition includes voice and data: X.25, frame relay, Internet services and voice messaging services.

Competitive Environment

Type of Service	Entire Market		Top Two Players		
	Market Size* (1997)	Number of Players**	Names	Annual Revenue (1997)	Ownership
Local	US$52.9 billion in local service plus US$32.3 billion for access	1,200 local exchange carriers, including more than 100 CLECs	Bell Atlantic SBC	US$13.11 billion US$9.6 billion	Publicly traded Publicly traded
Long Distance	US$76.8 billion	700 facilities-based carriers and resellers	AT&T MCI	US$46.17 billion US$18.5 billion (1996)	Publicly traded Publicly traded***
International	US$23.5 billion	Owned or leased facilities: 42 230 resellers of international message telephone service	AT&T MCI International	Included in long distance US$4.2 billion (1996)	Publicly traded Publicly traded
Cellular	US$32.5 billion	Several dozen facilities-based carriers; hundreds of resellers	Bell Atlantic AT&T	US$3.33 billion US$4.34 billion	Publicly traded Publicly traded
Paging	(Wireless: $25.4 billion; PCS: $510 million; Mobile Special Radio: $1.6 billion; Paging: $5.1 billion)	Several dozen large players	PageNet AirTouch Paging	US$839 million US$342 million (1996)	Paging Network, Inc.; publicly traded AirTouch Communications; publicly traded
Value-added****	US$13.5 billion	Hundreds, including CLECs, IXCs, Internet providers and others	AT&T MCI	Included within other revenue segments	Publicly traded Publicly traded

Sources: *1998 MultiMedia Telecommunications Market Review and Forecast* (formerly known as The North American Telecommunications Association); 1996 annual reports; 1997 annual reports.

* *1998 MultiMedia Telecommunications Market Review and Forecast* figures for 1997.

** Facilities-based carriers and resellers.

*** At press time, regulators were reviewing a bid by WorldCom to acquire MCI. British Telecom was expected to sell its shares in MCI.

**** Leased lines, ISDN (integrated services digital network), frame relay, ATM (asynchronous transfer mode), SMDS (switched multi-megabit data service).

Licensing Requirements

Telecommunications is regulated both by federal and state bodies. The FCC regulates U.S. telecommunications at the interstate level, and PUCs perform regulatory oversight at the state level.

Licenses for international service are granted by the FCC. Applications by foreign carriers from WTO countries, whether or not signatories to the Telecoms Agreement, are considered to be in the public interest and are given expedited approval. Foreign carriers from non-WTO countries must meet the "equivalent competitive opportunities" test before their applications can be approved. Competition in domestic long distance and local is open for facilities-based carriers and resellers. Interexchange carriers (IXCs) must get authorization from both the FCC and the PUC of any state in which they provide service. Local carriers, including CLECs, must get authorization from the PUC for local service and, if applicable, from the FCC for access services provided to long-distance carriers.

The FCC allocates frequencies for all radio-based transmissions and thus licenses cellular, mobile, satellite and other wireless services providers. The FCC has used auctions as the primary licensing mechanism for the last few years, with licenses being awarded to the highest bidders. No licenses are required for providers of value-added or on-line services.

Potential for Foreign Ownerships/Relationships

According to the commitments first submitted by the U.S. to the WTO, foreign interests would have been prohibited from operating in the U.S. domestic market unless there were a comparable business opportunity for U.S. carriers in the foreign country. Domestic corporations were limited to 20% foreign ownership (except with permission from the FCC). However, in November 1997, recognizing that the WTO agreement would substantially increase opportunities for U.S. carriers, the FCC withdrew its requirement for reciprocity with other signatories. Instead, it will rely on WTO safeguards against anti-competitive behavior.

Under the new FCC rules, operators from WTO countries will be authorized to provide end-to-end international services as well as local services. Even countries that are members of the WTO but have not signed the agreement will be allowed into U.S. international and local markets. Reciprocity is still an issue with non-WTO countries. For most telecommunications services, foreign ownership has been authorized on a case-by-case basis.

Cable & Wireless Plc was one of the earliest foreign carriers licensed to operate in the U.S.; subsequently, British Telecom's purchase of 20% of MCI was authorized. The FCC had approved British Telecom's proposed merger with MCI. But thereafter WorldCom made an offer for MCI, and at press time, regulators were reviewing the proposed acquisition. Industry observers expect BT to look for other investment opportunities with U.S. carriers.

Potential for Upcoming Liberalization/Investment Opportunities

Opportunities and open competition exist in all sectors of the U.S. telecommunications market. The market for wireless communications and the pace of investment in communications technology, telecommunications ventures, multimedia and Internet technologies will continue to flourish under the 1996 Telecommunications Act.

Forms of Doing Business

Permanent Establishment

In general, the business profits of a non-resident company may be subject to U.S. income tax only if the company has a taxable trade or business, or permanent establishment, in the U.S. The existence of a U.S. trade or business (USTB) is defined by U.S. domestic law, and a permanent establishment (PE) is defined by income tax treaties. Non-resident companies that benefit from tax treaties are subject to tax on their business profits only if such profits are attributable to the PE.

USTB under Domestic Law. For the business profits of a non-resident company to be subject to tax, the company must be engaged in a trade or business within the United States. The profits to be taxed must be effectively connected with that trade or business.

Case law has established that a foreign corporation is considered engaged in a USTB if it conducts substantial, regular and continuous business activity in the U.S. The level of U.S. activity required to constitute a U.S. trade or business is quite low, and includes the following:

- The sale of inventory on a regular basis

- The carrying on of business through a dependent agent

- The demonstration of products and the solicitation of orders in the U.S.

Except for certain categories of foreign-sourced income, a non-resident company's income is generally not considered as effectively connected income if it does not fall within the definition of U.S.-sourced income. A non-resident company's international communications income (ICI) is considered to be non-U.S.-sourced unless such income is attributable to the company's U.S. office or other fixed place of business, in which case it is treated as U.S.-sourced income. ICI includes all income derived from the transmission of communications or data from the U.S. to any foreign country or from any foreign country to the U.S., including wireless transmissions using satellites. Income from communications between two points in the U.S. is considered entirely U.S.-sourced income, even if the communications are routed through satellites. Moreover, income from communications between two foreign countries is entirely non-U.S.-sourced income. ICI can be considered either service, rent or intangible royalty income, depending on the type of communication involved. The law does not clearly define a number of aspects of income sourcing and, because of this, the taxation of non-resident communications companies is a developing area of the U.S. tax law.

PE under Tax Treaties. Although it varies by treaty, a PE is generally defined as a fixed place of business through which the business of an enterprise is carried on in whole or in part. Most treaties with the United States list examples of activities that constitute a PE. These generally include a fixed place of business, such as an office, branch, factory, mine, construction site, drilling operation, or other temporary project location (if the project continues for at least 12 months), and a dependent agent or employee. If a non-resident company's operations in the U.S. constitute a PE, the company will be taxed on its business profits that are attributable to such a PE. The business profits of the company will be considered attributable to a PE if the PE is a material factor in the realization of such profits and if they are realized in the ordinary course of the trade or business carried on through the PE. The activities of a PE are generally not considered to be a material factor in the realization of business profits unless the activities are an essential economic element in the realization of such profits.

Potential PEs under Tax Treaties. The types of activities in which foreign telecommunications companies are typically involved in the U.S. and their potential for treaty-based PE exposure are listed below (the particulars of the appropriate tax treaty would also have to be analyzed):

- The provision of long-distance services to local customers by a non-resident company without any local presence is unlikely to constitute a PE. The provision of these services by a non-resident company with physical equipment located in the U.S. will likely constitute a PE, particularly if, in addition to the physical presence of telecommunications equipment in the U.S., the non-resident company has other activities in the U.S., either directly or indirectly through an agent.

- The leasing or licensing by a non-resident company of telecommunications equipment or technology to a U.S. company for use outside of the U.S. is unlikely to constitute a PE if the non-resident company has no U.S. presence.

- The provision of technical assistance by a non-resident company to a U.S. company is unlikely to constitute a PE if the presence of foreign personnel in the U.S. is of relatively limited duration (e.g., six months) and the employees are sent only to advise and instruct a U.S. company (not to sell or license additional devices).

- The provision of call reorganization/turnaround services is unlikely to constitute a PE if a non-resident telecommunications company's activities in the U.S. are conducted through an independent agent and such agent's activities are limited to the solicitation of calling cards (and incidental related activities). A switch or server can be located within the territorial waters of the U.S. but be used exclusively for the provision of network management and services to subscribers outside the U.S. (the location of switches and servers is usually of no consequence to users). For call reorganization/turnaround services, for example, such equipment may be used primarily by non-resident customers calling abroad from inside the U.S., or such equipment may be used only for routing calls from outside the U.S. to non-U.S. destinations. Although a physical presence should be considered in determining whether a foreign service provider has a PE, it should not be the sole factor. However, the presence of such equipment combined with other types of activities, such as the performance of maintenance services and the provision of access to the switching equipment to U.S. customers for a fee, could constitute a PE.

- As long as an agent's activities are limited to solicitation, the provision of Internet access services is unlikely to constitute a PE. Because these services are in many ways similar to call reorganization/turnaround services, the physical presence of servers in the U.S. should not be the sole factor for assessing the presence of a PE. As mentioned above, additional factors, such as the use of an agent to accept local subscriptions for Internet service or the use of an agent for the maintenance of servers, combined with the physical presence of servers in the U.S., will likely constitute a PE.

- The laying of fiber optic cable and the construction of telecommunications switching equipment will generally constitute a PE unless the project takes place over a relatively short period (e.g., six months).

- Having a website located on a server within the U.S. or in a foreign country that can be accessed by customers in the U.S. should not, in and of itself, constitute a PE for the merchandiser (i.e., the person selling goods or services through the website).

Business Entities

A foreign investor can operate in the U.S. through a local branch or a U.S. subsidiary, or through various forms of joint venture.

Local Branch and Locally Incorporated Subsidiary of a Foreign Company. The key taxation consequences for local branches and locally incorporated subsidiaries of foreign companies are as follows:

- *Taxation of profits.* A U.S. subsidiary is taxed on its worldwide income. A branch is taxed only on the profits derived from its U.S. activities. Both branch and subsidiary profits are subject to federal, state and local taxation.

- *Taxation of amounts paid or deemed paid to owners.* A 30% withholding tax (or lower treaty rate) is applied to dividends and interest paid from a subsidiary to its foreign parent. Similarly, a branch is subject to branch taxes, which are designed to approximate the taxation of earnings distributed and interest paid by U.S. corporations to foreign shareholders and lenders.

- *Group filing.* A U.S. parent and its 80%-owned U.S. subsidiaries generally may file a consolidated return and be taxed as one corporation. Although a branch cannot be included in a U.S. consolidated group, branch losses from one activity can offset other branch profits from another activity of the same company. Some states and localities permit or require the filing of combined returns by related entities.

Joint Venture. A joint venture can be structured as either a corporation or a partnership. Under current regulations, certain specified entities, including a number of foreign limited liability entities, are automatically treated as corporations. All other business entities can elect to be treated as either corporations or partnerships. An entity that is 100%-owned by a single foreign corporation and that does not elect corporate treatment is taxed as a branch.

The key taxation differences between a corporation and a partnership are as follows:

- *A partnership mitigates double taxation.* A joint venture that is structured as a U.S. corporation is taxed on its worldwide income. Distributions to a foreign shareholder are subject to a 30% withholding tax (or a lower treaty rate). In contrast, a joint venture that is structured as a partnership is not subject to federal tax at the entity level. The income or loss of the partnership is passed through to the partners, who are taxed as if they operated a branch. The partnership as a whole, however, is required to withhold a 35% tax on the U.S. business profits allocated to a foreign corporate partner.

- *A partnership allows more flexibility.* Partnerships give investors great flexibility in allocating partnership income or loss and in making partnership distributions. A partner may be able to use the partnership's losses against its other income. In contrast, a corporation must make distributions in proportion to its shareholders' ownership with respect to a given class of stock, and the shareholders do not share in the corporation's losses. Along with this flexibility for the partnership, however, comes the prospect of more complex tax rules.

- *Liability.* Three types of entities can be structured as partnerships for tax purposes, each offering its members exposure to different levels of liability. In a general partnership, each partner is normally fully liable for the liabilities of the partnership. In a limited partnership, only the general partner is normally liable for the partnership's liabilities. In a limited liability company (LLC), none of the partners generally can be held liable for the company's liabilities. All three types of entities are required to file tax returns.

Local Funding Alternatives

Debt versus Equity

Debt financing is generally more favorable to the issuer than equity financing because, although dividends are not deductible, interest—whether paid to a U.S. or foreign lender—generally is deductible. Interest owed by a U.S. taxpayer to a related foreign person usually cannot be deducted until the interest is actually paid, regardless of the taxpayer's method of accounting. This rule applies even when the interest is exempt from U.S. tax under a treaty. In addition, interest deductions can be disallowed or deferred if a taxpayer does not satisfy thin capitalization requirements and the so-called earnings-stripping rules.

The thin-capitalization rules are aimed at ensuring that, based on the economic substance of the arrangement, an instrument that is labeled as debt is not recharacterized as equity. If debt is recharacterized as equity, a corporation will be denied an interest deduction. There are no safe-harbor rules to ensure debt characterization. Rather, various factors are considered in determining whether, for tax purposes, a debt instrument should be characterized as equity.

Under the earnings-stripping rules, when a U.S. subsidiary has a debt-to-equity ratio greater than 1.5 to 1, interest deductions can be deferred if the interest payments are made either to a foreign shareholder (or related party) who will not be subject to U.S. tax on the interest received, or on debt guaranteed by a foreign shareholder (or related party) if the interest is not subject to U.S. withholding tax.

The amount of interest expense incurred by a foreign corporation that can be deducted against the foreign corporation's U.S. business income generally is limited under a formula designed to approximate the amount of interest expense generated by the corporation's U.S. liabilities. The foreign corporation's U.S. liabilities are, in turn, determined under a formula that allocates to the U.S. a portion of the corporation's worldwide liabilities equal to the proportion of its worldwide assets considered to be U.S. assets. Interest paid to a foreign lender is subject to a 30% withholding tax, which may be reduced or eliminated under a tax treaty or under an exception available for loans made by certain unrelated lenders.

Foreign investors may prefer to receive interest income rather than a dividend if the interest is subject to a lower treaty withholding rate or if the interest is otherwise exempt from withholding.

Borrowers may have to include in their income foreign currency gains or losses on the repayment of debt instruments denominated in foreign currencies. Foreign currency gains and losses are realized only when the principal on the debt is actually repaid. Foreign currency gains are characterized as ordinary income.

Exchange Controls

There are no exchange controls in the U.S.

Business Acquisitions and Dispositions

Capital Contributions into an Existing Local Entity

With the exception of contributions of inventory, services or property for which depreciation deductions have been taken on a U.S. tax return, a capital contribution of property by a foreign corporation into a U.S. corporation is not taxable. There are no limitations on the value of intangibles that a foreign corporation may contribute into an existing U.S. entity. Certain intangibles, such as patents, trademarks and goodwill, constitute property and should qualify for tax-free treatment if most rights in such property are transferred.

It is not clear, however, whether the transfer of know-how will be treated as a transfer of property or of services. This determination generally will depend on the facts and circumstances of each transfer. If the transfer of know-how is treated as a transfer of services, the contributing foreign corporation will be treated as if the stock received in the exchange were compensation income. In this case, such income may be subject to U.S. tax if either the foreign corporation is engaged in a USTB (or has a PE under an applicable income tax treaty) and such income is effectively connected with such business and/or if the income is considered U.S.-sourced.

Purchase or Sale of Shares in a Local Entity

A target's U.S. shareholders generally will recognize a capital gain or loss on a stock sale unless the payment is in stock and the tax-free reorganization requirements are satisfied (see "Capital Gains Taxes"). A foreign seller of shares at a gain would not generally pay any U.S. tax.

In a taxable stock purchase, tax on the appreciation of the target's assets is avoided and the purchaser will not obtain a stepped-up basis in the target's assets (unless an election is made, as described below). The purchaser will receive a cost basis in the purchased shares.

For U.S. income tax purposes, and in some state and local jurisdictions, the buyer of stock can elect to treat a stock purchase as a purchase of assets for tax purposes so as to obtain a stepped-up basis in the target's assets. The target corporation is treated as if it had sold its assets to a new corporation. The new corporation would then take a stepped-up basis in the target's assets. The tax consequences of such an election depend on the tax status of the target.

Purchase or Sale of Assets

The aggregate tax basis of assets acquired in a taxable transaction is equal to the total purchase price paid for the assets. The total purchase price is allocated among the assets using the residual method, whereby the asset purchase price is first allocated to the cash (Class I assets) acquired. Next, the remainder of the purchase price is allocated to marketable securities and other types of highly liquid assets (Class II assets), then to all working capital and other tangible assets (Class III assets), and then to intangibles other than goodwill and going-concern value (Class IV assets). Finally, the residual, if any, is allocated to goodwill and going-concern value (Class V assets). (See "Depreciation/Cost-Recovery Conventions/Accelerated Deductions" for rules on the amortization of intangibles.) For the seller, whether U.S. or foreign, asset sales are always taxable.

A corporation that acquires assets in a tax-free transaction will get a carryover basis in such assets, and the seller will not report a gain or loss. Such a transaction could be tax-free when the consideration is the acquiring corporation's voting stock or the voting stock of its parent, and the acquisition is of substantially all of the assets of the selling corporation.

Purchase of a Partnership Interest. The acquirer of a partnership interest receives a cost basis in the partnership interest, and the basis of the underlying partnership assets does not change. In certain cases, purchasing partners can step up the basis of their share of the partnership's assets.

Start-up Business Issues

Pre-operating Losses and Start-up/ Construction Costs

Costs to Open Networks to Comply with the 1996 Telecommunications Act. The Act imposes numerous requirements on certain incumbent local exchange carriers (ILECs) and long-distance carriers to open their networks to competition. It is estimated that billions of dollars in direct and indirect costs to upgrade software and hardware will be spent to comply with the Act. The Act permits ILECs to enter new lines of business through separate subsidiaries. These businesses include long-distance telephony, equipment manufacturing, information services and cable TV.

Although software compliance costs will likely be recovered over three years, hardware investments will be recovered over their depreciable lives. The tax treatment of non-capital-type expenses is uncertain. Based on a case recently decided in the U.S. Supreme Court, the Internal Revenue Service (IRS) can be expected to argue that expenses that are otherwise deductible, ordinary and necessary business expenses, must be capitalized because compliance with the Act allows the BOC to remain in business and permits the BOC to enter other businesses, providing long-term benefits. There are other precedents in which the deductibility of costs to comply with government ordinances was disallowed. On the other hand, BOCs could argue that since many such costs are required to permit competition to occur that did not previously exist, the Act presents a detriment to them, rather than a long-term benefit. The benefits and detriments of the Act will vary depending on the local exchange in question.

Business Expansion Costs. Because of legal and regulatory requirements and business concerns, telcos typically form new companies to own any newly acquired licenses and to carry on these businesses. Start-up expenditures generally must be capitalized. Start-up expenditures include amounts paid or incurred in connection with the investigation of a new business, the creation of a new business, or activities occurring before a new business begins, if those expenses would be allowable as a deduction if paid or incurred in connection with an existing active trade or business. Start-up expenditures do not include interest expense, taxes, or research and experimentation (R&E) expenditures. However, a business can elect to amortize these expenses over 60 months (beginning with the month in which the active trade or business begins).

A taxpayer can elect either to deduct R&E expenditures immediately or to amortize them over a period of not less than 60 months. (See "Depreciation/Cost-Recovery Conventions/Accelerated Deductions.")

The costs of acquiring intangibles must be capitalized and amortized ratably over 15 years. For example, amounts paid to acquire licenses should be recovered over 15 years on a straight-line basis. There is some uncertainty over whether the 15-year amortization period begins in the month in which the intangible was acquired or when a trade or business begins. Both interpretations have statutory support. The IRS has issued proposed regulations that indicate the intention to delay the amortization period until the later of acquisition or commencement of a trade or business.

Interest must be capitalized if it is allocable to the construction or improvement of certain property, including real property and tangible personal property with specified class lives, and it is incurred after construction begins but before the property is placed in service.

Customs Duties and VAT

There is no value-added tax in the U.S. Generally, imported telephone and electronic equipment (including televisions and computers) are subject to customs duties, which range from 0% to 7.4%. Equipment imported from developing countries may be eligible for beneficial duty treatment under the General System of Preferences program. The U.S. is a signatory to the Information Technology Agreement (ITA) finalized in March 1997, which provides for the elimination of tariffs on information technology products by the year 2000. Countries will stage the majority of their tariff reductions to zero by 2000. The ITA also provides for a review of which products will be covered and for a continuing opportunity to pursue non-tariff measures that impede market access for information technology products.

Products originating in Canada and Mexico may be dutiable under the provisions of the North American Free Trade Agreement (NAFTA). The duty rates on qualifying products from these countries are lower than the normal rates under the General Agreement on Tariffs and Trade (GATT). Some of these products are already duty-free; others are in a phase-in period leading to eventual duty-free status.

The U.S. Customs Department will reject a price on a good if it believes that the price has been affected by a related-party relationship. In making such determinations, the Customs Department uses a methodology comparable in some respects to that used in the enforcement of Transfer Pricing Rules (see "Transfer Pricing Rules").

Strategies that help reduce customs duties include unbundling products into components that have more attractive duty rates. For example, software that would otherwise be a component of high-duty equipment can be unbundled from the equipment and treated as a separate item. Other customs strategies include first-sale and drawback. In a first-sale strategy, merchandise is appraised at the point of sale between the manufacturer and the distributor. This avoids the mark-ups that occur at later points in the supply chain. By obtaining the lower contract manufacturer's price, the duty paid on importation is lower.

Drawback is a refund of duties paid on goods imported into the U.S., which are later exported from the U.S. Thus, the duties paid on foreign-made parts that are included in the manufacture of a product (or which remain unused after importation), and which are later exported, will be refundable.

Loss Carryovers

A net operating loss incurred in a tax year prior to 1998 can generally be carried back for 3 years and carried forward for 15 years. A net operating loss incurred in 1998 and thereafter may be carried back for 2 years and forward for 20 years. A corporation can waive the carryback period. Capital losses can be carried back for three years and carried forward for five years. There is no waiver of the carryback period available in the case of capital losses. Both types of losses must first be carried back to the earliest year to which such losses may be carried, unless a carryback waiver has been made.

Generally, when the ownership of a corporation changes by more than 50% within a three-year period, the corporation's ability to use its pre-change tax attributes (i.e., net operating losses) to offset its post-change income may be subject to an annual limit. The formula for determining the annual limit is based on the corporation's equity value at the time the 50% ownership-change threshold is reached. The use of a loss carryover also may be limited to 90% of a corporation's alternative minimum taxable income if the corporation is subject to the alternative minimum tax (AMT). State and local rules regarding loss carryovers may be different.

There may be additional limits on the use of tax attributes when a corporation joins a consolidated group. In general, the separate-return-limitation-year (SRLY) rules may limit the use of a corporation's pre-consolidation losses within its new consolidated group.

Operating Considerations

Corporate Income Taxes

The U.S. taxes corporations and branches on their taxable income at the following rates:

Taxable Income		
More than	**But Not More than**	**Rate**
$0	$50,000	15%
$50,000	$75,000	25%
$75,000	$100,000	34%
$100,000	$335,000	39%
$10,000,000	$15,000,000	35%
$15,000,000	$18,333,333	38%
$18,333,333		35%

Alternative Minimum Tax. A corporation may be subject to an AMT, which is designed to ensure that taxpayers with substantial economic income do not avoid tax liability by using exclusions, deductions and other credits. The AMT liability is determined by computing a tentative minimum tax, equal to 20% of the corporation's alternative minimum taxable income (AMTI) in excess of $40,000. The AMT due is the amount by which the tentative minimum tax exceeds the corporation's regular tax liability. The AMTI is calculated by making certain adjustments to regular taxable income (for example, by adding back any accelerated depreciation deductions and limiting the use of net operating losses).

Withholding Taxes. U.S. payers of fixed annual or periodic income must withhold a 30% tax (which may be reduced by a tax treaty) on payments of such income to non-residents. Withholding is required on payments of interest, dividends, rents, royalties, salaries and compensation to the extent they are not connected to a U.S. business of the foreign payee. Also, a partnership doing business in the U.S. must withhold tax at the maximum applicable rate with respect to income allocated to its foreign partners. Certain states impose a withholding tax on dividends paid or partnership income allocated to a payee who is not a resident of that state and does not file an income tax return in that state.

Capital Gains Taxes

Corporate capital gains are generally taxed at the same rates as ordinary gains. Capital losses of corporations are deductible only to the extent of the capital gains. U.S. corporate sellers are limited in the amount of loss they can claim on the sale of stock of a subsidiary when the subsidiary is included in the seller's consolidated group.

Tax Holidays and Exemptions

Corporations can claim a federal tax credit for 20% of qualified research expenditures incurred between July 1, 1996, and June 30, 1998. To qualify for the research and experimentation (R&E) credit, the research activity must satisfy several tests. The development of software for a company's internal use can also qualify for the credit.

Qualified research expenditures may include:

- The cost of internally developed software, such as software used to test a telecommunications network, to track billing and accounts payable or receivable, or to open the local loop to competition

- The cost to develop new service offerings, such as caller ID and voice-recognition technologies

- The cost of developing new materials (e.g., cables, switches and transmission equipment)

- The cost of developing new capabilities, such as the compression of data onto existing lines

- The cost of building increased capability to handle new customer demand

Year 2000 Issues

As the year 2000 approaches, many corporations need to fix or replace software so that it recognizes date fields as four-digit fields. They will have to decide whether to enhance existing software or replace the software altogether. In addition to the technical considerations, because of the sizable costs involved, the accounting and tax treatment should be considered. Generally, the likely tax and accounting treatment favors replacement over enhancement:

Costs to Enhance — Accounting Treatment. It is likely that costs to enhance existing software will have to be expensed.

Costs to Enhance — Tax Treatment. The cost of fixing existing software can be deducted currently or amortized over a five-year period, at the election of the taxpayer. However, an R&E tax credit is available only in extraordinary circumstances and only if the services are performed in the U.S.

Costs to Replace — Accounting Treatment. Purchased software is amortized over its useful life for book purposes.

Costs to Replace — Tax Treatment. The cost of purchased software is amortized over three years if the cost is separately stated. If the cost is included in the cost of hardware, the software costs are depreciated over the same life as the computer.

Depreciation/Cost-Recovery Conventions/Accelerated Deductions

Tangible Property. Depreciation deductions are computed using a prescribed depreciation method and recovery period for each type of tangible depreciable property owned by a taxpayer. The assigned recovery periods are 3, 5, 7, 10, 15 and 20 years for tangible property other than real property; 27.5 years for residential real property; and 39 years for non-residential real property. The applicable depreciation method for 3-year, 5-year, 7-year or 10-year property is the 200% declining-balance method; for 15-year and 20-year property, the 150% declining-balance method is used. The straight-line method must be used for residential and non-residential real property. Listed below are the basic classes of telecommunications-related property and their recovery periods.

The allowance for depreciation begins when an asset is placed in service, which occurs when it is in a condition or state of readiness and able to perform its intended function. The asset does not actually have to be put to use, as long as every step necessary for its operation has been completed. However, no depreciation deduction is allowable for a business that has not yet commenced.

Cell Site Enclosures. These house the equipment used to operate cellular network transmission towers. The IRS has taken the unofficial position that such equipment falls within class 48.14 and is, therefore, 15-year property.

Intangibles. Certain intangibles acquired by a taxpayer in connection with a business acquisition can be amortized ratably over a period of 15 years. Intangibles that can be amortized include goodwill, going-concern value, business books and records, patents, copyrights, know-how, licenses and permits issued by the government, franchises, covenants not to compete, trademarks and trade names.

Computer Software. Computer software is generally depreciable on a straight-line basis over 36 months. Customized software that is acquired in the context of a business asset acquisition must be amortized over 15 years. The cost of computer software created by a taxpayer is deductible in the year incurred or, at the election of the taxpayer, amortized over a period of no less than five years.

Marketing and Advertising Costs. Marketing and advertising costs are generally deductible, even though they may be designed to produce long-term benefits. Advertising costs may have to be capitalized in the rare cases where the advertising is directed at obtaining future benefits significantly beyond those usually associated with ordinary advertising.

Sales Commission Expenses. It is unclear whether sales commission expenses paid to agents for signing clients onto a telecoms company's network are deductible or whether they must be capitalized. Generally, costs that secure benefits lasting beyond one year must be capitalized. IRS field agents are taking the position that commission costs paid to agents by cellular companies for signing customers onto their networks benefit the companies beyond one year even when subscriber agreements are for periods of one year or less, because the company has an expectation of a long-term contractual relationship with the customer. The IRS National Office is evaluating this position. A resolution is expected in 1998.

Asset Class	Property	Recovery Period (in years)
00.12	Information systems, including computers and peripheral equipment used in administering normal business transactions	5
00.11	Office furniture and fixtures	7
	Telephone communications:	
48.11	Telephone central-office buildings	20
48.12	Telephone central-office equipment	10
48.121	Computer-based switching equipment	5
48.13	Telephone-station equipment	7
48.14	Telephone distribution plant	15
	Telegraph, ocean cable and satellite communications:	
48.31	Power-generating and -distribution systems	10
48.32	High-frequency radio and microwave systems	7
48.33	Cable and long-line systems	20
48.34	Central-office control equipment	10
48.35	Computerized switching equipment	7
48.36	Satellite ground-segment property	7
48.37	Satellite space-segment property	5
48.38	Equipment installed on customer's premises	7
48.39	Support and service equipment	7

Transfer Pricing Rules

The IRS can, in accordance with transfer pricing rules, reallocate gross income, deductions, credits and allowances among businesses owned or controlled by the same interests in order to prevent evasion of taxes or to reflect income more clearly. Transfer pricing rules rely on the "arm's-length standard" to determine whether an income reallocation is warranted. States and some localities can also make reallocations.

U.S. corporations that are at least 25% foreign-owned and foreign corporations that operate U.S. branches are subject to extensive reporting requirements regarding related-party transactions. In addition, both must make available to the IRS their own books and records regarding related-party transactions, as well as the books and records of the related parties. Failure to document the arm's-length nature of inter-company transactions can result in significant penalties, sometimes as great as 40% of the underpayment of tax attributable to a transfer pricing adjustment. The penalties can be imposed on a transaction-by-transaction basis, under certain circumstances, or on a net adjustments basis.

Transfers of Patents, Trademarks and Software

Whether the transfer of an intangible asset (such as a patent or trademark) is treated as a sale or exchange or as a license for tax purposes will affect how the payment for the asset will be characterized. If the transfer is treated as a license, payments may be treated as royalty payments and generally will be deductible as business expenses unless they are required to be capitalized (e.g., when they are incurred as a start-up expense). Royalty payments paid to non-residents are generally subject to a 30% withholding tax if such payments provide the right to use the intangibles in the U.S. The withholding rate may be reduced under a treaty. If the transfer is treated as a sale or exchange, and the seller is not engaged in a U.S. trade or business, any gain realized on such a sale should not be subject to U.S. taxation. However, certain transactions legally referred to as licenses can be characterized for tax purposes as straight sales not subject to withholding.

Whether a transfer of technology is a sale or a license depends on whether all substantial rights in the intangible have been transferred. A transfer must not be limited to a particular field of use, to a duration of less than the entire remaining useful life of the property, or to a specific geographic region. Furthermore, the transferor must not retain the right either to terminate the agreement to transfer title at will or to prevent disclosure of technology. The tax authorities look to the substance, rather than the form, of the transaction to determine whether a sale or a license has occurred.

The transfer of a franchise, trademark or trade name will be treated as a license to the extent that the transferor retains significant rights or a continuing interest in the subject matter of the interest, such as the right to disapprove the assignment of the interest, the right to terminate the interest at will, or the right to prescribe standards of quality of products sold or services rendered. If the transferor does not retain significant rights in the transferred interest, the transfer may be characterized as a sale.

Under recently proposed regulations, the transfer of a computer program would be treated as a transfer of an intangible (i.e., a copyright) only if the transferee were granted certain special rights in the program including: (i) the right to reproduce copies of the computer program for sale to the general public, (ii) the right to prepare derivative works based on the copyrighted program, or (iii) the right to make public performance of or to display the computer program. If these rights were not granted, the transaction would be treated as a transfer of a copyrighted article. If the transaction were treated as a transfer of the copyright itself, the determination of whether the transfer was a license or a sale would be based on an analysis of whether "all substantial rights" had been transferred (similar to the transfer of technology analysis above). However, if the transaction were viewed as a transfer of a copyrighted article, the analysis of whether the transfer was a sale or lease would be based on case-law principles as to whether the "benefits and burdens" of ownership had actually been transferred. These proposed regulations also provide that certain software transactions could be characterized as the provision of services or, alternatively, of know-how. The determination of whether services are being provided is based on all the facts and circumstances. The provision of information will be treated as know-how only if it is related to computer programming techniques, is not capable of being copyrighted, and is subject to trade protection.

Service Fees

Fees paid for services performed by non-residents in the U.S. are generally subject to a 30% withholding tax. However, this tax is not required on fees paid for services performed in the U.S. by a non-resident who is subject to the regular graduated wage withholding rules applicable to all employees of U.S. businesses. Services performed outside the U.S. would be foreign sourced income and, therefore, not subject to withholding tax.

Value-Added Tax and Federal Excise Tax

The U.S. does not impose a VAT, nor does it impose a sales or use tax, except on gasoline, alcohol and tobacco. Sales and use taxes may be applied at the state and local levels (see "Local and Provincial Taxes"). The U.S. does impose a 3% excise tax on local and long-distance telephone services. The tax is paid by the user and collected and remitted by the service provider. Federal excise tax is imposed on both wireline and wireless telephone services.

Internet Access Services. There has been no ruling as to whether Internet access service should be subject to federal excise tax. Proposed tax legislation would exempt Internet access service, Internet access-related service, and on-line service from federal excise tax. Because the Internet is a packet-switched network that has been used primarily for data transmission, it can be argued that access fees related to it should not constitute telephony and should not be subject to the tax. Nevertheless, access to the Internet often involves connecting to the local telephone exchanges and thus some uncertainty exists on this issue.

Prepaid Telephone Cards. Prepaid telephone cards are taxed on their face value at the time the cards are transferred from a telecommunications provider to any person who is not a telecommunications provider.

Local and Provincial Taxes

Corporations are subject to state and local taxation. For partnerships and limited liability companies (LLCs), most states follow the federal rules when the entity is not subject to tax. Instead, the partners or LLC members are subject to tax on their allocable shares of partnership income in the states in which the partnership operates. Certain jurisdictions subject partnerships and LLCs to an entity-level tax.

Nexus. A company is taxable only in states in which it has nexus. Whether a company conducts a level of activity in a state sufficient to establish nexus depends on the nature, extent and regularity of the activities conducted. Activities such as owning or leasing real or tangible personal property within a state, having employees in a state, or licensing intangible property within a state can create nexus.

Apportionment. Most states apportion the business income of a U.S. company based on the ratio of its property, payroll and sales in that state to its total U.S. property, payroll and sales. States vary in the weights they attribute to each of the three factors. Some states, such as California, apportion the worldwide, rather than U.S., income of a business.

Telecommunications-Specific Taxes. Many states tax telecommunications service providers on their gross receipts. Among the specific telephone-related services that may be included in gross receipts are access charges, activation fees, call forwarding, data transmission charges, directory services, discounted cellular phones, installation fees, international toll charges, paging charges, telephone-number charge fees and voice-mail charges. Gross-receipts taxes may also be imposed on receipts from sales of telecommunications equipment.

States vary in their treatment of the different types of telecommunications companies. For instance, gross-receipts tax may not apply to cellular service providers in jurisdictions where it *is* imposed on long-distance resellers. Many states tax gross receipts on calls that originate or terminate in that state but provide a credit for taxes paid to other states for the same call. Double taxation may, nevertheless, result under such a regime because a particular state may not allow a credit for all the types of telecommunications taxes imposed in other states.

In determining the location of a call for gross-receipts tax purposes, many states look to the call's origination and termination, as well as the service or billing address. However, wireless carriers often find it difficult to determine the location of a call's origination or termination. For example, the signal from a call made from a car phone can cross state lines and be picked up by a cell site or a PCS antenna in a neighboring state. In addition, the states have not adopted uniform definitions of origination, termination and service/billing address. Consequently, multiple states can claim jurisdiction to tax a single call.

Sales and Use Taxes. Most state and local governments impose sales and use taxes. The products subject to tax vary by jurisdiction, and rates range up to 10%. State sales and use taxes are usually borne by the customer and collected by the provider. Providers generally must pay sales taxes on their purchases of equipment, products and services used in the provision of telecommunications services, subject to certain exemptions. Sales and use taxes may also be imposed on agent commissions, certain costs of a cell site, telecommunications central-office equipment, packaged software, engineering services, market research, printing, construction of cell towers, and tower and pole rentals.

Direct-to-Home Satellite Services. Under the Telecommunications Act of 1996, localities cannot levy new taxes on providers of direct-to-home satellite services.

Internet Access Services. Most states have not issued formal guidelines regarding the taxation of Internet access services. States that have issued guidelines vary in their treatment of these services. For example, New York State exempts Internet access charges from gross-receipts and sales tax. In New York, Internet access charges may also include items such as communications/navigation software, e-mail privileges, news headlines, and certain services. Conversely, Texas taxes Internet access service as an information service. Tennessee treats Internet access service as a taxable telecommunications service provided that such service originates or terminates in Tennessee and is provided to a location in Tennessee or is billed to a Tennessee address. The proposed Internet Tax Freedom Act would place a moratorium on subnational taxes on electronic commerce. The proposed moratorium would not repeal existing taxes applied consistently to electronic and traditional commerce. The bill would not pre-empt business taxes imposed on net income or fairly apportioned business license taxes.

Prepaid Telephone Cards. Some states consider prepaid telephone cards to be tangible personal property and thus tax the cards at the point of sale. Other states treat sales of such cards as sales of telecommunications services and impose tax on usage.

Property Taxes. State and local governments also impose taxes on real and personal property, generally based on the assessed value of the property (which is not necessarily the fair market value), at widely varying rates. Leased property may also be subject to property tax. Other telecommunications equipment, such as data processing equipment, and certain equipment used to create on-screen images, may also be subject to a personal property tax in some jurisdictions.

Many planning opportunities exist for minimizing property tax liabilities. Most important, property may be classified as realty or personalty to take advantage of particular rates or exemptions. Additionally, because of the rapid pace of technological change, telecommunications businesses will likely benefit from a careful analysis of valuation methods available for reducing a company's taxable property base.

Payroll Taxes. States assess unemployment and miscellaneous insurance taxes based on payroll. These taxes are often assessed on both employers and employees. Significant savings can result from careful planning around transactions involving mergers and acquisitions, divestments, workforce expansions or contractions, and office or site relocations.

Public Service Commission and FCC Fees and Taxes. Some state regulatory commissions impose a fee or tax on regulated service providers. The FCC levies a similar fee. Often these fees and taxes are levied to cover the cost of regulating the industry. Typically, they are imposed on a portion of a service provider's gross revenue.

Surcharges. Many states impose surcharges on telephony on a per-access-line basis or on a percentage of gross receipts. Receipts from the surcharges are used to fund state 911 (emergency services) and universal-service programs, and services for the hearing-impaired.

For Additional Information, Contact:

Dennis J. McCarthy
Tax Partner
1301 Avenue of the Americas
New York, NY 10019
USA
Telephone: 1 (212) 259 2585
Fax: 1 (212) 259 1316
E-mail: Dennis.McCarthy@us.coopers.com

Andrew B. Zimmerman
Telecoms & Media Consulting Partner
Address: same as above
Telephone: 1 (212) 259 2224
Fax: 1 (212) 259 1337
E-mail: Andy.Zimmerman@us.coopers.com

Venezuela

Telecommunications Tax Profile
by Eduardo Ramírez-Mendez
Tax Partner, Caracas

Overview of the Telecommunications Market

Historical Background

Because of a long history of strict government regulation under a telecommunications monopoly, liberalization of telecommunications arrived only recently in Venezuela. In 1991, the monopoly service provider, Compañía Anónima Nacional Teléfonos de Venezuela (CANTV), was partially privatized. At that time, 40% of CANTV's shares were sold to Venworld Telecom, C.A., which is a consortium formed by GTE, Telefónica de España, S.A., la Electricidad de Caracas, AT&T, and CIMA (which is partly owned by Banco Mercantil). In December 1996, an additional 39.99% was sold through public offerings on the Venezuelan and U.S. stock markets. The rest of the shares are held by the government (9.01%) and by CANTV workers (11%).

Although CANTV began limited cellular service in 1988, establishment of its cellular subsidiary, Movilnet, in 1992 has improved its position in the market by expanding geographic coverage, serving more cities, being the first of the two cellular companies currently rendering services in Venezuela to introduce digital technology, and increasing subscriber penetration with new rate plans and services. In 1991, the government provided CANTV with its first competition by creating a cellular duopoly. A 20-year license was granted to the Telcel Celular, C.A. (TELCEL) consortium, which consists of BellSouth Corporation, Racal, and Cisneros Group under three Venezuelan companies. The three Venezuelan companies in the consortium hold their shares through a single offshore holding company.

Due to the traditional lack of telecommunications infrastructure, many of Venezuela's largest companies have built their own private data networks over the years. Use of fiber, very small aperture terminals (VSAT), microwave and other transmission technologies has been authorized for these purposes. Although a monopoly still exists for basic voice services, competition has been opened in most other sectors.

Proposals to implement a new Telecommunications Law are also on the government's ambitious telecommunications agenda. Two draft versions of a new Telecommunications Law were presented to the Venezuelan National Congress in early 1997, and at the time of printing were undergoing committee discussion. The first version was presented by the National Telecommunications Council (CONINTEL), which comprises telecommunications companies. One of the most important aspects of the law is a proposal for a free regime in which anyone can install and exploit telecommunications systems and services as long as they meet outlined technical requirements. Only the administration of limited resources, such as radio spectrum, and the assignment of frequencies and numbers, would remain in the hands of the government.

The second version, presented by the National Telecommunications Commission (Comisión Nacional de Telecomunicaciones, or CONATEL), proposed that the telecommunications sector remain under the control of the state, which would grant concessions to private companies. The state, in CONATEL's version of the law, would maintain exclusive control of the radio spectrum and frequencies, and in event of emergency, be able to take over telecommunications equipment. CONATEL also wants the state to continue to determine regulations for each telecommunications service and the conditions under which each is to be delivered. In addition, it is CONATEL's position that only corporate citizens and private individuals based in Venezuela should be able to provide telecommunications services.

Current Status

The telecommunications sector is the rising star in the Venezuelan economy, and it is fast becoming one of Venezuela's most significant industries, second in size only to petroleum. Since 1992, the telecommunications sector has benefited from more than US$6 billion in investments. It currently contributes 6% to Venezuela's GNP and is expected to increase that contribution to 7% by the year 2000. To date, there are over 180 telecommunications companies operating in Venezuela. Profits are soaring in the communications-hungry market. Stimulated by the government's granting of concessions for private networks, value-added services and data services, the telecommunications sector has reported impressive annual growth of nearly 23.4% over the past five years, in spite of the 1994 Venezuelan economic crisis.

To prepare for competition and achieve profitability, CANTV has taken aggressive steps to improve its service, quality and penetration. In 1991, telephone line penetration was only 8% of the population. By 1995, penetration had increased to 14% of the population covering 40% of demand, with plans for reaching 18% of the population by the year 2000, when CANTV's monopoly on basic voice service will end. By that time, CANTV expects to have digitized 80% of its lines. Currently, CANTV utilizes INTELSAT and PanAmSat satellite systems for international communications. The incorporation of INMARSAT's mobile communications system will facilitate both rural telecommunications and a more powerful infrastructure in populated areas. To meet the growing demand for international services, CANTV has also made a Bs. 9.44 billion investment in the Columbus II Project, a submarine fiber optic cable consortium of 57 companies from 45 countries.

Currently undergoing a change of ownership and control under the direction of the Depositor's Guarantee Fund (el Fondo de Garantía de Depósitos Bancarios, or FOGADE), Telecomunicaciones Bantel, C.A. (Bantel) competes with CANTV in the telecommunications market. Bantel, a LATINET affiliate, provides voice, video and information services, markets electronic equipment and holds satellite assets.

In a move to globalize, restructure and advance technology in the petroleum field, PDVSA (Petróleos de Venezuela, S.A.) has chosen to outsource its telecommunications activities. The oil conglomerate has formed a partnership, INTESA, with the North American company SAIC (Science Applications International Corp.). This private network constitutes the second-largest network in the country after CANTV.

Due to the long wait for wireline phone installation, cellular phone use has grown 135% in the last two years. Cellular telephone subscriber penetration in Venezuela has now reached 2%. TELCEL and Movilnet are in the final stages of converting their networks to digital. In addition to opening the market to a third cellular service provider, CONATEL is contemplating a concession for a personal communications service (PCS) system.

In 1997, CONATEL granted two telephone licenses for local service in rural areas for towns with fewer than 5,000 inhabitants. In central provinces, a license was granted to DIGITEL, while ELCA received a license for eastern provinces. The bidding procedure has been the subject of criticism and is being discussed in the National Congress. In January 1998, ELCA signed the granted concession and announced an initial investment of between US$30 million and US$40 million in new equipment installation for third quarter 1998 and a beginning of operations for fourth quarter 1998.

Following complaints about system overcrowding, in 1997 the national government ordered cellular companies TELCEL and Movilnet to suspend the offering of services to new clients. This Administrative Resolution was later repealed by a court decision on constitutional grounds.

The value-added data service sector is the fastest-growing and most profitable segment of the Venezuelan telecommunications industry. Over 30 concessions are registered to provide value-added data. Currently, 38 companies also offer Internet services.

Current Liberalization Status

A new telecommunications law, currently under discussion by the Congress, is expected to modify the status of liberalization prevailing in Venezuela. This is one of the most significant changes currently underway in the country and is a clear sign that the growth of the telecommunications sector requires a new legal framework, considering the evolution the sector has experienced over the past few years. As part of that evolution, the Venezuelan telecommunications market has been opened to foreign investment, and the country has committed to an open telephone market by the year 2000, as well as full competition in all services, such as cellular, data and paging.

Type of Service	Degree of Liberalization	Key Legislation	Date of Actual or Expected Liberalization	Comments
Local	Private monopoly Concession required	Venezuelan Telecommunications Law of 1940	1999	There is a new Telecoms Law under consideration by Congress.
Long Distance	Private monopoly Concession required		1999	Same as above
International	Private monopoly Concession required		1999	Same as above
Cellular	Partially liberalized Limited concessions		By 2000	
Paging	Partially liberalized Limited concessions		By 2000	
Value-added	Partially liberalized Limited concessions		By 2000	

Competitive Environment

The prevailing monopoly held by CANTV in local, long-distance and international voice service is expected to cease by the year 2000, when a significant change in the competitive environment will occur with the entry of new players in the telecommunications market. The cellular duopoly will also be affected in the near future with the possible granting of two or three additional concessions.

| Type of Service | Entire Market | | Top Two Players | | |
	Market Size*	Number of Players	Names	Annual Revenue*	Ownership
Local and Long Distance	Bs. 463 billion	1	CANTV	Bs. 463 billion	Government (partially privately held and partially publicly traded)
International	Bs. 147 billion	1	CANTV	Bs. 147 billion	
Cellular	Bs. 179 billion	2	TELCEL	Bs. 102 billion	Privately held
			Movilnet	Bs. 77 billion	Privately held
Paging	Bs. 4 billion	78	Not available		
Value-added	Not available	33	T-NET (TELCEL)	Not available	18 concessions granted in 1997
			CANTV		

* 1996–1997 CONATEL statistics.

Licensing Requirements

Simultaneous with CANTV's privatization, CONATEL was created in September 1991 to plan, regulate and supervise telecommunications services; recommend the granting of concessions and permits; promote investment and technological innovation; and coordinate with national and international parties on the technical aspects of telecommunications.

Local and long-distance service will remain a monopoly until 2000. Currently, CONATEL is under pressure from the private sector to eliminate the concession requirements for value-added data services to facilitate easier entry into this growing market.

Potential for Foreign Ownerships/Relationships

Venezuela's privatization program is one of the principal objectives of the government's economic program to stabilize and stimulate greater efficiency and modernization of the country. With regard to permits and concessions, CONATEL and other regulatory agencies work to promote the best atmosphere for capital investment while enforcing industry regulations to promote a stable environment. To facilitate the application process, CONATEL has reduced the response period for concession requests from between five and eight months to one month and ten days.

Potential for Upcoming Liberalization/Investment Opportunities

The telecommunications sector is expected to remain a vibrant, growing sector of the Venezuelan economy throughout the rest of this decade and into the next. Investment is surging, as companies fight to capture a piece of their target markets. Further

granting of concessions and permits is expected, because CONATEL's budget is funded by a mandatory 0.5% contribution of the concessionaires' annual gross income, which allows the regulatory body to maintain its financial autonomy from the government.

Calling for widespread reforms by further deregulation of this sector, CONATEL initiated a triennial plan that was expected to bring in approximately Bs. 755.2 billion in investment in 1996 (not including the sale of CANTV) in digital radio and TV, satellite services, information transfer, and personal communications. By the year 2000, CONATEL has projected telecommunications to reach Bs. 4,248 billion with the awarding of seven new services, as follows: PCS, rural telecommunications (the CANTV monopoly does not include towns with a population of under 5,000), digital television, mobile satellite communication systems, mobile satellite-based systems (transmissions via artificial satellite networks), the Simón Bolívar Satellite Project and a third cellular telephone operator.

To spur further privatization of the telecommunications sector, CONATEL is working with the Investment Funds of Venezuela (FIV), the presidentially appointed body that coordinates and promotes further privatization offers to national and foreign investors. CANTV shares were offered to Venezuelan citizens through banks in November 1996. The stock began trading on the New York and Caracas Stock Exchanges in January 1997.

Forms of Doing Business

Permanent Establishment

A permanent establishment (PE) is a fixed place of business in which the activities of a business are carried out. Sites may include places of management, a branch, an office, a factory, a workshop, a building site or a construction or installation project lasting more than 12 months. According to the Organic Tax Code, foreign entities maintaining a PE in Venezuela are considered domiciled for tax purposes. A foreign corporation not domiciled in Venezuela will be subject to tax on Venezuelan-sourced income. There are no specific telecommunications provisions for income tax purposes.

Business Entities

Foreign investors are free to operate directly in Venezuela or through a subsidiary or branch. The Superintendency of Foreign Investments (Superintendencia de Inversiones Extranjeras, or SIEX), an agency under the Ministry of Finance, supervises and enforces rules governing foreign investments, including direct foreign investment (i.e., capital contributions), external credits, and importation of technology. For both branches and subsidiaries, an initial notice must be given to the Commercial Registry in the form of a petition for registration as a national, mixed or foreign-owned company, and must include documentation of foreign currency and intangible assets.

In addition, a local representative with power of attorney and notification of SIEX is required. A 1% registration fee based upon the parent company's authorized capital is required for registration. This expense might cause larger investors to open an intermediate main office having minimal capital, thereby reducing the registration fee.

Local Branch of a Foreign Company. A branch or PE of a foreign corporation is considered to be a separate legal entity for income tax purposes. As such, only the income attributable to the branch is considered taxable. The branch income is taxable under the same regulations applied to corporations, as discussed below. The net income is subject to corporate income tax. However, there is no additional tax on after-tax profits, even if the income is distributed to the foreign head office.

Locally Incorporated Subsidiary of a Foreign Company. An incorporated subsidiary of a foreign company is considered to be a separate legal entity in which each shareholder's liability is limited to the shareholder's capital subscription. The net income resulting from activities carried out in Venezuela is taxable according to the corporate income tax rate, while dividend distributions are non-taxable. An incorporated subsidiary is the entity structure most commonly used by foreign investors because it permits greater tax planning flexibility than operating as a branch. Foreign company subsidiaries are at liberty to establish other Venezuelan subsidiaries and to acquire an equity interest in existing Venezuelan companies without prior approval from SIEX.

As of fiscal year 1991, affiliated companies cannot file consolidated tax returns unless the companies form a single taxpaying economic unit (i.e., the companies have the same shareholders or owners, or the activities carried out between the companies constitute more than 50% of all operations). Even though the concept of an economic unit was introduced in the 1994 Income Tax Regulation, there are no provisions regulating its tax treatment. Although taxpayers have filed consolidated tax returns since the regulation was published, the tax authorities have not been in favor of accepting these returns and the general public is still awaiting a tax audit of such a return to set the standard.

Joint Venture. A joint venture (cuenta en participación) is a contract in which two or more parties agree to share in the profits and losses of a specific project. There is typically a managing partner who is fully liable and a partner who contributes capital or services in return for a share of the profits or losses from the venture. Unlike the formal requirements necessary to establish a branch or subsidiary, only a written agreement must be documented by the joint venture or consortium. Under Venezuelan law, neither a joint venture nor a consortium has legal personality; therefore, a joint venture has no rights, obligations or assets of its own even if it is jointly owned by the parties. The participating parties have no proprietary rights to the property in the agreement.

Frequently used as flow-through vehicles, joint ventures and consortia are becoming more common among foreign investors to divide both the gains and losses among participating parties. For tax purposes, the managing partner and the contributing partners are jointly liable and must include in their tax returns their share of profits or losses as specified in the joint venture contract. A joint venture is required to file an informative return allocating the percentage of profit and loss received by each participant, and then, accordingly, each participant will present respective profits and losses when filing.

Local Funding Alternatives

Debt versus Equity

Interest incurred from debt is deductible. The income tax withholding rate depends upon the classification of the receiving entity. The rate is 4.95% for a non-domiciled bank or financial institution; 34%, which is applied to 95% of the payment, for a non-resident individual or a non-domiciled company incorporated abroad; or 5% for a domiciled company. Dividends are not subject to either income tax withholding or income tax. However, as a result of the adjustment-for-inflation rules, a distribution of dividends may reduce taxable equity.

A capital contribution arising from assets or the capitalization of debt to a shareholder produces a tax deduction, which is adjusted for inflation. If the monetary deduction is less than the annual rate of inflation, the indebted company obtains a greater tax benefit when shareholders capitalize the debt they have in their favor. A capital contribution is subject to a 1% registration fee, which is applied to the amount capitalized. Non-monetary intangible assets are adjusted for inflation, thereby creating a taxable effect netted against the inflation adjustment of the capital contribution.

Exchange Controls

Although the Central Bank of Venezuela still has the authority to intervene, exchange controls were liberalized in April 1996. A floating exchange rate has been implemented. The Central Bank of Venezuela maintains a 7.5% fluctuation band (i.e., an established ceiling and floor), based upon the monthly inflation rate it sets.

Business Acquisitions and Dispositions

Capital Contributions into an Existing Local Entity

Capital contributions are subject to a 1% registration fee and nominal stamp taxes not exceeding Bs. 50,000 or Bs. 60,000. There are no limitations or restrictions on the contribution of intangibles by a foreign company into an existing local company.

Purchase or Sale of Shares in a Local Entity

A gain on a sale of shares is taxable at the general individual or corporate tax rates unless the sale is made through a Venezuelan securities market, in which case a 1% proportional income tax is imposed on the value of the stocks and withheld at the source. The gross amount of the sale of shares outside the Venezuelan Stock Exchange is subject to a withholding tax rate of 5% for domiciled and non-domiciled legal entities, 3% for resident individuals, and 34% for non-resident individuals. There is no mechanism allowing a foreign company to step-up the tax basis in assets owned by a local company.

Purchase or Sale of Assets

In a purchase of assets, the transaction is subject to the wholesale and luxury tax (WLT) at a rate of 16.5%. The sale of selected luxury goods and services is subject to an additional 10% to 20% surtax over and above the WLT (e.g., up to 20% for satellite dishes). As mentioned above, tangible and intangible assets are subject to the tax on business assets.

The party selling an asset should declare the gain between the fiscal cost and the sale price. The price paid will form part of the cost when the asset is sold at fair market value.

Start-up Business Issues

Pre-operating Losses and Start-up/ Construction Costs

Business investigation costs incurred within Venezuela in the start-up phase are deductible. If incurred outside Venezuela, such costs can only be deducted if they arise from a technical-assistance or technological-services contract duly registered with SIEX.

The following start-up expenditures are deductible:

- Organizational and pre-operating expenses that are capitalized and amortized over a period of three to five years

- A reasonable amortization allowance for the cost of intangible property

- All taxes paid during a fiscal year except for income taxes

- Depreciation of tangible fixed assets, amortization of intangible fixed assets and appreciation of fixed assets when inflation adjustments are authorized

- Research and development expenses

Customs Duties and VAT

Customs duties applicable to telecommunications equipment are as follows:

Description of Merchandise	General Tariff
Wireless telephone with microphone	15%
Videophone	15%
Telefax	10%
Teletypes	5%
Replacement apparatus for telephone or telegraph systems	10%
Other telecommunications apparatus for current carriers or digital telecommunications	10%
Emission apparatus for radiotelephone, radio-telegraph, broadcasting or television, including receiving, recording or reproduction of sound apparatus; television cameras; video cameras, including fixed images	5%
Receiving apparatus of radiotelephone, radio-telegraph, or broadcasting	20%
Identifiable parts for broadcasting and transmission apparatus	15%
Integrated circuits and microstructure electronics	5%
Lines, cables and other conductors for electricity; fiber optic cables	15%

Wholesale and luxury tax is similar to a value-added tax in that it applies to the sale of goods and services. Regular telephony and Internet telephony are considered services, and are therefore subject to WLT. Regular residential telephony is exempt up to 1,000 pulses. The WLT rate established as of August 1, 1996, is 16.5%. For exports to non-domiciled entities, the tax rate is 0%. The amount of WLT paid in the exporter's purchase price is used as a tax credit against WLT debits or prior authorization to be assigned to another taxpayer, to offset other tax liabilities, or to be refunded. Transactions between the same legal entity and transfers of goods or services between an agency or representative of the company and its national or foreign parent are excluded from WLT. For companies in the pre-operating period, WLT credits will accumulate and may be carried forward indefinitely until they are completely offset.

Regarding industrial projects that began prior to the July 25, 1996, publication of the Partial Reform of the Wholesale and Luxury Tax Law: if the pre-operating period lasts for more than one year, WLT credits will accumulate and be adjusted for inflation until the business commences, and may be carried forward indefinitely until they are completely offset.

In some cases, the importation and acquisition of capital goods and services received during the pre-operating stage by taxpayers executing industrial projects may be totally or partially exonerated from the wholesale and luxury tax for a period of up to five years. Currently this exoneration is under a modification proposal in order to allow a simplification of the system.

Loss Carryovers

Although net operating losses cannot be carried back, they may be carried forward for three years. Losses suffered by transparent entities may be used by partners as a deduction against taxable income.

Operating Considerations

Corporate Income Taxes

Venezuelan-sourced income for both domiciled and non-domiciled entities is subject to income tax. Foreign-sourced income is not taxable unless the statutes of the Income Tax Law state otherwise. Pressure from other countries is being applied for Venezuela to adopt the global income tax base.

Venezuelan-sourced income is defined as income, paid in cash or in-kind, from economic activities carried out in Venezuela or from property there. Income-producing activities include the formation, transfer, exchange or assignment of the use or the right to use tangible or intangible property. Interest paid by domiciled companies; rent and gains from the sale of movable and immovable, and tangible and intangible, goods located in Venezuela; royalties for intangible property used in Venezuela; fees paid for technical assistance and services used in Venezuela (regardless of where the services are performed); and the market price of property or services received in a barter transaction constitute Venezuelan income. All legal entities, whether domiciled or not, are subject to the income tax rates in the table below.

The withholding tax is creditable against the final income tax liability. Whenever there is an excess of withholding taxes, the taxpayer can either obtain a refund or use the excess tax as a credit against tax liabilities in subsequent years.

Capital Gains Taxes

Capital gains from the sale of property are subject to the ordinary income tax. If a sale of shares occurs through the Venezuelan Stock Exchange, a 1% tax, withheld at the source, is levied on the amount realized, regardless of the amount gained or lost.

Tax Holidays and Exemptions

No tax credits are available to new entities participating in telecommunications activities. However, a ruling in November 1997 issued by the Venezuelan tax authorities stated that the activity of cellular services rendered by TELCEL could be considered industrial in nature. Previously, telecommunications activities were not so considered. Consequently, TELCEL was given the right to enjoy a tax credit of 20% of the value of its investments in new fixed assets (other than land) applied to the increase of productivity. (The Venezuelan Income Tax Law provides for a 20% tax credit on the amount of new investments in new fixed assets for those taxpayers engaged in industrial and agro-industrial activities.)

This tax credit ruling is only applicable to TELCEL, and can be modified at any time by the tax authorities. However, TELCEL would not be subject to tax penalties if it were to use the above-

Income Bracket in Tax Units (TU)*				Income Bracket in Bs.	Tax Rate
Up to 2,000 TU				Bs. 0–10,800,000	15%
For the amount exceeding	2,000 TU	up to	3,000 TU	Bs. 10,800,000–16,200,000	22%
For the amount exceeding	3,000 TU			Bs. 16,200,000 and over	34%

* The income tax is calculated using tax units (TU). The TU conversion rate as of June 4, 1997 was Bs. 5,400 per TU.

mentioned tax credit to determine its income tax liability and the ruling were ultimately changed.

Other taxpayers engaged in the telecommunications sector activities can request from the Venezuelan tax authorities a formal opinion on the classification of their activities as industrial. This tax credit benefit would be applicable only until 1999.

Depreciation/Cost-Recovery Conventions/Accelerated Deductions

Normal and necessary costs incurred in Venezuela to produce taxable income are deductible for income tax purposes. If the income is taxed on an accrual base, expenses are deductible when incurred; if the income is taxed on a cash basis, expenses are deductible when paid. The following business expenses are deductible:

- Organizational and pre-operating expenses that are capitalized and amortized under the straight-line method over a period of three to five years

- Interest paid on borrowed funds, so long as a Venezuelan branch is not paying its foreign home office

- Royalties, fees and similar payment for technical assistance or services used in Venezuela, except fees paid to foreign entities when the same services are available in Venezuela

- All taxes for economic activities or income-producing property paid during a fiscal year, except income taxes

- Depreciation of tangible fixed assets and amortization of intangible fixed assets used to produce income, and appreciation of fixed assets when inflation adjustments are authorized. Depreciation methods include straight-line or unit-of-production methods depending on the business. A change in the method of depreciation and amortization must be authorized by the tax administration

- Rental payments for real or personal property used to generate income

- Research and development expenses

- Expenses for ordinary repairs, provided that the repairs are made in Venezuela and do not prolong the life of the asset or create an extension of the original structure

- Advertising expenses

Transfer Pricing Rules

Various tax laws (e.g., the Estate and Gift Tax, the Wholesale and Luxury Tax, and the Organic Customs Law) exist that use a fair market value concept, which is indirectly imposed on transfer pricing transactions. There are plans for additional legislation in this area. The tax administration presented a project containing transfer pricing rules drafted in the same language as the WLT. It was to be discussed in the 1998 Congressional sessions.

Transfers of Patents, Trademarks and Software

Though prior authorization is not required, licensing, technical assistance, and technological services agreements must be registered with the SIEX within 60 days of a contract's completion. The following ventures must be submitted to the SIEX:

- Use and distribution of trademarks with foreign ownership

- Use of patents pertaining to inventions, improvements, and industrial models and designs

- Supply of technical know-how via plans, models and personnel

- Engineering for installations, manufacturing or products, and execution of industrial and construction projects

- Technical assistance

- Management and operation consulting

The registration of these agreements ensures the right to remit royalties and fees abroad. Until the agreements are registered, the contracts are unenforceable and fees or royalties cannot be paid. Once the exclusivity of the property rights has expired, no royalties or similar payments are allowed for the use of trademarks, industrial procedures, patents or models. Moreover, following a Supreme Court decision, if the necessary registration is not filed, royalties paid by a Venezuelan licensee to a non-domiciled licensor may not be deductible for income tax purposes.

Costs incurred are deductible when duly registered with the SIEX and when income taxes are withheld and paid within the time period established in the legislation regulating such matters. While the granting of a license for the use of a brand is subject to withholding tax, the tax is applied to the sale of such intangible asset.

Service Fees

Services are subject to income tax withholding. Payments made by Venezuelan legal entities or consortia for non-mercantile professional activities are subject to a 5% withholding rate for domiciled legal entities, 3% for resident individuals and 34% for non-resident individuals. For payments originating from royalties, technical assistance and technological services supplied or rendered from abroad, the income tax withholding is calculated with a tax base of 90%, 30% and 50%, respectively. With regard to the same services, non-resident individuals are subject to a 34% withholding rate and non-domiciled entities follow the above-mentioned graduated tax schedule of 15%, 22% and 34%.

For payments made to contractors or subcontractors to perform construction or to render services in Venezuela, the same graduated tax rates described above apply to non-domiciled entities, while a rate of 34% is applied to non-resident individuals. Domiciled legal entities are subject to a 2% withholding rate and resident individuals to a 1% rate.

When a non-domiciled entity renders both technical assistance and technological services from abroad and the service contract does not specify the proportion of each service, 25% is considered to be technical assistance and 75% is deemed technological assistance. If the contract contains no provision stating what percentage of the services are rendered from abroad, 40% of the service fees is considered payment for services rendered within Venezuela.

Value-Added Tax, Sales Tax and/or Other Pertinent Taxes

Wholesale and Luxury Tax. The wholesale and luxury tax (WLT) replaced Venezuela's value-added tax (VAT) in August 1994. The WLT is a turnover tax imposed on the value added to the product at each stage of production, from the raw materials to the ultimate producer or wholesaler. Under the WLT, taxable activities include the sale of goods, rendering of independent services, import of goods and services, and transfer of these goods or services to affiliated companies. For imports, the receiving entity assumes responsibility for the WLT on behalf of the seller; likewise, when the seller is a non-domiciled entity, the purchaser is liable for the WLT. The WLT rate established as of August 1, 1996, is 16.5%. On the sale or import of specified luxury goods and services, an additional surtax at a rate of 10% to 20% may be imposed.

Foreign companies that incur costs subject to WLT can recover only the WLT paid, offsetting it with the WLT received from customers once the company is operational.

Tax on Business Assets. In an effort to curtail income tax evasion, the Tax on Business Assets (TBA) was enacted in 1993. All entities, whether or not domiciled, that are subject to the income tax must pay TBA at 1% on the average yearly inflation-adjusted value of the taxpayer's taxable assets. In the case of foreign capital taxpayers such as branches, agencies or subsidiaries, the net debits with the parent company or head office are deemed taxable assets. In the case of financial leases

governed by the General Banking Law, the lessees of the property are subject to the TBA. Because the tax serves as a minimum income tax, TBA liability may be credited against income tax or carried forward for up to three years. This tax may also be used as a U.S. foreign tax credit, although the use of the carry-forward provision may be detrimental to foreign tax credits. Exemptions to TBA are as follows:

•   New enterprises are exempt during the pre-operational period and two years subsequent. For companies planning to operate for three years or less, taxation begins on the date of the first sale.

•   Tax reductions of 50% apply to those companies that trade with public services regulated by the government.

•   Investments in shares of corporations or quotas of other legal entities are exempt.

•   In the case of the exportation of goods and services, the tax base is reduced.

Stamp Tax. To obtain concessions for commercial telecommunications, the following tax tariffs are paid:

Authorization for contracts for the transfer of technology	Bs. 108,000
Basic telecommunications services	Bs. 27,000,000
Services for public telecommunications terminals	Bs. 540,000
Television services and services of mobile telecommunications provided by satellite, in order to be rendered in cities: — Cities with more than one million inhabitants — Cities with fewer than one million inhabitants	 Bs. 54,000,000 Bs. 13,500,000
Satellite telecommunications systems coordinated by Venezuela	Bs. 5,400,000
International paging services	Bs. 810,000
National paging services	Bs. 162,000
Value-added, telematic and data line merger "trunking" services	Bs. 540,000
Information conversion network services and private network telecommunications services	Bs. 5,400,000
Rural and remote telecommunications services	Bs. 162,000
Permits to operate non-commercial telecommunications services	Bs. 54,000

Stamp tax tariffs are adjusted for inflation each calendar year in harmony with the change of value of the tax unit. The TU conversion rate as of June 4, 1997, was Bs. 5,400 per TU.

Other Telecommunications-Specific Taxes. Telecommunications services owned and operated by private entities also pay additional taxes. Telephone companies pay between 5%

and 10% of the revenue of the connections made and one Bolivar per kilometer per year for all telephone lines. The President has the authority to reduce this tax to Bs. 0.25 per kilometer per year if the expense is considerable.

Mobile cellular operators pay a tax on their gross income, beginning at 6% in year one of operation and increasing 1% for the following five years. Thus, from year five on, mobile operators pay a 10% tax.

Local and Provincial Taxes

Municipalities impose an annual business tax varying from 0.25% to 10% on the gross receipts of enterprises performing any commercial activity within the municipality. Since the municipalities establish their own rates, the licensing rate for telecommunications services typically ranges from 0.5% to 0.6% of the gross receipts. Because a clear definition of what constitutes gross receipts has not yet been established, each municipality attempts to tax every business activity taking place within its jurisdiction, often resulting in double taxation or more. In addition to various other municipal tariffs and fees, there is also an urban property tax based on the productivity of the property or its value.

However, a recent Supreme Court decision regarding the taxability of telecommunications activities (Telcel Celular, C.A. vs. Maracaibo Municipality) established that, in its particular case, such activity could only be taxed by the central government, denying any tax power to municipalities. This particular decision applied only to TELCEL, but other telecommunications companies could use it as a very important precedent in attempting to get a favorable decision on their behalf.

For Additional Information, Contact:

Eduardo Ramírez-Mendez
Tax Partner
and
Carlos Brown-García
Consulting Partner
Telecommunications Specialist
Multicentro Los Palos Grandes, Piso 8
Caracas, Miranda 1062
Venezuela
Telephone: 58 (2) 285 5722 or 283 7833 (Ramirez-Mendez)
            58 (2) 285 5722 or 284 7711 (Brown-Garcia)
Fax: 58 (2) 285 6960
E-mail: edur@telcel.net.ve (Ramirez-Mendez)
        cbrownclve@true.net (Brown-Garcia)

Appendixes

Acronyms, Abbreviations and Symbols

Companies, Agencies and Organizations

Acronyms, Abbreviations and Symbols

	Definition and Chapter(s) in Which Acronym, Abbreviation or Symbol Used
£	British Pound—currency
¥	Yen—Japanese currency
A.S.	Anonim Sirket—joint-stock company (Turkey)
a.s.	Akciová spolecnost—joint-stock company (Czech Republic, Slovakia)
ACA	Australian Communications Authority (Australia)
ACCC	Australian Competition and Consumer Commission (Australia)
ACE	Agrupamento Complementar de Empresas—complementary groupings of companies (Portugal)
ACT	Advance Corporation Tax (Ireland, UK)
ADSL	Asymmetric Digital Subscriber Line (New Zealand)
AE	Approved Enterprise (Israel)
AenP	Asociación en Participación (Mexico)
AG	Aktiengesellschaft—corporation (Austria, Germany)
AIL	Approved Issuer Levy (New Zealand)
AMPS	Advance Mobile Phone System (Hong Kong, Indonesia, Russia, Vietnam)
AMT	Alternative Minimum Tax (USA)
AMTI	Alternative Minimum Taxable Income (USA)

	Definition and Chapter(s) in Which Acronym, Abbreviation or Symbol Used
ANS	Ansvarlig Selskap—partnership with unlimited liability (Norway)
APA	Advanced Pricing Agreement (Canada)
ÁPV	Állami Privatizációs és Vagyonkezelô Részvénytársaság (Hungary)
ARP	Address Resolution Protocol (Finland)
ART	Autorité de Régulation des Télécommunications—Telecommunications Regulatory Authority (France)
AS	Aksjeselskap—private joint-stock company (Norway)
ASA	Almennaksjeselskap—public joint-stock company (Norway)
ATM	Asynchronous Transfer Mode (New Zealand, USA)
ATS	Austrian Schillings—currency
AUD	Australian Dollar—currency
AUSTEL	Australian Telecommunications Authority (Australia)
BAWAG	Bank für Arbeit und Wirtschaft AG (Austria)
Bayr.LB	Bayerische Landesbank AG (Austria)
BBV	Banco Bilbao Vizcaya (Spain)
BCC	Business Cooperation Contract (Vietnam)

Definition and Chapter(s) in Which Acronym, Abbreviation or Symbol Used

BCH	Banco Central Hispano (Spain)
BEF	Belgian Franc—currency
BIPT	Belgian Institute of Post and Telecommunications (Belgium)
BITT	Banking and Insurance Transactions Tax (Turkey)
BKPM	Badan Koordinasi Penanaman Modal—Investment Coordinating Board (Indonesia)
BMPT	Bundesminister für Post und Telekommunikation (Germany)
BNL	Banca Nazionale del Lavoro—National Bank of Lavoro (Italy)
BOC	Bell Operating Company (USA)
BOT	Build-Operate-Transfer (Indonesia, Vietnam)
BPI	Banco Português de Investimento, S.A. (Portugal)
Bs.	Bolívar—Venezuelan currency
BT	British Telecom (Belgium, Ireland, Italy, Portugal, Spain, UK)
BV	Besloten Vennootschap—limited liability company (Belgium, Hungary, Netherlands)
C$	Canadian Dollar—currency
C.A.	Compañía Anónima (Venezuela)
CANTV	Compañía Anónima Nacional Teléfonos de Venezuela (Venezuela)
CATV	Cable Television (UK)
CBR	Central Bank of Russia (Russia)
CDMA	Call Division Multiple Access (Chile, Czech Republic, Hong Kong, Korea, Russia, Ukraine, USA, Vietnam)
CEFTA	Central European Free Trade Association (Czech Republic, Hungary, Poland, Romania)
CGE	Compagnie Générale des Eaux (France)
CGT	Capital Gains Tax (Australia)
CGV	Compagnie Générale de Vidéocommunication (France)
CHF	Confédération Helvétique Francs—Swiss Francs—currency (Switzerland)

Definition and Chapter(s) in Which Acronym, Abbreviation or Symbol Used

CIE	Comisión Nacional de Inversiones Extranjeras—Foreign Investment Commission (Mexico)
CIF	Cost, Insurance and Freight (Austria, Belgium, China, Denmark, Finland, France, Germany, India, Ireland, Italy, Netherlands, Peru, Portugal, Spain, Sweden, UK)
CIS	Commonwealth of Independent States (Ukraine)
CJV	Cooperative Joint Venture (China)
CLEC	Competitive Local Exchange Carrier (USA)
CLP	Chilean Pesos—currency
CMRS	Cellular Mobile Radio Services (Canada)
CNC	Comisión Nacional de Comunicaciones—National Commission of Communications (Argentina)
COFETEL	Comisión Federal Telecomunicaciones—Federal Telecommunications Commission (Mexico)
CONATEL	Comisión Nacional de Telecomunicaciones—National Telecommunications Commission (Venezuela)
CPT	Compañía Peruana de Teléfonos Limitada (Peru)
CRTC	Canadian Radio-television and Telecommunications Commission (Canada)
CSG	Contribution Sociale Généralisée—supplementary social security contribution in aid of underprivileged (France)
CT	Consumption Tax (Japan)
CT-2 or CT2	Cordless Telephony Generation 2 (Korea, UK, Vietnam)
CTC	Chubu Telecommunications Company (Japan)
CTC	Compañía Telecomunicaciones de Chile S.A. (Chile)
CTI	Compañia de Teléfonos del Interior (Argentina)
CTU	Cesky Telekomunikaoní Úrad—Czech Telecommunications Office (Czech Republic)
CUFIN	Cuenta de Utilidad Fiscal Neta (Mexico)

Definition and Chapter(s) in Which Acronym, Abbreviation or Symbol Used

CUODE	Classification According to Usage or Economic Destination (Peru)
CUP	Comparable Uncontrolled Price (Poland)
CV	Capital Variable (Mexico)
CV	Commanditaire Vennootschap—limited partnership (Netherlands)
CWC	Cable & Wireless Communications (UK)
CZK	Czech Koruna—currency
DACOM	Data Communications Corporation of Korea (Korea)
D-AMPS	Digital Advanced Mobile Phone Service (New Zealand, Russia, Ukraine, Vietnam)
DASA	Daimler-Benz Aerospace AG (Argentina)
DBM	Declining-Balance Method (Japan)
DBP	Deutsche Bundespost (Germany)
DCC	Digital Cellular Communication (Ukraine)
DCS	Digital Cellular System (Austria, Finland, France, Germany, Hong Kong, Ireland, Italy, Netherlands, Malaysia, Norway, Poland, Portugal, Spain, Sweden, UK)
DDI	Daini Denden Inc. (Japan)
DECT	Digital European Cordless Telecommunication (Finland, Italy, Portugal)
DGPT	Department General of Posts and Telecommunications (Vietnam)
DGPT	Direction Générale des Postes et Télécommunications—Administration of Posts and Telecommunications (France)
DGT	Directorate General of Telecommunications (China)
DKK	Denmark Krone—currency
DL	Decreto Ley—Law Decree (Chile)
DM	Deutsche Mark—German currency
DOT	Department of Telecommunications (India)
D.S.	Decreto Supremo—Supreme Decree (Peru)
DTA	Double Tax Agreement (New Zealand)
DTAA	Double-Taxation Avoidance Agreement (India)

Definition and Chapter(s) in Which Acronym, Abbreviation or Symbol Used

EC	European Community (Belgium, Netherlands, Sweden)
ECB	External Commercial Borrowing (India)
EDI	Electronic Data Interchange (Australia, China, India)
EEA	European Economic Area (Austria, Finland, Norway)
EEC	European Economic Council (Belgium)
EEIG	European Economic Interest Group (Portugal)
EFTA	European Free Trade Association (Hungary, Norway, Poland, Romania)
EFT-POS	Electronic Funds Transfer at the Point of Sale (New Zealand)
EJV	Equity Joint Venture (China)
ENTEL	Empresa Nacional de Telecomunicaciones (Argentina, Chile)
ENTEL PERU	Empresa Nacional de Telecomunicaciones del Perú S.A. (Peru)
ERMES	European Radio Messaging System (Czech Republic, Portugal, Russia)
ETAC	Extended Total Access Communication (Malaysia)
ETB	Empresa de Teléfonos de Bogota (Colombia)
ETG	EDP, Transgás and Gás de Portugal—a consortium (Portugal)
EU	European Union (Austria, Belgium, Czech Republic, Denmark, Finland, France, Germany, Hungary, Ireland, Italy, Netherlands, Norway, Poland, Portugal, Romania, Slovakia, Spain, Sweden, Switzerland, Turkey, UK)
FCC	Federal Communications Commission (USA)
FCFS	First-Come-First-Served (Canada)
FCP	Fonds Communs de Placement—mutual fund (France)
FDI	Foreign Direct Investment (Korea, Portugal)
FECL	Foreign Exchange Control Law (Korea)
FEIT	Foreign Enterprise Income Tax (China)
FF	French Franc—currency

	Definition and Chapter(s) in Which Acronym, Abbreviation or Symbol Used
FI	Financial Institution (Hong Kong)
FID	Foreign Investment Directorate (Turkey)
FIE	Foreign Investment Enterprise (China)
FIM	Finnish Markka—currency
FIPB	Foreign Investment Promotion Board (India)
FIV	Investment Funds of Venezuela (Venezuela)
FLAG	Fiber-optic Link Around the Globe (Ukraine)
FLEX	Flexible high speed coding (Russia)
FOB	Free On Board (Australia)
FOGADE	el Fondo de Garantía de Depósitos Bancarios—Depositor's Guarantee Fund (Venezuela)
FTNS	Fixed Telecommunications Network Services (Hong Kong)
FY	Fiscal Year (Japan)
GAAP	Generally Accepted Accounting Principles (Japan, Colombia, India, Switzerland)
GATT	General Agreement on Tariffs and Trade (Australia, Austria, Belgium, Denmark, Finland, France, Germany, Hungary, Ireland, Italy, Japan, Netherlands, Portugal, South Africa, Spain, Sweden, UK, USA)
GbR	Gesellschaft bürgerlichen Rechts—partnership (Germany)
GKRcH	Gosudarstvennaya Komissia Radiochastot—State Radio Frequency Commission (Russia)
GmbH	Gesellschaft mit beschränkter Haftung—corporation (Austria, Germany)
GNP	Gross National Product (Mexico, Venezuela)
GSM	Global System for Mobile Communications (Australia, Austria, Belgium, China, Czech Republic, Denmark, Finland, France, Germany, Hong Kong, Hungary, India, Indonesia, Ireland, Israel, Italy, Malaysia, Netherlands, New Zealand, Norway, Poland, Portugal, Romania, Russia, Slovakia, South Africa, Spain, Sweden, Switzerland, Turkey, UK, Ukraine, Vietnam)

	Definition and Chapter(s) in Which Acronym, Abbreviation or Symbol Used
GSP	Generalized System of Preferences (Norway)
GST	Goods and Services Tax (Canada, New Zealand)
HK$	Hong Kong Dollar—currency
HKTC	Hong Kong Telephone Company Limited (Hong Kong)
HKTI	Hongkong Telecom International Limited (Hong Kong)
HST	Harmonized Sales Tax (Canada)
HTC	Hungarian Telecommunications Company Ltd. (Magyar Távközlési Részvénytársaság—MATÁV Rt.) (Hungary)
HUF	Hungarian Forint—currency
ICEP	Investimentos, Comércio e Turismo de Portugal—Foreign Trade Institute (Portugal)
ICI	International Communications Income (USA)
ICP	Instituto das Comunicações de Portugales—Portuguese Communications Institute (Portugal)
IDC	International Digital Communications (Japan)
ILEC	Incumbent Local Exchange Carrier (USA)
Inc.	Incorporated
INCOMEX	Instituto Colombiano de Comercio Exterior—Colombian Institute of Foreign Commerce (Colombia)
IPO	Initial Public Offering (Hungary, Israel)
IR£	Irish Pound—currency
IRAP	Imposta Regionale sulle Attivita Produttive—regional production tax (Italy)
IRPEG	Imposta sul Reddito delle Persone Giuridiche (Italy)
IRS	Internal Revenue Service (USA)
ISAF	Societatea de Automatizari si Semnalizari Feroviare (Romania)
ISDN	Integrated Services Digital Network (Japan, Korea, New Zealand, Norway, Ukraine, USA)

Definition and Chapter(s) in Which Acronym, Abbreviation or Symbol Used

ISP	Internet Service Provider (Austria, Portugal, Sweden, Turkey, UK)
ISR	International Simple Resale (Hong Kong, UK)
ITA	Information Technology Agreement (Austria, Belgium, Denmark, Finland, France, Germany, Ireland, Italy, Netherlands, Norway, Poland, Portugal, Spain, Sweden, UK, USA)
ITU	International Telecommunications Union (Hong Kong)
ITUR	Italy, Turkey, Ukraine and Russia—project (Ukraine)
IVAN	International Value-Added Network (Hong Kong)
IXC	Interexchange Carrier (USA)
JT	Japan Telecom (Japan)
JTM	Jabatan Telekom Malaysia (Malaysia)
JVC	Joint Venture Company (India)
KDD	Kokusai Denshin Denwa Co., Ltd. (Japan)
Kft.	Korlátolt Felelösségü Társaság—limited liability company (Hungary)
KG	Kommanditgesellschaft—partnership (Germany)
KK	Kabushiki Kaisha (Japan)
KPN	Koninklijke PTT Nederland NV (Ireland, Netherlands)
KS	Kommandittselskap—partnership with limited liability (Norway)
KSO	Kerja Sama Operasi—unincorporated joint venture/joint cooperation agreement (Indonesia)
KT	Korea Telecom (Korea)
Lda.	Limitada—limited liability company (Portugal)
LIBOR	London Interbank Offered Rate (Chile, Peru, South Africa)
LISR	Ley del Impuesto Sobre la Renta—Mexican Income Tax Law (Mexico)
Lit	Italian Lira—currency

Definition and Chapter(s) in Which Acronym, Abbreviation or Symbol Used

LLC	Limited Liability Company (USA)
LMCS	Local Multipoint Communications Systems (Canada)
Ltd.	Limited
M&E	Machinery and Equipment (Sweden)
M&P	Manufacturing and Processing (Canada)
MATÁV Rt	Magyar Távközlési Részvénytársaság—Hungarian Telecommunications Company Ltd. (HTC) (Hungary)
MCL	Mercury Communications Limited (UK)
MEI	Ministry of Electronics Industry (China)
METP	Ministry of Energy, Telecommunication and Posts (Malaysia)
MFE	Ministry of Finance and Economy (Korea)
MFJ	Modified Final Judgment (USA)
MFN	Most-Favored Nation (China)
MGTS	Moscow Telephone (Russia)
MHz	Megahertz
MIC	Ministry of Information and Communication (Korea)
MIMOS	Malaysian Institute of Microelectronic Services Bhd. (Malaysia)
MITI	Ministry of International Trade and Industry (Malaysia)
MOC	Ministry of Communications (Israel, Russia)
MODVAT	Modified Value-Added Tax (India)
MOF	Ministry of Finance (France, Indonesia)
MOST	Ministry of Science and Technology (Korea)
MPI	Ministry of Power Industry (China)
MPI	Ministry of Planning and Investment (Vietnam)
MPT	Ministry of Posts and Telecommunications (China, Japan)
MR	Ministry of Railways (China)
MSC	Multimedia Supercorridor (Malaysia)
MSS	Moscow Cellular Telecommunications (Russia)
MTN	Mobile Telephone Networks (Pty) Ltd (South Africa)

	Definition and Chapter(s) in Which Acronym, Abbreviation or Symbol Used
MTNL	Mahanagar Telephone Nigam Limited (India)
MTPT	Ministry of Tourism, Posts and Telecommunications (Indonesia)
NAFTA	North American Free Trade Agreement (Canada, Mexico, USA)
NAMPS	Narrowband Analog Mobile Phone Service (Israel)
NBP	National Bank of Poland (Poland)
NCC	New Common Carrier (Japan)
NLG	Netherlands Guilder—currency
NMT	Nordic Mobile Telephone (Czech Republic, Denmark, Finland, Indonesia, Malaysia, Norway, Romania, Russia, Slovakia, Turkey, Ukraine)
NOK	Norwegian Krone—currency
NRCWT	Non-Resident Contractors Withholding Tax (New Zealand)
NRWT	Non-Resident Withholding Tax (New Zealand)
NS	Nuevos Soles—Peruvian currency
NTP	National Telecommunications Policy (Malaysia)
NTT	Nippon Telegraph & Telephone Corporation (Indonesia, Japan, Russia, Vietnam)
NV	Naamloze Vennootschap—unlimited liability company (Ireland, Netherlands)
NZ$	New Zealand Dollar—currency
OECD	Organization for Economic Cooperation and Development (Argentina, Australia, Austria, Belgium, Colombia, Denmark, Finland, France, Germany, Hungary, India, Ireland, Israel, Italy, Japan, Netherlands, New Zealand, Portugal, Slovakia, Spain, Sweden, Switzerland)
OFCOM	Office Fédéral de la Communication (Switzerland)
OFTA	Office of the Telecommunications Authority (Hong Kong)
OFTEL	Office of Telecommunications (UK)
OHG	Offene Handelsgesellschaft—partnership (Germany)

	Definition and Chapter(s) in Which Acronym, Abbreviation or Symbol Used
OIC	Overseas Investment Commission (New Zealand)
OMP	Osaka Media Port (Japan)
ONP	Open Network Provision (Belgium)
OPI	Omnitel Pronto Italia (Italy)
OSIPTEL	Organismo Supervisor de Inversión Privada en Telecomunicaciones (Peru)
PBX	Private Branch Exchange (Belgium)
PCN	Personal Communications Network (Indonesia, Ireland, Korea, Malaysia, Turkey, UK)
PCS	Personal Communications Service (Argentina, Canada, Chile, Hong Kong, Korea, USA, Venezuela)
PDVSA	Petróleos de Venezuela, S.A. (Venezuela)
PE	Permanent Establishment (All Chapters)
PHS	Personal Handy-phone System (Indonesia, Japan)
Plc	Public Limited Company
PNET	Public Non-Exclusive Telecommunications service (Hong Kong)
POCSAG	Post Office Code Standard Advisory Group (Russia)
POSCO	Pohang Iron & Steel Co., Ltd. (Hong Kong)
PPI	Producer Price Index (Hungary)
PRC	People's Republic of China (China, Hong Kong)
PST	Provincial Sales Tax (Canada)
PSTN	Public Switched Telephony Network (Hong Kong, UK)
PSTS	Public Switched Telecommunications Services (South Africa)
PT	Portugal Telecom, S.A. (Portugal)
PT	Post-og Teletilsynet (Norway)
PTA	Post und Telekom Austria AG (Austria)
Pta	Peseta—Spanish currency
PTE	Portuguese Escudo—currency
PTIC	China National Posts and Telecommunications Industry Corp. (China)

	Definition and Chapter(s) in Which Acronym, Abbreviation or Symbol Used		**Definition and Chapter(s) in Which Acronym, Abbreviation or Symbol Used**
PTO	Public Telephony Operator (UK)	S.A.	Joint stock company (Poland)
PTT	Post Telephone and Telegraph (Finland, Hungary, Norway, Romania, Switzerland, Turkey)	S.A.	Sociedad anónima (Argentina, Chile, Colombia, Mexico, Spain); Sociedade anónima (Portugal)
PTT	Post und Telegraphanverwalt (Austria)	SA	Société Anonyme—joint stock company (France)
Pty	Proprietary		
PUC	Public Utility Commission (USA)	S.A. de C.V.	Sociedad anónima de capital variable (Mexico)
		SAEC	State Administration of Exchange Control (China)
QST	Quebec Sales Tax (Canada)	SAIC	Science Applications International Corp. (Venezuela)
		SANEF	Société des Autoroutes du Nord et de l'Est de la France (France)
R	Ruble—Russian currency		
R	Rand—South African currency	S.a.p.a.	Società in accomandita per azioni—incorporated partnership in which the liability of certain partners is without limit and is taxed as a corporation (Italy)
R&D	Research and Development (Australia, Belgium, Canada, Czech Republic, Finland, Netherlands, Portugal, Spain)		
R&E	Research and Experimentation (USA)	SAPRR	Société des Autoroutes Paris-Rhin-Rhône (France)
RASDAQ	Romanian Association of Securities Dealers Automated Quotation (Romania)	SARL	Société à Responsabilité Limitée—limited liability company (France)
RATP	Régie Autonome des Transports Parisiens (France)	SAS	Société par Actions Simplifiée—simplified joint stock company (France)
RBI	Reserve Bank of India (India)	S.a.s.	Società in accomandita semplice—partnership in which the liability of certain partners is limited by agreement to the amount of their capital contribution (Italy)
RBOC	Regional Bell Operating Company (USA)		
RCI	Rogers Communications Inc. (Canada)		
RDS	Remboursement de la Dette Sociale—social debt reimbursement (France)		
RDS	Radio Data System (Czech Republic)	SATRA	South African Telecommunications Regulatory Authority (South Africa)
RHQ	Regional Headquarters (Australia)	SBB	Schweizerische Bundesbahn—Swiss Railways (Switzerland)
RM	Malaysian Ringgit—currency	SCA	Société en Commandite par Actions—limited stock partnership (France)
Rmb	Renminbi—Chinese currency		
Rp	Rupiah—Indonesian currency	SCS	Société en Commandite Simple—limited partnership (France)
RPI	Retail Price Index (UK)		
RSC	Regional Services Council (South Africa)	SCT	Secretaria de Comunicaciones y Transportes—Secretary of Communications and Transport (Mexico)
RSS	Remote Subscriber Switch (Norway, Sweden)		
RSU	Remote Subscriber Unit (Norway)	SDH	Synchronous Digital Hierarchy (Slovakia)
Rt.	Részvénytársaság—a shareholding company, equivalent to Ltd. (Hungary)	SEC	Securities and Exchange Commission (USA)
		SEK	Swedish Krona—currency
RTT	Régie des Télégraphes et des Téléphones (Belgium)	SFR	Société Française du Radiotéléphone (France)
RUSF	Resource Utilization Support Fund (Turkey)	SG&A	Selling, General & Administrative (Indonesia)

	Definition and Chapter(s) in Which Acronym, Abbreviation or Symbol Used
SHCP	Secretaría de Hacienda y Crédito Publico (Mexico)
SICAV	Société d'Investissement à Capital Variable—investment company (France)
SIEX	Superintendencia de Inversiones Extranjeras—Superintendency of Foreign Investments (Venezuela)
SK	Slovakian Korina—currency
SLM	Straight-Line Method (Japan)
SMDS	Switched Multi-megabit Data Service (USA)
SNC	Société en Nom Collectif—general partnership (France)
S.n.c.	Società in nome colletivo—general partnership in which the liability of partners is not limited (Italy)
SNCF	Société Nationale des Chemins de Fer—National Railway Company (France)
Sp. z o.o.	Limited liability company (Poland)
S.p.A.	Società per Azioni—public limited liability company (Italy)
S.R.L.	Sociedad de Responsibilidad Limitada (Colombia, Mexico, Spain)
S.r.l.	Società per responsibilità limitata—private limited liability company (Italy)
SRLY	Separate Return Limitation Year (USA)
S.r.o.	Spolecnost s rucením omezeným (Czech Republic)
STC	Secondary Tax on Companies (South Africa)
STF	Statens Teleforvaltning—the telecommunications regulatory authority (Norway)
STM	Synchronous Transport Module (Ukraine)
SUBTEL	Subsecretariat of Telecommunications (Chile)
TAC	Telecommunications Administration Center (Finland)
TACS	Total Access Communications System (UK)
TBA	Tax on Business Assets (Venezuela)
TBL	Telecommunications Business Law (Japan, Korea)

	Definition and Chapter(s) in Which Acronym, Abbreviation or Symbol Used
TBT	Technical Barriers to Trade (TBT Agreement) (South Africa)
TC	Ministry of Transportation and Communications (Peru)
TD	Télécom Développement (France)
TDMA	Time Division Multiple Access (Chile, Czech Republic, Israel, USA)
TDP	Teledifusão de Portugal, S.A. (Portugal)
TDR	Société Française de Transmission de Données par Radio (France)
TERCL	Tax Exemption and Reduction Control Law (Korea)
TL	Turkish Lira—currency
TLM	Telemensagem—Chamada de Pessoaos, Lda. (Portugal)
TLP	Telefones de Lisboa e Porto, S.A. (Portugal)
TMB	Telekom Malaysia Berhad (Malaysia)
TMN	Telecomunicações Móveis Nacionais, S.A. (Portugal)
TP S.A.	Telekomunikacja Polska S.A. (Poland)
TRAI	Telecom Regulatory Authority of India (India)
TRIM	Trade Related Investment Measure (South Africa)
TRS	Trunked Radio System (Korea)
TTNet	Tokyo Telecommunications Network (Japan)
TU	Tax Units (Venezuela)
UAH	Ukrainian Hryvnia—currency
UBS	Union Bank of Switzerland (Switzerland)
UIT	Unidad Impositiva Tributaria—tax credit (Peru)
UKRTEC	Ukrainian Enterprise for International and Interurban Telecommunications and Broadcasting (Ukraine)
UMC	Ukrainian Mobile Communications (Ukraine)
URS	Ukrainian Radio Systems (Ukraine)
US$	United States Dollar—currency
USTB	U.S. Trade or Business (USA)

	Definition and Chapter(s) in Which Acronym, Abbreviation or Symbol Used		**Definition and Chapter(s) in Which Acronym, Abbreviation or Symbol Used**
UT	Union Temporal (Colombia)	VOF	Vennootschap Onder Firma—general partnership (Netherlands)
UTA	United Telecom Austria (Austria)	VPN	Virtual Private Network (Hong Kong)
UTE	Temporary Union of Companies (Argentina)	VSAT	Very Small Aperture Terminal (Argentina, Colombia, France, India, Indonesia, Mexico, Romania, Sweden, Venezuela, Vietnam)
UUCP	UNIX-to-UNIX Copy Program (Romania)		
		VSNL	Videsh Sanchar Nigam Limited (India)
VANS	Value-Added Network Services (Netherlands)		
VAS	Value-Added Services (Italy, Turkey)	WAN	Wide Area Network (Czech Republic)
VAT	Value-Added Tax (All Chapters)	WLL	Wireless Local-Loop—wireless in the local loop (UK)
VKW	Vorarlberger Kraftwerke AG (Austria)	WLT	Wholesale and Luxury Tax (Venezuela)
VMS	Vietnam Mobile Services (Vietnam)	WTO	World Trade Organization (All Chapters)
VNPT	Vietnam National Post and Telecommunications Corporation (Vietnam)		
		zl	Zlotys—Polish currency

Companies, Agencies and Organizations

This appendix does not purport to be a comprehensive listing of all telecommunications companies, agencies or organizations; nor does it purport to list all the countries in which these telecoms operate. This appendix includes only those companies, agencies and organizations mentioned in this book.

Company, Agency or Organization	Chapter in Which Mentioned	Company, Agency or Organization	Chapter in Which Mentioned
A2000 Holding	Netherlands	Alcatel Bell	Turkey
ABC Communications (Holdings) Ltd.	Vietnam	Alcatel Network Systems Romania	Romania
ACC TelEnterprises	Canada	Alestra	Mexico
ADSB Telecommunications B.V.	Belgium	Alfa Group	Mexico
Aéroports de Paris	France	Aliança Atlântica	Portugal
AIDC Fund	Australia	AliaTel, a.s.	Czech Republic
Airtel Móvil, S.A.	Spain	Állami Privatizációs és Vagyonkezelô Részvénytársaság (ÁPV)	Hungary
AirTouch Belgium	Belgium		
AirTouch Communications	Belgium, Germany, Romania, Spain	America Online	USA
		Ameritech	Belgium, Denmark, Hungary, New Zealand
AirTouch Europe BV	Portugal		
AirTouch Paging	USA	AMP Society	Australia
Albacom	Italy	Ana Industries SRL	Romania
Alcatel	Vietnam	Antenna Hungária Rt.	Hungary

Company, Agency or Organization	Chapter in Which Mentioned	Company, Agency or Organization	Chapter in Which Mentioned
Antimonopoly Committee	Russia	Bank of Spain	Spain
Arcor	Germany	Bankomsvyaz	Ukraine
Argentaria	Spain	Barak ITC	Israel
Argentine Central Bank	Argentina	Bayerische Landesbank AG (Bayr.LB)	Austria
AT&T	Argentina, Germany, Hong Kong, Ireland, Italy, Mexico, Netherlands, Russia, UK, Ukraine, USA, Venezuela	BC Telecom Inc.	Canada
		BCE Inc.	Canada
		BCE Mobile	Canada
		Beeper	Ukraine
AT&T Bell System	USA	Beeper Communications Israel Ltd.	Israel
AT&T Canada Long Distance Services Company	Canada	Beeper Pagecall Ltd.	Israel
AT&T World Partners	UK	Belgacom	Belgium
Atlantic West BV	Slovakia	Belgacom Mobile	Belgium
Audio-Info BV	Portugal	Belgacom Téléport	France
Audio-Info Portugal BV	Portugal	Belgian Institute of Post and Telecommunications	Belgium
Aurec Ltd.	Israel	Belgian National Bank	Belgium
Australian Capital Taxation Office	Australia	Bell Atlantic Corporation	Chile, Italy, Mexico, USA, New Zealand
Australian Capital Territory	Australia		
Australian Communications Authority	Australia	Bell Atlantic International	Czech Republic
Australian Competition and Consumer Commission	Australia	Bell CableMedia	UK
		Bell Canada	Canada
Australian Telecommunications Authority (AUSTEL)	Australia	Bell Canada International	UK
Austrian Parliament	Austria	BellSouth Celular	Chile
Autorità per le Garanzie nelle Comunicazioni	Italy	BellSouth Chile S.A.	Chile
Avantel	Mexico	BellSouth Corporation	Argentina, Chile, Denmark, Germany, Israel, Peru, USA, Venezuela
Baja Celular	Mexico	BellSouth Mobile	Belgium
Banca Nazionale del Lavoro (BNL)	Italy	BellSouth New Zealand	New Zealand
Banco Bilbao Vizcaya (BBV)	Spain	Bezeq—The Israel Telecommunications Corp. Ltd.	Israel
Banco Central Hispano (BCH)	Spain		
Banco Mercantil	Venezuela	BGH S.A.	Argentina
Banco Português de Investimento, S.A.	Portugal	Bilka	Turkey
Banco Santander	Spain	Bina Sat-Com Sdn. Bhd.	Malaysia
Bancomservice	Ukraine	Binariang Sdn. Bhd.	Malaysia
Bank für Arbeit und Wirtschaft AG (BAWAG)	Austria	Bip-a-Call	Israel
Bank Negara Malaysia	Malaysia	Board of Money Laundering	Turkey
Bank of Finland	Finland	Bouygues-STET Télécom (BS Télécom)	France
Bank of Israel	Israel	Bouygues Télécom	France

Company, Agency or Organization	Chapter in Which Mentioned
BPI, S.A. (Banco Português de Investimento)	Portugal
BPL Telecom	India
British Telecom (BT)	Belgium, France, Ireland, Italy, Netherlands, New Zealand, Portugal, Spain, Switzerland, UK, USA
British Telecom Belgium	Belgium
Budapest Stock Exchange	Hungary
Bundesminister für Post und Telekommunikation	Germany
Cable & Wireless Communications	UK
Cable & Wireless Plc	Australia, France, Germany, Hong Kong, Indonesia, Ireland, Israel, Italy, South Africa, Spain, UK, USA, Vietnam
CallLink	Vietnam
CallMax BV	Netherlands
Canadian Radio-television and Telecommunications Commission (CRTC)	Canada
Cantel	Canada
Cegetel	France
Celcom	Malaysia
Cellcom Israel Ltd.	Israel
Cellnet	UK
Cellular 8	Hong Kong
Cellular Communications Network (Malaysia) Sdn. Bhd. (Celcom)	Malaysia
Cellular Group	Japan
Celumovil	Colombia
CENTERTEL	Poland
Central Bank	Chile, Colombia, Hungary, Norway, Turkey
Central Bank of Brazil	Brazil
Central Bank of Denmark	Denmark
Central Bank of Russia	Russia
Central Bank of Venezuela	Venezuela
Central European Free Trade Association (CEFTA)	Czech Republic, Hungary, Poland, Romania

Company, Agency or Organization	Chapter in Which Mentioned
CERSA	Spain
Ceský telekomunikaoní úrad— Czech Telecommunications Office	Czech Republic
CESNET	Czech Republic
CETI CR, a.s.	Czech Republic
Chilesat S.A.	Chile
Chilquinta S.A.	Chile
China International Trust & Inv.	Hong Kong
China National Posts and Telecommunications Industry Corp. (PTIC)	China
China Telecom	China, Hong Kong
China Unicom (Lian Tong, or United Telecommunications Corporation Ltd.)	China
Chubu Telecommunications Company	Japan
CIMA	Venezuela
Cisneros Group	Venezuela
Citicorp	Argentina
City Com Austria Telekommunikation GmbH	Austria
Citynet	Vietnam
Claloom	Israel
Clear Communications Ltd.	New Zealand
Clearnet	Canada
Clearnet PCS	Canada
Colombian Institute of Foreign Commerce— Instituto Colombiano de Comercio Exterior (INCOMEX)	Colombia
COLT Telecommunications	France, Italy, Switzerland, UK
Columbus II Project	Venezuela
Comcast	USA
Comcell	Colombia
Comisión Nacional de Comunicaciones (CNC)	Argentina
Comisión Nacional de Telecomunicaciones— National Telecommunications Commission (CONATEL)	Venezuela
Comisión Reguladora de Telecomunicaciones (CRT)	Colombia
Commerce Commission	New Zealand
Commercial Registry	Venezuela
Commercial Registry Department	Portugal

Company, Agency or Organization	Chapter in Which Mentioned
Commission of the European Communities in Brussels	Belgium, Denmark, Finland, France, Germany, Ireland, Italy, Netherlands, Portugal, Spain, Sweden, UK
Commissioner of Inland Revenue	Hong Kong
Commissioner of Taxation	Australia
Committee of Science and Technology	Colombia
Commonwealth of Independent States (CIS)	Russia, Ukraine
Compagnie Générale de Vidéocommunication (CGV)	France
Compagnie Générale des Eaux (CGE)	France
Compañía de Radiocomunicaciones Móviles (Movicom)	Argentina
Companhia Portuguesa Radio Marconi, S.A.	Portugal
Compañía Anónima Nacional Teléfonos de Venezuela (CANTV)	Venezuela
Compañía de Telecomunicaciones de Chile S.A. (CTC)	Chile
Compañía de Teléfonos del Interior (CTI)	Argentina
Compañía Peruana de Teléfonos Limitada (CPT)	Peru
CompuServe	Spain, USA
Computer Land	Romania
Comsat	Argentina
Comvik International Vietnam AB	Vietnam
Comviq	Sweden
Conatel	Chile
Concert	Portugal, UK
Connect Austria GmbH	Austria
Consejo Nacional de Infomática, Telecomunicaciones y Electrónica—National Telecommunications Council (CONINTEL)	Venezuela
Constantia Privatbank	Austria
Contactel—Chamada de Pessoaos, Lda.	Portugal
Council of State	Finland
Court of Registration	Hungary
Credit Lyonnais Securities Asia	India
CTC-Celular	Chile
CTC Mundo	Chile
Cukurova Group	Turkey

Company, Agency or Organization	Chapter in Which Mentioned
CyberTron EDV-Netzwerkbetriebs GmbH (Austrian Digital Telecom)	Austria
Czech National Bank	Czech Republic
Czech On Line, a.s.	Czech Republic
Czech Post and Telecommunications	Czech Republic
Czech Radiocommunications	Czech Republic
Daewoo Telecom	Vietnam
Daimler-Benz Aerospace AG (DASA)	Argentina
Daimler-Benz Group	Germany
Daini Denden Inc. (DDI)	Japan
Danish Commerce and Companies Agency	Denmark
Data Communications Corporation of Korea (DACOM)	Korea
Data-Highway Burgenland GmbH	Austria
Datakom Austria AG	Austria
Dattel, a.s.	Czech Republic
DBKom	Germany
DBP Telekom	Germany
debitel	Germany
Department General of Posts and Telecommunications (DGPT)	Vietnam
Department of Finance	Canada
Department of Post and Telegraphs	Ireland
Department of Public Enterprise	Ireland
Department of Telecommunications	India
Department of Trade and Industry	UK
Department of Transport, Energy and Communications	Ireland
Depósito Central de Valores S.A.	Chile
Descarte Investment	South Africa
DeTeMobil	Austria, Germany, Indonesia
Deutsche Bahn AG	Germany
Deutsche Bundesbank	Germany
Deutsche Bundespost (DBP)	Germany
Deutsche Bundespost Telekom	Ukraine
Deutsche Telekom AG	Germany, Hungary, Israel, Italy, Malaysia, Russia, Turkey, UK, Ukraine

Company, Agency or Organization	Chapter in Which Mentioned	Company, Agency or Organization	Chapter in Which Mentioned
Magyar Államvasutak Részvénytársaság (MÁV)	Hungary	Microsystem	Hungary
MagyarCom	Hungary	Migros	Switzerland
Mahanagar Telephone Nigam Limited (MTNL)	India	Military Electronics and Telecommunications Company (Vietel)	Vietnam
Main Road Telecomunicações	Portugal	Miniphone	Argentina
Malaysian Institute of Microelectronic Services Bhd. (MIMOS)	Malaysia	Minister for Public Enterprise (also Department for Public Enterprise)	Ireland
Manitoba Telecom Services	Canada	Minister of Finance	New Zealand
Mannesmann AG	Germany, Italy	Minister of Posts, Telecommunications and Broadcasting	South Africa
Mannesmann Eurokom GmbH	Germany		
Mannesmann Mobilfunk	Germany	Ministry of Commerce	New Zealand
Maritime Telegraph and Telephone Company Ltd.	Canada	Ministry of Communications	Colombia, Israel, Italy, Romania, Russia, Ukraine
MATÁV Rt. (Magyar Távközlési Részvénytársaság)	Hungary, Israel	Ministry of Economics	Austria
Matrix Europe Ltd. (Matrix Telecommunication of Australia)	Poland	Ministry of Economics and Finance	Peru
		Ministry of Electronics Industry (MEI)	China
Max Mobil Telekoms	Austria	Ministry of Energy, Telecommunication and Posts (METP)	Malaysia
Maxitel—Serviços e gestão de Telecomunicações, S.A.	Portugal	Ministry of Finance	France, Germany, Indonesia, Italy, Japan, New Zealand, Poland, Turkey, Venezuela
MaxLink Communications Inc.	Canada		
Mayne Nickless Ltd.	Australia		
MCC (Mobile Communication Center)	Vietnam		
MCI	Ireland, Mexico, New Zealand, Portugal, UK, USA	Ministry of Finance and Economy (MFE)	Korea
		Ministry of Foreign Economic Relations and Trade	Ukraine
Measat Global Telecommunications Sdn. Bhd.	Malaysia	Ministry of Industry and Energy	Norway
Media Pro	Romania	Ministry of Information and Communication (MIC)	Korea
Mediaset	Italy	Ministry of International Trade and Industry (MITI)	Malaysia
MensaTel	Spain		
Mercosur (Common Market of the South)	Argentina, Chile	Ministry of Justice	Denmark
		Ministry of Planning and Investment (MPI)	Vietnam
Mercury Communications Limited (MCL)	UK	Ministry of Posts and Telecommunications	China, Japan, Russia
Mercury One 2 One	UK		
Merrill Lynch & Co.	Israel	Ministry of Power Industry (MPI)	China
Metro Group	Germany	Ministry of Public Works	Indonesia
MFS Communications	France, Italy, UK	Ministry of Public Works and Transport	Spain
MicroCell Network Inc.	Canada	Ministry of Railways (MR)	China
Microsoft Network	USA	Ministry of Science and Technology (MOST)	Korea

Company, Agency or Organization	Chapter in Which Mentioned
Ministry of Science, Technology and Environment	Vietnam
Ministry of Telecommunications	France, Poland
Ministry of Tourism, Posts and Telecommunications (MTPT)	Indonesia
Ministry of Transport and Communications	Czech Republic, Finland, Norway
Ministry of Transport and Public Works	Netherlands
Ministry of Transport and Telecommunications	Norway
Ministry of Transport, Communications and Construction	Hungary
Ministry of Transport, Communications and Water Management	Hungary
Ministry of Transport, Post and Telecommunications	Slovakia
Ministry of Transportation and Communications	Chile, Peru
Mitsubishi Corp.	Japan
Mitsui & Co.	Japan
MKM-Tel Távközlési és Kommunikációs Korlátolt Felelössegü Társaság	Hungary
MobiFon S.A.	Romania
Mobikom Sdn. Bhd.	Malaysia
Mobil Rom S.A.	Romania
Mobile Communication Center (MCC)	Vietnam
Mobile Telekom	Russia
Mobile Telephone Networks (Pty) Ltd (MTN)	South Africa
Mobility Canada	Canada
Mobilix	Denmark
Mobilkom Austria AG	Austria
Mobistar	Belgium
MOL Magyar Olaj és Gázipari Részvénytársaság	Hungary
Moscow Cellular Communications (MCC)	Russia
Moscow Telephone (MGTS)	Russia
Motorola	Australia, Argentina, Chile, Ireland, Israel, Japan, Mexico
Motorola Communications Israel Ltd.	Israel
Motorola Israel Ltd.	Israel

Company, Agency or Organization	Chapter in Which Mentioned
Movilnet	Venezuela
Mtel International	Argentina
Multitone CZ, s.r.o	Czech Republic
Mutiara Telecommunications Sdn. Bhd.	Malaysia
MV Komunikasyon	Turkey
NahuelSat	Argentina
Naray Mobile Telecom	Korea
Natel	Switzerland
National Bank of Poland (NBP)	Poland
National Bank of Slovakia	Slovakia
National Bank of Ukraine	Ukraine
National Mutual Holdings	Australia
National Property Fund	Czech Republic
National Telecommunications Council (CONINTEL)	Peru
NetCom AS	Norway
NetCom Systems AB	Sweden
Netia Telekom S.A.	Poland
New Brunswick Tel	Canada
New T&T	Hong Kong
New World Telephone Ltd.	Hong Kong
New York Stock Exchange	Hungary
NewTel Communications Ltd.	Canada
Newtelco/Sunrise	Switzerland
Nippon Telegraph & Telephone Corporation (NTT)	Indonesia, Japan, Russia, Vietnam
Nissan Motor Co.	Japan
Norwegian Telecom	Norway
NTT DoCoMo	Japan
Nuon International	Czech Republic
NYNEX CableComms	UK
NYNEX Corporation	Indonesia
o.tel.o	Germany
Office Fédéral de la Communication (OFCOM)	Switzerland
Office of Telecommunications (OFTEL)	UK

COMPANIES, AGENCIES AND ORGANIZATIONS

Company, Agency or Organization	Chapter in Which Mentioned
R.A. Posta Romana	Romania
R.P. Telekom	Poland
Racal	Venezuela
Radex-Heraklith International	Austria
Radiobip	Spain
Radiocom	Ukraine
Radiokontakt Operator, a.s	Czech Republic
Radiomobil	Czech Republic
Radiomóvel—Telecomunicações, S.A.	Portugal
Radiotel	Romania
RAM Mobile Data	Belgium
Rediffusion	Switzerland
Régie Autonome des Transports Parisiens (RATP)	France
Régle des Télégraphes et des Téléphones (RTT)	Belgium
Regional Services Council (RSC)	South Africa
Regional Telephone Company Intersvyaz Ltd	Ukraine
Regional Vision Inc.	Canada
Registrar of Companies	New Zealand, South Africa
Regulatory Commission for Telecommunications	Colombia
Regulierungsbehörde für Telekommunikation und Post, Bonn—Federal Regulator for Telecommunications and Postal Services, Bonn	Germany
Reliance Group of Industries	India
Reliance Telecom	India
Rembrandt Group	South Africa
Repart—Sistemas de Comunicações de Recursos Partilhados, S.A.	Portugal
Reserve Bank of Australia	Australia
Reserve Bank of India (RBI)	India
Resolutory Commission	Chile
Retevisión	Spain
Revenue Canada	Canada
Revenue Department	Australia
Robert Thomson Family	Australia

Company, Agency or Organization	Chapter in Which Mentioned
Rogers Cantel Mobile Communications Inc.	Canada
Rogers Communications Inc. (RCI)	Canada
Rom Post	Romania
Rom Post Telecom	Romania
Rom Radiocom	Romania
Rom Telecom	Romania
Romanian Association of Securities Dealers Automated Quotation (RASDAQ)	Romania
Romanian Trade Register	Romania
Rostelecom	Russia
RSLCOM New Telco Telecom AG (Com Austria)	Austria
Rumeli Holding	Turkey
RWE AG	Germany
RZB	Austria
Safra Brothers	Israel
Saigon ABC	Vietnam
Saigon Epro	Vietnam
Saigon Post and Telecommunications Joint Stock Corporation (Saigon Postel)	Vietnam
Saigon Telecom Co.	Vietnam
Samsung Chile Holding Ltda.	Chile
Samsung Group	Korea
Santander Investments	Chile
Santodomingo Group	Colombia
SaskTel	Canada
Satélites Mexicanos (Satmex)	Mexico
Satko	Turkey
Saturn Communications Limited	New Zealand
SBC Communications	Mexico, South Africa, Switzerland, USA
Schweizerische Bundesbahn (SBB)— Swiss Railways	Switzerland
Science Applications International Corp. (SAIC)	Venezuela
Secretaría de Hacienda y Crédito Publico (SHCP)	Mexico
Secretary for Economic Services	Hong Kong

Company, Agency or Organization	Chapter in Which Mentioned
Telenor A/S	Austria, Germany, Ireland, Norway
Telenor Invest A/S	Hungary
Telenor Link	Norway
Telenor Mobil A/S	Norway
Telepac—Serviços de Telecomunicações, S.A.	Portugal
Telepri	Portugal
Telering Telekom Service GmbH	Austria
Telesat Canada	Canada
Telespazio	Italy
Telesystem International Wireless Corporation NV	Netherlands
Telesystem International Wireless Inc.	Romania
Teletopia	Norway
Televisa de México (Televisa)	Mexico
Televoice—Consultadoria e Comércio Internacional, Lda.	Portugal
Televoz—Consultadoria em difusão, Lda.	Portugal
Teleway Japan	Japan
Telfort	Netherlands
Telia AB	Sweden
Telia Mobitel	Norway, Sweden
Telia Oy	Denmark, Finland, Ireland, Netherlands, Norway
Telindus	Belgium
Telinor	Mexico
Telintar	Argentina
Telivo Oy	Finland
Teljoy Holdings Limited	South Africa
Telkom SA Limited (Telkom)	South Africa
TELMOS Communications	Russia
TELNOR	Mexico
Telsim Mobil Telekomunikasyon Hizmeretleri AS (Telsim)	Turkey
TelSource	Czech Republic
Telstra Corporation Ltd.	Australia, Indonesia, New Zealand, Vietnam
TELUS Corporation	Canada

Company, Agency or Organization	Chapter in Which Mentioned
Temanet A/S	Ireland
The Island Telephone Company Ltd.	Canada
Thintana Communications LLC	South Africa
Time Telecommunications Sdn. Bhd.	Malaysia
T-Mobil	Czech Republic, Netherlands
T-NET	Venezuela
Tokyo Electric Power Company	Japan
Tokyo Telecommunications Network (TTNet)	Japan
Tomas Milmo	Mexico
Tomen Telecom Romania	Romania
Torch Telecom	UK
Town Khan	Hong Kong
Toyota Motor Corp.	Japan
Transgás	Portugal
Transnet Limited	South Africa
Transtel	South Africa
TriGem Computer, Inc.	Korea
Türk Telekomünikasyon A.S.	Turkey
Türkcell	Turkey
Türksat	Turkey
Turnet	Turkey
Ukrainian Enterprise for International and Interurban Telecommunications and Broadcasting (UKRTEC)	Ukraine
Ukrainian Mobile Communications (UMC)	Ukraine
Ukrainian Radio Systems (URS)	Ukraine
Ukrainian State Telecommunications Corporation (Ukrtelecom)	Ukraine
UkrPage	Ukraine
Ukrpak	Ukraine
Union Bank of Switzerland (UBS)	Switzerland
Unión Fenosa	Spain
Unisource	Austria, Germany, Hungary, Italy, Netherlands, UK
United Telecom Austria (UTA)	Austria
United Telecom Investment BV	Hungary